P9-CMF-826

Geo B. Johnson

THE EPISTLES OF ST JOHN.

THE EPISTLES OF ST JOHN:

THE GREEK TEXT

WITH NOTES AND ESSAYS

BY

BROOKE FOSS WESTCOTT, D.D., D.C.L.,

CANON OF WESTMINSTER, REGIUS PROFESSOR OF DIVINITY
AND FELLOW OF KING'S COLLEGE, CAMBRIDGE.

SECOND EDITION.

Cambridge and London:
MACMILLAN AND CO.
1886

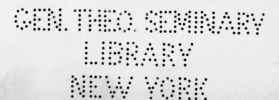

καὶ τὸ Πνεῦμα καὶ ἡ Νύμφη λέγουσιν Ἔρχου.
καὶ ὁ ἀκούων εἰπάτω Ἔρχου.
καὶ ὁ διψῶν ἐρχέσθω,
ὁ θέλων λαβέτω ὕδωρ ζωῆς δωρεάν.

Apoc. xxii. 17.

CAMBRIDGE: PRINTED BY C. J. CLAY, M.A. AND SON, AT THE UNIVERSITY PRESS.

In the present Commentary I have endeavoured to follow the plan which I sketched in the notes on the Gospel of St John in *The Speaker's Commentary*. It formed no part of my design to collect and discuss the conflicting opinions which have been held on the structure of the writings or on the interpretation of separate passages. Such a labour is indeed of the deepest interest and utility; but it appeared to me that I might help the student more by giving the results at which I have arrived, and by indicating the lines of inquiry by which they have been reached. In pursuing this end it has been my main desire to call attention to the minutest points of language, construction, order, as serving to illustrate the meaning of St John. I do not venture to pronounce that any variation is trivial or unimportant. The exact words are for us the decisive expression of the Apostle's thought. I have therefore, if I may borrow words which have been applied in a somewhat different sense, begun by interpreting the Epistles as I should 'interpret any other book', neglecting nothing which might contribute to a right apprehension of its full meaning. I do not feel at liberty to set aside the letter of a document till it has been found to be untenable.

Many writings, it is true, will not bear the consistent application of such a method of interpretation; but each day's study brings home to me more forcibly the conviction that in no other way can we hope to gain the living truth of apostolic teaching. The verification of the method lies in the result. If it discloses to patient investigation unsuspected harmonies and correspondences of thought: if it suggests good reasons for holding that views of faith which seem to be conflicting are really complementary: if it inspires with a vital power dogmatic statements which grow rigid by the necessities of controversy: if it opens on this side and that subjects of study which await fuller investigation : if it enables us to feel that the difficulties of our own time were not unnoticed by those who, under the guidance of the Holy Spirit, saw the Eternal: if it brings a sense of rest and confidence which grows firmer with increasing knowledge: then it seems to me that it needs no further justification.

It cannot but be that I have often erred in the application of the principles which I hold ; but no one, I trust, will condemn the method till he has tested it by personal labour. A few hours spent in tracing out the use of a word or a form, in comparing phrases often held to be synonymous, in estimating the force of different tenses of the same verb in regard to the contexts in which they are found, will bring assurance which no acceptance of another's work can give. Several notes in which I have sought to bring together materials serviceable for such inquiries will at least, I hope, encourage some to make the trial for themselves.

The study of Scripture is, I believe, for us the way by which God will enable us to understand His present revelation through history and nature. When once we can feel the divine power of human words, which gather in themselves the results of cycles of intellectual discipline, we shall be prepared to pass from the study of one book to the study of 'the Divine Library'. And the inquiries which thus come before us are not mere literary speculations. The fulness of the Bible, apprehended in its historical development, answers to the fulness of life. If we can come to see in it the variety, the breadth, the patience of the past dealings of God with humanity, we shall gain that courageous faith from a view of the whole world which is commonly sought by confining our attention to a little fragment of it.

The Bible is indeed the symbol and the pledge of the Catholicity of our Faith; and the real understanding of the Bible rests upon the acknowledgment of its Catholicity, of the universal range in which it includes in its records typical examples of the dealings of God with men under every variety of circumstance and being, social and personal. We are all so familiar with certain lessons which the Bible contains that we come to regard them, perhaps unconsciously, as the complete sum of its teaching. Special words, phrases, incidents, inspire our own souls and mould our own faith, and we forget that we are not the measure of the wants and powers of man. So it is that we pass over large sections of Scripture unstudied, or force them into unison with what we hear most easily. We neglect to take account of periods of silence in revelation scarcely less eloquent with instruction than the messages of prophets. We lose just those helps to knowing how God disciplines races, classes, individuals, who are most unlike ourselves, which we need sorest when we look on the sad spectacle of a disordered and divided world.

This Catholicity of the Bible is made more impressive by the fact that the Bible is in a large degree historical. It has pleased God to reveal Himself in and through life; and the record of the revelation is literary and not dogmatic. From first to last God is seen in the Bible conversing with man. He speaks to man as man can hear, and man replies as he can use the gift of the Spirit. But word and answer alike are according to the truth of life. All that has been written for us has been part of real human experience, and therefore it has an unending value. Thus in the main the Bible is the continuous unfolding in many parts and many ways of the spiritual progress of mankind. It may be a law, a narrative, a prophecy, a psalm, a proverb, but in each case it comes from life and enters into life; it belongs to a distinct epoch; it is only in its vital context, so to speak, that it can be perfectly understood.

In this long series of spiritual records the first Epistle of St John probably holds the last place. It is probably the final interpretation of the whole series of the divine revelations; and under this aspect it proclaims and satisfies the highest hope of man. It declares that in the Presence of Christ there has been given and there will be given that knowledge of God for which man was made, issuing in fellowship which is realised here in the Christian Society, and which reaches to the Source of all life. In this consummation the past finds accomplishment, and the sufferings and riddles of the present are shewn to be part of a sovereign counsel which passes beyond our sight. As we look back and look forward in the light thus thrown over the world we can work and wait.

The Son of God is come and hath given us an understanding that we may know Him that is true, and we are in Him that is true, even in His Son Jesus Christ.

That which we have seen and heard declare we unto you also, that ye also may have fellowship with us: yea, and our fellowship is with the Father and with His Son Jesus Christ.

Though I am quite unable to acknowledge or even to distinguish in detail my obligations to earlier writers in the course of a work which has been spread over more than thirty years, I cannot refrain from expressing my gratitude to three commentators who have helped me greatly in different ways. Bengel's notes always serve as a kind of standard of spiritual insight; and there is no one from whom I differ on a serious question of interpretation with more regret or more misgiving. Huther (4th edition, 1880) has given a most careful review of the opinions of previous editors to which I have been much indebted in revising my own notes. And Haupt has drawn at length a connected view of the Epistle which brings out into a clear light its theological significance. On many points of importance I am unable to accept his conclusions, but no one, I think, has shewn more impressively the true spirit of an interpreter of the New Testament.

There is a feeling of sadness in looking at that which must stand with all its imperfections as the accomplishment of a dream of early youth. The work might have answered better to the opportunity. But however greatly I have failed in other respects, I trust that at least I may have been allowed to encourage some students to linger with more devout patience, with more frank questionings than before, over words of St John.

CAMBRIDGE,
June 22, 1883.

W.   *b*

NOTICE TO THE SECOND EDITION.

THE truest gratitude which a writer can shew to his critics is, I think, to consider their criticisms silently and without the semblance of controversy or excuse to remove the faults which he is led to feel. On one criticism however which has been made on this volume I wish to offer a few words of explanation, lest I should seem to accept the assumption on which it rests. Several reviewers who have appreciated the work most generously have spoken of the Essays, ' as only loosely connected,' with the Commentary. I can only say that in my conception they are an essential part of it, and that as far as they appear to be merely accidental additions I have failed to make my purpose clear. If indeed I had regarded the Apostolic writings as addressed simply to the first age, it might have been enough to ascertain their literal meaning without touching on the problems of our own time as they are affected by them. But I believe that they still have a living voice for ourselves ; and I have endeavoured to indicate how we may interpret it. From the earliest time when I read the first Epistle of St John as a divine instruction for today I could not but ask What then is the world ? and What scope is left for Art ? The questions appeared to me to be of the highest practical importance. I could not have written a Commentary on the Epistle without striving to answer them, without having gained answers which were at least satisfactory to myself. And yet again : the characteristic revelation of the Epistle is 'God is love'. How, untold thousands have sadly inquired, can such a revelation be maintained in face of the facts of life ? 'The Gospel of Creation' points, I think, to the solution of this last enigma of our being.

I cannot suppose that my own experience in reading St John is in any way singular. I hope then that I have said enough to shew that the Essays are indeed most closely united with a living interpretation of his Epistles. We can each speak only as we feel. For others the same words may have other lessons.

In revising the notes I have made some transpositions which will, I trust, give greater coherence and clearness to them. For the same reason I have added a continuous translation to each section. In the interpretation of the Epistles I have not made any changes.

I have to thank many friends, old and new, for corrections of references. It is only by such generous help that approximate correctness can be gained.

B. F. W.

CAMBRIDGE,
   Oct. 10, 1885.

CONTENTS.

Contents.

INTRODUCTION
TO THE FIRST EPISTLE.

I. TEXT.

THE text of the Epistle is contained in the following authorities:

1. GREEK MSS.

   (*a*) *Primary uncials:*

   ℵ, Cod. Sin. sæc. IV.

   A, Cod. Alex. sæc. V.

   B, Cod. Vatic. sæc. IV.

   C, Cod. Ephr. sæc. V. from i. 1—iv. 2 ἐκ τοῦ θεοῦ.

   Secondary uncials:

   K, Cod. Mosq. sæc. IX.

   L, Cod. Angel. sæc. IX.

   P, Cod. Porphyr. sæc. IX.

   (*β*) *Cursives.* More than two hundred in number, including 13 (Cod. Colbert. sæc. XI. = 33 Gosp.), and 31 (Cod. Leicestr. sæc. XIV. = 69 Gosp.).

   D, *Codex Bezæ*, sæc. VI., has lost 67 leaves after Mark xvi. 15 (Gk.), in which there can be no doubt that the Epistle was contained, for after this gap follows the Latin translation of 3 John 11—15. The Book of the Acts comes immediately afterwards.

2. VERSIONS.

   (*a*) *Latin. Old Latin.*

   > A large and important fragment, iii. 8—end, has been published by L. Ziegler (1876) from a Munich MS. (cent. VII.), which gives an African text closely akin to that of Fulgentius (quoted as F or *Fris.*).

A nearly complete text of a different (Italic?) type has been preserved by Augustine in his Expository discourses on the Epistle (i. 1—v. 12). Many other fragments are preserved in quotations.

Vulgate Latin (V. lat. vg and vg).

(β) *Syriac.*

Peshito (syr. vg).

Harclean (syr. hl).

(γ) *Egyptian.*

Memphitic (Coptic) (me).

Thebaic (Sahidic) (the).

To these may be added the *Armenian* and the *Æthiopic*[1].

Character of the text.
The text does not present many difficult problems (ii. 20; iv. 3; v. 10). It was exposed to far fewer disturbing influences than that of the Gospels. There were no parallel texts or parallel traditions at hand (unless probably in iv. 3) to supply additions to the original words, or modifications of their form. The utmost amount of variation likely to find favour with critics of the most opposite schools is practically of very small extent, and, though no variation is without real significance, of comparatively small moment.

Collation with Stephens, 1550.
In the following table I have set down all the changes from the text of Stephens (1550) which I have adopted generally in accordance with the clear balance of the most ancient authority. The reader will be able to judge of their importance.

i. 3 add καὶ' ὑμῖν, *also* to you (אABC).

4 γρ. ἡμεῖς, write *we* (אA*B), for γρ. ὑμῖν, we write *to you*.

ἡ χ. ἡμῶν, *our* joy (אB), for ἡ χ. ὑμῶν (AC), *your* joy (doubtful).

5 ἔστιν αὕτη (אBC), for αὕτη ἐστίν (A).

ἀγγελία, *message* (אAB), for ἐπαγγελία (C), *promise*.

---

[1] I have given below the text a fairly complete view of the readings of the primary uncials and of the most ancient versions, but this limited summary, though it shews clearly the sources of the later texts, cannot supersede the study of a full *apparatus criticus*.

οὐκ ἔστιν ἐν αὐτῷ (B), for ἐν αὐτῷ οὐκ ἔστιν (אAC).

7 Ἰησοῦ, *Jesus* (אBC), omit Χριστοῦ, *Christ.*

ii.   4   add ὅτι ´ ἔγνωκα (אAB).

   6   om. οὕτω ´ περιπ. (AB) *to walk*, for *so to walk.*

   7   ἀγαπητοί, *Beloved* (אABC), for ἀδελφοί, *Brethren.*

       om. ἀπ᾽ ἀρχῆς (2°) (אABC), *ye heard*, for ye heard *from the beginning.*

   13   ἔγραψα, *I wrote* (אABC), for γράφω, *I write.*

   18   om. ὁ ´ ἀντίχριστος (א*BC).

   19   ἐξ ἡμῶν ἦσαν (BC), for ἦσαν ἐξ ἡμῶν.

   20   οἴδατε πάντες (B), ye *all* know, for καὶ οἴδατε πάντα, *and* ye know *all things* (doubtful).

   23   add ὁ ὁμολογῶν τὸν υἱὸν καὶ τὸν πατέρα ἔχει (אABC), *he that confesseth the Son hath the Father also.*

   24   om. οὖν (אABC), *therefore.*

   27   μένει ἐν ὑμῖν (א(A)BC), for ἐν ὑμῖν μένει.

       τὸ αὐτοῦ χρίσμα ((א)BC), *his* unction, for τὸ αὐτὸ χρ. *the same* unction.

       μένετε ((א)ABC), *abide*, for μενεῖτε, *ye shall abide.*

   28   ἐάν (אABC), *if* he shall, for ὅταν, *when* he shall.

       σχῶμεν (אᵒABC), for ἔχωμεν.

iii.   1   add καὶ ἐσμέν (אABC), *and such we are.*

   2   om. δέ (אABC), *but.*

   5   om. ἡμῶν (AB), *sins*, for *our* sins.

   13   om. μου (אABC), *brethren*, for *my* brethren.

   14   om. τὸν ἀδελφόν (אAB), *he that loveth not*, for he that loveth not *his brother.*

   16   θεῖναι (אABC) for τιθέναι.

   18   om. μου (אABC), *little children*, for *my* little children.

       add τῇ ´ γλώσσῃ (ABC).

       add ἐν ´ ἔργῳ (אABC).

   19   ἐν τούτῳ γνωσόμεθα (om. καὶ AB, γνωσόμεθα אABC), *in this* we *shall* perceive, for *and* in this we perceive.

       τὴν καρδίαν (A*B), our *heart*, for τὰς κ. our *hearts.*

21 om. ἡμῶν (twice) (1. AB, 2. BC).

22 ἀπ᾽ αὐτοῦ (ℵABC) for παρ᾽ αὐτοῦ.

iv. 3 om. Χριστὸν ἐν σαρκὶ ἐληλυθότα (AB), *Christ come in flesh.*

10 ἠγαπήκαμεν (B), *have* loved, for ἠγαπήσαμεν, love (doubtful).

12 ἐν ἡμῖν ἐστίν (ℵB) for ἐστὶν ἐν ἡμῖν.

15 add Χριστὸς (B), *Christ* (doubtful).

16 add μένει (ℵB), God *abideth* (doubtful).

19 om. αὐτόν (AB), we love, for we love *him.*

20 οὐ (ℵB) for πῶς, *cannot* love, for *how can he* love?

v. 1 om. καί (B), *also.*

2 ποιῶμεν (B), *do,* for τηρῶμεν, *observe.*

5 τίς ἐστιν δέ (B), *but* who is? for who is? (doubtful).

6 om. ὁ (ℵAB), Jesus Christ, for Jesus *the* Christ.

add ἐν᾽ τῷ αἵμ. and *in* the blood, for and the blood.

6, 7 om. ἐν τῷ οὐρανῷ...ἐν τῇ γῇ (ℵAB), *in heaven, the Father, the Word, and the Holy Ghost; and these three are one. And there are three that bear witness in earth.*

9 ὅτι (ℵAB), *that,* for ἦν, *which.*

10 αὐτῷ or αὑτῷ for ἑαυτῷ.

11 ὁ θεὸς ἡμῖν (B), for ἡμῖν ὁ θεός.

13 ἵνα...αἰώνιον, τοῖς πιστ....θεοῦ (ℵ*B) for τοῖς πιστ....θεοῦ, ἵνα αἰώνιον, that ye may know that ye have eternal life, *even* unto you that believe on the name of the Son of God, for unto you...God, that ye may...life.

om. καὶ ἵνα πιστ. εἰς τὸ ὄν. τοῦ υἱοῦ τοῦ θεοῦ (ℵAB), *and that* ye may believe on the name of the Son of God.

15 ὃ ἐάν for ὃ ἄν.

ἀπ᾽ αὐτοῦ (ℵB) for παρ᾽ αὐτοῦ.

18 τηρεῖ αὐτόν (A*B), keepeth *him,* for τηρεῖ ἑαυτόν, keepeth *himself.*

20 γινώσκομεν (ℵAB) for γινώσκωμεν.

om. ἤ (ℵAB).

21 ἑαυτά (ℵ*B) for ἑαυτούς.

om. Ἀμήν (ℵAB).

To these may be added a few variations which are more or less probable :

ii.   2 μόνων (B) for μόνον.

    10 οὐκ ἔστιν ἐν αὐτῷ (order) (אAC).

    25 ὑμῖν (B) for ἡμῖν.

    29 add καὶ πᾶς (אAC).

iii.   7 παιδία (AC) τεκνία.

    23 πιστεύωμεν (אAC) for πιστεύσωμεν.

iv.   2 ἐληλυθέναι (B) for ἐληλυθότα.

    3 λύει for μὴ ὁμολογεῖ.

v.   6 μόνῳ (B) for μόνον.

In v. 10 it may be questioned whether ὁ μὴ πιστεύων should not stand absolutely, τῷ θεῷ and τῷ υἱῷ being two attempts to define the sense.

It will be seen that there is in the majority of cases a clear preponderance if not a complete agreement of the most ancient Greek MSS. for the reading adopted. The mass of later Greek MSS. give in most cases the reading which is rejected, but not unfrequently they are fairly divided between the rival readings (e.g. ii. 4, 7, 13, 23, 24; iii. 1, 13, 16, &c.). The reading of the most ancient Greek MSS. is generally supported by important representatives of the early versions and by some later MSS. But in a very few cases a reading is taken on small ancient authority alone which would be inadequate if the reading were considered by itself (iv. 10, 15; v. 5).

Superiority of the most ancient text.

But not to enter now into the details of evidence it will be obvious upon a consideration of the contexts that the most ancient reading gives in very many cases that shade of colouring to the passage which at once approves itself to be original (e.g. i. 7; ii. 7, 19, 27; iii. 1, 2, 5, 14; iv. 3, 19; v. 6, 18). In other cases the most ancient reading easily explains the origin of the recent reading while the converse change is unintelligible (e.g. ii. 23; v. 13; see also i. 4, 5; ii. 4, 13, 18, 20, 24, 27, 28; iii. 13, 18; v. 2, 9). In one place only (iv. 20) does the reading of the more recent type of Greek MSS. appear at first sight to be intrinsically more likely.

The variants offer good examples of conflate readings (ii. 15 τοῦ θεοῦ καὶ πατρός; comp. 3 John 12 ὑπὸ αὐτῆς τῆς ἐκκλησίας καὶ τῆς ἀληθείας); of omissions by *homœoteleuton* (ii. 27 f.; iv. 6, 21; v. 2 f.; and especially ii. 23); of the addition and omission of the final ν, represented by a line over the vowel (ii. 13, 14); of *itacism* (iv. 2).

The text of Cod. Vat. B. **The text of B is, as elsewhere, of paramount excellence.** It appears to be in error in very few cases :

i. 2 + ὃ ´ ἑωράκαμεν.

ii. 14 τὸ ἀπ᾽ ἀρχῆς.

   25 ὑμῖν, comp. iii. 1.

   27 χάρισμα.

iii. 21 ἔχει.

Some of the readings which it gives are more or less doubtful :

ii. 2 μόνων.   Comp. v. 6.

   14 om. τοῦ θεοῦ.

   24 om. ἐν before τῷ πατρί.

   27 ἀλλά for ἀλλ᾽ ὥς.

   29 om. καί.

iii. 15 ἑαυτοῦ for αὐτοῦ.

   23 πιστεύσωμεν.

iv. 2 ἐληλυθέναι.

   10 ἠγαπήκαμεν.

   15 add Χριστός.

v. 5 τίς ἐστιν δέ.

   6 μόνῳ.   Comp. ii. 2.

It is not, as far as I can judge, ever in error (unless in iii. 7) when it is supported by some other primary uncial or version :

i. 5 οὐκ ἔστιν ἐν αὐτῷ Β 13 31 syr. vg me the.

ii. 6 om. οὕτως ΑΒ syr. vg latt the.

   20 om. καί (2°) Β the.

   πάντες אΒ the.

iii.　5　om. ἡμῶν AB 13 lat. vg syr. hl me.

　　19　om. καί (1°) AB lat. vg syr. hl me.

　　　　τὴν καρδίαν A*B syr. vg the.

　　21　om. ἡμῶν (1°) AB 13.

　　　　om. ἡμῶν (2°) BC.

iv.　3　om. Χρ. ἐν σ. ἐλ. AB lat. vg me.

　　12　ἐν ἡμῖν ἐστίν ℵB.

　　19　om. αὐτόν AB (the).

　　20　οὐ δύναται ℵB syr. hl the.

v.　1　om. καί (2°) B 13 (lat. vg) the.

　　2　ποιῶμεν B lat. vg syr me the.

　　18　αὐτόν A*B.

(iv. 21 is not a case in point.)

The text of ℵ contains many errors, some of which remain un-
corrected, and not a few peculiar false readings :

The text of
Cod. Sin.
ℵ.

i.　3　ὃ ἀκηκ. καὶ ἑωρ. καὶ ἀπαγγέλλ.

　　5　η απαγγελιας corrected to ἡ ἀγάπη τῆς ἐπαγγελίας.

ii.　3　φυλάξωμεν (1ᵃ m.).

　　4　om. ἐν τούτῳ.

　　　　ἡ ἀλ. τοῦ θεοῦ.

　　8　ἀλ. καὶ ἐν.

　　9　μισῶν, ψευστής ἐστιν καὶ ἐν τ. σκ.

　　13　τὸ πονηρόν.　Comp. v. 8 τὸν ἀλ.; v. 1.

　　24　ἀκηκόατε (twice).

　　　　ἐν τῷ π. καὶ ἐκ τῷ υἱῷ.

　　26　ταῦτα δέ.

　　27　πνεῦμα (1ᵃ m.).

　　　　ἀληθής.

　　28　om. καὶ νῦν...αὐτῶ.

　　　　ἐν τῇ παρ. ἀ. ἀπ᾽ αὐτοῦ.

iii.　5　οἴδαμεν.

　　　　οὐκ ἔ. ἐν αὐτῷ.

　　14　μεταβέβηκεν.

21 ἀδελφοί.

22 αἰτώμεθα.

iv.   2 γινώσκομεν.

    3 ὅτι ἀκηκ. ὅτι.

     ὁμ. Ἰησοῦν κύριον.   Comp. 1 Cor. xii. 3.

    8 om. ὁ μὴ ἀγ….θεόν (1ᵃ m.): om. τὸν θ. (אᶜ).

    9 ζῶμεν.

   17 μεθ᾽ ἡμῶν ἐν ἡμῖν.

     τῇ ἀγάπῃ τῆς κρ.

     ἐσόμεθα.

   20 om. ὅτι.

v.   1 τὸ γεγεννημένον.   Comp. v. 20; ii. 13.

    7 οἱ τρεῖς.

    9 τὴν μαρτ. τοῦ θεοῦ (1ᵃ m.).

   10 ἐμαρτύρηκεν.

     οὐκ ἐπίστευκεν.

   20 τὸ ἀληθινόν (1ᵃ m.).

In several cases it has false readings in common with A and with C respectively:

אA.

iii. 21 add ἡμῶν after καταγινώσκῃ.

v.   6 add καὶ πνεύματος after αἵματος.

אC.

i.   9 add ἡμῶν after ἁμαρτίας (2°).

ii.   6 add οὕτως.

iii. 5 add ἡμῶν after ἁμαρτίας.

   11 ἐπαγγελία.

   13 add καί.

   19 add καί.

   21 add ἡμῶν after καρδία.

The text of Cod. Alex. A.   The text of A, which represents a far more ancient type in this Epistle than in the Gospels, contains many peculiar readings, in which it has often the support of the Vulgate:

i.   6 ἐὰν + γάρ.

    7 μετ' αὐτοῖ (some lat).

ii. 2 ἐστ. ἰλ. lat. vg.

    8 σκιά.

    ἐν αὐτ. ἀλ.

    27 om. καί before καθώς.

iii. 20 om. ὅτι 2°, lat. vg me the.

    23 τῷ ὀν. αὐτοῦ 'Ι. Χ.

iv. 6 ἐν τούτῳ lat. vg me the.

    7 add τὸν θεόν.

    8 οὐ γινώσκει.

    10 ἐκεῖνος for αὐτός.

    15 ὁμολογῇ.

    16 πιστεύομεν (lat. vg) me.

    19 add οὖν lat. vg.

    ὁ θεός for αὐτός lat. vg.

    21 ἀπὸ τοῦ θεοῦ lat. vg.

v.   6 πνεύματι for αἵματι.

    10 add τοῦ θεοῦ lat. vg me.

    τῷ υἱῷ lat. vg.

    οὐκ ἐπίστευσεν.

    11 αὕτη ἐστὶν ἡ ζ.

    14 ὄνομα for θέλημα.

    16 μὴ ἁμαρτ. ἁμ. μὴ πρ. θ.

    20 ἀληθινὸν θεόν lat. vg me.

    om. 'Ιησοῦ Χριστῷ lat. vg.

The peculiar readings of C have no appearance of genuineness :   The text of Cod. Eph. C.

i.   4 add in fin. ἐν ἡμῖν.

    9 om. ἡμᾶς.

ii. 21 om. πᾶν.

iii. 20 κύριος (for θεός).

iv. 2 Χριστὸν 'Ιησοῦν.

W.   c

In several places it gives a correction which was adopted widely:

i.   3 om. δέ.

     5 ἐπαγγελία.

ii.   4 om. ὅτι.

iii. 14 add τὸν ἀδελφόν.

The *Latin Vulgate*.   The Vulgate Latin Version is for the most part very close to the early Greek text. It represents however in some cases readings which are not now noted from Greek MSS.:

ii.   1 *sed et si* : καὶ ἐὰν δέ (Did.).

     12 *remittuntur* (? ἀφίονται).

iii. 17 *qui habuerit* : om. δέ.

iv.   3 *qui solvit* (λύει) *Jesum Christum.*

        hic est antichristus, quod.

     4 *eum* : αὐτόν.

     16 *caritati* + *Dei.*

v.   6 *Christus* for τὸ πνεῦμα.

     7 *unum sunt* for εἰς τὸ ἕν εἰσιν.

     9 *test. Dei* + *quod majus est.*

     15 *et scimus* (ℵ*A omit καὶ ἐάν).

Other readings are preserved in some later copies:

ii. 10 *in nobis non est.*

     27 *maneat* : μενέτω.

iii. 6 + *et omnis.*

     16 + *Dei.*

iv.   2 *cognoscitur* : γνώσκεται.

v. 16 *scit* : εἰδῇ.

      ut roget quis : ἵνα ἐρωτήσῃ τις

     17 om. οὐ.

It agrees with ℵ alone in ii. 8 (+ *et in ipso*), and with B 31* in ii. 25 (*vobis*).

Some peculiarities of order may perhaps represent real variations:

i.   9 *fidelis et iustus est.*

ii.   5 *verbum eius.*

iv. 3 *nunc iam in mundo est.*

   12 *vidit umquam.*

   17 *nobiscum caritas.*

In three places '*sicut est*' represents ὥς, καθώς, i. 7 ; iii. 3, 7.

Variations in other passages may be simply due to interpretation:
i. 4 *scripsimus*, ii. 18 *nunc autem, id.* 20 *sed vos*, iii. 19 *suademus*,
iv. 20 *videt* (2).

The peculiarities of interpretation in the following places are
worthy of remark. Many of them are touched upon afterwards:

i.   3 *ut...sit.*

ii. 2 *pro totius mundi* [peccatis].

   16 *conc. carnis est...quæ non est.*

   21 *non...quasi ignorantibus...sed quasi scientibus....*

iii. 1 *ut nominemur et simus.*

   10 *qui non est iustus.*

   14 *translati sumus.*

v.   4 *quæ vincit.*

   15 *quas postulamus.*

   16 *petit.*

   18 *generatio dei* (? ἡ γέννησις τοῦ θεοῦ).

   20 *ut cognoscamus...ut simus.*

But caution is necessary in constructing the Greek text which
the version represents. The same words are not always rendered
in the same way in like contexts. Thus παράγεται is rendered
transierunt in ii. 8 and *transibit* (*transit*) (though both forms may
possibly represent *transiit*) in ii. 17 ; τηρεῖν is rendered in three
consecutive verses by *observare, custodire, servare* (ii. 3, 4, 5); φῶς
is rendered by *lux* (i. 5, 7; ii. 9), and by *lumen* (ii. 7, 10); γινώσκομεν in the same connexion is translated *scimus* (ii. 3, 5, 18; iii. 24),
cognoscimus (iii. 19; iv. 6; v. 2), and *intellegimus* (iv. 13).

II. TITLE.

In *Cod. Vat.* B and *Cod. Alex.* A the title is simply Ἰωάνου (-άννου) ᾱ, *Of John* 1. In *Cod. Sin.* ℵ this is further defined Ἰ. ἐπιστολή ᾱ, *The first Epistle of John;* and in *Cod. Angelicus* L (sæc. IX.) it becomes ἐπιστολὴ καθολικὴ τοῦ ἁγίου ἀποστόλου Ἰ., *The Catholic Epistle of the holy Apostle John;* while *Cod. Porphyr.* P (sæc. IX.) gives Ἰ. τοῦ εὐαγγελιστοῦ καὶ ἀποσ[τόλου ἐπιστολή] ᾱ, *The first Epistle of John the Evangelist and Apostle.*

One heading from a later MS. (f[scr]) is worth quoting: βροντῆς υἱὸς Ἰ. τάδε χριστιανοῖσιν, *John, a son of thunder [saith] these things to Christians.*

The Epistle is commonly spoken of as ἐπιστολὴ καθολική, 'a catholic, general, epistle.' The meaning of the epithet is well given by Œcumenius (sæc. X.). Καθολικαὶ λέγονται αὗται οἱονεὶ ἐγκύκλιοι. Οὐ γὰρ ἀφωρισμένως ἔθνει ἑνὶ ἢ πόλει ὡς ὁ θεῖος Παῦλος, οἷον Ῥωμαίοις ἢ Κορινθίοις, προσφωνεῖ ταύτας τὰς ἐπιστολὰς ὁ τῶν τοιούτων τοῦ κυρίου μαθητῶν θίασος, ἀλλὰ καθόλου τοῖς πιστοῖς, ἤτει Ἰουδαίοις τοῖς ἐν τῇ διασπορᾷ, ὡς καὶ ὁ Πέτρος, ἢ καὶ πᾶσι τοῖς ὑπὸ τὴν αὐτὴν πίστιν Χριστιανοῖς τελοῦσιν (*Præf. ad Comm. in Ep. Jac.*).

The word occurs in this connexion from the close of the second century onwards. Thus Clement of Alexandria (*Strom.* IV. c. 15, § 99, p. 606 P.) speaks of the letter contained in Acts XV. 23 ff. as ἡ ἐπιστολὴ ἡ καθολικὴ τῶν ἀποστόλων ἁπάντων...διακομισθεῖσα εἰς τοὺς πιστούς... Origen uses the epithet of the First Epistle of St Peter (cf. Euseb. *H. E.* VI. 25), 1 John, Jude (in the Latin translation), and of the (apocryphal) letter of Barnabas (*c. Cels.* I. 63). So also the word is used of letters with a general application (though specially addressed) which made no claim to canonical authority (Euseb. *H. E.* IV. 23; comp. V. 18).

In this sense the word was appropriately applied to the letters of James, 1 Peter, 1 John, which formed the centre of the collection of non-Pauline Epistles. It was then extended to 2 Peter and Jude, which are perfectly general in their address ; and so (less accurately) to 2, 3 John, which were taken in close connexion with 1 John.

By a singular error the group of letters was called in the later Western Church 'canonical' (*canonicæ*) in place of 'catholic.' Junilius (c. A. D. 550) had spoken of the letters of James, 2 Peter, Jude, 2, 3 John as added by very many to the collection of Canonical books (quæ apostolorum Canonicæ nuncupantur). Cassiodorus following shortly afterwards adopted the epithet apparently as a peculiar title of the whole group (*de inst. div. Litt.* 8), though he extends it also to the whole collection of apostolic epistles. From him it passed into common use in this limited sense (comp. *Decr. Gelas.* § 6 *vv. ll. Hist. of N. T. Canon*, p. 572).

The title Canonical.

III. FORM.

In catalogues of the Books of the New Testament the writing is always called a 'letter,' but the question arises In what sense can it be so called? It has no address, no subscription ; no name is contained in it of person or place : there is no direct trace of the author, no indication of any special destination. In these respects it is distinguished from the Epistle of St James and from the Epistles to the Ephesians and to the Hebrews, which come nearest to it. The Epistle of St James ends abruptly, but it has a formal salutation. The Epistle to the Ephesians has a salutation, though it is probable that in different copies the names of different churches were inserted, and it has a formal close : the Epistle to the Hebrews has a formal close with several personal details. The writing of St John is destitute of all that is local or special.

The writing has no specific marks of a letter;

But while this is so, the writing is at the same time instinct from first to last with intense personal feeling. The author is not dealing with abstractions but with life and living men. He is bound to them and they to him : the crown of his joy and their joy is the fulness of their faith (i. 4). He appeals to them as

but is full of personal relationship.

one who is acquainted both with their position and with their history (ii. 12 ff.).

He speaks in teaching and in counsel with the directness of personal experience (i. 1 ff.). He has a clear view of the dangers and of the strength of those whom he addresses (ii. 12 ff.; 7, 22, 27; iii. 2, 13 f.; iv. 1, 4 ff.; v. 13, 18 ff.). But all individual relationship and sympathy is seen in the light of a fellowship spiritual and eternal to which it is contributory.

A Pastoral.

Thus perhaps we can best look at the writing not as a Letter called out by any particular circumstances, but as a Pastoral addressed to those who had been carefully trained and had lived long in the Faith; and, more particularly, to those who were familiar either with the teaching contained in the Fourth Gospel or with the record itself. The substance of the Gospel is a commentary on the Epistle: the Epistle is (so to speak) the condensed moral and practical application of the Gospel.

IV. AUTHORSHIP, DATE, PLACE OF WRITING.

The authorship inseparable from that of the Gospel.

The question of the authorship of the Epistle cannot be discussed as an isolated question. The writing is so closely connected with the Fourth Gospel in vocabulary, style, thought, scope, that these two books cannot but be regarded as works of the same author (see § viii)[1]. The proofs which are given elsewhere to establish the fact that the Fourth Gospel was written by the Apostle St John extend to the Epistle also. Every paragraph of the Epistle reveals to the student its underlying dependence upon the record preserved in the Gospel. The teaching which it conveys is in every part the outcome of the life which is quickened by the Evangelist's witness to Christ. It is not that the author of the

---

[1] The arguments which have been alleged to support the opinion that the Books were by different authors, do not seem to me to need serious examination. They could not be urged if the books were not detached from life and criticised without regard to their main characteristics. Huther has examined them in detail. *Einl.* § 3.

Epistle directly uses the materials contained in the Gospel: he has found in them his starting-point and his inspiration, but at once he goes on to deal independently with problems which are before him.

A single illustration will suffice to shew the general relations of the two Books. Let any one compare the Introduction to the Gospel (John i. 1—18) with the Introduction to the Epistle (1 John i. 1—4), and it will be seen how the same mind deals with the same ideas in different connexions. No theory of conscious imitation can reasonably explain the subtle coincidences and differences in these two short crucial passages. And here a close comparison can be fairly made, because the Evangelist writes in this case not as a narrator of the Lord's words, but in his own person [1]. *The connexion between the two one of life not of external dependence.*

It may be added that the writer of the Epistle speaks throughout with the authority of an apostle. He claims naturally and simply an immediate knowledge of the fundamental facts of the Gospel (i. 1; iv. 14), and that special knowledge which was possessed only by the most intimate disciples of the Lord (i. 1 ἐψηλαφή-σαμεν).

But while the two writings are thus closely connected, there is no sufficient evidence to determine the relative dates of the Epistle and of the Gospel as written. The difference in the treatment of common topics and in the use of common language leads to no certain conclusion. Such variations are sufficiently accounted for by the different nature of the two writings; and there is every reason to believe that the Fourth Gospel was shaped by the Apostle in oral teaching long before it was published or committed to writing. It can only be said with confidence that the Epistle presupposes in those for whom it was composed a familiar acquaintance with the characteristic truths which are preserved for us in the Gospel. *The relative dates of the two Books uncertain.*

The conclusion as to the authorship of the Epistle which is obtained from internal evidence is supported by external evidence *External evidence.*

---

[1] Compare also i. 3 f., v. 13 with John xx. 31. See § ix.

as strong as the circumstances allow us to expect. It was used by Papias (Euseb. *H. E.* III. 39), by Polycarp (*ad Phil.* c. 7), and by Irenæus, the disciple of Polycarp (III. 16, 18). It is mentioned in the Muratorian fragment 'as received in the Catholic Church,' according to the more probable rendering, or as 'reckoned among the Catholic Epistles[1].' It was included in the oldest Versions of the East (Syriac) and West (Latin). It was quoted by the earliest fathers of Africa and Alexandria, whose writings have been preserved, Tertullian and Clement; and till recent times was 'universally acknowledged' (Euseb. *H. E.* III. 25; Hieron. *de virr. ill.* 9).

Probably written late and at Ephesus. There is no direct evidence to shew, when and where it was written. The circumstances of the Christian Society point clearly to a late date, and this may be fixed with reasonable likelihood in the last decade of the first century. The later years of St John were spent at Ephesus; and, in the absence of any other indication, it is natural to suppose that it was written there.

The specific form of false teaching which is directly condemned in the Epistle (iv. 3) suggests the same conclusion. Cerinthus, who is known to have maintained it, taught in Asia Minor at the end of the first century, and is placed by tradition in immediate connexion with St John (comp. § vi).

V. DESTINATION.

Addressed to a circle of Asiatic Churches. This being so, it seems to follow that the writing was addressed primarily to the circle of Asiatic Churches, of which Ephesus was the centre. Universal tradition and such direct evidence as there is from Asiatic writings alike confirm this view. Nor is there any evidence against it, for the strange statement which gained currency through Augustine (*Quæst. Evang.* II. 39) that the Epistle was addressed 'to the Parthians' (*epistola ad Parthos*) is obviously a blunder, and is wholly unsupported by any independent authority[2].

[1] Superscripti Johannis duas in catholica (all. catholicis) habentur. Comp. *Hist. of N. T. Canon*, p. 537.

[2] In one Latin MS., referred to by Sabatier, the Epistle is said to bear the title, *Epistola ad Sparthos*. This

VI. CHARACTER.

The exact destination of the Letter is however of no real moment. The colouring is not local but moral; and it offers a vivid picture of a Christian Society which is without parallel in the New Testament. The storm which St Paul foretold in his Pastoral Epistles (2 Tim. iii. 1; iv. 3), and in his address to the Ephesian elders (Acts xx. 29 f.), had broken over the Church. Jerusalem had been destroyed. The visible centre of the Theocracy had been removed. The Church stood out alone as the Body through which the Holy Spirit worked among men. And in correspondence with this change the typical form of trial was altered. Outward dangers were overcome. The world was indeed perilous; but it was rather by its seductions than by its hostility. There is no trace of any recent or impending persecution. Now the main temptations are from within. Perhaps a period of tranquillity gave occasion for internal dissensions as well as for internal development.

The Book answers to a new age of the Church.

Two general characteristics of the Epistle are due to this change in the position of the Church. On the one side the missionary work of the Society no longer occupies a first place in the Apostle's thoughts; and on the other, the topics of debate are changed.

At first sight there is something almost unintelligible in the tone in which St John speaks of 'the world.' He regards it without wonder and without sorrow. For him 'love' is identical with 'love of the brethren.' The difficulty however disappears when his

The world overcome.

has led to the conjecture that it was originally *epistola ad Sparsos* (comp. 1 Pet. i. 1). It is however more probable that the title is a corruption of πρὸς παρθένους. In a fragment of the Latin translation of the *Outlines* of Clement of Alexandria, it is said: *secunda Johannis epistola quæ ad virgines scripta simplicissima est* (p. 1010 P.); and a late cursive MS. (62) has for the subscription of the second Epistle, 'I. β πρὸς Πάρθους. This title may easily have been extended to the first Epistle, and then misinterpreted. So Cassiodorus extends the title *ad Parthos* to the Epistles of St John generally: Epistolæ Petri ad gentes …Johannis ad Parthos (*de instit. div. litt.* XIV.). Bede's statement that 'Athanasius, bishop of Alexandria,' was 'among the many ecclesiastical writers who affirm that it was written to the Parthians' (*Prol. super vii. Canon. Epp.*), cannot be accepted without corroborative evidence.

point of sight is realised.   According to his view, which answers
to the eternal order of things, the world exists indeed, but more as
a semblance than as a reality.   It is overcome finally and for ever.
It is on the point of vanishing.   This outward consummation is in
God's hands.   And over against 'the world' there is the Church,
the organised Christian society, the depository of the Truth and
the witness for the Truth.   By this therefore all that need be done
to proclaim the Gospel to those without is done naturally and
effectively in virtue of its very existence.   It must overcome the
darkness by shining.   There is therefore no need for eager exhortation to spread the word.   St Paul wrote while the conflict was
undecided.   St John has seen its close.

The Jew-
ish con-
troversy
closed.
This paramount office of the Church to witness to and to embody
the Truth, concentrated attention upon the central idea of its message in itself and not in its relation to other systems.   The first
controversies which fill the history of the Acts and St Paul's
Epistles are over.   There is no trace of any conflict between ad-
vocates of the Law and of the Gospel, between champions of works
and faith.   The difference of Jew and Gentile, and the question of
circumcision, have no place in the composition.   The names themselves do not occur (yet see 3 John 7).   There is nothing even to
shew to which body the readers originally belonged, for v. 21 cannot
The main
question
that of the
Person of
Christ.
be confined to a literal interpretation.   The main questions of
debate are gathered round the Person and Work of the Lord.   On
the one side He was represented as a mere man (Ebionism): on
the other side He was represented as a mere phantom (Docetism):
a third party endeavoured to combine these two opinions, and supposed that the divine element, Christ, was united with the man
Jesus at His Baptism and left Him before the Passion (Cerinth-
ianism).

The Epistle gives no evidence that St John had to contend with
Ebionistic error.   The false teaching with which he deals is Docetic
Docetism. and specifically Cerinthian.   In respect of the Docetic heresy generally Jerome's words are striking: apostolis adhuc in sæculo super-
stitibus, adhuc apud Judæam Christi sanguine recenti, phantasma

Domini corpus asserebatur (*Dial. adv. Lucifer.* § 23). Ignatius writes against it in urgent language :

Ad Trall. 9, 10, Κωφώθητε οὖν ὅταν ὑμῖν χωρὶς Ἰησοῦ Χριστοῦ λαλῇ τις, τοῦ ἐκ γένους Δαυίδ, τοῦ ἐκ Μαρίας, ὃς ἀληθῶς ἐγεννήθη, ἔφαγέν τε καὶ ἔπιεν, ἀληθῶς ἐδιώχθη ἐπὶ Ποντίου Πιλάτου, ἀληθῶς ἐσταυρώθη καὶ ἀπέθανεν...ὃς καὶ ἀληθῶς ἠγέρθη ἀπὸ νεκρῶν...Εἰ δέ, ὥσπερ τινὲς ἄθεοι ὄντες...λέγουσιν τὸ δοκεῖν πεπονθέναι αὐτὸν αὐτοὶ τὸ δοκεῖν ὄντες, ἐγὼ τί δέδεμαι ;

Ad Smyrn. 2, ἀληθῶς ἔπαθεν ὡς καὶ ἀληθῶς ἀνέστησεν ἑαυτόν· οὐχ ὥσπερ ἄπιστοί τινες λέγουσιν τὸ δοκεῖν αὐτὸν πεπονθέναι, αὐτοὶ τὸ δοκεῖν ὄντες. Comp. cc. 1, 5, 12.

Ad Ephes. 7, εἷς ἰατρός ἐστιν, σαρκικός τε καὶ πνευματικός, γεννη- τὸς καὶ ἀγέννητος, ἐν σαρκὶ γενόμενος θεός, ἐν θανάτῳ ζωὴ ἀληθινή, καὶ ἐκ Μαρίας καὶ ἐκ θεοῦ πρῶτον παθητὸς καὶ τότε ἀπαθής. Comp. c. 18.

So also Polycarp :

Ad Phil. c. 7, πᾶς γὰρ ὃς ἂν μὴ ὁμολογῇ Ἰησοῦν Χριστὸν ἐν σαρκὶ ἐληλυθέναι ἀντίχριστός ἐστι· καὶ ὃς ἂν μὴ ὁμολογῇ τὸ μαρτύριον τοῦ σταυροῦ ἐκ τοῦ διαβόλου ἐστί[1].

Irenæus characterises in particular the opinions of Cerinthus very clearly : [Cerinthus] Jesum subjicit non ex Virgine natum, impossibile enim hoc ei visum est; fuisse autem eum Joseph et Mariæ filium...et plus potuisse justitia et prudentia et sapientia præ omnibus, et post baptismum descendisse in eum Christum ab ea principalitate quæ est super omnia...in fine autem revolasse iterum Christum de Jesu, et Jesum passum esse et resurrexisse : Christum autem impassibilem perseverasse existentem spiritalem[2]. *Cerin- thianism.*

In the presence of these false views St John unfolds the Truth, *Against this false*

[1] The so-called 'Gospel according to Peter' is said to have favoured their views (Serapion, ap. Euseb. *H. E.* VI. 12).
[2] Iren. *adv. hær.* I. 26. I. Comp. Epiph. *Hær.* XXVIII. I. For the story of St John's refusal to be under the same roof with Cerinthus, see Iren. ap. Euseb. *H. E.* IV. 14 (Iren. *adv. hær.* III. 3. 4, on the authority of Polycarp). It is strange that either St John or Cerinthus should have visited the baths at Ephesus. This difficulty however was not felt by Irenæus. The Christology of Nes- torianism pressed to its logical con- sequences is not distinguishable, as it appears, from that of Cerinthus. The more extreme Docetæ regarded the manifestation of the Lord as being in appearance only (φαντασίᾳ), like the Theophanies in the Old Testament.

teaching
St John
proclaims
again the
Gospel

not in the form of argument but of announcement. He declares
that Jesus Christ has come (iv. 2), and is coming (2 Ep. 7) in the
flesh (comp. v. 6). He shews that the denial of the Incarnate Son
is practically the denial of the Father, the denial of God (ii. 22;
v. 20). It is the rejection of that power by which alone true life
is possible through a divine fellowship (i. 2 f.).

as the old
Truth.

But in insisting on these truths St John disclaims all appearance of bringing forward new points. His readers know implicitly
all that he can tell them. He simply pleads that they should yield
themselves to the guidance of the Spirit which they had received.
So they would realise what in fact they already possessed (ii. 7, 24;
iii. 11). Perhaps it may be inferred from the stress which St John
lays on the identity of the original word with the teaching which
he represented, that some had ventured to charge him also with
innovation. Such an accusation would have superficial plausibility;
and the Epistle deals with it conclusively either by anticipation or
in view of actual opponents.

The letter
specially
applicable
at present
from its
circum-
stances,
and

Thus this latest of the Epistles is a voice from the midst of the
Christian Church revealed at last in its independence. Many who
read it had, in all probability, grown up as Christians. A Christianity
of habit was now possible. The spiritual circumstances of those to
whom it was first sent are like our own. The words need no accom-
modation to make them bear directly upon ourselves.

from its
teaching.

And while the Christological errors which St John meets exist
more or less at all times, they seem to have gained a dangerous
prevalence now. Modern realism, which has found an ally in art,
by striving to give distinctness to the actual outward features of
the Lord's Life, seems to tend more and more to an Ebionitic Christology. Modern idealism, on the other hand, which aims at securing
the pure spiritual conception free from all associations of time and
place, is a new Docetism. Nor would it be hard to shew that
popular Christology is largely though unconsciously affected by
Cerinthian tendencies. The separation of Jesus, the Son of Man,
from Christ, the Son of God, is constantly made to the destruction
of the One, indivisible Person of our Lord and Saviour. We have

indeed no power to follow such revelations of Scripture into supposed consequences, but our strength is to hold with absolute firm-
ness the apostolic words as St John has delivered them to us.

The teaching of St John in his Epistle thus turns upon the
Person of Christ. Under this aspect it is important to observe that
it is intensely practical. St John everywhere presents moral ideas
resting upon facts and realised in life. The foundation on which
conviction is based is historical experience (i. 1 ff.; iv. 14). This,
as furnishing the materials for that knowledge which St John's
readers had 'heard from the beginning,' is set over against mere
speculation (ii. 24). Truth is never stated in a speculative form, but
as a motive and a help for action. The writer does not set before
his readers propositions about Christ, but the Living Christ Himself for present fellowship. And yet while this is so, the Epistle
contains scarcely anything in detail of Christ's Life. He came in
the flesh, 'by water and blood;' the Life was manifested; He
walked as we are bound to walk. He laid down His Life for us;
He is to be manifested yet again; this is all. There is no mention
of the Cross or of the Resurrection. But Christ having died lives
as our Advocate. (Compare Addit. Note on v. 6.)

The facts of the Gospel the basis and motive for action.

The apprehension of the historical manifestation of the Life of
Christ is thus pressed as the prevailing and sufficient motive for
godlike conduct; and at the same time mere right opinion, apart
from conduct, is exposed in its nothingness. Simply to say, 'we
have fellowship with God,' 'we are in the light,' we 'know God,'
is shewn to be delusion if the corresponding action is wanting
(i. 6, ii. 9, 4).

Intellec- tual assent in itself insuf- ficient.

The Epistle, as has been already said, comes from the midst of
the Christian Church to the members of the Church. It is the
voice of an unquestioned teacher to disciples who are assumed to be
anxious to fulfil their calling. In virtue of the circumstances of
its composition it takes the widest range in the survey of the Gospel,
and completes and harmonises the earlier forms of apostolic teaching.
St John's doctrine of 'love' reconciles the complementary doctrines
of 'faith' and 'works.' His view of the primal revelation 'that

Wide range of the Epi- stle.

which was from the beginning…concerning the word of life,' places Judaism in its true position as part of the discipline of the world, and vindicates for Christianity its claim to universality. His doctrine of 'Jesus Christ come in flesh' affirms at once the historical and the transcendental aspects of His Person. His exhibition of a present divine fellowship for man, issuing in a future transfiguration of man to the divine likeness, offers a view of life able to meet human weakness and human aspiration.

Silence as to Old Testament and ecclesiastical organisation. Two other peculiarities of the Epistle seem to be due to the same causes which determined this catholicity of teaching. Alone of all the writings of the New Testament except the two shorter letters and the Epistle to Philemon, it contains no quotations or clear reminiscences of the language of the Old Testament (yet see iii. 12). And again, while the Christian Society is everywhere contemplated in its definite spiritual completeness, nothing is said on any detail of ritual or organisation.

VII. OBJECT.

The object of the Epistle (as of the Gospel) positive. The object of the Epistle corresponds with its character. It is presented under a twofold form:

(i) i. 3, f. ὃ ἑωράκαμεν καὶ ἀκηκόαμεν ἀπαγγέλλομεν καὶ ὑμῖν, ἵνα καὶ ὑμεῖς κοινωνίαν ἔχητε μεθ᾽ ἡμῶν, καὶ ἡ κοινωνία δὲ ἡ ἡμετέρα μετὰ τοῦ πατρὸς καὶ μετὰ τοῦ υἱοῦ αὐτοῦ Ἰησοῦ Χριστοῦ· καὶ ταῦτα γράφομεν ἡμεῖς ἵνα ἡ χαρὰ ἡμῶν (v. ὑμῶν) ᾖ πεπληρωμένη.

That which we have seen and heard declare we unto you also, that ye also may have fellowship with us: yea, and our fellowship is with the Father, and with his Son Jesus Christ: and these things we write, that our joy may be fulfilled.

(ii) v. 13 ταῦτα ἔγραψα ὑμῖν ἵνα εἰδῆτε ὅτι ζωὴν ἔχετε αἰώνιον, τοῖς πιστεύουσιν εἰς τὸ ὄνομα τοῦ υἱοῦ τοῦ θεοῦ.

These things have I written unto you, that ye may know that ye have eternal life, even unto you that believe on the name of the Son of God.

With these must be compared the account given of the object of the Gospel :

(iii) John xx. 31 ταῦτα δὲ γέγραπται ἵνα πιστεύσητε ὅτι Ἰησοῦς ἐστὶν ὁ Χριστὸς ὁ υἱὸς τοῦ θεοῦ, καὶ ἵνα πιστεύοντες ζωὴν ἔχητε ἐν τῷ ὀνόματι αὐτοῦ.

But these are written, that ye may believe that Jesus is the Christ, the Son of God; and that believing ye may have life in his name.

There is a complete harmony between the three. The acceptance of the revelation of Jesus—the Son of man—as the Christ, the Son of God (iii), brings the power of life (ii), and this life is fellowship with man and with God in Christ (i). Life, in other words, life eternal, is in Christ Jesus, and is realised in all its extent in union with Him: it is death to be apart from Him.

The pursuit of such a theme necessarily involves the condemnation and refutation of corresponding errors. But St John's method is to confute the error by the exposition of the truth realised in life. His object is polemical only so far as the clear unfolding of the essence of right teaching necessarily shews all error in its real character. In other words St John writes to call out a welcome for what he knows to be the Gospel and not to overthrow this or that false opinion.

VIII. STYLE AND LANGUAGE.

The style of the Epistle bears a close resemblance to that of the Gospel both in vocabulary and structure. There is in both the same emphatic repetition of fundamental words and phrases,—'truth,' 'love,' 'light,' 'in the light,' 'being born of God,' 'being' or 'abiding in God'—and the same monotonous simplicity of construction. *General resemblance to the Gospel.*

The particles are singularly few. For example γάρ occurs only three times : ii. 19; iv. 20; v. 3 (2 John 11; 3 John 3, 7); δέ nine times (about one-third of its average frequency); μέν τε and οὖν (3 John 8) do not occur at all (the last is twice wrongly in common *Scantiness of particles.*

---

text). The absence of οὖν is the more remarkable because it is the characteristic particle of the narrative of the Gospel, where St John seems to dwell on the connexion of facts which might be overlooked; ὅτι, 'that' and 'because,' is very frequent; and it is constantly found where γάρ might have been expected.

The common particle of connexion is καί. This conjunction takes its peculiar colour from the sentences which are thus added one to the other: e.g. i. 5; ii. 3; and it is used not uncommonly when a particle of logical sequence might have been expected: e.g. iii. 3, 16.

Very frequently the sentences and clauses follow one another without any particles: e.g. ii. 22—24; iv. 4—6; 7—10; 11—13. See also ii. 5, 6; 9, 10; iii. 2; 4, 5; 9, 10.

Sometimes they are brought into an impressive parallelism by the repetition of a clause:

i. 6, 8, 10 (ἐὰν εἴπωμεν).

v. 18—20 (οἴδαμεν).

St John develops an idea by parallelism. These different usages are different adaptations of St John's characteristic principle of composition: he explains and develops his ideas by parallelism or (which answers to the same tone of thought) by antagonism.

It is not of course maintained that this method of writing is the result of studied choice. It is, as far as we may presume to judge, the spontaneous expression of the Apostle's vision of the Truth, opening out in its fulness before the eye of the believer, complete in its own majesty, requiring to be described and not to be drawn out by processes of reasoning.

In this respect and generally it will be felt that the writing is thoroughly Hebraistic in tone, and yet it does not contain one quotation or verbal reminiscence from the Old Testament.

Characteristic words. Of significant verbal coincidences of language between the Epistles and Gospel the following may be noticed. The words are either exceptionally frequent in these writings or peculiar to them:

κόσμος (moral) (John i. 10 note).

φῶς (1 John i. 5 note).

σκοτία (σκότος) (i. 6 note).

φανεροῦν (i. 2 note).

φαίνειν (ii. 8 note).

ἑωρακέναι (i. 1 note).

θεᾶσθαι (θεωρεῖν only once in the Epistles: 1 John iii. 17 (John i. 14 note).

θάνατος (spiritual) (iii. 14 note).

ζωὴ αἰώνιος (ἡ αἰώνιος ζ., ἡ ζ. ἡ αἰ.) (Add. note on v. 20).

ἡ ἀλήθεια (i. 6 note).

ὁ ἀληθινὸς θεός (v. 20 note).

τὸ πνεῦμα τῆς ἀληθείας (iv. 6 note).

μαρτυρεῖν, μαρτυρία (i. 2 note).

τεκνία (ii. 1 note).

παιδία (ii. 14 note).

ὁ μονογενὴς υἱός (Add. note on iv. 9).

ἀγαπᾶν ἀλλήλους, τὸν ἀδελφόν, τοὺς ἀδ. (iii. 11 note).

νικᾶν (ii. 13 note).

μένειν, εἶναι, ἔν τινι (ii. 5 note).

τὴν ψυχὴν τιθέναι (iii. 16 note).

The frequent use of ἵνα when the idea of purpose is not directly obvious; and the elliptical use of ἀλλ' ἵνα, are both characteristic of these books (iii. 11; ii. 19 notes).

In addition to these verbal coincidences there are also larger coincidences of expression. Of these the most important are the following :

Verbal coincidences with the Gospel.

1 EPISTLE OF ST JOHN.	GOSPEL OF ST JOHN.
i. 2, 3 ἡ ζωὴ ἐφανερώθη καὶ ἑωράκαμεν καὶ μαρτυροῦμεν...ὃ ἑωράκαμεν καὶ ἀκηκόαμεν ἀπαγγέλλομεν καὶ ὑμῖν.	iii. 11 ὃ ἑωράκαμεν μαρτυροῦμεν.
id. 4 ταῦτα γράφομεν ἡμεῖς ἵνα ἡ χαρὰ ὑμῶν ᾖ πεπληρωμένη.	xvi. 24 αἰτεῖτε καὶ λήμψεσθε ἵνα ἡ χαρὰ ὑμῶν ᾖ πεπληρωμένη.

w.

d

I Epistle of St John.	Gospel of St John.
ii. 11 ὁ μισῶν τὸν ἀδελφὸν αὐτοῦ ...ἐν τῇ σκοτίᾳ περιπατεῖ καὶ οὐκ οἶδεν ποῦ ὑπάγει.	xii. 35... ὁ περιπατῶν ἐν τῇ σκοτίᾳ οὐκ οἶδεν ποῦ ὑπάγει.
id. 14 ὁ λόγος τοῦ θεοῦ ἐν ὑμῖν μένει.	v. 38 τὸν λόγον αὐτοῦ οὐκ ἔχετε μένοντα ἐν ὑμῖν.
id. 17 ὁ ποιῶν τὸ θέλημα τοῦ θεοῦ μένει εἰς τὸν αἰῶνα.	viii. 35 ὁ υἱὸς μένει εἰς τὸν αἰῶνα.
iii. 5 ἁμαρτία ἐν αὐτῷ οὐκ ἔστιν.	viii. 46 τίς ἐξ ὑμῶν ἐλέγχει με περὶ ἁμαρτίας;
id. 8 ἀπ᾽ ἀρχῆς ὁ διάβολος ἁμαρτάνει.	viii. 44 ἐκεῖνος [ὁ διάβολος] ἀνθρωποκτόνος ἦν ἀπ᾽ ἀρχῆς.
id. 13 μὴ θαυμάζετε, ἀδελφοί, εἰ μισεῖ ὑμᾶς ὁ κόσμος.	xv. 18 εἰ ὁ κόσμος ὑμᾶς μισεῖ γινώσκετε ὅτι ἐμὲ πρῶτον ὑμῶν μεμίσηκεν.
id. 14 οἴδαμεν ὅτι μεταβεβήκαμεν ἐκ τοῦ θανάτου εἰς τὴν ζωὴν ὅτι ἀγαπῶμεν τοὺς ἀδελφούς.	v. 24 ὁ τὸν λόγον μου ἀκούων... μεταβέβηκεν ἐκ τοῦ θανάτου εἰς τὴν ζωήν.
id. 16 ἐκεῖνος ὑπὲρ ἡμῶν τὴν ψυχὴν αὐτοῦ ἔθηκεν.	x. 15 τὴν ψυχήν μου τίθημι ὑπὲρ τῶν προβάτων.
id. 22 ὃ ἂν αἰτῶμεν λαμβάνομεν ...ὅτι...τὰ ἀρεστὰ ἐνώπιον αὐτοῦ ποιοῦμεν.	viii. 29 οὐκ ἀφῆκέν με μόνον ὅτι ἐγὼ τὰ ἀρεστὰ αὐτῷ ποιῶ πάντοτε.
id. 23 αὕτη ἐστὶν ἡ ἐντολὴ αὐτοῦ ἵνα...ἀγαπῶμεν ἀλλήλους καθὼς ἔδωκεν ἐντολὴν ἡμῖν. Comp. iv. 11.	xiii. 34 ἐντολὴν καινὴν δίδωμι ὑμῖν ἵνα ἀγαπᾶτε ἀλλήλους καθὼς ἠγάπησα ὑμᾶς ἵνα...
iv. 6 ἡμεῖς ἐκ τοῦ θεοῦ ἐσμέν· ὁ γινώσκων τὸν θεὸν ἀκούει ἡμῶν, ὃς οὐκ ἔστιν ἐκ τοῦ θεοῦ (a) οὐκ ἀκούει ἡμῶν. (b)	viii. 47 ὁ ὢν ἐκ τοῦ θεοῦ τὰ ῥήματα τοῦ θεοῦ ἀκούει· ὑμεῖς οὐκ ἀκούετε (b) ὅτι ἐκ τοῦ θεοῦ οὐκ ἐστέ (a)

1 EPISTLE OF ST JOHN.

iv. 15 ὃς ἐὰν ὁμολογήσῃ ὅτι
Ἰησοῦς [Χριστός] ἐστιν ὁ υἱὸς τοῦ
θεοῦ,
ὁ θεὸς ἐν αὐτῷ μένει καὶ αὐτὸς ἐν
τῷ θεῷ. Comp. v. 16; iii. 24.

id. 16 ἐγνώκαμεν καὶ πεπιστεύκαμεν.

id. 16
ὁ μένων ἐν τῇ ἀγάπῃ ἐν τῷ θεῷ
μένει.

v. 4, f. αὕτη ἐστὶν ἡ νίκη
ἡ νικήσασα τὸν κόσμον, ἡ πίστις
ἡμῶν.
τίς ἐστιν ὁ νικῶν τὸν κόσμον...

id. 9 ἡ μαρτυρία τοῦ θεοῦ μείζων
ἐστίν, ὅτι αὕτη ἐστὶν ἡ μαρτυρία
τοῦ θεοῦ, ὅτι μεμαρτύρηκεν περὶ
τοῦ υἱοῦ αὐτοῦ.

id. 20 δέδωκεν ἡμῖν διάνοιαν
ἵνα γιγνώσκομεν τὸν ἀληθινόν·
καί ἐσμεν ἐν τῷ ἀληθινῷ, ἐν τῷ υἱῷ
αὐτοῦ [Ἰησοῦ Χριστῷ]. οὗτός ἐστιν ὁ ἀληθινὸς θεός, καὶ ζωὴ αἰώνιος.

GOSPEL OF ST JOHN.

vi. 56 ὁ τρώγων μου τὴν σάρκα
καὶ πίνων μου τὸ αἷμα

ἐν ἐμοὶ μένει κἀγὼ ἐν αὐτῷ. Comp.
xiv. 17.

vi. 69 πεπιστεύκαμεν καὶ
ἐγνώκαμεν.

xv. 10 ἐὰν τὰς ἐντολάς μου τηρή-
σητε
μενεῖτε ἐν τῇ ἀγάπῃ μου. Comp.
v. 9 μείνατε ἐν τῇ ἀ. τῇ ἐμῇ.

xvi. 33 θαρσεῖτε
ἐγὼ νενίκηκα τὸν κόσμον.

v. 32 ἄλλος ἐστὶν ὁ μαρτυρῶν
περὶ ἐμοῦ καὶ οἶδα ὅτι ἀληθής ἐστιν
ἡ μαρτυρία ἣν μαρτυρεῖ περὶ ἐμοῦ.

xvii. 3 αὕτη ἐστὶν ἡ αἰώνιος
ζωὴ
ἵνα γινώσκωσι σὲ τὸν μόνον
ἀληθινὸν θεὸν καὶ ὃν ἀπέστειλας
Ἰησοῦν Χριστόν.

IX. THE EPISTLES AND THE GOSPEL.

The last two passages (1 John v. 20; John xvii. 3), which
have been quoted, illustrate vividly the relation between the
Epistles and the Gospel. Both passages contain the same fundamental ideas: Eternal life is the progressive recognition (ἵνα γινώσκωσι) of God; and the power of this growing knowledge is given
in His Son Jesus Christ. But the ideas are presented differently

General
relation
of the
Epistles
to the
Gospel.

d 2

in the two places. The Gospel gives the historic revelation; the Epistle shews the revelation as it has been apprehended in the life of the Society and of the believer.

The two complementary.

This fundamental difference can be presented in another form. In the Epistle the aim of St John is to lay open what is the significance of the spiritual truths of the Faith for present human life. In the Gospel his aim is to make clear that the true human life of the Lord is a manifestation of divine love, that 'Jesus is the Christ, the Son of God.' Or, to put the contrast in an epigrammatic form, the theme of the Epistle is, 'the Christ is Jesus'; the theme of the Gospel is, 'Jesus is the Christ.' In the former the writer starts from certain acknowledged spiritual conceptions and points out that they have their foundation in history and their necessary embodiment in conduct. In the latter he shews how the works and words of Jesus of Nazareth establish that in Him the hope of Israel and the hope of humanity was fulfilled. So it is that the Gospel is a continuous record of the unfolding of the 'glory' of Christ. In the Epistles alone of all the books of the New Testament (except the Epistle to Philemon), the word 'glory' does not occur. Perhaps too it is significant that the word 'heaven' also is absent from them.

The differences answer to differences between a History and a Pastoral.

Several differences in detail in the topics or form of teaching in the books have been already noticed. These belong to the differences in the positions occupied by a historian and a preacher. The teaching of the Lord which St John has preserved was given, as He Himself said, 'in proverbs'; through the experience of Christian life, the Spirit, 'sent in His Name,' enabled the Apostle to speak 'plainly' (John xvi. 25).

The Coming (παρουσία).

Some other differences still require to be noticed. These also spring from the historical circumstances of the writing. The first regards the doctrine of 'the Coming,' 'the Presence' (ἡ παρουσία) of Christ. In the Gospel St John does not record the eschatological discourses of the Lord—they had found their first fulfilment when he wrote—and he preserves simply the general promise of a 'Coming' (xiv. 3; xxi. 22). By the side of these he records the references to the 'judgment' (v. 28 f.), and to 'the last day' (vi. 40, 44). In the Epistle he uses the term 'the Presence' (ii. 28), which is found in all the groups of New Testament writings, and speaks of a future 'manifestation' of the Ascended Christ (*l. c.*: iii. 2). As He 'came in flesh' (iv. 2), so He is still 'coming in flesh' (2 John 7). And the importance of this fact is pressed in its spiritual bearing. By denying it 'Antichrists' displayed their real nature. They sought to substitute a doctrine for a living Saviour.

St John's treatment of the present work of Christ stands in close connexion with this view of His future work. As the Holy Spirit is sent to believers as their Advocate on earth, so He is their Advocate with the Father in heaven (c. ii. 2). The two thoughts are complementary; and the heavenly advocacy of Christ rests upon His own promise in the Gospel (John xiv. 13 f.), though it must not be interpreted as excluding the Father's spontaneous love (John xvi. 26 f.). *The Advocacy of Christ.*

The exposition of the doctrine of 'propitiation' and 'cleansing' which is found in the Epistle (c. ii. 2; iv. 10 ἱλασμός; i. 7, 9 καθαρίζειν) is an application of the discourse at Capernaum (see especially John vi. 51, 56 f.); and it is specially remarkable that while the thoughts of the discourse are used, nothing is taken from the language. So again the peculiar description of the spiritual endowment of believers as an 'unction' (χρίσμα, c. ii. 20) perfectly embodies the words in John xx. 21 ff.; the disciples are in a true sense 'Christs' in virtue of the Life of 'the Christ' (John xiv. 19; comp. Apoc. i. 6). Once more, the cardinal phrase 'born of God' (c. ii. 29, &c.), which occurs in the introduction to the Gospel (i. 13), but not in the record of the Lord's words, shews in another example how the original language of the Lord was shaped under the guidance of the Spirit to fullest use. *The doctrine of Propitiation.*

It seems scarcely necessary to remark that such differences between the Epistles and the Gospel are not only not indicative of any difference of authorship, but on the contrary furnish a strong proof that they are the products of one mind. The Epistles give later *These differences shew the working of life.*

growths of common and characteristic ideas. No imitator of the
Gospel could have combined elements of likeness and unlikeness in
such a manner; and on the other hand, the substance of the Gospel
adequately explains the more defined teaching of the first Epistle.
The one writing stands to the other in an intelligible connexion of
life.

X. PLAN.

No plan can be complete.

It is extremely difficult to determine with certainty the structure
of the Epistle. No single arrangement is able to take account of
the complex development of thought which it offers, and of the
many connexions which exist between its different parts. The
following arrangement, which is followed out into detail in the
notes, seems to me to give on the whole the truest and clearest view
of the sequence of the exposition.

Outline followed.

INTRODUCTION.

The facts of the Gospel issuing in fellowship and joy (i. 1—4).

A. THE PROBLEM OF LIFE AND THOSE TO WHOM IT IS PRO-
POSED (i. 5—ii. 17).

I.   The Nature of God and the consequent relation of
man to God (i. 5—10).

II.   The remedy for Sin and the sign that it is effectual
(ii. 1—6).

III.   Obedience in love and light in actual life (ii.
7—11).

IV.   Things temporal and eternal (ii. 12—17).

B. THE CONFLICT OF TRUTH AND FALSEHOOD WITHOUT AND
WITHIN (ii. 18—iv. 6).

I.   The revelation of Falsehood and Truth (ii. 18—29).

II.   The children of God and the children of the Devil
(iii. 1—12).

III.   Brotherhood in Christ and the hatred of the world
(iii. 13—24).

IV.   The rival spirits of Truth and Error (iv. 1—6).

C. The christian life: the victory of faith (iv. 7—v. 21).

    I. The spirit of the Christian life: God and Love (iv. 7—21).

    II. The power of the Christian life: the Victory and Witness of Faith (v. 1—12).

    III. The activity and confidence of the Christian life: Epilogue (v. 13—21).

The thought of a fellowship between God and man, made possible *The main thought.* and in part realised in the Christian Church, runs through the whole Epistle. From this it begins: *Our fellowship is with the Father, and with His Son, Jesus Christ* (i. 3). In this it closes: *We are in Him that is True, in His Son Jesus Christ* (v. 20).

In the additional Notes I have endeavoured to illustrate the *Systematic illustration of its development.* main points in the development of this thought. These notes when taken in proper order will serve as an introduction to the study of the doctrine of St John. For this purpose they are most conveniently grouped in the following manner:

    I. The doctrine of God.

        The idea of God: note on iv. 8; comp. iv. 12.

        The Divine Name: 3 John 7.

        The Holy Trinity: v. 20.

        The Divine Fatherhood: i. 2.

    II. The doctrine of Finite Being.

        Creation: note on ii. 17.

        God and man: ii. 9.

        The nature of man: iii. 19.

        The Devil: ii. 13.

        Sin: i. 9; comp. v. 16.

        The world (note on Gospel of St John i. 10).

        Antichrist: ii. 18.

    III. The doctrine of Redemption and Consummation.

        The Incarnation: note on iii. 5.

        The titles of Christ: iii. 23; comp. iv. 9; v. 1.

        Propitiation: ii. 2.

The virtue of Christ's Blood : i. 7.

Divine Sonship : iii. 1.

Divine Fellowship : iv. 15.

The titles of believers : iii. 14.

Eternal Life : v. 20.

For St John's view of the Bases of Belief I may be allowed to refer to what I have said in regard to his teaching on 'the Truth,' 'the Light,' 'the Witness' in the Introduction to the Gospel, pp. xliv. ff.

INTRODUCTION

TO

THE SECOND AND THIRD EPISTLES.

I. TEXT.

The authorities for the text of the Epistles are enumerated in the Introduction to the first Epistle, § 1 (including the MSS. אAB(C)KLP). The text of *Cod. Ephr.* (C) is preserved for the third Epistle from *v.* 3—end.

The variations from the text of Stephens (1550) which I have adopted are set down in the following table:

THE SECOND EPISTLE.

3 om. Κυρίου, 'Jesus Christ' (AB), for '*the Lord* Jesus Christ.'

5 γράφων for γράφω (apparently an error).

6 αὕτη ἡ ἐντολή ἐστιν (AB), for αὕτη ἐστὶν ἡ ἐντολή.

7 ἐξῆλθαν, *are gone forth* (אAB), for εἰσῆλθον, *are entered*.

8 ἀπολέσητε, *ye lose* (אᶜAB), for ἀπολέσωμεν, *we lose*.
ἀπολάβητε, *ye receive* (אAB), for ἀπολάβωμεν, *we receive*.

9 προάγων, *goeth onward* (אAB), for παραβαίνων, *transgresseth*.
om. τοῦ χριστοῦ (2°), 'the teaching' (אAB), for 'the teaching *of the Christ*.'

11 ὁ λέγων γάρ (אAB) for ὁ γὰρ λέγων.

12 γενέσθαι (אAB) for ἐλθεῖν.
ὑμῶν (probably) (AB) for ἡμῶν.
πεπληρωμένη ᾖ (אB) for ᾖ πεπληρωμένη.

13 om. Ἀμήν (אAB).

THE THIRD EPISTLE.

4 χάριν (probably), *favour* (B), for χαράν, *joy*.
ἐν + τῇ ἀληθείᾳ (ABC*), 'in *the* truth,' for 'in truth.'

5 τοῦτο, *this* (אABC), for εἰς τούς, *to the*.

7 ἐθνικῶν (אABC) for ἐθνῶν.

8 ὑπολαμβάνειν (אABC*), *to welcome*, for ἀπολαμβάνειν, *to receive*.

9 ἔγραψά + τι′ (א*ABC), 'I wrote *somewhat*,' for 'I wrote.'

11 om. δέ, *but* (אABC).

12 οἶδας, *thou knowest* (אABC), for οἴδατε, *ye know*.

13 γράψαι σοι for γράφειν (אABC).

γράφειν for γράψαι (אABC).

14 σὲ ἰδεῖν for ἰδεῖν σε (ABC).

The text of B. The text of B maintains the first place as before. It has only one error in 2 John, the omission of τοῦ before πατρός in *v.* 4; and one error in 3 John, ἔγραψας for ἔγραψα in *v.* 9, in addition to two faults of writing, μαρτυρουν for μαρτυρούντων, *v.* 3 (at the end of a line), and ου for οὕς, *v.* 6.

The text of א.
2 John. The text of א has numerous errors and false readings:

THE SECOND EPISTLE.

3 ἀπὸ θεοῦ ..καὶ Ἰ. Χ. א*.

+ αὐτοῦ′ τοῦ πατρός, א* corr. אᶜ.

4 ἔλαβον.

5 ἀλλ’ + ἐντολὴν′ ἦν.

6 ἡ ἐντολὴ + αὐτοῦ′.

περιπατήσητε.

7 om. ὁ′ ἀντίχριστος.

8 ἀπόλησθε א* corr. אᶜ.

12 ἔχω א* Α*.

στόμα + τι′ א*.

3 John. THE THIRD EPISTLE.

8 ἐκκλησίᾳ for ἀληθείᾳ א* (so A).

10 om. ἐκ.

15 ἄσπασαι.

The text of A. There are, as in the first Epistle, many peculiar readings in A, some found also in the Latin Vulgate:

2 John. THE SECOND EPISTLE.

1 οὐκ ἐγὼ δέ.

2 ἐνοικοῦσαν for μένουσαν.

3 om. ἔσται μεθ’ ὑμῶν.

4 ἀπό for παρά.

9 τὸν υἱὸν καὶ τὸν πατέρα vg.

12 γράψαι.

ἐλπίζω γάρ vg.

THE THIRD EPISTLE.   3 JOHN.

3 om. σύ.

5 ἐργάζῃ.

8 ἐκκλησίᾳ (so ℵ*).

10 ἄν.

13 οὐκ ἐβουλήθην.

(15 οἱ ἀδελφοί).

There is also an unusual number of peculiar readings in the part of the third Epistle preserved in C : The text of C. 3 JOHN.

4 τούτων χαρὰν οὐκ ἔχω.

6 ποιήσας προπέμψεις.

7 ἐθνικῶν om. τῶν.

10 φλυαρῶν εἰς ἡμᾶς.

(ἐπιδεχομένους).

12 ὑπὸ αὐτῆς τῆς ἐκκλησίας καὶ τῆς ἀληθείας.

The readings of the Latin Vulgate do not offer anything of special interest : The text of the Latin Vulgate. 2 JOHN.

THE SECOND EPISTLE.

3 *Sit* nobiscum (vobiscum) gratia.

a Christo Jesu.

THE THIRD EPISTLE.   3 JOHN.

4 majorem horum non habeo gratiam.

5 et hoc *in*.

9 *scripsissem forsitan*.

Some Latin copies have a singular addition after 2 John 11 : *ecce prodixi vobis ne in diem domini condemnemini.*

II.   AUTHORSHIP.

The second and third Epistles of St John are reckoned by Eusebius among 'the controverted books' in the same rank as the These Epistles reckoned

<table>
<tr><td>among
'the con-
troverted
Books.'</td><td>Epistles of St James, St Jude and 2 Peter[1], 'as well known and recognised by most.' He does not give the authority or the exact ground of the doubt, but states the question generally as being 'whether they belong to the Evangelist, or possibly to another of the same name[2].'</td></tr>
<tr><td>External
evidence.</td><td>The Epistles are not contained in the Peshito Syriac Version, nor are they accepted by the Syrian Church. Origen was aware that 'all did not allow them to be genuine[3].' There is however no other ante-Nicene evidence against their authenticity. They are noticed as 'received in the Catholic Church' in the Muratorian Canon. This at least appears to be the most probable explanation of the clause. Comp. Hist. of N. T. Canon, p. 537. They were included in the Old Latin Version. Clement of Alexandria wrote short notes upon them[4]. Irenæus quotes the second Epistle as St John's, and once quotes a phrase from it as from the first Epistle[5]. There are no quotations from either of the Epistles in Origen, Tertullian, or Cyprian, but Dionysius of Alexandria clearly recognises them as the works of St John; and Aurelius, an African Bishop, quoted the second Epistle as 'St John's Epistle' at a Council where Cyprian was present.</td></tr>
<tr><td>The title
'the El-
der' likely
to create
confusion.</td><td>It is not difficult to explain the doubt as to their authorship, which was felt by some. They probably had a very limited circulation from their personal (or narrow) destination. When they were carried abroad under the name of John, the title of 'the elder' was not unlikely to mislead the readers. Papias had spoken of 'an elder John'; and so it was natural to suppose that the John who so styled himself in the Epistles was the one to whom Papias referred, and not the Apostle. Eusebius may refer to this conjecture, though it does not appear distinctly before the time of</td></tr>
</table>

[1] H. E. III. 25 τῶν δὲ ἀντιλεγομένων γνωρίμων δ' οὖν ὅμως τοῖς πολλοῖς.

[2] l. c. εἴτε τοῦ εὐαγγελιστοῦ τυγχάνουσαι εἴτε καὶ ἑτέρου ὁμωνύμου ἐκείνῳ. He argued from them himself as being written by St John: Demonstr. Ev. III. 5.

[3] In Joh. Tom. v. ap. Euseb. H. E. VI. 23.

[4] Euseb. H. E. VI. 14. Cf. Strom. II. 15.

[5] Adv. hær. III. 16. 8, in prædicta Epistola, having quoted in § 5, 1 John ii. 18 ff. Comp. I. 16. 3 Ἰωάννης ὁ τοῦ κυρίου μαθητής.

Jerome[1]. But this view of the authorship of the Epistles is purely conjectural. There is not the least direct evidence external or internal in its favour; and it is most unlikely that 'the elder John' would be in such a position as to be described by the simple title 'the elder,' which denotes a unique preëminence.

On the other hand, there is nothing in the use of the title ὁ πρεσβύτερος, 'the elder,' by the writer of the Epistles inconsistent with the belief that he was the Apostle St John. For too little is known of the condition of the Churches of Asia Minor at the close of the apostolic age to allow any certain conclusion to be formed as to the sense in which he may have so styled himself. The term was used by Irenæus of those who held the highest office in the Church, perhaps through Asiatic usage, as of Polycarp, and of the early Bishops of Rome[2]; and the absolute use of it in the two Epistles cannot but mark a position wholly exceptional. One who could claim for himself the title 'the elder' must have occupied a place which would not necessarily be suggested by the title of 'an apostle'; and it is perfectly intelligible that St John should have used the title in virtue of which he wrote, rather than that which would have had no bearing upon his communication. As an illustration of the superintendence exercised in the Asiatic Churches by St John, see Euseb. *H. E.* III. 23.

Not inapplicable to St John.

Internal evidence amply confirms the general tenor of external authority. The second Epistle bears the closest resemblance in language and thought to the first. The third Epistle has the closest affinity to the second, though from its subject it is less like the first in general form. Nevertheless it offers many striking parallels to constructions and language of St John: *v.* 3 ἐν ἀληθείᾳ; 4 μειζοτέραν τούτων...ἵνα... 6, 12 μαρτυρεῖν τινι, 11 ἐκ τοῦ θεοῦ ἐστίν...οὐχ ἑώρακεν τὸν θεόν, 12 οἶδας ὅτι ἡ μαρτ. ἡ. ἀληθής ἐστιν.

Internal evidence.

The use of the Pauline words προπέμπειν, εὐοδοῦσθαι and ὑγιαίνειν, and of the peculiar words φλυαρεῖν, φιλοπρωτεύειν, ὑπολαμβάνειν (in the sense of 'welcome'), has no weight on the other side.

[1] Jerome however speaks of the opinion as widely held in his time: *opinio a plerisque tradita (de virr. ill.* 18).

[2] Iren. ap. Euseb. *H. E.* v. 20. 24.

The complexion of the third Epistle is not Pauline; and the exceptional language belongs to the occasion on which it was written.

III. CHARACTER.

The letters contain no direct indication of the time or place at which they were written. They seem to belong to the same period of the Apostle's life as the first Epistle; and they were therefore probably written from Ephesus.

The destination of the second Letter is enigmatic. No solution of the problem offered by Ἐκλεκτῇ Κυρίᾳ is satisfactory. Nor does the Letter itself offer any marked individuality of address.

Picture of the Church in the third Epistle.

The third Letter, on the other hand, reveals a striking and in some respects unique picture of the condition of the early Church. There is a dramatic vigour in the outlines of character which it indicates. Gaius and Diotrephes have distinct individualities; and the reference to Demetrius comes in with natural force. Each personal trait speaks of a fulness of knowledge behind, and belongs to a living man. Another point which deserves notice is the view which is given of the independence of Christian societies. Diotrephes, in no remote corner, is able for a time to withstand an Apostle in the administration of his particular Church. On the other side, the calm confidence of St John seems to rest on himself more than on his official power. His presence will vindicate his authority. Once more, the growth of the Churches is as plainly marked as their independence. The first place in them has become an object of unworthy ambition. They are able and, as it appears, for the most part willing to maintain missionary teachers.

Altogether this last glimpse of Christian life in the apostolic age is one on which the student may well linger. The state of things which is disclosed does not come near an ideal, but it witnesses to the freedom and vigour of a growing faith.

ΙΩΑΝΟΥ Α

ΙΩΑΝΟΥ Α

Ο ΗΝ ΑΠ' ΑΡΧΗΣ, ὃ ἀκηκόαμεν, ὃ ἑωράκαμεν
τοῖς ὀφθαλμοῖς ἡμῶν, ὃ ἐθεασάμεθα καὶ αἱ χεῖρες ἡμῶν

1. Tertullian twice quotes the verse (omitting ὃ ἦν ἀπ' ἀρχῆς) as if he read
ὃ ἑωράκαμεν, ὃ ἀκηκόαμεν, τοῖς ὀφθαλμοῖς ἡμῶν ἐθεασάμεθα καὶ αἱ χεῖρες......(adv. Prax.
15, quod vidimus, quod audivimus, oculis nostris vidimus et manus......; de An. 17).
Probably the transposition came from v. 3. This being adopted, the omission of
ὃ before ἐθεασάμεθα became necessary. The same transposition occurs in the free
quotation contained in the Muratorian Fragment, quæ vidimus oculis nostris et
auribus audivimus et manus nostræ palpaverunt hæc scripsimus vobis (N. T. Canon,
p. 535). In v. 3 ℵ harl transpose conversely and read ὃ ἀκηκ. καὶ ἑωρ.

INTRODUCTION. THE FACTS OF THE
GOSPEL ISSUING IN FELLOWSHIP AND
JOY. (I. 1—4.)

This preface to the Epistle corresponds in a remarkable manner with
the preface to the Gospel (John i.
1—18); but the two passages are
complementary and not parallel. The
introduction to the Gospel treats of
the personal Word (ὁ λόγος), and so
naturally leads up to the record of
His work on earth: the introduction
to the Epistle treats of the revelation of life (ὁ λόγος τῆς ζωῆς) which
culminated in the Incarnation, and
leads up to a view of the position and
privileges and duties of the Christian.
In the former the Apostle sets forth
the Being of the Word in relation to
God and to the world (John i. 1, 2—
5), the historic manifestation of the
Word generally (6—13), the Incarnation as apprehended by personal experience (14—18). In the latter he
states first the various parts which
are united in the fulness of the
apostolic testimony (1 John i. 1); then
he dwells specially on the historic
manifestation of the Life (i. 2); and

lastly, he points out the personal
results of this manifestation (i. 3, 4).
Thus there is a harmonious correspondence between the two sections
regulated by the primary difference
of subject. In each the main subject
is described first (John i. 1, 2—5:
1 John i. 1): then the historical manifestation of it (John i. 6—13: 1 John
i. 2): then its personal apprehension
(John i. 14—18: 1 John i. 3 f.).
Comp. Introd. § 7.

¹ *That which was from the beginning, that which we have heard,
that which we have seen with our
eyes, that which we beheld and our
hands handled, concerning the word
of life—² and the life was manifested, and we have seen, and bear
witness, and declare unto you the
life,* even *the* life *eternal, which was
with the Father and was manifested
to us—³ that which we have seen and
heard* (I say) *declare we unto you
also, that you also may have fellowship with us; yea and our fellowship
is with the Father, and with his Son
Jesus Christ; ⁴ and these things write
we that our* (your) *joy may be fulfilled.*

St John throughout this section uses the plural (contrast ii. 1, 7, &c.) as speaking in the name of the apostolic body of which he was the last surviving representative.

1—3. *That which was...that which we have seen and heard declare we...* The construction of the passage is broken by the parenthesis of *v.* 2, which may for the moment be dismissed from consideration. The beginning of *v.* 3 (ὁ ἑωράκ. καὶ ἀκηκ.) thus stands out clearly as a resumption of the construction and (in part) of the words of *v.* 1. The relatives in the two verses (ὁ ἀκηκ., ὁ ἑωράκ.) must therefore be identical in meaning; and the simple resumptive clause gives the clue to the interpretation of the original more complex clause. Now in *v.* 3 there can be no doubt that the relative ὅ is strictly neuter, 'that which': it can have no direct personal reference. The sense is perfectly simple: '*that which we have... heard, we declare...*' If to such a sentence the phrase, '*concerning the word of life*' (περὶ τοῦ λόγου τῆς ζωῆς) be added, there can still be no doubt as to the meaning. '*The word of life*' is the subject as to which the Apostle has gained the knowledge which he desires to communicate to others: '*that which we...have heard concerning the word of life we declare...*' So far the general interpretation of the passage appears to be quite clear; nor can the addition of other clauses in *v.* 1 alter it. Whatever view be adopted as to the meaning of the phrase, '*the word of life*,' it can only be taken, according to the natural structure of the sentence, as the object of the various modes of regard successively enumerated. The apparent harshness of combining the clause '*concerning the word of life*' with '*that which was from the beginning*,' and '*that which...our hands handled*,' is removed by the intervening phrases; and the preposition (περί) 'concerning,' 'in regard to,' is

comprehensive in its application. The ordinary construction by which the clause is treated as co-ordinate with the clauses which precede: '*that which was from the beginning, that which we have heard...even concerning the word of life...we declare to you,*' seems to be made impossible (1) by the resumptive words in *v.* 3, (2) by the break after *v.* 1, (3) by the extreme abruptness of the change in the form of the object of *we declare*.

1. The contents of this verse correspond closely with John i. 1, 9, 14 *In the beginning was the Word... There was the Light, the true Light, which lighteth every man, coming into the world... And the Word became flesh...* But, as has been already noticed, here the thought is of the revelation and not of the Person.

ὃ ἦν...ὃ ἀκηκ., ὃ ἑωρ., ὃ ἐθ....ἐψηλά-φησαν] *That which was...that which ..., that which...that which...handled.* These four clauses, separated by the repeated relative, which follow one another in a perfect sequence from the most abstract (ὃ ἦν ἀπ' ἀρχῆς) to the most material aspect of divine revelation (ὃ ἐθ....αἱ χ. ἐψηλάφησαν), bring into distinct prominence the different elements of the apostolic message. Of this, part extended to the utmost limits of time, being absolutely when time began: part was gradually unfolded in the course of human history. The succession of tenses marks clearly three parts of the message: *that which was* (ἦν)... *that which we have heard* (ἀκηκόαμεν) ..., *that which we beheld...*(ἐθεασά-μεθα...). That which we understand by the eternal purpose of God (Eph. i. 4), the relation of the Father to the Son (John xvii. 5), the acceptance of man in the Beloved (Eph. i. 6), *was* already, and entered as a factor into the development of finite being, when the succession of life began (ἦν ἀπ' ἀρχῆς, *was from the beginning*). But these truths were gradually realised in the course of ages, through the teaching of patriarchs, lawgivers, and prophets, and lastly of the Son Himself, Whose words are still pregnant with instruction (ὃ ἀκηκόαμεν, *which we have heard*); and above all, through the Presence of Christ, the lessons of Whose Life abide unchangeable with the Church and are realised in its life (ὃ ἑωράκαμεν τοῖς ὀφθαλμοῖς ἡμῶν, *which we have seen with our eyes*). And this Presence of Christ itself, as a historic fact, was the presence of One truly man. The perfection of His manhood was attested by the direct witness of those who were sensibly convinced of it (ὃ ἐθεασάμεθα, κ.τ.λ., *which we beheld and our hands handled*). All the elements which may be described as the eternal, the historical, the personal, belong to the one subject, to the fulness of which they contribute, even '*the word of life*.'

As there is a succession of time in the sequence of the clauses, so there is also a climax of personal experience, from that which was remotest in apprehension to that which was most immediate (*that which was from the beginning...that which our hands handled*).

ἀπ᾿ ἀρχῆς] *from the beginning.* Comp. c. ii. 7 note. '*From the beginning*' is contrasted with *in the beginning* (John i. 1). The latter marks what *was* already at the initial point, looking to that which is eternal, supra-temporal: the former looks to that which starting at the initial point has been operative in time. The latter deals with absolute being (ὁ λόγος ἦν πρὸς τὸν θεόν); the former with temporal development. Compare ἀπὸ καταβολῆς κόσμου (Apoc. xiii. 8, xvii. 8; Heb. iv. 3, ix. 26) as contrasted with πρὸ κατ. κ. (John xvii. 24; 1 Pet. i. 20).

The absence of the definite article both here and in John i. 1 is to be traced back finally to Gen. i. 1 (LXX.). The beginning is not regarded as a definite concrete fact, but in its character, according to man's apprehension, 'that to which we look as beginning.' The use of ἐσχάτη ὥρα in c. ii. 18, ἔσχαται ἡμέραι 2 Tim. iii. 1 is similar. Compare iii. 10 ποιεῖν δικ. note.

The Greek commentators justly dwell on the grandeur of the claim which St John makes for the Christian Revelation as coeval in some sense with creation: θεολογῶν ἐξηγεῖται μὴ νεώτερον εἶναι τὸ καθ᾿ ἡμᾶς μυστήριον, ἀλλ᾿ ἐξ ἀρχῆς μὲν καὶ ἀεὶ τυγχάνειν αὐτὸ νῦν δὲ πεφανερῶσθαι ἐν τῷ κυρίῳ, ὅς ἐστι ζωὴ αἰώνιος καὶ θεὸς ἀληθινός (Theophlct. *Argum.*). And again in a note upon the verse: τοῦτο καὶ πρὸς Ἰουδαίους καὶ πρὸς Ἕλληνας οἳ ὡς νεώτερον διαβάλλουσι τὸ καθ᾿ ἡμᾶς μυστήριον (id. *ad loc.*).

The 'hearing' 'concerning the word of life' is not to be limited to the actual preaching of the Lord during His visible presence, though it includes this. It embraces the whole divine preparation for the Advent provided by the teaching of Lawgiver and Prophets (comp. Heb. i. 1) fulfilled at last by Christ. This the Apostles had 'heard' faithfully when the Jewish people had not heard (John v. 37; Luke xvi. 29). So also the 'seeing,' as it appears, reaches beyond the personal vision of the Lord. The condition of Jew and Gentile, the civil and religious institutions by which St John was surrounded (Acts xvii. 28), the effects which the Gospel wrought, revealed to the eye of the Apostle something of 'the Life.' 'Hearing' and 'seeing' are combined in the work of the seer: Apoc. xxii. 8.

The clear reference to the Risen Christ in the word '*handled*,' makes it probable that the special manifestation indicated by the two aorists (ἐθεασάμεθα, ἐψηλάφησαν) is that given to the Apostles by the Lord after the Resurrection, which is in fact the revelation of Himself as He remains with His Church by the Spirit. The two words are united with one relative, and they express in ascending order the ground of the Apostle's personal belief in the reality of the true humanity of Christ as He is (*we beheld...and handled*).

Thus there is a survey of the whole course of revelation in the four clauses, more complete than has been already indicated. The personal experience of the Presence of Christ is crowned by the witness to the Risen Christ. This witness of what he had actually experienced is part of the message which the Apostle had to give (comp. Acts i. 22). The Resurrection was the final revelation of life. At the same time the four clauses bind together inseparably the divine and human. There is, as we have seen, but one subject whether this is revealed as eternal (*that which was from the beginning*), or through the experience of sense (*that which our hands handled*).

ἀκηκόαμεν] *have heard*, *vv.* 3, 5, iv. 3; John iv. 42, v. 37, xviii. 21. The perfect in every case preserves its full force.

ἑωράκ. τ. ὀφθ.] *have seen with our eyes*. The addition *with our eyes*, like *our hands* below, emphasises the idea of direct personal outward experience in a matter marvellous in itself. The vision was not of the soul within, but in life. Comp. Deut. iii. 21, iv. 3, xi. 7, xxi. 7; Zech. ix. 8; Ecclus. xvi. 5. See also John xx. 27. On sight and hearing, see Philo, *de Sacr. A. et C.* § 22, i. 178.

ὃ ἑωράκαμεν...ὃ ἐθεασάμεθα...] *quod vidimus...quod perspeximus* V., *which we have seen...which we beheld*. The general relation of these clauses has been touched upon already. They offer also contrasts in detail. The change of tense marks the difference between that which was permanent in the lessons of the manifestation of the Lord, and that which was once shewn to special witnesses. The change of the verbs also is sig-

nificant. Θεᾶσθαι, like θεωρεῖν, expresses the calm, intent, continuous contemplation of an object which remains before the spectator. Comp. John i. 14 n. On the other hand the emphatic addition of τοῖς ὀφθαλμοῖς ἡμῶν to ἑωράκαμεν emphasises the personal nature of the witness as ἐθεασάμεθα emphasises its exactness. Generally the first two verbs (*heard, seen*) express the fact, and the second two (*beheld, handled*) the definite investigation by the observer.

Bede (*ad loc.*) brings out the moral element in ἐθεασάμεθα: Non solum quippe corporalibus oculis sicut ceteri Dominum viderunt sed et perspexerunt, cujus divinam quoque virtutem spiritualibus oculis cernebant.

ἐψηλάφησαν] *contrectaverunt* V. (all. *tractaverunt, palpaverunt, perscrutatæ sunt*), *handled*. There can be no doubt that the exact word is used with a distinct reference to the invitation of the Lord after His Resurrection: *Handle me...* (Luke xxiv. 39 ψηλαφήσατέ με). The tacit reference is the more worthy of notice because St John does not mention the fact of the Resurrection in his Epistle; nor does he use the word in his own narrative of the Resurrection. From early times it has been observed that St John used the term to mark the solid ground of the Apostolic conviction: οὐ γὰρ ὡς ἔτυχε συγκατετέθεμεθα τῷ ὀφθέντι (Theophlct. *ad loc.*).

περὶ τοῦ λόγου τῆς ζωῆς] *de verbo vitæ* V. (*de sermone vitæ*, Tert.), *concerning the word of life*, that is *the message of life*, or, according to the more modern idiom, *the revelation of life*. The *word* (ὁ λόγος) conveys the notion of a connected whole (*sermo*), and is not merely an isolated utterance (ῥῆμα· comp. John vi. 68 ῥήματα ζωῆς αἰωνίου). Hence *the word of life* is the whole message from God to man, which tells of life, or, perhaps, out of which life springs, which beginning to be spoken by the prophets, was at last fully proclaimed by one who was His Son (Hebr. i. 1, 2). Christ is, indeed, Himself THE WORD, but in the present passage the obvious reference is to the whole *Gospel*, of which He is the centre and sum, and not to Himself personally. This follows both from the context and from the appended genitive (τῆς ζωῆς). It is *the life* and not *the word* which is said to have been manifested; and again in the four passages where ὁ λόγος is used personally (John i. 1 ter, 14) the term is absolute. On the other hand we have ὁ λόγος τῆς βασιλείας (Matt. xiii. 19), ὁ λόγος τῆς σωτηρίας ταύτης (Acts xiii. 26), ὁ λόγος τῆς χάριτος αὐτοῦ (Acts xx. 32), ὁ λόγος ὁ τοῦ σταυροῦ (2 Cor. i. 18), ὁ λόγος τῆς καταλλαγῆς (2 Cor. v. 19), ὁ λόγος τῆς ἀληθείας τοῦ εὐαγγελίου (Col. i. 5), ὁ λόγος τῆς ἀληθείας (2 Tim. ii. 15; comp. λόγ. ἀληθείας James i. 18), in all of which the genitive describes the subject of the tidings or record. There can then be no reason for departing from the general analogy of this universal usage here, since it gives an admirable sense, and the personal interpretation of '*the word of life*' is not supported by any parallel. Moreover, a modification of the phrase itself occurs in St Paul, λόγον ζωῆς ἐπέχειν (Phil. ii. 16: compare also Titus i. 2, 3 ἐπ' ἐλπίδι ζωῆς αἰωνίου ἣν ἐπηγγείλατο...ἐφανέρωσεν δὲ... τὸν λόγον αὐτοῦ...: John vi. 68; Acts v. 20). The personal interpretation could not fail to present itself to later readers, in whose speculation 'the Word' occupied a far larger place than it occupies in the writings of St John, and to become popular. In a most true sense Christ is the gospel; and the name of the triumphant conqueror in Apoc. xix. 13 (ὁ λόγος τοῦ θεοῦ· comp. Acts vi. 7, xv. 6 &c.) shews the natural transition in meaning from 'the Word of God' to Him who is 'the Word of God.' Comp. John x. 35.

The Peshito Syriac (not Harcl.) appears to support the interpretation which has been given: *that which is the word of life*.

The sense of the genitive τῆς ζωῆς, *of life*, is doubtful. According to general usage noticed above, it would specify the contents of the message: 'the revelation which proclaims and presents life to men.' It must however be noticed that in other connexions St John uses the words (τῆς ζωῆς) to describe the character of that to which they are applied, as life-giving, or life-sustaining: τὸ ξύλον τῆς ζωῆς (Apoc. ii. 7 &c.), ὁ στέφανος τῆς ζωῆς (Apoc. ii. 10), ζωῆς πηγαὶ ὑδάτων (Apoc. vii. 17), τὸ ὕδωρ τῆς ζωῆς (Apoc. xxi. 6 &c.), ἡ βίβλος τῆς ζωῆς (Apoc. iii. 5 &c.), and more particularly ὁ ἄρτος τῆς ζωῆς (John vi. 35), τὸ φῶς τῆς ζωῆς (John viii. 12), which suggest such a sense as 'the life-containing, life-communicating word.' The context here, which speaks of the manifestation of *the life*, appears at first sight to require the former interpretation; for it is easy to pass from the idea of *the life* as the subject of the divine revelation to *the life* made manifest, while the conception of *life* as characteristic of the word does not prepare the way for the transition so directly. On the other side the usage of the Gospel is of great weight; and it is not difficult to see how the thought of the revelation, which from first to last was inspired by and diffused life, leads to the thought that the life itself was personally manifested.

It is most probable that the two interpretations are not to be sharply separated. The revelation proclaims that which it includes; it has, announces, gives life. In Christ life as the subject and life as the character of the Revelation were absolutely united. See Additional Note on v. 20.

The preposition (περί) is used in a wide sense, 'in regard to,' 'in the

ἐψηλάφησαν, περὶ τοῦ λόγου τῆς ζωῆς,—²καὶ ἡ ζωὴ

matter of.' Comp. John xvi. 8. The subject is not simply a message, but all that had been made clear through manifold experience 'concerning' it.

If we now look back over the verse it is not difficult to see why St John chose the neuter form (*that which was* and not *Him that was*), and why he limited the record of his experience by the addition *concerning the word of life.* He does not announce Christ or the revelation of life, but he announces something relating to both. Christ is indeed the one subject of his letter, yet not the Person of Christ absolutely but what he had himself come directly to know of Him. Nor yet again does the apostle write all that he had come to know of Christ by manifold intercourse, but just so much as illustrated the whole revelation of life (comp. John xx. 30 f.). His pastoral is not a Gospel nor a dogmatic exposition of truth, but an application of the Truth to life.

2. The whole verse is parenthetical. Elsewhere St John interrupts the construction by the introduction of a reflective comment (*v.* 3 b; c. ii. 27, John i. 14, 16, iii. 1, 16 ff., 31 ff., xix. 35, 2 John 2), and pauses after some critical statement to consider and realise its significance. And so here the mention of the whole 'revelation of life,' which extends throughout time, leads him to rest for a moment upon the one supreme fact up to which or from which all revelation comes. 'Concerning the word of life,' he seems to say, 'Yes, concerning that revelation which deals with life and which brings life in all its manifold relations; and yet while our thoughts embrace this vast range which it includes, we may never forget that the life itself was shewn to us in a personal form. What we have to declare is not a word (λόγος) only: it is a fact.'

The simple statement is given first (*the life was manifested*), and then subject and predicate are more fully explained ('*the life eternal which was with the Father,*' '*was manifested to us*'). The phrase, *the life was manifested,* recals the corresponding phrase in the prologue to the Gospel, *the Word became flesh.* The latter regards the single fact of the Incarnation of the Word Who 'was God'; this regards the exhibition in its purity and fulness of the divine movement. And yet further, in the Gospel St John speaks directly of a Person: here he is speaking of the revelation which he had received of the energy of a Person. The full difference is felt if for a moment the predicates are transferred. The reality of the Incarnation would be undeclared if it were said: 'the Word was manifested'; the manifoldness of the operations of life would be circumscribed if it were said: 'the life became flesh.' The manifestation of the life was a consequence of the Incarnation of the Word, but it is not co-extensive with it.

καὶ ἡ ζωή] *and the life....* This use of the simplest conjunction (καί) is characteristic of St John. It seems to mark the succession of contemplation as distinguished from the sequence of reasoning. Thought is added to thought as in the interpretation of a vast scene open all at once before the eyes, of which the parts are realised one after the other.

ἡ ζωή] *the life,* John xiv. 6 n., xi. 25 n. The usage of the word in John i. 4 is somewhat different. Here life is regarded as final and absolute: there life is the particular revelation of life given in finite creation. Christ *is* the life which He *brings,* and which is realised by believers *in* Him. In Him 'the life' became visible. Comp. c. v. 11, 12, 20; Col. iii. 4; Rom. v. 10, vi. 23; 2 Cor. iv. 10;

ἐφανερώθη, καὶ ἑωράκαμεν καὶ μαρτυροῦμεν καὶ ἀπαγ-

2. καὶ ὃ ἑωράκαμεν, B (ἑορ.); καὶ ὃ ἑωρ. μαρτ. Dion Alex. (Migne, P. Gr. x. 1248).
The insertion or omission of o before ΕΟΡΑΚΑΜΕΝ (so B) was equally easy; but
ἐφανερώθη seems to require the direct connexion of ἑωράκαμεν with τὴν ζ. τ. αἰ.

2 Tim. i. 1. But the term 'the life'
is not to be regarded as simply a personal name equivalent to the Word :
it expresses one aspect of His Being
and Working. Looking to Him we
see under the conditions of present
human being the embodied ideal of
life, which is fellowship with God and
with man in God.

ἐφανερώθη] manifestata est V. (below apparuit), was manifested. The
word is used of the revelation of the
Lord at His first coming (c. iii. 5, 8;
John i. 31; comp. c. iv. 9; John vii.
4; 1 Pet. i. 20; 1 Tim. iii. 16; Heb.
ix. 26); of His revelation after the
Resurrection (John xxi. 14, 1; [Mark]
xvi. 12, 14); and of the future revelation (c. ii. 28; comp. 1 Pet. v. 4; Col.
iii. 4). In all these ways the Word
Incarnate and glorified is made known
as 'the Life.'

ἑωράκαμεν...μαρτυροῦμεν...ἀπαγγέλ-
λομεν...] seen...bear witness...de-
clare... The three verbs give in due
sequence the ideas of personal experience, responsible affirmation, authoritative announcement, which are
combined in the apostolic message.
The first two verbs are probably used
absolutely, though the object of the
third (the life eternal) is potentially
included in them. Comp. John i. 34,
xix. 35. So Augustine, et vidimus et
testes sumus.

ἑωράκαμεν] John xix. 35, i. 34, xiv.
7, 9. It is worthy of notice that this
is the only part of the verb which is
used by St John in the Gospel and
Epistles (ὅρα μή, Apoc. xix. 10; xxii.
9: not xviii. 18; nor John vi. 2);
and in these books it is singularly
frequent.

Severus (Cramer Cat. ad loc.), comparing these words with iv. 12 θεὸν

οὐδεὶς πώποτε τεθέαται, no man hath
beheld God at any time, remarks : τῷ
σεσαρκῶσθαι καὶ ἐπηνθρωπηκέναι θεατὸς καὶ ψηλαφητὸς γενέσθαι εὐδόκησεν
[ὁ λόγος], οὐχ ὃ ἦν θεαθεὶς καὶ ψηλα-
φηθεὶς ἀλλ' ὃ γέγονεν· εἰς γὰρ ὑπάρχων
καὶ ἀδιαίρετος ὁ αὐτὸς ἦν καὶ θεατὸς καὶ
ἀθέατος καὶ ἁφῇ μὴ ὑποπίπτων καὶ ψη-
λαφώμενος...

μαρτυροῦμεν] Comp. iv. 14; John
xxi. 24. For the characteristic use of
the idea of witness in St John see
Introd. to Gospel of St John, pp.
xliv. ff.

Augustine dwells on the associations of the Greek μάρτυρες which
were lost in the Latin testes : Ergo
hoc dixit Vidimus et testes sumus :
Vidimus et martyres sumus; testimonium enim dicendo...cum displiceret
ipsum testimonium hominibus adversus quos dicebatur, passi sunt omnia
quae passi sunt martyres (ad loc.).

ἀπαγγέλλομεν] adnunciamus V., we
declare. The word occurs again in
St John's writings in John xvi. 25
(it is falsely read iv. 51, xx. 18). In
the Synoptists and Acts it is not un-
common in the sense of 'bearing back
a message from one to another.' This
fundamental idea underlies the use
here and in John xvi. 25. The message comes from a Divine Presence
and expresses a Divine purpose.

Comp. 1 Cor. xiv. 25; Heb. ii. 12
(LXX.); v. 5 note.

The application of the words must
not be confined to the Epistle, which
is in fact distinguished from the general proclamation of the Gospel (v. 4,
καὶ ταῦτα γράφομεν), but rather understood of the whole apostolic ministry.
More particularly perhaps we may see
a description of that teaching which
St John embodied in his Gospel.

γέλλομεν ὑμῖν τὴν ζωὴν τὴν αἰώνιον ἥτις ἦν πρὸς τὸν

τὴν ζ. τὴν αἰ.] *the eternal life*, more exactly, *the life*, even *the* life *eternal*. The phrase used in the beginning of the verse is first taken up and then more fully developed. This form of expression in which the two elements of the idea are regarded separately is found in the N. T. only here and in ii. 25. The simpler form ἡ αἰώνιος ζωή is also very rare (John xvii. 3; Acts xiii. 46; I Tim. vi. 12), and in each case where it occurs describes the special Messianic gift brought by Christ (*the eternal life*) as distinguished from the general conception (ζωὴ αἰώνιος, *life eternal*).

This 'eternal life' is seen in this passage to be the divine life, the life that *is* and which was visibly shewn in Christ, and not merely an unending continuance (Heb. vii. 16, ζ. ἀκατάλυτος). Comp. John xvii. 3. The equivalent phrase appears to occur first in Dan. xii. 2 (לְחַיֵּי עוֹלָם). Comp. 2 Macc. vii. 9 εἰς αἰώνιον ἀναβίωσιν ζωῆς ἡμᾶς ἀναστήσει.

For the use of the article (ἡ ζ. ἡ αἰ.) see c. ii. 7 (ἡ ἐντ. ἡ π.) note; and for the idea of 'eternal life' the Additional Note on v. 20.

ἥτις ἦν...] *which was*.... This clause not only defines but in part confirms the former statement. The relative is not the simple relative (ἥ), but the 'qualitative' relative (ἥτις). Comp. John viii. 53 (ὅστις ἀπέθανεν); Apoc. i. 7; ii. 24; xi. 8; xx. 4. 'We declare with authority'—such is the apostle's meaning—'the life which is truly eternal, *seeing that* the life of which we speak was with the Father, and so is independent of the conditions of time; and it was manifested to us apostles, and so has been brought within the sphere of our knowledge.'

ἦν πρὸς τ. π.] *erat apud patrem V., was with the Father*. Comp. John i. 1, 2. The life was not '*in* the Father,' nor in fellowship (μετά) or in

combination (σύν) with Him, but realised with Him for its object and law (ἦν πρός). That which is true of the Word as a Person, is true necessarily of the Word in action, and so of the Life which finds expression in action. The verb (ἦν) describes continuous and not past existence; or rather, it suggests under the forms of human thought an existence which is beyond time (Apoc. iv. 11 ἦσαν; John i. 3 f.).

τὸν πατέρα] *The Father*, the title of God when regarded relatively, as the 'One God, of whom (ἐξ οὗ) are all things' (I Cor. viii. 6). The relation itself is defined more exactly either in reference to the material world: James i. 17 ὁ πατὴρ τῶν φώτων; or to men: Matt. v. 16 ὁ πατὴρ ὑμῶν, &c.; or, more commonly and peculiarly, to our Lord, '*the Son*': Matt. vii. 21 ὁ πατήρ μου, &c. The difference of the paternal relation of the One Father to Christ and to Christians is indicated in a very remarkable manner in John xx. 17 (ἀναβαίνω πρὸς τὸν πατέρα μου καὶ πατ. ὑμῶν) where the unity of the Person is shewn by the one article common to the two clauses, and the distinctness of the relations by the repetition of the title with the proper personal pronoun. The simple title ὁ πατήρ occurs rarely in the Synoptic Gospels, and always with reference to 'the Son': Matt. xi. 27∥Luke x. 22; Matt. xxiv. 36∥Mark xiii. 32; Luke ix. 26; Matt. xxiii. 19. (But comp. Luke xi. 13 ὁ π. ὁ ἐξ οὐρανοῦ; the usage in Matt. xi. 26∥Luke x. 21; Mark xiv. 36 is different.) In the Acts it is found only in the opening chapters; i. 4, 7; ii. 33. In St Paul only Rom. vi. 4 (ἠγέρθη...διὰ τῆς δόξης τοῦ π.); I Cor. viii. 6 (εἰς θεὸς ὁ πατήρ); Eph. ii. 18 (τὴν προσαγωγὴν...πρὸς τὸν πατέρα); and not at all in the Epistles of St Peter, St James or St Jude, or in the Apocalypse. In St John's Gospel, on the contrary, and in his Epistles (i. ii.) the term is very frequent.

πατέρα καὶ ἐφανερώθη ἡμῖν,—³ὃ ἑωράκαμεν καὶ ἀκηκόαμεν ἀπαγγέλλομεν καὶ ὑμῖν, ἵνα καὶ ὑμεῖς κοινωνίαν

3. ὁ ἀκηκ. καὶ ἑωρ. ℵ harl: see v. 1.   +καί ἀπαγγ. ℵ am.   –καί
ὑμῖν, ⸆ vg me.   – δέ ⸆ C*.   Hence Aug. Ambr. vg et societas nostra sit
(ἵνα…ἔχητε καὶ ᾖ ἡ κοινωνία ἡ ἡμετέρα…)

Comp. John iv. 21 add. note; and the
additional note on this passage.

In this place the idea of Fatherhood comes into prominence in connexion with life (*the life was with the
Father*). In the Gospel the absolute
idea of Godhead is placed in connexion with the Word (John i. 1 ὁ λ. ἦν
πρὸς τὸν θεόν, *the Word was with
God*). In both passages a glimpse
is given of the essential relations of
the Divine Persons, and we learn that
the idea of Father lies in the Deity
itself and finds fulfilment in the
Deity. The simplest conception which
we can form of God in Himself as
absolutely perfect and self-sufficing
includes Tripersonality.

ἐφαν. ἡμῖν] *apparuit nobis* V. (*manifestata est in nobis* Aug., *palam
facta est*, &c. all.) *was manifested to
us.* The general statement given before (*was manifested*) is made personal. Actual experience is the foundation of St John's testimony.

3. In the parenthesis (v. 2) St John
has described the subject of his message as '*the life eternal*': he now
describes it as '*that which we have
seen and heard.*' The fulness of apostolic experience, the far-reaching
knowledge of the Son of God, is indeed identical with the life. By ap-
propriating that knowledge of the
Son the life is appropriated.

Life is manifested in fellowship;
and in regarding the end of his message St John looks at once to a twofold fellowship, human and divine, a
fellowship with the Church and with
God. He contemplates first the fellowship which exists in the Christian
body itself, and then rises from this
to the thought of the wider privileges

of such fellowship as resting on a
divine basis. Manifeste ostendit B.
Johannes quia quicunque societatem
cum Deo habere desiderant primo
ecclesiæ societati debent adunari....
(Bede).

ὃ ἑωρ. καὶ ἀκηκ.] *that which we
have seen and heard...* The transposition of the verbs in this resumptive
clause (v. 1 *heard...seen...*) is natural
and significant. Before the Apostle
was advancing up to the Incarnation,
now he is starting from it. At the
same time the two elements of experience are brought together and
not (as before) separated by the repeated relative (v. 1 *that which...that
which...*).

καὶ ὑμῖν] *unto you also.* The revelation was not for those only to whom
it was first given; but for them also
who 'had not seen.' The message
was for 'them also' that 'they also'
might enjoy the fruits of it. There is
no redundance in the repeated καί.

This thought is well brought out
by Augustine, who asks the question:
Minus ergo sumus felices quam illi
qui viderunt et audierunt? and answers it by recalling the history of St
Thomas (John xx. 26 ff.) who rose by
Faith above touch: Tetigit hominem,
confessus est Deum. Et Dominus
consolans nos qui ipsum jam in cælo
sedentem manu contrectare non possumus sed fide contingere, ait illi
*Quia vidisti credidisti, beati qui non
viderunt et credunt.* Nos descripti
sumus, nos designati sumus. Fiat
ergo in nobis beatitudo quam Dominus prædixit futuram: manifestata est
ipsa vita in carne...ut res quæ solo
corde videri potest videretur et oculis,
ut corda sanaret (Aug. *ad loc.*).

ἔχητε μεθ' ἡμῶν· καὶ ἡ κοινωνία δὲ ἡ ἡμετέρα μετὰ τοῦ
πατρὸς καὶ μετὰ τοῦ υἱοῦ αὐτοῦ Ἰησοῦ Χριστοῦ· ⁴καὶ

ἵνα...μεθ' ἡμῶν] ut et vos societatem habeatis nobiscum V., *that ye also may have fellowship with us, i.e.* 'may be united with us, the apostolic body, in the bonds of Christian communion' (comp. *vv.* 6, 7; iv. 6) by the apprehension of the fulness of the truth; that you may enjoy to the uttermost by spiritual power what we gained in the outward experience of life (John xx. 29). The last of the apostles points to the unbroken succession of the heritage of Faith. It will be observed that St John always assumes that 'knowledge' carries with it the corresponding action (*e.g.* ii. 3). The words cannot without violence be made to give the sense: 'that ye may have the same fellowship [with God and Christ] as we have.'

The phrase κοινωνίαν ἔχειν, as distinguished from the simple verb κοινωνεῖν (2 John 11; 1 Pet. iv. 13; Phil. iv. 15), expresses not only the mere fact, but also the enjoyment, the conscious realisation, of fellowship. Comp. *v.* 8 (ἁμαρτίαν ἔχειν) note.

κοιν. μεθ' ἡμῶν] *fellowship with.* The preposition (μετά) emphasises the mutual action of those who are united. Κοινωνία is also used with a genitive of the person (1 Cor. i. 9), as in the case of things (1 Cor. x. 16; Phil. iii. 10), when the thought is of a blessing imparted by fellowship in the person, or of a fellowship springing from the person (2 Cor. xiii. 13). The word is also used absolutely Acts ii. 42.

καὶ ἡ κοιν. δέ...] *et societas nostra sit* V., Aug., *yea and our fellowship...* The connecting particles (καί...δέ) and the possessive pronoun (ἡ κ. ἡ ἡμετέρα) are both emphatic. The particles lay stress on the characteristics of the fellowship which are to be brought forward: the possessive in place of the personal pronoun marks that which peculiarly distinguishes Chris-

tians rather than simply that which they enjoy. 'And the fellowship itself in fact to which we call you, the fellowship which is truly Christian fellowship, &c.'

For καί...δέ... compare John vi. 51; viii. 16, 17; xv. 27; 3 John 12. The combination occurs sparingly throughout the N. T. The δέ serves as the conjunction, while καί emphasises the words to which it is attached.

For ἡ κοιν. ἡ ἡμετέρα compare John xv. 9 n. (ἡ ἀγ. ἡ ἐμή), 11, 12; xvii. 13, 24; xviii. 36, &c.; c. ii. 7 note.

The insertion of the δέ makes the false construction (*Latt.*) 'and that our fellowship may be...' impossible. The whole clause is like *v.* 2 (see note), a development of the preceding idea over which the apostle lingers as it were in personal reflection. For the foundation of the thought see John xvii. 20 f.

μετὰ τοῦ π....Ἰ. X.] *with the Father... his Son Jesus Christ....* The thought prepared in *vv.* 1, 2 now finds full expression. The revelation of 'the life' had brought men into connexion with 'the Father.' 'The life' was apprehended in a true human personality in virtue of the Incarnation, and so men could have fellowship with the life and with the source of life. Through the Son God was revealed and apprehended as Father. It must also be observed that 'fellowship with the Father' and 'fellowship with His Son' are directly co-ordinated (*with... and with...*). Such co-ordination implies sameness of essence. And yet further: the fellowship with the Father is not only said to be established *through* the Son: the fellowship with the Father is involved in fellowship with the Son (comp. ii. 23). The consummation of this fellowship is the 'being in God' (c. v. 20) 'a quo fontaliter omnia pro-

ταῦτα γράφομεν ἡμεῖς ἵνα ἡ χαρὰ ἡμῶν ᾖ πεπληρωμένη.

4. ἡμεῖς ℵA*B the: ὑμῖν ς A**C vg syrr me. In such a case the evidence of verss. is of little weight.

(ἡ χ.) ἡμῶν ℵB the; ὑμῶν ςAC me. The later MSS. and the Latin and Syriac verss. are divided. The confusion of ἡμ. and ὑμ. in the best authorities is so constant that a positive decision on the reading here is impossible. It may be noticed that C*, reading ὑμῶν, adds ἐν ἡμῖν and some verss. reading ἡμῶν add ἐν ὑμῖν at the end of the clause. Comp. ii. 8, 25; iii. 1; v. 4.

Some copies of Vulg. read ut+gaudeatis et' gaudium vestrum (nostrum) sit plenum.

cedunt, in quo finaliter omnes sancti fruibiliter requiescunt' (Th. Kemp. i. 15. 2).

τοῦ υἱοῦ αὐ. 'I. X.] *His Son Jesus Christ.* By the use of this full title St John brings out now both aspects of the Lord's Person ('His Son,' 'Jesus Christ') which he had indicated before ('*which was with the Father*,' '*our hands handled*'). The full title is found again in iii. 23; v. 20 (?); 2 John 3; 1 Cor. i. 9; 2 Cor. i. 19. Compare also i. 7 (iv. 15; v. 5); 1 Thess. i. 10; Heb. iv. 14. In each case it will be seen to be significant in all its elements.

4. καὶ ταῦτα] *and these things.* The apostolic message which had been regarded before in its unity (ὅ *that which*) is now regarded in some special aspects of its manifold power. St John embraces in 'the vision of his heart' (Eph. i. 18) all that his letter contains, though it was then unwritten.

The phrase, *these things,* is not however co-extensive with *that which.* St John has present to his mind both the general revelation of the Gospel (*we declare*) of which the end was to create spiritual fellowship between God and man and men; and the particular view of it which he purposes to lay before his readers (*we write*) with a view to establishing the fulness of joy in the Church.

γράφομεν ἡμεῖς] *write we.* Both the pronoun and the verb are emphatic. The proclamation (*vv.* 2, 3)

was presented in an abiding form: not spoken only but written, so far as there was need, that it might work its full effect. And it was written by those who had full authority to write. Nor is it fanciful to suppose that by the stress laid on the word *write,* which is emphasised by the absence of a personal object (the *to you* of the common text is to be omitted), St John looks forward to his apostolic service to later ages.

The plural (γράφομεν) which belongs to the form of the apostolic message stands in contrast with the personal address (γράφω) which immediately follows in c. ii. 1. Elsewhere in the epistle the verb occurs only in the singular (ii. 7 f., 12 ff., 21, 26; v. 13).

ἵνα ἡ χ. ἡμῶν (v. ὑμῶν) ᾖ πεπληρ.] *that our* (or *your*) *joy may be fulfilled.* The fulfilment of Christian joy depends upon the realisation of fellowship. The same thought underlies the other passages where the phrase occurs (see next note). Fellowship with Christ, and fellowship with the brethren, fellowship with Christ in the brethren, and with the brethren in Christ, is the measure of the fulness of joy. Both readings (ἡμῶν and ὑμῶν) are well supported and both give good sense. The object of the apostle may be regarded either as to the fulfilment of his work relatively to himself, or as to the fulfilment of his work relatively to his disciples. The joy of the apostle as well as the joy

⁵Καὶ ἔστιν αὕτη ἡ ἀγγελία ἣν ἀκηκόαμεν ἀπ' αὐτοῦ

5. καὶ ἔστιν αὕτη ℵBC; καὶ αὕτη ἐστίν ς A vg.

ἡ ἀγγελία ℵᶜAB vg: ἡ ἐπαγγελία ς C me the.

ℵ had originally η απαγγελιας, which the scribe himself altered by letters
written above to ἡ ἀγάπη τῆς ἐπαγγελίας. Comp. iii. 11; ii. 25.

of the disciples is secured by the same
result.

ἡμῶν γὰρ ὑμῖν (Œcum. ὑμῶν...ἡμῖν)
κοινωνούντων πλείστην ἔχομεν τὴν χάριν
(l. χαρὰν) ἡμῶν, ἣν τοῖς θερισταῖς ὁ
χαίρων σπορεὺς ἐν τῇ τοῦ μισθοῦ ἀπο-
λήψει βραβεύσει χαιρόντων καὶ τούτων
ὅτι τῶν πόνων αὐτῶν (l. αὐτοῦ) ἀπο-
λαύουσι (Theophlct.).

πεπληρωμένη] *plenum* (V., Aug.) *fulfilled*. The phrase is characteristic.
Comp. 2 John 12; John iii. 29, xv. 11,
xvi. 24; xvii. 13. For the use of the
resolved form see iv. 12 n. Gaudium
doctorum fit plenum cum multos præ-
dicando ad sanctæ ecclesiæ societatem...perducunt (Bede). Comp. Phil.
ii. 2.

A. THE PROBLEM OF LIFE AND
THOSE TO WHOM IT IS PROPOSED (i. 5—
ii. 17).

I. 5—10. THE NATURE OF GOD
AND THE CONSEQUENT RELATION OF
MAN TO GOD.

The section contains 1 the description of the Being of God (*v.* 5); and
then 2 the description of man's relation to God as thus made known (6—
10), in answer to the three typical
false pleas (i) of the indifference of
moral action in regard to spiritual
fellowship (6, 7); (ii) of the unreality
of sinfulness as a permanent consequence of wrong action (8, 9); and (iii)
of actual personal freedom from sinful deeds (10). These pleas are shewn
to depend (1) on immediate denial of
what is distinctly known (6); (2) on
self-deception (8); and (3) on disregard of divine revelation (10).

1. *The Nature of God* (i. 5).

5. *⁵And this is the message which
we have heard from him and*

announce to you, that God is light,
and in him is no darkness at all.
The connexion of this verse with
what precedes is not at once obvious.
The declaration which it contains as
to the nature of God is not, as
far as we know, a direct repetition
of any words of the Lord; nor is
it clear at first sight how it gathers
up what has been already said of
'the revelation of life' as apprehended
in apostolic experience. Fuller consideration appears to shew that the
idea of spiritual fellowship furnishes
the clue to the course of St John's
thought. Fellowship must repose
upon mutual knowledge. If we have
fellowship with God we must know
truly what He is and what we are,
and the latter knowledge flows from
the former. The revelation of life
from first to last is the progressive
manifestation of God and the progressive assimilation to God. The
revelation through the Incarnation
completes all that was revealed before: Christ came 'not to destroy but
to fulfil': and this revelation is briefly
comprehended in the words 'God is
light,' absolutely pure, glorious, self-
communicating from His very nature.
He imparts Himself, and man was
made to receive Him; and, in spite of
sin, man can receive Him. Thus the
fundamental ideas of Christianity lie
in this announcement: 'God is light';
and man turns to the Light as
being himself created in the image of
God (Gen. i. 27; 1 Cor. xi. 7) and re-
created in Christ (Eph. ii. 10; Col.
iii. 10). This message is really 'the
Gospel.'

Hac sententia B. Johannes...divinæ
puritatis excellentiam monstrat quam
nos quoque imitari jubemur dicente

καὶ ἀναγγέλλομεν ὑμῖν, ὅτι ὁ θεὸς φῶς ἐστιν καὶ σκοτία

ipso: *Sancti estote quoniam ego sanctus Dominus Deus vester* Lev. xix. 2 (Bede).

καί...] *And...* The declaration is the simple development of the statement in *v.* 3: 'We declare unto you what we have seen and heard, in order to establish your fellowship with us, and to fulfil our joy. And this *is* the message which has such divine power.'

ἔστιν αὕτη] *this is the message.* The original order (lost in V. *et hoc est*) in which the substantive verb stands first with unusual emphasis (καὶ ἔστιν αὕτη), marks the absoluteness, the permanence, of the message. The '*is*' is not merely a copula, but predicates existence in itself. Comp. c. v. 16, 17; ii. 15 note; John v. 45, viii. 50, 54. The exact form of expression is unique. On the other hand see c. ii. 25; iii. 11, 23; v. 4, 9, 11, 14 and 2 John 6.

ἀγγελία] *adnuntiatio* V., *message.* The word occurs only here and iii. 11 in the N. T., and it is rare in the LXX. The corresponding verb occurs in the N. T. only in John xx. 18. The simplest word appears to be chosen to describe the divine communication. The announcement as to the nature of God is a personal revelation and not a discovery. God gives tidings of Himself and so only can man know Him.

ἀπ᾽ αὐτοῦ] *from him,* that is, the Son of the Father, Jesus Christ, in whom the life was manifested, and who has been the main subject of the preceding verses.

The 'from' (ἀπ᾽ αὐτοῦ) marks the ultimate and not necessarily the immediate source (παρ᾽ αὐτοῦ). The phrase ἀκούειν ἀπό is not found elsewhere in St John (but see Acts ix. 13) while ἀκούειν παρά is frequent: John i. 40; vi. 45; vii. 51; viii. 26, 38, 40; xv. 15. The 'message' which the Apostle announces had been heard not only from the lips of Christ but in fact also from all those in whom

He had spoken in earlier times (1 Pet. i. 11). He was the source even where He was not the speaker. Comp. 1 Cor. xi. 23 παρέλαβον ἀπό, and c. ii. 27 note.

ἀναγγέλλομεν] *adnuntiamus,* V., *we announce.* The simple verb and its derivatives convey shades of meaning which cannot be preserved in a version. Ἀγγέλλειν simply '*to bring tidings*' occurs only John xx. 18. Ἀναγγέλλειν to report, with the additional idea of bringing the tidings *up to* or *back to* the person receiving them. Ἀπαγγέλλειν to announce with a distinct reference to the *source* or *place from* which the message comes. Καταγγέλλειν to proclaim with authority, as commissioned to spread the tidings *throughout* those who hear them. In ἀναγγέλλειν the recipient, in ἀπαγγέλλειν the origin, in καταγγέλλειν the relation of the bearer and hearer of the message, are respectively most prominent. (1) Thus ἀναγγ. has in nine cases a personal pronoun (ὑμῖν, ἡμῖν) after it, and in the two remaining places where it occurs (Acts xv. 4; xix. 18) the persons to whom the announcement is made are placed in clear prominence. The word is not found in the Synoptic Gospels (Mark v. 14, 19 false readings). For its meaning compare 1 Pet. i. 12 ἃ νῦν ἀνηγγέλη ὑμῖν, tidings which were lately brought as far as up to you. Acts xx. 20, 27 τοῦ μὴ ἀναγγεῖλαι ὑμῖν, not to extend my declaration of the Gospel even to you; John xvi. 13, 14, 15; Acts xv. 4; 2 Cor. vii. 7; Acts xiv. 27. (2) The proper sense of ἀπαγγ., again, is seen clearly Matt. ii. 8 ἀπαγγ. μοι, from the place where you find the Christ, Mark xvi. 13 ἀπηγγ. τοῖς λοιποῖς, from Emmaus where the revelation was made; [John iv. 51 ἀπηγγ. λέγοντες, from his house where the sick child lay;] 1 Cor. xiv. 25 ἀπαγγ., from the assembly at which he was moved. The word is frequent in the Synoptic

Gospels and in the Acts; elsewhere, in addition to the places quoted, it occurs only 1 Thess. i. 9; 1 John i. 2, 3. (Heb. ii. 12 LXX.) Comp. *v.* 2 note. (3) Καταγγέλλειν is found only in Acts (καταγγελεύς Acts xvii. 18) and St Paul. Its force appears Acts xvi. 21 καταγγέλλουσιν ἔθη, xvii. 3 ὃν ἐγὼ καταγγέλλω, &c.

In connexion with these words it may be noticed that St John never uses in his Gospel or Epistles εὐαγγέλιον (or cognates). Cf. Apoc. xiv. 6; x. 7.

ὅτι...ἐστὶν καί...ιοὐκ ἔστιν...] The combination of the positive and negative statements brings out (1) the idea of God's nature, and (2) the perfect realisation of the idea: He is light essentially, and in fact He is perfect, unmixed, light. The form of the negative statement is remarkable: 'Darkness there is not in Him, no, not in any way.' Οὐδείς is added similarly to a sentence already complete in John xix. 11 (vi. 63; xii. 19). The double negative is lost in the Latin: *tenebræ in eo non sunt ullæ.*

Positive and negative statements are combined *vv.* 6, 8; ii. 4, 27; v. 12. John i. 3, 5, 20; ii. 25; iii. 16 (20).

ὁ θεὸς φῶς ἐστίν] *Deus lux est,* V., *God is light.* The statement is made absolutely as to the nature of God, and not directly as to His action: as to what He *is,* and not as to what He *does.* It is not said that He is 'a light,' as one out of many, through Whom or from Whom illumination comes; nor again, that He is 'the light,' in relation to created beings. But it is said simply 'He is light.' The words are designed to give us some conception of His Being. Comp. Philo *de Somn.* i. p. 632 πρῶτος μὲν ὁ θεὸς φῶς ἐστί...καὶ οὐ μόνον φῶς ἀλλὰ καὶ παντὸς ἑτέρου φωτὸς ἀρχέτυπον, μᾶλλον δὲ ἀρχετύπου πρεσβύτερον καὶ ἀνώτερον....

Thus the phrase is at once distinguished from the cognate phrases which are defined by some addition; as

when creation, so far as it is a manifestation of the life of the Word, that is, as Life, is spoken of as being '*the light of men*' (John i. 4 f.): or when '*the light, the true light, which lighteth every man*' is spoken of as '*coming into the world*' (John i. 9; comp. c. ii. 8); or when Christ—the Incarnate Word—declares Himself to be '*the light of the world*' (John viii. 12; ix. 5; comp. xii. 46); or '*the light*' (John iii. 19 f., xii. 35 f.); or when Christians, as representing Christ, are also called by Him '*the light of the world*' (Matt. v. 14).

On the other hand it is closely parallel with two other phrases in St John's writings with which it must be compared and combined: *God is spirit* (John iv. 24) and *God is love* (c. iv. 8, 16).

To a certain degree this phrase unites the two others. It includes the thought of immateriality, which finds its most complete expression in the idea of 'spirit,' and that of 'diffusiveness,' which finds its most complete expression in the idea of 'love.' But to these thoughts it adds those of purity and glory, which find their most complete expression in relation to man as he is in the idea of 'fire' (Heb. xii. 29).

In order to enter into the meaning of the revelation given in the words, it is necessary to take account both of the biblical application of the term 'light' and of the thoughts which are naturally suggested by a consideration of the nature of light.

In each region of being 'light' represents the noblest manifestation of that energy to which it is applied. Physically 'light' embodies the idea of splendour, glory: intellectually of truth: morally of holiness.

Again: in virtue of light, life and action become possible. Light may exist close beside us and yet we ourselves be in darkness, wholly unconscious of its presence, unless some object intervene and itself become visible by reflecting into our eyes that which we had not before seen. Comp. Philo *de prœm. et pœn.* ii. 415 ὁ θεὸς ἑαυτοῦ φέγγος ὢν δι' αὐτοῦ μόνου θεωρεῖται. See also Ps. xxxvi. 10. As light it cannot but propagate itself; and, as far as its own nature is concerned, propagate itself without bound. All that limits is darkness.

It must not however be supposed that in speaking of God as 'light' St John is speaking metaphorically, as if earthly 'light' were the reality to which God is likened. On the contrary according to his thought the earthly light, with all its associations, is but a reflection in the finite and sensible world of the heavenly light. Through the reflection we rise, according to our power, to the reality.

This being so, the description of God as 'light' is fitted to bring before us the conception that He is in Himself unapproachable, infinite, omnipresent, unchangeable, the source of life, of safety, of the transfiguration of all things.

And yet more than this the phrase has a direct bearing upon the economy of Redemption. It implies that God in Himself is absolutely holy; and at the same time that it is His nature to impart Himself without limit.

The first fact carries with it the condition of man's fellowship with Him. The second fact suggests that He will make some provision for the redemption and atonement of man fallen, in accordance with the purpose of creation.

The revelation of the Word, the Life, of 'Jesus, the Son of God,' fulfils the condition and the hope. By this we apprehend in all fulness that God is light, self-communicating, making the darkness felt to be what it is, conquering the darkness, while He claims from man complete self-surrender to His influence.

Here then as in every other place the revelation of the nature of God is not

W.

a satisfaction of speculative questionings: it is the groundwork of practical results.

God is light: therefore men must walk in the light.

God is spirit: therefore men must worship in spirit (John iv. 24).

God is love: therefore the manifestation of love is the sign of divine childship (iv. 7, 8, 16).

Comp. Heb. xii. 29.

See Additional Note on iv. 8.

The general opposition of light and darkness, which occurs throughout all Scripture, as throughout all literature, in its manifold partial applications, gives additional meaning to the phrase.

Category of Light.	Category of Darkness.
truth	falsehood.
good	evil.
joy	sorrow.
safety	peril.
life	death.

Compare Matt. iv. 16; Luke i. 79; xi. 35 f.; John iii. 19, 20; 1 Pet. ii. 9; 2 Cor. iv. 6; vi. 14; Ps. xxvii. 1 (and Hupfeld's note).

καὶ σκοτία...] The light which God is, is infinite, unbounded by any outline, and absolutely pure. It follows that all that is in darkness, all that is darkness, is excluded from fellowship with God by His very nature. There is in Him nothing which has affinity to it.

In speaking of 'light' and 'darkness' it is probable that St John had before him the Zoroastrian speculations on the two opposing spiritual powers which influenced Christian thought at a very early date. Comp. Basilides, *fragm.* Quidam enim [barbarorum] dixerunt initia omnium duo esse quibus bona et mala associaverunt, ipsa dicentes initia sine initio esse et ingenita: id est, in principiis lucem fuisse ac tenebras, quæ ex semetipsis essent non quæ esse dicebantur (ap. Iren. Stieren, i. p. 901).

2

οὐκ ἔστιν ἐν αὐτῷ οὐδεμία.   ⁶Ἐὰν εἴπωμεν ὅτι

οὐκ ἔστιν ἐν αὐτῷ B me the: ἐν αὐτῷ οὐκ ἔστιν ⸉ ℵAC vg.   6. ἐὰν + γάρ A.

2. *The relation of men to God* (i. 6—10).

The revelation of what God is determines man's relation to Him; for it is assumed that man knows (or can know) what he himself is in himself. The declaration of the majesty of God therefore raises the question of the possibility of man's fellowship with Him; of the possibility, that is, of the fulfilment of the Apostle's purpose (*v.* 3). How can the message '*God is light*' issue in our *communion with the Father and with His Son Jesus Christ?* The answer lies, as we have seen, in the fact that it is of the essence of light-nature to communicate itself. The true sense of what God is takes us out of ourselves. He gives Himself: we must welcome Him; and so reflecting His glory we become like Him (2 Cor. iii. 18; 1 John iii. 2).

But this 'assimilation to God' (ὁμοίωσις τῷ θεῷ κατὰ τὸ δυνατόν) requires a frank recognition of what we are. St John therefore considers the three false views which man is tempted to take of his position. He may deny the reality of sin (6, 7), or his responsibility for sin (8, 9), or the fact of sin in his own case (10). By doing this he makes fellowship with God, as He has been made known, impossible for himself. On the other hand, God has made provision for the realisation of fellowship between Himself and man in spite of sin.

The contrasts and consequences involved in this view of man's relation to God can be placed clearly in a symmetrical form (*vv.* 6, 8, 10):
⁶*If we say We have fellowship with Him, and walk in the darkness,*
    we lie, *and*
        we do not the truth.

⁸*If we say We have no sin,*
    we deceive ourselves *and the truth is not in us.*
¹⁰*If we say We have not sinned,*
    we make Him a liar *and His word is not in us.*

On the other hand (*vv.* 7, 9):
But if we walk in the light, as He is in the light,
        we have fellowship one with another, and the blood of Jesus His Son cleanseth us from all sin.
⁹*If we confess our sins,*
        He is faithful and righteous to forgive us our sins, and
        to cleanse us from all unrighteousness.

The third contrast passes into a different form (ii. 1 f.).

The whole description refers to the general character and tendency of life, and not to the absolute fulfilment of the character in detail.

The progress in the development of the thought is obvious from the parallelisms. '*We lie,*' '*we deceive ourselves,*' '*we make Him a liar*': we are false, that is, to our own knowledge; we persuade ourselves that falsehood is truth; we dare to set ourselves above God. And again: '*we do not the truth,*' '*the truth is not in us,*' '*His word is not in us*': we do not carry into act that which we have recognised as our ruling principle; the Truth, to which conscience bears witness, is not the spring and law of our life; we have broken off our vital connexion with the Truth when it comes to us as 'the Word of God' with a present, personal force.

Corresponding to this growth of falsehood we have a view of the general character of the Christian

Κοινωνίαν ἔχομεν μετ᾽ αὐτοῦ καὶ ἐν τῷ σκότει περιπατῶμεν, ψευδόμεθα καὶ οὐ ποιοῦμεν τὴν ἀλήθειαν.

life, a life of spiritual fellowship and
sanctification; and then of its detailed
realisation in spite of partial failures.

6. ἐὰν εἴπωμεν] St John considers only the case of professing
Christians. In doing this he unites
himself with those whom he addresses ; and recognises the fact that
he no less than his fellow-Christians
has to guard against the temptations
to which the three types of false doctrine correspond.

The exact form of expression (ἐὰν
εἴπωμεν) is found only in this passage
(vv. 6, 8, 10; comp. iv. 20 ἐάν τις εἴπῃ).
It contemplates a direct assertion of
the several statements, and not simply
the mental conception of them.

ὅτι] The particle here and in vv.
8, 10 seems to be recitative. Comp.
ii. 4; iv. 20; John i. 20, 32; iv. 17,
25; vi. 14; vii. 12; ix. 9, 23, 41.

κοιν. ἔχομεν μετ᾽ αὐτοῦ] with Him,
i.e. with God (the Father), the subject which immediately precedes.

The statement is the simple assertion of the enjoyment of the privileges
of the Christian faith, v. 3, note: "If
we claim to have reached the end of
Christian effort..."

καὶ ἐν τῷ σκ. περ.] The compati-
bility of indifference to moral action
with the possession of true faith has
been maintained by enthusiasts in all
times of religious excitement. Comp.
c. ii. 4 ; iii. 6; 3 John 11.

For early forms of the false teach-
ing see Iren. i. 6, 2; Clem. Alex.
Strom. iii. 4 §§ 31 f.; 5 § 40. Comp.
Jude v. 4.

ἐν τῷ σκ. περ.] walk in the darkness, choose and use the darkness
as our sphere of action. The question is not directly of the specific
character of special acts, but of the
whole region of life outward and inward. The darkness (τὸ σκότος) is
the absolute opposite of 'the light.'

To choose this as our sphere of movement is necessarily to shun fellowship
with God. Part of the thought included in 'walking in darkness' may
be expressed by saying that we seek
to hide part of our lives from ourselves, from our neighbour, from God.
Comp. John iii. 20.

For the phrase see Is. ix. 2; John
viii. 12 (ἐν τῇ σκοτίᾳ). Comp. Matt. iv.
16; Luke i. 79; Rom. ii. 19. Σκότος
occurs in St John only here and John
iii. 19 note.

The image of 'walking,' resting on
the Old Testament הָלַךְ, LXX. περιπατεῖν, is not found applied to conduct
in classical writers, but is common in
St John and St Paul. The word is
not found in this sense in St James
or St Peter, and in the Synoptic
group of writings only in Mark vii. 5;
Acts xxi. 21. St John, it may be
added, does not use ἀναστροφή, ἀνα-
στρέφεσθαι, which are common in St
Peter and occur in St Paul and St
James; nor πορεύεσθαι, which is found
in St Luke (Gosp. Acts), St Peter (1,
2), and St Jude. Such 'walking' is
not to be limited to mere outward
conduct, but covers the whole activity
of life.

ψευδόμεθα...οὐ ποιοῦμεν...] The combination of the positive and negative
expressions here again (v. 5) presents
the two sides of the thought. Men
who profess to combine fellowship
with God with the choice of darkness
as their sphere of life, actively affirm
what they know to be false; and on
the other hand, they neglect to carry
out in deed what they claim to hold.
The two clauses (lie...do) correspond
with the two which precede (say...
walk).

ψευδόμεθα] The assertion is not
only false in fact, but known to be
false: it is at variance with man's
nature. Comp. James iii. 14.

^{7}ἐὰν δὲ ἐν τῷ φωτὶ περιπατῶμεν ὡς αὐτὸς ἔστιν ἐν τῷ

οὐ ποιοῦμεν τὴν ἀλήθειαν] *non facimus veritatem* V., *we do not the truth* (syr vg gives *do not advance in...*). Truth is not only in thought and word, but also in action. 'The Truth' (ἡ ἀλήθεια) which reaches to every part of human nature—the sum of all that 'is'—must find expression in a form answering to the whole man. 'I act,' in the words of Whichcote, 'and therefore I am.' Comp. John iii. 21 note; Neh. ix. 33 (LXX.).

In the Old Testament the phrase 'to do mercy and truth' (LXX.) occurs not unfrequently: Gen. xlvii. 29; Josh. ii. 14; 2 Sam. ii. 6; xv. 20, &c. Contrast ποιεῖν ψεῦδος, Apoc. xxi. 27.

7. 'Walking in the darkness' is fatal to fellowship with God, but such fellowship is still possible. The Christian can in his measure imitate God (Eph. v. 1); and as he does so, he realises fellowship with the brethren, which is the visible sign of fellowship with God. At the same time Christ's Blood cleanseth him constantly, and little by little, from all sin. The chosen rule of life—the 'walking in light'—is more and more perfectly embodied in deed. The failure which is revealed in the presence of God is removed.

God *is* in the light absolutely and unalterably: man moves in the light from stage to stage as he advances to the fulness of his growth; and under the action of the light he is himself transfigured.

The process of this great change is written significantly in the N. T. Christ by resurrection from the dead first proclaimed light (Acts xxvi. 23), that is life reflecting the divine glory; to this God has called us (1 Pet. ii. 9); and opened our eyes *to look on the illumination of the gospel of the glory of Christ who is the image of God* (2 Cor. iv. 4); who *made us meet to be partakers of the inheritance of the*

saints in the light (Col. i. 12). By *believing on the light* we *become sons of light* (John xii. 36: comp. Luke xvi. 8; 1 Thess. v. 5); and finally are ourselves *light in the Lord* (Eph. v. 8).

'Walking in the light' brings two main results in regard to our relation to men and to God. We realise fellowship one with another, and in the vision of God's holiness we become conscious of our own sin. That fellowship is the pledge of a divine fellowship: that consciousness calls out the application of the virtue of Christ's life given for us and to us.

ἐὰν δέ...] *but if we walk...* There is a sharp contrast between the vain profession of fellowship and godlike action. *But,* setting aside mere words, *if we walk in the light...*

ἐν τῷ φ. περιπ.] The one absolute light is opposed to the darkness. To choose the light as the sphere of life is to live and move as in the revealed presence of God. Comp. Is. ii. 5; li. 4.

The thought of walking in light and in darkness soon found expression in the allegory of 'The two ways.' Barn. *Ep.* xviii. ff. *Doctrine of the Apostles*, 1—6.

ὡς αὐτός...] *sicut et ipse* Latt., *as He Himself is in the light.* God is light, and He is in the light. Being light He radiates (as it were) His glory and dwells in this light unapproachable (1 Tim. vi. 16). The realm of perfect truth and purity in which He is completely corresponds to His own nature. Under another aspect light is His garment (Ps. civ. 2), which at once veils and reveals His Majesty.

Bede expresses well the contrast of περιπατεῖν and εἶναι: Notanda distinctio verborum... Ambulant...justi in luce cum virtutum operibus servientes ad meliora proficiunt... Deus autem sine aliquo profectu semper bonus, justus, verusque existit.

φωτί, κοινωνίαν ἔχομεν μετ᾽ ἀλλήλων καὶ τὸ αἷμα
Ἰησοῦ τοῦ υἱοῦ αὐτοῦ καθαρίζει ἡμᾶς ἀπὸ πάσης ἁμαρ-

7. μετ᾽ ἀλλήλων: A* (appy) tol Cl Al Tert (followed by *J. C. domini nostri*)
read μετ᾽ αὐτοῦ; harl has *cum deo*. The readings are evidently interpretative
glosses.

Ἰησοῦ ℵBC syrr the: + χριστοῦ ς A vg me.

καθαρίζει: some auths., including A, read the future (καθαρίσει or καθαριεῖ).

αὐτός] He Himself, our Lord and
King. Comp. Deut. xxxii. 39; Is.
xli. 4 (Cheyne); xliii. 10; Jer. v. 12;
Ps. cii. 28 (הוא).

κοιν. ἔχ. μετ᾽ ἀλλ.] *societatem habemus ad invicem* V., *we have fellowship one with another,* that is brother
with brother: we enjoy the fulness of
Christian communion. The transcendental fellowship with God which the
false Christian claimed becomes for us
a practical fellowship in actual life.
True fellowship with God comes
through men. Love of the brethren is
the proof of the love of God: fellowship with the brethren is the proof of
fellowship with God.

St John does not repeat the phrase
which he has quoted from the vain
professors of Christianity (*we have
fellowship with Him, v. 6*), but gives
that which is its true equivalent according to the conditions of our being.
Comp. *v.* 3.

The supposition that μετ᾽ ἀλλήλων
means 'we with God and God with
us' is against the apostolic form of
language (John xx. 17), and also a-
gainst the general form of St John's
argument, for he takes the fellowship
of Christians as the visible sign and
correlative of fellowship with God:
iv. 7, 12. Comp. iii. 11, 23.

καὶ τὸ αἷμα...] *and the blood...*
This clause is coordinate with that
which goes before. The two results
of 'walking in the light' are inti-
mately bound together. Active fellowship shews the reality of that
larger spiritual life, which is life in
God; and at the same time the action
of Christ upon the members of His

Body brings about that real sinlessness
which is essential to union with God.

The case taken is that of those who
are in Christ's Body. The question
is not of 'justification,' but of 'sanctification.' 'Walking in the light' is
presupposed, as the condition for this
application of the virtue of Christ's
Life and Death. See Additional Note.

Ἰησοῦ τοῦ υἱοῦ αὐτοῦ] *Jesus His
Son.* The union of the two natures
in the one Person is clearly marked
by the contrast *'Jesus'* (not *Jesus
Christ,' 'His Son.'* Compare (iv. 15);
v. 5; Heb. iv. 14; (Gal. iv. 4 ff.);
and for the full title *v.* 3 note. Here
the human name (*Jesus*) brings out the
possibility of the communication of
Christ's Blood; and the divine name
brings out its all-sufficing efficacy.

Mire... ait *et sanguis Jesu filii
eius:* Filius quippe Dei in divinitatis
natura sanguinem habere non potuit;
sed quia idem Filius Dei etiam Filius
hominis factus est recte propter unitatem personæ eius Filii Dei sanguinem appellat ut verum eum corpus
assumpsisse, verum pro nobis sanguinem fudisse demonstraret (Bede).
So Ignatius (*ad Eph.* 1) ventures to
write ἐν αἵματι θεοῦ. Comp. Lightfoot on Clem. Rom. i. 2 παθήματα
αὐτοῦ, and the Additional Note in the
Appendix, pp. 400 ff.

For the title see Additional Note
on. iii. 23.

καθαρίζει] *emundat* V., *purgabit*
Aug., *cleanseth.* Comp. John xiii. 10.
The thought is not of the forgiveness
of sin only, but of the removal of sin.
The sin is done away; and the puri-
fying action is exerted continuously.

τίας.   ⁸Ἐὰν εἴπωμεν ὅτι Ἁμαρτίαν οὐκ ἔχομεν, ἑαυτοὺς

The idea of 'cleansing' is specially connected with the fitting preparation for divine service and divine fellowship. Ritual 'cleanness' was the condition for the participation in the privileges of approach to God, under the Old Covenant. So 'the blood of Christ' cleanses the conscience for service to Him Who is a Living God (Heb. ix. 13 f., 22 f.). He gave Himself for us, to cleanse for Himself a peculiar people (Tit. ii. 14). He cleansed the Church to present it to Himself in glory (Eph. v. 26 f.).

The fulness of the thought is expressed in Matt. v. 8, were the blessing of 'the clean (καθαροί) in heart' is that they shall see God (comp. 1 John iii. 2).

ἀ. πάσης ἁμ.] *from all sin*, so that men are made like to God, in Whom is no darkness (*v.* 5). The thought here is of 'sin' and not of 'sins': of the spring, the principle, and not of the separate manifestations. For the singular compare c. iii. 8 f.; John i. 29: for the plural *v.* 9; ii. 2, 12; iv. 10; Apoc. i. 5.

The sing. and plur. are used in significant connexion, John viii. 21, 24.

For the use of πᾶς with abstract nouns (π. ἁμ. 'sin in all its many forms') see James i. 2 πᾶσα χαρά, 2 Cor. xii. 12 πᾶσα ὑπομονή, Eph. i. 8 πᾶσα σοφία, 2 Pet. i. 5 πᾶσα σπουδή. Contrast 1 Pet. v. 7 πᾶσα ἡ μέριμνα, John v. 22 (τὴν κρίσιν πᾶσαν), xvi. 13 (τὴν ἀλήθειαν πᾶσαν).

8. The mention of sin at the end of *v.* 7 leads on to a new thought and a new plea. 'How,' it may be asked, 'has the Christian anything more to do with sin? How does it still continue?' The question has real difficulty.

Some who do not venture to affirm the practical indifference of action, may yet maintain that sin does not cleave to him who has committed it,

that man is not truly responsible for the final consequences of his conduct. This is the second false plea: *We have no sin;* sin is a transient phenomenon which leaves behind no abiding issues: it is an accident and not a principle within us.

The issue of this second false plea is also presented in a positive and negative form. By affirming our practical irresponsibility 'we lead ourselves astray' positively, and negatively we shew that 'the truth is not in us' as an informing, inspiring power.

ἁμ. οὐκ ἔχομεν] *we have no sin*. The phrase ἁμαρτίαν ἔχειν is peculiar to St John in the N. T. Like corresponding phrases ἔχειν πίστιν (Matt. xvii. 20; xxi. 21, &c.), ζωὴν ἔχειν (John v. 26, 40, &c.), λύπην ἔχειν (John xvi. 21 f.), &c., it marks the presence of something which is not isolated but a continuous source of influence (comp. κοινωνίαν ἔχειν *v.* 3).

Thus 'to have sin' is distinguished from 'to sin' as the sinful principle is distinguished from the sinful act in itself. 'To have sin' includes the idea of personal guilt: it describes a state both as a consequence and as a cause.

Comp. John ix. 41; xv. 22, note, 24; xix. 11.

The word 'sin' is to be taken quite generally and not confined to original sin, or to sin of any particular type. A tempting form of this kind of error finds expression in a fragment of Clement of Alexandria (*Ecl. Proph.* § 15, p. 993 P.) ὁ μὲν πιστεύσας ἄφεσιν ἁμαρτημάτων ἔλαβεν παρὰ τοῦ κυρίου, ὁ δ' ἐν γνώσει γενόμενος ἅτε μηκέτι ἁμαρτάνων παρ' ἑαυτοῦ τὴν ἄφεσιν τῶν λοιπῶν κομίζεται.

ἑαυτοὺς πλαν.] *ipsi nos seducimus* V., *we deceive ourselves*, or rather, *we lead ourselves astray.* Our fatal error is not only a fact (πλανώμεθα

πλανῶμεν καὶ ἡ ἀλήθεια οὐκ ἔστιν ἐν ἡμῖν. ⁹ἐὰν ὁμολογῶμεν τὰς ἁμαρτίας ἡμῶν, πιστός ἐστιν καὶ δίκαιος

8. οὐκ ἔστιν ἐν ἡμῖν ℵB me the: ἐν ἡμῖν οὐκ ἔστιν ς AC vg.   Comp. v. 10.

Matt. xxii. 29; John vii. 47), but it is
a fact of which we are the responsible
authors. The result is due to our
own efforts. We know that the assertion which we make is false (ψευδόμεθα); and, more than this, we persuade ourselves that it is true.

The phrase does not occur again in
N. T. For the use of ἑαυτούς with
the first person see Acts xxiii. 14;
Rom. viii. 23; xv. 1; 1 Cor. xi. 31;
2 Cor. i. 9, &c. St John uses it with
the second person c. v. 21; 2 John 8;
John v. 42; vi. 53; xii. 8.

The idea of πλάνη (c. iv. 6) is in all
cases that of straying from the one
way (James v. 19 f.): not of misconception in itself, but of misconduct.
Such going astray is essentially ruin-
ous.

The cognate terms are used of
the false christs and prophets (Matt.
xxiv. 4 ff.; Apoc. ii. 20; xiii. 14; xix.
20; comp. c. iv. 6; 2 Ep. 7); of
Satan (Apoc. xii. 9; xx. 3 ff.), of
Babylon (Apoc. xviii. 23), of Balaam
(Jude 11).

Ἀπατάω, ἀπάτη (φρεναπατάω, φρενα-
πάτης) are not found in the writings
of St John. In this group of words
the primary idea is that of 'decep-
tion,' the conveying to another a false
belief.

καὶ ἡ ἀλ. οὐκ ἔ. ἐν ἡμ.] and the truth
is not in us. According to the true
reading the pronoun is unemphatic
(so v. 10). The thought of 'the Truth'
prevails over that of the persons. In
St John 'the Truth' is the whole
Gospel as that which meets the re-
quirements of man's nature. Comp.
John viii. 32 ff.; xviii. 37. Introd.
to Gospel of St John, p. xliv.

The same conception is found in
the other apostolic writings; 2 Thess.
ii. 12; Rom. ii. 8; 2 Cor. xiii.;

(Gal. v. 7); 1 Tim. iii. 15; iv. 3; vi. 5;
2 Tim. ii. 15, 18; (Tit. i. 1); Heb. x.
26; 1 Pet. i. 22; James iii. 14; v. 19.

The Truth may therefore in this
most comprehensive sense be regarded
without us or within us: as something outwardly realised (v. 6 do the
truth), or as something inwardly efficacious (the truth is in us). Comp. v.
10 note. With this specific statement
ἡ ἀλ. οὐκ ἔστιν ἐν ἡμῖν (comp. ii. 4) contrast the general statement οὐκ ἔστιν
ἀλ. ἐν αὐτῷ John viii. 44 ('there is no
truth in him').

9. How then, it may be asked, can
consequences be done away? If sin
is something which clings to us in this
way, how can it be 'effaced'? The
answer is that the same attributes of
God which lead to the punishment of
the unrepentant lead to the forgiveness and cleansing of the penitent. He
meets frank confession with free blessing. And the divine blessing connected with the confession of sins is
twofold. It includes (1) the remission
of sins, the remission of the consequences which they entail, and (2)
the cleansing of the sinner from the
moral imperfection which separates
him from God: 1 Cor. vi. 9; Luke
xiii. 27.

ἐὰν ὁμολ.] There is no sharp opposition in form between this verse and
v. 8, as there is between 7 and 6 (if
we say—but if (ἐὰν δέ) we walk). Open
confession and open assertion are acts
of the same order.

ὁμολ. τὰς ἁμ.] confess our sins, not
only acknowledge them, but acknowledge them openly in the face of men.
Comp. ii. 23; iv. 2, 3, 15; Apoc. iii. 5;
John i. 20; ix. 22; xii. 42; Rom. x. 9,
&c. The exact phrase is not found elsewhere in N.T.; but the kindred phrase
ἐξομολογεῖσθαι ἁμαρτίας (παραπτώματα)

ἵνα ἀφῇ ἡμῖν τὰς ἁμαρτίας καὶ καθαρίσῃ ἡμᾶς ἀπὸ

9. τὰς ἁμ. (2) AB: + ἡμῶν ℵC vg syrr the me.   om. ἡμᾶς C.

occurs Matt. iii. 6 ‖ Mk. i. 5; James v. 16. Comp. Acts xix. 18.

Comp. Ecclus. iv. 26 μὴ αἰσχυνθῇς ὁμολογῆσαι ἐφ᾽ ἁμαρτίαις σου, Sus. v. 14 ὡμολόγησαν τὴν ἐπιθυμίαν.

Nothing is said or implied as to the mode in which such confession is to be made. That is to be determined by experience. Yet its essential character is made clear. It extends to specific, definite acts, and not only to sin in general terms. That which corresponds to saying 'we have no sin' is not saying 'we have sin,' but 'confessing our sins.' The denial is made in an abstract form: the confession is concrete and personal.

Augustine says with touching force: Ista levia quæ dicimus noli contemnere. Si contemnis quando appendis, expavesce quando numeras. And again : Vis ut ille ignoscat? tu agnosce.

πιστός ἐστιν...] The subject (God) is necessarily supplied from the context, vv. 5 ff. The form of the sentence (πιστός...ἵνα) presents the issue as that which is, in some sense, contemplated in the divine character. Forgiveness and cleansing are ends to which God, being what He is, has regard. He is not, as men are, fickle or arbitrary. On the contrary, He is essentially 'faithful' and 'righteous.' Comp. 1 Clem. ad Cor. c. 27.

Ἵνα is construed with adjectives in other cases: John i. 27 ἄξιος ἵνα...; Luke vii. 6 ἱκανὸς ἵνα..., but these are not strictly parallel; see c. iii. 11 note.

The epithet 'faithful' (πιστός) is applied to God not unfrequently in the Pauline epistles as being One who will fulfil His promises (Heb. x. 23; xi. 11), and complete what He has begun (1 Thess. v. 24; 1 Cor. i. 9), and guard those who trust in Him

(1 Cor. x. 13; comp. 1 Pet. iv. 19), because this is His Nature (2 Tim. ii. 13). With these passages those also must be compared in which Christ is spoken of as 'faithful' (2 Thess. iii. 3), and that both in regard to God (Heb. iii. 2) and to man (Heb. ii. 17).

God (the Father) again is spoken of in the New Testament as 'righteous' (δίκαιος) in Apoc. xvi. 5; John xvii. 25; Rom. iii. 26; and so also Christ, c. ii. 1, iii. 7; 1 Pet. iii. 18 (the usage in Matt. xxvii. 19, 24; Luke xxiii. 47 is different). The subject in c. ii. 29 is doubtful.

The essence of righteousness lies in the recognition and fulfilment of what is due from one to another. Truth passing into action is righteousness. He is said to be righteous who decides rightly, and he also who passes successfully through a trial.

Righteousness is completely fulfilled in God both in respect of what He does and of what He is. Here action and character (as we speak) absolutely coincide. And yet further, the 'righteousness' of God answers to His revealed purpose of love; so that the idea of righteousness in this case draws near not unfrequently to the idea of 'mercy.' Compare the use of 'righteousness' in the second part of Isaiah (e.g. xlii. 6, Cheyne).

It may indeed be said most truly that the righteousness of God is His love seen in relation to the discipline of man; and that love is righteousness seen in relation to the purpose of God.

So far as righteousness is manifested in the life of one whose powers and circumstances change, the principle, which is unchanging, will receive manifold relative embodiments from time to time.

The forgiveness and the cleansing

πάσης ἀδικίας. ¹⁰Ἐὰν εἴπωμεν ὅτι Οὐχ ἡμαρτήκαμεν,

of those who 'confess their sins' are naturally connected with God's faithfulness and righteousness. They answer to what He has been pleased to make known to us of His being in Scripture and life and history. He has laid down conditions for fellowship with Himself which man can satisfy and which He will satisfy.

It is not difficult to see how this view of God's action is included in the fundamental message : *God is light*. Light necessarily imparts itself (πιστός), and imparts itself as light (δίκαιος).

The two epithets are applied to God as 'a righteous and faithful witness,' Jer. xlii. 5.

ἀφῇ ἡμῖν τὰς ἁμ.] The verb ἀφιέναι occurs in this connexion in St John c. ii. 12; John xx. 23. The phrase ἄφεσις ἁμαρτιῶν (Synn., Acts, Eph., Col., Heb.) is not found in his writings. The image of 'remission,' 'forgiveness,' presents sin as a 'debt,' something external to the man himself in its consequences, just as the image of 'cleansing' marks the personal stain.

The repetition of the pronoun (ἡμῖν, ἡμᾶς) is to be noticed.

ἀφῇ...καθαρίσῃ] *remittat...emundet ab...* V., *dimittat...purget ex...* Aug., *forgive...cleanse...* Both acts are here spoken of in their completeness. The specific sins (αἱ ἁμαρτίαι) are forgiven (see Additional Note): the character (ἀδικία) is purified. The Christian character (*righteousness*) depends on a distinct relation to God in Christ. This admits of no degree; but there is a progressive hallowing of the Christian which follows after to the end of life (*v.* 7).

The two parts of the divine action answer to the two aspects of righteousness already noticed. As judging righteously God forgives those who stand in a just relation to Himself: as being righteous He communicates His nature to those who are united with Him in His Son.

Hence it is said that 'God cleanses' —there can be no doubt as to the subject—as before that 'the blood of Christ cleanses.' The Father, the one Fountain of Godhead, cleanses by applying the blood of the Son to believers. It is significant also that 'sin' (as distinguished from 'sins') is here regarded under the relative aspect of duty as 'unrighteousness' (c. v. 17).

ἀδικίας] *iniquitate* V., *unrighteousness.* The word occurs elsewhere in St John only in c. v. 17; John vii. 18. Generally the kindred words (δικαιοσύνη, &c.) are rare in his writings. Righteousness and unrighteousness are regarded by him characteristically under the aspect of truth and falsehood: that is, under the form of being rather than under the form of manifestation.

The correspondence of *righteous* and *unrighteousness* is lost in the Latin (*justus...iniquitate*), and hence in A.V.

10. So far the Apostle has dealt with the two main aspects of the revelation *God is light*. He has shewn what is the character which it fixes for the man who is to have fellowship with Him (*if we walk in the light*); and he has shewn also how that character can be obtained (*if we confess our sins*). Man must become like God; and to this end he must recognise his natural unlikeness to Him.

A third plea still remains. He who recognises the true character of sin, and the natural permanence of sin as a power within, may yet deny that he personally has sinned. This plea is suggested by the words 'our sins' in *v.* 9, just as the plea in *v.* 8 was suggested by 'all sin' in *v.* 7. Conviction in this case is sought not primarily in consciousness (*we lie, v.* 6;

ψεύστην ποιοῦμεν αὐτὸν καὶ ὁ λόγος αὐτοῦ οὐκ ἔστιν
ἐν ἡμῖν.

we deceive ourselves, v. 8), but in the voice of God (*we make Him a liar*).

The consequences of this assertion of sinlessness are stated in the same form as before (*vv.* 6, 8). By making it we affirm (positively) that God deals falsely with men; and (negatively) we are without the voice of God within us which converts His revelation for each one into a living Word.

Thus divine revelation is regarded first from without and then from within. God speaks; and (it is implied) His word enters into the soul of the believer, and becomes in him a spring of truth (John iv. 14) and a power of life (c. ii. 14). By claiming sinlessness we first deny generally the truth of the revelation of God; and, as a consequence of this denial, we lose the privilege of 'converse' with Him : *His word is not in us.*

Philo in an interesting passage (*Leg. Alleg.* i. 13: i. p. 50 M) notices the grounds on which men seek to escape the charge of sin : ὁ μὴ ἐμπνευσθεὶς (Gen. ii. 7) τὴν ἀληθινὴν ζωὴν ἀλλ' ἄπειρος ὢν ἀρετῆς κολαζόμενος ἐφ' οἷς ἥμαρτεν εἶπεν ἂν ὡς ἀδίκως κολάζεται, ἀπειρίᾳ γὰρ τοῦ ἀγαθοῦ σφάλλεσθαι περὶ αὐτό...τάχα δὲ μηδ' ἁμαρτάνειν φήσει τὸ παράπαν εἴ γε τὰ ἀκούσια καὶ τὰ κατὰ ἄγνοιαν οὐδὲ ἀδικημάτων λόγον ἔχειν φασί τινες.

οὐχ ἡμαρτήκαμεν] *we have not sinned.* The statement is quite unlimited. It is an absolute denial of the fact of past sin as carrying with it present consequences.

ψ. ποιοῦμεν αὐτόν] *mendacem facimus eum* V., *we make Him a liar*, that is God (the Father) who is the main subject of the whole section 6—10 (*with Him, v.* 6 ; *as He is, v.* 7 ; *He is faithful, v.* 9). The conclusion follows from a consideration of the nature of divine revelation. Revelation is directed in the first instance

to making clear the position of man towards God. Such an office St Paul assigns to law, and to the Law particularly. And generally all the communications of God to men presuppose that the normal relations between earth and heaven have been interrupted. To deny this is not only to question God's truth in one particular point, but to question it altogether; to say not only 'He lieth' in the specific declaration, but 'He is a liar' in His whole dealing with mankind. Comp. c. v. 10.

The peculiar phrase ψ. ποιοῦμεν is characteristic of St John (John v. 18; viii. 53; x. 33; xix. 7, 12), and carries with it the idea of overweening, unrighteous self-assertion.

ὁ λόγος αὐτοῦ] *His word*, the word of God, ii. 14. Comp. John viii. 55; x. 35; xvii. 6, 14, 17.

The phrase is used specially for the Gospel message, which is the crown of all revelation: Luke v. 1; viii. 11, 21; xi. 28; and habitually in the Acts : iv. 31; vi. 2, 7; viii. 14; xi. 1; xii. 24; xiii. 5, 7, 44, 46, &c.

The 'word' here differs from the 'truth' in *v.* 8 as the process differs from the result. The 'truth' is the sum considered objectively of that which the 'word' expresses. The word as a living power makes the truth real little by little to him who receives it (John viii. 31, 32). And further, the 'word' is personal: it calls up the thought of the speaker : it is 'the word of God.' The truth on the other hand is abstract, though it is embodied in a Person.

The word, like the truth, can be regarded both as the moving principle which stirs the man and as the sphere in which the man moves. The 'word abides in him' (John v. 38, comp. viii. 37), and conversely he 'abides in the word' (John viii. 31).

Additional Note on i. 2. The Fatherhood of God.

The idea of the Divine Fatherhood, answering to that of human sonship TheDivine
and childship (see Additional Note on iii. 1), occupies an important place Father-
in the writings of St John. It cannot be rightly understood without hood.
reference to its development in the Old Testament and in the Synoptic
Gospels.

In the Old Testament the general notion of Fatherhood was made i. In the
personal by the special covenants which He was pleased to establish with Old Testa-
representative men. He thus became the 'Father' of the chosen people ment.
in a peculiar sense (Ex. iv. 22; Deut. xxxii. 6; comp. i. 31, viii. 5; Is. lxiii.
16, lxiv. 8; comp. xliii. 1, 6, 21, xliv. 2, 24, xlvi. 3 ff.; Jer. xxxi. 9, 20; Hos.
xi. 1; Mal. ii. 10; comp. i. 6); and each member of the nation was His
child (Deut. xiv. 1; Is. i. 2, xxx. 1, 9, xliii. 6, lxiii. 8; Jer. iii. 4, 19; comp.
Matt. xv. 24, 26). But this sonship was regarded as an exceptional blessing.
It belonged to the nation as 'priests and kings' to the Lord; and so we
find that the relationship of privilege, in which all the children of Israel
shared in some manner, was in an especial degree the characteristic of the
theocratic minister (comp. Ps. lxxxii. 6). Of the king, the representative
head of the royal nation, God said '*Thou art my Son, this day,*' that is at
the moment of the solemn consecration, '*have I begotten thee*' (Ps. ii. 7):
and again, '*He shall cry unto me : Thou art my Father, my God, and the
rock of my salvation. Also I will make him my firstborn, higher than
the kings of the earth*' (Ps. lxxxix. 26 f.; comp. 2 Sam. vii. 12 ff.). Comp.
Ecclus. xxiii. 1, 4.

It will however be observed on a study of the passages that the idea of This idea
Fatherhood in the Old Testament is determined by the conceptions of an limited.
Eastern household, and further that it is nowhere extended to men generally. God is the great Head of the family which looks back to Him as its
Author. His 'children' owe Him absolute obedience and reverence : they
are 'in His hand': and conversely He offers them wise counsel and protection. But the ruling thought throughout is that of authority and not
of love. The relationship is derived from a peculiar manifestation of God's
Providence to one race (Ex. iv. 22; Hos. xi. 1), and not from the original
connexion of man as man with God. If the nobility of sonship is to be
extended to Gentiles, it is by their incorporation in the chosen family (Ps.
lxxxvii).

So far the conception of a Divine Fatherhood is (broadly speaking) ii. The
national among the Jews as it was physical in the Gentile world. But in idea of
the Gospels the idea of Sonship is spiritual and personal. God is revealed as Divine
the Giver and Sustainer (Matt. vii. 9 ff.) of a life like His own, to those who hood in the
were created in His image, after His likeness, but who have been alienated Synoptic
from Him (Luke xv. 11 ff.). The original capacity of man to receive God is Gospels.
declared, and at the same time the will of God to satisfy it. Both facts
are set forth once for all in the person of Him who was both the Son of
man and the Son of God.

This idea realised in Christ,

The idea of the Divine Fatherhood and of the Divine Sonship as realised in Christ appears in His first recorded words and in His dedication to His public ministry. The words spoken in the Temple : '*Wist ye not that I must be in my Father's house ?*' (Luke ii. 49 ἐν τοῖς τοῦ πατρός) appear to mark in the Lord, from the human side, the quickened consciousness of His mission at a crisis of His life, while as yet the local limitations of worship are fully recognised (contrast John iv. 21). The voice at the Baptism declares decisively the authority of acknowledged Sonship as that in which He is to accomplish His work (Matt. iii. 17 and parallels; comp. John i. 34).

Declared in the Sermon on the Mount.

In the Sermon on the Mount the idea of God's Fatherhood in relation both to Christ and to the disciples is exhibited most prominently. The first notice of the sonship of men is remarkable and if rightly interpreted most significant: '*Blessed are the peacemakers for they shall be called sons of God*' (Matt. v. 9). This benediction is seen in its true light by comparison with the angelic hymn : '*On earth peace among men of well-pleasing*' (Luke ii. 14). The peace of which Christ speaks is that of reunited humanity (comp. Eph. ii. 14 ff.). The blessing of sonship is for those who, quickened by God's Spirit (Rom. viii. 14), help to realise on earth that inward brotherhood of which He has given the foundation and the pledge.

The teaching which follows the beatitude enforces and unfolds this thought. The sign of Sonship is to be found in god-like works which cannot but be referred at once to their true and heavenly origin (Matt. v. 16). These are to be in range no less universal than the most universal gifts of God, the rain and the sunshine (v. 44 ff.; Luke vi. 35 ff.), in order that the fulness of divine sonship may be attained and manifested (*v.* 45 ὅπως γένησθε υἱοὶ τοῦ π. ὑ. τοῦ ἐν οὐρ.; Luke vi. 35 ἔσεσθε υἱοὶ ὑψίστου). At the same time the standard of judgment, even all-knowing love, impresses a new character upon action (Matt. vi. 1, 4, 6, 18). The obligations of kindred to others follow from the privilege of kindred with the common Father (Matt. vi. 14 f.; Mark xi. 25 f.). The Father's knowledge anticipates the petitions of the children (Matt. vi. 8 ; Luke xii. 30), and duly provides for their wants (Matt. vi. 26 ff.; Luke xii. 24 ff.). Here and elsewhere the laws of natural affection are extended to spiritual relations (Matt. vii. 9 ff.; Luke xi. 11 ff.).

The elevation of the idea in the New Testament.

From these passages it will be seen how immeasurably the conception of Fatherhood is extended by the Lord beyond that in the Old Testament. The bond is moral, and not physical : it is personal and human, and not national. It suggests thoughts of character, of duty, of confidence which belong to a believer as such and not peculiarly to those who stand in particular outward circumstances. In the few other passages in the Synoptic Gospels in which the title 'your Father' occurs, it has the same force : it conveys implicitly grounds of trust and the certainty of future triumph (Matt. x. 20, 29; Luke xii. 32). The 'name' of Him whom the Lord made known was, it may be said truly, 'the Father,' even as the name of Him who sent Moses was 'Jehovah,' 'the absolute,' 'the self-existent[1].' And in this con-

---

[1] There is really no strict representative of the name Jehovah in the New Testament except in the ὁ ὤν of the Apocalypse, and even there it is modified: Apoc. i. 4, 8, iv. 8 (ὁ ὤν καὶ ὁ ἦν καὶ ὁ ἐρχ.), xi. 17, xvi. 5 (ὁ ὤν καὶ ὁ ἦν).

nexion the first petition of the Lord's Prayer gains a new meaning : *Our Father which art in heaven, hallowed be Thy name*—the supreme revelation of Fatherhood (Matt. vi. 9; comp. Luke xi. 2).

The revelation of the Father is indeed distinctly claimed by the Lord for Himself alone (Matt. xi. 27; Luke x. 22). True discipleship to Him is the fulfilment of 'His Father's' will (Matt. vii. 21). He pronounces with authority upon the divine counsels and the divine working, as being of 'His Father' (Matt. xv. 13, xvi. 17, xviii. 10, 14, 19, 35, xxv. 34, xxvi. 29; Luke xxii. 29). He speaks of 'His Father's promise' (Luke xxiv. 49), and of 'His Father's presence' (Matt. x. 32 f.) with the confidence of a Son. But with the confidence of a Son the Lord maintains also the dependence of a Son. Every prayer which He makes will be answered (Matt. xxvi. 53), yet He places Himself wholly in 'His Father's' hands (Matt. xxvi. 39, 42) ; and He reserves some things for His Father alone (Matt. xx. 23).

The revelation of theFather, the work of Christ.

Such a revelation of the Divine Fatherhood through the Son to sons definitely distinguishes the Christian doctrine of God from Pantheism and Theism. As against Pantheism it shews God as distinct from and raised immeasurably above the world; as against Theism it shews God as entering into a living fellowship with men, as taking humanity into personal union with Himself. The unseen King of the divine Kingdom is made known as One to whom His people can draw near with the confidence of children[1].

Distinctive features of the revelation.

The revelation of God as the Father is specially brought out by St John; but in a somewhat different form from that in which it is found in the Synoptists. Two titles occur commonly in the Gospel in relation to Christ : (a) The Father; and (β) My Father. Both of these occur in the Synoptists each nine or ten times. But on the other hand St John never uses the phrases ὁ πατήρ μου ὁ ἐν οὐρανοῖς (ὁ οὐράνιος), ὁ πατὴρ ὑμῶν ὁ ἐν οὐρανοῖς, which occur each nine times in the Synoptic Gospels; nor does he use the phrase ὁ πατὴρ ὑμῶν except xx. 17 (in contrast); nor yet the Pauline phrase ὁ πατὴρ ἡμῶν in his own writings. In the Epistles he uses

iii. The revelation of Fatherhood in St John,

---

[1] The simple title 'my Father' is comparatively rare in the Synoptic Gospels. It is not found in St Mark (comp. viii. 38‖Matt. xvi. 27). It occurs in St Luke :

ii. 49 (ἐν τοῖς τοῦ π. μ.)

x. 22 (parallel to Matt. xi. 27)

xxii. 29 (καθὼς διέθετό μοι ὁ π. μ. βασιλείαν)

xxiv. 49 (τὴν ἐπαγγελίαν τοῦ π. μ.)

In St Matthew it is found more frequently

xi. 27 πάντα μοι παρεδόθη ὑπὸ τοῦ π. μ.

xx. 23 οἷς ἡτοίμασται ὑπὸ τοῦ π. μ.

xxv. 34 οἱ εὐλογημένοι τοῦ π. μ.

xxvi. 29 ἐν τῇ βασιλείᾳ τοῦ π. μ.

—— 39, 42 Πάτερ μου

xxvi. 53 παρακάλεσαι τὸν πατέρα μου.

But most frequently with the addition ὁ ἐν (τοῖς) οὐρανοῖς (ὁ οὐράνιος).

vii. 21, xii. 50 τὸ θέλημα τοῦ π. μ. τοῦ ἐν (τοῖς) οὐρ.

x. 32, 33 ἔμπροσθεν τοῦ π. μ. τοῦ ἐν (τοῖς) οὐρ.

xv. 13 ἣν οὐκ ἐφύτευσεν ὁ π. μ. ὁ οὐράνιος

xvi. 17 οὐκ ἀπεκάλυψεν ἀλλ' ὁ π. μ. ὁ ἐν οὐρ.

xviii. 10 τὸ πρόσωπον τοῦ π. μ. τοῦ ἐν οὐρ.

—— 19 γενήσεται αὐτοῖς παρὰ τοῦ π. μ. τοῦ ἐν οὐρ.

—— 35 οὕτως καὶ ὁ π. μ. ὁ οὐράνιος ποιήσει ὑμῖν.

uniformly the absolute title ὁ πατήρ (comp. 2 John 3) without any addition;
and in the Apoc. ὁ πατὴρ αὐτοῦ (μου) but not ὁ πατήρ.

in contrast with that in the Synoptists. These differences though minute are really significant. St John in his latest writings regards the relation of the Divine Fatherhood in its eternal, that is, in its present, realisation, and not in regard to another order. Or to look at the truth from another point of view, St John presents to us the Sonship of Christ, the foundation of the sonship of men, from its absolute side, while the Synoptists connect it with the fulfilment of the office of the Messianic King.

The title 'the Father.' The full sense of the title 'the Father' will be seen by an examination of the passages in which the titles ὁ πατήρ and ὁ θεός occur in close connexion:

John i. 18 θεόν... εἰς τὸν κόλπον τοῦ πατρός.

— iii. 34 ff. ὁ θεός...τὰ ῥήματα τοῦ θεοῦ...ὁ πατὴρ ἀγαπᾷ...ἡ ὀργὴ τοῦ θεοῦ.

— iv. 21 ff. τῷ πατρί...τῷ πατρί...ὁ πατήρ...πνεῦμα ὁ θεός.

— vi. 27 ὁ πατήρ, ὁ θεός.

— 45 f. θεοῦ...τοῦ πατρός...τὸν πατέρα...τοῦ θεοῦ...τὸν πατέρα.

— xiii. 3 ὅτι πάντα ἔδωκεν αὐτῷ ὁ πατήρ...καὶ ὅτι ἀπὸ θεοῦ ἐξῆλθεν καὶ πρὸς τὸν θεὸν ὑπάγει.

— xiv. 1, 2, 9 τὸν θεόν...τοῦ πατρός μου...τὸν πατέρα.

1 John ii. 13 ff. τὸν πατέρα...τοῦ θεοῦ...τοῦ πατρός...τοῦ πατρός...τοῦ θεοῦ.

— iii. 1 ὁ πατήρ...θεοῦ.

— iv. 14 ff. ὁ πατήρ...τοῦ θεοῦ...ὁ θεός...τῷ θεῷ.

The title 'my Father.' The title 'my Father' as used by the Lord marks the special relation of God to the Son Incarnate, and so, mediately, to man in virtue of the Incarnation, and to all revelation as leading up to it. It is found John ii. 16, v. 17, 43, vi. 32, 40, viii. 19, 49, 54, x. 18, 25, 29, 37, xiv. 2, 7, 20, 21, 23, xv. 1, 8, 15, 23, 24, xx. 17.

The relation of the two titles. As to the relation of the two titles 'the Father' and 'my Father,' it may be said generally that 'the former suggests those thoughts which spring from the consideration of the moral connexion of God and man in virtue of the creation of man 'in the image of God,' while the latter points to those which spring from what has been made known to us in the course of the history of the world, the revelation of the connexion of the Incarnate Son with God and with man. 'The Father' corresponds under this aspect with the group of ideas gathered up in the Lord's title 'the Son of man' (comp. John vi. 27, viii. 28); and 'my Father' with those which are gathered up in the titles, 'the Son of God,' 'the Christ.'

The first instances in which the Lord uses the two titles seem to mark their meaning.

ii. 16 ὁ οἶκος τοῦ π. μου, comp. Luke ii. 49.

iv. 21, 23 προσκυνεῖν τῷ πατρί, comp. Matt. xi. 27.

And the first great discourse which lays the foundation of the Lord's claims unfolds the relation of the Son to the Father and to men, and so of men to the Father (John v. 19 ff.).

In this discourse it will be noticed that the title 'my Father' is found at the beginning and the end (*vv.* 17, 43), but elsewhere only the absolute titles 'the Father,' 'the Son.'

The two titles occur not unfrequently in close connexion, *e.g.* :

John v. 43 ἐλήλυθα ἐν τῷ ὀνόματι τοῦ πατρός μου.

— 45 μὴ δοκεῖτε ὅτι ἐγὼ κατηγορήσω ὑμῶν πρὸς τὸν πατέρα.

— vi. 27 τοῦτον ὁ πατὴρ ἐσφράγισεν.

— 32 ὁ πατήρ μου δίδωσιν ὑμῖν τὸν ἄρτον ἐκ τοῦ οὐρανοῦ.

— x. 27 διὰ τοῦτό με ὁ πατὴρ ἀγαπᾷ.

— 28 ταύτην τὴν ἐντολὴν ἔλαβον παρὰ τοῦ πατρός μου.

— 29 ὁ πατήρ μου ὃ δέδωκεν...ἁρπάζειν ἐκ τῆς χειρὸς τοῦ πατρός.

— xiv. 7 τὸν πατέρα μου ἂν ᾔδειτε.

— 9 ὁ ἑωρακὼς ἐμὲ ἑώρακεν τὸν πατέρα.

— xx. 17 οὔπω ἀναβέβηκα πρὸς τὸν πατέρα.

— ἀναβαίνω πρὸς τὸν πατέρα μου...

They are found also in phrases otherwise identical to which they give a sensible difference of colour.

John xiv. 11 ἐγὼ ἐν τῷ πατρὶ καὶ ὁ πατὴρ ἐν ἐμοί.

— 20 ἐγὼ ἐν τῷ πατρί μου καὶ ὑμεῖς ἐν ἐμοί.

— 31 ἐντολὴν ἔδωκέν μοι ὁ πατήρ.

— x. 18 ταύτην τὴν ἐντολὴν ἔλαβον παρὰ τοῦ πατρός μου.

If we try to go a little further into detail we notice the title 'the Father': *Use of the title 'the Father.'*

(1) In relation to men :

John iv. 21—3 προσκυνεῖν τῷ πατρί.

— v. 45 μὴ δοκεῖτε ὅτι ἐγὼ κατηγορήσω ὑμῶν πρὸς τὸν π.

— vi. 45 πᾶς ὁ ἀκούσας παρὰ τοῦ π.

— 46 οὐχ ὅτι τὸν π. ἑώρακέν τις.

— 65 ἐὰν μὴ ᾖ δεδομένον αὐτῷ ἐκ τοῦ π.

— x. 29 ἁρπάζειν ἐκ τῆς χειρὸς τοῦ π.

— 32 ἔδειξα ὑμῖν καλὰ ἐκ τοῦ π.

— xii. 26 τιμήσει αὐτὸν ὁ π.

— xiv. 6 οὐδεὶς ἔρχεται πρὸς τὸν π.

— 8 δεῖξον τὸν π...ἑώρακεν τὸν π.

— xv. 16 ὅτι ἂν αἰτήσητε τὸν π.

— xvi. 23 ἄν τι αἰτήσητε τὸν π.

— 26 ἐρωτήσω τὸν π. περὶ ὑμῶν.

— 27 ὁ π. φιλεῖ ὑμᾶς.

1 John ii. 1 παράκλητον ἔχομεν πρὸς τὸν π. (note).

— 14 ἐγνώκατε τὸν π.

— 15 ἡ ἀγάπη τοῦ π.

— 16 οὐκ ἔστιν ἐκ τοῦ π.

— iii. 1 δέδωκεν ἡμῖν ὁ π.

2 John 4 ἐντολὴν ἐλάβομεν παρὰ τοῦ π.

(2) In relation to the Son absolutely :

John i. 18 ὁ ὢν εἰς τὸν κόλπον τοῦ π.

— iii. 35 ὁ π. ἀγαπᾷ τὸν υἱόν (comp. xv. 9).

— v. 26 ὁ π....τῷ υἱῷ ἔδωκεν.

John vi. 46 οὗτος ἑώρακεν τὸν π.
— 57 κἀγὼ ζῶ διὰ τὸν π.
— x. 29 ἐγὼ καὶ ὁ π. ἕν ἐσμεν.
— xiv. 28 ὁ π. μείζων μού ἐστιν.
— xvi. 15 πάντα ὅσα ἔχει ὁ π. ἐμά ἐστιν.
1 John i. 2 ἥτις ἦν πρὸς τὸν π.
2 John 3 τοῦ υἱοῦ τοῦ π.
— 9 καὶ τὸν π. καὶ τὸν υἱὸν ἔχει (comp. 1 John ii. 22 ff.).

(3) In relation to the Mission of the Son—'the Father that sent me':

John v. 23 ὁ π. ὁ πέμψας αὐτόν.
— 36 ἃ δέδωκέν μοι ὁ π....μαρτυρεῖ ὅτι ὁ π. με ἀπέσταλκεν.
— 37, viii. 16, 18, xii. 49, xiv. 24 ὁ πέμψας με πατήρ.
— vi. 44 ὁ π. ὁ πέμψας με.
— x. 36 ὃν ὁ π. ἡγίασεν καὶ ἀπέστειλεν.
— xx. 21 καθὼς ἀπέσταλκέν με ὁ π.
Comp. xvi. 27 f. παρὰ τοῦ π., ἐκ τοῦ π. ἐξῆλθον.
1 John iv. 14 ὁ π. ἀπέσταλκεν τὸν υἱόν.
— i. 3, ii. 22, 23, 24 ὁ π., ὁ υἱός.

(4) More particularly in relation to the form of the Mission:
John v. 36 ἃ δέδωκέν μοι ὁ π. ἵνα τελειώσω αὐτά.
— vi. 27 ὁ υἱὸς τοῦ ἀνθρώπου...τοῦτον ὁ π. ἐσφράγισεν.
— viii. 28 καθὼς ἐδίδαξέν με ὁ π. ταῦτα λαλῶ.
— 38 ἃ ἐγὼ ἑώρακα παρὰ τῷ π. λαλῶ.
— xii. 50 καθὼς εἴρηκέν μοι ὁ π. οὕτως λαλῶ.
— xiv. 31 καθὼς ἐντολὴν ἔδωκέν μοι ὁ π. οὕτως ποιῶ.
— xv. 10 καθὼς ἐγὼ τοῦ π. τὰς ἐντολὰς τετήρηκα.
— xviii. 11 τὸ ποτήριον ὃ δέδωκέν μοι ὁ π.

(5) And also to the active communion between the Father and the Son in the accomplishment of it:
John v. 19 ff. ἂν μή τι βλέπῃ τὸν π. ποιοῦντα, ὁ π. πάντα δείκνυσιν αὐτῷ.
— vi. 37 ὃ δίδωσίν μοι ὁ π.
— x. 15 γινώσκει με ὁ π. κἀγὼ γινώσκω τὸν π.
— 38 ἐν ἐμοὶ ὁ π. κἀγὼ ἐν τῷ π.
— xiv. 10 ὁ π. ἐν ἐμοὶ μένων ποιεῖ τὰ ἔργα αὐτοῦ.
— 11 ἐγὼ ἐν τῷ π. καὶ ὁ π. ἐν ἐμοί.
— 31 ἀγαπῶ τὸν π.
— xvi. 32 ὁ π. μετ' ἐμοῦ ἐστίν.

(6) And to the consummation of the Mission:
John x. 17 διὰ τοῦτό με ὁ π. ἀγαπᾷ ὅτι ἐγὼ τίθημι τὴν ψυχήν μου.
— xiv. 12 ἐγὼ πρὸς τὸν π. πορεύομαι.
— 13 ἵνα δοξασθῇ ὁ π. ἐν τῷ υἱῷ.
— 16 ἐρωτήσω τὸν π. καὶ ἄλλον παράκλητον δώσει.
— 28, xvi. 28 πορεύομαι πρὸς τὸν π.
— xvi. 10 πρὸς τὸν π. ὑπάγω.
— 17 ὑπάγω πρὸς τὸν π.
Comp. xiii. 1 ἵνα μεταβῇ...πρὸς τὸν π.

(7) And to the Mission of the Spirit:

John xiv. 26 τὸ πνεῦμα τὸ ἅγιον ὃ πέμψει ὁ π. ἐν τῷ ὀνόματί μου.

— xv. 26 ὁ παράκλητος ὃν ἐγὼ πέμψω ὑμῖν παρὰ τοῦ π., το πνεῦμα...ὃ
παρὰ τοῦ π. ἐκπορεύεται.

— xvi. 25 περὶ τοῦ π. ἀπαγγελῶ ὑμῖν.

In each respect the particular relation is traced up to the primal
relation of the perfect divine love expressed in the idea of Fatherhood and
Sonship.

The title 'my Father' is far more rare than 'the Father,' though it Use of the
has been not unfrequently substituted for it in the later texts in order to title 'My
bring out a more obvious sense. It fixes attention, as has been already Father.'
remarked, upon the actual circumstances of Christ as the Incarnate Son,
as serving to convey the true idea of God as Father.

Hence it is used

(1) Specially in connexion with the office of Christ as the Fulfiller
of the old Covenant, the Interpreter of the God of Israel Who had
been misunderstood by the Jews. Looking to Christ, to His acts and
words, Israel might see the true character of the Lord. The Son was the
revelation of His Father:

John ii. 16 τὸν οἶκον τοῦ π. μ.

— v. 17 ὁ π. μ. ἕως ἄρτι ἐργάζεται.

— vi. 32 ὁ π. μ. δίδωσιν ὑμῖν τὸν ἄρτον ἐκ τοῦ οὐρανοῦ.

— viii. 19 οὔτε ἐμὲ οἴδατε οὔτε τὸν π. μ.

— 49 τιμῶ τὸν π. μ.

— 54 ἔστιν ὁ π. μ. ὁ δοξάζων με.

— x. 37 εἰ οὐ ποιῶ τὰ ἔργα τοῦ π. μ.

— xv. 1 ὁ π. μ. ὁ γεωργός ἐστιν.

— 8 ἐν τούτῳ ἐδοξάσθη ὁ π. μ.

— 23 ὁ ἐμὲ μισῶν καὶ τὸν π. μ. μισεῖ.

— 24 μεμισήκασιν καὶ ἐμὲ καὶ τὸν π. μ.

(2) And more widely of the particular aspect under which Christ presented the divine character in His own Person and Life:

John vi. 40 τὸ θέλημα τοῦ π. μ.

— x. 18 ταύτην τὴν ἐντολὴν ἔλαβον παρὰ τοῦ π. μ.

— 29 ὁ π. μ. ὃ δέδωκέν μοι.

— xiv. 2 ἐν τῇ οἰκίᾳ τοῦ π. μ.

— 7 εἰ ἐγνώκειτέ με καὶ τὸν π. μ. ἂν ᾔδειτε.

— 20 γνώσεσθε ὅτι ἐγὼ ἐν τῷ π. μ.

— 21 ἀγαπῶν ἐμὲ ἀγαπηθήσεται ὑπὸ τοῦ π. μ.

— 23 ὁ π. μ. ἀγαπήσει αὐτόν.

— xv. 15 ἃ ἤκουσα παρὰ τοῦ π. μ. ἐγνώρισα ὑμῖν.

— xx. 17 ἀναβαίνω πρὸς τὸν π. μ. καὶ πατέρα ὑμῶν.

Thus we can see the full force of the phrase 'I came in My Father's
name,' and not simply 'in the Father's name.' Christ consummated the

W. 3

earlier teaching and presented in a pattern of complete sacrifice the fulfilment of that love which is the source of being:

John v. 43 ἐλήλυθα ἐν τῷ ὀνόματι τοῦ π. μ.

— x. 25 τὰ ἔργα ἃ ἐγὼ ποιῶ ἐν τῷ ὀνόματι τοῦ π. μ.

Comp. xvii. 6, 11, 12, 26 (τὸ ὄνομα τοῦ π.).

'My Father' in the revelation of Christ brings 'the Father' close to
us (comp. Heb. ii. 11 ff.).

'The living   Still one other title must be noticed 'the living Father,' John vi. 57.
Father.'   This phrase is unique, though it corresponds to the common title 'the
living God' (Apoc. vii. 2 θεοῦ ζῶντος, xv. 7 τοῦ θεοῦ τοῦ ζῶντος εἰς τοὺς αἰ.
Matt. xvi. 16 ὁ υἱὸς τοῦ θ. τοῦ ζ. &c.). In the view which it gives of the
continuous activity of the divine love it completes the view of the divine
sovereignty given by the phrase ὁ βασιλεὺς τῶν αἰώνων, 1 Tim. i. 17; Apoc.
xv. 3.

Additional Note on i. 7.   *The idea of Christ's Blood in the
New Testament*[1].

The idea   The interpretation of the passages in the New Testament which refer
of Blood in to the blessings obtained by the 'Blood' of Christ must rest finally upon
the O. T.   the interpretation given to the use of Blood in the sacrificial system of the
O. T. Our own natural associations with Blood tend, if not to mislead, at
least to obscure the ideas which it suggested to a Jew.

And here it is obvious that the place occupied by Blood in the Jewish
sacrifices was connected with the general conception attached to it through-
The seat of out the Pentateuch. The Blood is the seat of Life in such a sense that it
Life; and can be spoken of directly as the Life itself (נֶפֶשׁ Gen. ix. 4; Deut. xii. 23).
More exactly the Life is said to be 'in the Blood' (Lev. xvii. 11). Hence it
was forbidden to eat flesh with the blood (Gen. ix. 4; Lev. vii. 26 f.; xvii.
11 ff.; Deut. xii. 23 f.): a man might not use another's life for the support
of his physical life.

living   For. it must be observed that by the outpouring of the Blood the life
when shed. which was in it was not destroyed, though it was separated from the
organism which it had before quickened: Gen. iv. 10; comp. Heb. xii.
24 (παρὰ τὸν ῎Αβελ); Apoc. vi. 10.

Appointed   This prohibition of the use of Blood as food gave occasion for the
for an   clearest declaration of its significance in sacrifice (Lev. xvii. 11): *I will
atone-   even set my face against that soul that eateth blood, and will cut him off
ment.   from among the people. For the soul—life—*(נֶפֶשׁ) *of the flesh is in the
blood; and I have given it to you upon the altar to make an atonement
for your souls—lives—*(עַל־נַפְשֹׁתֵיכֶם)*, for the Blood, it atones through
the soul—life* (בַּנֶּפֶשׁ יְכַפֵּר)*,* i.e. its atoning virtue lies not in its material
substance but in the life of which it is the 'vehicle.' Moreover, the

[1] On the subject of this note I may   Milligan, *The Resurrection of our Lord*,
refer to the very suggestive note of Dr   pp. 263 ff.

Blood already shed is distinctly treated as living. When it is sprinkled 'upon the altar' it makes atonement in virtue of the 'life' which is in it.

Thus two distinct ideas were included in the sacrifice of a victim, the death of the victim by the shedding of its blood, and the liberation, so to speak, of the principle of life by which it had been animated, so that this life became available for another end[1]. The ritual of sacrifice took account of both these moments in the symbolic act. The slaughtering of the victim, which was properly the work of the offerer, was sharply separated from the sprinkling of the blood, which was the exclusive work of the priest. The death was inflicted by him who in his representative acknowledged the due punishment of his sin; the bringing near to God of the life so rendered up was the office of the appointed mediators between God and men. Death and life were both exhibited, death as the consequence of sin, and life made by the divine appointment a source of life. And it is worthy of notice that these two thoughts of the shedding and of the sprinkling of the Blood, which embrace the two elements in the conception of atonement, were equally expressed by the one word αἱματεκχυσία, *sanguinis effusio (fusio)* V., *outpouring of blood* (Heb. ix. 22). Thus the life was first surrendered and then united with God.

Two aspects of its use: (1) shedding, (2) sprinkling.

So far the thoughts suggested by the Jewish animal sacrifices seem to be clear; but they were necessarily imperfect and transitional. The union between the offerer and the offering was conventional and not real. The victim was irrational, so that there could be no true fellowship between it and the offender. Its death was involuntary, so that it could not embody in the highest form surrender to the divine will.

The Levitical use necessarily symbolical and imperfect.

All that was foreshadowed by the Mosaic sacrificial system, all that was from the nature of the case wanting in it, Christ supplied. With Him, the Son of Man, all men are made capable of vital union: in Him all men find their true life. His sacrifice of Himself, through life and through death, was in every part a reasonable service. He endured the Cross at the hands of men. He was at once 'offered' and 'offered Himself' (Heb. ix. 14, 28); *and by His own blood He entered in once for all into the holy place, having obtained eternal redemption for us* (Heb. ix. 12).

The idea fulfilled in Christ.

Thus in accordance with the typical teaching of the Levitical ordinances the Blood of Christ represents Christ's Life (1) as rendered in free self-sacrifice to God for men, and (2) as brought into perfect fellowship with God, having been set free by death. The Blood of Christ is, as shed, the Life of Christ given for men, and, as offered, the Life of Christ now given to men, the Life which is the spring of their life (John xii. 24). In each case the efficacy of the Life of Christ depends, from man's side, on the incorporation of the believer 'in Christ.'

Christ's Blood (1) shed (Death), (2) offered to God (Life).

It will be evident from what has been said that while the thought of Christ's Blood (as shed) includes all that is involved in Christ's Death, the Death of Christ, on the other hand, expresses only a part, the initial part,

The idea of Christ's Blood always includes that of Christ's Life. Usage of St John.

---

[1] Compare Philo, *qu. det. pot. ins.* § 23, i. 207 M.: ἡ μὲν οὖν κοινὴ πρὸς τὰ ἄλογα δύναμις οὐσίαν ἔλαχεν αἷμα· ἡ δὲ ἐκ τῆς λογικῆς ἀπορρυεῖσα πηγῆς, τὸ πνεῦμα... τύπον τινὰ καὶ χαρακτῆρα θείας δυνάμεως, ἣν ὀνόματι κυρίῳ Μωυσῆς εἰκόνα καλεῖ...

of the whole conception of Christ's Blood. The Blood always includes the thought of the life preserved and active beyond death.

This conception of the Blood of Christ is fully brought out in the fundamental passage, John vi. 53—56. Participation in Christ's Blood is participation in His life (v. 56). But at the same time it is implied throughout that it is only through His Death—His violent Death—that His Blood can be made available for men.

In the other passages of St John's writings, where reference is made to the Blood of Christ, now one part of the whole conception and now the other predominates. In Apoc. i. 5 τῷ ἀγαπῶντι ἡμᾶς καὶ λύσαντι ἡμᾶς ἐκ τῶν ἁμαρτιῶν ἡμῶν ἐν τῷ αἵματι αὐτοῦ, and in Apoc. v. 9 ὅτι ἐσφάγης καὶ ἠγόρασας τῷ Θεῷ ἐν τῷ αἵματι, the idea of the single act, the pouring out of blood in death, is most prominent and yet not exclusively present. In the one case the present participle (ἀγαπῶντι) seems to extend the act beyond the moment of accomplishment; and in the other ἐν τῷ αἵματι is felt to add something to ἐσφάγης which is not included in it. The Blood is not simply the price by which the redeemed were purchased but the power by which they were quickened so as to be capable of belonging to God.

On the other hand in Apoc. xii. 11 ἐνίκησαν αὐτὸν διὰ τὸ αἷμα τοῦ ἀρνίου, Apoc. vii. 14 ἐλεύκαναν αὐτὰς [τὰς στολάς] ἐν τῷ αἵματι τοῦ ἀρνίου, 1 John i. 7 τὸ αἷμα Ἰησοῦ τοῦ υἱοῦ αὐτοῦ καθαρίζει ἡμᾶς ἀπὸ πάσης ἁμαρτίας, the conception of the Blood as an energetic power, as a fountain of life, opened by death and flowing still, is clearly marked.

This latter thought explains the stress which St John lays on the issue of the blood and the water from the side of the Lord after the Crucifixion (John xix. 34; 1 John v. 6 ff. notes). That which was outwardly, physically, death, was yet reconcileable with life. Christ lived even in Death and through Death.

The simple idea of the Death of Christ, as separated from His Life, falls wholly into the background in the writings of St John (John xi. 50 f.; xviii. 14; xii. 24 f., 33; xviii. 33). It is only in the words of Caiaphas that the virtue of Christ's death is directly mentioned. In this respect his usage differs from that of St Paul and St Peter (πάσχειν). If the Good Shepherd 'lays down His life for the sheep' (John x. 11), this last act only reveals the devotion of His care for them.

Usage of the Epistle to the Hebrews. In the Epistle to the Hebrews the manifold efficacy of Christ's Blood is directly illustrated by a parallel with two representative sacrifices, the Covenant Sacrifice by which Israel was brought into fellowship with God (Heb. ix. 15 ff.), and the Service of the Day of Atonement, by which the broken fellowship was again restored (Heb. ix. 11 ff.).

The Blood of Christ is the Blood of the New Covenant: Heb. ix. 15 ff. See Matt. xxvi. 28; Mk. xiv. 24; Lc. xxii. 20; 1 Cor. xi. 25, 27 (comp. 1 Cor. x. 16); and it is the Blood through which He as our High Priest enters into the Presence of God for us: Heb. ix. 12, 23 ff.; comp. xiii. 12, i. 3. These two aspects of the truth need to be carefully regarded. By 'sprinkling' of Christ's Blood the believer is first brought into fellowship with God in Christ; and in the imperfect conduct of his personal life, the life of Christ is continually communicated to him for growth and cleansing. He himself enters into the Divine Presence 'in the Blood of Jesus' (Heb. x. 19) surrounded, as it were, and supported by the Life which flows from Him[1]. Similar thoughts find expression in the other writings of the New Testament. Thus we read with predominant reference to the initial act of salvation: Usage in other books of N. T.

Acts xx. 28 τὴν ἐκκλησίαν τοῦ Θεοῦ ἣν περιεποιήσατο διὰ τοῦ αἵματος τοῦ ἰδίου.

1 Pet. i. 18 f. ἐλυτρώθητε...τιμίῳ αἵματι ὡς ἀμνοῦ ἀμώμου καὶ ἀσπίλου Χριστοῦ.

Col. i. 20 εἰρηνοποιήσας διὰ τοῦ αἵματος τοῦ σταυροῦ αὐτοῦ.

But even in such cases the first act is not regarded as an isolated act of forgiveness. It is the beginning of a state which continues:

Rom. v. 9 δικαιωθέντες νῦν ἐν τῷ αἵματι αὐτοῦ σωθησόμεθα δι' αὐτοῦ.

Eph. i. 7 ἐν ᾧ ἔχομεν τὴν ἀπολύτρωσιν διὰ τοῦ αἵματος αὐτοῦ.

Eph. ii. 13 ἐγενήθητε ἐγγὺς ἐν τῷ αἵματι τοῦ Χριστοῦ.

In other places the thought of the continuous efficacy of Christ's Blood as a power of life is even more conspicuous:

1 Pet. i. 2 (ἐκλεκτοῖς) εἰς ὑπακοὴν καὶ ῥαντισμὸν αἵματος Ἰησοῦ Χριστοῦ.

Heb. ix. 14 τὸ αἷμα τοῦ Χριστοῦ...καθαριεῖ τὴν συνείδησιν ἡμῶν ἀπὸ νεκρῶν ἔργων εἰς τὸ λατρεύειν Θεῷ ζῶντι.

Heb. x. 19 ἔχοντες...παρρησίαν εἰς τὴν εἴσοδον τῶν ἁγίων ἐν τῷ αἵματι Ἰησοῦ...προσερχώμεθα...

Heb. xii. 24 (προσεληλύθατε) αἵματι ῥαντισμοῦ κρεῖττον λαλοῦντι παρα τὸν Ἄβελ.

The two elements which are thus included in the thought of Christ's 1 John i. 9. Blood, or, in the narrower sense of the word, of Christ's Death and Christ's Blood, that is of Christ's Death (the Blood shed) and of Christ's Life (the Blood offered), are indicated clearly in *v.* 9 [*God*] *is faithful and righteous to forgive us our sins* (the virtue of Christ's Death); *and to cleanse us from all unrighteousness* (the virtue of Christ's Life).

Additional Note on i. 9. *The idea of sin in St John.*

The treatment of the doctrine of sin by St John requires to be con- The idea of sin in St John. sidered briefly in its main features for the understanding of many details in the Epistle. 'Sin,' St John says in a phrase of which the terms are made convertible, 'is lawlessness' (c. iii. 4 ἡ ἁμαρτία ἐστὶν ἡ ἀνομία, *peccatum est iniquitas* V.). The description is absolutely exhaustive. Man is constituted with a threefold relation, a threefold obligation to self, to the world, to God. To violate the 'law' by which this relation is defined in life is 'to sin.' Each conscious act by which the law is broken

---

[1] Compare a remarkable passage of Clement of Alexandria: διττὸν δὲ τὸ αἷμα τοῦ κυρίου, τὸ μὲν γάρ ἐστιν αὐτοῦ σαρκικόν, ᾧ τῆς φθορᾶς λελυτρώμεθα, τὸ δὲ πνευματικόν, τουτέστιν ᾧ κεχρίσμεθα. καὶ τοῦτ' ἔστι πιεῖν τὸ αἷμα τοῦ Ἰησοῦ τῆς κυριακῆς μεταλαβεῖν ἀφθαρσίας· ἰσχὺς δὲ τοῦ λόγου τὸ πνεῦμα, ὡς αἷμα σαρκός (*Pæd.* ii. 2, § 19).

is 'a sin': the principle which finds expression in the special acts is 'sin' (ἡ ἁμαρτία, John i. 29)[1].

Sin is self-assertion, selfishness, hatred.

When traced back to its last form this 'sin' is the self-assertion of the finite in violation of the limits which guide the harmonious fulfilment of the idea of its being. Every such act, being in its essence self-regarding, self-centred, must be a violation of 'love.' Thus lawlessness is under another aspect selfishness; or as it is characterised by St John, 'hatred' in opposition to love (1 John ii. 9; iii. 14 f.; iv. 20). There can be essentially no middle term.

The revealed law.

The 'law' which determines man's right conduct finds manifold declaration, through special divine utterances (John xvii. 8, ῥήματα), commandments (c. ii. 3 ἐντολαί), which are gathered up in the unity of one revelation (λόγος) without and within (c. ii. 7, 14). To disregard any of these is to sin.

'Sin.' 'sins.'

It follows that ἁμαρτία ('a sin,' 'sin') and ἁμαρτάνειν ('to sin') have two distinct meanings. Ἁμαρτία may describe a single act impressed by the sinful character (1 John v. 16 f.), or sin regarded in the abstract (John xvi. 8 f.). And again ἁμαρτάνειν may be 'to commit a sinful act' (c. i. 10) or 'to present a sinful character' (c. iii. 6). The plural ἁμαρτίαι offers no ambiguity (John viii. 24; xx. 23; 1 John i. 9; ii. 2, 12; iii. 5; iv. 10; comp. Apoc. i. 5; xviii. 4 f.).

The sinful character.

This distinction between the principle, the power, of sin and the manifestation of the power in individual sins is of primary importance. The wrong-doer embodies sin in deed (c. iii. 4, 8 ὁ ποιῶν τὴν ἁμαρτίαν, comp. John viii. 34), just as the right-doer embodies the Truth (c. i. 6 ποιεῖν τὴν ἀλήθειαν); and by so doing he contracts a character corresponding to his deeds (c. i. 8 ἔχει ἁμαρτίαν).

All men as sinful need salvation.

Sin, as a fact, is universal (1 John i. 10); and the end of sin is death (James i. 15). Or, as St John states the case, looking at the eternal relations of things, man in his natural state is 'in death' (1 John iii. 14 μεταβεβήκαμεν ἐκ τοῦ θανάτου εἰς τὴν ζωήν; comp. John v. 24, 40; Matt. viii. 22 ‖ Lc. ix. 60; Lc. xv. 24). 'The wrath of God abideth upon him' (John iii. 36 μένει ἐπ' αὐτόν; comp. Eph. ii. 3 τέκνα φύσει ὀργῆς). He needs 'salvation' (σῴζειν John iii. 17; v. 34; x. 9; xii. 47; σωτήρ John iv. 42, 1 John iv. 14; ἡ σωτηρία John iv. 22; comp. Apoc. vii. 10; xii. 10; xix. 1).

It may come to pass that 'sin' and 'sins' surround the sinner and become as it were the element in which he exists (John viii. 21 ἐν τῇ ἁμαρτίᾳ, 24 ἐν ταῖς ἁμαρτίαις, comp. 1 John v. 19 ἐν τῷ πονηρῷ κεῖται). He who sins 'has not seen God' (1 John iii. 6). 'Darkness' not only hinders the use of sight but destroys the organ of sight (1 John ii. 11). There is even in the Christian body a sin unto death (c. v. 16 ἁμαρτία πρὸς θάνατον,

---

[1] This use of ἡ ἁμαρτία is not found in the Synoptic Gospels nor in the Acts. It occurs in St Paul: Rom. v. 12, &c.

Many of the special terms which are used for sin in different aspects in other writings of the New Testament, are wanting in St John, e.g. ἀσεβεῖν, ἀσέβεια (St Paul, St Peter, St Jude), παραβαίνειν, παράβασις, παραβάτης (St Matthew, St Paul, Hebrews, St James; in 2 John 9 read προάγων); (παρανομεῖν, παρανομία); παράπτωμα (παραπίπτειν) (St Matthew, St Mark, St Paul). He commonly speaks of sin under the terms 'darkness,' 'hatred,' 'wandering.'

peccatum ad mortem V.) which excludes from the privileges of the Christian society, the natural forces of the Christian life.

The efficacy of Christ's work extends both to sin and sins. As 'the Lamb of God' 'He taketh away the sin of the world' (John i. 29 ὁ ἀμνὸς τοῦ θεοῦ, ὁ αἴρων τὴν ἁμαρτίαν τοῦ κόσμου, V. *Agnus Dei...qui tollit peccatum mundi*); and again 'He was manifested that he may take away sins,' not simply 'our sins' (1 John iii. 5 ἐφανερώθη ἵνα ἄρῃ τὰς ἁμαρτίας, *apparuit ut peccata tolleret* V.). Under another aspect this 'removal of sins' is an 'undoing,' an 'abrogation of the works of the devil' (c. iii. 8 ἐφανερώθη ὁ υἱὸς τοῦ θεοῦ ἵνα λύσῃ τὰ ἔργα τοῦ διαβόλου, *apparuit Filius Dei ut dissolvat opera diaboli* V.). *Christ deals with sin and sins.*

The consequences of sin once committed place the need of the sinner in a clear light. Sin unless it be taken away 'abideth' (John ix. 41); and its consequences fall under three main heads. The sinner incurs a debt; he falls into bondage; and he is estranged from God. The particular act calls for a proportionate reparation, the moral discipline of the debtor coinciding with the satisfaction due to the broken law; the wrong-doing impairs so far the powers of the doer; and it also places a barrier between him and God. The notion of debt (Matt. vi. 12) is recognised in that of the 'remission' of sins (c. i. 9; John xx. 23): the notion of bondage finds a most emphatic exposition in John viii. 32 ff.: 'the love of the Father' is incompatible with the love of the world, out of which sin springs (1 John ii. 15 ff.; comp. Eph. iv. 18; Col. i. 21). *Sin brings debt, bondage, alienation from God.*

Thus it is that man needs forgiveness, redemption, reconciliation. Forgiveness in order to be complete involves not only the remission of the penalty of the deed but the removal of the direct results of the act on the doer. As long as a debtor finds that his debt is remembered though the payment of it will not be exacted, forgiveness is not complete. The exercise of such a power of forgiveness corresponds with a new creation. Thus when the Lord claims as Son of man the power of the forgiveness of sins He offers as a sign of it a creative act (Matt. ix. 5 f.; comp. John v. 14). And so St John appeals to the divine promise assured to the penitent to 'forgive their sins and cleanse them from all unrighteousness' (1 John i. 9). *Forgiveness.*

Redemption again includes two elements, the deliverance of the sinner from thraldom to a foreign power, and the restoration of his lost strength. St John does not use the group of words connected with λύτρον (λυτροῦσθαι, λυτρωτής, λύτρωσις, ἀντίλυτρον), but he has the simple λύω (Apoc. i. 5); and in the Apocalypse he carries out the notion yet further, representing Christians as 'bought' for God (v. 9; xiv. 3 f.). *Redemption.*

Man's estrangement from God by sin can also be regarded in two ways. Sin cannot but be a bar to God's love; and conversely man as sinful cannot love God. He requires a change in condition and a change in feeling, propitiation and reconcilement. The latter thought finds its plainest expression in the group of words καταλλάσσειν, ἀποκαταλλάσσειν, καταλλαγή, which are peculiar to St Paul: the former in the group ἱλάσκομαι, ἱλασμός, ἱλαστήριον. The change in the personal relation of man to God, from the side of man, indicated by 'reconcilement' (2 Cor. v. 18—20; Rom. v. 10 f.), is referred to its source by St John, who shews that *Reconciliation.*

the love of God in the Mission of His Son calls out man's love (1 John iv. 10). On the other hand God looks with good pleasure on man in Christ: Christ is 'the propitiation for our sins' (c. ii. 2). 'He loosed us from our sins in His blood' (Apoc. i. 5). 'His blood cleanseth from all sin' (i. 7; comp. Heb. i. 3 καθαρισμὸν ἁμ. ποιησάμενος, Acts xxii. 16 ἀπόλουσαι τὰς ἁμ.)[1].

All flow from fellowship in Christ.

The last phrases lead at once to St John's view of the way in which the work of the Word Incarnate avails for forgiveness, for redemption, for reconcilement. By dying on the Cross He made His Life—His blood—available for all who believe in Him. The gift of God is eternal, divine, life, 'and this life is in His Son' (1 John v. 11 f.). The possession of such life is the destruction of past sin, and safety from sin to come (1 John iii. 9). By incorporation with Christ the believer shares the virtue of His humanity (John vi. 51, 57). Thus finally unbelief in Him is the test of sin (John xvi. 9).

Compare additional notes on i. 7; ii. 2, 13.

It may be added that it will be evident from this sketch of the teaching of the N. T. on sin, according to which the fundamental conception of sin is the self-assertion of the finite against the infinite, that the relation of good to evil is not one which exists of necessity in the nature of things. The difference is not metaphysical, inherent in being, so that the existence of evil is involved in the existence of good; nor physical, as if there were an essential antagonism between matter and spirit; but moral, that is recognised in the actual course of life, so that evil when present is known to be opposed to good.

---

[1] It will be of interest to put together without any discussion the various phrases which describe the action of Christ with regard to sin and sins.

(1) As to sin itself, He brought condemnation by His Incarnation; Rom. viii. 3 ὁ Θεὸς τὸν ἑαυτοῦ υἱὸν πέμψας...κατέκρινε τὴν ἁμαρτίαν ἐν τῇ σαρκί.

disannulling by His sacrifice: Heb. ix. 26 εἰς ἀθέτησιν τῆς ἁμαρτίας, διὰ τῆς θυσίας αὐτοῦ πεφανέρωται... Comp. Rom. vi. 7 ὁ ἀποθανὼν δεδικαίωται ἀπὸ τῆς ἁμ.

(2) As to the sins of men Christ makes propitiation for them: Heb. ii. 17...ἀρχιερεύς...εἰς τὸ ἱλάσκεσθαι τὰς ἁμαρτίας τοῦ λαοῦ.

forgives them: Matt. ix. 2 ff.: ἀφίενταί σου αἱ ἁμαρτίαι. Comp. Col. ii. 13 χαρισάμενος τὰ παραπτώματα.

takes them away, by bearing them: 1 John iii. 5 ἵνα ἄρῃ τὰς ἁμαρτίας; John i. 29 ὁ αἴρων τὴν ἁμαρτίαν τοῦ κόσμου. Comp. Heb. x. 4 ἀφαιρεῖν ἁμ.; x. 11 περιελεῖν ἁμ.

looses men from them: Apoc. i. 5 τῷ...λύσαντι ἡμᾶς ἐκ τῶν ἁμ. ἐν τῷ αἵματι αὐτοῦ. Comp. Rom. vi. 22 ἐλευθερωθέντες ἀπὸ τῆς ἁμ.

cleanses men from all sin: 1 John i. 7 τὸ αἷμα Ἰησοῦ...καθαρίζει ἡμ. ἀπὸ π. ἁμ.

saves from sins: Matt. i. 21 σώσει ...ἀπὸ τῶν ἁμ.

II. ¹ Τεκνία μου, ταῦτα γράφω ὑμῖν ἵνα μὴ ἁμάρ-

II. THE REMEDY FOR SIN AND THE
SIGN THAT IT IS EFFECTUAL (ii.
1—6).

Having dealt with the fact of sin
and the false pleas by which man en-
deavours to do away with its significance, St John states

1 The divine remedy for sin (vv. 1, 2).
2 The sign that the remedy is effectual in any particular case (vv. 3—6).

The first sub-section answers to the
counter-statements made in relation to
the first two pleas of men (i. 7, 9), but
it has a prominent distinctness of form,
as giving the complete answer to the
problem raised in i. 5—10. The assurance of the forgiveness of sin when
combined with the fact of its universality might lead some to underrate
its evil. In order to remove the last
semblance of support for such an
error, St John shews that the nature of the remedy for sin is such as
to move men most powerfully to
shrink from all sin and to help them
to avoid it.

This connexion is partly indicated
by Augustine: Male vis esse securus,
sollicitus esto. Fidelis enim est et
justus ut dimittat nobis delicta nostra
si semper tibi displiceas et muteris
donec perficiaris. Ideo quid sequitur?
*Filioli mei, hæc scribo vobis ut non
peccetis.*

1. *The divine remedy for sin*
(ii. 1, 2).

¹*My little children, these things I
write to you that ye may not sin.
And if anyone sin, we have an advocate with the Father, Jesus Christ,
the righteous;* ²*and himself is a
propitiation for our sins, and not for
ours only, but also for the whole
world.*

The fact of sin as something which
is irreconcileable with God and fruitful in consequences raises the questions of propitiation and mediation.

How, it may be asked, is that forgiveness, that cleansing, already spoken
of (i. 7, 9), brought about? The answer
is given in the summary description
of Christ's work. Christ is a universal
propitiation for sins; and He is an
advocate for the Christian. He has
accomplished a work on earth for all:
He is accomplishing a work in heaven
for those who are united with Him.
Both in Person (*righteous*) and in
work (*propitiation*) He is fitted to
fulfil the office which our necessities
require. These thoughts are treated
in the inverse order, because the apostle approaches the subject from the
side of believers (*we have*).

It has been already noticed that
the third plea (i. 10, *we have not
sinned*) is not treated exactly as the
two former. Symmetry would have
required a clause answering to the
assertion '*we have not sinned.*' St
John might, for example, have continued: 'if we sin....' But he shrinks
naturally from regarding sin as a
normal element in the Christian life;
and therefore he changes the mode
of dealing with the subject. Before
touching on the fact of sin, as indeed
part of the believer's experience to
the last, he asserts the end of his
teaching, which is sinlessness. This
is the end; and even if it cannot be
gained by the believer's effort and
directly, it can be gained through the
Saviour's work. That which is true
of the past (i. 9) is true throughout.

1. τεκνία μου] *filioli mei* V., *my
little children.* The form adopted in
i. 7, 9 is changed for one more direct
and personal. The thought of sin as a
reality for each one moves the apostle
to address with the utmost tenderness
those to whom he stands in the relation of a father. The title τεκνία occurs in John xiii. 33 and c. ii. 12, 28;
iii. 7, 18; iv. 4; v. 21 (Gal. iv. 19 τεκνία
μου is uncertain). The full title τεκνία

τητε.   καὶ ἐάν τις ἁμάρτῃ, παράκλητον ἔχομεν πρὸς

μου is found only here (c. iii. 18 is a
false reading). A commentary on St
John's use of the word is given by
the story (μῦθος οὐ μῦθος) of the
young Robber (Euseb. *H. E.* iii. 23).

ταῦτα γράφω] *these things I write*,
not only all that has been already said
as to the nature of God and as to the
reality, the nature, and the fact of sin
(i. 5—10), but, as i. 4, all that is present to the mind of the apostle as the
substance of his letter, though indeed
the preceding section includes all by
implication.

The use of the singular, *I write* (*vv.*
7, 8, 12, 13, 14, 21, 26; v. 13; contrast
i. 4) follows from 'my dear children.'

ἵνα μὴ ἁμάρτητε] *ut non peccetis* V.,
that ye may not sin. The phrase
is absolute. The thought is of the
single act (ἁμάρτητε) not of the state
(ἁμαρτάνητε); and the tense is decisive
against the idea that the apostle is
simply warning his disciples not to
draw encouragement for licence from
the doctrine of forgiveness. His aim
is to produce the completeness of the
Christ-like life (*v.* 6).

The difference of the aor. and pres.
conj. in connexion with ἵνα is well
illustrated by John v. 20, 23; vi. 28 f.

καὶ ἐάν τις...] *sed et si quis* V., i.e. ἐὰν
δὲ καί, *si quis* Aug., *and if any...* The
declaration of the remedy for sin is
placed as part of the main declaration of St John. It is not set as a
contrast (i. 7 ἐὰν δέ), nor simply as a
parallel clause (i. 9 ἐὰν ὁμολογῶμεν);
but as a continuous piece of the one
message. Here again the thought is
of the single act (ἁμάρτῃ), into which
the believer may be carried against
the true tenor of his life (i. 7), as
contrasted with the habitual state
(ἁμαρτάνει iii. 6, 8, 9; v. 18). Nothing
is said in one direction or the other
of the possibility of a Christian life
actually sinless.

The change of construction in the
sentence is remarkable. St John
writes *if any one...we...* and not *if
ye sin...ye...*, nor yet *if we sin...
we...*or *if any one...he...*, in order
to bring out the individual character
of the offence, and then to shew that
he is speaking of the Christian body
with which he identifies himself,
and to which Christ's promises are
assured. This is forcibly pointed out
by Augustine: Non dixit *habetis*, nec
me habetis dixit, nec *ipsum Christum
habetis* dixit; sed et Christum posuit
non se, et *habemus* dixit non *habetis*.
Maluit se ponere in numero peccatorum ut haberet advocatum Christum quam ponere se pro Christo advocatum et inveniri inter damnandos
superbos.

ἔχομεν] *we have* as a divine gift.
Comp. ii. 23; v. 12; 2 John 9.

παράκλητον] *advocatum* V., *an advocate.* This is the uniform rendering of the Latin and English Versions in this place, and is unquestionably correct, although the Greek
fathers give to it, as in the Gospel, an
active sense, 'consoler,' 'comforter.'
Christ as Advocate pleads the cause
of the believer against his 'accuser'
(κατήγωρ Apoc. xii. 10; comp. Zech.
iii. 1; ἀντίδικος 1 Pet. v. 8). In this
work the 'other Advocate' (John xiv.
16), the Spirit of Christ, joins (Rom.
viii. 26, 34).

One aspect of the Advocate's office
was foreshadowed by the entrance of
the High Priest into the Holy of
Holies on the Day of Atonement
(Heb. ix. 11 ff., 24; vii. 25).

For the meaning of the term παράκλητος in the Gospel of St John (xiv.
16, 26; xv. 26; xvi. 7) see note on
xiv. 16.

It will be noticed that in the context of the passage in which the Lord
promises 'another Advocate' (John
xiv. 16) he sets forth his own advocacy (xiv. 12 ff.).

τὸν πατέρα Ἰησοῦν Χριστὸν δίκαιον, ²καὶ αὐτός

Augustine applies the legal image in a striking parallel : Si aliquando in hac vita committit se homo disertæ linguæ et non perit, committis te Verbo et periturus es ?

The reference to the Advocate implies that the Christian on his part has effectually sought His help. This is assumed, and indicated by the change of person (*we* Christians *have*).

Clement of Rome (i. 36) speaks of the Lord under a corresponding title : ...εὕρομεν τὸ σωτήριον ἡμῶν Ἰησοῦν Χριστόν, τὸν ἀρχιερέα τῶν προσφορῶν ἡμῶν, τὸν προστάτην (*patronum*) καὶ βοηθὸν τῆς ἀσθενείας ἡμῶν.

πρὸς τὸν πατέρα] *apud patrem* V., *ad patrem* Aug. (*apud deum patrem* Tert.), *with the Father*, not simply in His Presence, but turned toward Him, addressing Him with continual pleadings. Comp. c. i. 2 ; John i. 1.

Christ's advocacy of man is addressed to God in that relation of Fatherhood which has been fully revealed in the Son who has taken manhood to Himself (πρὸς τὸν πατέρα not πρός τὸν θεόν).

Comp. i. 2 ἦν πρὸς τὸν πατέρα ; i. 3 μετὰ τοῦ πατρὸς καὶ μετὰ τοῦ υἱοῦ αὐτοῦ ; ii. 14 ἐγνώκατε τὸν πατέρα ; ii. 15 ἡ ἀγάπη τοῦ πατρός ; ii. 16 οὐκ ἔστιν ἐκ τοῦ πατρός ; ii. 22 ὁ ἀρνούμενος τὸν πατέρα καὶ τὸν υἱόν ; ii. 23 ὁ ὁμολογῶν τὸν υἱὸν καὶ τὸν πατέρα ἔχει ; ii. 24 ἐν τῷ υἱῷ καὶ [ἐν] τῷ πατρί ; iii. 1 δέδωκεν ἡμῖν ὁ πατήρ ; iv. 14 ὁ πατὴρ ἀπέσταλκεν τὸν υἱόν.

In every case this special conception is important for the fulness of the argument. See Additional Note on i. 2.

And on the other side man's Advocate is described by that compound name *Jesus Christ*, which presents Him in His humanity and also as the promised Saviour and King of mankind, the Son of man, and the Son of David. See Additional Note on iii. 23.

δίκαιον] *the righteous*. The adjective is not a simple epithet but marks predicatively ('being as he is righteous') that characteristic of the Lord which gives efficacy to His advocacy of man.

This rests (so to speak) not on His divine nature as Son of God, but on His human character (comp. 1 Pet. iii. 18).

He has Himself fulfilled and pleads for the fulfilment of that which is right according to the highest law. He is not an advocate who wishes to set aside the law but to carry it out and apply it. In Him the idea of manhood has obtained its absolute satisfaction, and in turn He claims that the virtue of this satisfaction be extended to all in fellowship with Himself.

The righteousness of Christ as presented here answers to the righteousness of the Father brought forward in i. 9 : He accomplishes perfectly all that is set forth in the revelation of the Father's Nature. By this righteousness He fulfils in fact the conditions which the High Priest fulfilled in symbol. Comp. Heb. vii. 26.

The thought of righteousness as a divine attribute belongs peculiarly to St John : John xvii. 25 πατὴρ δίκαιε ; c. i. 9 ; ii. 29 ; iii. 7. Comp. Rom. iii. 26.

Nothing is said of the manner of Christ's pleading : that is a subject wholly beyond our present powers. It is enough that St John represents it as the act of a Saviour still living (Heb. vii. 25) and in a living relation with His people. His work for them continues as real as during His earthly life (Lc. xxii. 32 ; xxiii. 34 ; John xvii. 24), though the conditions of it are changed. He is still acting personally in their behalf, and not only by the unexhausted and prevailing power of what He has once done. He Himself uses for His people the virtue of

ἱλασμός ἐστιν περὶ τῶν ἁμαρτιῶν ἡμῶν, οὐ περὶ τῶν
ἡμετέρων δὲ μόνον ἀλλὰ καὶ περὶ ὅλου τοῦ κόσμου.

2 ἰλ. ἐστιν ℵBC: ἐστ. ἰλ. A vg.　　μόνον ℵAC vg: μόνων B me the; comp.
Rom. iii. 29.

that work which He accomplished on
earth.

Bede says well: Unigenito Filio
pro homine interpellare est apud co-
æternum Patrem se ipsum hominem
demonstrare; eique pro humana natura rogasse est eandem naturam in
divinitatis suæ celsitudine suscepisse.
Interpellat ergo pro nobis Dominus
non voce sed miseratione, quia quod
damnare in electis noluit suscipiendo
servavit.

2. καὶ αὐτός...] *et ipse* V., *and He,*
or rather, *and He Himself* (Matt. i.
21). The emphatic pronoun enforces
the thought of the efficacy of Christ's
advocacy as 'righteous.' He who
pleads our cause, having fulfilled the
destiny of man, is at the same time
the propitiation for our sins. Comp.
v. 25; c. i. 7; iv. 10, 19 (3 John 10);
John ii. 25; iv. 44; v. 20; vi. 6 (xii.
49); 1 Pet. ii. 24.

The ideas of 'advocacy' and 'propitiation' are distinct, and yet in close
connexion. The latter furnishes the
basis of the former: the latter is
universal, while the former, so far
as it is revealed, is exercised for believers. It is to be noticed further
that the 'propitiation' itself is spoken
of as something eternally valid (*He is*)
and not as past (*He was;* comp. iii. 16
τὴν ψυχὴν ἔθηκεν).

ἱλασμός] *propitiatio* V., *a propitiation.* Comp. iv. 10. The Latin
renderings are unusually numerous.
Besides *propitiatio* which prevailed,
exoratio, deprecatio, placatio are
found, and also the verbal renderings
(*ipse*) *exorat, interpellat, postulat
pro....* And Augustine has in some
places *propitiator.* Christ is said to
be the 'propitiation' and not simply
the 'propitiator' (as He is called

the 'Saviour' iv. 14), in order to
emphasise the thought that He is
Himself the propitiatory offering as
well as the priest (comp. Rom. iii. 25).
A propitiator might make use of
means of propitiation outside himself.
But Christ is our propitiation, as He
is 'our life' (Col. iii. 4), our 'righteousness, sanctification and redemption' (1 Cor. i. 31). He does not
simply guide, teach, quicken: He is
'the Way, the Truth, the Life' (John
xiv. 6). It follows that the efficacy of
His work for the individual depends
upon fellowship with Him. See Additional Note.

Qui per humanitatem interpellat
pro nobis apud Patrem idem per di-
vinitatem propitiatur nobis cum Patre
(Bede *ad loc.*).

περὶ τῶν ἁμ. ἡ.] *pro peccatis nostris* V., *peccatorum nostrorum* Aug.,
for our sins. The privilege of Christians (ἡμῶν) is noticed first. And it
is natural that in the first case the
stress is laid on 'sins' (περὶ τῶν ἁμ.
ἡμῶν) and in the second case on 'our'
(περὶ τῶν ἡμετέρων).

The propitiation of Christ is here
described as being 'for,' 'in the matter of (περί) our sins' (comp. כִּפֶּר עַל),
and not as 'in behalf of us' (ὑπὲρ
ἡμῶν). On the phrases περὶ (ὑπέρ)
ἁμαρτίας (-ιῶν) see Hebr. xiii. 11
note.

οὐ π. τ. ἡ. δέ] The particle (δέ) marks
the clause as guarding against error,
not merely adding a new thought.

περὶ ὅλου τοῦ κόσμου] *pro totius
mundi* [sc. *peccatis*] V., (*sed et*) *totius
mundi* Aug., *for the whole world.*
The variation in the construction (*for
our sins...for the whole world*) is full
of meaning (comp. Heb. ix. 7). Christians as such are holy but still not

³ Καὶ ἐν τούτῳ γινώσκομεν ὅτι ἐγνώκαμεν αὐτόν, ἐὰν

3 Aug. reads simply *et in hoc cognoscimus eum*. φυλάξωμεν (for τηρῶμεν) א*.

unstained by sins contracted 'in the walk of life' (John xiii. 10); the world, all outside the Church, as such is sinful (c. v. 19). But for all alike Christ's propitiation is valid. The propitiation extends as far as the need of it (*l. c.*), through all place and all time. Comp. iv. 14 (John iv. 42; xii. 32; xvii. 22—24).

The supposition that περὶ ὅλου τοῦ κόσμου is an elliptical expression for περὶ τῶν ἁμαρτιῶν ὅλου τοῦ κόσμου (so Latt.) is not justified by usage, and weakens the force of the passage. Philo in a noble passage (*de Monarch.* ii. 6, ii. p. 227 M.) contrasts the special offerings of other forms of worship with the universal intercession of the Jewish High-priest: ὁ τῶν Ἰουδαίων ἀρχιερεὺς οὐ μόνον ὑπὲρ ἅπαντος ἀνθρώπων γένους ἀλλὰ καὶ ὑπὲρ τῶν τῆς φύσεως μερῶν, γῆς ὕδατος ἀέρος καὶ πυρός, τάς τε εὐχὰς καὶ τὰς εὐχαριστίας ποιεῖται, τὸν κόσμον, ὅπερ ἐστὶ ταῖς ἀληθείαις, πατρίδα εἶναι ἑαυτοῦ νομίζων, ὑπὲρ ἧς ἱκεσίαις καὶ λιταῖς εἴωθεν ἐξευμενίζειν τὸν ἡγεμόνα ποτνιώμενος τῆς ἐπιεικοῦς καὶ ἵλεω φύσεως αὐτοῦ μεταδιδόναι τῷ γενομένῳ.

Comp. 1 Clem. R. c. 7 ἀτενίσωμεν εἰς τὸ αἷμα τοῦ Χριστοῦ καὶ ἴδωμεν ὡς ἔστιν τίμιον τῷ θεῷ καὶ πατρὶ αὐτοῦ, ὅτι διὰ τὴν ἡμετέραν σωτηρίαν ἐκχυθὲν παντὶ τῷ κόσμῳ μετανοίας χάριν ὑπήνεγκεν.

2. *The signs of the personal efficacy of the divine remedy for sin* (ii. 3—6).

³*And in this we perceive that we know him, if we observe his commandments, ⁴He that saith I know him and observeth not his commandments, is a liar, and in this man the truth is not; ⁵but whosoever observeth his word, verily in this man the love of God hath been perfected.*

The first two verses of the chapter

declare the nature of the divine remedy for sin; in these next four St John indicates the sign of its personal efficacy. The sign is twofold, and corresponds with two aspects of the spiritual life; there is the sign of knowledge (*vv.* 3—5 *a*); and there is the sign of union (*vv.* 5 *b*, 6). The sign of knowledge is (shortly) obedience; and the sign of union is imitation.

3. The new form of false doctrine which St John meets corresponds with and grows out of the first of those which he has already analysed. Some claimed a knowledge of God, as some claimed fellowship with God (i. 6), irrespective of a Christ-like life. Knowledge no less than fellowship involves real likeness (comp. John viii. 32; c. iii. 7).

vv. 3—5 *a. The sign of knowledge.* The sign of knowledge is developed characteristically by the Apostle. He first states generally that it lies in obedience (*v.* 3), and then follows out this statement further negatively and positively, shewing the issues of the want of obedience (*v.* 4), and of the activity of obedience (*v.* 5 *a*).

3. Under one aspect this verse is connected with i. 5. But between the declaration of God's nature and man's knowledge of Him there comes in the episode of sin. This fatal interruption breaks the natural development of thought. The connexion of i. 1, 3, 5 (καί), ii. 3 (καί), corresponds with that of John i. 1, 14.

ἐν τούτῳ γινώσκομεν] *in hoc scimus* V., *in hoc cognoscimus* Aug., *in this we perceive*. The phrase '*in this*' is characteristic of the Epistle and occurs with slight variations of form.

(1) *In this* (ἐν τούτῳ) *we perceive* (γινώσκομεν): ii. 5; iii. 24; iv. 13; v. 2 and so also '*in this we know* (ἐγνώκαμεν)' iii. 16; and '*in this we*

shall know (γνωσόμεθα)' iii. 19; and '*in this ye perceive*' (γινώσκετε) iv. 2. Comp. John xiii. 35 (xv. 8; xvi. 30).

(2) *From this* (ἐκ τούτου) *we perceive:* iv. 6.

(3) *Whence* (ὅθεν) *we perceive:* ii. 18.

Generally '*this*' (τοῦτο) marks something which has been already expressed, though it is further developed in what follows (comp. e.g. διὰ τοῦτο... ὅτι, iii. 1; John v. 16, 18; vi. 65; viii. 47; x. 17; xii. 18; xvi. 15). But here the reference appears to be to that which is clearly apprehended in the mind of the Apostle and present to him, though it has not yet been brought forward; *in this*...namely *if* .... Perhaps however even here the '*this*' really rests upon the whole relation of the Christian to Christ which is implied in *vv.* 1, 2. That relation furnishes the test of knowledge; if the relation be vital it will include obedience. Comp. *v.* 2.

The experience to which the Apostle appeals here and in the parallel passages (γινώσκομεν) is present and immediate, confirmed from moment to moment in the actual course of life. So far it is distinguished from the knowledge of an absolute fact (οἴδαμεν, iii. 2 note).

ἐγνώκαμεν...] *cognovimus* V., *know Him*, or, more exactly, *have come to a knowledge of Him*. Knowledge of a person involves sympathy (c. iii. 1 n.); and in this particular case includes the striving after conformity with Him who is known. To know God as God is to be in vital fellowship with Him, to love Him, to fulfil that relation towards Him for which we are born. And conversely to be known by God, to be the object of His knowledge, is to be in harmony with Him. Comp. Gal. iv. 9; 1 Cor. viii. 2; xiii. 12; John x. 14 f.; and negatively Matt. vii. 23; 2 Cor. v. 21.

This knowledge of God gained by experience (γινώσκειν), and so contrasted with the knowledge which is imme-diate and absolute (οἶδα), is presented in its different stages in the Gospel and Epistles of St John. It is regarded

(1) In reference to the point of acquisition (ἔγνων John i. 10; x. 38; xvi. 3; xvii. 8, 25; c. iii. 1; iv. 8).

(2) As a result of the past realised in the present (ἔγνωκα, John viii. 55; xiv. 9; xvii. 7; *vv.* 4, 13, 14; iii. 6, 16; 2 John 1). And

(3) As being actually realised at the moment (γινώσκω, John viii. 43; x. 14 f., 27, 38; xiv. 7, 17; xvii. 3, 23; c. iv. 2, 6, 7; v. 20).

These three aspects of the knowledge of God offer a view of the beginning, the strength and the aim of life.

It is worthy of remark that St John nowhere uses γνῶσις (St Luke, St Paul, St Peter), nor the compound forms ἐπιγινώσκειν (Synn., Acts, St Paul, 2 Peter), ἐπίγνωσις (St Paul, Heb., 2 Peter). He confines himself, as he does almost exclusively in dealing with faith (πιστεύειν εἰς), to the simple verb. This form of expression brings out most distinctly the personal character of the energy.

In this context it is not clearly defined to Whom the pronoun (ἐγν. αὐτόν) refers. The Divine Being fills the apostle's vision, but the Person is not distinctly named. It has been supposed that the reference is to Christ, the main subject of the preceding verses. In favour of this view it is urged that in i. 6 ff. the αὐτοῦ refers to the last subject of i. 5, and that the construction of this section is similar; that the occurrence of the phrase the *love of God* in *v.* 5 implies a reference of the preceding αὐτοῦ to the Son and not to the Father; that Christ Himself speaks of the 'keeping of His Commandments' as the proof of love (John xiv. 15, &c.). On the other hand it is said that in this Epistle 'the Commandments' referred to are always the Commandments of God (i.e. the Father) as iii. 22, 24; v. 2, 3; and that God is the great under-

τὰς ἐντολὰς αὐτοῦ τηρῶμεν. ⁴ ὁ λέγων ὅτι Ἔγνωκα
αὐτόν καὶ τὰς ἐντολὰς αὐτοῦ μὴ τηρῶν ψεύστης
ἐστίν, καὶ ἐν τούτῳ ἡ ἀλήθεια οὐκ ἔστιν· ⁵ ὃς δ' ἂν τηρῇ

4 ὁ λέγων ὅτι ℵAB syrr: –ὅτι ϚC.   – καὶ' ἐν τ. A.   – ἐν τούτῳ ℵ:
ἡ ἀλ. +τοῦ Θεοῦ ℵ.

lying subject of all, the 'He' (αὐτός)
which is self-defined ; so that in point
of fact αὐτός generally refers to ' God,'
while ἐκεῖνος always refers to Christ
(v. 6 note).

The sense remains substantially the
same in both cases. It is in the Son
that the Father is known (John xiv.
9). And perhaps it is best to suppose
that St John assumes a general antecedent ' Him to whom we turn as
God ' without special distinction of
Persons. In other places he does not
seem to draw any sharp distinction
between the Father and the Son, but
in the One God looks now to the revelation of the Father in the Son and
now to the revelation of the Son
(comp. iii. 1—3, 5, 6; v. 20).

ἐάν...τηρῶμεν] si observemus V., si
servaverimus Aug., if we keep his
commandments. Comp. v. 4; iii. 22,
24; v. 3; John xiv. 15, 21; xv. 10;
Apoc. xii. 17; xiv. 12. The phrase
(τηρεῖν τὰς ἐντολάς) is only found elsewhere in New Testament in Matt.
xix. 17; 1 Tim. vi. 14 (τηρεῖν τὴν ἐντ.).
Comp. 1 Cor. vii. 19. It appears to
be distinguished from the phrase
which follows 'keep his word' as
being an observance of definite in-
structions, while that is the observance
of a principle which is ever taking a
new embodiment in the very process
of life.

The phrase ποιεῖν τὰς ἐντολάς, which
is found in the common text of Apoc.
xxii. 14, is a false reading.

The idea of τηρεῖν, as distinguished
from φυλάσσειν in this connexion
(John xii. 47; Matt. xix. 20; Luke
xi. 28) appears to be that of watchful
heed to an object which claims, so to
speak, a living observance, a service

not of the letter but of the spirit.
A definite, unchangeable, deposit is
'guarded' (φυλάσσεται, 1 Tim. vi. 20):
a vital, growing, word is 'observed'
(τηρεῖται, John xiv. 22). The two
verbs occur in juxtaposition in John
xvii. 12 (note).

4. ὁ λέγων] He that saith. This in-
dividualising of the statement stands
in contrast with the comprehensive
form cited before If we say (i. 6, 8,
10) and that used in v. 5. It occurs
again vv. 6, 9.

ἔγνωκα αὐτόν] se nosse eum V.,
quia cognovit (cognovi) eum Aug., I
know him. The direct personal assertion (ὁ λέγων ὅτι) is bolder in form
than the oblique construction in vv.
6, 9 (ὁ λέγων μένειν, εἶναι). Comp.
Hos. viii. 2.

In the words which follow St John
significantly takes up again phrases
which he has used already in connexion
with the three false pleas in regard
to sin (ψεύστης ἐστίν ‖ ψεύδεται v. 6;
ἐν τούτῳ ἡ ἀλ. οὐκ ἔστιν ‖ ἡ ἀλ. οὐκ
ἔστιν ἐν ἡμῖν v. 8; (ὃς δ' ἂν τηρῇ) αὐτοῦ
τὸν λόγον ‖ ὁ λόγος αὐτοῦ (οὐκ ἔστιν ἐν
ἡμῖν v. 10).

ψεύστης...οὐκ ἔστιν] a liar...in this
man. The whole character is false.
See i. 10 note. The clause is very
similar to i. 6 b, but differs from it in
being general while that is special.
Here we have two characteristics of a
permanent state (is a liar, the truth
is not in him), and there two separate
manifestations of the state (we lie, we
do not the truth).

ἐν τούτῳ...οὐκ ἔστιν] in him the
truth is not. Or more literally in
this man thus definitely characterised
and brought before us. See v. 5.
This use of the demonstrative pro-

αὐτοῦ τὸν λόγον, ἀληθῶς ἐν τούτῳ ἡ ἀγάπη τοῦ θεοῦ

noun is characteristic of St John (John v. 38; i. 2 note); and the emphatic order adds to its force.

The truth is said to be in a man as an active principle within him regulating his thoughts and judgments (c. i. 8; John viii. 44; comp. John viii. 32); and again a man is said to be in the truth, as the sphere in which he moves (2 John 4; 3 John 3, 4; John viii. 44; comp. John xvii. 17).

5. ὃς δ' ἂν τηρῇ...] qui autem servat V., qui a. servaverit Aug., but whosoever keepeth. The indefinite form (iii. 17; iv. 15) marks the breadth of the assertion. The apostle does not here, as before and after, either single out a special example (ὁ λέγων, v. 4), or join himself with others (ἐὰν εἴπωμεν, i. 6). He makes the statement in the most general terms.

It will be noticed that the opposite to the vain assertions of false claimants to the Christian name is not given in a counter assertion but, as always, in action (i. 7 if we walk; i. 9 if we confess; v. 10 he that loveth).

τηρῇ αὐτοῦ τὸν λόγον] keepeth his word. The phrase expresses not only the fulfilment of specific injunctions (keep his commandments, v. 3) but also the needful regard to the whole revelation made by Christ as a living and active power, of which the voice is never silent. The unity of the many 'commandments' is not in a 'law' but in a 'word': it answers to the spirit and not to the letter. Comp. John viii. 51 f., 55; xiv. 23; xv. 20; xvii. 6. The passage John xiv. 21—24 is of singular interest as illustrating the full meaning of the phrase.

The position of the pronoun here (αὐτοῦ τὸν λόγον), as contrasted with that which it has in v. 3 (τὰς ἐντολὰς αὐτοῦ), emphasises the personal idea. The main thought is that the word is His word, the word of God. There is emphasis also on the 'keeping' ὃς δ'

ἂν τηρῇ contrasted with ὁ...τὰς ἐντ. μὴ τηρῶν).

ἀληθῶς ἐν τούτῳ] verily in him, in this man, v. 4 note.

In the description of the state of the watchful believer the form of expression is changed significantly. St John does not say of him (v. 4) that 'he is true and the truth is in him'; but he rather regards his character from the divine side, and points out not what such a man is, but what such a man has received from Him who is unchangeable: in this man the love of God hath been perfected. By doing this he passes at the same time from that which may be a part of life to the fulness of life. Truth may be only a right conception realised in thought: love is the Truth realised in a personal relation. The love which God gives (iii. 1) becomes an active, divine power in the man who welcomes it.

ἡ ἀγάπη τοῦ θεοῦ] caritas Dei V., dilectio Dei Aug., the love of God. The phrase, which occurs in the Epistle first here and henceforth throughout it, is ambiguous and may mean, according as the gen. is taken subj. or obj., either (1) the love which God shews, or (2) the love of which God is the object. It may also mean more generally (3) the love which is characteristic of God whether it is regarded as shewn by God or by man through His help. Generally the genitive after ἀγάπη in the N.T. is subj., and defines those who feel or shew love: 1 Thess. iii. 6; 2 Thess. i. 3; Phil. i. 9; Col. i. 8; Philem. 5, 7; Apoc. ii. 4, 19. Once it marks the object of love: 2 Thess. ii. 10 ἡ ἀγ. τῆς ἀληθείας. But the object is more commonly expressed by εἰς: 1 Thess. iii. 12; Col. i. 4; 1 Pet. iv. 8. Comp. Ign. Mart. 1; [Clem. R.] fragm. 1 (Jacobson).

In St Paul 'the love of God,' with

τετελείωται. Ἐν τούτῳ γινώσκομεν ὅτι ἐν αὐτῷ ἐσμέν·

5 ἐν τούτῳ...ἐσμέν: Aug. reads *in hoc cognoscimus quia in ipso sumus si in ipso perfecti fuerimus.*

the doubtful exception of 2 Thess. iii. 5, always means the love which is shewn by God, which comes from God: 2 Cor. viii. 14; Rom. v. 5; viii. 39; Eph. ii. 4; and so also 'the love of Christ' is the love which Christ has shewn and shews: 2 Cor. v. 14; Rom. viii. 35; Eph. iii. 19. Comp. Ign. *ad Trall.* 6; *ad Rom.* inscr. In like manner 'the love of the Spirit' (Rom. xv. 30) is that love which the Spirit kindles and sustains. The phrase 'the love of God' does not occur in the LXX.

The usage of St John is less simple than that of St Paul. In 1 John iv. 9 '*the love of God*' is evidently the love which God has shewn (comp. c. v. 9 ἡ μαρτυρία τοῦ θεοῦ), and this love is declared to be the spring of all love. '*His love*' (*v.* 12) becomes effective in man. This conception of the love of God as communicated by God to man is plainly expressed in 1 John iii. 1 *the Father hath given to us love* (comp. c. iv. 7, 16). Love such as God Himself feels—'divine love'—becomes therefore an endowment of the Christian. In this sense 'the love of God' in the believer calls for deeds of love to the brethren (c. iii. 17). At the same time God is Himself the object of the love of which He is the source and the rule: c. v. 3 (comp. John xiv. 15, 31); ii. 15 (ἡ ἀγ. τοῦ πατρός).

It appears therefore most probable that the fundamental idea of 'the love of God' in St John is 'the love which God has made known, and which answers to His nature.' This love communicated to man is effective in him towards the brethren and towards God Himself. But however it may be manifested the essential conception that it is a love divine in its origin and character is not lost. Comp. John xv. 9 f.

W.

According to this interpretation the phrase corresponds with the 'righteousness of God' (Rom. i. 17, &c.), the 'peace of God' (Phil. iv. 7).

The phrase occurs twice only in the Gospels: Luke xi. 42; John v. 42. In each case the rendering 'love to God' is admissible, but this rendering does not seem to exhaust the meaning (comp. Clem. R. 1 *Cor.* 49).

In the present passage there can be little doubt that c. iv. 9 defines the meaning. 'The love of God' is God's love towards man welcomed and appropriated by man. The thought of action is throughout connected with the thought of what God has done. The Christian 'knows the love of God and it becomes in him a spring of love, attaining its complete development in human life through vital obedience.

On the use of ἀγάπη by St John see additional note on c. iii. 16.

ἀληθῶς] *vere* V., *verily*, in very truth, and not in word only (c. iii. 18). Comp. John i. 47 (48); viii. 31. The word qualifies the whole clause which follows. This practical result is contrasted by implication with the idle assertions of false Christians.

The perfection of love is conditioned by the completeness of obedience.

τετελείωται] *perfecta est* V., *consummata est* Lucf., *hath been perfected.* Comp. c. iv. 12 (note), 17, 18 where the thought is presented in different lights. Comp. Clem. R. 1 *Cor.* 50 οἱ ἐν ἀγάπῃ τελειωθέντες. *Doctr. Apost.* x. 5 μνήσθητι, κύριε, τῆς ἐκκλησίας σου...τελειῶσαι αὐτὴν ἐν τῇ ἀγάπῃ σου. The potential fulfilment of the love of God in the Christian lies in his absolute readiness to learn and to do God's will (comp. Rom. xiii. 10). Each Christian according to his

4

$^{6}\dot{o}$ λέγων ἐν αὐτῷ μένειν ὀφείλει καθὼς ἐκεῖνος περιε-
πάτησεν καὶ αὐτὸς περιπατεῖν.

6 καὶ αὐτὸς περιπ. AB vg the: καὶ αὐτ. + οὕτως' περιπ. ℵ°C me syr hcl.

measure is perfected as a member of Christ (Eph. iv. 16). He receives from Christ what Christ has Himself received. Comp. John xvii. 25 f. On this idea of 'perfection,' "consummation,' see Heb. ii. 10; ix. 9; xii. 23 and notes. Contrast τελεῖται 2 Cor. xii. 9.

Both τελειοῦν and ἐπιτελεῖν are used of Christian action (Phil. iii. 12; Gal. iii. 3). But in τελειοῦν there is the idea of a continuous growth, a vital development, an advance to maturity (τελειότης, Heb. v. 13; vi. 1). In ἐπιτελεῖν the notion is rather that of attaining a definite end (τέλος). Contrast James ii. 22 ἐκ τῶν ἔργων ἡ πίστις ἐτελειώθη with 2 Cor. vii. 1 ἐπιτελοῦντες ἁγιωσύνην, and Acts xx. 24 τελειῶσαι τὸν δρόμον with 2 Tim. iv. 7 τὸν δρόμον τετέλεκα. In 2 Cor. xii. 9 τελειοῦται has been substituted in later authorities for τελεῖται.

v. 5 b, 6. *The sign of union.* The sign of union with God is found in the imitation of Christ. As the sign of knowledge is to be seen in the keeping of the divine commandments in their unity (v. 3) and in the keeping of the divine word in its unity (v. 5), so the sign of fellowship is to be seen in the copying the divine life.

In this we perceive that we are in him: ⁶he that saith he abideth in him, ought himself also to walk even as he walked.

Ἐν τούτῳ] *Hereby, in this,* in the realisation of this spirit of obedience which is the gift of love: v. 3 note.

γινώσκομεν] Comp. v. 3; c. v. 2 notes.

ἐν αὐτῷ ἐσμέν] *are in Him.* The idea finds a full expression in Acts xvii. 28 ἐν αὐτῷ ζῶμεν καὶ κινούμεθα καὶ ἐσμέν. It is prominent in St John's writings in its spiritual form, and is presented under several different as-

pects. The fellowship of believers with God is accomplished in Christ (John xiv. 20; xvii. 21, 23). They have in Him the unity and foundation of their being, even as 'the world' 'lies in the evil one' (c. v. 19 f.). The connexion finds a twofold fulfilment in 'heaven' and on 'earth,' 'we in Him and He in us' (iv. 15 note).

For the phrase 'being in God' St John more commonly, as in the following clause, uses the phrase 'abiding in God,' which adds the conception of personal determination and effort: vv. 24, 27, 28; iii. 6, 24; iv. 12 f.; 15 f. John vi. 56 note; xv. 4 ff.

Thus there is a progressive closeness of relation in the three phrases used in this section: ἐγνωκέναι αὐτόν, εἶναι ἐν αὐτῷ, μένειν ἐν αὐτῷ ('cognitio, communio, constantia,' Bengel).

6. ὁ λέγων] *he that saith.* v. 4. The open, personal profession carries with it a paramount obligation.

ἐν αὐτῷ μένειν] v. 5 note.

The construction of λέγω with the infin. occurs again in v. 9. Comp. 2 Tim. ii. 18; and v. 4 note.

ὀφείλει] *debet* V., *ought,* is bound. The obligation is represented as a debt (Luke xvii. 10). The life which is from God and in God must be manifested after the pattern of the divine life which has been shewn upon earth. As contrasted with δεῖ, an obligation in the nature of things (John xx. 9), which is not found in the Epistles of St John, though it is not unfrequent in the Gospel (c. iii. 14 note) and the Apocalypse, ὀφείλειν expresses a special, personal obligation.

Comp. c. iii. 16; iv. 11; 3 John 8. The image is frequent in St Paul. Comp. Rom. i. 14; Gal. v. 3.

καθὼς ἐκεῖνος] *even as he*, i.e. Christ.
The pronoun ἐκεῖνος occurs iii. 3, 5, 7,
16; iv. 17, and is always used of
Christ. He stands out as the one
figure seen in full perfection of His
humanity. Comp. John i. 18; 2 Tim.
ii. 13. For the omission of οὗτως see
c. iv. 17 note.

περιεπάτησεν] *walked*, i. 6 note.
Even in the contemplation of the
loftiest thoughts St John fixes a
practical standard. The divine fellowship to which he points is realised
on earth in corresponding action.

The pattern of Christ, as set before
us in the New Testament, is in every
case a pattern of humiliation, suffering, sacrifice. Comp. Matt. xi. 29;
John xiii. 15; Rom. xv. 2 f.; Eph. v.
1 ff.; Phil. ii. 5 ff.; 1 Pet. ii. 21;
Heb. xii. 2.

Augustine points out that 'walking'
may be 'bearing' only: [Christus]
fixus in cruce erat et in ipsa via am-
bulabat: ipsa est via caritatis.

III. Obedience in love and light in actual life (ii. 7—11).

The declaration of the test of knowledge of God and fellowship with God,
which St John has given in *vv.* 3—6,
leads to a view of the practical fulfilment of the test indicated already in
v. 6. The Life of Christ, a Life of complete love, of complete self-sacrifice, is
the type of the Christian's Life; and
the significance of Christ's Life in
this aspect is gathered up in the
one commandment of love, which expresses what is meant by 'keeping
His commandments' (*v.* 3) and 'walking even as He walked' (*v.* 6). This
commandment is first set forth in its
twofold character as old and yet new
(*vv.* 7, 8); and then traced out in its
issues (*vv.* 9—11).

1. *The Commandment old and
new* (ii. 7, 8).
The commandment, which is the
rule of the Christian Life, is as old as
the first message of the Gospel and

yet as new as the latest realisation of
its power. It lies included in what
we first hear, and is illuminated by
the growing experience of life.

⁷*Beloved, it is no new commandment I write to you, but an old commandment which ye had from the
beginning: the commandment, the
old* commandment, *is the word which
ye heard.*

⁸*Again, a new commandment I
write to you,* even *that which is true
in him and in you, because the darkness is passing away and the light,
the true* light, *already shineth.*

The 'commandment' to which the
apostle refers has not been formally
stated, but it is implied in the 'ought'
('is bound' ὀφείλει) of *v.* 6. The idea
of the imitation of Christ is identical
with the fulfilment of love. And the
word ὀφείλει carries us back to the
Lord's interpretation of His example:
John xiii. 14 (ὑμεῖς ὀφείλετε). We
have already seen that the many
'commandments' (*v.* 3) are included
in 'the word' (*v.* 5). Now the 'commandments' are summed up in the
one 'commandment' (John xiii. 34;
comp. c. iii. 22 f.).

This commandment is spoken of as
'not new but old.' In this connexion
'old' may mean either (1) old relatively: one which belonged to the
first stage of the Christian Church,
while perhaps as yet it was unsepa-
rated from the old order: one of
which believers had been in possession
from the beginning, from the first
origin of their faith; or (2) old absolutely: one which was included in the
very constitution of man *from the
beginning:* one which the Jew had
recognised in the injunctions of the
Law, and the Gentile in the prompt-
ings of his heart.

The clause which immediately follows, and the identification of the
commandment with 'the word' which
the disciples heard, seem to determine that the first sense is undoubtedly right.

4—2

⁷Ἀγαπητοί, οὐκ ἐντολὴν καινὴν γράφω ὑμῖν, ἀλλ'
ἐντολὴν παλαιὰν ἣν εἴχετε ἀπ' ἀρχῆς· ἡ ἐντολὴ ἡ

7 ἀγαπητοί ℵABC vg the me syrr: ἀδελφοί ⸂.

7. Ἀγαπητοί] *Carissimi* V., *Dilectissimi* Aug., *Beloved.* This is the first
occurrence of the title. It is suggested by the thought of the last few
verses, just as the paternal address
My little children (*v.* 1) was suggested by i. 10. The love of God and
the love of Christ calling out man's
love presents Christians in their new
relation one to another. St John
while enforcing the commandment of
love gives expression to love. Comp.
iii. 2, 21 ; iv. 1, 7 note, 11 ; and in
the sing. 3 John 2, 5, 11. In each
case the use of the title illustrates the
apostle's thought. So also the title
ἀδελφοί brings out the point of his
teaching in the one place where he
adopts it: iii. 13.

With ἀγαπητοί contrast ἠγαπημένοι
Col. iii. 12 ; 1 Thess. i. 4 ; 2 Thess. ii.
13. Comp. Eph. i. 6.

οὐκ ἐντ. κ. γ.] Comp. 2 John 5 οὐχ
ὡς ἐντ. γράφων σοι κ.

ἀπ' ἀρχῆς] *ab initio* V., *from the
beginning.* The words are, as has
been already indicated, ambiguous.
The phrase is used both absolutely
and relatively.

1. It is used absolutely: c. iii. 8
ἀπ' ἀρχῆς ὁ διάβολος ἁμαρτάνει, when
first the present order of being is
disclosed.

vv. 13, 14 ὁ ἀπ' ἀρχῆς.

c. i. 1 ὁ ἦν ἀπ' ἀρχῆς.

Matt. xix. 4, 8 ἀπ' ἀρχῆς. ‖ Mc. x. 6
ἀπ' ἀρχῆς κτίσεως. 2 Pet. iii. 4.

2. Again it is used relatively in
different connexions :

John xv. 27 ἀπ' ἀρχῆς μετ' ἐμοῦ
ἐστέ, from the beginning of my public
ministry. Comp. ἐξ ἀρχῆς John vi. 64,
xvi. 4 ; Acts xxvi. 4 τὴν ἀπ' ἀρχῆς
γενομένην [βίωσιν] from the beginning
of my life.

Luke i. 2 οἱ ἀπ' ἀρχῆς αὐτόπται.
Comp. Acts i. 22.

c. ii. 24 ὁ ἀπ' ἀρχῆς ἠκούσατε, from
the beginning of your Christian faith.
Comp. c. iii. 11 ; 2 John 6.

These last passages, which are closely
parallel, decide that the reference here
is to the beginning of the Christian
faith of the readers.

Comp. Is. lxiii. 16 (LXX.).

The article is omitted as in the corresponding phrases ἀπὸ καταβολῆς
κόσμου, πρὸ καταβολῆς κόσμου. See
c. i. 1 note.

ἡ ἐντολὴ...ἠκούσατε] *the commandment,* the commandment of which I
speak, *the old* commandment, *is the
word which ye heard.* The form of
expression used emphasises the two
thoughts which have gone before (*the
commandment, the old* commandment). Comp. i. 2, ii. 25 ἡ ζωὴ ἡ αἰώνιος
(*the life, the eternal* life) ; i. 3 ἡ κοινωνία ἡ ἡμετέρα (the fellowship of which
I speak, the fellowship which is our
blessing); *v.* 8 τὸ φῶς τὸ ἀληθινόν ; iv.
9 ὁ υἱὸς ὁ μονογενής : 2 John 11 τοῖς
ἔργοις αὐτοῦ τοῖς πονηροῖς : 13 τῆς ἀδελφῆς σου τῆς ἐκλεκτῆς.

On the other hand St John writes
c. iv. 18 ἡ τελεία ἀγάπη : 3 John 4 τὰ
ἐμὰ τέκνα.

ὁ λόγος] The old commandment,
the commandment of love, was included in the 'Gospel' which the
apostles proclaimed. The record of
the Lord's work, *the word of life,* was
a continuous call to love.

ὃν ἠκούσατε] *which ye heard, v.* 24,
iii. 11. Contrast the perfect: i. 1, 3,
5, iv. 3. The change of tenses in εἴχετε,
ἠκούσατε, is significant. The commandment was a continuous power :
the hearing of the word was at once
final in its obligation.

παλαιά ἐστιν ὁ λόγος ὃν ἠκούσατε. ⁸ πάλιν ἐντολὴν
καινὴν γράφω ὑμῖν, ὅ ἐστιν ἀληθὲς ἐν αὐτῷ καὶ ἐν ὑμῖν,

ἠκούσατε ℵABC vg the me syrr : +ἀπ᾽ ἀρχῆς ϛ.   8 ἀλ. καὶ ἐν αὐτῷ ℵ:
ἐν αὐτῷ ἀλ. A.   ἐν ὑμῖν ℵBC vg the me syrr : ἐν ἡμῖν A syr hcl mg (lat).

8. πάλιν] iterum V., again. The
apostle has given one side of the
Truth : he now turns to the other.
The πάλιν answers exactly to our
'again' when we enter on a new line
of argument or reflection, starting
afresh. Comp. John xvi. 28 ; 1 Cor.
xii. 21 ; 2 Cor. x. 7 ; xi. 16.

ἐντολὴν καινήν] mandatum novum
V., a new commandment. Comp.
John xiii. 34. The commandment of
love was new to the disciples who
had followed Christ when He gave it
them on the eve of the Passion in a
new form and with a new sanction.
It was new also to the believers whom
St John addressed in proportion as
they were now enabled to apprehend
with fresh power the Person and Life
of Christ. The 'newness' is relative
to the position of those to whom St
John writes. While life advances the
Gospel must be always new. Contrast
Hebr. viii. 13.

ὅ ἐστιν ἀληθές...] quod verum est...
V., even that which is true... The
whole sentence admits of several different translations : (1) As a new
commandment I write unto you that
which is true... (2) A new commandment write I unto you, namely, that
which is true... (3) A new commandment write I unto you, a fact (i.e.
that it is new as well as old) which is
true.... The symmetry of the structure seems to be decisive against (1) :
'Εντολὴν καινὴν γράφω cannot but be
strictly parallel to οὐκ ἐντολὴν καινὴν
γράφω—'a new commandment do I
write,' 'not a new commandment do
I write.' It is more difficult to decide
between (2) and (3). If (2) be taken
the sense will be: 'A new commandment write I unto you, new no less
than old, new in its shape and in its

authority, even that which, while it was
enjoined upon us from the first, has
been found to correspond more closely
than we then understood with the facts
of Christ's Life, with the crowning
mystery of His Passion, and with the
facts of the Christian life.' If on the
other hand (3) be taken then we have
this line of thought : 'A new commandment write I unto you, new, I
say, as well as old, an assertion which
is proved true in Christ, so far as His
works and words have become more
fully known; and in you, so far as the
actual experience of life has shewn
this duty of love in a new light,
more comprehensive and more con-
straining.'

On the whole the second interpretation appears to fall in best with the
context and with the reason which follows (because...the true light already
shineth). That which gave novelty to
the commandment was found in the
larger and deeper views of Christ's
Person and of the work of the Church
which had been unfolded since 'the
beginning.' Old words, St John could
affirm, and appeal to his readers for
the confirmation of the statement, had
become new. Comp. 2 Cor. v. 17.

ὅτι ἡ σκοτία...] because the darkness...The apostle justifies his paradox
by calling attention to the change
which had taken place in the face of
the world since the Gospel was first
preached. The outward establishment
of the Church gave a clearer distinctness to the Christian character. It had
become possible to point to that which
was openly before men's eyes. At the
same time the Person of Christ Himself, with its infinite significance, was
illuminated by the experience of believers. The meaning of 'the word'

ὅτι ἡ σκοτία παράγεται καὶ τὸ φῶς τὸ ἀληθινὸν ἤδη

σκιά Α.

(for example) was made clearer than before by the Gospel of St John as compared with the earlier Gospels.

The clause may be taken as an explanation of the reason for which the apostle is repeating the command, even that it was the 'last hour.' But this interpretation appears improbable.

παράγεται...φαίνει] transierunt... lucet V., is passing away...already shineth. The change is pictured as in process. The darkness is being withdrawn (παράγεται) as a curtain from the face of the world, and the light is beginning (ἤδη) to have free course.

For παράγεται see v. 17. The intrans. παράγει occurs 1 Cor. vii. 31; Ps. cxliv. (cxliii.) 4. The idea seems to be that God is removing the veil in order to lay open the better things which it conceals.

τὸ φῶς τὸ ἀληθινόν] verum lumen V., lux vera Aug., the light, the true light. The addition of the epithet ἀληθινόν (c. v. 20) which is found only here and John i. 9 (note) with φῶς, marks the light as that which fulfilled all that had been promised by the preparatory, partial, even fictitious, lights which had existed in the world before. If we endeavour to fix the meaning of 'the light' here it can be best done by the help of the parallel John i. 9. Before the Incarnation 'the Word,' 'the true Light' was ever 'coming into the world.' Now by the mission of the Holy Spirit, sent in His name, He was shining with a steady beam. The darkness had not eclipsed it. In the Christian Society, seen in the midst of the world, there was an evident manifestation of the light defining the lines of Christian conduct.

God 'is light' absolutely (i. 5): the revelation of God in Christ by the

Spirit is 'the light, the true light' for men; and in His light the believer is enabled to see all things.

φαίνει] lucet V., shineth. Comp. John i. 5 (note). The idea is of a luminary giving out its brightness: Apoc. i. 16, viii. 12, xxi. 23; 2 Pet. i. 19.

For the image generally compare Rom. xiii. 11 ff.; Tit. ii. 11; iii. 4.

2.　The issues of the commandment of love (ii. 9—11).

The fulfilment of the commandment of love is regarded in its general nature (v. 9) and then more in detail in the effects of love and hatred (vv. 10, 11). A state of love is the condition of being in light; and this state carries with it a clear certainty of right action which is otherwise unobtainable. Hatred on the other hand involves complete ignorance of the way and of the end of life. This must be so; for dwelling in darkness destroys the very power by which the light is discerned.

⁹He that saith he is in the light and hateth his brother is in the darkness until now. ¹⁰He that loveth his brother abideth in the light, and there is none occasion of stumbling in him; ¹¹but he that hateth his brother is in the darkness, and walketh in the darkness, and knoweth not whither he goeth, because the darkness hath blinded his eyes.

9. The link of transition lies in the last words of v. 8. The thought of 'the light already shining' naturally suggests the question, Who then is in the light? St John's account of the obligations and issues of love explains this and is an answer to the false claims of knowledge separated from the action which embodies it (comp. v. 4).

Ὁ λέγων...] He that saith. v. 4. It

φαίνει.　　　⁹ Ὁ λέγων ἐν τῷ φωτὶ εἶναι καὶ τὸν
ἀδελφὸν αὐτοῦ μισῶν ἐν τῇ σκοτίᾳ ἐστὶν ἕως ἄρτι.

9 μισῶν: +ψεύστης ἐστὶν καὶ ℵ Cypr Lcfr.

is always easy to mistake an intellectual knowledge for a spiritual knowledge of the Truth. Real knowledge
involves, at least potentially, corresponding action.

ἐν τῷ φωτὶ εἶναι] *is in the light*,
surrounded, as it were, by an atmo-
sphere of divine glory. Comp. i. 7 (iv.
15 note).

μισῶν...] *hateth....* Indifference is
impossible. Comp. Luke xi. 23. There
is no twilight in this spiritual world.
'The brother' stands in a relation
towards us which makes some feeling
on our part inevitable. In such a case
there is a simple choice between 'for'
and 'against,' that is essentially between 'love' and 'hatred.' 'Hatred'
is the expression of a want of sympathy. Where sympathy exists hatred
is impossible (John vii. 7); where
sympathy does not exist hatred is
inevitable (John xv. 18 ff., xvii. 14,
iii. 20).

There is however a certain ambiguity
in the word 'hate' for it serves as the
opposite both to the love of natural
affection (φιλεῖν), and to the love of
moral judgment (ἀγαπᾶν). In the
former case 'hatred,' which may become a moral duty, involves the sub-
jection of an instinct (John xii. 25,
xv. 18 f.; comp. Luke xiv. 26); in
the latter case 'hatred' expresses a
general determination of character (c.
iii. 15, iv. 20; comp. Matt. v. 43, vi.
24; Eph. v. 28 f.).

τὸν ἀδελφόν] *his brother*, that is,
his fellow-Christian, and not more
generally his fellow-man. It is only
through the recognition of the relation to Christ that the wider relation
is at last apprehended. The idea of
brotherhood under the new dispensation (comp. Acts ii. 37, iii. 17, vi. 3,
ix. 30, &c.: Rom. i. 13, &c.) is nor-

mally thus limited (yet see Acts xxii.
1, xxviii. 17; Rom. ix. 3). 'Brethren'
are those who are united together in
Christ to God as their Father (John
xx. 17, xxi. 23; comp. Matt. xii. 50).
The title occurs significantly in the
first record of the action of the Church
(Acts i. 15 ἐν μέσῳ τῶν ἀδελφῶν;
comp. ix. 30, &c.) and then throughout
the apostolic writings (1 Thess v. 26;
Gal. i. 2; 1 Cor. v. 11; Rom. xvi. 14
&c.; 1 Tim. vi. 2; James i. 9; 1 Pet. v.
12 &c.; c. iii. 14, 16; 3 John 3, 5, 10.

The singular is characteristic of this
epistle (*vv.* 10, 11, iii. 10, 15, 17, iv.
20 f., v. 16). Comp. Rom. xiv. 10 ff.;
1 Cor. viii. 13. Compare Additional
Note on c. iii. 14.

There is, as far as it appears, no
case where a fellow-man, as man, is
called 'a brother' in the N. T. Such
passages as Matt. v. 22 ff., Luke vi.
41 ff., presuppose a special bond of
'brotherhood.' The 'love of the
brotherhood' (φιλαδελφία· 1 Thess. iv.
9; Rom. xii. 10; Heb. xiii. 1; 1 Pet.
i. 22 (iii. 8); 2 Pet. i. 7) leads up to
'love' (ἀγάπη). But this widest love
is expressly assigned in its full extent
only to God (John iii. 16, c. iv. 10 f.).

Augustine makes a striking application of the words to the Donatists :
Offendit te nescio quis sive malus,
sive ut tu putas malus, sive ut tu
fingis malus, et deseris tot bonos ?
Qualis dilectio est fraterna ? Qualis
apparuit in istis [Donatistis]. Cum
accusant Afros deseruerunt orbem
terrarum.

And again he points out the ground
of the Christian's love of enemies: Sic
dilige inimicos ut fratres optes. Sic
dilige inimicos ut in societatem tuam
vocentur. Sic enim dilexit ille qui in
cruce pendens ait Pater ignosce illis,
quia nesciunt quid faciunt.

¹⁰ ὁ ἀγαπῶν τὸν ἀδελφὸν αὐτοῦ ἐν τῷ φωτὶ μένει, καὶ
σκάνδαλον ἐν αὐτῷ οὐκ ἔστιν· ¹¹ ὁ δὲ μισῶν τὸν ἀδελφὸν
αὐτοῦ ἐν τῇ σκοτίᾳ ἐστὶν καὶ ἐν τῇ σκοτίᾳ περιπατεῖ,

10 ἐν αὐτῷ οὐκ ἔστιν B vg: οὐκ ἔστιν ἐν αὐτῷ אAC (me) the.

ἐν τῇ σκ. ἐστίν] *is in the darkness.*
Comp. i. 6 note. The assertion is not
simply characterised as false (i. 6 *we
lie*) or as revealing a false nature (*v.* 4
he is a liar): it involves the existence
of a moral state the exact opposite of
that which is claimed.

ἕως ἄρτι] *usque adhuc* V., *until
now,* though the light is actually
shining, and he affirms that he is in
it, yea even that he has been in it
from the first.

10. ὁ ἀγαπῶν...] *He that loveth...*
The reality of the fact is set against
the assertion in *v.* 9 (*He that saith...*).
Comp. *vv.* 4, 5 note.

ἐν τῷ φωτὶ μένει] *abideth* (and not
simply *is* as in *v.* 9) *in the light.*
The idea of stability is added to that
of simple 'being' (comp. *vv.* 5, 6).
The position of the false brother and
of the true brother is referred to the
initial point of faith. Love testifies
to the continuance of a divine fellowship on man's part but does not create
it: the absence of love shews that the
fellowship has never been realised.
For the use of '*abide*' in various
connexions see *v.* 6, iii. 14, iv. 16; 2
John 9; John xii. 46.

By love the disciple 'follows' his
Master and has 'the light of life'
(John viii. 12).

σκάνδαλον...ἔστιν] *scandalum in eo
non est* V., *there is none occasion of
stumbling in him.* The image occurs
elsewhere in St John's writings in
John vi. 61, xvi. 1; Apoc. ii. 14;
comp. John xi. 9 f. It is at first
sight doubtful whether the occasion of
stumbling is that which may be in the
way of others or in the way of the
believer himself. A man may cause
others to fall through want of love or

he may by the same defect create
difficulties in his own path.

The parallel in *v.* 11 favours the
second view. Love gives the single
eye which commands a clear prospect
of the course to be followed, while if
love be absent doubts and questionings arise which tend to the overthrow of faith (2 Pet. i. 10). But on
the other hand the general use of
σκάνδαλον points to the first meaning,
and it is quite in St John's manner to
regard love in its twofold working in
relation to the man who loves and to
others, while he regards hatred only
in its subject. The triumph of love is
that it creates no prejudice against
the Truth. Want of love is the most
prolific source of offences.

ἐν αὐτῷ] *in him.* If the 'offence'
is that which stands in a man's own
way, then he is regarded as offering
in himself the scene of his spiritual
advance: his progress, his dangers, are
spiritual, internal. If the offence is
that which lies in another's way, then
he who gives the offence presents
the cause of stumbling in his own
person.

11. Of the fruits of love it is sufficient to say that 'he that loveth
abideth in the light, and there is
none occasion of stumbling in him.'
The issues of hatred are traced in different directions. They are regarded
both in respect of present being (*is
in*) and action (*walketh in*) and in
respect of the final goal (*knoweth
not whither*) to which life is directed.
He who hates has lost the faculty of
seeing, which requires light and love,
'so that his whole life is a continual
error' (Howe).

ἐστίν...περιπατεῖ...] Comp. i. 7. The

καὶ οὐκ οἶδεν ποῦ ὑπάγει, ὅτι ἡ σκοτία ἐτύφλωσεν

phrase πορεύεσθαι ἐν σκότει is used in a different sense in Is. l. 10.

οὐκ οἶδεν...] *knoweth not*... John xii. 35; Prov. iv. 19. On the other hand that which was true of Christ (John viii. 12, xiii. 3) is true also of the believer (comp. John xiv. 4, 5). He knows what is the end of life.

ὑπάγει] *goeth*. The idea is not that of proceeding to a definite point (πορεύεσθαι), but of leaving the present scene.

ἐτύφλ. τοὺς ὀφθαλμούς] The image comes from Is. vi. 10 (John xii. 40), which is the fundamental description of God's mode of dealing with the self-willed. Comp. Rom. xi. 10 (Ps. lxix. 24); and for the opposite Eph. i. 18 πεφωτισμένους τοὺς ὀφθ. τῆς καρδίας. (Clem. 1 *Cor.* 36.)

ἐτύφλωσεν] The English idiom will not bear the exact rendering *blinded*. The original tense (comp. 2 Cor. iv. 4 and contrast John xii. 40) marks the decisive action of the darkness at the fatal moment when it once for all 'overtook' the man (John xii. 35 ἵνα μὴ καταλάβῃ, i. 5 οὐ κατέλαβεν). This darkness not only hindered the use of vision but (as darkness does physically) destroyed the spiritual organ.

IV. ii. 12—17. THINGS TEMPORAL AND ETERNAL.

Hitherto St John has stated briefly the main scope of his Epistle. He has shewn what is the great problem of life, and how the Gospel meets it with an answer and a law complete and progressive, old and new. He now pauses, as it were, to contemplate those whom he is addressing more distinctly and directly, and to gather up in a more definite form the charge which is at once the foundation and the end of all he writes.

The section is divided into two parts. The apostle first gives the ground of his appeal (*vv.* 12—14); and then he gives the appeal itself (15—17).

1. *The ground of the appeal* (ii. 12—14).

The ground of the apostle's appeal lies in the character and position of those whom he is addressing. He regards his readers first under their common aspect as all alike believers, and then under a twofold aspect as 'fathers' and 'young men,' separated one from another by the length of their Christian experience. This he does twice, first in respect of the actual work in which he is at the moment engaged, and then again in respect of a work looked upon as finished and complete. He shews with an impressive iteration that from first to last, in all that he writes or has written, one unchanging motive is supreme. Because his readers are Christians and have in part experienced the power of their faith he moves them to nobler efforts; his object is that their 'joy may be fulfilled' (c. i. 4).

The exact relation of γράφω to ἔγραψα has been variously explained. It may be a reference to some other writing which has not been preserved, or, as some think, to the Gospel (comp. 3 John 9; 1 Cor. v. 9; 2 Cor. ii. 3 f., vii. 12); but the use of ἔγραψα in *vv.* 21, 26 is unfavourable to this view.

It may mark a contrast between the former part of the letter, and that part which the apostle is now writing, as if he resumed his work after an interval and looked back upon the words already written (comp. 1 Cor. ix. 15; Rom. xv. 15).

Or it may indicate simply a change of mental position in accordance with which St John transfers himself to the place of his readers, and regards the whole letter as they would do, as belonging to a past date.

Or yet again, to put this mode of

τοὺς ὀφθαλμοὺς αὐτοῦ.   ¹² Γράφω ὑμῖν, τεκνία,

explanation in another form, St John may look at his letter first as it is in the process of transcription still incomplete (1 Cor. xiv. 37; 2 Cor. xiii. 10), and then as it is ideally complete. This appears to be the true explanation of the 'epistolary aorist.' Comp. *vv.* 21, 26, v. 13; 2 John 12; 1 Pet. v. 12 ; Gal. vi. 11; Philem. 19, 21.

The Latin renderings of γράφω and ἔγραψα are alike *scribo*.

The symmetry of the corresponding clauses is remarkable.

(1) *I write to you*, little children (τεκνία), *because*
> your sins are forgiven you for His name's sake.

(a) *I write to you, fathers, because*
> ye know Him that is from the beginning.

(β) *I write to you, young men, because*
> ye have overcome the evil one.

(2) *I have written (I wrote) to you*, little ones (παιδία), *because*
> ye know the Father.

(a) *I have written (I wrote) to you, fathers, because*
> ye know Him that is from the beginning.

(β) *I have written (I wrote) to you, young men, because*
> ye are strong and the word of God abideth in you and ye have overcome the evil one.

The common title of address is different in the two cases (1) *little children;* (2) *little ones.* And in correspondence with this the aspect of the common ground of addressing those who are thus designated is also different (1) *because your sins are forgiven for His name's sake;* (2) *because ye know the Father.* The special ground of addressing 'the fathers' is the same in each case:

that of addressing 'the young men' is not changed in the second case but more fully developed.

The causes of these variations will appear as we examine the text.

Augustine, like many others, supposes that three classes of readers are addressed. On this assumption he characterises them vigorously :

Filii sunt, patres sunt, juvenes sunt. Filii quia nascuntur : patres quia principium agnoscunt : juvenes, quare? Quia vicistis malignum. In filiis nativitas, in patribus antiquitas, in juvenibus fortitudo.

12. Γράφω] *I write.* Compare *v.* 1, and contrast i. 4 (*we write*). For the present tense compare Gal. i. 20; 1 Cor. xiv. 37 ; 2 Cor. i. 13; 1 Tim. iii. 14.

τεκνία] *filioli* V., *little children.* Comp. *v.* 1 *my little children.* The simple title occurs again *v.* 28 (iii. 7), iv. 4, v. 21. The word which expresses fellowship of nature is connected with that which is the sign of it, the forgiveness of sins. Comp. John iii. 5. Both from the symmetry of the structure (*little children, fathers, young men*), and from the general scope of the passage, it is evident that the title (here as elsewhere) is addressed to all St John's readers and not to a particular class of children in age.

ὅτι] *quoniam* V., *quia* Aug., *because.* There can be no doubt that the particle is causal (*because*) and not declarative (*that*). St John does not write to make known the privileges of Christians, but to enforce the duties which follow from the enjoyment of them.

ἀφέωνται ὑ. αἱ ἁμ.] *remittuntur vobis peccata* V., *your sins are forgiven, i.e.* have been forgiven. The present of the Latin is misleading though the past forgiveness of sin carries with it the constant applica-

ὅτι ἀφέωνται ὑμῖν αἱ ἁμαρτίαι διὰ τὸ ὄνομα αὐτοῦ.

tion of the grace to which it was due:
John xiii. 10. In parallel narra-
tives, it may be added, ἀφίενται is
used by St Matthew (ix. 2, 5) and St
Mark (ii. 5, 9), and ἀφέωνται by St
Luke (v. 20, 23). In Luke vii. 47 f.
ἀφέωνται is practically undisturbed.
The reading in John xx. 23 is somewhat doubtful (ἀφέωνται, ἀφίενται).

The proclamation of the forgiveness
of sins was the message of the Gospel:
Luke xxiv. 47; Acts xiii. 38. This
includes potentially the fulfilment of
man's destiny as man. Comp. i. 9 note.
For Christ's sake the Father (v. 14) forgives those who are united with Him.

διὰ τὸ ὄνομα αὐτοῦ] propter nomen
ejus V., per n. e. Aug., for his name's
sake. There is no direct antecedent;
but from v. 6 the thought of Christ as
the perfect exemplar of divine love
has been present to the mind of the
apostle; and the pronoun clearly refers to Him. Forgiveness is granted
to men because Christ is indeed what
He is revealed to be and what His
'name' expresses. It is of course
assumed that Christians acknowledge
Him as being what He is (Matt. xxviii.
19).

Redemption is referred to Christ as
He has been made known, both in
respect of the fact that that revelation
contains the force through which as
the means (διά gen.) and the ground
for the sake of which as the cause
(διά acc.) it is accomplished. See c. iv.
9 ζήσωμεν δι' αὐτοῦ; John vi. 57 ζήσει
δι' ἐμέ. The latter construction is
very rare. Comp. John xv. 3 καθαροί
ἐστε διὰ τὸν λόγον; Apoc. xii. 11 ἐνίκησαν διὰ τὸ αἷμα τοῦ ἀρνίου.

For διὰ τὸ ὄνομα see Matt. x. 22,
xxiv. 9 and parallels; John xv. 21;
Apoc. ii. 3.

διὰ τοῦ ὀνόματος Acts iv. 30, x. 43;
1 Cor. i. 10.

In two other places of the Epistle
'the name' of Christ is mentioned as

the object of faith in different aspects.
The commandment of God is that we
believe the name (πιστεύειν τῷ ὀν.) of
His Son Jesus Christ (iii. 23), that
is, that we accept the revelation conveyed in that full title as true. And
again those who believe in the name
(πιστεύειν εἰς τὸ ὄν.) of the Son of
God (v. 13), who cast themselves
wholly upon the revelation, are assured of the possession of life eternal
(comp. John i. 12 note). With these
passages must be compared John xx.
31, where St John says that the object of his Gospel was that his readers
may believe that Jesus is the Christ,
the Son of God, and believing may
have life in His name (ἐν τῷ ὀν.), in
fellowship with Him as He has thus
been made known.

The pregnant use of 'the name' as
summing up that which is made known
of Christ, explains how it came to be
used as equivalent to 'the faith': 3
John 7 ὑπὲρ τοῦ ὀνόματος ἐξῆλθαν.
See Additional Note on iii. 23.

13. Believers, who are one in the
possession of the gift of forgiveness,
are distinguished by the circumstances of life. Differences of experience correspond generally to differences of age. Mature Christians, in
a society like that which St John addressed, would be 'fathers' in years.
The difference of 'fathers' and 'young
men' answers to that of 'the thinkers,
and the soldiers in the Christian
army,' to the two main applications of
the Faith. It is a spring of wisdom;
and it is also a spring of strength. In
the natural sequence action is the
way to that knowledge through which
wisdom comes. Christian wisdom is
not speculative but first the fruit of
work and then the principle of work.

The characteristic of 'fathers' is
knowledge, the fruit of experience
(ἐγνώκατε): that of 'young men,'
victory, the prize of strength. St

¹³ γράφω ὑμῖν, πατέρες, ὅτι ἐγνώκατε τὸν ἀπ᾽ ἀρχῆς·
γράφω ὑμῖν, νεανίσκοι, ὅτι νενικήκατε τὸν πονηρόν.

13 τὸ πονηρόν ℵ.

John bases his appeal to each class on that which they had severally gained.

πατέρες] The word, like אָב, *Abba*, *pater*, *papa*, is used naturally of those who stand in a position of responsible authority. Thus it is applied in the O. T. to prophets (2 K. ii. 12; vi. 21; xiii. 14), priests (Jud. xvii. 10; xviii. 19), teachers (Prov. i. 8). Comp. Matt. xxiii. 9; (1 Cor. iv. 15;) Acts vii. 2; xxii. 1. Here the natural characteristic of age is combined with that of eminence in the Christian body.

ὅτι ἐγνώκατε] *quoniam (quia) cognovistis* V., *because ye know*.... The essence of wisdom lies in the recognition of the unity of purpose which runs through the whole development of being, and of that unity of life which exists in all. This truth is brought home through the deeper understanding of the age-long revelation of God consummated in the Incarnation and interpreted by the Spirit.

For the idea of knowledge see *v.* 3 note. God can be known only in His Son. The knowledge here spoken of is that which is the result of the past still abiding (ἐγνώκατε) and not that which marked a crisis in growth (ἔγνωτε) or which is still in continuous advance (γινώσκετε).

τὸν ἀπ᾽ ἀρχῆς] *eum qui ab initio* (*a principio* Aug.) *est* V., *Him that is from the beginning*, the Word, that is, brought near to us in the Person of Christ Jesus. The title sums up shortly what is expressed in its successive stages in John i. 1—14, the Word through Whom all things were made, and in Whom all things consist, Who, as Life, was the Light of men, Who was ever coming into the world which He made, Who became Flesh. *The word of life* (c. i. 1) is the record of the revelation of *Him that is from the beginning*. The whole course of history is, when rightly understood, the manifestation of one will. To know this in Christ is the prerogative of a 'father,' and the knowledge is the opportunity for the completest life.

νεανίσκοι] *adulescentes* V., *juvenes* Aug., *young men* in the full vigour of opening life. Comp. Matt. xix. 20; Luke vii. 14.

νενικήκατε] *have overcome*, not 'overcame' simply (c. v. 4 ἡ νίκη ἡ νικήσασα). The past remains effective. The image, based on John xvi. 33, is characteristic of the Apocalypse (ii. 7 ff., xii. 11, xxi. 7) and of this Epistle: *v.* 14, iv. 4, v. 4 f.

τὸν πονηρόν] *malignum* V., *the evil one*, *v.* 14, iii. 12, v. 18 f.; John xvii. 15; Matt. vi. 13, xiii. 19, 38 (v. 37, 39). The personal aspect of the Christian conflict on its spiritual side is naturally brought out now. Darkness has its prince: John xii. 31, xiv. 30, xvi. 11. It is assumed that a conflict is inevitable unless men passively yield to the power of evil (c. v. 19). Comp. Eph. ii. 2, vi. 12. The abruptness with which the idea of 'the evil one' is introduced shews that it was familiar. See Additional Note.

14. At the close of *v.* 13 there is a pause in thought if not a break in the composition of the letter. Looking back on the record of his purpose the apostle appears to resume the thread of his argument: 'I write, yea I have written, because you have had experience of the Faith.'

παιδία] *infantes* V., *pueri* Aug., *little ones*. This title, *little ones*, which like τεκνία is applied to the whole

¹⁴ἔγραψα ὑμῖν, παιδία, ὅτι ἐγνώκατε τὸν πατέρα·
ἔγραψα ὑμῖν, πατέρες, ὅτι ἐγνώκατε τὸν ἀπ᾽ ἀρχῆς·
ἔγραψα ὑμῖν, νεανίσκοι, ὅτι ἰσχυροί ἐστε καὶ ὁ λόγος

14 ἔγραψα ὑ. π. ℵABC the me syrr: γράφω ὑ. π. ς.   τὸ ἀπ᾽ ἀρχῆς B.
ὁ λόγος τοῦ θεοῦ ℵAC vg syrr: – τοῦ θεοῦ B the.

Christian body, differs from *little children* by emphasising the idea of subordination and not that of kinsmanship. St John speaks not as sharing the nature of those to whom he writes, but as placed in a position of authority over them. Comp. *v.* 18 (John xxi. 5).

In correspondence with this difference in the address St John gives a different reason for his writing: *because ye know the Father.*

The sense of an immediate personal relationship to God (comp. John xiv. 7) gives stability to all the gradations of human authority. In this respect 'knowing the Father' is different from 'knowing Him that is from the beginning.' The former involves a direct spiritual connexion: the latter involves besides an intellectual apprehension of the divine 'plan.' The knowledge 'of the Father' is that of present love and submission: the knowledge of Him 'that is from the beginning' is sympathy with the Divine Thought which is fulfilled in all time.

At the same time the two titles 'little children,' 'little ones,' indicate a twofold spiritual position. As 'little children' we are all bound one to another by the bond of natural affection: as 'little ones' we all recognise our equal feebleness in the presence of the One Father. It may be added that the relation of the readers of the letter to the Apostle really determined their relation to God (c. i. 3).

There is a difference in the general ground for writing (*v.* 12 *because your sins are forgiven...*, *v.* 14 *because ye*

know *the Father*), but in writing to 'the fathers' specially there is no change, no development, in St John's language. The knowledge of Christ as the Word, active from the beginning of Creation, includes all that we can know. At the same time this knowledge is regarded in two different aspects corresponding to the two general ideas of forgiveness and Fatherhood (*vv.* 12, 14); even as the Incarnation satisfies man's need of redemption and his need of consummation.

In writing to 'the young men' St John makes no change in his reason (*because ye have overcome the evil one*) but he develops what he has said. He adds the twofold permanent ground of the Christian's victory to the assertion of the fact which he made before. The young soldier is '*strong*' (ἰσχυρός comp. Eph. vi. 10; Matt. xii. 29) as having the personal qualifications for his work; and '*the word of God abideth in him,*' so that he is in living contact with the source of life. The natural endowment of energetic vigour is consecrated to a divine end by a divine voice.

ὁ λόγος...μένει...] *the word...abideth...* Comp. *vv.* 24, 27; John xv. 7 (*v.* 3). The converse thought occurs John viii. 31. Comp. c. i. 10 note.

2. *The appeal* (ii. 15—17).

In the preceding verses St John has set forth the privileges of Christians both generally in their sense of forgiveness and of a Divine Fatherhood, and specially in the far-reaching wisdom of the old, and the victorious strength of the young: he now goes

[τοῦ θεοῦ] ἐν ὑμῖν μένει καὶ νενικήκατε τὸν πονηρόν.

on to enforce the consequence which is made possible. A great 'love not' follows on the command to love.

The structure of the passage is simple and regular. The prohibition (15 *a*) is followed by a view of its overwhelming necessity. The love of the world is incompatible with the love of the Father (15 *b*), for the objects of love determine its character (16). And further: there is between them the contrast of time and eternity, of transition and abiding (17).

¹⁵ *Love not the world nor the things in the world. If any one love the world, the love of the Father is not in him:* ¹⁶ *because all that is in the world, the desire of the flesh, and the desire of the eyes, and the vainglory of life, is not of the Father, but is of the world.* ¹⁷ *And the world is passing away, and the desire thereof, but he that doeth the will of God abideth for ever.*

The three false tendencies under which St John ranges 'all that is in the world' cover the whole ground of worldliness, of the temptation to set up the creature as an end. They offer typical tests of man's real state as to himself, as to things external, and (specially) as to his fellow-men. Or, if we follow the division suggested by the words (ἐπιθυμία, ἐπιθυμία, ἀλαζονία), they indicate prevailing false views in regard to want and to possession. We desire wrongly and we glory wrongly in what we have.

The 'wants' which man feels can be divided into two great classes. Some things he desires to appropriate personally: some things he desires to enjoy without appropriation. The desire of the flesh embraces the one class (*e.g.* gratification of appetites); the desire of the eyes the other (*e.g.* pursuit of art as an end).

The wrong use of possession lies in

the empty and ostentatious assertion of advantages which are placed in a wrong light. A superiority is asserted on external grounds which cannot be justified in the face of the true issues of life. The ἀλάζων is in this case 'one who lays claim to blessings which are not truly his for the sake of renown' (comp. Theophr. *Char.* § 23; [Plat.] *Def.* p. 416 ἀλαζονεία ἕξις προσποιητικὴ ἀγαθοῦ ἢ ἀγαθῶν τῶν μὴ ὑπαρχόντων.

The three tendencies naturally recall the three Temptations of the Lord, with which they have obvious points of contact. The first Temptation corresponds to the first and most elementary form of ἐπιθυμία τῆς σαρκός, the desire of the simplest support of natural life. A divine word is sovereign over this: the means which God uses are not limited to one form (Luke iv. 4). The offer of the kingdoms of the civilized world (τῆς οἰκουμένης) and their glory, which is placed second in St Luke's order seems to answer in the loftiest shape to ἐπιθυμία τῶν ὀφθαλμῶν, the power of commanding all that is fairest and most attractive in the world. Here also Scripture shews that no aim however true and noble can be allowed to trench on the absolute homage due to God (Luke iv. 8). And again the call to claim an open manifestation of God's protecting power touches the root of ἀλαζονία τοῦ βίου, in which endowments and gifts are used arbitrarily for personal ostentation. Such use is a tempting of God from Whom man dares to isolate himself (Luke iv. 12).

It has been felt no less natural to look for some correspondence between the threefold worldly tendencies of St John and the three master vices which occupy a prominent place in ancient and mediæval ethics, φιληδονία, πλεονεξία, φιλοδοξία, voluptas, avaritia, superbia.

¹⁵ Μὴ ἀγαπᾶτε τὸν κόσμον μηδὲ τὰ ἐν τῷ κόσμῳ. ἐάν τις ἀγαπᾷ τὸν κόσμον, οὐκ ἔστιν ἡ ἀγάπη τοῦ πατρὸς

15 ἡ ἀγάπη τοῦ πατρός ℵB vg syrr the me: ἡ ἀγ. τοῦ θεοῦ AC.

The correspondence is so far real, though not direct, that the germs of these special vices lie in the feelings which St John characterises. Comp. Just. M. *Dial.* 82, p. 308 D διὰ δεὸς οὖν [Ezech. iii. 17 ff.) καὶ ἡμεῖς σπουδάζομεν ὁμιλεῖν κατὰ τὰς γραφάς, οὐ διὰ φιλοχρηματίαν ἢ φιλοδοξίαν ἢ φιληδονίαν· ἐν οὐδενὶ γὰρ τούτων ἐλέγξαι ἡμᾶς ὄντας δύναταί τις.

The enumeration does not include spiritual sins. These are not, under the present aspect, 'of the world' or 'in the world.' St John has dwelt before on the relation of man to man —love and hatred; and he dwells afterwards on the relation of man to true opinion. Here he is considering the relation of man to the κόσμος as an external system which has lost its true character: Rom. viii. 19 f.

15. Μὴ ἀγαπᾶτε] *Nolite diligere* V., *Love not.* The command is not given to any particular class (as to the young) but to all. That which man may not do, being what he is, God can do, John iii. 16 (ἠγάπησεν τὸν κόσμον). God looks through the surface of things by which man is misled to the very being which He created.

τὸν κόσμον] *mundum* V., *the world*, the order of finite being regarded as apart from God. The Roman empire with its idolatry of the Emperor as the representative of the State, presented the idea in a concrete and impressive form. See Essay I.

The system as an organised whole (κόσμος) is in other places considered as the dominant form of life, the age (ὁ αἰὼν οὗτος, ὁ νῦν αἰών). Comp. Rom. xii. 2; 2 Tim. iv. 2.

For the use of κόσμος see John i. 10 note.

With 'the world' are joined 'the things in the world,' all, that is, which

finds its proper sphere and fulfilment in a finite order and without God. 'To be in the world' is the opposite to 'being in God.' The question is not of the present necessary limitations of thought and action but of their aim and object. Whatever is treated as complete without reference to God is so far a rival to God. This thought is brought out in the words which follow.

Augustine illustrates the idea in respect of the love of nature : Non te prohibet Deus amare ista sed non diligere ad beatitudinem, sed ad hoc probare et laudare ut ames creatorem. Quemadmodum......si sponsus faceret sponsæ suæ annulum et illa acceptum annulum plus diligeret quam sponsum qui illi fecerit annulum ; nonne in ipso dono sponsi anima adultera deprehenderetur quamvis hoc amaret quod dedit sponsus ?

ἐάν τις...] There can be but one supreme object of moral devotion. All secondary objects will be referred to this. The love of the finite as an absolute object necessarily excludes the love of the Creator (*the Father*). Comp. Rom. i. 25 ; James iv. 4 (ἡ φιλία τοῦ κόσμου). Unum cor duos tam sibi adversarios amores non capit : Matt. vi. 24 (Bede, *ad loc.*).

Here as elsewhere St John places the contrast before his readers in its ultimate essential form, as of light and darkness, love and hatred. He assumes that there cannot be a vacuum in the soul. So Augustine writes : Noli diligere mundum. Exclude malum amorem mundi ut implearis amore Dei. Vas es sed adhuc plenus es ; funde quod habes ut accipias quod non habes.

It will be observed also that he speaks here of *the love of the Father*

ἐν αὐτῷ· ¹⁶*ὅτι πᾶν τὸ ἐν τῷ κόσμῳ· ἡ ἐπιθυμία τῆς*

and not of *the love of God* (c. ii. 5 note).
The phrase is unique (comp. Col. i.
12 f.), and suggests as the object of
man's love God as He has been
pleased to bring Himself within the
range of man's knowledge (John xiv.
9; comp. c. i. 2 note). Thus it expresses primarily the love of 'the
children' of God to God; but this
love answers to and springs out of the
love shewn to them by 'the Father'
whom 'they know' (*v.* 14.)

By the 'love of the world, and of the
things in the world' the sense of the
personal relationship to God is lost,
and not merely the sense of a divine
presence. Of the man who is swayed
by such a passion it must be said that
the love of the Father is not in him
as an animating, inspiring power (c. i.
10). This phrase expresses more than
'he loveth not God' or 'he loveth not
the Father.' That form of expression would describe a simple fact: this
presents the fact as a ruling principle.
The exact order of the Greek is
remarkable: 'there exists not, whatever he may say, the love of the
Father in him.' Comp. c. i. 5; iv. 16 f.;
John v. 45; vi. 45; vii. 28; viii. 44,
50, 54; ix. 16; x. 12, 34; xiii. 10, 16.

The thought finds a striking expression under the imagery of St John in
a fragment of Philo quoted by John
of Damascus (*Parall. Sacra* A, *Tit.*
xxx. p. 370): *ἀμήχανον συνυπάρχειν
τὴν πρὸς κόσμον ἀγάπην τῇ πρὸς τὸν
θεὸν ἀγάπῃ, ὡς ἀμήχανον συνυπάρχειν
ἀλλήλοις φῶς καὶ σκότος.*

16. *ὅτι...*] *because...* In moral
and spiritual things there is a law of
equilibrium. Nothing rises higher
than its source. The desire of things
earthly as ends in themselves comes
from the world and is bounded by the
world. It is therefore incompatible
with the love of the Father.

The point of sight from which 'all
that is in the world' is regarded here

is more distinctly defined than in *v.*
15. In themselves all finite objects,
'the things that are in the world,' are
'of the Father.' It is the false view
of them which makes them idols.
Hence St John defines 'that which is
in the world,' that which, as now regarded, finds its consummation 'in the
world,' from the human side. The
feeling which misuses the object determines and shews by its misuse
what there is defective in the object
which gives occasion to the wrong-
doing.

This general aspect of the question
determines the exact form of language. St John writes *πᾶν τὸ ἐν τ. κ.*
and not *πάντα τὰ ἐν τ. κ.* He looks at
'all' in its unity in relation to the
feeling man. Comp. c. v. 4: Eph. v.
13 (*πάντα, πᾶν*). The world as such
has nothing more to offer than what
is summed up in the three typical
phrases by which *πᾶν* is defined. This
thought has been made wrongly the
main thought of the sentence by the
Latin versions: *omne quod in mundo
est concupiscentia (desiderium) carnis est....*

ἡ ἐπιθυμία τῆς σαρκός] *concupiscentia (desiderium* Aug.) *carnis* V.,
the desire of the flesh, the desire of
which the flesh is the seat. The genitive with *ἐπιθυμία* is in the N. T.
characteristically subjective (John viii.
44; Rom. i. 24; Apoc. xviii. 14).
Comp. Gal. v. 16, 24; Eph. ii. 3; 1
Pet. ii. 11 (*αἱ σαρκικαὶ ἐπιθυμίαι*), Rom.
xiii. 14; 1 Pet. iv. 2 (*ἀνθρώπων ἐπιθυ-
μίαις*); Tit. ii. 12 (*αἱ κοσμικαὶ ἐπιθυμίαι*).

Under this category are included
all desires which involve the appropriation of the object to which they
are directed. By the separate mention of *οἱ ὀφθαλμοί* the sense of *σάρξ*
is proportionately limited.

In St John generally *σάρξ* is used
to express humanity under the present

σαρκὸς καὶ ἡ ἐπιθυμία τῶν ὀφθαλμῶν καὶ ἡ ἀλαζονία
τοῦ βίου, οὐκ ἔστιν ἐκ τοῦ πατρός, ἀλλὰ ἐκ τοῦ κόσ-

conditions of life (c. iv. 2; 2 John 7; John i. 14; vi. 51—55; xvii. 2). Once the θέλημα σαρκός is set by the side of θέλημα ἀνδρός as distinct from it (John i. 13); twice σάρξ is opposed to πνεῦμα (John iii. 6; vi. 63); and once κατὰ τὴν σάρκα is used to describe a judgment which is external, superficial, destitute of moral insight (John vii. 15). The desire of the σάρξ as σάρξ is necessarily for that which is like itself. It cannot include any spiritual element.

Compare Additional Note on iii. 19.

ἡ ἐπιθ. τῶν ὀφθ.] concupiscentia (desiderium Aug.) oculorum V., the desire of the eyes, the desire of which the eyes are the organ: not the pleasure of the miser only or characteristically (Eccles. iv. 8; v. 11), but all personal vicious indulgence represented by seeing. The desire of appropriation enters into 'the desire of the flesh': the 'desire of the eyes' is satisfied by enjoyment which comes under the general form of contemplation. So far it is true that in the former the thought of physical pleasure is dominant, as the object of desire, while in the latter forms of mental ('psychical') pleasure find place. The 'eyes' are the typical example of the organs to which art ministers.

Augustine gives a singular illustration of what he holds to be 'the desire of the eyes,' which is worth quoting as giving a vivid trait in the Christian feeling of his time: Aliquando tentat etiam [curiositas] servos Dei, ut velint quasi miraculum facere: tentare utrum exaudiat illos Deus in miraculis. Curiositas est; hoc est desiderium oculorum; non est a patre.

ἡ ἀλαζ. τοῦ βίου] superbia vitae V., ambitio saeculi Aug. (other Latin au-

thorities give jactantia hujus vitae, vitae humanae), the vainglory of life, the vainglory which springs out of and belongs to our visible earthly life. The genitive is subjective, as in the two other cases. The ἀλάζων (comp. Rom. i. 30; 2 Tim. iii. 2) is closely connected with the ὑπερήφανος; but his vice centres in self and is consummated in his absolute self-exaltation, while the ὑπερήφανος shews his character by his overweening treatment of others. 'The ἀλάζων sins most against truth: the ὑπερήφανος sins most against love.' Ἀλαζόνεια (-ία) may be referred to a false view of what things are in themselves, empty and unstable: ὑπερηφανία to a false view of what our relations to other persons are. Comp. Mk. vii. 22; Luke i. 51; James iv. 6; 1 Pet. v. 5. See also Wisd. v. 8; xvii. 7; 2 Macc. ix. 8, xv. 6; Prov. xxv. 6.

Such 'vainglory,' such a false view of the value of our possessions, belongs to life (ὁ βίος) in its present concrete manifestation and not to life in its essential principle (ἡ ζωή). Comp. Luke viii. 14 (ἡδοναὶ τοῦ βίου); 1 Tim. ii. 2 (βίον διάγειν); 2 Tim. ii. 4 (ταῖς τοῦ βίου πραγματείαις); (in 1 Pet. iv. 3 τοῦ βίου is an addition, but βιῶσαι occurs in v. 2). Hence ὁ βίος is used for 'the means of life': Mk. xii. 44; Luke [viii. 43], xv. 12, 30; c. iii. 17. Compare also βίωσις, Acts xxvi. 4; and βιωτικός, Luke xxi. 34; 1 Cor. vi 3 f.

These characteristic feelings of want and of wealth, the desire of the flesh and the desire of the eyes, and the vainglory of life, are said to be, as man now is naturally, of the world (c. iv. 5 note; John xv. 19; xvii. 14, 16; xviii. 36). The declaration marks the false position into which man has come. In his original

W.

5

μου ἐστίν· ¹⁷καὶ ὁ κόσμος παράγεται καὶ ἡ ἐπιθυμία
[αὐτοῦ], ὁ δὲ ποιῶν τὸ θέλημα τοῦ θεοῦ μένει εἰς τὸν
αἰῶνα.

17 ἡ ἐπιθ. αὐτοῦ: – αὐτοῦ A. Many Latin authorities and (in sense) the Thebaic version add: *quomodo* (*sicut et*) *deus* (*ipse*) *manet in æternum*.

constitution the desire was good, because it was directed consciously towards the fulfilment of his office in
regard to the whole order and to God:
the exultation was good, because it
was an acknowledgment of divine
bounty. Now the desire is suggested
by the creature and not by the Creator, by the object separated from the
Living Author of all, not by the Living
Author to whom the child should
look (ἐκ τοῦ πατρός not simply ἐκ τοῦ
θεοῦ). Thus each typical false tendency is the corruption of a noble
instinct, the longing for support and
for beauty, the joy of thankfulness.

The phrase εἶναι ἐκ (*v.* 21; iii. 19;
iv. 5) *to be of* is characteristic of St
John expressing derivation and dependence. Compare John iii. 31 note;
and Additional Note on iii. 1.

17. This clause contains a second
ground for the prohibition in *v.* 15.
Not only is the love of the world irreconcileable with the love of the Father ; but also, yet further, the fate
of the world is included in its essential character. The world—the external system which occupied the
place of God—was already when St
John wrote in the act of dissolution
and vanishing.

The words can also be taken as a
second proof of the antagonism of the
love of the Father and of the love of
the world, so far as these are at variance in their issue no less than in
their source. But this connexion
appears to be less natural than the
other.

παράγεται] *is passing away:* see
v. 8. The word describes not the
general character of the world as

transitory but its actual condition in
the face of the church, 'the Kingdom
of God.' The whole sum of finite
things, regarded in itself as complete,
is (as it were) a screen which hides
the presence of God. By the declaration of the Truth this was in St John's
time beginning to be removed. Compare *v.* 8; 1 Cor. vii. 31; and contrast
the ideal view from the divine side:
τὰ ἀρχαῖα παρῆλθεν, ἰδοὺ γέγονεν καινά
(2 Cor. v. 17: comp. Apoc. xxi. 4).

In the thanksgiving after the
Eucharist in *The Doctrine of the
Apostles* the clause occurs: ἐλθέτω
χάρις καὶ παρελθέτω ὁ κόσμος οὗτος (c.
x. 6).

ἡ ἐπιθυμία αὐτοῦ] *concupiscentia*
(*desideria* Aug.) *ejus* V., *the desire
thereof,* the desire which belongs to
it and which it stimulates. Comp.
Tit. ii. 12 αἱ κοσμικαὶ ἐπιθυμίαι. The
gen. is subjective as in *v.* 16, though
it is true that the desire which the
world fosters is in turn directed to
the world as its object. A verb corresponding to παράγεται must be supplied. The world which is the source
and the object of the desire is shewn
to be by itself unsubstantial and evan-
escent. The desire therefore is shewn
in its utter vanity (καταργεῖται). But
the desire remains as an aching void.

The contrast to this 'desire' which
is earth-born and empty is 'the will
of God.' That alone is permanent of
which this will is the ground.

ὁ δὲ ποιῶν...μένει...] *qui autem
facit* (*fecerit* Aug.) V., *but he that
doeth...abideth...* While the fabric of
'the world' is being removed the
Christian suffers no disturbance. The
present in this sense is eternal. When

all else changes the obedience of love continues unchanged. This abides in the new order to which indeed it properly belongs. The contrast to the world converted into an idol is not God, but the believer who in action strives to do God's will. Hence St John does not say 'he that loveth God,' which might have been suggested by *v.* 15, but *he that doeth the will of God abideth for ever.* Such a one is truly akin to the Son of man: Mk. iii. 35.

Compare John iv. 34; vi. 38; vii. 17; ix. 31.

The will of God expresses the true end of all things, and is opposed to 'the desire' which springs from a finite source as its ultimate origin. At the same time 'the will of God' includes the right use of all natural powers, faculties, instincts, which in their essential nature answer to it: Apoc. iv. 11. Compare 1 Thess. iv. 3.

In speaking of the divine will St John says 'the will of God' and not 'the will of the Father' as might seem to be suggested by *v.* 16. Stress is laid upon the divine majesty rather than upon the divine love. 'The will of the Father' is found only in St Matthew (vi. 10 *our Father,* vii. 21: xii. 50 *my Father;* comp. xviii. 14; xxvi. 42). *The will of our God and Father* occurs Gal. i. 4 (comp. Eph. i. 5, 9, 11). *The will of God* is not unfrequent: 1 Pet. ii. 15; iii. 17; iv. 19; Rom. i. 10; xii. 2; Heb. x. 36. In the Gospel of St John the phrase which is always used by the Lord is *the will of Him that sent me:* iv. 34; v. 30; vi. 38 ff. (vii. 17).

μένει εἰς τ. αἰ.] *abideth for ever.* Comp. John viii. 35; xii. 34; 2 Cor. ix. 9 (LXX); 1 Pet. i. 25 (LXX). The absolute use of μένειν is not unfrequent: John xv. 16; 1 Pet. i. 23; Heb. x. 34.

εἰς τὸν αἰῶνα] *in æternum* V. This is the only form in which αἰών occurs in the Epistles (here and 2 John 2)

and Gospel (12 times) of St John, except the correlative ἐκ τοῦ αἰῶνος (John ix. 32). The phrase occurs independently of the LXX (1 Pet. i. 25; 2 Cor. ix. 9; Hebr. v. 6; vi. 20; vii. 17 ff.) only (with negative) in Matth. xxi. 19‖Mk. xi. 14; Mk. iii. 29; 1 Cor. viii. 13 (Jude 13 εἰς αἰῶνα). [1 Pet. i 23 and 2 Pet. ii. 17 are false readings.] It is very common in the LXX. as the rendering of עַד עוֹלָם, לְעוֹלָם, עוֹלָם. The thought contained in the words here is given by the addition which is found in *Theb.* and *Old Lat.* 'as God also abideth for ever' (*sicut et ipse manet in æternum*). Augustine reads the addition and remarks on the whole passage: Voluit te amor mundi, tene Christum. Propter te factus est temporalis ut tu fias æternus; quia et ille sic factus est temporalis ut maneret æternus.

And again: Terram diligis, terra eris. Deum diligis: quid dicam, Deus eris? Non audeo dicere ex me: scripturas audiamus *Ego dixi, dii estis et filii altissimi omnes.*

B.   THE CONFLICT OF TRUTH AND FALSEHOOD WITHOUT AND WITHIN (ii. 18—iv. 6).

The broad contrast which has been drawn in the last section between things temporal and eternal, between the world and the Church, leads to the central subject of the Epistle, the great conflict of life, which is treated of in ii. 18—iv. 6. In this the hostile power is seen to arise from within the Christian society. The world has found expression in an anti-Christian system which lays claim to spiritual endowment and authority. False prophetic power (Apoc. xiii. 1 ff.) takes its place by the side of the imperial power (Apoc. xii. 1 ff.). These false teachers, this 'spirit of antichrist,' are 'of the world' (iv. 4 f.).

Characteristic marks of this conflict appear throughout: ἀντίχριστος ii. 18,

5—2

¹⁸Παιδία, ἐσχάτη ὥρα ἐστίν, καὶ καθὼς ἠκούσατε

20; τὸ πνεῦμα τοῦ ἀντιχρίστου iv. 3; ψευδοπροφῆται iv. 1; οἱ πλανῶντες ii. 26, comp. iii. 7; τὸ πνεῦμα τῆς πλάνης iv. 6. And underneath the false spiritual teaching lies 'the hatred' of the world: iii. 13. The question is no longer of false opinion or vicious practice within the Church, but of temptations to yield allegiance to a rival power.

The view which St John gives of the Christian conflict falls into four sections:

I. The Revelation of Falsehood and Truth (ii. 18—29).

II. The Children of God and the children of the devil (iii. 1—12).

III. Brotherhood in Christ and the hatred of the world (iii. 13—24).

IV. The Rival spirits of Truth and Error (iv. 1—6).

Step by step the strength of the Christian is shewn in his firm hold upon the Truth, in the consciousness and the character of Sonship, in the activity of Love, in the power of Spiritual Discernment. So the conflict passes to victory.

I. The Revelation of Falsehood and Truth (ii. 18—29).

This section is separable into three parts:

1. *Antichrists and Christians* (18—21).

2. *The essence and the power of the Truth* (22—25).

3. *Abiding in the Truth* (26—29).

The progress of thought is simple. The fact of apostasy from the Christian body is recognised as a characteristic of the crisis. This fact serves to remind Christians of the gift which they have received for the discernment of the Truth. The essence of the Truth lies in the acknowledgment

of the Messiahship of Jesus. The confession of the Son gives fellowship with the Father; issuing in the life eternal. This knowledge of God then Christians have to keep firmly, that they may face their Lord at His appearance. And true knowledge has the seal of righteousness, likeness to God, the mark of divine sonship.

1. *Antichrists and Christians* (18—21.

The necessity of conflict which has been laid down on general grounds in *vv.* 15—17 is enforced by the special circumstances of the age. It is 'a last hour,' and as such marked by divisions, errors, temptations in the Christian society itself (18, 19). At the same time, as answering to this special peril, Christians have a gift of spiritual discernment which it is their privilege to use as a decisive criterion of error (20, 21).

¹⁸*My little ones, it is a last hour, and as ye heard that Antichrist cometh, even now many Antichrists have arisen; whence we perceive that it is a last hour.* ¹⁹*They went out from us, but they were not of us; for if they had been of us, they would have remained with us; but they went out that they may be made manifest that they all are not of us.* ²⁰*And ye have an unction from the Holy One; and ye all know—*²¹*I have not written to you because ye know not the faith, but because ye know it, and because no lie is of the truth.*

18. Παιδία] *Filioli (Pueri)* V., *My little ones.* See *v.* 14. The apostle addresses his readers with the authority of age and experience, and not as dwelling on the thought of spiritual kinship (τεκνία).

In the sentence which precedes he had spoken of 'the world' as 'passing away.' He now points out the decisive sign of the coming change in the condition of the Christian society. It is 'a last hour.'

The conception of 'a last time,' 'a last season,' the 'last days,' rests upon the O. T., in which the phrase אַחֲרִית הַיָּמִים is used for the distant future, on which the prophet's eye is fixed. Thus in Gen. xlix. 1; Num. xxiv. 14 (ἐπ᾽, ἐσχάτων [-του] τῶν ἡμερῶν) it points to the time when Israel had entered upon the possession of Canaan, the first stage in the fulfilment of the divine promise. In Is. ii. 2; Mic. iv. 1; Hos. iii. 5; Jerem. xxiii. 20; xxx. 24; xlviii. 47; xlix. 39, it describes the time when Zion shall be restored and the people shall fear and obey the Lord. In Ezek. xxxviii. 16 it regards some particular season of signal deliverance. Thus the phrase in its biblical sense includes in part the notion of 'the age to come' and the immediate preparation for it.

In post-biblical times 'the age to come' was sharply distinguished from the period of trial by which it was to be ushered in; and 'the latter days' came to be regarded as a season of conflict and suffering through which the divine victory should be accomplished. This appears to be the ruling idea of the phrase in the N.T.: Acts ii. 17 ἐν ταῖς ἐσχ. ἡμ. (Joel iii. 1, ἐσχάταις being an explanatory gloss); James v. 3 ἐν ἐσχ. ἡμ.; 1 Pet. i. 20 ἐπ᾽ ἐσχάτων τῶν χρόνων.

But in this interpretation the successive partial dawnings of 'the age to come' give a different force to the words 'the last days' which usher in the age according to the context in which they occur. In one sense 'the age to come' dated from Pentecost; in another from the destruction of Jerusalem; in another it was still the object of hope. So also 'the last days' are found in each of the seasons of fierce trial which precede the several comings of Christ. The age in which we live is, under one aspect, 'the last days,' and in another it is 'the age to

come,' which was prepared by the travail-pains of the old order. As we look forward a season of sore distress separates us from that which is still to be revealed (2 Tim. iii. 1; 2 Pet. iii. 3; Jude 18; 1 Pet. i. 5, contrast v. 20): as we look back we have entered on an inheritance now though struggles of 'a last time.'

But while the great counsel of God goes forward to fulfilment the date of the consummation is not revealed: Acts i. 7; Matt. xxiv. 36.

The calculation which Severus (Cramer, Cat. in loc.) makes is interesting in the face of our present knowledge of the world's history: πεντακισχιλίων ἐνιαυτῶν παραδραμόντων ἐξ οὗ γέγονεν ὁ κόσμος...καὶ ἀπὸ τῆς Χριστοῦ παρουσίας οὔπω πεπληρωμένων ἑξακοσίων ἤγουν ἑπτακοσίων ἢ χιλίων ἐτῶν, δῶμεν γὰρ οὕτω, πῶς [οὐκ] (dele) ἔξω λόγου φανήσεται τῶν ἑξακοσίων ἐτῶν ἢ χιλίων, εἰ τύχοι, τὰς ἡμέρας πρὸς τὰς τῶν πεντακισχιλίων παρεξεταζομένας ἐσχάτας καλεῖν;

In this passage the anarthrous phrase ἐσχάτη ὥρα, novissima hora V., seems to mark the general character of the period and not its specific relation to 'the end.' It was a period of critical change 'a last hour,' but not definitely 'the last hour.' The exact phrase is not found elsewhere in the N.T. (comp. 1 Pet. i. 5; 2 Tim. iii. 1). The use of 'hour' recals that in the Gospel: iv. 21, 23; v. 35, 38; xvi. 2, 4, 25, 32. Compare ii. 4; vii. 30; viii. 20; xii. 23, 27; xiii. 1; xvii. 1; and the idea of 'a last hour' corresponds with the characteristic phrase of St John 'the last day' (vi. 39 f., 44, 54; xi. 24; xii. 48). The definiteness of this latter phrase (ἡ ἐσχ. ἡ.) justifies the wider sense given to the former (comp. iv. 17, ἡ ἡμέρα τῆς κρίσεως note). Comp. Ign. ad Ephes. c. 11. The true reading in 1 Thess. v. 2 (ἡμ. not ἡ ἡμ.) illustrates ἐσχ. ὥρα here.

καθὼς ἠκούσατε] as ye heard in general terms as part of the evangelic message (Mk. xiii. 6 ff.; Matt. xxiv. 5,

ὅτι Ἀντίχριστος ἔρχεται, καὶ νῦν ἀντίχριστοι πολλοί

18 ὅτι Ἀντ.: – ὅτι A.   Ἀντίχριστος ℵ*BC: ὁ ἀντίχριστος ℵ°A.

24), and in the teaching of apostles (Acts xx. 30). Comp. 1 Tim. iv. 1. These general predictions of false Christs and false teachers were concentrated in the thought of a typical adversary: 2 Thess. ii. 3.

Ἀντίχριστος] The term *Antichrist* is peculiar to St John in the N.T. It occurs again *v.* 22; iv. 3 and 2 John 7. The absence of the article shews that it had become current as a technical (proper) name.

The word means far more than simply 'an adversary of Christ.' As far as the form is concerned it may describe 'one who takes the place of Christ' (ἀντιβασιλεύς, ἀντιταμίας, ἀνθύπατος), or 'one who under the same character opposes Christ' (ἀντιδιδάσκαλος, ἀντιστρατιώτης). There is a similar ambiguity in the word ἀντιστράτηγος, which means both 'one who occupies the place of στρατηγός, *proprætor*,' and also 'an opposing general.' It seems to be most consonant to the context to hold that Ἀντίχριστος here describes one who assuming the guise of Christ opposes Christ. In this sense it embodies an important truth. That hostility is really formidable in which the adversary preserves the semblance of the characteristic excellence which he opposes (comp. 2 Cor. xi. 13; Apoc. ii. 2). The Antichrist assails Christ by proposing to do or to preserve what He did while denying Him (comp. John v. 43). The false Christ on the other hand (ψευδόχριστος Matt. xxiv. 24) is simply a pretender to the Messianic office. In St John's use of 'Antichrist' it will be seen that the sense is determined by the full Christian conception of 'Christ' and not by the Jewish conception of the promised Saviour.

Under one aspect it may be said that the work of the Incarnation was to reveal the true divine destiny of man in his union with God through Christ; while the lie of Antichrist was to teach that man is divine apart from God in Christ.

The passages in which the term occurs are not decisive as to St John's teaching in regard to the coming of one great Antichrist, of which the others were preparatory embodiments. As far as his words are concerned 'Antichrist' may be the personification of the principle shewn in different antichrists, or the person whose appearance is prepared by these particular forms of evil. The former is however the most natural interpretation: *v.* 22; 2 John 7. The spirit of evil comes in those whom he inspires. Contrast 2 Thess. ii. 3 ff.

The essential character of 'Antichrist' lies in the denial of the true humanity of Messiah (*v.* 22 ὁ ἀρνούμενος ὅτι Ἰησοῦς οὐκ ἔστιν ὁ χριστός. iv. 3 πν. ὃ μὴ ὁμολογεῖ (λύει) τὸν Ἰησοῦν. 2 John 7 οἱ μὴ ὁμολογοῦντες Ἰησοῦν Χριστὸν ἐρχόμενον ἐν σαρκί).

This denial involves the complete misunderstanding of Christ's past and future work, and takes away the knowledge of the Father, which is brought to us by the Incarnate Son. The teaching of Antichrist leaves God and the world still ununited. The proclamation of the union is the message of the Gospel.

It may be added that St John's description of 'Antichrist' (c. iv. 3) is made use of by Polycarp (*ad Phil.* 7); and Irenæus, the disciple of Polycarp, first developed the teaching. The word does not occur in the other Apostolic Fathers, or Justin Martyr, who does however refer to ὁ τῆς ἀνομίας ἄνθρωπος (*Dial.* 32, p. 250 A ὁ τῆς ἀποστασίας ἄνθρωπος *Dial.* 110, p. 336 D). It appears therefore to be characteristic of the school of St John. See Additional Note.

γεγόνασιν· ὅθεν γινώσκομεν ὅτι ἐσχάτη ὥρα ἐστίν.
¹⁹ἐξ ἡμῶν ἐξῆλθαν, ἀλλ᾽ οὐκ ἦσαν ἐξ ἡμῶν· εἰ γὰρ ἐξ

19 ἐξ ἡμῶν ἦσαν (2⁰) BC syrr me the: ἦσαν ἐξ ἡμῶν ςℵA vg.

ἔρχεται] venit (sit venturus) V.,
cometh. The same term is used of
Christ and of His adversary. Comp.
c. iv. 3; John xiv. 3; xxi. 22 f.; Apoc.
xxii. 20. In both cases it implies
something more than one advent,
though it includes this. The rival
power finds a personal expression as
often as Christ comes. Comp. v. 6
note.

καθώς...καὶ νῦν] as...even so now.
Comp. John xv. 9; xvii. 18; xx. 21.

γεγόνασιν] facti sunt V., have
arisen, and fulfilled the expectation.
The use of a different word for their
advent (γεγόνασιν not ἐληλύθασιν) connects their appearance with the actual conditions of the development of
the Church. Comp. Heb. ii. 17 note.
The use is the more remarkable as the
verb is not used elsewhere in the
epistle (yet 3 John 8). The tense
shews that these antichrists are
spoken of as being still active. They
are not simple types of Antichrist but
revelations of him in many parts : c.
iv. 3.

For the absolute use of γίνεσθαι see
2 Pet. ii. 1; John i. 6; Mk. i. 4.

ὅθεν γινώσκομεν...] whence we perceive... because this form of trial is
connected with each critical conflict
which comes before an end. A full
manifestation of (good and) evil is the
condition of a divine judgment.

Ὅθεν is found here only in the
writings of St John. It is characteristic of the Epistle to the Hebrews
(see ii. 17 note), but is not found in
the Epistles of St Paul.

19. ἐξ ἡμ. ἐξ.] Ex nobis prodierunt
(exierunt) V., They went out from us
they proceeded from our midst. They
belonged at first to our outward communion and shared all our privi-

leges. Till the moment of separation
they were undistinguishable from the
rest of the Christian society; but they
were not of us, they did not draw
their life from our life (c. i. 3) and so
form living members of the body.
Comp. Heb. vi. 4 ff.

The change in the position of ἐξ
ἡμῶν in the successive clauses varies
the emphasis: 'From us, it is true,
they went out, but they were not of
us; for if they had been of us really...'
For εἶναι ἐκ see v. 16 note.

The phrase ἐξελθεῖν ἐξ may describe
either removal (Apoc. xviii. 4; John
viii. 59) or origin (Apoc. ix. 3; xiv.
13 ff.; xix. 5, 21; John iv. 30). The
correspondence with οὐκ ἦσαν ἐξ ἡμῶν
decides here in favour of the latter
sense (comp. Acts xx. 30), though it
necessarily leads to the other. This
trait in the Antichrists indicates one
ground of their influence. They professed to speak with the voice of the
Christian Body. Διὰ τί ἀπὸ τῶν τοῦ
Κυρίου μαθητῶν οἱ ἀντίχριστοι; ἵν᾽ ἔ-
χοιεν τὸ πιστὸν τοῖς πλανωμένοις κο-
μίζειν ὡς ἀπὸ τῶν μαθητῶν ὄντες...
(Theophlct.)

εἰ γὰρ...] If they had in the truest
sense shared our life, the life would
have gone forward to its fruitful consummation (μεμενήκεισαν ἂν perman-
sissent utique V.). The fact of separation revealed the imperfection of their
fellowship. The words will not admit
of any theoretical deductions. The test
of experience is laid down as final.
Non audio quid sonet, Augustine
says, sed video quid vivat. Opera
loquuntur; et verba requirimus?

Here, looking upon the manifest
apostasy, St John denies the truth of
the life; from another point of sight,
in regard to the uncertain future, the

ἡμῶν ἦσαν, μεμενήκεισαν ἂν μεθ' ἡμῶν· ἀλλ' ἵνα φανερω-

life is presented as real, but liable to an abrupt close (John xv. 1 ff.). The two views are perfectly harmonious. The end of life is fruitfulness. The life which is barren or worse than barren is not life and yet potentially it was life.

Thus Augustine can say truly in reference to the actual Church: Si antequam exirent non erant ex nobis, multi intus sunt, non exierunt, et tamen Antichristi sunt. And again: Sic sunt in corpore Christi quomodo humores mali. Compare also the striking language of Ignatius, *ad Trall.* 11 οὗτοι οὐκ εἰσὶ φυτεία πατρὸς ἀλλ' ἔγγονα κατηραμένα. πᾶσα δέ, φη-σὶν ὁ κύριος, φυτεία ἣν οὐκ ἐφύτευσεν ὁ πατήρ μου ὁ ἐπουράνιος ἐκριζωθήτω. εἰ γὰρ ἦσαν τοῦ πατρὸς κλάδοι οὐκ ἂν ἦσαν ἐχθροὶ τοῦ σταυροῦ τοῦ Χριστοῦ ἀλλὰ τῶν ἀποκτεινάντων τὸν τῆς δόξης κύριον.

It may be added that γάρ, *for,* is very rarely used in the Epistles ; c. iv. 20; v. 3; 2 John 11; 3 John 3, 7. As distinguished from ὅτι, *because,* it will be seen that γάρ expresses a reason or explanation alleged (subjective), while ὅτι marks a distinct fact (objective) which is itself an adequate cause or explanation of that with which it is connected. Comp. c. v. 3, 4; John ii. 25; iii. 16—21; iii. 23 f.; ix. 22, &c.

μεθ' ἡμῶν] It might have been expected that St John would have written ἐν ἡμῖν, according to his characteristic usage which is all but universal in his Epistles; but the thought is not of absolute unity in one body but of personal fellowship one with another: John xiv. 16; Luke xxiv. 29.

ἀλλ' ἵνα...] *but they went out* (or this separation came to pass) *that they may be made manifest* (*ut manifesti sint* [*manifestarentur*] V.), *that they all are not of us* i.e. that none of them are of us. For this ellipse see John i. 8; ix. 3; xiii. 18; xiv.

31; xv. 25. The departure of these false teachers after a temporary sojourn in the Christian society was brought about that they might be shewn in their true character, and so seen to be not of it. The last clause is rather irregular in form. The πάντες is inserted as it were by an afterthought; 'they went out that they may be made manifest that they are not, no not in any case, however fair their pretensions may be, of us.'

The separation of these teachers from the Christian Body was, without exception, a decisive proof that they did not belong truly to it. The clear revelation of their character was a divine provision for the avoidance of further evil. By 'going out' they neutralised the influence which they would otherwise have exercised. Comp. 1 Cor. xi. 19.

When the πᾶς is separated by the verb from the οὐ the negation according to the usage of the New Testament, is always universal (*all...not*), and not partial (*not all*). Comp. *v.* 21; iii. 15; Apoc. xxii. 3; Matt. xxiv. 22 (οὐ...πᾶς); Luke i. 37 (οὐ πᾶς); Acts x. 15; Rom. iii. 20 (οὐ...πᾶς); Gal. ii. 16 (οὐ...πᾶς); Eph. v. 5; and in dependent negations, John iii. 16 (πᾶς ...μή); vi. 39 (πᾶς...μή); xii. 46 (*id.*); 1 Cor. i. 29 (μή...πᾶς); Eph. iv. 29 (πᾶς...μή). Comp. Apoc. xxi. 27 (οὐ μή...πᾶς).

On the other hand see Matt. vii. 21; Rom. ix. 6; 1 Cor. x. 23; xv. 39 (οὐ πᾶς).

In the face of this usage it is impossible to translate the words '*that they may be made manifest* themselves, and that it may be made manifest in them *that not all* who are outwardly united with the Church *are of us,* in true fellowship with Christ.'

For φανερ. ὅτι οὐκ εἰσίν compare 2 Cor. iii. 3 φανερούμενοι ὅτι ἐστέ.

20. Even without this revelation

θῶσιν ὅτι οὐκ εἰσὶν πάντες ἐξ ἡμῶν. ²⁰καὶ ὑμεῖς χρίσμα
ἔχετε ἀπὸ τοῦ ἁγίου· οἴδατε πάντες—²¹οὐκ ἔγραψα

20 οἴδατε πάντες: καὶ οἴδατε πάντα ϛ. See Additional Note.

in outward fact, the readers of the Epistle had the power of discerning the real character of 'Antichrists.' 'Christians' are themselves in a true sense 'Christs,' anointed ones, consecrated to God as 'prophets,' 'priests,' and 'kings' (1 Pet. ii. 5 (9); Apoc. i. 6; v. 10; xx. 6); and in virtue of that consecration endowed with corresponding blessings. So Severus (Cramer, *Cat.* in loc.) writes: χριστοί εἰσίν οὐχ οἱ προφῆται μόνον...ἀλλ᾽ ἐξαιρέτως καὶ πάντες οἱ εἰς τὸν μέγαν καὶ μόνον καὶ ἀληθῆ Χριστὸν καὶ σωτῆρα Θεὸν πιστεύσαντες...καὶ ἐν τῷ θείῳ...βαπτίσματι συμβολικῶς τῷ μύρῳ χριόμενοι...

καὶ ὑμεῖς...] *Sed (et) vos*...V., *And further you yourselves*, in virtue of your position as contrasted with them, *have an unction* (comp. *v.* 27 χρίσμα ὃ ἐλάβετε) *from the Holy One.* Comp. *vv.* 24, 27; iv. 4.

χρίσμα] *unctionem* V. (*unguentum* Hier.), *an unction.* The word, which expresses not the act of anointing, but that with which it is performed ('anointing oil' Ex. xxix. 7; xxx. 25; xl. 15 (LXX); comp. Dan. ix. 26), marks the connexion of Christians with their Head. As He was 'anointed' for His office (Luke iv. 18 [Is. lxi. 1]; Acts iv. 27 [Ps. ii. 2]; x. 38; Heb. i. 9 [Ps. xlv. 7]); so too are they (2 Cor. i. 21 f.). The verb χρίω (answering to מָשַׁח) in LXX. is employed generally, though not exclusively, of the anointing of things for sacred use. In the New Testament it is found only in the places quoted above, and thus always of the impartment of a divine grace.

Here the outward symbol of the Old Testament—the sacred oil—is used to signify the gift of the Spirit *from the Holy One* which is the characteristic endowment of Christians. This gift is referred to a definite time (*v.*

27 ὃ ἐλάβετε); and the narrative of the Acts fixes this normally at the imposition of hands which followed on Baptism (Acts viii. 14 ff.). But the context shews that the word χρίσμα is not to be understood of the material sign, but of the corresponding spiritual reality. There is not indeed any evidence to shew that 'the chrism' was used at confirmation in the first age. Perhaps, as has been suggested, St John's language here may have tended to fix the custom, which represented the communication of the divine grace in an outward rite. Tertullian speaks of the custom as habitual in his time: Egressi de lavacro perungimur benedicta unctione de pristina disciplina, qua ungi oleo de cornu in sacerdotium solebant (*de Bapt.* 7).

Unctio spiritualis ipse Spiritus Sanctus est cujus sacramentum est in unctione visibili (Bede).

This 'unction,' this gift of the Spirit, is said to come finally (ἀπὸ see c. i. 5, note) *from the Holy One.* The title is chosen with direct reference to the gift, for all hallowing flows from 'the Holy One,' but in itself it is ambiguous, and has been understood of God (the Father) and of Christ. In support of the former view reference is made to 1 Cor. vi. 19; John xiv. 16; but ὁ ἅγιος seems to be more naturally referred to Christ; Apoc. iii. 7; John vi. 69; Acts iii. 14; iv. 27, 30; and Christ Himself 'sends' the Paraclete (John xvi. 7).

οἴδατε πάντες] *ye all know*, i.e. the Truth. If this reading be adopted the statement must be taken in close connexion with the clause which follows: 'ye all know—I have not written to you because ye do not know—the Truth.' With οἴδατε τὴν ἀλ. contrast 2 John 2 οἱ ἐγνωκότες τὴν ἀλ.

ὑμῖν ὅτι οὐκ οἴδατε τὴν ἀλήθειαν, ἀλλ᾽ ὅτι οἴδατε
αὐτήν, καὶ ὅτι πᾶν ψεῦδος ἐκ τῆς ἀληθείας οὐκ
ἔστιν.　　　²²Τίς ἐστιν ὁ ψεύστης εἰ μὴ ὁ ἀρ-

21 – πᾶν C.

The common reading καὶ οἴδατε πάντα gives an explanation of the actual force of χρίσμα ἔχετε: 'ye have an unction, and, in virtue of that gift of the Holy Spirit, ye know all things; ye have potentially complete and certain knowledge: no false teaching can deceive you if ye are faithful to yourselves.' Comp. v. 27; Jude 5 (εἰδότας ἅπαξ πάντα); John xiv. 26, xvi. 13. See Additional Note.

21. The object of the apostle in writing was not to communicate fresh knowledge, but to bring into active and decisive use the knowledge which his readers already possessed. For ἔγραψα see vv. 14 note, 26.

ἀλλ᾽ ὅτι...καὶ ὅτι...] sed quasi scientibus...et quoniam...(sed quia... quia) V., but because...and because... The ὅτι in the second clause appears to be coordinated with that in the first clause. St John gives two grounds for his writing:
1. Because his readers know the truth.
2. Because no lie is of the truth.

The first witnesses to the necessary sympathy between writer and readers: the second explains the occasion of the particular warning.

The second ὅτι can however also be translated 'that' thus defining a second feature in Christian knowledge: 'ye know the truth and know that no lie is of the truth.' In this case the words indicate the practical consequences which follow from the revelation of the antichrists.

According to both views the absolute irreconcileableness of any falsehood with 'the Truth' is laid down as a clear rule for the protection of Christians in the presence of seductive teachers. It was, on the other hand,

the office of the Paraclete to guide them 'into all the Truth' (John xvi. 13).

πᾶν ψ....οὐκ ἔστιν] see v. 19 note.

ψεῦδος] mendacium V. Error is regarded in its positive form as part of 'the lie' (τὸ ψεῦδος) which is the opposite of 'the Truth.' Compare John viii. 44; 2 Thess. ii. 11; Rom. i. 25; Eph. iv. 25. See also Apoc. xxi. 27, xxii. 15.

ἐκ τῆς ἀλ. ἔστιν] c. iii. 19; John xviii. 37. See v. 16 note. The source of falsehood is marked in John viii. 44.

2. *The essence and the power of the Truth* (22—25).

The mention of 'lies' in v. 21 leads directly to the question as to the essential character of him who maintains them, and by contrast of him who holds the Truth (22, 23). Then follows the portraiture of the power of the Truth firmly held, which brings fellowship with God, even eternal life (24, 25).

²²*Who is the liar but he that denieth that Jesus is the Christ? This is the Antichrist, even he that denieth the Father and the Son.* ²³*Every one that denieth the Son hath not even the Father: he that confesseth the Son hath the Father also.* ²⁴*As for you, let that which ye heard from the beginning abide in you. If that abide in you which ye heard from the beginning, ye also shall abide in the Son and in the Father.* ²⁵*And this is the promise that he himself promised us, even the life eternal.*

22. τίς ἐστιν...] Quis est mendax ...? V. Who is the liar...'? The abrupt question (comp. c. v. 5) corresponds with a brief mental pause after

νούμενος ὅτι Ἰησοῦς οὐκ ἔστιν ὁ χριστός; οὗτός
ἐστιν ὁ ἀντίχριστος, ὁ ἀρνούμενος τὸν πατέρα καὶ τὸν

v. 21. 'I have spoken of lies: *what*, nay rather, *who* is their source? Who is the liar?' The abruptness of *vv.* 22 f. is remarkable. Clause stands by clause in stern solemnity without any connecting particles.

ὁ ψεύστης] *the liar*, who offers in his own person the sum of all that is false; and not simply 'a liar' who is guilty of a particular sin. The denial of the fact 'Jesus is the Christ' when grasped in its full significance—intellectual, moral, spiritual—includes all falsehood: it reduces all knowledge of necessity to a knowledge of phenomena: it takes away the highest ideal of sacrifice: it destroys the connexion of God and man.

τίς...εἰ μή] c. v. 5; 1 Cor. ii. 11; 2 Cor. ii. 2, &c.

ὁ ἀρνούμενος ὅτι...οὐκ ἔστιν] *that denieth that...* The insertion of the negative in the original (preserved in the Old Latin, *qui negat quod Jesus non est Christus*) gives a positive, aggressive, character to the negation. The adversary denies that Jesus is the Christ when the claim is made; and on his own part he affirms that He is not. Comp. Luke xx. 27; Gal. v. 7; Heb. xii. 19. For the converse see John i. 20.

The phrase by which St John describes the master-falsehood as the 'denial that Jesus is the Christ,' itself marks the progress of Christian thought. In the earliest stage of the Church the words would have expressed a denial of the Messiahship of Jesus from the Jewish point of view (Acts v. 42, ix. 22, xvii. 3, xviii. 28). They now answer to a later form of opinion. A common 'Gnostic' theory was that 'the æon Christ' descended upon the man Jesus at His Baptism, and left Him before the Passion. Those who held such a doctrine denied that 'Jesus was the Christ'; and in so denying, denied the union of the divine and human in one Person. This heresy then St John signalises here, the direct contradiction to the fundamental truth which he proclaimed, *the Word became flesh.*

οὗτος] *this* liar, this maintainer of the central falsehood in regard to revelation, as to God and man, *is the antichrist*, even *he that denieth the Father and the Son.* The denial of the personal union of true manhood and true Godhead in Christ involves the denial of the essential relations of Fatherhood and Sonship in the Divine Nature. The conception of this relation in the immanent Trinity prepares the way for the fact of the Incarnation; and conversely, the fact of the Incarnation gives reality to that moral conception of God as active Love without which Theism becomes a formula.

ὁ ἀντίχριστος] The term expresses the embodiment of a principle, and is not to be confined to one person. The character of 'the antichrist' is described in the words which follow (even *he that...Son*), which are not simply a resumption of οὗτος.

ὁ ἀρνούμενος τ. π.] To deny the Father is to refuse to acknowledge God as Father. Comp. Matt. x. 33; Acts iii. 13 f.; 2 Tim. ii. 12; 2 Pet. ii. 1; Jude 4.

τὸν πατέρα] The title *the Father* occurs in the Epistles of St John, as in the Gospel, in connexion with 'the Son' (*vv.* 22, 23, 24, i. 3, iv. 14; 2 J. 3, 9), and in relation to men (ii. 1, 14, 15 f., iii. 1; 2 J. 4) in virtue of the revelation of Christ. It is used also in relation to 'the Life' (i. 2 note).

The title always stands in the Epistles in its simple form. 'His Father'

υἱόν. ²³πᾶς ὁ ἀρνούμενος τὸν υἱὸν οὐδὲ τὸν πατέρα ἔχει·
ὁ ὁμολογῶν τὸν υἱὸν καὶ τὸν πατέρα ἔχει. ²⁴῾Υμεῖς ὃ

23 ὁ ὁμολ....ἔχει ℵABC me syrr. om ς.   24 ὑμεῖς ℵABC vg: ὑμ. +οὖν ς.
Other conjunctions are inserted in versions.

or 'our Father,' or 'the Father in
heaven' do not occur. See additional
note on i. 2.

τὸν υἱόν] By the use of the absolute
term *the Son* (comp. John v. 19 note),
which occurs in the Epistle first here
(comp. iv. 14, v. 12), St John brings out
distinctly what is involved in the fact
that the Christ and Jesus are personally one. There is no passage in the
mind of the Apostle from one personality to another, from the human
to the divine, nor yet from the conception of 'the man Christ Jesus' to
that of 'the Word': the thought of
'the Son' includes both these conceptions in their ideal fulness.

23. πᾶς ὁ ἀρν. τ. υἱ....] *Qui negat
Filium nec Patrem habet* V. The
original is compressed : *Every one
that denieth the Son hath not even
the Father* (οὐδὲ τ. π. ἔ.) or, according
to our idiom, *No one that denieth the
Son hath even the Father.* Such a
one hath not the Son, whom he re-
jects, nor yet the Father, whom he
professes to regard. The translation
quoted by Augustine completes the
sentence : *qui negat Filium nec
Filium nec Patrem habet.*

The 'denial of the Son' expresses
in another form that which has been
more fully described before as 'the
denial of Jesus as the Christ.'

The denial of the Son involves the
loss of the Father, not only because the
ideas of sonship and fatherhood are
correlative, but because the Son alone
can reveal the Father (Matt. xi. 27;
John xiv. 9), and it is, in other words,
only in the Son that we have the
revelation of God as Father.

The οὐδέ retains its full force 'has
not even the Father,' though this result may seem to be against expecta-

tion, and contrary to the claim of the
false teachers. Comp. John v. 22,
viii. 42; Gal. ii. 3; 1 Tim. vi. 7.

For the use of πᾶς ὁ ἀρν. in place of
the simple ὁ ἀρν. see c. iii. 3 note.

οὐδὲ ἔχει...ἔχει] *hath not even...
hath...* The second clause in each
case is more than a simple repetition
of the first. It is not said of him
'that denieth the Son' that he denieth
the Father also; but that he 'hath
not even the Father.' Such a man
might shrink from denying the Father
in words, and even claim to do Him
honour, but yet St John says 'he hath
not even the Father,' as one who enjoys the certain possession of a living
Friend. And conversely he ' that confesseth the Son' not only confesses
the Father in an act of faith, but also
lives in conscious communion with
Him.

ἔχει] Comp. v. 12; 2 John 9.

Augustine has an interesting discussion on the application of the test
to Catholics and Donatists. His conclusion is : 'Quisquis factis negat
Christum Antichristus est,' adding
the words quoted on *v.* 19. And Bede
says of this confession : confessionem
hic cordis vocis et operis inquirit qualem quærebat Paulus (1 Cor. xii. 3).

ὁ ὁμολογῶν τὸν υἱόν] *qui confitetur Filium* V., *he that confesseth the
Son*, he that openly acknowledges that
Jesus is the Christ, the Son of God.
The constructions of ὁμολογεῖν in N.T.
are numerous. The simplest are those
with the *infin.* and with ὅτι which
serve for the affirmation of a definite
fact past, present or future (*infin.*
c. iv. 2; Tit. i. 16; Matt. xiv. 7; ὅτι
c. iv. 15; John i. 20; Acts xxiv. 14;
Heb. xi. 13). From the construction
with the *infin.* that with the *accus.*

ἠκούσατε ἀπ' ἀρχῆς, ἐν ὑμῖν μενέτω· ἐὰν ἐν ὑμῖν μείνῃ
ὃ ἀπ' ἀρχῆς ἠκούσατε, καὶ ὑμεῖς ἐν τῷ υἱῷ καὶ [ἐν]

ἀκηκόατε (bis) אּ.　ὃ ἀπ' ἀρχ. ἀκηκ. אּ (vg) mg the.　ἐν τῷ π. אּAC: − ἐν B vg.
ἐν τῷ π. καὶ ἐν τῷ υἱῷ אּ syr vg.

follows, either a simple *accus.* Acts
xxiii. 8 (comp. c. i. 9) ; or an *accus.*
with a secondary predicate 2 John 7 ;
John ix. 22. Here and in c. iv. 3 the
predicate which gives the substance
of the confession is supplied from the
context. Elsewhere the verb is used
absolutely: John xii. 42 ; with cogn.
accus. 1 Tim. vi. 12 ; with the substance of the confession added in the
direct: Rom. x. 9 (Κύριος 'Ιησοῦς).
More remarkable is the construction
with ἐν Matt. x. 31 f.; Luke xii. 8,
which suggests the idea of an acknowledged fellowship.

To know the Son as Son is to have
such knowledge as we can have at
present of the Father (John xiv. 7 ff.).
Hence *he that confesseth the Son
hath the Father also* as well as the
Son whom he directly acknowledges.

24 f. The view of the true nature
of the confession and denial of Christ
is followed by a view of the power
of the confession. The knowledge to
which it witnesses carries with it
eternal life.

24. Ὑμεῖς...] *As for you...* The
pronoun stands at the head of the
sentence in contrast with the false
teachers of whom the apostle has
spoken (*v.* 22): comp. Matt. xiii. 18.
For the irregular construction see *v.*
27; John vi. 39; vii. 38; xiv. 12 ; xv.
2 ; Luke xxi. 6, &c.

The construction is broken, because
the thought of St John is turned from
that which the disciples had to do to
that which was done for them. 'As
for you, do you keep' is changed to
'As for you, let that abide in you.'
The final strength of the Christian
lies not in his own effort, but in the
Truth by which he is inspired. That
is the power of life which he is charged

not to hinder. Comp. John xv. 7. For
the double divine fellowship, 'God in
us, we in God,' see iv. 15 note.

ὃ ἠκούσατε...] *that which ye
heard...(v.* 7). The first simple message of the Gospel apprehended in its
unity (ὃ not ἃ ; comp. John xiv. 23).
This 'word' taken into the heart becomes a power fashioning the whole
man (John viii. 31 f.; xv. 7).

ἐν ὑμῖν μενέτω] *let that...abide in
you.* The Gospel is described both as
a medium in which the believer lives
(John viii. 31), and as a quickening
spirit which dwells in him (Col. iii.
16 ; 2 John 2).

ὃ ἠκ. ἀπ' ἀρχῆς...ὃ ἀπ' ἀρχ. ἠκ....]
The change of order marks a change
of emphasis. In the first clause the
stress lies on the fact that the readers had received a divine message
(*ye heard*): in the second, on the
coincidence of that message in time
with the origin of their faith (*from
the beginning*). Comp. iii. 8 note.

καὶ ὑμεῖς...] *ye also...*i.e. 'then ye
on your side...' not 'ye as well as
others....' The presence of the divine
life carries with it of necessity the
possession of divine fellowship. Thus
one fact is correlative to the other
(comp. i. 3). This correlation is made
clearer by the correspondence in the
pronouns : ἐὰν ἐν ὑμῖν...καὶ ὑμεῖς.
Comp. iii. 24.

For the use of καί to mark a corresponding issue, see iv. 11.

ἐν τῷ υἱῷ καὶ ἐν τ. π.] The order, as
contrasted with that in *v.* 22 (τ. π. καὶ
τ. υἱ.) is significant. Here the thought
is that of rising through the confession of the Son to the knowledge of
the Father; there the thought is of
the issue of denial culminating in the
denial of the Father.

τῷ πατρὶ μενεῖτε. ²⁵καὶ αὕτη ἐστὶν ἡ ἐπαγγελία
ἣν αὐτὸς ἐπηγγείλατο ἡμῖν, τὴν ζωὴν τὴν αἰώνιον.   ²⁶Ταῦτα ἔγραψα ὑμῖν περὶ τῶν πλα-

---

25 ἡμῖν: ὑμῖν B (lat).   26 ταῦτα + δέ ℵ syrvg.

---

25.   καὶ αὕτη ἐστίν...] *And this is...*
The pronoun may refer either to that
which precedes or to that which follows. The promise may be that of
abiding communion with the Father
and the Son (John xvii. 21), which is
explained by the words added in apposition 'the life eternal'; or it may
be simply 'the life eternal.' In either
case 'the life eternal' consists in union
with God by that knowledge which is
sympathy (John xvii. 3), so that there
is no real difference of sense in the
two interpretations. The usage of
St John in the Epistle is decidedly in
favour of the second view (i. 5, iii. 23,
v. 11, 14), nor is there any sufficient
reason for departing from it.

ἐπαγγελία] *repromissio* V., *polli-
citatio* Aug. This is the only place
where the word occurs in the writings
of St John (not c. i. 5). Contrast
ἐπάγγελμα (*promissum* V.) 2 Pet. i. 4;
iii. 13.

ἣν αὐτός...] *that He...* He himself,
Christ our Master. The *nom.* (αὐτός)
is always emphatic: see *v.* 2 note.
There is not any special saying of the
Lord recorded in which this promise
is expressly contained (yet comp.
James i. 12; Apoc. ii. 10); but it was
the whole aim and scope of His
teaching to lead men to seek 'life.'
And a divine charge is a divine
promise.

τὴν ζ. τὴν αἰ.] See c. i. 2 note. For
the attraction compare Phil. iii. 18.
Winer, p. 665.

3. *Abiding in the Truth* (ii. 26—29).
The view which St John has given
of the nature and power of the Truth
is followed by a fresh application of
the teaching to the readers of the
Epistle. An affirmation (μένετε, *indic.*,

v. 27) leads to a command (μένετε,
imper., *v.* 28). Thus the paragraph
falls into two parts which deal (1)
with the divine teaching as permanent and progressive (*vv.* 26 f.) and
(2) with human effort directed to the
future (*vv.* 28 f.).

²⁶ *These things have I written to
you concerning them that would lead
you astray.* ²⁷ *And as for you, the
unction which ye received from him
abideth in you, and ye have no need
that any one teach you; but as his
unction teacheth you of all things
(and it is true and is no lie), and
even as it taught you, ye abide in
him.*
²⁸ *And now, little children, abide
in him, that, if he shall be manifested,
we may have boldness and not shrink
in shame from him at his presence.*
²⁹ *If ye know that he is righteous,
know (notice) that every one that doeth
righteousness hath been begotten of
him.*

26 f. In the preceding verses (*vv.*
24 f.) St John had appealed to the
original apostolic message which his
readers had received (ὃ ἠκούσατε) in
contrast with all false teaching. He
now appeals to the inward voice of the
Spirit whose first teaching (ἐδίδαξεν)
and whose present teaching (διδάσκει)
is one.

26. Ταῦτα] *These things*, the clear
unfolding of the true character and
significance of the false teachers in
relation to the church (*vv.* 18—25).

ἔγραψα] See *v.* 14 note.

τῶν πλανώντων] *qui seducunt vos*
V., *them that would lead you astray*,
who are actively engaged in the effort:
c. iii. 7; Apoc. xiii. 14, xii. 9.

St John has spoken of the false

νώντων ὑμᾶς. ²⁷καὶ ὑμεῖς τὸ χρίσμα ὃ ἐλάβετε ἀπ᾽
αὐτοῦ μένει ἐν ὑμῖν, καὶ οὐ χρείαν ἔχετε ἵνα τις διδάσκῃ
ὑμᾶς· ἀλλ᾽ ὡς τὸ αὐτοῦ χρίσμα διδάσκει ὑμᾶς περὶ

27 χρίσμα (1): χάρισ μα B.	μέν. ἐν ὑμ. אABC vg me the: ἐν ὑμ. μέν. ϛ:
μενέτω vg.	ἀλλ᾽ ὡς אAC vg the: ἀλλά B.	τὸ αὐτοῦ אBC vg the
syr hl.: τὸ αὐτό ϛA me.	χρίσμα (2): πνεῦμα א*me (χρεῖσμα B).

teachers under their spiritual aspect as 'antichrists'; he now speaks of them under their outward aspect as leading men away from the fellowship of the Christian Society.

27. καὶ ὑμεῖς...] *And as for you...* The construction is like that in *v.* 24. The pronoun is set at the head of the sentence in order to bring out sharply the contrast between believers and their adversaries.

τὸ χρίσμα] *v.* 20 note.

ὃ ἐλάβ. ἀ. αὐ.] *which ye received from Him* 'the Holy One' (*v.* 20), even Christ (*v.* 25). The gift which before (*v.* 20) was simply described as a possession (ἔχετε) is now referred to its source. The personal relation to which it witnesses is a ground of confidence.

ἐλάβ. ἀπ᾽ αὐ.] The use of ἀπό to mark the source in this connexion has been already touched on (c. i. 5). The distinction of the 'source' (ἀπό) and the 'giver' (παρά) is illustrated by the combination of the prepositions ἀπό and παρά with different verbs:

(1) λαμβάνειν παρά John v. 41, 44; x. 18; 2 John 4; Apoc. ii. 27; Mk. xii. 2; Acts ii. 33; iii. 5; xvii. 9; xx. 24; James i. 7; 2 Pet. i. 17. λαμβάνειν ἀπό 1 John iii. 22; 3 John 7; Matt. xvii. 25.

(2) παραλαμβάνειν παρά 1 Thess. ii. 13; iv. 1; 2 Thess. iii. 6; Gal. i. 12. παραλαμβάνειν ἀπό 1 Cor. xi. 23.

(3) ἔχειν παρά Acts ix. 14. ἔχειν ἀπό c. ii. 20; iv. 21; 1 Tim. iii. 7. ἔχειν ἐκ 1 Cor. vii. 7; 2 Cor. v. 1.

For ἀκούειν παρά, ἀπό see c. i. 5 note.

μένει] *abideth.* The apostle so writes as looking at the divine side of the

truth. The gifts of God are sure on His part.

οὐ χρείαν ἔχ....] *ye have no need...* The outpouring of the Spirit, the characteristic of the last days (Jer. xxxi. 34; Joel ii. 28; Heb. viii. 11; Acts ii. 17 ff.), gave to each one who received it a sure criterion of truth. Christians needed not fresh teaching even from apostles, still less from those who professed to guide them into new 'depths.'

οὐ χρ. ἔχ. ἵνα...] *non necesse habetis ut* V., *non habetis necessitatem ut* Aug. The same construction occurs in John ii. 25, xvi. 30. The phrase χρείαν ἔχειν is used absolutely in several places: Mk. ii. 25; Acts ii. 45, iv. 35; 1 Cor. xii. 24; Eph. iv. 28, as in this Epistle c. iii. 17. This usage supplies a probable explanation of the construction: 'Ye are not in need such that you require....'

ἀλλ᾽ ὡς...καὶ καθὼς...ἐν αὐτῷ] *but as His unction teacheth you...and even as it taught you, ye abide in Him.* These words serve to establish the statement just made. 'You need no one to teach you, but on the contrary you remain firm in that direct divine fellowship established by the teaching which you are continually receiving and which at first you received once for all.' Impatience drives men to look without for the guidance which in due time will be recognised within. Such impatience is the opposite to the steadfastness of the Christian.

But while so much is clear the construction of the sentence is uncertain. The last clause (*and even as...in Him*) may be either a resumption or

πάντων, καὶ ἀληθές ἐστιν καὶ οὐκ ἔστιν ψεῦδος, καὶ

27 ἀληθής ℵ.   καὶ καθώς: om. καὶ A the.

rather a continuation of the former words (*as His...no lie*), or a new and distinct clause. In the latter case the first apodosis will be in the words '*so is it true and no lie*,' 'but as His unction teacheth you, even so is it true and no lie.' This use of καὶ in the apodosis is however rare in St John; nor does there appear to be any special force in making the affirmation of the perfect truth of the divine teaching a substantive conclusion. It is therefore more natural to suppose that there is only one apodosis (*ye abide in Him*), and that the sentence as originally shaped (*but, on the contrary, as His unction teacheth you concerning all things, ye abide in Him*) was afterwards enlarged by the addition of the reflection '*and it is true and is no lie*,' which again led to the further statement that the present progressive teaching is essentially the same as the first teaching *as His unction teacheth...and even as it taught you, ye abide in Him*.

The reading of B gives a plain and simple sense, but it is difficult to understand how it could have been altered if it had been the original reading.

το αὐ. χρ.] *His unction*, the unction which ye received from Christ. Comp. John xvi. 7.

The most unusual order τὸ αὐ. χρ. (for τὸ χρ. αὐ.) throws a strong emphasis on the pronoun. Comp. 1 Thess. ii. 19 (contrast 1 Cor. xv. 23; 2 Cor. vii. 7); Rom. iii. 24 (in 2 Pet. iii. 7 τῷ αὐτοῦ λ. is probably a false reading). As might be expected this is the normal order with ἐκεῖνος: John v. 47; 2 Pet. i. 16; 2 Cor. viii. 9, 14; 2 Tim. ii. 26; Tit. iii. 7.

διδ. ὑ. π. π.] *teacheth you of all things*. The application and interpretation of the truth is continuous.

The Spirit of Truth sent in Christ's name (John xiv. 26), sent, that is, to make the meaning of the Incarnation fully known, is ever bringing out something more of the infinite meaning of His Person and Work, in connexion with the new results of thought and observation (περὶ πάντων). Comp. John xvi. 13 f.

καὶ ἀληθές ἐστιν...] *and it is true...* The 'unction,' the gift of the Spirit, is now identified with the results of the gift. The Spirit is the Spirit of Truth (John xiv. 17); and its teaching is true, and admits no element of falsehood (*v.* 21).

Parenthetical reflections like this are found elsewhere in St John's writings. Comp. c. i. 2 note.

οὐκ ἔ. ψεῦδος] *non est mendacium* V., *is no lie*. By the use of ψεῦδος (not ψευδές) St John implies that the false teachers practically represented the Gospel as 'a lie' in its concrete form, and not simply as 'false' (comp. *v.* 21 note).

The combination of the positive and negative is characteristic of St John: i. 5 note.

καὶ καθὼς ἐδίδαξεν...] *and even as it taught....* The first teaching contained implicitly all that is slowly brought to light in later times (comp. ii. 7). The believer abides in Christ as the Spirit makes Him known, and even as it made Him known in the simple Gospel 'Jesus is the Christ.' This clause excludes all 'developments' of teaching which cannot be shewn to exist in germ in the original message; and at the same time leaves no room for the inventions of fanaticism. That which was taught first is the absolute standard.

The use of καθώς marks this idea of a definite and fixed standard: *vv.* 6, 18, iii. 2, 3, 7, 12, &c.

καθὼς ἐδίδαξεν ὑμᾶς, μένετε ἐν αὐτῷ. ²⁸ Καὶ νῦν,
τεκνία, μένετε ἐν αὐτῷ, ἵνα ἐὰν φανερωθῇ σχῶμεν παρ-

μένετε ℵABC vg syrr me the: μενεῖτε ς.   28 – καὶ νῦν...αὐτῷ ℵ.
ἵνα ἐάν ℵABC the: ἵνα ὅταν ς syrr.   σχῶμεν ℵᶜABC: ἔχωμεν ς ℵ*.

μένετε ἐν αὐτῷ] *ye abide in Him*,
i.e. Christ. The verb may be indicative or imperative (as in *v*. 28, so
Vulg. *manete in eo*), but the parallelism with μένει (*the unction abideth...ye abide*) is decisive in favour of
the indicative. In this verse St John
assumes the fulfilment of the conditions which he presses upon his
readers in *v*. 28.

For the general thought compare
John vi. 56, xv. 4 ff. Elsewhere the
Christian is said to 'abide in God':
iii. 24, iv. 12 ff. So in *vv*. 28 f. 'Christ'
and 'God' are treated as interchange-
able.

At first sight it might appear most
natural to take ἐν αὐτῷ of the 'teaching of the Spirit' (χρίσμα) as is done
by the Latin translation used by
Augustine (*permanete in ipsa* sc.
unctione) according to John viii. 31;
but the personal reference cannot be
questioned in *v*. 28, and that must decide the interpretation here. Christ—
God in Christ—is the subject constantly present to the mind of the
Apostle.

Augustine contrasts finely the human and divine teachers: Sonus verborum nostrorum aures percutit,
magister intus est. Nolite putare
quemquam hominem aliquid discere
ab homine. Admonere possumus per
strepitum vocis nostræ; si non sit intus qui doceat inanis fit strepitus
noster.... Magisteria forinsecus ad-
jutoria quædam sunt et admonitiones.
Cathedram in cælo habet qui corda
docet.

28 f. St John turns from the ideal
view of the believer to the practical
enforcement of duty: 'I have said
that God's gift is unchangeable; and
that the Christian continues living in

that which he received, and so abides
in his Lord; and now, in the face of
your enemies, realise your life: do
you abide in Him, and prove your fellowship by your action.'

The verses serve also to prepare
the way for the next section, introducing ideas which are afterwards developed (φανεροῦσθαι, παρρησίαν ἔχειν,
ποιεῖν τὴν δικ., γεγεννῆσθαι ἐξ αὐτοῦ).

28. καὶ νῦν...] *And now*... For this
connexion see John xvii. 5; 2 John
5; Acts iii. 17, x. 5, xiii. 11, xx. 25,
xxii. 16.

τεκνία] *filioli* V., *my little children*.
The tenderness of the address (τεκνία)
commends the charge.

ἐν αὐτῷ] *in Him*, i.e. in Christ, *v*. 27.
ἐὰν φανερωθῇ] *cum apparuerit* V.,
cum manifestatus fuerit Aug., *if he
shall be manifested*, c. iii. 2. The hy-
pothetic form does not throw doubt
upon the fact in itself (see *v*. 29), but
marks the uncertainty of the circumstances under which the fact will be
realised: the manifestation might be
while they all still lived. Comp. John
xxi. 22 f.; c. iv. 17 ἐν τῇ ἡμ. τῆς κρίσεως.

The same word φανερωθῆναι is used
for the first manifestation of the Lord
in the flesh (c. i. 2, iii. 5, 8; 1 Tim. iii.
16; 1 Pet. 1. 20); and for that manifestation which is still looked for (c.
iii. 2; Col. iii. 4; 1 Pet. v. 4). It is
used also for the manifestations of the
Risen Lord ([Mark] xvi. 12, 14; John
xxi. 14 (1)), and for His 'manifestation to Israel' (John i. 31: comp. vii.
4).

It is worthy of notice that St John
nowhere uses ἀποκαλύπτεσθαι of the
revelation of Christ.

σχῶμεν παρρ.] *we may*... St John
again identifies himself with his

W.   6

ρησίαν καὶ μὴ αἰσχυνθῶμεν ἀπ᾽ αὐτοῦ ἐν τῇ παρουσίᾳ
αὐτοῦ. ²⁹ἐὰν εἰδῆτε ὅτι δίκαιός ἐστιν, γινώσκετε ὅτι
πᾶς ὁ ποιῶν τὴν δικαιοσύνην ἐξ αὐτοῦ γεγέννηται.

28 ἐν τῇ παρ. ἀ. ἀπ᾽ αὐτοῦ ℵ.   29 εἰδῆτε ℵBC vg syrr: ἴδητε A me.   –ὅτι
πᾶς B me syr hl: ὅτι + καὶ πᾶς ℵAC the syr vg.

children: comp. v. 1. All form one body. It is possible to understand the words as referring to the Apostle's joy in the crown of his work (comp. 1 Thess. ii. 19 f.; Phil. iv. 1). The parallel with 1 Thess. ii. 19 f. is certainly close; but it seems to be more natural to suppose that the apostle made himself **one** with those who shared his life, and the absence of the personal pronoun seems to exclude the notion of any contrast between him and them.

The use of ἔχειν παρρησίαν (c. iii. 21, iv. 17, v. 14; comp. Heb. iii. 6, x. 19; Phil. 8) in connexion with the manifestation of Christ suggests St Paul's thought of the judgment-seat of Christ (2 Cor. v. 10) or of God (Rom. xiv. 10), where man must 'render account' (Rom. xiv. 12) of his life. The idea of open, unreserved utterance is never lost. See John vii. 4 note. The difference in order here (σχ. παρρ.) and in iii. 21, iv. 17 (παρρ. ἔχειν) indicates a different emphasis on the elements of the phrase: comp. Eph. iii. 12.

μὴ αἰσχυνθῶμεν ἀπ᾽ αὐτοῦ] non confundamur ab eo V., *not shrink with shame from Him*, 'as a guilty thing surprised.' The same thought of separation is found more plainly expressed 2 Thess. i. 9. The construction αἰσχύνεσθαι ἀπό is used in the same sense in the LXX: Is. i. 29; Jer. ii. 36, xii. 13 (בּוֹשׁ כָּמוֹ); Ecclus. xxi. 22, xli. 17 ff.

παρουσίᾳ] adventu V., *presence* (coming). The word does not occur elsewhere in St John's writings. Its single occurrence here, where it might easily have been omitted, in exactly

the same sense as it bears in all the other groups of apostolic writings (Matt., James, 2 Peter, 1, 2 Thess., 1 Cor.) is a signal example of the danger of drawing conclusions from the negative phenomena of the books of the New Testament. The fact is the more worthy of notice as the subject of eschatology falls into the background in the Gospel and Epistles of St John. Comp. John xxi. 22.

It may be added that St John does not use the Pauline word ἐπιφάνεια (2 Thess., 1, 2 Tim., Tit.).

29. ἐὰν εἰδῆτε...γινώσκετε...] si scitis ...scitote (Vig. Taps. scitis)... V. If *ye know...perceive, observe, notice....* Knowledge which is absolute (εἰδῆτε) becomes the basis of knowledge which is realised in observation (γινώσκετε). Comp. John ii. 24 note. The distinction is lost in the Latin and can hardly be preserved in an English version.

The second verb (γινώσκετε) may be either indicative or imperative. Both renderings are found in early Latin authorities. In favour of the imperative it is urged that it stands between two imperatives (μένετε, and iii. 1 ἴδετε). On the other hand it is said that v. 29 contains a general reason for the command in v. 28. 'Abide in Him in fruitful well-doing, for the first article of your faith teaches you that right action is the sign of a divine birth.'

A decision is difficult; but upon the whole the general structure of vv. 28 f. favours the imperative. It seems to be more in accordance with the context that St John should here charge his readers to apply practically the truth which they had inwardly mastered, than that he should appeal to them as having done thus.

The use of ἐάν with the subj. (ἐὰν εἰδῆτε), when there is no intention of questioning the fact or treating it as uncertain, often serves to turn the thoughts of the hearer or reader upon it in the way of self-interrogation: 'if, as I assume to be the case, as you profess, as by silent inquiry you can assure yourselves....' Comp. c. iv. 12 (v. 15); John xiv. 15.

δίκαιος... ἐξ αὐ. γεγένν.] *He is righteous...begotten of Him....* Great difficulty has been felt in determining whether the pronoun refers to 'God' or to 'Christ.' There can be no doubt that Christ is the subject in *v.* 28 (*abide in Him...at His presence*). It is therefore most natural to suppose that He is the subject in this verse also, unless the context makes such an interpretation impossible. This probability is strengthened by the fact that no personal pronoun is introduced in *v.* 29. And there is a further presumption that the same subject is continued from the fact that in iii. 1 a new subject is distinctly named (*the Father*). The application of the epithet 'righteous' to Christ is supported by *v.* 1. But it is argued on the other side that the Christian cannot be said '*to be born of Christ.*' It is certainly true that the exact phrase does not occur elsewhere, while '*to be born of God*' (who is called 'righteous' c. i. 9) is a characteristic phrase of St John (γενν. ἐκ θεοῦ John i. 13, γενν. ἐκ τοῦ θεοῦ c. iii. 9; iv. 7; v. 1, 4, 18). But this argument does not seem to be conclusive. Christians are said equally to '*abide in God*' and to '*abide in Christ*' (*v.* 27). They are also said to be '*born of the Spirit*' (John iii. 6, 8). The word of Christ is in them as a quickening power (comp. 1 Pet. i. 23; James i. 18). There is then nothing against the tenour of Scripture in saying that Christians are 'born of

Christ,' who is 'God only-begotten' (John i. 18).

The true solution of the difficulty seems to be that when St John thinks of God in relation to men he never thinks of Him apart from Christ (comp. c. v. 20). And again he never thinks of Christ in His human nature without adding the thought of His divine nature. Thus a rapid transition is possible from the one aspect of the Lord's divine-human Person to the other. Here the passage is from 'Christ' to 'God' (ἐὰν φανερωθῇ, ἐν τῇ παρουσίᾳ αὐτοῦ, δίκαιός ἐστιν, ἐξ αὐτοῦ γεγέννηται); and conversely in iii. 1—4 the passage is from 'God' to 'Christ' (τέκνα θεοῦ, οὐκ ἔγνω αὐτόν, ἐὰν φανερωθῇ, ὅμοιοι αὐτῷ ἐσόμεθα, καθὼς ἐκεῖνος), yet without any change of Person.

This appears to be the view of Augustine who writes: ex ipso natus est, ex Deo, ex Christo. Bede writes simply 'id est, ex Christo.'

δίκαιος] *righteous.* The epithet is used of Christ ii. 1; iii. 7. Comp. Acts iii. 14, vii. 52, xxii. 14; and of God (the Father) c. i. 9 (see note); John xvii. 25; Apoc. xvi. 5.

ὅτι πᾶς...γεγέννηται] *that every one...hath been begotten of Him.* The presence of righteous action is the sure sign of the reality of the divine birth. We are often tempted, according to our imperfect standards of judgment, to exclude some (comp. *v.* 23 πᾶς ὁ ἀρν. note), but the divine law admits no exception. It must be further observed that righteousness is not the condition but the consequence of Sonship. God is the one source of righteousness. Apart from God in Christ there is no righteousness. It follows therefore that the presence of active righteousness is the sign of the divine Sonship, and the sign of that abiding power of Sonship which brings final confidence. Other tests of Sonship are offered in the Epistle: 'love' (iv. 7) and belief 'that Jesus is the

Christ' (v. 1). Each one, it will be found, includes the others. See v. 1 note.

The apostle's argument might have appeared more direct if the clauses had been inverted : 'know (take note of the fact) that every one that is born of God doeth righteousness.' But the present order includes a promise, and leaves the power of Sonship in its amplitude. The outwardly witnessed fact of righteousness points to the reality of a relation which includes blessings not yet fully grasped.

ὁ ποιῶν τὴν δικ.] *qui facit justitiam* V., *who doeth righteousness*, who realises in action little by little the righteousness which corresponds with the Divine Nature (τὴν δικ. compare c. iii. 7 note). The tense (ποιῶν) is full of meaning, as Theophylact observes : ἐπισημαντέον ὅτι οὐκ εἶπε Πᾶς ὁ ποιήσας δικαιοσύνην ἢ, Ὁ ποιήσων ἀλλ' Ὁ ποιῶν. πρακτικαὶ γὰρ [αἱ] ἀρεταὶ καὶ ἐν τῷ γίνεσθαι ἔχουσι τὸ εἶναι· παυσάμεναι δὲ ἢ μέλλουσαι οὐδὲ τὸ εἶναι ἔχουσι.

Bede thus marks the beginning and the end of this realisation of righteousness: Cœpisti non defendere peccatum tuum, jam inchoasti justitiam. Perficietur autem in te quando te nihil aliud facere delectabit.

Compare also ποιεῖν τὴν ἀλήθειαν c. i. 6 note.

ἐξ αὐτοῦ γεγέννηται] *ex ipso natus est* V., *is begotten of Him*. Comp. c. iii. 9 note. The phrase occurs here first in the Epistle. The order emphasises the fact that such a one has *God* for his Father, and not that he has a new life. Compare iii. 9 *b*; iv. 7; v. 1; John i. 13.

Additional Note on ii. 2.	*The use of* ἱλασμός *and cognates in
the Greek Scriptures.*

The word ἱλασμός occurs in the N.T. only here and in a parallel passage
iv. 10.

In the LXX. it is found with the corresponding ἐξιλασμός more frequently,
where one or other of the two words is the usual representative of כִּפֻּרִים :

Lev. xxv. 9 ἡ ἡμέρα τοῦ ἱλασμοῦ.

— xxiii. 27 f. ἡ ἡμέρα τοῦ ἐξιλασμοῦ.

Num. v. 8 ὁ κριὸς τοῦ ἱλασμοῦ δι᾽ οὗ ἐξιλάσεται.

— xxix. 11 τὸ περὶ τῆς ἁμαρτίας τῆς ἐξιλάσεως.

Exod. xxix. 36 ἡ ἡμέρα τοῦ καθαρισμοῦ.

Vat. A. Σ. Θ. ἐξιλασμοῦ.

— xxx. 10 ἀπὸ τοῦ αἵματος τοῦ καθαρισμοῦ.

Vat. A. ἐξιλασμοῦ.

The two words used also for חַטָּאת :

Ezek. xlv. 19 λήψεται ἀπὸ τοῦ αἵματος τοῦ ἐξιλασμοῦ.

xliv. 27 προσοίσουσιν ἱλασμόν.

Comp. Ezek. xliii. 23 (Amos viii. 14 is a false rendering of אַשְׁמָה).

2 Macc. iii. 33 ποιουμένου τοῦ ἀρχιερέως τὸν ἱλασμόν (the sacrifice offered
for the recovery of Heliodorus).

2 Macc. xii. 45 περὶ τῶν τεθνηκότων τὸν ἐξιλασμὸν ἐποιήσατο τῆς ἁμαρτίας
ἀπολυθῆναι.

In Ps. cxxix. (cxxx.) 4 and Dan. ix. 9 ἱλασμός (-οί) is used to translate
סְלִיחָה.

The words are always used absolutely without any addition to mark the
person to or for whom, or the offence for which the propitiation is offered.

In Ecclus. xviii. 12 ἐπλήθυνε (κύριος) τὸν ἐξιλασμὸν αὐτοῦ the sense is that
of Ps. cxxix. 4 'mercifulness.' Comp. c. xvi. 11 ἐξιλασμοί.

The corresponding verb ἱλάσκομαι is found twice in the N.T.:

(1)	With the dat. of person sinning,

Luke xviii. 13 ἱλάσθητί μοι τῷ ἁμαρτωλῷ.

(2)	With the accus. of the sin,

Heb. ii. 17 εἰς τὸ ἱλάσκεσθαι τὰς ἁμαρτίας τοῦ λαοῦ.

Ἱλάσκομαι is comparatively rare in the LXX. It occurs as a translation
of כָּפַר :

(1)	With accus. of the sin,

Ps. lxiv. 3 ἱλάσῃ τὰς ἀσεβείας.

(2)	With dat. of the sin,

Ps. lxxvii. 38 ἱλάσεται ταῖς ἁμαρτίαις.

— lxxviii. 38 ἱλάσθητι ταῖς ἁμ.

Marginal notes:

Use of ἱλασμός in N. T. and LXX.

Use of ἱλάσκομαι.

9

It occurs also as a translation of סָלַח for which ἵλεως εἶναι is commonly used :

(1) With the dat. of person,
4 (2) K. v. 18 ἱλάσεται [ἱλασθήσεται] τῷ δούλῳ.

(2) With the dat. of the sin,
Ps. xxiv. 12 ἱλάσθητι τῇ ἁμαρτίᾳ.

(3) Absolutely,
Lam. iii. 42 οὐχ ἱλάσθης.
Dan. ix. 19 ἱλάσθητι.

ἐξιλάσ-
κομαι.

The compound ἐξιλάσκομαι, which is the usual representative of כִּפֶּר, is more common. This is found

(1) With the accusative

(a) of the object cleansed :
Ezek. xliii. 26 τὸ θυσιαστήριον.
— xlv. 18 τὸ ἅγιον.
— xlv. 20 τὸν οἶκον.
— xliii. 20, 22 τὸ θυσιαστήριον (וְחִטֵּא).

(b) and specially of sin,
Dan. ix. 24 τοῦ ἐξιλάσασθαι ἀδικίας.
Ecclus. iii. 30 ἁμαρτίας.

Comp. Ps. lxiv. 4.

In this case the subject (he who expiates, atones, cleanses) may be either

(a) God,
Ecclus. v. 6 πλῆθος ἁμαρτιῶν.
— xxxi. (xxxiv.) 23 οὐδὲ ἐν πλήθει θυσιῶν ἐξιλάσκεται ἁμαρτίας,
or

(b) the human agent,
Ecclus. iii. 3 ὁ τιμῶν πατέρα ἐξιλάσεται ἁμαρτίας.
— xx. 28, xxviii. 5.

So also the word is found in the passive,
1 Sam. iii. 14 εἰ ἐξιλασθήσεται ἡ ἀδικία...ἐκ θυσίας (יִתְכַּפֵּר).

Comp. Deut. xxi. 8 ἐξιλασθήσεται αὐτοῖς τὸ αἷμα.

(2) With περί gen.

(a) of the sin,
Ex. xxxii. 30, &c.
or

(b) of the person sinning,
Lev. i. 4.
— iv. 20, &c.

Comp. Ecclus. xvi. 7 οὐκ ἐξιλάσατο περὶ τῶν ἀρχαίων γιγάντων.

So also with ὑπέρ,
Ezek. xlv. 17.

The word is also used absolutely,
Lev. xvi. 17.　Comp. Lam. iii. 42; Dan. ix. 19.

(3) Passive with ἀπὸ,

Num. xxxv. 33 οὐκ ἐξιλασθήσεται ἡ γῆ ἀπὸ τοῦ αἵματος.

(4) The accusative of the person 'propitiated' is found only,

Gen. xxxii. 20 (בִּפֶּר) ἐξιλάσομαι τὸ πρόσωπον αὐτοῦ ἐν τοῖς δώροις (for ἐν comp. Levit. vi. 37; 1 Sam. iii. 14).

Zech. vii. 2 (חִלָּה) ἐξιλάσασθαι τὸν κύριον.

These constructions stand in remarkable contrast with the Classical and Hellenistic[1] usage in which the accus. of the person propitiated is the normal construction from Homer downwards; a usage which prevails in patristic writers. Contrast of Biblical and Classical usage.

They shew that the scriptural conception of ἱλάσκεσθαι is not that of appeasing one who is angry, with a personal feeling, against the offender; but of altering the character of that which from without occasions a necessary alienation, and interposes an inevitable obstacle to fellowship. Such phrases as 'propitiating God' and God 'being reconciled' are foreign to the language of the N. T. Man is reconciled (2 Cor. v. 18 ff.; Rom. v. 10 f.). There is a 'propitiation' in the matter of the sin or of the sinner. The love of God is the same throughout; but He 'cannot' in virtue of His very Nature welcome the impenitent and sinful: and more than this, He 'cannot' treat sin as if it were not sin.

This being so, the ἱλασμός, when it is applied to the sinner, so to speak, neutralises the sin. In this respect the idea of the efficacy of Christ's propitiation corresponds with one aspect of the Pauline phrase 'in Christ.' The believer being united with Christ enjoys the quickening, purifying, action of Christ's 'Blood,' of the virtue of His Life and Death, of His Life made available for men through Death.

Compare additional note on i. 9.

Additional Note on ii. 9. St John's view of the state of man.

St John assumes that the actual state of man and of the world is known by experience, from what we see about us and from history and from consciousness.

Naturally 'darkness' (comp. c. i. 5, note) is the sphere in which man abides (John xii. 46; 1 John ii. 9 ἕως ἄρτι) until it is dispelled. (Comp. John viii. 12; 1 Pet. ii. 9; Eph. vi. 12; Col. i. 13.) Under one aspect this darkness has wrought its work, and the crisis is past (c. ii. 11, ἐτύφλωσεν, note). Under another aspect there are times when the darkness falls afresh over men with a thicker gloom (John xii. 35, ἵνα μὴ σκ. ὑ. καταλάβῃ). Viewed from a different point of sight this darkness is death (John v. 24). Man by nature in darkness and death.

---

[1] E.g. Clem. ad Cor. i. 7 οἱ δὲ (the Ninevites) μετανοήσαντες ἐπὶ τοῖς ἁμαρτήμασιν ἐξιλάσαντο τὸν θεὸν ἱκετεύσαντες. Herm. Vis. i. 2 πῶς ἐξιλάσομαι τὸν θεὸν περὶ τῶν ἁμαρτιῶν μου τῶν τελείων; Test. xii. Patr. Levi 3 οἱ ἄγγελοι...οἱ λειτουρ-γοῦντες καὶ ἐξιλασκόμενοι πρὸς Κύριον ἐπὶ πάσαις ταῖς ἀγνοίαις τῶν δικαίων. Philo, de plantat. § 39 (i. 354) εὐξάμενοι καὶ θυσίας ἀναγαγόντες, καὶ ἱλασάμενοι τὸ θεῖον. Comp. Leg. Alleg. iii. § 61 (i. 121 M).

<table>
<tr><td>

This state due to external influence.

</td><td>

This present state of man is due to a mysterious interruption of the Divine plan which is noticed abruptly (John i. 5) and came from another order (c. iii. 8). It is not due to a physical or metaphysical necessity, and is foreign to the essence of man. As the creature of God man was made good not absolutely but relatively. Sin has disturbed his normal development (c. iii. 4). Nothing however is said by St John of the Fall; nor does he mention Adam (yet comp. Apoc. xii. 9 ff.; xx. 2 ὁ ὄφις ὁ ἀρχαῖος). The sin of Cain, the manifestation of sin in the realm of human life, and not the sin of Adam, is treated as the archetypal sin (c. ii. 12).

</td></tr>
</table>

Man failed to see God.

As a necessary consequence of his state, man failed of himself to gain a knowledge of God in the way of nature (John i. 10; comp. iii. 3), though he was not left unvisited (John i. 4, 9).

The mission of the Son of God revealed man to himself.

Under these circumstances God sent His Son to save the world, giving in this the measure of His love (John iii. 16 f.; c. iv. 10). But the coming of Christ was in effect a judgment, shewing to men what they had become (John ix. 39; comp. Apoc. iii. 17 ff.; Luke ii. 34 f.). For they were not without the power of recognising this Divine revelation (John xv. 22, 24; v. 36). The will to recognise God and not the capacity was wanting (John v. 40; vii. 17; viii. 44; xii. 48 ἔχει τὸν κρίνοντα; comp. iii. 18; vi. 67; ix. 41). The manifestation of love called out, as a necessary consequence, the opposition of selfishness, hatred (John iii. 19 f.; vii. 7; xv. 18 f., 23 f.; xvii. 14; comp. c. ii. 9, 11; iii. 10, 15; iv. 20). But this hatred was in despite of man's real nature. It is true still that if he violates moral law he 'lies,' and 'deceives himself' (c. i. 6, 8; ii. 4, 22; iv. 20).

The actual state of man shewn in contrasts.

These several traits combine to give a striking view of the grandeur and powerlessness of man ('un roseau pensant'). He is made for God: he is unable of himself to attain to God: God claims his concurrence with the activity of Divine love. And it is most worthy of notice that St John simply declares the antithetic facts in their simple solemnity. He shews no desire to resolve the discords which he accentuates. He leaves them for a state of fuller knowledge and larger life.

Man is in darkness and death (John v. 24; c. iii. 14). On the other side the true Light shineth (John i. 5; xii. 36; c. ii. 8); and Christ offers ' His flesh for the life of the world' (John vi. 51).

The world 'lieth in the Evil One' (c. v. 19). On the other side 'the Prince of the world' is judged and cast out (John xii. 31; xvi. 11; comp. xiii. 40; c. v. 4 ἡ νίκη ἡ νικήσασα). There is a human will which is responsible and therefore in that sense 'free' (John v. 40; iii. 19 ff.; vii. 17). On the other side there is a Divine will which we cannot conceive to be finally ineffective (vi. 44 ff., 65; v. 21).

In the opening of the Gospel, John i. 12 f., these contrasts find a concurrent affirmation. On the one side the human element is seen in ἔλαβον, πιστεύουσιν, γενέσθαι. On the other side the Divine element is seen in ἐγεννήθησαν, ἔδωκεν ἐξουσίαν, τέκνα θεοῦ. Comp. John vi. 27 ff. (ἐργάζεσθε, δώσει).

The wide extent of these contrasts.

The same clear assertion of truths which appear to be in opposition extends to other parts of the region of Divine and human relations. There is one absolute message (John xii. 48); and yet concessions are made that

men may embrace it more readily (John v. 34 ; comp. viii. 17). There is a
group whom Christ speaks of as His own (John x. 27, 4); and yet He
appeals generally to all, for the image of thirst expresses a universal want
which Christ alone can satisfy (John vii. 37). A new birth is necessary for
the perception of the Divine Kingdom and entrance into it (John iii. 3 ff.) ;
and yet there are, as still without it, those who 'are of the truth' (John
xviii. 37), who 'do the truth' (iii. 21), who are 'children of God' (xi. 52).

In part we can see perhaps where the reconciliation of these statements
can be found. In part they finally go back to the fundamental antithesis
of the finite and infinite before which our present powers fail. The teaching
of St John helps us to see that it is enough that we hold the fulness of the
truth as it is presented to us in complementary fragments.

Additional Note on ii. 13. The powers of evil.

St John speaks comparatively little of subordinate spiritual powers in his Gospel and Epistles. The ministry of angels is essential to the whole structure of the Apocalypse, which contains also characteristic references to 'the Serpent,' 'the ancient Serpent,' 'the dragon' (xii. 3 ff. ; xiii. 2 ff. ; xvi. 13 ; xx. 2), 'who is called the Devil and Satan' (xii. 9) ; compare also ix. 20 (τὰ δαιμόνια); xvi. 14 (πν. δαιμονίων). But into these notices we do not now inquire.

Few references to subordinate powers and evil in St John.

The only references to angels in the Gospel are in i. 51 (52); xx. 12 (v. (3) 4, embodies an early tradition, but is no part of the original text). They have no place in the Epistles. In the Gospel 'demons' are only spoken of by the Jews or in direct reference to their words (vii. 20 ; viii. 48 ff. ; x. 20 f.). In the first epistle 'spirits' of antichrist are described as influencing men (c. iv. 2 ff. note, 6).

But the notices of the representative power of evil are of great importance. He is spoken of as 'the Devil' (ὁ διάβολος John viii. 44 ; xiii. 2 ; c. iii. 8, 10), the false accuser (John vi. 70 note) ; 'Satan' (ὁ Σατανᾶς John xiii. 27), the adversary (comp. ὁ κατήγωρ Apoc. xii. 10); 'the evil one' (ὁ πονηρός xvii. 15, note ; c. ii. 13 f. ; iii. 12 ; v. 18 f.); 'the ruler of this (the) world' (ὁ ἄρχων τοῦ κόσμου τούτου John xii. 31 ; xvi. 11 ; ὁ τοῦ κ. ἄρχ. John xiv. 30).

The Evil One.

Of his origin nothing is specially said. But enough is laid down to exclude the notion of two coordinate or absolute or original beings, good and evil. He was originally good, but 'he stood not (John viii. 44 οὐκ ἔστηκεν, note) in the truth.' This is all that we are concerned to know. For the rest he appears 'from the beginning' on the scene of human activity (c. iii. 8). Thus he stands in opposition to the Word (c. i. 1), and finally to the Incarnate Son (c. iii. 8 note ; v. 18 f. ; John xiv. 30 f.).

A fallen being.

In this respect he is directly at variance with Christ in His essential character. Christ is 'the truth' (John xiv. 6): the devil is a liar (John viii. 44; comp. c. ii. 22). Christ is 'the life' (John xiv. 6): the devil is a murderer (John viii. 44; comp. c. iii. 15). In each case a personal an-

The antagonist of the Son.

tagonist is set over against the absolute idea. In relation to the reality of things, and in relation to human fellowship : in the regions of thought, feeling, action ; the devil conflicts with the Son of God.'

His present influence on men. For the present, as the title 'the ruler of this world' implies, the devil exercises a wide influence over men (c. iii. 8 ff. ; John viii. 44 ; xiii. 2, 27). They may become his 'sons,' his 'children' (c. iii. 10 note); they may be 'of him' (c. iii. 8). But they are never said to be 'born of him,' as they are born of God (c. ii. 29 &c).

Already overthrown. And in relation to the work of Christ he is already finally defeated (John xvi. 11 ; xii. 31 ; xiv. 30 ; c. v. 4, 18). It remains to secure the fruits of the victory.

Additional Note on ii. 17. *St John's teaching on creation.*

St John's conception of creation. The main conception of creation which is present in the writings of St John is expressed by the first notice which he makes of it : '*all things came into being (ἐγένετο) through* [the Word]' (John i. 3). This statement sets aside the notions of eternal matter and of inherent evil in matter. 'There was when' the world 'was not' (John xvii. 5, 24) ; and, by implication, all things as made were good. The agency of the Word 'who was God' again excludes both the Gnostic idea of a Demiurge, a creator essentially inferior to God ; and the idea of an abstract Monotheism, in which there is no living relation between the creature and the Creator ; for as all things come into being 'through' the Word, so they are supported 'in' Him (John i. 3 ὃ γέγ. ἐν αὐτῷ ζωὴ ἦν note; comp. Col. i. 16 f. ; Heb. i. 3). And yet more the use of the term ἐγένετο, 'came into being,' as distinguished from ἐκτίσθη 'were created,' suggests the thought that Creation is to be regarded (according to our apprehension) as a manifestation of a Divine law of love. Thus Creation (πάντα ἐγένετο δι' αὐτοῦ) answers to the Incarnation (ὁ λόγος σὰρξ ἐγένετο). All the unfolding and infolding of finite being to the last issue lies in the fulfilment of His will Who is love.

An order unfolded in spite of the irruption of darkness. A Divine 'must.' The irruption of darkness, however, has hindered the normal progress of the counsel of God. This is obvious in 'the world' which falls within the range of man's observation. But in spite of the violation of the Divine order by man there is still a fulfilment of the counsel of God in the world. This is seen most distinctly in the record of the Lord's work. In the accomplishment of this there is a Divine necessity, a 'must' and a 'cannot' in the very nature of things ; and also a Divine sequence in the unfolding of its parts.

This Divine 'must' (δεῖ) extends to the relation of the Forerunner to Christ (iii. 30); to the fulfilment of the work of God during an allotted time (ix. 4) ; to the Passion and Exaltation (iii. 14 ; xii. 34) ; to the Rising again (xx. 9) ; to the execution of a wider office (x. 16) (comp. Apoc. i. 1 ; iv. 1 ; xxii. 6 ; xvii. 10 ; xx. 3).

A Divine 'cannot.' On the other hand there is also a 'cannot,' a moral, and not an external or arbitrary, impossibility in life. This defines, while it does not limit, the action of the Son : v. 19, 30 (comp. Mark vi. 5). And so also it fixes the conditions of discipleship (iii. 5 ; vi. 44, 65 ; vii. 34, 36 ; viii. 21 f.; comp. xiii. 33, 36); of understanding (iii. 3 ; viii. 43 f.; xiv. 17); of faith (xii. 39 ; comp. v. 44); of fruitfulness (xv. 4 f.); of progress (xvi. 12); of character (1 John iii. 9).

These terms ('must,' 'cannot') lay open the conditions (so to speak) of A Divine the Lord's life. The Divine sequence in the course of its events is no less 'hour.' distinctly marked by the term 'hour.' The crises of the manifestations of the Lord are absolutely fixed in time (ii. 4 ; comp. xi. 9 f.; ix. 4). Till this hour comes His enemies are powerless (vii. 30 ; viii. 20). When it has come He recognises its advent (xii. 27 ; xvii. 1) ; and it is appointed with a view to the issue to which it leads (xii. 23 ; xiii. 1 ἵνα).

Compare iv. 21, 23 ; v. 25, 28 ; 1 John ii. 18 ; Apoc. xiv. 7, 15 (ὥρα); John vii. 6, 8 (καιρός) ; Eph. i. 10 τὸ πλήρωμα τῶν καιρῶν ; Gal. iv. 4 τὸ πλήρωμα τοῦ χρόνου.

Under this same aspect the 'works' of the Lord are said to have been The life of 'given' to Him (v. 36 ; xvii. 4). The circumstances which furnished Christ, occasion for them are shewn to enter into the scheme of providence (ix. 3 ἵνα; xi. 4 ἵνα). Even unbelief was a necessity in regard of the history of mankind (xii. 38 ; xiii. 18 ; xv. 25 ; xvii. 12). This being so, Christ knew all 'the things that were coming upon Him' (xviii. 4 ; comp. xiii. 1, 11 ; vi. 64 ; comp. xviii. 9, 32). He laid down His life 'in order to take it again' (x. 17). This was His Father's will.

The whole life of Christ was thus a 'fulfilment,' 'a bringing to a perfect accomplishment' of all that had been shadowed forth or begun[1].

The same Divine appointment is extended to the discipline of the Church. and the The extremity of persecution is part of the revelation of the counsel of God life of the (John xvi. 2 ἵνα, note), as even was the failure of the disciples at their Church ac- Master's suffering (John xvi. 32 ἵνα, note). The birth of the Church has a law. real correspondence with the birth of the man (John xvi. 21 ff.). And in the work of service there is an appointed difference of function with a common end (John iv. 36 ff.).

The life of Christ and the life of the Church, as presented by St John, thus A true become revelations of a perfect order even in the disorder of the world nature lying beneath the surface of things, and veiled by suffering and by the under- workings of evil. In the same way he seems to indicate that below the neath ap- transitory appearances of nature there is that which is Divine and abiding. pearances. 'The world passeth away (παράγεται) and the desire thereof' (1 John ii. 17, 8), but at the same time he looked for a new heaven and a new earth (Apoc. xxi. 1).

He recognised most sharply the difference between the natural and the unnatural in what we call Nature as a whole, and saw in the complete

---

[1] The use of the two words πληρόω, τελειόω is worth study :

(a) πληρῶσαι
vii. 8 ὁ ἐμὸς καιρὸς οὔπω πεπλήρωται.

Of Holy Scripture and Divine words: ἵνα πληρωθῇ xii. 38 ; xiii. 18 ; xv. 25 ; xvii. 12 ; xviii. 32 ; xix. 24, 36. Comp. Apoc. vi. 11.

(b) τελειῶσαι
iv. 34 τελ. αὐτοῦ τὸ ἔργον; v. 36 τὰ ἔργα ἃ δέδ. ἵνα τελ.; xvii. 4 τὸ ἔργον τελ. ὃ δέδωκάς μοι.

Of Holy Scripture: xix. 28 ἵνα τελ. ἡ γρ. Comp. τετέλεσται, xix. 28, 30; and Apoc. x. 7.

destruction of the unnatural, the restoration of Nature. In this position he stands alike removed from the Hellenic worship of nature and from the Gnostic degradation of nature. (Comp. Lutterbeck, *Lehrb. d. Apost.* ii. 270 f.)

Additional Note on ii. 18. Antichrist.

Elements in the conception of Antichrist.

Different elements entered into the conception of 'Antichrist' in early patristic literature. Of these the chief were Dan. vii. 7 ff.: Matt. xxiv. 23 ff.; 2 Thess. ii. 3 ff.; Apoc. xiii.

But the aspects under which the opposing power is presented by St Paul and St John (Epistle) are distinct. The portraiture in St Paul is based on that of Daniel and presents a single adversary claiming personal worship, while St John dwells upon the spiritual element in his claims, and the spiritual falsehood which gave him the semblance of strength.

IRENÆUS.

IRENÆUS, the earliest writer who treats of the subject in detail, combines the name of Antichrist with the description in 2 Thess. ii. 3 ff. and the cognate passages in Daniel, St Matthew and the Apocalypse (Iren. v. 25 ff.; compare iii. 6, 4 ; 7, 2 ; 16, 5, 8 ; 23, 7).

CLEMENT OF ALEXANDRIA is silent on Antichrist. But the teaching on Antichrist attracted the attention of CELSUS, though Origen says that he had not read what was said of him by Daniel or Paul (*c. Cels.* vi. 45). In reply

ORIGEN.

to Celsus ORIGEN explains his own view, which is briefly that the Son of God and the son of the evil one, of Satan, of the devil, stand at the opposite poles of humanity, presenting in direct opposition the capacity of man for good and for evil. Elsewhere Origen draws out at length a comparison of Christ and Antichrist. All that Christ is in reality Antichrist offers in false appearance (*Comm. Ser. in Matt.* § 27); and so all false teaching which assumes the guise of truth, among heretics and even among heathen, is in some sense 'Antichrist' (*id.* § 47).

TERTUL-LIAN.

TERTULLIAN speaks several times of Antichrist and Antichrists. Quoting 2 Thess. ii. 3 he writes '*homo delinquentiæ*, id est, *antichristus*' (*de Res. carnis*, 24; cf. 27). Again referring to Matt. xxiv. 24, he asks : 'qui pseudoprophetæ sunt nisi falsi prædicatores ? qui pseudapostoli nisi adulteri evangelizatores ? qui antichristi nisi Christi rebelles ? (*de præscr. hær.* 4). And again in reference to 1 John ii. 18 he writes : in epistola sua eos maxime antichristos vocat qui Christum negarent in carne venisse, et qui non putarent Jesum esse filium dei. Illud Marcion, hoc Ebion vindicavit (*id.* 33).

One feature in the conception of Antichrist ought not to be overlooked. Just as Moses was the type of the Christ in His prophetic character,

Balaam.

Balaam, 'the anti-Moses,' was regarded as a type of the Antichrist. This explains the enigmatic references in Apoc. ii. 14 (6); Jude 11 ; 2 Pet. ii. 15.

Armillus.

In late Rabbinic traditions an Antichrist (Armillus, Armalgus) was represented as killing the Messiah of the stock of Ephraim, and then himself slain by the Messiah of the stock of David (Targ. on Is. xi. 4 ; comp. 2 Thess. ii. 8).

The Epistles to the Seven Churches form a commentary on the idea of *The Apo-calypse.* the many antichrists.

Apoc. ii. 2 (Ephesus) τοὺς λέγοντας ἑαυτοὺς ἀποστόλους. *id.* 6 τὰ ἔργα τῶν Νικολαιτῶν.

ii. 9 (Smyrna) τῶν λεγόντων Ἰουδαίους εἶναι.

ii. 13 (Pergamum) ὅπου ὁ θρόνος τοῦ Σατανᾶ. 14 τὴν διδαχὴν Βαλαάμ. 15 τὴν διδαχὴν Νικολαιτῶν.

ii. 20 (Thyatira) Ἰεζέβελ, ἡ λέγουσα ἑαυτὴν προφῆτιν. 24 τὰ βαθέα τοῦ Σατανᾶ (cf. I Cor. ii. 10).

iii. 3 (Sardis) μνημόνευε πῶς εἴληφας καὶ ἤκουσας καὶ τήρει.

iii. 8 f. (Philadelphia) τῆς συναγωγῆς τοῦ Σατανᾶ, τῶν λεγόντων ἑαυτοὺς Ἰουδαίους εἶναι.

Additional Note on the reading of ii. 20.

There is a remarkable variety of readings in the last words of this verse:

(1) καὶ οἴδατε πάντα
    AC MSS mss
    Memph Vulg.

The Syriac reads πάντα but translates it as if it were masc. (*and know every man*).

(2) καὶ οἴδατε (-αι ℵ) πάντες ℵP 9.

Hesych. Presb. (sæc. vii) *in Lev.* i. 5 ff. (Migne *P. Gr.* XCIII. p. 796) Et vos unctionem habetis a sancto et scitis omnes.

(3) οἴδατε πάντες B Theb.

The rendering which is given without variation in the Discourses of Augustine (ad loc.) *ut ipsi vobis manifesti sitis* can hardly be correct. His comment suggests πάντες: hanc unctionem Christi dicit omnes qui habent cognoscere malos et bonos; nec opus esse ut doceantur quia ipsa unctio docet eos.

The Latin translation of Irenæus, in a continuous quotation of *vv.* 18—22, omits *v.* 20 and part of *v.* 21 : ...sed ut manifestarentur quoniam non sunt ex nobis. Cognoscite ergo quoniam omne mendacium extraneum est et non est de veritate. Quis est mendax...(Iren. iii. 16. 5).

The combination for πάντες ℵBP 9 Theb. is very strong; and the shorter reading without καί readily explains how the others arose. When once the connexion of οἴδατε with τὴν ἀλήθειαν was lost, the insertion of καί and the change of πάντες to πάντα was almost inevitable, especially with the apparent parallel in *v.* 27 περὶ πάντων.

The occurrence of 9 (Cambr. Univ. Libr. Kk. vi. 4) in the small group of authorities which have preserved the main element of the true reading may serve as an excuse for directing attention to that remarkable MS, which has been strangely overlooked.

It was pointed out by Porson and Marsh that this MS is that marked ιγ´ in Stephens' edition of 1550; and apparently the capricious selection of readings quoted from it by Stephens has been the limit of the knowledge of the MS preserved by later editors. Mill's generalisations from the readings in Stephens (*Proleg.* 1170) might well have caused it to be more carefully examined.

The following readings in 1 John are worthy of notice:

i. 2 ἐφανερώθη ἐν ἡμῖν.
— 4 ἡμῶν.
— 9 τὰς ἁμαρτίας ἡμῶν.
ii. 1 γράφομεν.
— 8 ἐν ἡμῖν.
— 11 ἐτύφλωσεν αὐτὸν καὶ τοὺς ὀφθαλμοὺς αὐτοῦ.
— 17 ἡ ἐπιθυμία *om.* αὐτοῦ.
— 18 νῦν *om.* καί.
— 20 καὶ οἴδατε πάντες.
iii. 1 ἔδωκεν.
— — κληθῶμεν καὶ ἐσμέν.
— 5 τὰς ἁμαρτίας ἡμῶν.
— 7 τέκνα.
— 8 τοῦ διαβόλου ἐστίν *om.* ἐκ.
— — ὁ διάβολος ἀπ' ἀρχῆς.
— 19 γινωσκόμεθα.
— 21 καταγινώσκῃ *om.* ἡμῶν.
— 23 πιστεύωμεν.
iv. 2 γινώσκομεν.
— 3 Ἰησοῦν *om.* τόν.
— 8 ὁ μὴ ἀγαπῶν ἐκ τοῦ θεοῦ οὐκ ἔστιν.
— 10 ἠγαπήκαμεν.
v. 4 ὑμῶν.
— 20 ἡ ζωὴ ἡ αἰώνιος.

The title of the Epistle is ἐπιστολὴ Ἰωάννου ā and the subscription τοῦ ἁγίου ἀπ. Ἰω ἐπιστολὴ ā.

III.　¹Ἴδετε ποταπὴν ἀγάπην δέδωκεν ἡμῖν ὁ πατὴρ

1 δέδωκεν ℵBC: ἔδωκεν A.　　　ἡμῖν: ὑμῖν B.

II. THE CHILDREN OF GOD AND THE CHILDREN OF THE DEVIL (iii. 1—12).

The section seems to fall most naturally into three parts:

1. *The position present and future of the children of God* (iii. 1—3).

2. *The essential character of the children of God* (4—9).

3. *The outward manifestation of the children of God* (10—12).

The thoughts are unfolded throughout in contrast with the corresponding thoughts as to the position, character, and manifestation of 'the children of the devil.' The world knows not Christians. Sin is incompatible with Sonship of God. Active hatred is the sign of hostility to right.

1. *The position present and future of the children of God* (1—3).

The position of Christians is considered in regard both to the present (*v.* 1) and to the future (*v.* 2). They stand now to 'the Father' in the relation of 'children of God' in title and in reality: on the other hand 'the world' fails to recognise them. Their future is as yet unrevealed; but so much is known that it will answer to the open, transfiguring vision of God in Christ. Meanwhile therefore the thought of this transfiguration is the rule and inspiration of Christian effort (*v.* 3).

¹ *Behold (See) what manner of love the Father hath given to us, that we should be called children of God:—and such we are. For this cause the world knoweth us not, because it knew him not.* ² *Beloved, now are we children of God, and it is not yet manifested what we shall be. We know that if he shall be manifested, we shall be like him, because we shall see him even as he is.*
And every one that hath this hope

on him purifieth himself even as he is pure.

1. Ἴδετε] *Videte* V., *Ecce* Aug., *Behold, See.* The use of the plural is remarkable, and elsewhere it is used only of something actually visible (Gal. vi. 11; yet comp. Acts xiii. 41, LXX). The image at the close of the last chapter (*born of Him*) seems to fill St John's vision, and, as he pauses to dwell upon it himself, he invites his readers to contemplate the same truth as present before them in an intelligible shape.

ποταπὴν ἀγάπην] *qualem caritatem (dilectionem* Aug.) V., *what manner of love* truly divine in its nature. The word ποταπός, which is not found in the LXX, is rare in the New Testament. It is used to call attention to the character both of persons (Matt. viii. 27; Luke vii. 39; 2 Pet. iii. 11) and of things (Mk. xiii. 1; Luke i. 29).

ὁ πατήρ] *the Father.* This title is chosen in order to illustrate and (in some degree) to explain the gift of love which God has bestowed on men.

δέδωκεν ἡ.] *dedit nobis* V., *hath given to us.* Comp. John xiv. 27. The love is not simply exhibited towards believers, but imparted to them. The divine love is, as it were, infused into them, so that it is their own, and becomes in them the source of a divine life (Rom. xiii. 10). In virtue of this gift therefore they are inspired with a love which is like the love of God, and by this they truly claim the title of children of God, as partakers in His nature. Comp. c. iv. 7, 19. See also Leo, *Serm.* xii. § 1 (Migne, *Patrol. Lat.* LIV. p. 169): Diligendo itaque nos Deus ad imaginem suam nos reparat et, ut in nobis formam suæ bonitatis inveniat, dat unde ipsi quoque quod operatur operemur, accendens

ἵνα τέκνα θεοῦ κληθῶμεν, καὶ ἐσμέν. διὰ τοῦτο ὁ

καὶ ἐσμέν ℵABC vg me the syrr: om. ς. The Latt. by a natural error read *et simus* (as depending on *ut*). Compare c. v. 20.

scilicet mentium nostrarum lucernas, et igne nos suæ caritatis inflammans, ut non solum ipsum sed etiam quidquid diligit diligamus.

With δέδωκεν, which regards the endowment of the receiver, contrast κεχάρισται (Gal. iii. 18), ἐχαρίσατο (Phil. ii. 9) which regards the feeling of the giver.

ἡμῖν (ὑμῖν)] St John is here considering the blessing of love as actually realised in the Christian society. Contrast John iii. 16 ἠγάπησεν ὁ θεὸς τὸν κόσμον.

ἵνα...κληθῶμεν...] *ut...nominemur* (*vocemur* Aug.) V., *that we should be called*. The final particle has its full force. The divine gift of love which is appropriated by the believer forms the basis, the justification, of the divine title. The end of the blessing is that sonship may be real. For ἵνα compare v. 11 note.

Pelagii...condemnatur hæresis in eo quod dicitur a Deo nobis caritatem... dari qua adoptionem filiorum accipiamus (Bede).

τέκνα θεοῦ] *filii Dei* V., *children of God* not *sons of God* which comes from the Latin. The thought here is of the community of nature with the prospect of development (τέκνον, comp. 2 Pet. i. 4), and not of the position of privilege (υἱός). The only place in St John's writings where 'son' is used of the relation of man to God is Apoc. xxi. 7 in a free quotation from Zech. viii. 8.

The use of υἱός is characteristic of St Paul's Epistles to the Romans and Galatians: Rom. viii. 14, 19; Gal. iii. 26; iv. 6, 7. Comp. Heb. ii. 10, xii. 5 ff.; Rom. ix. 26; 2 Cor. vi. 18; Matt. v. 9, 45, xvii. 26; Luke vi. 35, xx. 36.

On the other hand the idea of 'children of God' (τέκνα θεοῦ) is not unfrequent in St John: vv. 2, 10, v. 2; John i. 12, xi. 52. See Additional Note.

By using θεοῦ in place of the simple pronoun αὐτοῦ St John, reciting the full name of Christians (v. 10; v. 2; John i. 12, xi. 52; Rom. viii. 16 ff., ix. 8; Phil. ii. 15), emphasises the idea of the nobility of the Christian's position ('children of Him who is God').

κληθῶμεν] *be called*. The privilege is already enjoyed in the present and not only anticipated in the future. Christians are outwardly recognised as 'God's children' in their services and intercourse with others. Such an open recognition of the title gives a solemn dignity to it.

It is worthy of notice that St John never uses καλεῖν of the Divine 'call' (John x. 3 φωνεῖ). Comp. John ii. 2.

καὶ ἐσμέν] *and such we are.* This parenthetical addition is an emphatic expression of the Apostle's own faith. He has stated the historic position of Christians in the world, which depends on the Father's gift of love. He affirms now that that historic position corresponds with a real fact. The name represents an absolute truth. For such an introduction of a reflective comment see i. 2 note; 2 John 2. The Latin by a natural error connects the ἐσμέν with ἵνα, *ut nominemur...et simus*.

διὰ τοῦτο] *propter hoc* V., *For this cause* (iv. 5), i.e. because we are children of God, and so share His nature, *the world knoweth us not*, seeing that it has shewn decisively its inability to recognise Him. The reference to the world at first sight seems to interrupt the current of thought, but St John's whole argument proceeds on the supposition that men stand between two powers, God and the

κόσμος οὐ γινώσκει ἡμᾶς ὅτι οὐκ ἔγνω αὐτόν. ²Ἀγα-
πητοί, νῦν τέκνα θεοῦ ἐσμέν, καὶ οὔπω ἐφανερώθη τί

ἡμᾶς: ὑμᾶς ℵ*.

world. He has shewn the relation in which they stand to God : he now shews the relation in which they stand to the world. At the same time the clause meets an objection which is likely to rise from a consideration of the character of Christians. If they are children of God, righteous and loving, may they not look for an immediate and decisive victory? So we are inclined to argue; and therefore the apostle at once points out that their likeness to God becomes the occasion of misunderstanding.

οὐ γινώσκει...οὐκ ἔγνω...] non novit...non novit...V., non cognoscit... non cognovit...Aug., the world knoweth us not does not enter into, come to understand, our principles and methods and character, for true knowledge of men requires sympathy (c. ii. 3 note). The conduct of Christians must be more or less a riddle to those who do not take account of that which is to them the spring of action. This follows from the fact that when the opportunity was given to the world for recognising the great features of the divine character it knew Him not (comp. c. iv. 8 note). The world failed to recognise God so far as He was manifested in creation and history (1 Cor. i. 21); and its failure was still more conspicuous when He was manifested in His Son (John xvi. 3). It is to this revelation specially that the Apostle refers. The 'Him' is God in Christ, as in ii. 29.

Augustine says, using an impressive image : [homines] amando delectationes peccatorum non agnoscebant Deum : amando quod febris suadebat injuriam medico faciebant.

2. Ἀγαπητοί] Carissimi V., Dilectissimi Aug., Beloved. The title (ii. 7 note) embodies the thought

which has been just expressed. St John in the spirit of love addresses those who with him look forward to the issue of love. In doing this he takes up the words which he has just used, half in personal reflection (καὶ ἐσμέν); 'Yes, now are we children, children with the promise of mature development.' The change to which he thus looks forward will not be in the position of children, but in the conditions under which the relation will be shewn. The Christian has now, even in the present life, that which carries with it potentially infinite blessings, but the manifestation of his sonship is hindered by the circumstances in which he is placed. He will not be anything essentially different hereafter, but he will be what he is now essentially more completely, though in ways wholly beyond our powers of imagination.

νῦν...ἐσμέν, καὶ...] now are we and... The thought of what Christians are and the thought of what they will be are treated as parts of the same thought and not placed in contrast. The fact and the hope are both powerful for life.

οὔπω ἐφανερώθη...ἐὰν φανερωθῇ...] nondum apparuit...cum apparuerit...V., nondum manifestatum est (and apparuit)...cum apparuerit (and manifestatum fuerit) Aug., manifestatum est...si manifestaverit (one MS. manifestatus fuerit) Tert., nondum revelatum est...cum revelatum fuerit Ambr.

The main difficulty in this passage lies in the interpretation of the clause ἐὰν φανερωθῇ. The subject is not expressed; and the clause can be rendered either (1) if it shall be manifested i. e. what we shall be; or (2) if he shall be manifested. In

W.

7

ἐσόμεθα. οἴδαμεν ὅτι ἐὰν φανερωθῇ ὅμοιοι αὐτῷ ἐσόμεθα, ὅτι ὀψόμεθα αὐτὸν καθώς ἐστιν. ³ καὶ πᾶς ὁ

2 οἴδαμεν ℵABC vg the syrhl: + δέ ϛ me syrvg.

favour of the first interpretation it is
urged that the clause must refer back
to the corresponding words (οὔπω
ἐφανερώθη) which have immediately
gone before: *it is not yet manifested…
if it shall be manifested…;* unless
such an explanation be obviously
excluded by other considerations;
and on the other hand it is answered
rightly, I think, that this is in fact
the case; that the words *if it shall
be manifested* are altogether without
force; or rather that they obscure the
meaning. The knowledge which is
affirmed is not dependent on any
manifestation, but absolute. Christians
already possess it; and their certainty
so far is not conditioned by anything
future. Or to put the thought somewhat differently: it cannot be said
that the knowledge that we shall be
like Christ (which is assumed) depends upon the manifestation of what
we shall be. On the other hand there
is an inspiring power in the assurance
that our likeness to the Lord will be
a likeness to His glorified Being,
which will hereafter be shewn, though
as yet we cannot understand what it
is.

And further in support of the rendering *if he shall be manifested* it is to
be noticed that the same phrase has
been used in ii. 28 where the meaning
is beyond all doubt. It may be added
that this use of φανεροῦσθαι appears
to rule the whole line of the apostle's
thought (ii. 28, iii. 8). Christ has been
(was) manifested and He will be
manifested. The past manifestations
made some things clear and left some
things dark (iii. 5, 8). The future
manifestation will remove this darkness (comp. Col. iii. 4).
Even in the foregoing clause there
is, as will be seen, something of this

same thought. The manifestations of
the Risen Christ have not completely
illuminated our future.

οὔπω ἐφανερώθη] *it is not yet made
manifest.* The aorist (ἐφανερώθη) appears to point back to some definite
occasion on which the revelation
might have been expected (compare
ἔγνω v. 1). Perhaps it is best to
refer the word to the manifestations
(comp. ii. 28 note) of the Risen Lord.
These revelations of a changed and
glorified humanity do not make
known to us what we shall be. They
only serve to shew that the limitations of the present mode of existence
will be removed.

τί ἐσόμεθα] For the use of the
direct interrogation, see Moulton's
Winer, pp. 210 f.

οἴδαμεν] *We know.* Comp. c. v. 2, 18
notes. There is no opposition between
this clause and that which immediately precedes such as is suggested
by the δέ of the common text. The
knowledge corresponds with the
whole consciousness of the position
of children.

ὅμοιοι αὐτῷ] *similes ei,* V., *like him,*
like God in Christ. The image in which
we were made will then be consummated in the likeness to which it was
the divine purpose that we should
attain. Compare the Essay on *The
Gospel of Creation,* III. 1 (*a*).

This likeness of man redeemed and
perfected to God is the likeness of
the creature reflecting the glory of
the Creator. Contrast Phil. ii. 6 τὸ
εἶναι ἴσα θεῷ, said of the Son. Dispar
est res, sed *sicut* ad similitudinem
dicitur. Habemus ergo et nos imaginem Dei, sed non illam quam habet
Filius æqualis patri (Aug).

ὅτι ὀψόμεθα…] *quoniam videbimus…* V., *because we shall see….* The

causal particle is ambiguous.... The likeness to God may be either (1) the necessary condition, or (2) the actual consequence of the Divine Vision. The argument may be : We shall see God, and therefore, since this is possible, we must be like Him; or, We shall see God, and in that Presence we shall reflect His glory and be transformed into His likeness. Both thoughts are scriptural; and perhaps the two thoughts are not very sharply distinguished here. It is true that likeness is, in this case, the condition of vision ; and it is true also that likeness is the consequence of vision. We see that which we have the sympathetic power of seeing and we gain greater power of seeing, that is greater sympathy with the object of sight, by exercise of the power which we have. Augustine dwells upon this idea : Tota vita Christiani boni sanctum desiderium est. Quod autem desideras nondum vides; sed desiderando capax efficeris ut cum venerit quod videas implearis. ....Deus differendo extendit desiderium, desiderando extendit animum, extendendo facit capaciorem. And again: Hæc est vita nostra ut desiderando exerceamur.

At the same time it may be urged that the verb (ἐσόμεθα), which describes a being and not a becoming (γενησόμεθα 1 Cor. xv. 37, 54; John x. 16), appears to mark a state which co-exists with the divine manifestation at the first, and does not follow from it. On the other hand the thought of the transfiguring virtue of the divine vision is familiar. Comp. 2 Cor. iii. 18; v. 4; Iren. IV. 38. 3 (a very fine passage).

In either case the central truth is the same. The great confidence of the believer is that he will see the full revelation of the glory of God in Christ, and therefore that when that is made he will be like Him. Time, indeed, before and after, has no place in the eternal.

Augustine strives to emphasise the thought of the verse : Ergo visuri sumus quandam visionem...præcellentem omnes pulcritudines terrenas, auri, argenti, nemorum atque camporum, pulcritudinem maris et aeris, pulcritudinem solis et lunæ, pulcritudinem stellarum, pulcritudinem angelorum : omnia superantem quia ex ipsa pulcra sunt omnia. Quid ergo nos erimus quando hæc videbimus ? Quid nobis promissum est ? *Similes ei erimus, quoniam videbimus eum sicuti est.* Quomodo potuit lingua sonuit: cetera corde cogitentur.

Philo in a remarkable passage (*de Abr.* § 12, ii. pp. 9 f. M.) speaks of the vision of the 'Father of all things,' as man's highest blessing : ὅτῳ ἐξεγένετο μὴ μόνον τὰ ἄλλα ὅσα ἐν τῇ φύσει δι' ἐπιστήμης καταλαμβάνειν ἀλλὰ καὶ τὸν πατέρα καὶ ποιητὴν τῶν συμπάντων ὁρᾶν, ἐπ' ἄκρον εὐδαιμονίας ἴστω προεληλυθώς. οὐδὲν γὰρ ἀνωτέρω θεοῦ πρὸς ὃν εἴ τις τὸ τῆς ψυχῆς τείνας ὄμμα ἔφθακε μονὴν εὐχέσθω καὶ στάσιν.

The main elements in the idea of the 'vision' of God seem to be a real knowledge, a direct knowledge, a continuous knowledge, a knowledge which is the foundation of service. The seat of the organ of spiritual sight is the 'heart,' the part of man which is representative of personal character (Eph. i. 18; Matt. v. 8). The 'vision' of God's face appears in the hope of the righteous in the Psalms (Ps. xvii. 15; xi. 7 Hupfeld), while it is recognised as unattainable and unbearable by man in the present earthly life (Ex. xxxiii. 18 ff.). In the new Jerusalem it finds accomplishment, Apoc. xxii. 4, *His servants* (δοῦλοι) *shall do Him service* (λατρεύσουσιν) *and they shall see His face and His name shall be on their foreheads.* As He is light, they shall be made light (comp. Eph. v. 13), and when the sons of God are thus revealed the end of creation will be reached (Rom. viii. 18 ff.).

In treating of this final transfigu-

ἔχων τὴν ἐλπίδα ταύτην ἐπ᾽ αὐτῷ ἁγνίζει ἑαυτὸν καθὼς

ration the Greek Fathers did not scruple to speak of men as being 'deified' (θεοποιεῖσθαι), though the phrase sounds strange to our ears (Athan. *de Inc. Verbi* IV. § 22).

καθώς ἐστιν] *sicuti est* V., *even as He is.* Hitherto the Divine in Christ has been veiled. Hereafter the Godhead will be plain as the Manhood, when, according to Christ's prayer, His disciples shall see His Glory (John xvii. 24). It may be doubted whether it could be said of the Father that men shall see Him 'as He is.' Comp. I Cor. xiii. 12, ἄρτι δι᾽ ἐσόπτρου ἐν αἰνίγματι τότε πρόσωπον πρὸς πρόσωπον. Thomas Aquinas discusses at length (*Sum. Theol. Suppl. Qu.* xcii. art. 1) the question whether the human intellect can attain to seeing God in essence (ad videndum Deum per essentiam), and concludes in the affirmative.

'The last words with which [Dr Arnold] closed his last lecture on the New Testament were in commenting on [this verse]. "So too," he said, " in the Corinthians, *For now we see through a glass darkly, but then face to face.* Yes," he added, with marked fervency, "the mere contemplation of Christ shall transform us into His likeness" ' (*Life* ii, 329 f.).

3. καὶ πᾶς...ἐπ᾽ αὐτῷ] *et omnis qui habet hanc spem in eo* (*ipso* Aug.) V., *And every one that hath this hope on Him.* The practical conclusion from the great Christian hope of the assimilation of the believer to his Lord is given as a coordinate thought (καί). The conclusion itself is involved in the hope. He who looks forward to becoming like God hereafter must strive after His likeness now : Matt. v. 8; Gal. v. 5, ἐλπίδα δικαιοσύνης ἀπεκδεχόμεθα.

By employing the universal form of expression (πᾶς ὁ ἔχων) instead of the simply descriptive (ὁ ἔχων), St John deals with the exceptional presump-

tion of men who regarded themselves as above the common law. In each case where this characteristic form of language occurs there is apparently a reference to some who had questioned the application of a general principle in particular cases (*vv.* 4, 6, 9, 10, 15 ; c. ii. 23, 27 ; iv. 7 ; v. 1, 4, 18 ; 2 John 9).

It is remarkable that this is the only place in which St John speaks of the Christian 'Hope,' a characteristic thought of St Paul and St Peter. St Peter speaks of a 'living hope' as the result of a new birth (1 Pet. i. 3).

ἐπ᾽ αὐτῷ] *on Him*, that is, as before, on God in Christ.

The phrase ἔχειν ἐλπίδα ἐπί τινι is not found elsewhere in the N. T. It is distinguished from ἐλπ. ἔχειν εἰς (Acts xxiv. 15) by the idea of 'hope resting upon' in place of 'reaching unto': and from the simple 'hoping on' (ἐλπίζειν ἐπί Rom. xv. 12 ; 1 Tim. iv. 10) by that of the enjoyment of possession. Comp. i. 3 note (κοινωνίαν ἔχειν).

ἁγνίζει ἑαυτόν] *purifieth himself.* Personal effort is necessarily called out by a definite object of personal devotion. The believer's act is the using what God gives. So Augustine writes: Quis nos castificat nisi Deus ? Sed Deus te nolentem non castificat. Ergo quod adjungis voluntatem tuam Deo castificas teipsum. Castificas te non de te sed de illo qui venit ut habitet in te. Tamen quia agis ibi aliquid voluntate ideo et tibi aliquid tributum est. Comp. James iv. 8; 1 Pet. i. 22; 2 Cor. vii. 1 ; 1 Tim. v. 22.

ἁγνίζει] *sanctificat* V., *castificat* Aug., *purifieth*. The thought probably is derived from the ceremonial purification required before the appearance in the Divine presence. Comp. John xi. 55 (Acts xxi. 24 ff.) ; Ex. xix. 10. The spiritual correlative is marked Heb. x 19 ff.

ἐκεῖνος ἁγνός ἐστιν.

⁴ Πᾶς ὁ ποιῶν τὴν ἁμαρ-

It is not easy to lay down sharply the distinction between ἁγνός, ἁγνίζειν and καθαρός, καθαρίζειν. As far as the usage of the N. T. is concerned, ἁγνός has a personal, an internal, reference which is wanting in καθαρός. Ἁγνός suggests the notion of shrinking from contamination, of a delicate sensibility to pollution of any kind, while καθαρός expresses simply the fact of cleanness. Ἁγνός marks predominantly a feeling, and καθαρός a state. Ἁγνεία comes as the result of an inward effort, καθαρότης by the application of some outward means. He of whom it is said that he ἁγνίζει ἑαυτόν not only keeps himself actually 'pure,' but disciplines and trains himself that he may move more surely among the defilements of the world (1 Tim. v. 22; 1 Pet. iii. 2). Both ἁγνός and καθαρός differ from ἅγιος in that they admit the thought or the fact of temptation or pollution; while ἅγιος describes that which is holy absolutely, either in itself or in idea. God can be spoken of as ἅγιος but not as ἁγνός, while Christ can be spoken of as ἁγνός in virtue of the perfection of His humanity. A man is ἅγιος in virtue of his divine destination (Heb. x. 10) to which he is gradually conformed (ἁγιάζεται, Heb. x. 14); he is ἁγνός in virtue of earthly, human discipline.

καθὼς ἐκ. ἁγνός ἐστιν] *even as He (Christ) is pure.* The pronoun ἐκεῖνος, as throughout the Epistle (ii. 6 note), refers to Christ. It is chosen here, though the preceding αὐτός refers to the same divine-human Person, in order to emphasise the reference to the Lord's human life. It is in respect of this only that He can be spoken of as ἁγνός; and in respect of His true humanity it can be said of Him that "He *is* pure," and not only that "He *was* pure." The result of the perfection of His earthly discipline (Heb. v. 7 ff.) still abides in His

glorified state. For the change of pronouns compare *v.* 5; John v. 39; xix. 35.

2. *The essential character of the children of God* (iii. 4—9).

The character of children of God is seen in relation to sin and righteousness. Sin is in its nature irreconcileable with Christianity (*vv.* 4—6). Sin marks a connexion with the devil as righteousness with Christ (*vv.* 7, 8). Sin is impossible for the child of God (*v.* 9). The underlying thought of the action of false teachers (*v.* 7), who placed salvation in knowledge, is everywhere present.

4—6. The nature of sin is considered in itself as to its manifestation and its essence (*v.* 4); as to Christ both in His Work and in His Person (*v.* 5); and as to man negatively and positively (*v.* 6).

⁴ *Every one that doeth sin doeth also lawlessness; and sin is lawlessness.* ⁵ *And ye know that he was manifested, that he may take away sins; and in him is no sin.* ⁶ *Every one that abideth in him sinneth not; every one that sinneth hath not seen him neither knoweth him.*

4. The transition of thought from *vv.* 1—3 lies in the idea of 'purification.' This effort corresponds with the fulfilment of man's true destiny, which Christ has again made possible. He who commits sin does in fact violate the divine law; and, more than this, sin and violation of the divine law are absolutely identical. The first clause deals with the practical manifestation of sin and the second with the innermost essence of it.

In *vv.* 4, 5 the successive clauses are coordinated by καί...καί...καί. In *vv.* 6—8 clause follows clause without any conjunction.

4. Πᾶς ὁ ποιῶν...] *Every one that...*

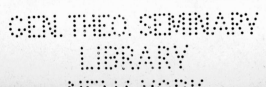

τίαν καὶ τὴν ἀνομίαν ποιεῖ, καὶ ἡ ἁμαρτία ἐστὶν ἡ

Comp. *v.* 3 note. The constant repetition of this form in this group of verses is very impressive.

ὁ ποιῶν τὴν ἁμ.] *qui facit peccatum (delictum* Tert.) V., *that doeth sin.* The phrase is distinguished from the simple term 'that sinneth' (ὁ ἁμαρτάνων *v.* 6) by adding the conception of the actual realisation of sin as something which is definitely brought about. This conception is emphasised by the addition of the article (τὴν ἁμαρτίαν). The man does not simply commit a sin (πᾶς ὁ ἁμαρτίαν ποιῶν comp. *v.* 9; 1 Pet. ii. 22; 2 Cor. xi. 7), but realises sin in its completeness.

Compare *vv.* 8, 9, John viii. 34 (τὴν ἁμ.); and contrast James v. 15 κἂν ἁμαρτίας ᾖ πεποιηκώς. . . . .

The corresponding phrase is ὁ ποιῶν τὴν δικαιοσύνην *v.* 7 (10), ii. 29. Sin as a whole (ἡ ἁμαρτία) answers to righteousness as a whole (ἡ δικαιοσύνη). For ἡ ἁμαρτία compare Rom. v. 12 (ἁμαρτία *v.* 13), 20; vi. 1 ff.

καὶ τὴν ἀνομ. ποιεῖ] *et iniquitatem facit* V., *doeth also lawlessness,* violates a law which claims his loyal obedience (comp. Matt. xiii. 41 ; vii. 23 οἱ ἐργαζόμενοι τὴν ἀνομ.). And, yet more than this,

ἡ ἁμαρτία ἐστὶν ἡ ἀνομία, *peccatum est iniquitas* V., *sin is lawlessness.* Sin and lawlessness are convertible terms. Sin is not an arbitrary conception. It is the assertion of the selfish will against a paramount authority. He who sins breaks not only by accident or in an isolated detail, but essentially the 'law' which he was created to fulfil.

This 'law' which expresses the divine ideal of man's constitution and growth has three chief applications. There is the 'law' of each man's personal being: there is the 'law' of his relation to things without him : there is the 'law' of his relation to God. To violate any part of this threefold law is to sin, for all parts are divine. (James ii. 10).

The Mosaic Law was directed in a representative fashion to each of these spheres of duty. It touched upon man's dealing with himself : upon his treatment of creation (of men, animals and crops) : upon his duty towards God. In this way it was fitted to bring home to men the divine side of all action.

The origin of sin in selfishness is vividly illustrated by St James (i. 14 f.), who shews also that the neglect of duty, the violation of the law of growth, is sin (James iv. 17). So St John lays down that 'unrighteousness,' the failure to fulfil our obligations to others, is sin (c. v. 17).

Other examples of the use of the article with both subject and predicate, when the two are convertible, occur : Apoc. xix. 10 ἡ μαρτυρία Ἰησοῦ ἐστὶν τὸ πνεῦμα τῆς προφητείας ; Matt. vi. 22 ; 1 Cor. x. 4 ; xv. 56 ; Phil. iii. 19 ; comp. John i. 4 ; xv. 1 ; 2 Cor. iii. 17. The variations in Matt. xiii. 38 f. are instructive (ὁ ἀγρός ἐστιν ὁ κόσμος... ὁ θερισμὸς συντέλεια αἰῶνος).

It is interesting to notice that Bede observes the inadequacy of the Latin rendering : Virtus hujus sententiæ, he says, facilius in lingua Græcorum, qua edita est epistola, comprehenditur, siquidem apud eos *iniquitas ἀνομία* vocatur... Omnes enim qui peccant prævaricationis (Ps. cxix. 119 Lat.) rei sunt, hoc est non solum illi qui datam sibi scriptæ legis scientiam contemnunt, sed et illi qui innocentiam legis naturalis quam in protoplasto omnes accepinus sive infirmitate sive negligentia sive etiam ignorantia corrumpunt.

For the change of order in the two clauses see v. 2 note.

5. Not only is sin a violation of the law of man's being: it sets at

ἀνομία. ⁵ καὶ οἴδατε ὅτι ἐκεῖνος ἐφανερώθη ἵνα τὰς
ἁμαρτίας ἄρῃ, καὶ ἁμαρτία ἐν αὐτῷ οὐκ ἔστιν. ⁶ πᾶς

5 οἴδατε: οἴδαμεν ℵ the (lat).   τὰς ἁμ. AB vg me syrhl: +ἡμῶν ⌜ℵC the (lat).
ἐν αὐ. οὐκ ἔ.: οὐκ ἔ. ἐν αὐ. ℵ me the   6 πᾶς ὁ ἁμ.: +καί vg syrvg.

naught Christ's mission. His work
was to take away sins : He Himself
was sinless. Thus the most elementary
knowledge shews that sin is utterly
alien from the faith.

οἴδατε] scitis V., ye know. This
appeal to the knowledge of Christians
is characteristic of St John, though it
is found also in St Paul : c. ii. 20 f.,
iv. 2, 14 f., v. 15, 18 f. note ; 3 John 12.

ἐκεῖνος ἐφαν.] ille apparuit V.,
manifestatus est Aug., He was manifested. The subject is not defined
under any particular aspect (Lamb of
God John i. 29, Son of God v. 8), but
left in its fulness. For ἐκεῖνος see c.
ii. 6 note. It will be observed that in
this verse ἐκεῖνος and αὐτός are naturally referred to the same subject.
Comp. John xix. 35.

ἐφανερώθη] was manifested. Comp.
i. 2 ; ii. 28 notes. The 'manifestation'
of the Lord includes the whole of His
historical Life with its consequences :
His Birth, and Growth, and Ministry,
and Passion, and Resurrection, and
Ascension. Each part of the Revelation contributed in some way to the
removal of sins. The Redemption
and Atonement were wrought out by
His living as well as by His dying.
Compare Matt. viii. 17.

The idea of 'manifestation' in this
connexion involves a previous being.
Thus the term includes not only ὁ ἦν
ἀπ' ἀρχῆς but also ἦν ἐν ἀρχῇ.

For the different phrases used by
St John to describe the Incarnation
see Additional Note.

ἵνα...ἄρῃ] ut peccatum (-ta Tert.) au-
ferat Aug., ut peccata nostra tolleret
V., that He may take away sins, not
simply do away with the punishment
of them. Comp. i. 9 note.

Tollit autem et dimittendo quæ

facta sunt et adjuvando ne fiant et
perducendo ad vitam ubi fieri omnino
non possint (Bede).

For the sense of αἴρειν compare John
i. 29 note ; and Heb. x. 4 (ἀφαίρειν
ἁμ.) ; id. 11 (περιελεῖν ἁμ.) notes. The
dominant thought here is not that of
the self-sacrifice of Christ, but of His
utter hostility to sin in every shape.
He came to remove all sins even as
He was Himself sinless. It is true
that Christ 'took away' sins by
'taking them upon Him,' by 'bearing
them,' but the simple sense of 'bearing' appears to be foreign to the
context here, though it has found
strong support in the parallel passage
in the Gospel.

The use of the plural 'sins' (τὰς ἁμ.)
distinguishes the exact conception of
Christ's work here from that given in
John i. 29 ('the sin of the world').
The idea is that of the manifold personal realisations of the sin of humanity
which Christ takes away. The phrase
stands without further definition (sins
not our sins) in order to include the fulness of the truth expressed in c. ii. 2.

For the plural used absolutely see
Rom. vii. 5; Col. i. 14; Heb. i. 3 ;
(James v. 16; 1 Pet. ii. 24). [The
common reading in Eph. ii. 1 is
wrong.]

ἁμαρτία ἐν αὐτῷ οὐκ ἔστιν] The clause
is independent and can be connected with ὅτι. Fo: the statement
and the form of expression compare
John vii. 18 ἀδικία ἐν αὐτῷ οὐκ ἔστιν.
This fact at once explains how Christ
could take away sin, and how sin is incompatible with fellowship with Him.
The tense (is not was) marks the
eternal character of the Redeemer.
All that belongs to His 'perfected'
manhood (Heb. ii. 10, v. 9) 'is' in Him

ὁ ἐν αὐτῷ μένων οὐχ ἁμαρτάνει· πᾶς ὁ ἁμαρτάνων οὐχ

no less than His unchanged Divinity. The 'purity' of *v.* 3 is traced back to its inherent source.

The emphasis is thrown upon 'sin,' so that the literal rendering would be: 'sin in Him there is not.'

6. This verse flows directly from the last clause of *v.* 5. True fellowship with Christ, Who is absolutely sinless, is necessarily inconsistent with sin; and, yet further, the practice of sin excludes the reality of a professed knowledge of Christ. 'No one that abideth in Him sinneth.'

μένων] St John speaks of 'abiding' in Christ and not simply of 'being' in Christ, because his argument rests on the efficacy of continuous human effort. Comp. ii. 5 note.

οὐχ ἁμαρτάνει] *sinneth not*. The commentary on this phrase is found in c. i. 6. It describes a character, 'a prevailing habit' and not primarily an act. Comp. Tit. iii. 11 ; Hebr. x. 26. Each separate sinful act does as such interrupt the fellowship, and yet so far as it is foreign to the character of the man, and removed from him (ii. 1), it leaves his character unchanged. This is the truth which Augustine partially expresses when he says that the sin spoken of is the violation of love; for love may be taken fairly to express the essence of the Christian character. Comp. c. v. 18 note.

Compare John xiii. 10.

Bede describes the fact as it is practically embodied when he says: in quantum in eo manet in tantum non peccat ; but he leaves out of sight the internal spiritual character.

πᾶς ὁ ἁμ....οὐδὲ ἔγνωκεν αὐτόν] The interruption of the formal parallelism is characteristic of St John. Instead of saying 'every one that sinneth abideth not in (is cut off from) Him,' he substitutes a predicative clause which carries back the mind of the reader to an earlier stage of the fatal failure, as if he would say: 'In such a case there is no question of 'abiding.' The conditions of fellowship have never been satisfied. Such a one hath not seen Christ (God in Christ) nor yet come to know Him.'

Compare i. 6 f. ('fellowship with Him,' 'fellowship one with another') ; i. 8, 9, ii. 4 f. ('the truth is not in us,' 'the love of God is perfected'); *vv.* 7, 8 ; iv. 5, 6 a ; 7 b, 8 ; v. 10. In ii. 23 there is a perfect correspondence.

οὐχ ἑώρ....αὐτόν] *non vidit eum nec cognovit eum* V., *hath not seen... neither knoweth*. The first word describes the immediate and direct vision of Christ; and the second the personal and detailed appropriation of the truth so presented to the eyes. 'Seeing' expresses briefly the fullest exertion of our utmost faculties of gaining new elements of truth from without : 'knowing' (ἐγνωκέναι), the apprehension and coordination of the truth within. 'Knowing' is less direct and immediate and therefore forms the climax here.

ἑώρακεν] Comp. c. iv. 20 ; 3 John 11 ; John i. 18, v. 37, vi. 46, xiv. 7, 9 (Heb. xi. 27).

The use of the word here in connexion with Christ seems to point to some teachers who appealed to their personal sight of the Lord (comp. i. 1 ff.; John xix. 35, xx. 29) as giving authority to their false doctrine. Of such in spite of outward intercourse it could be said that 'they had not seen Christ' (comp. 2 Cor. v. 16).

οὐδὲ ἔγνωκεν] 'neither hath come to know,' i.e. *neither knoweth*. The point regarded is present and not past. Comp. ii. 3 note.

The statement leaves on one side the question of the indefectibility of grace. It deals with the actual state of the man. Past sight and past knowledge cease to be unless they go forward.

ἑώρακεν αὐτὸν οὐδὲ ἔγνωκεν αὐτόν. 7 Τεκνία, μηδεὶς πλανάτω ὑμᾶς· ὁ ποιῶν τὴν δικαιοσύνην δίκαιός ἐστιν,

7 τεκνία אB vg syrr; παιδία AC me syrhlmg.   μή τις A.   – τὴν΄ δικ. א*.

Luther expressed the truth when he said 'He who is a Christian is no Christian.'

7, 8. From considering the nature of sin St John passes on to consider the personal spiritual source with which it is connected as righteousness is connected with Christ. Sin is the sign of dependence on the devil whose works Christ came to abolish.

7 *Little children, let no one lead you astray: he that doeth righteousness is righteous, even as he is righteous:* 8 *he that doeth sin is of the devil, because the devil sinneth from the beginning. Unto this end the Son of God was manifested that he may destroy the works of the devil.*

7. Τεκνία] *Filioli* V., *Little children.* See ii. 12 note. The tenderness of the address is called out by the peril of the situation.

μηδεὶς πλανάτω] *nemo vos seducat* V., *let no one,* even with the most plausible signs of authority (ii. 26), *lead you astray.* The question is one of action not of opinion. Comp. i. 8 note.

ὁ ποιῶν τὴν δικ.] *he that doeth righteousness,* he who gives effect to it in life, who realises it in conduct (c. ii. 29). Compare '*doeth sin*' (*v.* 4 note), '*doeth the truth*' (c. i. 6 note). 'To do righteousness' is more than 'to do righteous acts' (ποιεῖν δίκαια, comp. 1 Pet. iii. 12 ποιεῖν κακά, James iv. 17 καλὸν π.), or even than 'to do the acts of righteousness' (ποιεῖν τὰ δίκαια, comp. *v.* 22 π. τὰ ἀρεστά, Rom. iii. 8 π. τὰ κακά); and it differs from 'doing that which is righteous' (π. τὸ δίκαιον, comp. Rom. xiii. 3 f. π. τὸ ἀγαθόν, τὸ κακόν) by presenting the idea in a less abstract form. Compare Col. iv. 1 (τὸ δίκαιον, τὴν ἰσότητα) ; iii. 5 (ἀκαθαρσίαν, τὴν πλεονεξίαν).

The exact phrase is different in form from the negative phrase (*v.* 10 note). 'Righteousness' here is the virtue in its completeness and unity (τὴν δικαιοσύνην): in *v.* 10 δικαιοσύνη expresses any particular manifestation of righteousness. Comp. ii. 29; Matt. v. 5.

δίκαιός ἐστιν] Righteousness is the sign of divine sonship (c. ii. 29). The 'doing righteousness' reveals the character and does not create it. The man who is righteous is recognised by his actions. The personal character underlies the deeds. The form of the sentence may be compared with John iii. 31 *he that is of the earth is of the earth and speaketh of the earth.*

καθώς] *sicut* V., *even as.* Christ (ἐκεῖνος c. ii. 6 note) is the One Type of righteousness. The Christian's righteousness, like that of his Master, must extend to the fulness of life. Comp. *v.* 3; ii. 6; iv. 17; John xiii. 15; xv. 12; xvii. 14.

Augustine (whom Bede transcribes) remarks on this comparison between the righteousness of the believer and the righteousness of Christ (see *v.* 2): Videtis quia non semper *sicut* ad parilitatem et æqualitatem refertur... Habemus et nos imaginem Dei, sed non illam quam habet Filius æqualis Patri.

δίκαιός ἐστιν] ii. 29; iv. 17; *v.* 3 notes. Christ gave the complete example of the fulfilment of all man's offices. In Him righteousness was and is the expression of love.

8. The opposite to *v.* 7 is expressed with characteristic variations in the parallelism:

(a) ὁ π. τὴν δικ. ‖ ὁ ποιῶν τὴν ἁμ.

(b) δίκαιός ἐστιν ‖ ἐκ τοῦ διαβ. ἐστίν.

(c) καθὼς ἐ. δ. ἐ.‖ ὅτι...ὁ διάβ. ἁμ.

The spiritual affinity (b) is in the

καθὼς ἐκεῖνος δίκαιός ἐστιν· ⁸ὁ ποιῶν τὴν ἁμαρτίαν ἐκ
τοῦ διαβόλου ἐστίν, ὅτι ἀπ' ἀρχῆς ὁ διάβολος ἁμαρτάνει. εἰς τοῦτο ἐφανερώθη ὁ υἱὸς τοῦ θεοῦ ἵνα λύσῃ

8 ὁ ποιῶν: ὁ δὲ π. A me (lat).

one case described by the personal
character, in the other, directly; while
man's character is shewn to be in each
case though under different relations
(καθώς, ὅτι), a reflection of his spiritual master (c).

ὁ π. τὴν ἁμ.] v. 4 note.

ἐκ τοῦ διαβ. ἐστίν] ex (de, a, all.)
diabolo est V., is of the devil, draws
from him the ruling principles of his
life, as his child. Comp. ii. 16 note;
and Additional Note on v. 1. The
phrase finds a parallel in was of the
evil one, v. 12; and John viii. 44 ye
are of your father, the devil. Compare 'to be of the things below' John
viii. 23; to be of the world xvii. 16, &c.,
c. ii. 16. Additional Note on v. 10.

It will be noticed that as St Paul
traces back sin to the act of the typical representative of mankind, Adam
(Rom. v. 14; 1 Cor. xv. 22), so St
John traces it back yet further to a
spiritual origin.

Augustine remarks that the devil
is not treated in Scripture as the
author of any being : Neminem fecit
diabolus, neminem genuit, neminem
creavit. Sed quicunque fuerit imi-
tatus diabolum quasi de illo natus
sit filius diaboli imitando non proprie
nascendo. In this connexion it is remarkable that Origen, while he distinctly notices that in relation to the
devil St John says ἐστίν ἐκ and not
γεγέννηται ἐκ (γεγεννημένος ἐστὶν ἐκ) (in
Joh. xx. § 13, iv. 325), elsewhere gives
ἐκ τοῦ διαβόλου γεγέννηται (γεγέννηται)
(Hom. ix. in Jer. § 4, iii. 181; Sch. in
Jer. xii. 10, iii. 290; Hom. vi. in
Ezech. § 3, iii. 377, Lat.) in quoting
the verse freely.

For St John's teaching on the powers
of evil see Additional Note on ii. 13.

ὅτι...ἁμαρτάνει] because...the begin-

ning. The force of the argument lies in
the recognition of the state of things
at the first dawn of human history.
From the very beginning we see a
power in action hostile to God. Between these two, as between light and
darkness, there can be no middle
term. He who does not belong to
the one belongs to the other. Character reveals the choice. The position of ἀπ' ἀρχῆς at the head of
the clause emphasises the thought.
Contrast i. 1; ii. 7; iii. 11; and compare ii. 24 note.

ἀπ' ἀρχῆς] ab initio V., a primor-
dio Tert., from the beginning. Comp.
i. 1; ii. 7 notes. Sin exists before
man.

ἁμαρτάνει] sinneth. See v. 6 note.
His sinful action is continuous and
present : subjunxit verbum praesentis
temporis quia ex quo ab initio coepit
diabolus peccare nunquam desiit
(Bede).

εἰς τοῦτο] in hoc V. (ideo, idcirco
all.), unto this end, which has been
included in the preceding clauses and
is defined by what follows.

ἐφανερώθη] See v. 5 note.

ὁ υἱὸς τοῦ θεοῦ] the Son of God.
The title of dignity is now expressed
for the first time in the Epistle to
bring out the nature of the conflict (c.
iv. 4). Hitherto the Christ has been
spoken of under the title 'the Son'
(ii. 22, 23, 24), or more fully 'His (i.e.
the Father's) Son' (i. 3). Hencefor-
ward 'the Son of God' is His most
common name (iv. 15; v. 5, 9 ff., 20).
The spiritual adversary of man has
a mightier spiritual antagonist. A
second Adam answers to the first
Adam: the Son of God to the devil.

λύσῃ] dissolvat V., solvat Aug.,
destroy. 'The works of the devil' are

τὰ ἔργα τοῦ διαβόλου. ⁹ πᾶς ὁ γεγεννημένος ἐκ τοῦ
θεοῦ ἁμαρτίαν οὐ ποιεῖ, ὅτι σπέρμα αὐτοῦ ἐν αὐτῷ

represented as having a certain con-sistency, and coherence. They shew a kind of solid front. But Christ by His coming has revealed them in their complete unsubstantiality. He has 'undone' the seeming bonds by which they were held together.

The word λύειν occurs literally in this sense Acts xxvii. 41. Comp. Eph. ii. 14; John ii. 19, and 2 Pet. iii. 10—12; and Acts v. 38; Gal. ii. 18; Rom. xiv. 20 &c. (καταλύειν).

The transition to the figurative sense is seen in Acts xiii. 43 (λυθείσης τῆς συναγωγῆς), ii. 24. Comp. Ign. *Eph.* 13 καθαιροῦνται αἱ δυνάμεις τοῦ Σατανᾶ καὶ λύεται ὁ ὄλεθρος αὐτοῦ ἐν τῇ ὁμονοίᾳ ὑμῶν τῆς πίστεως.

The two objects of the 'manifesta-tion' of Christ (*vv.* 5, 8) cover the whole work of redemption, 'to take away sins,' 'to destroy the works of the devil.'

In this connexion 'the works of the devil' are gathered up in 'sin' which is their spring. This the devil has wrought in men and in the world, and men make his works their own. Comp. John viii. 41. These works under different aspects are spoken of as 'works of darkness' (Rom. xiii. 12; Eph. v. 11), and 'of the flesh' (Gal. v. 19). They stand opposed to 'the works of God' (John ix. 3) and 'the works of the Christ' (Matt. xi. 2). Au-gustine brings the thought of 'de-stroying the works of the devil' into connexion with man's natural and spi-ritual births: Si cum nullo peccato nascimur, quid est quod cum infanti-bus ad baptismum curritur ut absol-vantur? Ergo duas nativitates at-tendite fratres, Adam et Christi... Nativitas illa trahit secum peccatum, nativitas ista liberat a peccato.

9. The antagonism of the Christian to sin is now placed in its last and de-cisive aspect. Two things are affirm-ed of him : 'he doeth no sin' and 'he cannot sin.' The first fact follows from the permanence of the vital power by which he is animated. The second from the nature of that power, that it is of God. In the second case the ἐκ τοῦ θεοῦ is placed emphatically first; "he cannot sin, because it is of God, and of no other, that he hath been born."

⁹ *Every one that is begotten of God doeth no sin, because his seed abideth in him; and he cannot sin because he is begotten of God.*

ὁ γεγεννημένος ἐκ τοῦ θεοῦ] qui natus est ex Deo V., *that is begotten of God.* Comp. ii. 29. The phrase occurs here first in the epistle in its full form. Comp. iv. 7, v. 1 (4), 18. John i. 13. (iii. 3, 5 ff.). The exact form is important. The perfect (ὁ γεγεννημένος) marks not only the single act (*aor.* ἐγεννήθησαν John i. 13; c. v. 18) but the continuous presence of its efficacy. 'He that hath been born and still remains a child of God.' See Additional Note on *v.* 1.

ἁμαρτίαν οὐ ποιεῖ] Compare *v.* 4 note. A fine phrase of Athenagoras will serve as a comment on this view of the Christian life: οἷς ὁ βίος ὡς πρὸς στάθμην τὸν θεὸν κανονίζεται ('Christians for whom the conception of God is the ideal standard of life') ...ὥστε τούτους, μηδ᾽ εἰς ἔννοιάν ποτε τοῦ βραχυτάτου ἐλευσομένους ἁμαρτήματος (*Leg. pro Christ.* c. 31).

σπέρμα αὐτοῦ] semen ipsius V., *his seed,* the principle of life which He has given continues to be the ruling principle of the believer's growth. God gives, as it were, of Himself to the Christian. He does not only work upon him and leave him. The germ of the new life is that out of which the mature man will in due time be developed. Comp. John i. 13.

μένει, καὶ οὐ δύναται ἁμαρτάνειν, ὅτι ἐκ τοῦ θεοῦ
γεγέννηται.   ¹⁰ Ἐν τούτῳ φανερά ἐστιν τὰ τέκνα
τοῦ θεοῦ καὶ τὰ τέκνα τοῦ διαβόλου· πᾶς ὁ μὴ ποιῶν

The instrument by which this vital element is conveyed is the 'word': James i. 18; 1 Pet. i. 23; Luke viii. 12, 15.

The absence of the article (σπέρμα not τὸ σπέρμα) directs attention to the character of the divine principle and not to the divine principle communicated in the particular case. See *v.* 10 note.

οὐ δύναται ἁμ.] *he cannot sin.* The ideas of divine sonship and sin are mutually exclusive. As long as the relationship with God is real (ὅτι ἐκ θεοῦ γεγένν.) sinful acts are but accidents. They do not touch the essence of the man's being. The impossibility of sinning in such a case lies in the moral nature of things. Comp. John v. 19, 30, xii. 39, xiv. 17, &c.

Augustine again insists that the reference is to the great commandment of love : Est quoddam peccatum quod non potest admittere ille qui natus est ex Deo, et quo non admisso solvuntur cetera, quo admisso confirmantur cetera. Quod est hoc peccatum? Facere contra mandatum Christi, contra testamentum novum (John xiii. 34). The explanation is true so far as love is the determining element in the Christian character.

3. *The outward manifestation of the children of God* (10—12).

The spiritual affinities of men are shewn by two patent signs, righteousness and love (*v.* 10); and these signs correspond to two archetypal patterns, the Gospel, that is, the Life of Christ (*v.* 11), and the history of Cain (*v.* 12).

¹⁰ *In this the children of God are manifest and the children of the devil: every one that doeth not*

righteousness is not of God, and he that loveth not his brother. ¹¹ *Because this is the message which ye heard from the beginning that we should love one another:* ¹² *not as Cain was of the wicked one and slew his brother; and wherefore slew he him? because his own works were evil and his brother's righteous.*

10. Life reveals the children of God. They bear characteristic marks which stamp their action and their feeling, their conduct and the motive of their conduct. They embody righteousness in deed. They acknowledge the ties which Christ has established among Christians and so potentially among men. They practically realise the law of man's original constitution, and the law of man's redemption.

Ἐν τούτῳ] *In hoc* V. (*Ex hoc* F.), *In this*, in this fact of the essential sinlessness of the Christian's life, which is followed out into its main aspects in the verse which follows (comp. *c.* ii. 3 note).

τὰ τέκνα τοῦ θεοῦ] *filii Dei* V., *the children of God.* See *v.* 1 note.

St John divides the world sharply into two classes. Looking at the spiritual characteristics of life he admits no intermediate class. For him there is only light and darkness, and no twilight. He sees only 'life' and 'death.'

φανερά] *manifesti* V., *manifestati* Aug., *manifest*, so that all men may see what they are: Matt. xii. 16; Acts vii. 13; 1 Cor. xi. 19. That which is in its essence secret is thus revealed before the eyes of men. Comp. Mark iv. 22; 2 Cor. v. 10 f.

τὰ τέκνα τοῦ διαβόλου] *filii diaboli* V., *the children of the devil.* The phrase is unique. Compare Eph. ii. 3 τέκνα φύσει ὀργῆς. 2 Pet. ii. 14 κατάρας τέκνα. And also: Matt. xiii. 38

δικαιοσύνην οὐκ ἔστιν ἐκ τοῦ θεοῦ, καὶ ὁ μὴ ἀγαπῶν
τὸν ἀδελφὸν αὐτοῦ. ¹¹ ὅτι αὕτη ἐστὶν ἡ ἀγγελία ἣν

10 ὁ μὴ ποιῶν δικ. אABC me syrr (lat): ὁ μὴ ὢν δίκαιος vg the syrhlmg.
δικαιοσύνην אB : τὴν δικ. AC.   Comp. v. 7.   11 ἀγγελία AB vg : ἐπαγγελία אC me
the syrr (lat).   Comp. i. 5.

οἱ υἱοὶ τοῦ πονηροῦ ; xxiii. 15 υἱὸς γεέν-
νης ; Acts xiii. 10 υἱὲ διαβόλου.
πᾶς ὁ μὴ π. δ.] *Every one*... Compare *v.* 3 note. By expressing the
characterisation of Divine sonship in
a negative form, St John enforces the
necessary universality of the condition which he lays down, and gives a
pointed warning against those who
trusted in the Christian name. It is
not only true that every one that
doeth righteousness 'hath been born
of God' (ii. 29) and 'is of God' (3 John
11) and shares the character of Christ
(*v.* 7), but it is true also that to do
righteousness is a necessity for him
who is of God. A Christian must be
active and not passive only. To fail
either in deed or in word (c. iv. 3 ὁ μὴ
ὁμολογεῖ) is fatal to the reality of the
divine connexion.

ὁ μὴ ποιῶν δικ.] *qui non est justus*
V. (*qui non facit justitiam* F.), *that
doeth not righteousness.* It has been
already noticed (*v.* 7 note) that the
phrase used here is different from
that used in *v.* 7, ii. 29. Here 'righteousness' (δικαιοσύνη) expresses that
which bears a particular character: in
the former passage 'righteousness'
(ἡ δικαιοσύνη) expresses the idea
realised in its completeness. The
same general distinction is to be
observed in the use of other like
words in the Epistle: ἁμαρτία *vv.*
5, 9, v. 16 f.; ἡ ἁμαρτία *vv.* 4, 8;
ἀγάπη iv. 8, 16 ; ἡ ἀγάπη (ii. 5, 15),
iii. 16, iv. 7, 10, 12, 16 ff. (v. 3); ζωή
v. 15. v. 11, 13, 16, 20 ; ἡ ζωή i. 2, ii.
25, iii. 14, v. 12 ; ἀλήθεια 3 John 3 ;
ἡ ἀλήθεια i. 6, 8, ii. 4, 21, iii. 19, iv. 6,
v. 6 ; 2 John 1, 2 ; 3 John 8.
The full force of the article will also
be felt in the following places : i. 6 ἐν

τῷ σκότει, ii. 9 ἐν τῷ φωτί, iii. 4 ἡ
ἀνομία, iv. 18 τῇ γλώσσῃ, v. 10 τὴν
μαρτυρίαν (v. 21 τῶν εἰδώλων). On the
other hand the absence of the article
in the following places is significant:
in ii. 18 ἐσχάτη ὥρα, v. 9 σπέρμα.
From the nature of the case anarthrous forms occur in predicates and
negative sentences : yet see iii. 4, v. 6.
οὐκ ἔ. ἐ. τ. θ.] Comp. iv. 3 note ;
Additional Note on *v.* 1.
καὶ ὁ μὴ ἀγ. τ. ἀδ.] *and he that loveth
not his brother.* Comp. ii. 10 note.
This clause is not a mere explanation
of that which precedes but the expression of it in its highest Christian
form. Righteousness involves the fulfilment of all law, of relations to God
and to man, both personally and
socially. The love of Christian for
Christian, resting on the sense of a
divine fellowship (c. i. 3) carries forward to its loftiest embodiment the
righteousness which man can reach.
Augustine says in striking words
which were adopted by Bede : Quidquid vis habe ; hoc solum [caritatem]
non habeas : nihil tibi prodest. Alia
si non habeas hoc habe, et implesti
legem.

11, 12. The revelation of character
is traced back to the type given in
the portraiture of the first fulfilment
of man's ideal in the Gospel, and of
the first sin after the Fall.

11. ὅτι...] *Because...* The whole
aim of the Gospel is the creation and
strengthening of love. To this Christ's
life of sacrifice pointed from first to
last. The record of His life is the
message of the Gospel.

ἡ ἀγγελία] *adnuntiatio* V., *mandatum* F., *repromissio* (ἐπαγγελία) Lucf.,
the message. Comp. i. 5 note.

ἠκούσατε ἀπ᾽ ἀρχῆς, ἵνα ἀγαπῶμεν ἀλλήλους· ¹²οὐ καθὼς Καὶν ἐκ τοῦ πονηροῦ ἦν καὶ ἔσφαξεν τὸν ἀδελφὸν
αὐτοῦ· καὶ χάριν τίνος ἔσφαξεν αὐτόν; ὅτι τὰ ἔργα
αὐτοῦ πονηρὰ ἦν, τὰ δὲ τοῦ ἀδελφοῦ αὐτοῦ δίκαια.

ἀπ᾽ ἀρχῆς] *from the beginning.* See
ii. 7 note. The first tidings of Christianity contain this lesson.

ἵνα ἀγαπῶμεν ἀλλ.] *ut diligatis alterutrum* V., *diligamus invicem* Aug.,
that we love one another... The
words do not simply give the contents of the message, but its aim, its
purpose. The fundamental declaration of Christ's Life and Work is
directed to this end, that men should
be moved by it to self-sacrifice. For
this use of ἵνα see *v.* 23; iv. 21;
John xiii. 34; xv. 12, 17. The particle not unfrequently expresses an
effort or an aim suggested by the
words which precede: c. v. 3; iv.
17; 2 John 6; John iv. 34; vi. 29;
viii. 56; xv. 13; xvii. 3. Sometimes
it indicates a divine purpose which is
not at once obvious: *v.* 1; i. 9; John
xii. 23; xvi. 2, 32.

The phrase '*to love one another*'
(*v.* 23 note) differs in shade of meaning from 'loving the brethren' (*v.* 14).
'Loving one another' expresses the
full social energy of the Christian
life: 'loving the brethren' points to
the personal feeling of one towards
the body.

12. οὐ καθώς...] *not as*... The construction is irregular and elliptical.
Comp. John vi. 58. The clause without the negative would have run on
naturally with *v.* 10 ...'that loveth
not his brother, even as Cain was of
the evil one and slew his brother.'
Cain shewed his dependence on the
devil by want of love and hatred
of righteousness. But the insertion
of *v.* 11, the positive rule of Christians, leads to the insertion of the
negative before the typical example
of the opposite character. 'We do
not (or We shall not) present the

type of selfishness, even as Cain was
of the evil one...' 'The case is not
with us as it was with Cain; he
was of the evil one...' The use of
the direct negative οὐ requires that
the sentence should be treated as
independent and not connected with
ἵνα (μηδὲ ὦμεν ἐκ τοῦ πονηροῦ καθὼς
Καίν...).

The history of the first death naturally attracted wide attention as
presenting in a representative and impressive form the issues of selfishness,
self-will, sin. Comp. Jude 11; Heb.
xi. 4; xii. 24. Philo discusses the
history in a special book. In Clem.
Hom. iii. 25 it is said of Cain: φονεὺς
ἦν καὶ ψεύστης καὶ μετὰ ἁμαρτίων ἡσυ-
χάζειν μηδὲ ἐπὶ τῷ ἄρχειν θέλων.

ἐκ τοῦ πονηροῦ ἦν] *ex maligno erat*
V., *was of the evil one.* Comp. *v.* 8 ἐκ
τοῦ διαβόλου ἐστίν note; ii. 13 τὸν
πονηρόν note. The name is chosen
here in order to connect the works of
Cain (πονηρὰ ἦν) with their spiritual
source.

ἔσφαξεν] *occidit* V., *slew.* The word
occurs elsewhere in the N.T. only in the
Apocalypse. It expresses properly the
slaughter of a victim. Here it seems
to point to the deliberate determination of the murder.

καὶ χάριν τίνος...] *et propter quid*
V., *and wherefore*... This unusual
mode of expression (comp. *v.* 17),
appears to be adopted in order to bring
out sharply that the murder of a
brother came from hatred of righteousness. Cain lost practical sympathy
with his brother; and so in the end
he slew him.

This use of χάριν occurs in this
place only in the writings of St John.
Elsewhere in the N. T. it stands (as
generally) after its case. It expresses

¹³ Μὴ θαυμάζετε, ἀδελφοί, εἰ μισεῖ ὑμᾶς ὁ κόσμος.

13 μὴ θαυμ. ABCᶜᵒʳʳ vg me the syrhl: +καὶ' μὴ θαυμ. אC* syrvg.   ἀδελφοί
אABC vg: +μου ᧕ me the syrr.

commonly an object aimed at (Eph.
iii. 1, 14; 1 Tim. v. 14; Gal. iii. 19,
Lgtft. &c.), but also an antecedent
ground (Luke vii. 47).

ὅτι...] *because*... The explanation
given is an interpretation of the history in Gen. iv. The sacrifices (Heb.
xi. 4) answered to the characters of
the brothers, and God's judgment
upon them gave occasion for the open
revelation of character which followed.

Augustine traces the temptation of
Cain to envy: Qui invidet non amat.
Peccatum diaboli est in illo... Cecidit
enim et invidit stanti. Non ideo voluit dejicere ut ipse staret sed ne
solus caderet.

III. Brotherhood in Christ and the Hatred of the World (iii. 13—24).

There appear to be three main divisions of the section:

1. *Hatred and love* (13—15).
2. *The manifestation of love* (16 —18).
3. *The fruit of love* (19—24).

St John starts from the thought of
hatred as the characteristic of the
world. Over against this is love, the
necessary sign of the presence of the
new life of Christians. This love must
be moulded on the pattern of Christ's
sacrifice, and extend to the fulness of
life. And the fruit of love is confidence,
which issues in perfect sympathy.

i. *Hatred and love* (13—15).

The thought of Cain leads to the
consideration of the Cain-like character. Hatred is the mark of the world,
which is 'dead' (13). Love among
Christians is the sign of a new life
(14). And consequently hatred among
Christians is the sign not only of the
absence of life but of the destruction
of life (15).

¹³ *Marvel not, brethren, if the world
hateth you.* ¹⁴ *We know that we have
passed out of death into life, because
we love the brethren: he that loveth
not abideth in death.* ¹⁵ *Every one that
hateth his brother is a murderer;
and ye know that no murderer hath
eternal life abiding in him.*

13. Love has been presented as
the necessary mark of the Christian.
Still it is met by hatred. This however cannot but be so. Love is the
sign of a change from death to life.
They who remain in death must shew
their real nature (hatred) towards the
living. Terrible as Cain's history is,
it is still realised in essence.

Μὴ θαυμάζετε] *Nolite mirari* V.,
Marvel not. For the thought compare John xv. 18 ff., xvi. 1 ff.

The words occur again John v. 28,
and in another form John iii. 7 μὴ
θαυμάσῃς. The latter place is the only
example in the Gospel or Epistles
(John xix. 24 is not strictly parallel)
of the imperative construction of μή
with aor. subj. which occurs more frequently than the construction with
pres. imp. in the Apocalypse (vi. 6, vii.
3, x. 4, xi. 2, xxii. 10). A comparison
of John iii. 7 with the present passage
brings out the difference of meaning
in the two constructions. There the
thought is of the special feeling a-
roused by the single statement, here
of the continuous feeling stirred by
the whole temper of men (comp. ii.
15, iv. 1). Comp. 1 Pet. ii. 17; John
ii. 16 note.

For θαυμάζειν εἰ see Mark xv. 44.

ἀδελφοί] *brethren.* This is the only
place in the Epistle where this title of
address is used (ii. 7 is a false reading).
It contains an implicit argument. By
emphasising the new relation in which
Christians stand one to another it implies that this position of necessary

¹⁴ἡμεῖς οἴδαμεν ὅτι μεταβεβήκαμεν ἐκ τοῦ θανάτου εἰς
τὴν ζωήν, ὅτι ἀγαπῶμεν τοὺς ἀδελφούς· ὁ μὴ ἀγαπῶν

14 τοὺς ἀδ. +ἡμῶν ℵ syr vg.
me syrr.

ὁ μὴ ἀγ. ℵAB vg.: +τὸν ἀδελφόν [αὐτοῦ] 5°C

mutual affection is characteristic of
them as distinguished from other men
('the world'). The title is common
in St James (ἀδελφοί, ἀδελφοί μου),
and not unfrequent in St Paul and in
the Epistle to the Hebrews. It is not
found in the first Epistle of St Peter
or St Jude.

The three forms which St John
borrows from the family to express
Christian relations preserve each their
proper meaning. 'Brethren' expresses
the idea of Christian equality in virtue
of the common life: 'Children' (τεκνία)
that of spiritual dependence in the
order of the new life with the prospect of growth: 'Little ones' (παιδία)
that of subordination and immaturity.
In contrast with these 'Beloved' is
simply the personal manifestation of
feeling.

εἰ μισεῖ] si odit V., if...hateth you.
This is assumed as a fact (comp. c. iv.
11; v. 9; John xv. 18); and by the
order the stress is thrown here upon
the verb and not (as in John xv.
18 ff.) upon the pronoun or the subject. Hatred is characteristic of 'the
world' (mundus V., hic mundus F.).

14. ἡμεῖς οἴδαμεν] nos scimus V.
We (ἡμεῖς) as distinguished from the
world, know by the essential nature
of our faith, by our own inward experience....The fact that we are conscious
of a love for Christians as Christians
is a proof to us that we have entered
upon a new life: that we now first
truly live. The passage has been
made: the new sphere of being has
been gained. Life is not future but
present. Compare the simple οἴδαμεν
in v. 2.

μεταβεβήκαμεν] translati sumus V.,
have passed... Comp. John v. 24 (xiii.
1). This love was indeed the accept-

ance in faith of Christ's 'word' (c. ii.
7, iii. 11).

ἐκ τοῦ θ. εἰς τὴν ζ.] de morte in vitam
V., out of death into life. Death and
life are regarded as the two spheres
in which men move, and they are presented in their substantive fulness
'the death which is truly death,' 'the
life which is truly life' (ὁ θάνατος, ἡ
ζωή). Ὁ θάνατος is found here and
in the following clause in St John's
Epistles; in the Gospel it occurs only
in the parallel v. 24 (xi. 13 is different).
Ὁ θάνατος is personified in Apoc. i. 18.
vi. 8, ix. 6, xx. 13 f. (xxi. 4). Compare
Acts ii. 24; Rom. v. 12 ff., viii. 2; 1
Cor. xv. 21 ff.; 2 Cor. iv. 12; 2 Tim. i.
10 (opposed to ζωή); Heb. ii. 14. For
ἡ ζωή compare i. 2 note; John v. 24;
Matt. vii. 14 (opposed to ἡ ἀπώλεια),
xviii. 8 f., xix. 17; (Mark ix. 43, 45);
Acts iii. 15; 2 Cor. v. 4. The depth
of the expression is lost both in Latin
and in English.

'To enter into life' (εἰσελ. εἰς τὴν ζ.) is
a phrase characteristic of St Matthew
(xviii. 8 f., xix. 17; comp. vii. 14) and
of St Mark (ix. 43, 45). In this
largest sense 'life' (ἡ ζωή) is the fulfilment of the highest idea of being:
perfect truth in perfect action. Compare 2 Tim. i. 10 καταργήσαντος μὲν
τὸν θάνατον φωτίσαντος δὲ ζωὴν καὶ
ἀφθαρσίαν, where in the second member the thought is of 'life' in the
abstract and not of the Christian fulfilment of the whole conception of life.

ὅτι...ὅτι...] quoniam...quoniam...
V., that...because... Active love is the
sign of life and not the ground of life.
Comp. Luke vii. 47. The connexion
is 'we know because...' and not 'we
have passed because...'.

τοὺς ἀδ.] the brethren. The simple
phrase (3 John 5, 10) is more expres-

μένει ἐν τῷ θανάτῳ. ¹⁵πᾶς ὁ μισῶν τὸν ἀδελφὸν αὐτοῦ ἀνθρωποκτόνος ἐστίν, καὶ οἴδατε ὅτι πᾶς ἀν- θρωποκτόνος οὐκ ἔχει ζωὴν αἰώνιον ἐν αὐτῷ μένου-

15 ἑαυτοῦ B.   αυτω B: ἑαυτῷ אAC.

sive than 'our brethren.' This is the only place in which the exact words occur (ἀγ. τοὺς ἀδελφούς). Elsewhere St John says ἀγ. ἀλλήλους (v. 11 note). Ἀγ. τὸν ἀδ. occurs ii. 10; iii. 10; iv. 20.

See Additional Note.

In view of the imperfection of Christians Augustine says: Viget [gloria caritatis] sed adhuc in hieme : viget radix sed quasi aridi sunt rami. Intus est medulla quæ viget, intus sunt folia arborum, intus fructus; sed æstatem expectant.

ὁ μὴ ἀγαπῶν] qui non diligit V., he that loveth not. The omission of his brother, according to the true text, strengthens the thought. The feeling is regarded in its completest form.

μένει ἐν τῷ θ.] abideth (permanet F.) in death. There is a moral vis inertiæ. It is not said that he dies. Death is his natural state. It fol- lows that love and life are convertible terms.

Compare John iii. 36.

15. The hatred of 'the world' can cause no marvel : it is, in a certain sense, natural. But hatred may find place among 'the brethren' (ii. 9, 11). There are Cains in the new family. Such hatred is essentially identical with murder, not simply as being the first step towards it but as involving the same moral position. It is more- over in the man himself the destruc- tion of that life which is love.

πᾶς ὁ...] Every one that hateth... though he bear the name of Christ. Comp. c. iii. 3.

ἀνθρωποκτόνος] homicida V., mur- derer. The word is used of the devil, John viii. 44. Among men Cain is the type.

οἴδατε] ye know. Comp. c. v. 18 note.

πᾶς...οὐκ...] Comp. ii. 19 note.

πᾶς ἀνθρωποκτόνος] Omnis inquit homicida: scilicet non solum ille qui ferro verum et ille qui odio fratrem insequitur (Bede).

ζ. αἰ. ἐν αὐτῷ μέν.] eternal life abiding in him. The addition of the last words brings out the thought that 'eternal life' must (under the circumstances of our present life) be a continuous power, and a communicat- ed gift (comp. John vi. 53).

The whole phrase is unique. Else- where 'the word' (ii. 14; John v. 38; comp. xv. 7), the 'unction' (ii. 27), 'the seed of God' (iii. 9), 'the love of God' (iii. 17), 'the truth' (2 John 2), are said to 'abide' in the believer; and so also God (v. 24, iv. 12, 13, 15 f.) and Christ (John vi. 56, xv. 5). Even to the last man has not 'life in himself.' This is the divine prerogative alone.

2. The manifestation of love (vv. 16—18).

It has been shewn that love is the sign of the Christian life. It is now shewn that love must be fashioned after the pattern of Christ who made it known in sacrifice (v. 16). Such love extends to the common inter- course of life (v. 17); and must be at once active and real (v. 18).

¹⁶ In this we know love, because he laid down his life for us; and we ought to lay down our lives for the brethren. ¹⁷ But whosoever has the world's goods, and beholdeth his brother in need, and shutteth up his heart from him, how abideth the love of God in him? ¹⁸ Little children, let us not love in word, neither with the tongue, but in deed and truth.

σαν.   ¹⁶Ἐν τούτῳ ἐγνώκαμεν τὴν ἀγάπην, ὅτι
ἐκεῖνος ὑπὲρ ἡμῶν τὴν ψυχὴν αὐτοῦ ἔθηκεν· καὶ ἡμεῖς
ὀφείλομεν ὑπὲρ τῶν ἀδελφῶν τὰς ψυχὰς θεῖναι.   ¹⁷ὃς
δ᾽ ἂν ἔχῃ τὸν βίον τοῦ κόσμου καὶ θεωρῇ τὸν ἀδελφὸν

16 τὴν ἀγ. +τοῦ θεοῦ vg.   θεῖναι ℵABC: τιθέναι ς

16. Ἐν τούτῳ] *In this*, see c. ii. 3
note. The truth which has been
enunciated, the self-sacrificing character of love, as opposed to the murder-
ous character of hatred, opens the way
to the most complete revelation of love.
The 'this,' as elsewhere, looks both
backwards and forwards.

ἐγνώκαμεν] *cognovimus* V., *cognoscimus* Aug., *we know* as the result of
divine teaching: we have learnt and
now hold the lesson for ever. This
knowledge of experience is contrasted
with the knowledge of intuition (οἴδατε) in *v.* 15. Comp. John xv. 13.

τὴν ἀγάπην] See Additional Note.

ἐκεῖνος] *He*, Christ. See ii. 6 note.

τὴν ψυχὴν αὐτοῦ ἔθηκεν] *animam
suam posuit* V., *laid down His life*.
The phrase is peculiar to St John,
John x. 11 (note), 15, 17 ff., xiii. 37 ff.,
xv. 13.

This is the only passage in the
Epistle in which St John uses ὑπέρ *in
behalf of* (comp. 3 John 7). It occurs
in the Gospel in similar connexions not
unfrequently: vi. 51 ; x. 11, 15 ; xi. 50
ff. ; xiii. 37 f. ; xv. 13 ; xvii. 19 ; xviii.
14. Contrast περί c. ii. 2 ; iv. 10.

The image appears to be that of
divesting oneself of a thing (John xiii.
4). Compare 'animam ponere,' 'de-
ponere.'

καὶ ἡμεῖς ὀφείλομεν] *and we ought…*
as a consequence of this knowledge ;
but St John regards the duty as included in the knowledge (*and we
ought*) and not as logically deduced
from it (*wherefore we ought*). Comp.
v. 3. The obligation lies in the perception of the relation in which we
stand to one another and to Christ.
That which constrains us is not only

His example, but the truth which
that example reveals. Comp. *v.* 7.
For ὀφείλομεν see ii. 6 note. Ignatius
speaking of himself in the spirit of
this passage says to the Ephesians :
ἀντίψυχον ὑμῶν ἐγώ (*ad Eph.* 21 ;
comp. *ad Smyrn.* 10 ; *ad Polyc.* 2, 6).
The words addressed by St John to
the young Robber sound like an echo
of it: ἂν δέῃ τὸν σὸν θάνατον ἑκὼν ὑπο-
μενῶ, ὡς ὁ Κύριος τὸν ὑπὲρ ἡμῶν· ὑπὲρ
σοῦ τὴν ψυχὴν ἀντιδώσω τὴν ἐμήν
(Euseb. *H. E.* iii. 23).

17. St John turns from considering
the greatness of our obligation to notice
the ordinary character of failure. By
the transition he suggests that there
is a danger in indulging ourselves in
lofty views which lie out of the way of
common experience. We may therefore try ourselves by a far more home-
ly test. The question is commonly
not of dying for another but of communicating to another the outward
means of living. If we are found
wanting here, we need look no further
for judgment.

ὃς δ᾽ ἂν ἔχῃ] *Qui habuerit* V. Comp.
ii. 5 note.

τὸν βίον τοῦ κόσμου] *substantiam
vitæ* V., *facultates mundi* Aug., *the
life of the world* 'the substance of
the world' as contrasted with 'life
eternal' (*v.* 15). Comp. Luke xv. 12
(τὸν βίον) ; ii. 16 note. The phrase
includes all the endowments which
make up our earthly riches, wealth,
station, intellect. It has been finely
said of a great teacher that 'he was
tender to dulness as to all forms of
poverty.'

θεωρῇ] *behold* as a spectacle on
which he allows his eyes to rest. This

αὐτοῦ χρείαν ἔχοντα καὶ κλείσῃ τὰ σπλάγχνα αὐτοῦ
ἀπ᾽ αὐτοῦ, πῶς ἡ ἀγάπη τοῦ θεοῦ μένει ἐν αὐτῷ;
¹⁸ Τεκνία, μὴ ἀγαπῶμεν λόγῳ μηδὲ τῇ γλώσσῃ ἀλλὰ

18 τεκνία ℵABC (vg) syrhl: +μου ⱔ syrvg me the (vg).   τῇ γλ. ABC:
−τῇ ⱔℵ.

is the only place where the verb occurs in St John's Epistles; and elsewhere in the Epistles it is found only
in Heb. vii. 4. Comp. Apoc. xi. 11 f.
The word is common in the Gospel of
St John and is always used with its
full meaning. See John ii. 23 note.

χρείαν ἔχοντα] necesse habere V.,
egere F., esurientem, egentem Aug.
The rendering of the Vulgate is
suggested by ii. 27. See note there
for the absolute use of χρ. ἔχειν.

κλείσῃ τὰ σπλ.] clauserit viscera sua
ab eo V., shuts up his heart from him
so that the destitute brother can find
no access to his sympathy. The phrase
'to shut up the heart' is apparently
unique. It expresses the interposition of a barrier between the sufferer
and the tender feelings of his brother.
Comp. Ps. lxxvii. 10 (קִפֵּץ רחֲ συνέχειν
τοὺς οἰκτιρμούς LXX.). Τὰ σπλάγχνα is
found here only in the writings of St
John (it occurs in St Luke and St
Paul).

πῶς... ;] how doth... ? The interro-
gative construction is similar to that
in v. 12.

ἡ ἀ. τοῦ θ.] caritas Dei V., dilectio
Dei Aug., the love of God, the love of
which God is at once the object and
the author and the pattern. Comp.
ii. 5 note.

μένει] abide...as a continuous active
power. Comp. v. 15.

18. Τεκνία] Filioli V., Little children. The word of address is changed
(v. 13). The father now pleads with
those who draw their being from him.

μὴ...λόγῳ μηδὲ τῇ γλ.] not...with
word, neither with the tongue, in
theory as opposed to action; with
mere outward expression as opposed

to the genuine movement of our whole
being.

λόγῳ...ἐν ἔργῳ...] with word...in
deed... The slight change of construction marks the difference between the
instrument and the sphere of the manifestation of love. It must find scope
in our true and full life. For ἐν ἔργῳ
καὶ ἀλ. compare John iv. 23 f. ἐν
πνεύματι καὶ ἀληθείᾳ.

'If love depends on a word, when
the word ceaseth the love ceaseth.
Such was the love of Balak and Balaam' (Jalkut Reub. 145. 4: Schoettgen). The passage quoted from Aboth
v. 22 is wholly different in sense.

3.   The fruit of love (vv. 19—24).

As St John has spoken of the necessity and of the pattern of love so
now he goes on to speak of its fruit.
The fruit of love is confidence. Such
confidence stills the condemnation
which the heart pronounces against
the believer (vv. 19, 20). It finds
its expression in prayers, which are
necessarily answered, because they are
the voice of obedient love (vv. 21—23).
It issues in the fulness of sympathy
(v. 24).

¹⁹ In this we shall know that we
are of the truth, and shall assure our
heart before him, ²⁰ whereinsoever
our heart may condemn us; because
God is greater than our heart and
knoweth all things. Beloved, if our
heart condemn us not, we have boldness towards God, ²² and whatsoever
we ask we receive from him, because
we observe his commandments and
do the things that are pleasing in his
sight. ²³ And this is his commandment, that we should believe the name

8—2

ἐν ἔργῳ καὶ ἀληθείᾳ.   ¹⁹Ἐν τούτῳ γνωσόμεθα
ὅτι ἐκ τῆς ἀληθείας ἐσμέν, καὶ ἔμπροσθεν αὐτοῦ πείσομεν τὴν καρδίαν ἡμῶν ²⁰ὅτι ἐὰν καταγινώσκῃ ἡμῶν

ἐν ἔ. ℵABC: – ἐν ς.   19 ἐν τ. AB vg me syrhl: +καὶ ἐν τ. ℵC the syrvg.
γνωσόμεθα ℵABC me the: γινώσκομεν ς vg syrr.   τὴν κ. A*B the syrvg: τὰς
κ. ℵA**C vg me syrhl.

*of his Son Jesus Christ and love one
another, even as he gave us commandment.* ²⁴ *And he that observeth his
commandments abideth in him and
he in him; and in this we know that
he abideth in us, from the Spirit
which he gave us.*

19. Ἐν τούτῳ] *In this,* the consciousness of active and sincere love
of the brethren, resting upon and
moulded by the love of Christ.

γνωσόμεθα] *cognoscemus* V., *we shall
know, perceive.* The future expresses
the dependence of the knowledge upon
the fulfilment of the specified condition. Again it is to be noticed that
the knowledge which comes through
outward experience stands in contrast
with the knowledge which belongs to
the idea of faith *v.* 14 (οἴδαμεν).

ἐκ τῆς ἀλ. ἐσμέν] *ex veritate sumus*
V., *are of the truth,* draw the power
of our being from the Truth as its
source. Comp. ii. 16. Christ Himself
is revealed as the Truth, in whom the
right relations of man to man and to
God and to the world are perfectly
presented (comp. John xviii. 37). So
far then as the Christian is like Him,
he is 'of the truth.' The conception
of being 'a child of the Truth' is different from that of being 'a child
of God,' though practically the two
are identical. In the latter case the
thought is of the presence of the divine
principle as divine: in the former, of
the fulfilment of all the offices of man.

καὶ ἔμπροσθεν αὐτοῦ...] *and,* as a
consequence of the knowledge of our
complete dependence upon the Truth,
we shall assure our hearts before Him,
i.e. in the presence of God. The antecedent is supplied by the reader.

The simple pronoun (αὐτός) naturally
describes the one Sovereign Lord,
just as the isolating and defining pronoun (ἐκεῖνος) describes Christ.

The phrase 'before Him' (*in con-
spectu ejus* V., *coram ipso* Aug.) stands
emphatically first in order to mark
the essential character of the Christian
life. It is lived out in the very sight
of God. The believer feels himself to
be always before His eyes. In that
Presence (comp. ii. 28) if not before,
he comes to find what he is. Comp.
2 Cor. v. 10 (φανερωθῆναι); 1 Thess.
iii. 13.

πείσομεν...ὅτι ἐὰν καταγινώσκῃ...ὅτι
μείζων...πάντα] *suademus (suadeamus,
suadebimus) quoniam si reprehenderit nos (male senserit* Aug.) *cor nostrum major est Deus corde nostro et
novit omnia* V., (*we*) *shall assure our
heart before Him whereinsoever our
heart condemn us, because God is
greater than our heart and knoweth
all things.* The many conflicting interpretations of this passage spring
out of the different translations of (1)
the verb πείσομεν, and (2) the double
conjunction or relative ὅτι (ὅ τι).

1. Thus if we take the sense *persuade* for the verb, there are two
groups of renderings possible: the
first (*a*) in which the clauses which
follow give the substance of that of
which we are satisfied; and the second (β) in which this substance is
supposed to be supplied by the reader.

(*a*) In the first case there are two
possible views:

(a) The second ὅτι may be simply
resumptive: *We shall persuade our
heart, that, if our heart condemn us,
that,* I say, *God is greater...*

ἡ καρδία, ὅτι μείζων ἐστὶν ὁ θεὸς τῆς καρδίας ἡμῶν

20 ὅτι μ. ℵBC syrvg: om. ὅτι A vg me the.   κύριος (for θεὸς) C.

(b) Or the first ὅτι may be taken as the relative: *We shall persuade our heart, whereinsoever our heart condemn us, that God is greater...*

Against both these interpretations it may be urged, as it seems with decisive force, that the conclusion is not one which flows naturally from the premiss. The consciousness of a sincere love of the brethren does not furnish the basis of the conviction of the sovereign greatness of God.

(β) If the substance of that of which we shall be persuaded is mentally supplied, as, 'that we are of the truth,' or 'that our prayers are heard,' there are again two possible interpretations:

(a) The second ὅτι may be taken as resumptive in the sense *because: we shall persuade our heart, because if our heart condemn us, because I say God is greater...*

(b) Or again the first ὅτι may be taken as the relative: *we shall persuade our heart whereinsoever our heart condemn us, because God is greater...*

It appears to be a fatal objection to both these views that just that has to be supplied which the sense given to the verb leads the reader to expect to be clearly expressed. And further it may be remarked that while the use of a resumptive ὅτι is quite intelligible after the introduction of a considerable clause it is very unnatural after the insertion of a few words.

2. If on the other hand the verb be taken in the sense 'we shall assure,' 'we shall still and tranquillise the fears and misgivings of our heart,' there are yet two modes of completing the sentence:

(a) The second ὅτι may be taken as resumptive in the sense of *because: we shall assure our hearts, because if our heart condemn us, because, I say,*

God is greater. Such a resumptive use of the particle has however been shewn to be very harsh.

(β) There remains then the adoption of the first ὅτι as the relative: *We shall assure our heart, whereinsoever our heart condemn us, because God is greater...*

This sense falls in completely with the context and flows naturally from the Greek.

But an ambiguity still remains. In what sense is the superior greatness of God to be understood? Is it the ground of our exceeding need? or of our sure confidence? Both interpretations can be drawn from the words. (1) We shall then, and then only, still our heart, in whatsoever it may condemn us, because we know that the judgment of God must be severer than our own judgment, and so apart from fellowship with Him we can have no hope. Or (2) We shall then still our heart in whatsoever it may condemn us, because we are in fellowship with God, and that fact assures us of His sovereign mercy. The latter sense seems to be required by the whole context. See below.

πείσομεν] The nearest parallel in the N. T. to the sense of the word which has been adopted here is Matt. xxviii. 14. Comp. 2 Macc. iv. 45.

τὴν καρδίαν] *our heart*, the seat of the moral character. It occurs only in this passage in the Epistles of St John. Comp. Rom. ii. 15; Eph. i. 18.

The singular (which St John always uses in the Gospel and Epistle) fixes the thought upon the personal trial in each case. See Additional Note.

20. ὅτι ἐάν] *whereinsoever*. The words balance the 'all things' which follows. The form ὅτι ἐάν does not occur as the true text elsewhere in N. T. (Col. iii. 23 ὃ ἐάν), but always

καὶ γινώσκει πάντα. ²¹Ἀγαπητοί, ἐὰν ἡ καρδία μὴ
καταγινώσκῃ, παρρησίαν ἔχομεν πρὸς τὸν θεόν, ²²καὶ

21 ἀγαπητοί: ἀδελφοί א.   ἡ κ. AB (lat): + ἡμῶν ﬞאC vg syrr me the.
μὴ κατ. BC: +ἡμῶν ﬞאA vg me the syrr.   ἔχομεν: ἔχει B.

ὅτι ἄν (John ii. 5, xiv. 13, xv. 16). This
however does not appear to be a decisive objection. In John ii. 5, xv. 16
ἐάν is an early variant (אA).

καταγινώσκῃ] reprehenderit V.,
male senserit Aug., condemn. The
word is used of the internal judgment
of conscience (Ecclus. xiv. 2) as distinguished from the formal sentence
of the judge (κατακρίνω).
Comp. Gal. ii. 11.

μείζων ἐ. ὁ θ. τῆς κ. ἡ.] major est
Deus corde nostro V., God is greater
than our heart, justly able to sway
and control it. He is the Supreme
Sovereign over the whole man. Nothing in man can stand against His
judgment and will. The context requires that this sovereignty should be
regarded under the aspect of love, as
exercised for the calming of human
doubts. The supposition that 'greater'
means more searching and authoritative in condemnation than the heart
is at variance with the tenor of the
passage and also with the natural sense
of 'greater.'

γινώσκει π.] novit omnia V., knoweth all things, watches (to use human
language) the course and spring of
action (John ii. 25 note), not only this
failure and that on which the heart
dwells, but these and all else, and
with this knowledge offers us His
love and assures us of it.

Thus the meaning of the whole
passage will be: The sense within us
of a sincere love of the brethren, which
is the sign of God's presence with us,
will enable us to stay the accusations
of our conscience, whatever they may
be, because God, who gives us the
love, and so blesses us with His fellowship, is greater than our heart; and
He, having perfect knowledge, for-

gives all on which the heart sadly
dwells.

21. Ἀγαπητοί] Carissimi V., Dilectissimi Aug. Comp. c. ii. 7 note. The
tender address follows naturally from
the thought of the fears and hopes of
Christians. The sense of misgiving
(the condemnation of the heart) and
the sense of duty done (the acquittal
of the heart) severally involve special
applications of the divine revelation.
In the one case this revelation brings
assurance, and in the other effectual
prayer.

ἐὰν ἡ καρδία μὴ καταγ.] si cor nostrum
non reprehenderit V. (male senserit
Aug.), if our heart condemn us not.
This evidently is the converse case to
'if our heart condemn us.' It does
not imply a claim to sinlessness, nor
yet an insensibility to the heinousness
of sin, but the action of a lively faith
which retains a real sense of fellowship with God, and this carries with it
confidence and peace.

The change in the order of the
words in the parallel clauses marks
a change of emphasis. In the first
clause stress is laid on the fact of
condemnation (ὅτι ἐὰν καταγινώσκῃ ἡ
καρδία): in the second on the moral
faculty which pronounces no condemnation (ἐὰν ἡ καρδία μὴ καταγ.).

παρρησίαν ἔχομεν] fiduciam habemus V., we have boldness, so as
to express without reserve all our
wants. Compare c. v. 14 (ii. 28, iv.
17); John vii. 4 note. The thought
here is of the boldness with which the
son appears before the Father, and
not of that with which the accused
appears before the Judge.|

πρὸς τ. θ.] ad Deum V., towards
God. Compare Acts xxiv. 16; Rom. iv.
2 (πρὸς θ.), v. 1; 2 Cor. iii. 4; Phil. iv. 6.

ὃ ἂν αἰτῶμεν λαμβάνομεν ἀπ' αὐτοῦ, ὅτι τὰς ἐντολὰς
αὐτοῦ τηροῦμεν καὶ τὰ ἀρεστὰ ἐνώπιον αὐτοῦ ποιοῦμεν.
²³καὶ αὕτη ἐστὶν ἡ ἐντολὴ αὐτοῦ, ἵνα πιστεύσωμεν τῷ

22 αἰτώμεθα ℵ. Comp. v. 14 f.   λαμβάνωμεν A: comp. for similar confusion c. iv. 17 (ℵ) 13: accipiemus vg the syrhl.   ἀπ' αὐ. ℵABC: παρ' αὐ. Ϛ.
τηρῶμεν ℵA.   23 πιστεύσωμεν ϚB: πιστεύωμεν ℵAC.   τῷ ὄν. τοῦ υἱ. αὐ.
'I. X. ℵBC vg me the syrr: τῷ ὄν. αὐ. 'I. Χριστῷ A (all. τῷ υἱῷ αὐ. 'I. X.).

22. καὶ ὃ ἂν αἰτῶμεν] et quodcunque
petierimus V., and whatsoever we
ask... The expression of our wants is
followed by the satisfying of them.
The words describe the actual present
experience of the believer (αἰτῶμεν)
and the assertion is absolute. Every
prayer is granted. But Augustine
rightly adds: Discernamus exaudi-
tiones Dei. Invenimus enim quosdam
non exauditos ad voluntatem exauditos ad salutem ; et rursus quosdam
invenimus exauditos ad voluntatem
et non exauditos ad salutem.

Here the thought is of the actual
perception of the gift by the believer
in time (λαμβάνομεν): in St Mark xi.
24 (ἐλάβετε) the thought is of the
divine response in the eternal order.
For λαμβ. ἀπό see c. ii. 27 note.

ὅτι...τηροῦμεν] because we observe...
Obedience is not alleged as the ground
but as the assurance of the fulfilment.
The answer to prayer is given not as
a reward for meritorious action, but
because the prayer itself rightly understood coincides with God's will
(comp. John viii. 29, xi. 42). The sole
object of the believer is to do thoroughly the part which has been assigned
to him: his petitions are directed to
this end and so are necessarily granted.
Comp. John xv. 7.

τηροῦμεν...ποιοῦμεν] keep...do...The
eyes of the believer are turned watch-
fully to discern (τηροῦμεν) the will of
God for the future, and at the present
he is engaged in executing that which
is pleasing to Him. Under this twofold aspect right action is presented
both as a work of obedience and as a

work of freedom, as enjoined and also
as spontaneous.

For the sense of τηρεῖν see John
xvii. 12 note, and for τηρεῖν τ. ἐντ. c.
ii. 3 note. Τηρεῖν and ποιεῖν occur
again together in v. 2, 3.

τὰ ἀρεστά] ea quæ sunt placita V.,
the things that are pleasing... not
simply 'things pleasing,' but definitely
those which correspond with our position and duty.

Compare John viii. 29.

ἐνώπιον αὐτοῦ] coram eo V., in His
sight. Comp. Hebr. xiii. 21; Acts iv.
19; 1 Pet. iii. 4; 1 Tim. ii. 3; v. 4.
But we find ἀρεστὰ αὐτῷ John viii. 29.
The slight shade of difference between ἔμπροσθεν αὐτοῦ (v. 19) and ἐνώπιον αὐτοῦ seems to be expressed by
the phrases 'in His presence' and 'in
His sight.' The latter phrase accentuates the thought of the Divine
regard. Comp. John xii. 37 (ἔμπ. αὐ.)
and xx. 30 (ἐνώπ. τ. μ.).

23. καὶ αὕτη ἐ. ἡ ἐντ. αὐ.] And this
is his commandment. The 'things
that are pleasing,' the many 'commandments' are summed up in one
commandment, which includes faith
and practice, the power of action and
the form of action, faith and love.
Comp. ii. 4 f.; 2 John 6.

ἡ ἐντολή...ἵνα...] Comp. John xiii.
34, xv. 12, 17.

ἵνα πιστεύσωμεν...] that we believe
... Faith also is a work, John vi. 29,
and therefore the proper object of
command; and it may be regarded
either as unceasingly continuous and
progressive (πιστεύωμεν) or as exercised at a critical moment when the

ὀνόματι τοῦ υἱοῦ αὐτοῦ Ἰησοῦ Χριστοῦ καὶ ἀγαπῶμεν

whole tenor of life is determined (πιστεύσωμεν). This is the first place in the Epistle in which the exercise of faith is mentioned. Afterwards πιστεύω occurs not unfrequently. On the whole the reading πιστεύσωμεν is the more likely here. In this case the decisive act of faith is treated as the foundation of the abiding work of love; at the same time the present πιστεύωμεν gives an excellent sense, faith and love being presented as simultaneous in their present development.

The tenses of the verb (πιστεύω) appear to be used with significant exactness by St John; and the instances of the occurrence of the different forms will repay examination.

1 *Present:* the immediate, continuous exercise of faith:

John x. 38 (dat.), vi. 29, xvi. 9 (εἰς), xx. 31 (ὅτι), iv. 42, x. 25 f., xii. 39 (xix. 35), xx. 31 (abs.).

imper.: John iv. 21, x. 37, xiv. 11; 1 John iv. 1 (dat.); John xii. 36, xiv. 1 (εἰς).

partic. (ὁ πιστεύων, οἱ πιστεύοντες): John v. 24; 1 John v. 10 (dat.); John iii. 16, 18, 36, vi. 35, 40, 47, vii. 38 f., xi. 25 f., xii. 44, 46, xiv. 2, xvii. 20; 1 John v. 10, 13 (εἰς), 1 John v. 1, 5 (ὅτι); John iii. 15, vi. 64 (abs.).

2 *Imperfect:* the continuous exercise of faith in the past:

John v. 46 (dat.), vii. 5, xii. 11, 37 (εἰς).

3 *Aorist:* the definite, decisive act of faith:

John ii. 22, iv. 50, vi. 30, x. 38; 1 John iii. 23 (dat.); John ii. 11, 23, iv. 39, vii. 31, 48, viii. 30, ix. 36, x. 42, xi. 45, xii. 42 (εἰς); John viii. 24, ix. 18, xi. 42, xiii. 19, xvii. 8, 21 (ὅτι); John i. 7, iv. 4, 53, v. 44, xi. 15. 40, xiv. 29 (abs.).

partic.: John xx. 29 (abs.).

4 *Perfect:* the past exercise of faith continued into the present:

John viii. 31 (dat.); John iii. 18, 1 John v. 10 (εἰς); John vi. 69, xi. 27, xvi. 27 (ὅτι); John xx. 29; 1 John iv. 16 (?) (abs.).

The differences come out clearly where different tenses stand in close connexion; e.g. John vi. 29 f., vii. 5, 31, xii. 37, 42 ; 1 John v. 10.

πιστ. τῷ ὀνόματι] *believe the name...* The phrase is remarkable. It is equivalent to 'believe as true the message which the name conveys.' The full title, *His Son Jesus Christ* (c. i. 3 note), is a compressed Creed. Contrast 'believe in the name' v. 13; John i. 12, ii. 23, iii. 18. Comp. v. 10. The translation of A. V. probably comes from the Vulgate which gives *credamus in nomine,* the rendering elsewhere of πιστεύειν εἰς τὸ ὄνομα (John i. 12, ii. 23, iii. 18). See Additional Note on the names of Christ in this Epistle.

ἀγαπῶμεν ἀλλ.] *diligamus alterutrum* V., *love one another: v.* 11 note, iv. 7, 11, 12; 2 John 5; John xiii. 34 (ἐντολὴν καινὴν δίδωμι); xv. 12, 17. The exact words are used (contrast *v.* 14) in which Christ Himself gave the commandment on the eve of His Passion, when He fulfilled the ideal of love. The subject to ἔδωκεν is supplied naturally from the preceding clause.

Compare Rom. xiii. 10.

Multum facit qui multum diligit... Bene facit qui communitati magis quam suæ voluntati servit (Thom. a Kempis, *De Imit.* 1. 15, 2).

24. The obedience, which is the rule of the Christian life, issues in abiding fellowship with God. This verse is closely connected with *v.* 22, while *v.* 23 is in thought parenthetical.

ἀλλήλους, καθὼς ἔδωκεν ἐντολὴν ἡμῖν. ²⁴καὶ ὁ τηρῶν
τὰς ἐντολὰς αὐτοῦ ἐν αὐτῷ μένει καὶ αὐτὸς ἐν αὐτῷ·
καὶ ἐν τούτῳ γινώσκομεν ὅτι μένει ἐν ἡμῖν, ἐκ τοῦ πνεύματος οὗ ἡμῖν ἔδωκεν.

ἡμῖν ℵABC vg me the syrr: om. ϛ.   24 καὶ ἐν τ.: om. καί ℵ* the.   οὗ
ἡμ. ἔδ. ABC (lat): οὗ ἔδ. ἡμ. ℵ vg me the syrr.

καὶ ὁ τηρῶν...] *And he that observeth...* These words take up ὅτι τὰς
ἐντολὰς αὐτοῦ τηρ. in *v.* 22, so that the
reference is to 'the commandments of
God,' and not directly to the one commandment of Christ *v.* 23. Our prayers
are granted because they spring out
of that spirit which strives after perfect sympathy; and, more than this,
our obedience is the pledge of a personal fellowship.

ἐν αὐτῷ μένει...] i.e. in God. See
c. iv. 15 note.

Bede says with singular force: Sit
ergo tibi domus Deus et esto domus
Dei: mane in Deo, et maneat in te
Deus.

ἐν τούτῳ γινώσκομεν] *in this we
know, perceive...* The love which the
Christian feels and which is the spring
of his obedience, assures him of God's
fellowship with him. In other words,

God has given him of His Spirit.
The use of the two prepositions '*in*
(ἐν) *this,*' '*from* (ἐκ) the Spirit,' shews
that the two clauses are not in apposition. Γινώσκομεν is repeated in
thought before ἐκ τοῦ πν. c. iv. 6.

ἐκ τοῦ πνεύματος] This is the first
mention of the Spirit in the Epistle.
Afterwards the references are not unfrequent. It is remarkable that the
Name never occurs with the epithet
'Holy' in the Epistles or Apocalypse
of St John.

οὗ...ἔδωκεν] *which he gave* when
we became Christians. Comp. c. iv. 13;
John xiv. 16; Acts v. 32, viii. 18, xv.
8; 2 Cor. i. 21 f.

Augustine draws a striking conclusion from the truth that the Spirit of
God is the source of man's life: Con-
temne te cum laudaris. Ille in te
laudetur qui per te operatur.

Additional Note on iii. 1. Children of God.

The three phrases by which St John describes the new life. St John uses several phrases to describe the relation of believers to God which require to be carefully considered in connexion with the contexts in which they occur. The initial fact of the communication of the divine life is expressed by γεννηθῆναι ἐκ τοῦ θεοῦ (i). The essential connexion existing in virtue of this quickening is expressed by εἶναι ἐκ τοῦ θεοῦ (ii). In virtue of this connexion the believer becomes and is a τέκνον θεοῦ (iii).

i. 'To be born (begotten) of God,' (1) in the Perfect, i. (1) The phrase γεννηθῆναι ἐκ τ. θ. is used commonly in the perfect (γεγέννηται, γεγεννημένος); that is, the initial fact of the new life is regarded in its abiding power.

This communicated life is

(a) shewn by certain signs, faith in Jesus as the Christ, righteousness and love:

1 John v. 1 πᾶς ὁ πιστεύων ὅτι Ἰησοῦς ἐστὶν ὁ χριστὸς ἐκ τοῦ θεοῦ γεγέννηται.

— ii. 29 πᾶς ὁ ποιῶν τὴν δικαιοσύνην ἐξ αὐτοῦ γεγέννηται.

— iv. 7 πᾶς ὁ ἀγαπῶν ἐκ τοῦ θεοῦ γεγέννηται.

and

(β) carries with it certain consequences, freedom from sin and victory:

1 John iii. 9 πᾶς ὁ γεγεννημένος ἐκ τοῦ θεοῦ ἁμαρτίαν οὐ ποιεῖ ὅτι σπέρμα αὐτοῦ ἐν αὐτῷ μένει.

— οὐ δύναται ἁμαρτάνειν ὅτι ἐκ τοῦ θεοῦ γεγέννηται.

— v. 18 πᾶς ὁ γεγεννημένος ἐκ τοῦ θεοῦ οὐχ ἁμαρτάνει.

— 4 πᾶν τὸ γεγεννημένον ἐκ τοῦ θεοῦ νικᾷ τὸν κόσμον.

Compare

John iii. 6 τὸ γεγεννημένον ἐκ τοῦ πνεύματος.

— 8 ὁ γεγεννημένος ἐκ τοῦ πνεύματος.

(2) in the Aorist. (2) The fact of the communication of the divine life is specially noticed:

John i. 12 f. ἔδωκεν αὐτοῖς ἐξουσίαν τέκνα θεοῦ γενέσθαι...οἳ...ἐκ θεοῦ ἐγεννήθησαν.

Compare

1 John v. 18 ὁ γεννηθεὶς ἐκ τοῦ θεοῦ.

— 1 πᾶς ὁ ἀγαπῶν τὸν γεννήσαντα...

Compare also

John iii. 3 (7) ἐὰν μή τις γεννηθῇ ἄνωθεν.

— 5 ἐὰν μή τις γεννηθῇ ἐξ ὕδατος καὶ πνεύματος.

The *aorist* and *perfect* occur together 1 John v. 18; John iii. 5—8. See also Gal. iv. 23, 29.

The form of expression is not found in any of the other writers of the N.T. Yet compare St Paul's use of γεννᾶν 1 Cor. iv. 15; Philem. 10; and St Peter's use of ἀναγεννᾶν, 1 Pet. i. 3, 23.

ii. The phrase εἶναι ἐκ τοῦ θεοῦ is connected with a considerable group ii. *'To be* of similar phrases, εἶναι ἐκ τοῦ διαβόλου (c. iii. 8), ἐκ τοῦ πονηροῦ (iii. 12), ἐκ *of God,'* τοῦ κόσμου (ii. 16, note), ἐκ τῆς ἀληθείας (ii. 21, note), ἐκ τῆς γῆς (John iii. 31, note), ἐκ τῶν κάτω, ἐκ τῶν ἄνω (viii. 23). It expresses the ideas of derivation and dependence, and so of a moral correspondence between the issue and the source.

(1) The characteristics of him who is thus vitally dependent upon God (1) signs (1 John v. 19, iv. 4, 6) are expressed both in a positive and in a negative in men; form.

(a) positively:

3 John 11 ὁ ἀγαθοποιῶν ἐκ τοῦ θεοῦ ἐστίν.

John viii. 47 ὁ ὢν ἐκ τοῦ θεοῦ τὰ ῥήματα τοῦ θεοῦ ἀκούει.

(β) negatively:

1 John iii. 10 πᾶς ὁ μὴ ποιῶν δικαιοσύνην οὐκ ἔστιν ἐκ τοῦ θεοῦ.

— iv. 6 ὃς οὐκ ἔστιν ἐκ τοῦ θεοῦ οὐκ ἀκούει ἡμῶν.

(2) And corresponding declarations are made with regard to spirits (2) signs (1 John iv. 1): in spirits.

1 John iv. 2 πᾶν πνεῦμα ὃ ὁμολογεῖ Ἰησοῦν Χριστὸν ἐν σαρκὶ ἐληλυθότα ἐκ τοῦ θεοῦ ἐστίν.

— 3 πᾶν πνεῦμα ὃ μὴ ὁμολογεῖ τὸν Ἰησοῦν ἐκ τοῦ θεοῦ οὐκ ἔστιν.

Compare

1 John iv. 7 ἡ ἀγάπη ἐκ τοῦ θεοῦ ἐστίν.

John vii. 17 ...περὶ τῆς διδαχῆς πότερον ἐκ τοῦ θεοῦ ἐστίν...

1 John ii. 16 πᾶν τὸ ἐν τῷ κόσμῳ...οὐκ ἔστιν ἐκ τοῦ πατρός...

The nearest parallels in other writings of the N.T. are:

Acts v. 38 f. εἰ ἐκ θεοῦ ἐστίν.

1 Cor. i. 30 ἐξ αὐτοῦ [τοῦ θεοῦ] ὑμεῖς ἐστὲ ἐν Χριστῷ Ἰησοῦ.

— xi. 12 τὰ δὲ πάντα ἐκ τοῦ θεοῦ.

iii. The familiar title τέκνον θεοῦ, which describes the relation established iii. *'Child* by the new life, is of rarer occurrence in St John's writings. *of God.'*

(1) The power of duly becoming a 'child of God' is given by the (1) The communication of the divine life. beginning.

John i. 12 f. ἔδωκεν αὐτοῖς ἐξουσίαν τέκνα θεοῦ γενέσθαι, τοῖς πιστεύουσιν εἰς τὸ ὄνομα αὐτοῦ, οἱ...ἐκ θεοῦ ἐγεννήθησαν.

(2) The position is realised through the gift of love. (2) The

1 John iii. 1...ἀγάπην δέδωκεν ἡμῖν ὁ πατὴρ ἵνα τέκνα θεοῦ κληθῶμεν... growth

— 2 νῦν τέκνα θεοῦ ἐσμέν. and

(3) Thus 'the children of God' form a distinct body marked by right- (3) The eousness and love. signs.

1 John iii. 10 ἐν τούτῳ φανερά ἐστιν τὰ τέκνα τοῦ θεοῦ...

Comp. c. v. 2; John xi. 52.

The idea of τέκνον as it is thus presented by St John includes the two The idea notions of the presence of the divine principle and the action of human of 'chil-growth. The child is made to share in his Father's nature (comp. 2 Pet. i. dren' 4), and he uses in progressive advance the powers which he has received.

This thought of progress will be traced through the whole picture which St John draws of the spiritual life. 'From strength to strength' is the law by which it is shaped.

distinct from that of 'sons.' It is therefore easily intelligible why St John never uses the title υἱός, the name of definite dignity and privilege, to describe the relation of Christians to God. He regards their position not as the result of an 'adoption' (υἱοθεσία), but as the result of a new life which advances from the vital germ to full maturity.

Additional Note on iii. 5. *Aspects of the Incarnation.*

Different aspects of the Incarnation. The phrases which St John uses to describe the Incarnation fall into different groups corresponding with different aspects of the Fact. In regard to the Father, it is a 'Sending,' a 'Mission' (1). In regard to the Son, it is a 'Coming' (2). In regard to the form, it is in 'Flesh' (3). In regard to men, it is a 'Manifestation' (4).

1. Mission. 1. The idea of the Mission of Christ, the Son, by the Father is expressed by two verbs, πέμπω, ἀποστέλλω. The former describes the simple relation of the Sent to the Sender: the last adds 'the accessory notions of a special commission and so far of a delegated authority in the person sent.'

(a) The use of πέμπω. Πέμπω is not found in this connexion in the Epistles of St John (comp. Rom. viii. 3 only); and it is used in the Gospel only by the Lord in the participial form in three phrases ὁ πέμψας με (αὐτόν), ὁ πέμψας με πατήρ, ὁ πατὴρ ὁ πέμψας με.

i. ὁ πέμ-ψας με. Of these phrases the simple ὁ πέμψας με is by far the most common. It is used in two connexions to express (a) some relation of Christ to Him Who sent Him, and (β) some relation of men to Christ as so sent.

    (a) John iv. 34 ἐμὸν βρῶμα...ἵνα ποιήσω τὸ θέλημα τοῦ π. μ.
    — v. 30 ζητῶ...τὸ θέλημα τοῦ π. μ.
    — vi. 38 καταβέβηκα...ἵνα ποιῶ...τὸ θέλημα τοῦ π. μ.
    —   39 τοῦτό ἐστιν τὸ θέλημα τοῦ π. μ. ἵνα...μὴ ἀπολέσω...
    — vii. 16 ἡ ἐμὴ διδαχή...ἐστίν...τοῦ π. μ.
    —   26 ὁ π. μ. ἀληθής ἐστιν κἀγὼ ἃ ἤκουσα...λαλῶ.
    — ix. 4 δεῖ ἐργάζεσθαι τὰ ἔργα τοῦ π. μ.
    — viii. 29 ὁ π. μ. μετ' ἐμοῦ ἐστιν.
    — vii. 33, xvi. 5 ὑπάγω πρὸς τὸν π. μ.
  Comp. vii. 18 ὁ ζητῶν τὴν δόξαν τοῦ π. αὐτὸν ἀληθής ἐστιν.

    (β) John v. 24 ὁ...πιστεύων τῷ π. μ.
    — xii. 44 ὁ πιστεύων εἰς ἐμέ...πιστεύει...εἰς τὸν π. μ.
    —   45 ὁ θεωρῶν ἐμὲ θεωρεῖ τὸν π. μ.
    — xiii. 20 ὁ ἐμὲ λαμβάνων λαμβάνει τὸν π. μ.
    — xv. 21 ταῦτα ποιήσουσιν διὰ τὸ ὄνομά μου ὅτι οὐκ οἴδασιν τὸν π. μ.
  Comp. vii. 28 ἔστιν ἀληθινὸς ὁ π. μ. ὃν ὑμεῖς οὐκ οἴδατε.

The phrase ὁ πέμψας με πατήρ adds to the notion of 'sending' that of ii. ὁ πέμ-
the essential relation which gives authority to the mission. ψας με πατήρ.

John v. 37 ὁ π. μ. π. ἐκεῖνος μεμαρτύρηκεν.

— [viii. 16 (doubtful reading: comp. viii. 29) μόνος οὐκ εἰμί, ἀλλ'
    ἐγὼ καὶ ὁ π. μ. π.]

— viii. 18 μαρτυρεῖ περὶ ἐμοῦ ὁ π. μ. π.

— xii. 49 ὁ π. μ. π....ἐντολὴν δέδωκεν τί εἴπω...

— xiv. 24 ὁ λόγος ὃν ἀκούετε...ἐστίν...τοῦ π. μ. π.

In the phrase ὁ πατὴρ ὁ πέμψας με the two notions of natural authority iii. ὁ πατὴρ
and mission are dwelt on separately. It occurs   ὁ πέμψας
                                           με.
John vi. 44 ἐὰν μὴ ὁ π. ὁ π. μ. ἑλκύσῃ αὐτόν.

Comp. v. 23 ὁ μὴ τιμῶν τὸν υἱὸν οὐ τιμᾷ τὸν π. τ. π. αὐτόν.

The use of ἀποστέλλω differs from that of πέμπω by the fact that in St (b) The
John (yet see Matt. x. 40; Mark ix. 37; Luke ix. 48, x. 16) it is found only use of
in the finite forms, ἀπέστειλα, ἀπέσταλκα.   ἀποστέλ-
                                              λω.
The aorist is by far the most common tense. This is used to describe i. Aorist.
the fact of the specific Mission in some particular aspect:

John iii. 17 ἀπέστειλεν ὁ θεὸς τὸν υἱὸν εἰς τὸν κόσμον...ἵνα σωθῇ ὁ κόσμος
    δι' αὐτοῦ.

— x. 36 ὃν ὁ πατὴρ ἡγίασεν καὶ ἀπέστειλεν εἰς τὸν κόσμον.

1 John iv. 10 [ὁ θεὸς] ἀπέστειλεν τὸν υἱὸν αὐτοῦ ἱλασμὸν περὶ τῶν ἁμαρτιῶν
    ἡμῶν.

Compare

John vi. 57 καθὼς ἀπέστειλέν με ὁ ζῶν πατήρ...

— xvii. 18 καθὼς ἐμὲ ἀπέστειλας εἰς τὸν κόσμον...

— vii. 29 παρ' αὐτοῦ εἰμὶ κἀκεῖνός με ἀπέστειλεν.

— viii. 42 οὐδὲ ἀπ' ἐμαυτοῦ ἐλήλυθα ἀλλ' ἐκεῖνός με ἀπέστειλεν.

And this Mission is presented as the object (a) of recognition (knowledge), or (β) of faith:

  (a) John xvii. 3 ἵνα γινώσκωσιν...ὃν ἀπέστειλας Ἰησοῦν Χριστόν.

        — 23 ἵνα γινώσκῃ ὁ κόσμος ὅτι σύ με ἀπέστειλας.

        — 25 οὗτοι ἔγνωσαν ὅτι σύ με ἀπέστειλας.

  (β) John v. 38 ὅτι ὃν ἀπέστειλεν ἐκεῖνος τούτῳ ὑμεῖς οὐ πιστεύετε.

        — vi. 29 τὸ ἔργον τοῦ θεοῦ ἵνα πιστεύητε εἰς ὃν ἀπέστειλεν
           ἐκεῖνος.

        — xi. 42 ἵνα πιστεύσωσιν ὅτι σύ με ἀπέστειλας.

        — xvii. 21 ἵνα ὁ κόσμος πιστεύῃ ὅτι σύ με ἀπέστειλας.

Comp. John iii. 34 ...ἐσφράγισεν ὅτι...ὃν γὰρ ἀπέστειλεν ὁ θεός...

The perfect, which occurs but rarely, describes the Mission in its ii. Perfect.
abiding continuance:

John v. 36 τὰ ἔργα ἃ ποιῶ μαρτυρεῖ...ὅτι ὁ πατήρ με ἀπέσταλκεν.

1 John iv. 9 τὸν υἱὸν αὐτοῦ τὸν μονογενῆ ἀπέσταλκεν ὁ θεὸς εἰς τὸν κόσμον
    ἵνα ζήσωμεν δι' αὐτοῦ.

— 14 τεθεάμεθα καὶ μαρτυροῦμεν ὅτι ὁ πατὴρ ἀπέσταλκεν τὸν υἱὸν
    σωτῆρα τοῦ κόσμου.

John xx. 21 καθὼς ἀπέσταλκέν με ὁ πατήρ, κἀγὼ πέμπω ὑμᾶς.

2. COMING.   2. The Coming of Christ, like the Mission, is regarded both as a simple fact realised historically once for all (ἦλθον), and as an abiding fact (ἥκω, ἐλήλυθα). It is also set forth as a present fact being realised at the moment, and as a future fact of which the fulfilment is potentially begun (ἔρχομαι)[1].

(a) Aor. ἦλθον.

The simple fact of Christ's Coming is affirmed by St John both in respect of His true Divinity as the Word, and of His true humanity:

John i. 11 εἰς τὰ ἴδια ἦλθεν [τὸ φῶς τὸ ἀληθινόν].

1 John v. 6 ὁ ἐλθὼν δι' ὕδατος καὶ αἵματος Ἰησοῦς Χριστός.

In the discourses of the Lord the fact of His Coming, the fact of the Incarnation, is connected with the manifold issues which it involved:

John ix. 39 εἰς κρίμα ἐγὼ εἰς τὸν κόσμον τοῦτον ἦλθον ἵνα οἱ μὴ βλέποντες ...καὶ οἱ βλέποντες....

— x. 10 ἐγὼ ἦλθον ἵνα ζωὴν ἔχωσιν καὶ περισσὸν ἔχωσιν.

— xii. 47 οὐκ ἦλθον ἵνα κρίνω τὸν κόσμον ἀλλ' ἵνα σώσω τὸν κόσμον.

— xv. 22 εἰ μὴ ἦλθον καὶ ἐλάλησα οὐκ ἂν εἶχον ἁμαρτίαν.

And the Lord bases the truth of His witness on His consciousness of the fact:

John viii. 14 ἀληθής ἐστιν ἡ μαρτυρία μου ὅτι οἶδα πόθεν ἦλθον καὶ ποῦ ὑπάγω (contrasted with πόθεν ἔρχομαι).

ἐξῆλθον.

The divine relation implied in this use of 'came' is expressed more distinctly by the verb 'came forth' (ἐξῆλθον). This is used in the Lord's words with different prepositions (ἐκ, παρά):

John viii. 42 ἐγὼ ἐκ τοῦ θεοῦ ἐξῆλθον καὶ ἥκω.

— xvi. 28 ἐξῆλθον ἐκ τοῦ πατρὸς καὶ ἐλήλυθα εἰς τὸν κόσμον.

—   27 πεπιστεύκατε ὅτι ἐγὼ παρὰ τοῦ πατρὸς ἐξῆλθον.

— xvii. 8 ἔγνωσαν...ὅτι παρὰ σοῦ ἐξῆλθον.

And it is significant that St John and the disciples use the word with a yet different turn of thought (ἀπό):

John xiii. 3 εἰδὼς...ὅτι ἀπὸ θεοῦ ἐξῆλθεν.

— xvi. 30 πιστεύομεν ὅτι ἀπὸ θεοῦ ἐξῆλθες[2].

(b) Perf. ἐλήλυθα.

The perfect (ἐλήλυθα) serves to bring out the abiding significance of the fact of Christ's Coming, the necessary effects which it has as distinguished

---

[1] The usage in John i. 9 ἦν τὸ φῶς τὸ ἀληθινόν......ἐρχόμενον is unique. See note.

[2] It is of interest to compare the instances of the use of ἦλθον, ἐλήλυθα in the Synoptic Gospels:

Matt. v. 17 οὐκ ἦλθον καταλῦσαι ἀλλὰ πληρῶσαι.

—— ix. 13 ‖ Mark ii. 17 οὐκ ἦλθον καλέσαι δικαίους ἀλλὰ ἁμαρτωλούς·

Luke v. 32 οὐκ ἐλήλυθα κ. δ. ἀ. ἀ. εἰς μετάνοιαν.

—— x. 34 οὐκ ἦλθον βαλεῖν εἰρήνην

ἀλλὰ μάχαιραν. ἦλθον γὰρ διχάσαι......

Luke xii. 49 πῦρ ἦλθον βαλεῖν ἐπὶ τὴν γῆν.

Matt. xi. 19 ‖ Luke vii. 33 ἦλθεν (Lk. ἐλήλυθεν) ὁ υἱὸς τοῦ ἀνθρώπου ἐσθίων καὶ πίνων.

—— xx. 28 ‖ Mark x. 45 ὁ υἱὸς τοῦ ἀνθρώπου οὐκ ἦλθεν διακονηθῆναι...

Luke xix. 10 ἦλθεν ὁ υἱὸς τοῦ ἀνθρώπου ζητῆσαι καὶ σῶσαι τὸ ἀπολωλός.

from its general issues. So St John uses the tense in connexion with the testing power of Christ revealed as 'light' and 'in flesh':

John iii. 19 τὸ φῶς ἐλήλυθεν εἰς τὸν κόσμον καὶ ἠγάπησαν οἱ ἄνθρωποι μᾶλλον τὸ σκότος...

1 John iv. 2 πᾶν πνεῦμα ὃ ὁμολογεῖ 'Ι. Χ. ἐν σαρκὶ ἐληλυθότα ἐκ τοῦ θεοῦ ἐστίν.

And the Lord thus speaks of the special character of His Coming:

John v. 43 ἐγὼ ἐλήλυθα ἐν τῷ ὀνόματι τοῦ πατρός μου.

— xii. 46 ἐγὼ φῶς εἰς τὸν κόσμον ἐλήλυθα.

— xviii. 37 ἐλήλυθα εἰς τὸν κόσμον ἵνα μαρτυρήσω τῇ ἀληθείᾳ.

and generally:

John vii. 28 καὶ ἀπ᾽ ἐμαυτοῦ οὐκ ἐλήλυθα (viii. 42 οὐδὲ ἀπ᾽ ἐμ. ἐλ.).

— xvi. 28 ἐξῆλθον ἐκ τοῦ πατρὸς καὶ ἐλήλυθα εἰς τὸν κόσμον.

The verb ἥκω is used in this connexion twice only: *ἥκω.*

John viii. 42 ἐκ τοῦ θεοῦ ἐξῆλθον καὶ ἥκω.

1 John v. 20 ὁ υἱὸς τοῦ θεοῦ ἥκει.

It occurs also in quotations from the LXX. Hebr. x. 7, 9 (ἥκω); Rom. x. 26; Hebr. x. 37 (ἥξει); and of the future Coming of Christ; Apoc. ii. 25, iii. 3.

The present ἔρχομαι occurs to describe a Coming realised at the (c) Pres. moment: *ἔρχομαι.*

John viii. 14 πόθεν ἔρχομαι (contrasted with πόθεν ἦλθον), and as a future fact potentially included in the present:

John xiv. 3 πάλιν ἔρχομαι.

— 18, 28 ἔρχομαι πρὸς ὑμᾶς.

— xxi. 22 f. ἕως ἔρχομαι.

2 John 7 οἱ μὴ ὁμολογοῦντες 'Ι. Χ. ἐρχόμενον ἐν σαρκί.

Comp. John iii. 31 f. ὁ ἄνωθεν (ἐκ τοῦ οὐρανοῦ) ἐρχόμενος.

See also Apoc. i. 7, ii. 6, iii. 11, xxii. 7, 12, 20.

The passages John viii. 14, 42, xvi. 27 f. will repay particular study as illustrating the different forms.

3. The mode of Christ's Coming is exhaustively set forth in the three 3. INCAR-phrases in which it is connected with 'flesh.' First there is the fundamental NATION. statement:

John i. 14 ὁ λόγος σὰρξ ἐγένετο.

And then this fact is connected with the past and present:

1 John iv. 2 (ὁμολογεῖν) Ἰησοῦν Χριστὸν ἐν σαρκὶ ἐληλυθότα (ἐληλυθέναι),

and with the future:

2 John 7 (ὁμολογεῖν) Ἰησοῦν Χριστὸν ἐρχόμενον ἐν σαρκί.

The 'manifestation' (φανερωθῆναι) of the Lord is noticed by St John 4. MANI-in regard to the great crises in His progressive revelation. Thus it is said FESTATION. that He was 'manifested' by the Incarnation:

1 John i. 2 ἡ ζωὴ ἐφανερώθη.

— iii. 5 ἐκεῖνος ἐφανερώθη ἵνα τὰς ἁμαρτίας ἄρῃ.

— 8 ἐφανερώθη ὁ υἱὸς τοῦ θεοῦ ἵνα λύσῃ τὰ ἔργα τοῦ διαβόλου.

and when He was openly presented to the people: .

John i. 31 ἵνα φανερωθῇ τῷ Ἰσραὴλ διὰ τοῦτο ἦλθον.

So also 'He was manifested' and 'He manifested Himself' in the new life after the Resurrection :

John xxi. 14 ἐφανερώθη Ἰησοῦς τοῖς μαθηταῖς.

— 1 ἐφανέρωσεν ἑαυτὸν Ἰησοῦς τοῖς μαθηταῖς.

and Christians still look for a manifestation in the future :

1 John ii. 28 ἵνα ἐὰν φανερωθῇ σχῶμεν παρρησίαν...ἐν τῇ παρουσίᾳ αὐτοῦ.

— iii. 2 ἐὰν φανερωθῇ ὅμοιοι αὐτῷ ἐσόμεθα.

Completeness of the teaching. It is not necessary to draw out in detail the teaching of these pregnant words. They offer the fullest view which man can gain of the Person of the Lord in its absolute unity, truly human and truly divine. St John says both 'the Word became flesh' and 'Jesus Christ came in flesh'; and further he speaks of 'Jesus Christ coming in flesh.' Again he says equally 'the Life was manifested,' 'the Life which was with the Father,' and 'He [Jesus Christ] was manifested,' and 'the Son of God was manifested.' Now one aspect of the Lord's Person, now another is brought forward without change. There is nothing in the least degree formal in the different statements: they spring directly out of the immediate context as answering to one sovereign conception : and when put together they combine to produce a final harmony, the fulness of apostolic teaching, upon the central Truth of the Gospel. The least variation adds something to the completeness of the idea; and the minute correspondences bring an assurance that the result which the combination of the different phrases suggests answers to the thought of the Apostle which underlay all that he wrote.

Additional Note on iii. 14.   *Titles of believers.*

The titles of believers in the New Test. Christians. The different names which are given to Christians in the Apostolic writings offer an instructive study of the original conception of the Gospel. The origin of the historic Gentile name 'Christians' (Χριστιανοί, comp. *Pompeiani*) is noticed in Acts xi. 26 ; and it is used as familiarly known by Agrippa (Acts xxvi. 26) and by St Peter (1 Pet. iv. 16; comp. Tac. *Ann.* xv. 44). From the time of Ignatius this name, with the correlative for 'Christianity' (Χριστιανισμός), passed into general use (comp. Ign. *ad Magn.* 4, 10; *ad Rom.* 3 ; *Mart. Polyc.* 10); but it was natural that in the first age of the Church it should not be used by believers among themselves.

Four titles: disciples, brethren, saints, believers. Four terms find more or less currency in the N. T. which express different aspects of the Christian view of the Christian position : 'the disciples' (οἱ μαθηταί), 'the brethren' (οἱ ἀδελφοί), 'the saints' (οἱ ἅγιοι), 'the believers' (οἱ πιστοί, οἱ πιστεύοντες). These fall into two pairs, of which the first pair, 'disciples,' 'brethren,' marks predominantly traits of personal relationship, and the second pair, 'saints,' 'faithful,' traits of general character.

The earliest title is that of 'the disciples.' This answers to 'master,' 1. *The*
'teacher' (διδάσκαλος), and passed from the Jewish schools to the followers *disciples.*
of Christ during His lifetime. It was used both in a wider sense for all
who attached themselves to Him (John ii. 11 ff. ; vi. 61, 66; vii. 3) and also
in a narrower sense for 'the twelve' (John xiii. 5 ff.). After the Ascension
it is still employed absolutely in the narrative of the Acts to describe
believers generally (vi. 1, 2, 7; ix. 19, 25, 38; xi. 26, 29; xiii. 52; xiv. 20,
22, 28; xviii. 23, 27; xix. 9, 30; xx. 1 ; xxi. 4, 16); and so it is found in
the record of a speech of St Peter (xv. 10) and of a speech of St Paul (xx.
30). The discipleship is once connected with the human teacher (ix. 25 οἱ
μ. αὐτοῦ) and once with the Lord (ix. 19). It is remarkable that in one
place (xix. 1) those who had only received John's Baptism are spoken of as
disciples. The title does not occur in the Epistles or in the Apocalypse.

It is significant that the first title given to the body of believers after 2. *The*
the Ascension is 'the brethren' (Acts i. 15 true text); and from this time *brethren.*
onwards it occurs in all the groups of Apostolic writings. Thus in the Acts
it is found in the narrative: ix. 30; x. 23 ; xi. 29; xiv. 2; xv. 1, 3, 22, 32 f.,
40; xvi. 2, 40; xvii. 10; xviii. 18, 27; xxi. 7, 17 ; xxviii. 14 f.; and once in
the record of St Paul's words: xv. 36. Twice in the same book it is used
of unconverted Jews: xxii. 5 (St Paul's words); xxviii. 21. St Paul uses
the title throughout his Epistles: 1 Thess. iv. 10; v. 26 f.; 1 Cor. viii. 12;
xvi. 20; Gal. i. 2; Rom. xvi. 14; Phil. iv. 21; Eph. vi. 23; Col. iv. 15;
1 Tim. iv. 6; 2 Tim. iv. 21. In the writings of St John it occurs: 1 John iii.
14; 3 John 5, 10; John xxi. 23. St Peter uses the abstract term 'the
brotherhood' (ἡ ἀδελφότης, 1 Pet. ii. 17; v. 9). The singular is not
uncommonly used (*e.g.* Rom. xvi. 23; 1 Cor. vii. 15), and especially with a
personal pronoun, 'thy brother,' 'his brother' (*e.g.* Rom. xiv. 10; 1 John
ii. 9 ff.). Compare c. ii. 9 note.

The general idea of 'the believers' is expressed in three different forms 3. *The*
which convey shades of difference in the application of the common mean- *believers.*
ing: 'the believers' (οἱ πιστοί), 'they that believe' (οἱ πιστεύοντες), 'they
that believed' (οἱ πιστεύσαντες). The first (οἱ πιστοί) is found Acts x. 45
(οἱ ἐκ περιτομῆς πιστοί) ; 1 Tim. iv. 12; comp. Eph. i. 1; 1 Tim. iv. 3;
1 Pet. i. 21. 'They that believe' (οἱ πιστεύοντες) occurs: 1 Pet. ii. 7; 1 Thess.
i. 7; ii. 10 f.; 1 Cor. i. 21 ; Rom. iii. 22 ; Eph. i. 19. 'They that believed'
(οἱ πιστεύσαντες) occurs: Acts ii. 44; iv. 32; 2 Thess. i. 10; Hebr. iv. 3.
In the two last phrases the historic reference to the act of belief still
remains.

The title 'the saints' is characteristic of St Paul and of the Apocalypse. 4. *The*
It occurs four times in the Acts, twice in connexion with St Paul's conver- *saints.*
sion (Acts ix. 13 τοὺς ἁγίους σου; xxvi. 10), and twice in connexion with the
episode of St Peter's visit to Lydda (ix. 32) and Joppa (ix. 41). It is found
also once in St Jude (Jude 3); but not in any other of the Catholic Epistles
(comp. 1 Pet. ii. 5, 9). In St Paul it is frequent and distributed throughout
his Epistles: 1 Thess. iii. 13; 2 Thess. i. 10 ; 1 Cor. vi. 1 f.; xiv. 33; xvi. 1,
15; 2 Cor. i. 1; viii. 4; ix. 1, 12; xiii. 12; Rom. xii. 13; xv. 25 f., 31;
xvi. 2, 15; Phil. i. 1; iv. 22; Eph. i. 1, 15, 18; iv. 12; vi. 18; Col. i. 2, 4,
12, 26; Philem. 5, 7. It is found also in Hebr. vi. 10; xiii. 24. In the

Apocalypse it is found: v. 8; viii. 3 f.; xi. 18; xiii. 7, 10: xiv. 12; xvii. 6;
xviii. 20; xix. 8.

General
relation of
the titles.

The main differences of conception between the four titles are evident.
Christians stand in the position of learners in the school of their Lord.
The lesson which they have to learn surpasses all others. But the relation
to the Divine Master is at once embodied in a new relation to fellow-
believers. So the title 'the disciples' is soon lost in that of 'the brethren.'
In the same way the title of 'the faithful,' which corresponds to 'disciples,'
is far less common and characteristic than 'the saints' ('the holy'), which
marks the recognised consecration of believers.

The titles
in con-
nexion.

But while these broad distinctions are obvious, it is not easy to seize
the exact force of the particular titles except that of 'the faithful' on each
occasion, or even when they come near together, as 'disciples' and
'brethren;' Acts xi. 29; xviii. 27; xxi. 16 f. : 'disciples' and 'saints;' Acts
ix. 38, 41: 'brethren' and 'saints;' 1 Cor. xvi. 15, 20; Rom. xvi. 14 f.;
Eph. vi. 18, 23. It seems not unlikely that the title 'the brethren,' was
carried over from the 'Israel according to the flesh' to the spiritual Israel,
and was specially used of the Jewish congregations. This view is supported
by Acts xxii. 5; xxviii. 21. But in any case the title was soon extended
more widely: Acts xv. 1.

Additional note on iii. 16. *St John's conception of love*
(ἀγάπη).

1. The verb ἀγαπᾶν occurs throughout Greek literature from Homer
downwards. The noun ἀγάπη belongs to Biblical literature exclusively.
It occurs first in the LXX., where it is found in 2 Sam. xiii. 15, thirteen
times in Eccles. and Cant., and in Jer. ii. 2. It is not found in the
Pentateuch; nor is it quoted from Philo or Josephus. The word is used
in all the books of the New Testament except the Gospel of St Mark, Acts,
and the Epistle of St James (in the Synoptic Gospels only Matt. xxiv. 12;
Luke xi. 42). The collateral form ἀγάπησις occurs in the LXX. and later
Greek writers but not in the New Testament.

The one compound of ἀγαπ- which is recorded is the Homeric ἀγαπήνωρ.

2. The words ἀγαπᾶν, ἀγάπη are used to describe the feeling of

I.   God (the Father) for

(1)   *The Son:*

John iii. 35 ὁ πατὴρ ἀγαπᾷ τὸν υἱόν.
—   x. 17 διὰ τοῦτό με ὁ πατὴρ ἀγαπᾷ ὅτι...
—   xv. 9 καθὼς ἠγάπησέ με ὁ πατήρ, κἀγώ...
—   — 10 μένω αὐτοῦ ἐν τῇ ἀγάπῃ.
—   xvii. 23 ...καθὼς ἐμὲ ἠγάπησας.
—   — 24 ἠγάπησάς με πρὸ καταβολῆς κόσμου.
—   — 26 ἵνα ἡ ἀγάπη ἣν ἠγάπησάς με ἐν αὐτοῖς ᾖ...

(2) *The world:*

John iii. 16 οὕτως ἠγάπησεν ὁ θεὸς τὸν κόσμον ὥστε...

(3) *Men:*

John xiv. 21 ὁ ἀγαπῶν με ἀγαπηθήσεται ὑπὸ τοῦ πατρός μου.

— — 23 ὁ πατήρ μου ἀγαπήσει αὐτόν.

— xvii. 23 ἠγάπησας αὐτοὺς καθὼς ἐμὲ ἠγάπησας.

1 John iv. 10 αὐτὸς [ὁ θεὸς] ἠγάπησεν ἡμᾶς.

— — 11 εἰ οὕτως ὁ θεὸς ἠγάπησεν ἡμᾶς...

Comp. Apoc. xx. 9 τὴν πόλιν τὴν ἠγαπημένην.

Φιλεῖν is found in a corresponding connexion in regard to

(1) *The Son:*

John v. 20 ὁ πατὴρ φιλεῖ (v.l. ἀγαπᾷ) τὸν υἱόν.

(2) *Men:*

John xvi. 27 ὁ πατὴρ φιλεῖ ὑμᾶς.

II. The Son, for

(1) *The Father:*

John xiv. 31 ἵνα γνῷ ὁ κόσμος ὅτι ἀγαπῶ τὸν πατέρα.

(2) *The disciples:*

severally

xi. 5 ἠγάπα δὲ ὁ Ἰησοῦς τὴν Μάρθαν...

xiii. 23; xix. 26; xxi. 7, 20 (εἷς τῶν μαθητῶν) ὃν ἠγάπα ὁ Ἰησοῦς.

xiv. 21 ἐγὼ ἀγαπήσω αὐτόν...

Apoc. iii. 9 ὅτι ἐγὼ ἠγάπησά σε.

generally

xiii. 1 ἀγαπήσας τοὺς ἰδίους τοὺς ἐν τῷ κόσμῳ εἰς τέλος ἠγάπησεν αὐτούς.

xiii. 34; xv. 9, 12 ἠγάπησα ὑμᾶς· μείνατε...

[— 9 μείνατε ἐν τῇ ἀγάπῃ τῇ ἐμῇ]?

— 10 μενεῖτε ἐν τῇ ἀγάπῃ μου καθώς...

Apoc. i. 5 τῷ ἀγαπῶντι ἡμᾶς.

Compare the use of φιλεῖν for the feeling of Christ towards men severally.

John xi. 3 ἴδε ὃν φιλεῖς ἀσθενεῖ.

— — 36 ἴδε πῶς ἐφίλει αὐτόν.

— xx. 2 μαθητὴς ὃν ἐφίλει ὁ Ἰησοῦς.

Apoc. iii. 19 ἐγὼ ὅσους ἐὰν φιλῶ, ἐλέγχω.

III. Men for

(1) *God (the Father):*

John v. 42 τὴν ἀγάπην τοῦ θεοῦ οὐκ ἔχετε ἐν ἑαυτοῖς.

1 John ii. 15 οὐκ ἔστιν ἡ ἀγάπη τοῦ πατρὸς ἐν αὐτῷ.

— iv. 10 οὐχ ὅτι ἡμεῖς ἠγαπήκαμεν τὸν θεόν.

— — 20 f. ἐάν τις εἴπῃ ὅτι Ἀγαπῶ τὸν θεόν.

— v. 1 πᾶς ὁ ἀγαπῶν τὸν γεννήσαντα...

— — 2 ...ὅταν τὸν θεὸν ἀγαπῶμεν.

(2) *Christ:*

John viii. 42 εἰ ὁ θεὸς πατὴρ ὑμῶν ἦν ἠγαπᾶτε ἂν ἐμέ.

— xiv. 15 ἐὰν ἀγαπᾶτέ με...

— — 21 .. ἐκεῖνός ἐστιν ὁ ἀγαπῶν με· ὁ δὲ ἀγαπῶν με...

— — 23 ἐάν τις ἀγαπᾷ με...

— — 24 ὁ μὴ ἀγαπῶν με...

— — 28 εἰ ἠγαπᾶτέ με ἐχάρητε ἄν...

[— xv. 9 μείνατε ἐν τῇ ἀγάπῃ τῇ ἐμῇ...]?

— xxi. 15 f. Σίμων Ἰωάνου ἀγαπᾷς με... ;

(3) *The brethren:*

John xiii. 34; xv. 17 (ἐντολήν) ἵνα ἀγαπᾶτε ἀλλήλους.

— — 35 ...ἐὰν ἀγάπην ἔχητε ἐν ἀλλήλοις.

— xv. 12 ἵνα ἀγαπᾶτε ἀλλήλους καθὼς ἠγάπησα ὑμᾶς.

1 John ii. 10; iv. 21 ὁ ἀγαπῶν τὸν ἀδελφόν...

— iii. 10, 14; iv. 20 ὁ μὴ ἀγαπῶν τὸν ἀδελφόν.

— — 11, 23; iv. 7, 11; 2 John 5 (ἀγγελία) ἵνα ἀγαπῶμεν ἀλλήλους.

— — 14 ...ὅτι ἀγαπῶμεν τοὺς ἀδελφούς.

— v. 1 ...ἀγαπᾷ καὶ τὸν γεγεννημένον ἐξ αὐτοῦ.

— — 2 ὅτι ἀγαπῶμεν τὰ τέκνα τοῦ θεοῦ.

2 John 1 οὓς ἐγὼ ἀγαπῶ.

3 John 1 ὃν ἐγὼ ἀγαπῶ.

(4) *Life:*

Apoc. xii. 11 οὐκ ἠγάπησαν τὴν ψυχὴν αὐτῶν ἄχρι θανάτου.

(5) *Evil (darkness):*

John iii. 19 ἠγάπησαν...μᾶλλον τὸ σκότος ἢ τὸ φῶς.

— xii. 43 ἠγάπησαν τὴν δόξαν τῶν ἀνθρώπων...

1 John ii. 15 μὴ ἀγαπᾶτε τὸν κόσμον μηδὲ τὰ ἐν τῷ κόσμῳ· ἐάν τις ἀγαπᾷ τὸν κόσμον...

So φιλεῖν is used of the feeling of men for

(1) *Christ:*

John xvi. 27 ὑμεῖς ἐμὲ πεφιλήκατε.

— xxi. 15 ff. σὺ οἶδας (γινώσκεις) ὅτι φιλῶ σε.

— — 17 φιλεῖς με ;

Comp. 1 Cor. xvi. 22 εἴ τις οὐ φιλεῖ τὸν κύριον.

(2) *Life:*

John xii. 25 ὁ φιλῶν τὴν ψυχήν.

(3) *Evil:*

Apoc. xxii. 15 ὁ φιλῶν...ψεῦδος.

Comp. John xv. 19 ὁ κόσμος ἂν τὸ ἴδιον ἐφίλει.

Φιλεῖν is not used by St John of the feeling of man for the Father or for man (Matt. x. 27; Tit. iii. 15).

Φιλία occurs only James iv. 4 ἡ φιλία τοῦ κόσμου ἔχθρα τοῦ θεοῦ ἐστίν.

3. The words ἀγαπᾶν, ἀγάπη are also used absolutely.

1 John iii. 1 ποταπὴν ἀγάπην δέδωκεν ἡμῖν ὁ θεός...
— — 16 ἐν τούτῳ ἐγνώκαμεν τὴν ἀγάπην...
— — 18 μὴ ἀγαπῶμεν λόγῳ...
— iv. 7 ἡ ἀγάπη ἐκ τοῦ θεοῦ ἐστίν.
— — id. πᾶς ὁ ἀγαπῶν ἐκ τοῦ θεοῦ γεγέννηται.
— — 8 ὁ μὴ ἀγαπῶν οὐκ ἔγνω τὸν θεόν.
— — id., 16 ὁ θεὸς ἀγάπη ἐστίν.
— — 10 ἐν τούτῳ ἐστὶν ἡ ἀγάπη, οὐχ ὅτι...
— — 16 ὁ μένων ἐν τῇ ἀγάπῃ.
— — 17 ἐν τούτῳ τετελείωται ἡ ἀγάπη μεθ᾽ ἡμῶν, ἵνα...
— — 18 φόβος οὐκ ἔστιν ἐν τῇ ἀγάπῃ.
— — id. ἡ τελεία ἀγάπη ἔξω βάλλει τὸν φόβον.
— — id. ὁ φοβούμενος οὐ τετελείωται ἐν τῇ ἀγάπῃ.
— — 19 ἡμεῖς ἀγαπῶμεν, ὅτι...
2 John 3 ἐν ἀληθείᾳ καὶ ἀγάπῃ.
— 6 αὕτη ἐστὶν ἡ ἀγάπη, ἵνα...
3 John 6 ἐμαρτύρησάν σου τῇ ἀγάπῃ.

4. From a consideration of these passages it will be seen that ἀγαπᾶν, ἀγάπη are an expression of character, determined, as we are forced to conceive of things, by will, and not of spontaneous, natural emotion. In this sense 'love' is the willing communication to others of that which we have and are; and the exact opposite of that passion which is the desire of personal appropriation (ἐρᾶν, ἔρως).

5. God Himself is love. The creation and preservation of the world are in essence a continuous manifestation of His love; but, as things are, His love is characteristically made known through redemption, that is the consummation of the divine counsel of creation in spite of the intrusion of sin (1 John iii. 16; iv. 9). So it is that the revelation of the divine love is referred to an absolute (eternal) moment (ἠγάπησας, ἠγάπησεν) both in relation to the Son and also to the world and to men.

6. At the same time God who is love is also the source of love (1 John iv. 7). He endows believers with love (1 John iii. 1, 16 f.; iv. 9, 12, 16; 2 John 6); and this love becomes in them a fountain of moral energy, issuing necessarily in self-sacrifice (John xv. 13; 1 John iii. 16).

On the other hand the love of evil is so far moral suicide.

7. It is of interest to notice that 'love' is connected by St Paul with each Person of the Holy Trinity :

ἡ ἀγάπη τοῦ θεοῦ· 2 Thess. iii. 5; 2 Cor. xiii. 13; Rom. v. 5; (Eph. ii. 4).
ἡ ἀγάπη τοῦ χριστοῦ· 2 Cor. v. 14; Rom. viii. 35; Eph. iii. 19.
ἡ ἀγάπη τοῦ πνεύματος· Rom. xv. 30.

In each case the thought appears to be of the love of which God is the source rather than the object. But the love of God in man becomes in him a spring of love. On the idea of 'the love of God' see c. ii. 5 note.

Additional Note on iii. 19.   *The nature of man.*

Limita-
tion of St
John's
view of
man's
nature.

St John does not, like St Paul, give any definite analysis of the constitution or of the spiritual experience of man.   But he recognises the same
elements in human nature.   Like St Paul, he distinguishes 'the flesh,'
'the soul,' 'the spirit,' 'the heart.'   But it is worthy of notice that the
characteristic intellectual faculties are rarely noticed by him.   'Understanding' (διάνοια) occurs only once in the most remarkable passage 1 John
v. 20; and 'mind' (νοῦς) is found only in the Apocalypse (xiii. 18 ; xvii. 9).
'Conscience' (συνείδησις) is nowhere mentioned by St John (contrast
[John] viii. 8).   In St Paul these words are not unfrequent.   For St John's
use of γινώσκειν see c. ii. 3 note.

i. *Flesh*
(σάρξ).

The term 'flesh' (σάρξ) describes the element with the characteristics
of the element (comp. 1 Cor. xv. 39).   It includes all that belongs to the
life of sensation, all by which we are open to the physical influences of
pleasure and pain, which naturally sway our actions.

As applied to human nature 'flesh' describes humanity so far as it
is limited and defined by earthly conditions.   In 'flesh' lies the point of
connexion between man and the lower world.   Through flesh come the
temptations which belong to sense.

The word is used of mankind (as in O. T.) John xvii. 2 (πᾶσα σάρξ) to
describe them under the aspect of earthly transitoriness.

'Flesh' is contrasted with 'spirit,' not as evil with good, but as the
ruling element of one order with the ruling element of another : John iii.
6 ; vi. 63.

By 'flesh' we are united to earth ; and by 'spirit' to heaven.

'The will of the flesh' (John i. 13) is the determination which belongs
to the earthly powers of man as such.

'The desire of the flesh' (1 John ii. 16) is the desire which, as it springs
out of man's present earthly constitution, is confined within the earthly
sphere and rises no higher.

'Judgment after the flesh' (John viii. 15) is external, superficial,
limited by what catches the senses (comp. 2 Cor. v. 16).

Thus the idea of evil attaches to the flesh not in virtue of what it is
essentially, but from the undue preponderance which is given to it.   The
flesh serves for the manifestation of character.   It ministers to other powers.
It becomes evil when it is made supreme or dominates.   It does not
include the idea of sinfulness, but it describes human personality on the
side which tends to sin, and on which we actually have sinned.

Use of
'flesh' in
relation to
Christ.

The essential conception of σάρξ is seen in its application to Christ
(1) in His Person :

John i. 14 ὁ λόγος σὰρξ ἐγένετο.
1 John iv. 2 ἐληλυθὼς ἐν σαρκί.
2 John 7 ἐρχόμενος ἐν σαρκί.
Compare 1 Tim. iii. 16 ἐφανερώθη ἐν σαρκί.
Col. i. 22 τὸ σῶμα τῆς σαρκὸς αὐτοῦ.

And

(2) in His Work :

John vi. 51 ἡ σάρξ μου ὑπὲρ τῆς τοῦ κόσμου ζωῆς.

— 53 φαγεῖν τὴν σάρκα τοῦ υἱοῦ τοῦ ἀνθρώπου καὶ πιεῖν αὐτοῦ τὸ αἷμα.

— 56 ὁ τρώγων μου τὴν σάρκα καὶ πίνων μου τὸ αἷμα.

In these passages 'flesh' is seen to describe the element of Christ's perfect humanity
It may be added that while σῶμα is found in St John (John ii. 21 ; xx. 12, &c.), it is never used metaphorically, and it does not occur in the epistles (Apoc. xviii. 13 = mancipiorum). In the Apocalypse σάρξ is found only in the plural.

The sense of the word represented by 'soul,' 'life' (ψυχή) is often ii. Soul obscure in other apostolic writers from the complex nature of the living 'life' man ; but in St John it is used only for the personal principle of our (ψυχή). present earthly life, the vital energy of the σάρξ (yet notice John x. 24).

It is used

(1) of men generally :

John xii. 25 (comp. Luke xiv. 26 ; xvii. 33).

— xiii. 37 f. τιθέναι τὴν ψυχήν.

— xv. 13 id. ; I John iii. 16 id. ; 3 John 2.

And

(2) of Christ :

John xii. 27 ; x. 11, 15, 17 τὴν ψ. τιθέναι.

1 John iii. 16 id.

With the phrase τιθέναι τὴν ψυχὴν ὑπέρ (x. 11, 15; comp. Matt. xx. 28) must be contrasted (δοῦναι) τὴν σάρκα ὑπέρ (vi. 51).

In the Apocalypse ψυχή is used in the most unusual sense of disembodied 'souls'; vi. 9; xx. 4.

While the 'soul' (ψυχή) expresses the sum of man's present vital iii. Spirit powers, the 'spirit' (πνεῦμα) describes the quickening element which (πνεῦμα). belongs to a heavenly sphere (comp. Rom. viii. 10) as the flesh describes the earthly element : John iii. 6 (5); vi. 63.

It is used of the Lord : John xiii. 21 (comp. xii. 27); xi. 33.

Compare the phrases 'to become in spirit,' 'in spirit,' found in the Apocalypse: i. 10 (ἐγενόμην ἐν πνεύματι); iv. 2 (id.); xvii. 13 (ἐν πνεύματι); xxi. 10 (id.).

The sense the 'breath of life' is wholly distinct: John xix. 30 (comp. Matt. xxvii. 50; Lk. viii. 55); Apoc. xi. 11 (πνεῦμα ζωῆς); xiii. 15 (δοῦναι πν. τῇ εἰκόνι).

The seat of individual character, of personal feeling and moral determi- iv. 'Heart' nation, is the 'heart' (καρδία). The elements already considered are (καρδία). morally colourless in themselves, they are generic and not individual. The mention of the heart is comparatively rare in St John. But he shews that it is the seat of sorrow (John xvi. 6), of joy (xvi. 22), of distress generally (xiv. 1, 27), and also of purpose (xiii. 3), and spiritual discernment (xii. 40, LXX.).

The most remarkable passage in which he describes the office of the heart is in 1 John iii. 19—21. In this the heart appears as representing the whole conscious moral nature of man. The heart in fact includes the conscience, and covers the whole range of life. It takes account not only of the abstract rule but of all the personal circumstances which go to characterise action.

Compare Apoc. ii. 23; xvii. 17; xviii. 7.

Additional Note on iii. 23. The Names of the Lord.

The names of the Lord in the Epistles.

Something has been already said on the use of the Divine Names in the Epistles of St John (Additional Note on i. 2). It is however of deep interest to study in detail the exact relation of the several Names of the Lord to the contexts in which they occur. Such an inquiry will leave, I believe, a strong conviction in the mind of the student that each Name is perfectly fitted to present that aspect of the Lord's Person which is dominant at the particular point in the Apostle's exposition of the Truth.

The idea of 'the Name.'

Here, as elsewhere in the Bible, the Name has two distinct and yet closely connected meanings. It may express the revelation of the Divine Being given by a special title; or the whole sum of the manifold revelations gathered up together so as to form one supreme revelation. It is used in the latter sense in regard to the revelation of God in Christ in 3 John 7 ὑπὲρ τοῦ ὀνόματος, where τὸ ὄνομα, 'the Name' absolutely, includes the essential elements of the Christian Creed, the complete revelation of Christ's Person and Work in relation to God and man (comp. Acts v. 41; John xx. 31). In ii. 12 διὰ τὸ ὄνομα αὐτοῦ the term is more limited. The Person Who is present to St John through the paragraph is Christ as He lived on earth and gave Himself for those whom He called brethren (ii. 6; comp. Hebr. ii. 11 ff.). In iii. 23, v. 13 the exact sense of 'the Name' is defined by the words which follow.

The special names: His Son Jesus Christ,

From the Name thus generally referred to or defined we pass to the actual Names used. The full title *His Son Jesus Christ* (ὁ υἱὸς αὐτοῦ Ἰησοῦς Χριστός) is found i. 3, iii. 23, v. 20. The divine antecedent is differently described in the three cases, and this difference slightly colours the phrase. In i. 3 it is 'the Father' (compare 2 John 3 παρὰ θεοῦ πατρός, καὶ παρὰ Ἰησοῦ Χριστοῦ τοῦ υἱοῦ τοῦ πατρός); in iii. 23, 'God'; and in v. 20, 'He that is true.' Thus in the three cases the Sonship of Jesus Christ is regarded in relation to God as the Father, to God as God, and to God as perfectly satisfying the divine ideal which man is able to form. Bearing these secondary differences in mind we see that the whole phrase includes the two elements of the confession, or the two confessions, which St John brings into prominence: 'Jesus [Christ] is the Son of God' (iv. 15, v. 5); and 'Jesus is the Christ' (v. 1; comp. ii. 22). It is in other words 'the Name' written out at length.

The constituents of this compressed phrase are all used separately by St John:

(1) *Jesus:*

ii. 22 ὁ ἀρνούμενος ὅτι Ἰησοῦς οὐκ ἔστιν ὁ χριστός.

v. 1 ὁ πιστεύων ὅτι Ἰησοῦς ἐστὶν ὁ χριστός.

iv. 3 ὃ μὴ ὁμολογεῖ τὸν Ἰησοῦν.

In these passages it is obvious that the central thought is of the Lord in His perfect, historical, humanity. The use of the definite article in the last example probably conveys a reference to *v.* 2.

(2) *Christ:*

2 John 9 ἡ διδαχὴ τοῦ χριστοῦ.

The title seems to point back to the long preparation under the Old Covenant which checks impatience (προάγων) under the New.

(3) *Jesus Christ:*

ii. 1 παράκλητον ἔχομεν...Ἰησοῦν Χριστὸν δίκαιον.

v. 6 ὁ ἐλθὼν δι᾿ ὕδατος καὶ αἵματος, Ἰησοῦς Χριστός.

2 John 7 οἱ μὴ ὁμολ. Ἰησοῦν Χριστὸν ἐρχόμενον ἐν σαρκί.

Here the idea of the Messianic position of the Lord is no less important for the full sense than that of His true humanity.

In iv. 15 ὅτι Ἰησοῦς [Χριστός] ἐστιν ὁ υἱὸς τοῦ θεοῦ the reading is doubtful. The adoption of Χριστός adds to the completeness of the thought.

For the clause iv. 2 ὁμολ. Ἰησοῦν Χριστὸν ἐν σαρκὶ ἐλ. see note. In spite of the close verbal parallel of these words with 2 John 7 the use of Ἰησοῦς Χριστός here seems to be differentiated from the sense there by ἐληλυθότα as contrasted with ἐρχόμενον.

(4) *the Son:*

ii. 22 ὁ ἀρνούμενος τὸν πατέρα καὶ τὸν υἱόν.

— 23 ὁ ἀρν. τὸν υἱὸν οὐδὲ τὸν πατέρα ἔχει.

— 23 ὁ ὁμολογῶν τὸν υἱὸν καὶ τὸν πατέρα ἔχει.

— 24 ἐν τῷ υἱῷ καὶ ἐν τῷ πατρὶ μενεῖτε.

iv. 14 ὁ πατὴρ ἀπέσταλκεν τὸν υἱόν.

v. 12 ὁ ἔχων τὸν υἱὸν ἔχει τὴν ζωήν.

In all these cases the central thought is that of the absolute relation of sonship to fatherhood. The argument turns upon essential conceptions of son and father. Comp. John v. 19 note.

(5) *the Son of God:*

iii. 8 ἐφανερώθη ὁ υἱὸς τοῦ θεοῦ ἵνα λύσῃ τὰ ἔργα τοῦ διαβόλου.

v. 10 ὁ πιστεύων εἰς τὸν υἱὸν τοῦ θεοῦ.

— 12 ὁ μὴ ἔχων τὸν υἱὸν τοῦ θεοῦ.

— 13 τοῖς πιστ. εἰς τὸ ὄνομα τοῦ υἱοῦ τοῦ θεοῦ.

— 20 οἴδαμεν ὅτι ὁ υἱὸς τοῦ θεοῦ ἥκει.

With these passages must be compared

iv. 10 ἀπέστ. τὸν υἱὸν αὐτοῦ,

v. 9 ff. ὁ υἱὸς αὐτοῦ,

where the immediate antecedent is ὁ θεός. In all these cases the idea of

Christ's divine dignity is equally prominent with that of sonship in relation to a father.

Compare also v. 18 ὁ γεννηθεὶς ἐκ τοῦ θεοῦ.

Jesus His Son,

(6) *Jesus His* (God's) *Son:*

i. 7 τὸ αἷμα Ἰησοῦ τοῦ υἱοῦ αὐτοῦ.

The double title brings out the two truths that 'the blood' of Christ can be made available for men and is efficacious.

His Son, His only Son.

(7) *His* (God's) *Son, His only Son:*

iv. 9 τὸν υἱὸν αὐτοῦ τὸν μονογενῆ.

The uniqueness of the gift is the manifestation of love.

In connexion with these titles it must be added that the title 'the Son' in various forms is eminently characteristic of the first and second Epistles, in which it occurs 24 (or 25) times (22 or 23 + 2), more times than in all the Epistles of St Paul.

It is remarkable that the title 'Lord' (κύριος) is not found in the Epistles (not 2 John 3). It occurs in the narrative of the Gospel and is frequent in the Apocalypse. It occurs also in all the other epistles of the N. T. except that to Titus.

The absence of the title may perhaps be explained by the general view of the relation of Christ to the believer which is given in the Epistles. The central thought is that of fellowship. For the same reason the conception of external organization is also wanting in the Epistle.

IV.   ¹Ἀγαπητοί, μὴ παντὶ πνεύματι πιστεύετε,
ἀλλὰ δοκιμάζετε τὰ πνεύματα εἰ ἐκ τοῦ θεοῦ ἐστίν,

IV. The rival spirits of Truth
and Error (iv. 1—6).

This section is closely connected
both with what precedes and with
what follows; and corresponds with
the first section of this great division
of the Epistle: ii. 18—29. It contains
three main thoughts:

1 *There are many spiritual influences at work (v.* 1).

2 *The test of spirits lies in the
witness to the incarnation (vv.* 2, 3).

3 *The test of men lies in the
recognition of the Truth (vv.* 4, 5).

The progress of thought is parallel
to that in ii. 18—29 (see p. 67), but
the argument of St John has passed
to a new stage. There his teaching
was centred in the Messiahship, the
Sonship of Jesus: here in the Incarnation of Jesus Christ. There he
insisted on the original message of the
Gospel: here he appears to regard
the fuller interpretation of the message. This section in fact presents
the conflict of the Faith with its
counterfeits in the last form, as a conflict of spiritual powers, unseen and
real.

1 *The many spiritual influences
(v.* 1).

The 'many false prophets' stand
in a relation towards the Spirit like
that which the 'many Antichrists' occupy towards Christ (ii. 18). Through
them evil spiritual powers find expression. Spirits therefore must be
proved.

¹*Beloved, believe not every spirit,
but prove the spirits, whether they
are of God; because many false
prophets are gone out into the world.*

1. Ἀγαπητοί] Comp. ii. 7 note. The
existence of a subtle spiritual danger
calls out the tenderness of love.

μὴ παντὶ πν. πιστ.] *nolite omni*

spiritui credere V., *believe not every
spirit.* The mention of a spirit as the
characteristic endowment of Christians leads to a definition of true and
false spirits. There are many spiritual
powers active among men, and our
first impulse is to believe and to obey
them. They evidently represent that
which is not of sight. But some of
these are evil influences belonging to
the unseen order. They come to us
under specious forms of ambition,
power, honour, knowledge, as distinguished from earthly sensual enjoy-
ments. All such spirits are partial
revelations of the one spirit of evil
which become (so to speak) embodied
in men.

Comp. *Doctr. App.* 11 οὐ πᾶς ὁ
λαλῶν ἐν πνεύματι προφήτης ἐστίν, ἀλλ'
ἐὰν ἔχῃ τοὺς τρόπους κυρίου.

δοκιμάζετε τὰ πν.] *probate spiritus* V.,
prove the spirits. As we are charged
to 'prove' the season (Luke xii. 56),
ourselves (1 Cor. xi. 28; 2 Cor. xiii. 5),
what is the will of God (Rom. xii. 2;
Eph. v. 10), our work (Gal. vi. 4), our
fellow-workers (2 Cor. viii. 8, 22; 1
Cor. xvi. 3; 1 Tim. iii. 10), all things
(1 Thess. v. 21, notice *vv.* 19, 20), so
we are charged to 'prove the spirits.'
Elsewhere the discrimination of spirits
is referred to a special gift (1 Cor. xii.
10 διακρίσεις πνευμάτων). Here however the injunction to 'prove' them
is given to all Christians. Comp. ii.
20. Man maintains his personal supremacy and responsibility in the presence of these powers: 1 Cor. xiv. 32.

εἰ ἐκ τοῦ θ. ἐστίν] *whether they are
of God,* whether they derive from Him
their characteristic being and their
power.

For εἶναι ἐκ see ii. 16 note; and for
δοκιμ. εἰ compare 2 Cor. xiii. 5; Mk.
iii. 2; Lk. xiv. 28, 31 (Matt. xii. 10
parallels).

ὅτι πολλοὶ ψευδοπροφῆται ἐξεληλύθασιν εἰς τὸν κόσμον. ²Ἐν τούτῳ γινώσκετε τὸ πνεῦμα

2 γινώσκετε ℵ°ABC me the syr hl: γινώσκεται vg syr vg: γινώσκομεν ℵ*.

ὅτι π. ψευδ....] Such watchful care is required *because many false prophets*, through whom the false spirits speak, as the Spirit speaks through the true prophets (2 Pet. i. 21, ii. 1), *are gone out into the world*. 'The spirit of antichrist' inspires them. So 'false Christs' and 'false prophets' are joined together (Matt. xxiv. 24). The use of the term ψευδοπροφήτης in the N. T. is suggestive. It is applied to the rivals of the true prophets under the old dispensation (Luke vi. 26; 2 Pet. ii. 1); and to the rivals of the apostles under the new dispensation (Matt. vii. 15, xxiv. 11, 23 f. || Mk. xiii. 22 ; Acts xiii. 6); and especially, in the Apocalypse, to the embodied power of spiritual falsehood (Apoc. xvi. 13, xix. 20, xx. 10). The false-prophet is not only a false-teacher (2 Pet. ii. 1 ψευδοπροφῆται, ψευδοδιδάσκαλοι), but a false-teacher who supports his claims by manifestations of spiritual power (Matt. xxiv. 24 δώσουσιν σημεῖα μεγάλα καὶ τέρατα ; Acts xiii. 6 ἄνδρα τινὰ μάγον; Apoc. xix. 20 ὁ ποιήσας τὰ σημεῖα).

ἐξεληλύθασιν] exierunt V. (*prodierunt* F.), *are gone out* on a mission of evil from their dark home. The tense, as contrasted with ii. 19, 2 John 7, ἐξῆλθαν, expresses the continuance of their agency as distinguished from the single fact of their departure. Comp. John viii. 42, xiii. 3, xvi. 27 &c.

εἰς τὸν κόσμον] *into the world* as the scene of their activity. John iii. 17, ix. 39, x. 36 &c.

The words evidently refer to external circumstances vividly present to St John's mind. They point, as it appears, to the great outbreak of the Gentile pseudo-Christianity which is vaguely spoken of as Gnosticism, the endeavour to separate the 'ideas' of the Faith from the facts of the historic Redemption.

2 *The test of spirits lies in the witness of the Incarnation* (2, 3).

2, 3. The test of the presence of the Divine Spirit is the confession of the Incarnation, or, more exactly, of the Incarnate Saviour. The Gospel centres in a Person and not in any truth, even the greatest, about the Person. The Incarnate Saviour is the pledge of the complete redemption and perfection of man, of the restoration of 'the body' to its proper place as the perfect organ of the spirit. Hence the Divine Spirit must bear witness to Him. The test of spirits is found in the confession of a fact which vindicates the fulness of life. The test of antichrist was found in the confession of a spiritual truth (ii. 22 f.).

²*In this ye know the Spirit of God; every spirit which confesseth Jesus Christ come in flesh is of God;* ³*and every spirit which confesseth not Jesus is not of God. And this is the spirit* (revelation) *of Antichrist whereof ye heard that it cometh ; and now is it in the world already.*

2. Ἐν τούτῳ] *In hoc* V. (*Hinc* F.), *Hereby*. The idea of the process of testing passes directly into that of the test itself.

γινώσκετε] cognoscitur (i.e. γινώσκεται) V., *ye know*, i.e. perceive, recognise the presence of. The Vulgate rendering is evidently derived from a common itacism (-αι for -ε) and may be dismissed at once. Throughout the Epistle St John speaks personally (*we know, ye know*), and not in an abstract form (*it is known*). It is more difficult to decide whether γι-

τοῦ θεοῦ· πᾶν πνεῦμα ὃ ὁμολογεῖ Ἰησοῦν Χριστὸν ἐν
σαρκὶ ἐληλυθότα ἐκ τοῦ θεοῦ ἐστίν, ³καὶ πᾶν πνεῦμα

2 Ἰν Χν: Χν Ἰν C.　　　ἐληλυθότα אAC: ἐληλυθέναι B (vg).

νώσκετε is *indic.* (*ye know*), or *imper.*
(*know ye*). In every other place in
the Epistle ἐν τούτῳ is joined with a
direct statement. On the other hand
it is always elsewhere used with the
first person in combination with γινώσκω (ἐν τούτῳ γινώσκομεν, ἐγνώκαμεν). The change of person may
therefore be connected with a change
of mood ; and in this case the imperative carries on the charge *believe not,
prove.* Compare John xv. 18. So far
there is nothing in usage to determine
the question ; but on the whole it
seems more likely that St John would
appeal to the results of actual experience which had been hitherto decisive (*ye discern, recognise*) than
seem to enjoin a new and untried
rule (*discern, recognise*). Comp. *v.* 4.

τὸ πν. τοῦ θ.] *the Spirit of God,* the
one Holy Spirit who reveals Himself
in many ways and in many parts. He
must be recognised as the inspirer of
all who speak from God ; and all that
is truly spoken is from Him.

In *v.* 13 St John speaks of ' His
Spirit ' (i. e. of God), and in c. v. 6, 8
of 'the Spirit,' but, as has been noticed,
the title ' the Holy Spirit ' is not found
in the Epistles or in the Apocalypse.
Comp. *v.* 6.

πᾶν πν. ὃ...] *every spirit which...*
There is an endless variety in the
operations of the Spirit (1 Cor. xii. 4).
These severally appear to find cha-
racteristic organs in ' spirits ' which
are capable of acting on man's spirit.
Comp. 1 Cor. xii. 10 ; xiv. 12, 32 ;
Hebr. i. 14 (xii. 9, 23), (1 Pet. iii. 19),
(Apoc. xxii. 6); τὰ ἑπτὰ πν. Apoc. i.
4 ; iii. 1 ; iv. 5 ; v. 6.

ὁμολογεῖ] *confitetur* V., *confesseth,*
openly and boldly acknowledges the
Person of the Incarnate Saviour and
not only the fact of the Incarnation.

Comp. ii. 23 note. The question
here is not of inner faith, but of outward confession. Faith, if it is real,
must declare itself. Active love must
be connected with a distinct recognition of its source. Ergo, Augustine
says, followed by Bede, *ipse est spiritus Dei qui dicit Jesum in carne venisse ; qui non dicit lingua sed factis ;
qui dicit non sonando sed amando.*

Ἰ. Χ. ἐν σ. ἐλ.] The construction of
these words is not quite clear. Three
ways of taking them are possible. (1)
The direct object may be Ἰησοῦν and
χριστὸν ἐν σ. ἐλ. a secondary predicate : ' confesseth Jesus as Christ and
a Christ come in flesh ' ; (2) The direct
object may be Ἰησοῦν Χριστὸν and ἐν
σ. ἐλ. a secondary predicate : ' confesseth Jesus Christ, Him who is known
by this full name, as come in flesh.'
(3) The whole phrase may form a compound direct object : ' confesseth Him,
whose nature and work is described
by the phrase, ' Jesus Christ come in
flesh.'.' The corresponding clause in
v. 3 Ἰησοῦν which gives the person
and not any statement about the person as the object of confession is in
favour of the last view.

ἐληλυθότα] The construction with
the participle gives a different thought
from that with the infinitive (ἐληλυθέναι). It does not express the acknowledgment of the truth of the fact
but the acknowledgment of One in
whom this fact is fulfilled and of whom
it is predicated. Comp. 2 John 7 (ὁμολ.
ἐρχόμενον). For the sense of ἔρχεσθαι
see c. v. 6 note.

ἐν σαρκὶ ἐληλ.] *come in flesh,* manifested under this special form. The
order (ἐν σαρκὶ ἐλ.) and the tense of
the verb (ἐληλ.) lay emphasis on the
mode rather than on the fact of
Christ's coming. 'The Word became

ὃ μὴ ὁμολογεῖ τὸν Ἰησοῦν ἐκ τοῦ θεοῦ οὐκ ἔστιν· καὶ

3 ὃ μὴ ὁμολογεῖ: ὃ λύει vg.　See Additional Note.　　τὸν Ῑν AB (vg) me syrr;
Ῑν Χ̄ν (vg) (others read τὸν Ῑν Χ̄ν).　　＋ἐν σαρκὶ ἐληλυθότα ℵ syrr (lat): om. AB
vg me the.

flesh' (i. 14); and that not tempo-
rarily, but so that He is still coming
in it (2 John 7). The Christ 'who
should come' came, and coming in
this way fulfilled and still fulfils the
promises of the past. For the confession is not only of One who 'came'
(ἐλθόντα) but of One who 'is come'
(ἐληλυθότα), whose 'coming' is an
abiding fact. And yet further He
came 'in flesh,' as revealing the nature
of His mission in this form, and not
only 'into flesh' (εἰς σάρκα), as simply
entering on such a form of being.

ἐκ τοῦ θ. ἐ.] Comp. 1 Cor. xii. 3;
and Additional Note on iii. 1.

3. καὶ πᾶν πν.] The negative statement is here directly joined to the
positive. In ii. 23 the positive and
negative statements are placed in
simple parallelism.

ὃ μὴ ὁμ. τὸν Ἰ.] The substance of
the confession which has been given
in detail in the former verse is gathered up in the single human name of
the Lord. To 'confess Jesus,' which
in the connexion can only mean to
confess 'Jesus as Lord' (1 Cor. xii. 3,
Rom. x. 9), is to recognise divine
sovereignty in One Who is truly man,
or, in other words, to recognise the
union of the divine and human in one
Person, a truth which finds its only
adequate expression in the fact of the
Incarnation.

The very ancient reading ὃ λύει τὸν
Ἰησοῦν (qui solvit Jesum V., qui
destruit Lcfr.: see Additional Note)
expresses this view more directly.
The meaning which it is designed to
convey must be 'which separates the
divine from the human, which divides
the one divine-human Person.' But
it may well be doubted whether

Ἰησοῦς would be used in this comprehensive sense. In Scripture 'Jesus'
always emphasises the humanity of
the Lord considered in itself. The
thought would be conveyed by ὃ λύει
Ἰησοῦν Χριστόν or even by ὃ λύει τὸν
χριστόν. It seems likely that the
verb was transferred to this context
from some traditional saying of St
John in which it was applied to false
teachers, such as οἱ λύοντες τὸν χριστόν, or the like. The words of Polycarp which appear only indirectly, and
yet certainly, to refer to the phrase
in the Epistle indicate that St John
dwelt upon the thought in various
aspects: πᾶς γὰρ ὃς ἂν μὴ ὁμολογῇ Ἰησοῦν Χριστὸν ἐν σαρκὶ ἐληλυθέναι ἀντίχριστός ἐστι, καὶ ὃς ἂν μὴ ὁμολογῇ τὸ
μαρτύριον τοῦ σταυροῦ ἐκ τοῦ διαβόλου
ἐστί (ad Phil. c. vii.).

ὃ μὴ ὁμολογεῖ] The use of μή marks
the character of the spirit which leads
to the denial ('such that it confesseth
not') as distinguished from the simple
fact of the failure to confess (ὃ οὐχ
ὁμολογεῖ: v. 6 ὃς οὐκ ἔστιν).

τὸν Ἰ.] Comp. i. 7 note. For the use
of this simple human name of the Lord
in similar connexions see Rom. iii. 26;
(x. 9;) 2 Cor. xi. 4; Eph. iv. 21; Phil.
ii. 10; Hebr. ii. 9 note. Comp. 2 Cor.
iv. 10 f.

ἐκ τοῦ θεοῦ οὐκ ἔ.] The denial of
the Incarnation is in fact the denial
of that which is characteristic of
the Christian Faith, the true union of
God and man (comp. ii. 22 ff.). By
this form of statement (as distinguished from 'is of the devil,' or the
like) St John meets the specious
claims of the false prophets: such a
spirit, whatever appearances may be,
is not of God.

τοῦτό ἐστιν τὸ τοῦ ἀντιχρίστου, ὃ ἀκηκόατε ὅτι ἔρχεται, καὶ νῦν ἐν τῷ κόσμῳ ἐστὶν ἤδη.   ⁴ Ὑμεῖς

ὃ ἀκηκ.: ὅτι ἀκηκ. א.

The antagonists regarded here are not mere unbelievers but those who knowing Christianity fashion it into a shape of their own.

Augustine (ad loc.) remarks characteristically that the denial of the Incarnation is the sign of the absence of love: Caritas illum adduxit ad carnem. Quisquis ergo non habet caritatem negat Christum in carne venisse. And so he goes on to interpret 'solvit' of the spirit of the schismatic: Ille venit colligere, tu venis solvere. Distringere vis membra Christi. Quomodo non negas Christum in carne venisse qui disrumpis Ecclesiam Dei quam Ille congregavit?

It is of interest to notice the two negative signs which St John gives of 'not being of God.' In c. iii. 10 he writes πᾶς ὁ μὴ ποιῶν δικαιοσύνην οὐκ ἔστιν ἐκ τοῦ θεοῦ: here πᾶν πνεῦμα ὃ μὴ ὁμολογεῖ τὸν Ἰησοῦν ἐκ τοῦ θεοῦ οὐκ ἔστιν. In the case of men the proof of the absence of the divine connexion is found in the want of active righteousness: in the case of spirits in the failure to confess the Incarnation. The two tests exactly correspond to one another in the two spheres to which they severally belong. The confession of the Incarnation embodied in life must produce the effort after righteousness which finds its absolute spiritual support in the belief in the Incarnation.

καὶ τοῦτο...] et hic est antichristus quod audistis V., hoc est illius antichristi quod aud. F., 'and this whole manifestation of false, ungodly, spiritual powers is the manifestation of antichrist, whereof (ὃ not ὄν) ye have heard....' The omission of πνεῦμα in the phrase τὸ τοῦ ἀντιχρίστου gives greater breadth to the thought, so that the words include the many

spirits, the many forces, which reveal the action of antichrist.

τοῦ ἀντιχρίστου] The spiritual influence is not only negatively 'not of God': it is positively 'of antichrist.'

ἀκηκόατε] Compare καθὼς ἠκούσατε ii. 18. The difference in tense places the two warnings in a somewhat different relation to the hearers. For the perfect see c. i. 1, 3, 5; for the aorist, ii. 7, 18, 24, iii. 11; 2 John 6.

ἔρχεται] The same word is used of the advent of the power of evil as of the advent of the Lord. Comp. ii. 18; v. 6, notes.

καὶ νῦν...ἤδη] et nunc jam V., and now...already. For the position of ἤδη see John ix. 27 (not iv. 35). The prophecy had found fulfilment before the Church had looked for it.

3. The test of men lies in the recognition of the Truth (4—6).

4—6. In the verses which precede (2, 3) St John has considered the teaching of spirits as the test of their character. He now regards the subject from another point of view and considers the teaching of spirits as the test of men.

⁴ Ye are of God, little children, and have overcome them, because greater is he that is in you than he that is in the world. ⁵ They are of the world: for this cause speak they of the world and the world heareth them. ⁶ We are of God: he that knoweth God heareth us; he who is not of God heareth not us. By this we know the spirit of truth and the spirit of error.

4. Ὑμεῖς] You as contrasted with the world; you who are in possession of spiritual endowments. Comp. ii. 20 καὶ ὑμεῖς χρίσμα ἔχετε, ii. 24, 27.

ἐκ τοῦ θεοῦ ἐστε] Comp. Additional note on iii. 1.

ἐκ τοῦ θεοῦ ἐστέ, τεκνία, καὶ νενικήκατε αὐτούς, ὅτι
μείζων ἐστὶν ὁ ἐν ὑμῖν ἢ ὁ ἐν τῷ κόσμῳ· ⁵αὐτοὶ ἐκ τοῦ

The hearers of St John have that divine connexion which the false spirits have not (v. 3 ἐκ τοῦ θ. οὐκ ἔ.).

τεκνία] c. iii. 18. The father in Christ speaks again. The address 'beloved' has been used twice in the interval (iii. 21, iv. 1).

νενικήκατε αὐτούς] vicistis eum V., eos F., have overcome them. The personal reference goes back to v. 1 (ψευδοπροφῆται). The intervening verses are structurally parenthetical, though they contain the ruling thought of the section.

The false spirits, whose characteristic has now been defined, must have their organs through whom to speak; and Christians must wage war against them. In this conflict the virtue of their Master's Victory (John xvi. 33) is granted to them. They have to claim the fruits of a triumph which has been already gained.

Comp. ii. 13 (νενικήκατε) note. The thought of a spiritual conflict is developed in Eph. vi. 12 ff.

ὅτι...] The ground and the assurance of the victory of Christians lie in the Power by which they are inspired (c. iii. 24). The strength of men is proportioned to the vital force of which they are the organs.

Vicistis eum, inquit. Sed unde vicerunt? Numquid liberi virtute arbitrii? Non utique. Taceat Pelagius, dicat ipse Johannes: Quoniam major est qui in vobis est... (Bede). So Augustine; ...qui audit Vicistis erigit caput, erigit cervicem, laudari se vult. Noli te extollere: vide quis in te vicit.

μείζων] greater. See iii. 20.

ὁ ἐν ὑμῖν] qui in vobis est V., he that is in you, that is in the Christian Society. The Church appears to be set over against the world; so that here the thought is of the body, and not (as in iii. 24) of the individual. The Divine Person is undefined. We think naturally of God in Christ. Comp. John vi. 56, xiv. 20, xv. 4 f., xvii. 23, 26. Elsewhere 'the word of God' (c. ii. 14), 'the unction received from Him' (ii. 27), 'His seed' (iii. 9) is said to 'abide' in believers, as here He himself is in them. See note on v. 15. St Paul expresses the same thought in relation to the individual: Gal. ii. 20.

ὁ ἐν τῷ κόσμῳ] he that is in the world. The many false spirits represent one personal power of falsehood, 'the prince of the world' (John xii. 31, xiv. 30), the devil whose 'children' the wicked are (iii. 10). The world occupies in regard to him the same twofold position which Christians occupy with regard to God: 'the world lieth in the wicked one' (c. v. 19) and he 'is in the world.' The natural opposite to 'in you,' taken personally, would have been 'in them'; but St John wishes to shew that these false prophets are representatives of the world. The conflict, as has been said above, is regarded socially.

Comp. Eph. ii. 2.

5. αὐτοί...] ipsi V., they, the false prophets, through whom the false spirits work.

The nom. pl. αὐτοί, which occurs here only in the Epistles, emphasises the contrast. Comp. James ii. 6, 7; Hebr. xiii. 17; Luke xi. 48. See c. ii. 25 note.

ἐκ τ. κ. εἰσίν] de mundo sunt V., are of the world and not simply of the earth (John iii. 31). The 'earth' expresses the necessary limitations of the present order: the 'world' the moral characteristics of the order, as separated from God. For the phrase compare c. ii. 16; John xv. 19, xvii.

κόσμου εἰσίν· διὰ τοῦτο ἐκ τοῦ κόσμου λαλοῦσιν καὶ
ὁ κόσμος αὐτῶν ἀκούει. ⁶ἡμεῖς ἐκ τοῦ θεοῦ ἐσμέν· ὁ
γινώσκων τὸν θεὸν ἀκούει ἡμῶν, ὃς οὐκ ἔστιν ἐκ τοῦ

6 ὃς οὐκ...ἡμῶν: om. A.

14, 16 and the cognate phrase 'to be of this world': John viii. 23, xviii. 36.

διὰ τοῦτο] *ideo* V., *for this cause.* The character of their speech and the character of their hearers are determined by their own character. They draw the spirit and the substance of their teaching from (out of) the world and therefore it finds acceptance with kindred natures. The words 'of the world' answer to 'the world' in the order of the original: '*it is of the world they speak, and the world heareth them.*'

For the threefold repetition of 'the world' see John iii. 17, 31; 2 Macc. vii. 11.

ἀκούει] Comp. John xv. 19.

6. ἡμεῖς ἐκ τ. θ. ἐ.] *we are of God.* The apostle has spoken of Christian hearers (*v.* 4 ὑμεῖς ἐκ τ. θ. ἐ.): he now speaks of Christian teachers. In each case living dependence upon God produces its full effect. The hearer discerns the true message. The teacher discovers the true disciple. And this concurrence of experience brings fresh assurance and deeper knowledge.

The opposition of ἡμεῖς to ὑμεῖς and the use of ἀκούει shew that St John is not speaking here of Christians generally but of those whose work it is to unfold the divine message.

The description of the true teachers is not exactly parallel with that of the false teachers. It is not directly said of these that 'they speak of God' because the conclusion does not admit of being put in the same form as in the former case ('they speak of the world and the world heareth them'). The world listens to those who express its own thoughts; the Christian listens to those who teach him more

W.

of God, new thoughts which he makes his own. Thus the argument which in the former clause lies in 'speak of the world,' in this clause lies in 'he that knoweth God.' The readiness to hear springs from a living, growing, knowledge, which welcomes and appropriates the truth.

Comp. John viii. 47.

ὁ γινώσκων τ. θ.] *qui novit Deum* V., *he that knoweth God.* The Latin and English renderings both fail to express the force of the original phrase which describes a knowledge apprehended as progressive and not complete, a knowledge which answers to the processes of life. Comp. *v.* 7, v. 20; John xvii. 3. Contrast ii. 3 f., 13 f., iii. 1.

So St Paul speaks of 'the call' of God as continuous; 1 Thess. v. 24. Comp. Phil. iii. 12 ff.

St John appears to choose this most expressive phrase in place of the more general one 'he that is of God' in order to illustrate the position of the true disciple as one who is ever advancing in the knowledge of God, and whose power of hearing and learning is given by this attitude of faithful expectancy.

So it is that when he passes to the negative side it is sufficient to say 'he that is not of God' without bringing into prominence the special energy which flows from this divine dependence in regard to the fuller exposition of the Gospel.

The contrast which is marked here between him 'that *knoweth God*' and the man 'who *is not of God*' is given under a slightly different form in *v.* 7 where it is said 'he that loveth *hath been born of God and knoweth God,*'

10

θεοῦ οὐκ ἀκούει ἡμῶν. ἐκ τούτου γινώσκομεν τὸ πνεῦμα
τῆς ἀληθείας καὶ τὸ πνεῦμα τῆς πλάνης.

ἐκ τούτου ℵB syrr: ἐν τούτῳ A vg me the.

while 'he that loveth not *knew not God.'*

οὐκ ἀκούει] Comp. John xiv. 17 note.

ἐκ τούτου] *in hoc* V., *hereby, from this.* The phrase does not occur again in the Epistle and must be distinguished from the common ἐν τούτῳ (see c. ii. 3 note). It is found twice in the Gospel marking a connexion partly historical and partly moral (vi. 66, xix. 12). ᾽Εν τούτῳ seems to note a fact which is a direct indication in itself of that which is perceived: ἐκ τούτου suggests some further process by which the conclusion is obtained. The consideration of the general character of those who receive and of those who reject the message, and again of the teaching which is received and rejected by those who are children of God, leads to a fuller discernment of the spirit of the Truth and of the spirit of the opposing error. The power to recognise and accept the fuller exhibition of the Truth must come from the Spirit of Truth: the rejection of the Truth reveals the working of the spirit of error.

γινώσκομεν] *cognoscimus* V., *we know, recognise, perceive.* This power of recognition belongs to all believers. It is not limited to teachers by an emphatic pronoun as before; but expresses what is learnt in different ways by hearers and teachers.

τὸ πν. τῆς ἀλ.] *spiritum veritatis* V., *the Spirit of Truth.* Comp. John xiv. 17 note; 1 Cor. ii. 12 ff.

τὸ πν. τῆς πλάνης] *spiritum erroris* V., *the spirit of error.* The phrase is unique in the N. T. Comp. 1 Cor. ii. 12 τὸ πνεῦμα τοῦ κόσμου. 1 Tim. iv. 1 πνεύμασι πλάνοις. In contrast to ἡ ἀλήθεια 'the Truth' stands ἡ πλάνη (Eph. iv. 14) 'the error,' in which lie

concentrated the germs of all manifold errors. Compare τὸ ψεῦδος 2 Thess. ii. 11; Rom. i. 25; Eph. iv. 24 f.; John viii. 44.

'The seven spirits of error' occupy an important place in *The Testaments of the XII Patriarchs,* Reuben 2 ff. The two spirits of truth and error are described as attending man, and it is added, τὸ πνεῦμα τῆς ἀληθείας μαρτυρεῖ πάντα καὶ κατηγορεῖ πάντων, καὶ ἐμπεπύρισται ὁ ἁμαρτήσας ἐκ τῆς ἰδίας καρδίας. Judah, 20.

C. THE CHRISTIAN LIFE: THE VICTORY OF FAITH.
(iv. 7—v. 21.)

The consideration of Antichrists and of the spirit of Antichrist and error is now over, and St John lays open the fulness of the Christian life. In doing this he takes up in a new connexion thoughts which he has before touched upon, and groups them in relation to the final revelation *God is love* (iv. 8, 16).

The whole division of the Epistle seems to fall most naturally into three sections:

I. THE SPIRIT OF THE CHRISTIAN LIFE: GOD AND LOVE.
    (iv. 7—21.)

II. THE POWER OF THE CHRISTIAN LIFE: THE VICTORY AND WITNESS OF FAITH.
    (v. 1—12.)

III. THE ACTIVITY AND CONFIDENCE OF THE CHRISTIAN LIFE: EPILOGUE.
    (v. 13—21.)

I. THE SPIRIT OF THE CHRISTIAN LIFE: GOD AND LOVE (iv. 7—21).

This section deals in succession with

*᾽Αγαπητοί, ἀγαπῶμεν ἀλλήλους, ὅτι ἡ ἀγάπη ἐκ
τοῦ θεοῦ ἐστίν, καὶ πᾶς ὁ ἀγαπῶν ἐκ τοῦ θεοῦ γεγέν-*

7 ὁ ἀγαπῶν : +τὸν θεόν A (*fratrem* is also added).

1. *The ground of love* (7—10).
2. *The inspiration of love* (11—16 a).
3. *The activity of love* (16 b—21).

In the first paragraph the subject is regarded mainly from its abstract, and in the second mainly from its personal side: in the third it is treated in relation to action.

1. *The ground of love* (7—10).

The Christian Society has been shewn to be clearly distinguished from the world, even when the world obtains the support of spiritual powers. St John therefore passes on to consider the spirit of the Christian life as seen in the Christian Body. This spirit is love, the presence of which is the proof of divine sonship, seeing that God is love (*vv.* 7, 8); and in the Incarnation we have set before us the manifestation (*v.* 9) and the essence of love (*v.* 10).

⁷ *Beloved, let us love one another, because love is of God, and every one that loveth is begotten of God and knoweth God.* ⁸ *He that loveth not, knoweth not (knew not) God, because God is love.* ⁹ *In this was manifested the love of God in us, that God hath sent his Son, his only Son, into the world that we may live through him.* ¹⁰ *In this is love, not that we have loved God, but that he loved us, and sent his Son a propitiation for our sins.*

7. The transition of thought appears to lie in the implied efficiency of love as a moral test of knowledge. The twofold commandment of faith and love is essentially one commandment (iii. 23 f.). Love in the region of action corresponds to the confession of the Incarnation in the region of thought. The Christian spirit then is proved by love. Comp. John x. 14 ff. note.

᾽Αγαπητοί] The title and the charge go together. See ch. ii. 7 note.

The title occurs comparatively frequently in 2 Peter, Jude, and sparingly in the other Epistles of the New Testament: 2 Pet. iii. 1, 8, 14, 17; Jude 3, 17, 20; 1 Pet. ii. 11; iv. 12; 2 Cor. vii. 1; xii. 19; Rom. xii. 19; Phil. iv. 1; Hebr. vi. 9. ᾽Αγαπητοί μου occurs 1 Cor. x. 14; and ἀδελφοί μου ἀγαπητοί, James i. 16, 19; ii. 5; 1 Cor. xv. 58.

ἀγαπῶμεν ἀλλήλους] *diligamus invicem*, V., *let us love one another.* Comp. ch. iii. 11 note. St John deals with the love of Christians for Christians (φιλαδελφία, St Paul, Hebr., St Peter) as the absolute type of love. There is no longer any distinction of 'ye' and 'we' (*vv.* 4 ff.); nor any emphasis on the pronoun. Compare iii. 14, 18, 23; iv. 12, 19; v. 2. St John never says ἀγαπᾶτε, though he does say μὴ ἀγαπᾶτε (ii. 15).

ὅτι...] *because...* The charge is based upon a twofold argument: (1) Love is of God, and therefore since it proceeds from Him, it must be characteristic also of those who partake in His Nature, as His children; and, again, (2) Active love becomes to him who exercises it the sign of his sonship (iii. 19).

ἐκ τ. θ. ἐ.] *is of God*, flows from Him, as the one spring, and in such a way that the connexion with the source remains unbroken. See Additional Note on iii. 1.

πᾶς ὁ ἀγαπῶν...] *every one that loveth...* The clause appears at first sight to be inverted in form. It might have seemed to be a more

νηται καὶ γινώσκει τὸν θεόν.   ⁸ὁ μὴ ἀγαπῶν οὐκ ἔγνω
τὸν θεόν, ὅτι ὁ θεὸς ἀγάπη ἐστίν.   ⁹ἐν τούτῳ ἐφανερώθη ἡ ἀγάπη τοῦ θεοῦ ἐν ἡμῖν, ὅτι τὸν υἱὸν αὐτοῦ

8 ὁ μὴ ἀγ....θεόν: om. א* (om. τὸν θεὸν אᶜ).
οὐκ ἔγνωκεν אᶜ.

οὐκ ἔγνω: οὐ γινώσκει Α:

direct argument to say 'let us love one another because...every one that is born of God loveth.' But as it is, the words bring out the blessing as well as the implied necessity of love. Every one that loveth hath in the consciousness of that spirit the proof of his divine sonship. Comp. c. iii. 19.

πᾶς ὁ...] every one that... Comp. iii. 3 note. St John does not say simply 'he that loveth.' He insists on the supreme characteristic of love as overpowering in whomsoever it is realised difficulties which men might discover in subordinate differences.

ἐκ τοῦ θ. γεγέννηται] hath been begotten of God. Compare Additional Note on iii. 1. The combination of γεγέννηται with γινώσκει (not ἔγνωκεν) is significant. Living knowledge is regarded only in its present activity. The active principle of sonship is referred to its origin.

γινώσκει] cognoscit V., knoweth. See v. 6 note. The present is sharply contrasted with the aor. (ἔγνω, novit, V.) which follows (v. 8).

The idea of 'knowledge' is introduced here in connexion with the action of the Spirit of Truth in the fuller unfolding of the mystery of Christ's Person. He that loveth derives his spiritual being from God, and of necessity therefore is in sympathy with him, and knows Him, that is, recognises every revelation which shews more of Him (v. 6).

8. As the presence of active love is the pledge of advancing knowledge, so the absence of love is the proof that apparent knowledge was not real. 'He that loveth not, knew not God' (οὐκ ἔγνω τ. θ., non novit V.,

ignorat F.) when he made profession of knowing Him. His acknowledgment of God (as at Baptism) was based on no true recognition of His nature. The aor. (ἔγνων) always has its full force. Compare iii. 1; John x. 38, xvi. 3.

ὅτι...] because. It is assumed that knowledge involves practical sympathy. Compare ii. 3 note.

Bede puts well one side of the truth; Quisquis [Deum] non amat, profecto ostendit quia quam sit amabilis non novit (ad c. ii. 5). This conception of the nature of knowledge corresponds with the view of the Gospel as 'the Truth.'

ὁ θ. ἀγάπη ἐστίν] Deus caritas est V. See Additional Note.

9. ἐν τούτῳ...ὅτι...] In hoc...quoniam... V. In this...that... So v. 10, John ix. 30.

ἐν τ. ἐφαν...] The manifestation and the essence of love (v. 10 ἐν τ. ἐστὶν ἡ ἀ.) are distinguished, though both are seen in the Incarnation. The manifestation of love was shewn in the fact (τ. υἱ. τ. μον. ἀπέστ.) and in the end (ἵνα ζήσ.) of the Mission of the Son. The essence of love was shewn in this that the Mission of the Son was absolutely spontaneous (αὐτὸς ἠγάπησεν ἡ.). Comp. Rom. viii. 32.

ἐφανερώθη] apparuit V.,manifestata est Aug., was manifested. That which 'was' eternally was made known in time. Compare c. i. 2 note. In the retrospect of His completed work on earth the Lord says: ἐφανέρωσά σου τὸ ὄνομα (John xvii. 6), that is 'the Father's name,' the revelation of love. See also 2 Tim. i. 9 f.

τὸν μονογενῆ ἀπέσταλκεν ὁ θεὸς εἰς τὸν κόσμον ἵνα
ζήσωμεν δι᾽ αὐτοῦ. ¹⁰ἐν τούτῳ ἐστὶν ἡ ἀγάπη, οὐχ

9 ζήσωμεν: ζῶμεν ℵ*.   10 ἡ ἀγ.: +τοῦ θεοῦ ℵ me the.

ἐν ἡμῖν] in nobis V., in us: not
simply 'towards us' as the objects
to whom the love was directed, but
'in us,' in us believers, as the medium in which it was revealed and
in which it was effective (that we
may live through Him). Comp. v.
16. The Christian shares the life of
Christ, and so becomes himself a
secondary sign of God's love. There
is a sense in which creation shews
God's love, but this revelation becomes clear through the new creation. The manifestation of the love
of God to man becomes a living power
as a manifestation of His love in man.

The sense in our case, or among
us (John i. 14), is excluded by the constant use of the preposition in the
context to express the presence of
God in the Christian body (v. 12).

τὸν υἱὸν αὐ. τὸν μον.] filium suum
unigenitum V., His Son, His only
Son. The exact form occurs only here
and John iii. 16. Comp. ii. 7; John i.
14 notes; and Additional Note on iii.
23. The order of the words in the
whole clause is most impressive: 'in
this that His Son, His only Son, hath
God sent into the world,' into the
world, though alienated from Him.

ἀπέσταλκεν] He hath sent, and we
now enjoy the blessings of the Mission:
v. 14; John v. 36, xx. 21. Comp.
John v. 33; Luke iv. 18; 2 Cor. xii.
17, &c. The aorist (ἀπέστειλα) occurs v. 10; John iii. 17, 34, vi. 29, &c.,
xvii. 3, &c. See Additional Notes on
iii. 5; John xx. 21.

Both here and in John iii. 16 the
Mission of the Son is referred to
'God' and not to 'the Father.' The
central idea is that of the divine
majesty of the Son and not that of
the special relation in which the

Father stands to the Son and, through
the Son, to men. Contrast v. 14, and
see Additional Note on i. 2.

ἵνα ζήσωμεν...] that we may live...
The natural state of men is that of
death: c. iii. 14. It is perhaps strange
that this is the only place in the
Epistles in which the verb ζῆν occurs.
Compare John v. 25; vi. 51, 57 f.;
xi. 25; xiv. 19. The term is used
because the Apostle lays stress upon
the activity of the Christian and not
upon his safety only (that we may be
saved: John iii. 17). In him, as he
lives, the love of God is seen visibly
working. As compared with John
iii. 16 f., which should be closely
examined with this passage, the object of the Mission of Christ is here
set forth in its personal working and
not in its general scope.

δι᾽ αὐτοῦ] per eum V., through
Him, as the efficient cause of life.

Elsewhere the Christian is said to
live 'on account of' Christ; John vi.
57 (δι᾽ ἐμέ).

St Paul speaks of Christ as living
in the Christian; Gal. ii. 20. 'The
life of Jesus' is that which the believer strives to manifest: 2 Cor. iv.
10 f.; and Christ is his life: Col. iii.
4 (comp. 1 John v. 12, 20); while
hereafter the Christian will live with
Him (σὺν αὐτῷ): 1 Thess. v. 10. So
Christ is the aim of the Christian's
life: Rom. xiv. 8 (τῷ κυρίῳ ζ.); comp.
Rom. vi. 10 f.; Gal. ii. 19; and the
substance of his life (τὸ ζῆν): Phil.
i. 21.

It is to be noticed that the Christian
is not said in the New Testament to
'live in Christ' (contrast Acts xvii.
28); though the Christian's life is
'in Him': 1 John v. 11; Rom. vi. 23;
2 Tim. i. 1. This phrase however

ὅτι ἡμεῖς ἠγαπήκαμεν τὸν θεόν, ἀλλ᾽ ὅτι αὐτὸς ἠγάπησεν ἡμᾶς καὶ ἀπέστειλεν τὸν υἱὸν αὐτοῦ ἱλασμὸν
περὶ τῶν ἁμαρτιῶν ἡμῶν.   ¹¹ Ἀγαπητοί, εἰ
οὕτως ὁ θεὸς ἠγάπησεν ἡμᾶς, καὶ ἡμεῖς ὀφείλομεν ἀλλή-

ἠγαπήσαμεν ℵA (ἠγάπησεν ℵ*) : ἠγαπήκαμεν B.   αὐτός : ἐκεῖνος A.
ἀπέστειλεν : ἀπέσταλκεν ℵ.

occurs in Polyc. *ad Phil.* 8, δι᾽ ἡμᾶς,
ἵνα ζήσωμεν ἐν αὐτῷ, πάντα ὑπέμεινε.

10. ἐν τούτῳ ἐστίν...ὅτι...] *in this
is...that...*] In this we can see a
revelation of the true nature of love.
The source of love is the free will of
God Himself. He loved us because
'He is love,' and in virtue of that love
sent His Son. The origin of love lies
beyond humanity.

ἡ ἀγάπη] *caritas* V., *love*, in its
most absolute sense, not farther defined as the love of God or of man.

οὐχ ὅτι...ἀλλ᾽ ὅτι...] *non quasi...sed
quoniam* V., *not that...but that...*
The negative clause is brought forward to emphasise the thought of
man's inability to originate love. For
somewhat similar forms of expression
see 2 John 5; John vi. 38; vii. 22;
xii. 6. Non illum dileximus prius:
nam ad hoc nos dilexit ut diligamus
eum (Aug., Bede).

αὐτός] *ipse* V., *He*, of His own free
will. Compare ii. 25 note.

ἠγάπησεν] *loved us.* The love is
viewed in regard to its historic manifestation, John iii. 16; Eph. ii. 4;
2 Thess. ii. 16. Comp. Gal. ii. 20;
Eph. v. 2, 25; Apoc. iii. 9.

ἱλασμόν] *propitiationem* V., *litatorem* Aug.; in quibusdam codicibus...
legitur...*litatorem*... Bede; *expiatorem*
Lcfr., *a propitiation.* Comp. ii. 2 note.
The idea is introduced here to mark
the preparation of men for fellowship
with God. God was pleased to make
men fit to share His nature. The life
(*v.* 9) followed on the removal of sin.

2. *The inspiration of love* (11—16 *a*).

St John has shewn that love must

come from God Who has revealed in
the Incarnation what it is essentially,
the spontaneous communication of the
highest good. He now considers what
must be the effect upon men of this
manifestation of love, which is the
assurance and the revelation of the
Divine Presence.

The character of God's love carries
with it an obligation to love (*v.* 11)
through the fulfilment of which by
the Spirit we gain the highest possible
assurance of fellowship with God (*vv.*
12, 13). And the experience of the
Church attests equally the love of
God and the effects of His love
among men (14—16 *a*).

¹¹ *Beloved, if God so loved us, we
also ought to love one another.* ¹² *No
man hath ever yet beheld God: if we
love one another, God abideth in us
and his love is perfected in us.* ¹³ *In
this we know that we abide in him
and he in us, because he hath given
us of his Spirit.* ¹⁴ *And we have
beheld and bear witness that the
Father hath sent the Son as Saviour
of the world.* ¹⁵ *Whosoever shall
confess that Jesus [Christ] is the Son
of God, God abideth in him and he
in God.* ¹⁶ *And we know and have
believed the love which God hath in us.*

11. Ἀγαπητοί] *v.* 7 note.

εἰ οὕτως...] *si sic Deus dilexit nos,
if it was so,* as we see in the mission
of His Son, *God loved us....* The
order of the words throws a stress
upon the particular manifestation of
God's love (ἠγάπησεν, John iii. 16);
and the repetition of ὁ θεός emphasises the Majesty of Him Who thus
revealed His love.

λους ἀγαπᾶν. ¹²θεὸν οὐδεὶς πώποτε τεθέαται· ἐὰν ἀγαπῶμεν ἀλλήλους, ὁ θεὸς ἐν ἡμῖν μένει καὶ ἡ ἀγάπη αὐτοῦ

καὶ ἡ. ὀφ.] et nos debemus V., we
also ought... See iii. 16 note. The love
which God has not only shewn but
given to us (v. 1) becomes a con-
straining motive for action.
ἀλλ. ἀγ.] alterutrum diligere V.,
invicem diligere Aug. (F.). The
phrase marks the mutual fulness of
love. Comp. iii. 11 note. Of the love
itself Augustine says: Noli in homine
amare errorem, sed hominem : hominem enim Deus fecit, errorem ipse
homo fecit.

It is of importance to observe that
the obligation which St John draws
from the fact of God's love is not that
we should 'love God' but that we
should 'love one another.' It is
through human affections and duties
that the spiritual, when once apprehended in its sublime purity, gains
definiteness and reality under the
conditions of our present state (comp.
v. 20; c. i. 3 note). The thought of
'the love of God' (i.e. of which God
is the object) as distinct from the
'love of Christ' (John xiv. 15, 21, 23 f.,
28 ; xxi. 16; Eph. vi. 24) is very rare
in the N. T. (v. 21; c. v. 2 ; Rom. viii.
28 ; 1 Cor. ii. 9, LXX.; viii. 3 εἴ τις
ἀγαπᾷ τὸν θεόν, οὗτος ἔγνωσται ὑπ᾽ αὐτοῦ). The command to love God is
quoted from the Law (Matt. xxii. 37
and parr. from Deut. vi. 5). Gradually by the elevation of thought God
seemed to be withdrawn from men;
and then in the Person of His Son,
who took humanity to Himself, God
gave back to man that in which
human feeling can find inspiration
and rest.

12. θεόν...τεθέαται] Deum nemo
vidit unquam V., God hath no man
ever beheld. Comp. John i. 18 note. In
both passages θεόν stands first and
without the article, 'God as God';
and in both passages the object is

directly followed by the subject : God
hath no man ever (seen). But the
verbs are different. In John i. 18
the thought is of the vision which
might be the foundation of revelation
(ἑώρακεν): here the thought is of the
continuous beholding which answers to
abiding fellowship (τεθέαται). Comp.
John xvi. 16 note. On θεός and ὁ
θεός see Additional Note.

οὐδεὶς πώποτε...] no man ever yet....
In these words St John seems to call
up all the triumphs of the saints in
past time. However close their fellowship with God had been, yet no
one had beheld Him as He is. The
question here is not one of abstract
power but of actual experience.

ἐὰν ἀγαπῶμεν ...] if we love......
Though God is invisible He yet is not
only very near to us but may be in
us, the Life of our lives. The words,
as Bede points out, meet the implied
question : Quo solatio utendum ubi
divina visione nondum licet perfrui ?

The manifestation of active love by
men witnesses to two facts : (1) the
abiding of God in them, and (2) the
presence of divine love in them in its
completest form. There is both the
reality of fellowship and the effectiveness of fellowship.

ὁ θ. ἐν ἡμ. μένει] abideth in us. See
Additional Note on v. 15. Generally
this fellowship is described under its
two aspects ('God in us, we in God'),
but here the idea is that of the power
of the divine indwelling. Comp. John
xvii. 23, 26.

The question has been asked (Bede),
How the highest blessedness is attached to the mutual love of Christians while in the Gospel the love of
enemies is enjoined (Matt. v. 43 ff.)?
The answer lies in the recognition of
the essence of Christian love. This
resting upon the Incarnation regards

τετελειωμένη ἐν ἡμῖν ἐστίν. ¹³ἐν τούτῳ γινώσκομεν ὅτι ἐν αὐτῷ μένομεν καὶ αὐτὸς ἐν ἡμῖν, ὅτι ἐκ τοῦ

12 τετ. ἐν ἡμῖν ἐ. אB: ἐν ἡμῖν τετ. ἐ. A vg: τετ. ἐ. ἐν ἡμῖν me the syrr.

all men in the light of that fact. The Christian can separate in man that which belongs to his true nature from the disease which corrupts it: Sævit in te homo. Ille sævit, tu deprecare: ille odit, tu miserere. Febris animæ ipsius te odit: sanus erit et gratias tibi aget (Aug. *in* 1 *Joh. Tract.* viii. § 11).

The love of the brethren is indeed the recognition of God in men by the exercise of that in man which is after the image of God. Ubi factus est ad imaginem Dei? Augustine asks on this passage, and replies: In intellectu, in mente, in interiore homine, in eo quod intellegit caritatem, dijudicat justitiam et injustitiam, novit a quo factus est, potest intellegere Creatorem suum, laudare Creatorem suum (*Tract.* viii. § 6).

He afterwards adds a profound test of love: Hoc naturale habes: semper melior eris quam bestia. Si vis melior esse quam alius homo, invidebis ei quando tibi esse videbis æqualem. Debes velle omnes homines æquales tibi esse (§ 8).

ἡ ἀγ. αὐτοῦ] *caritas ejus* V., *His love,* the love which answers to His nature and with which He has endowed us. Comp. ii. 5 note. Man receives the love of God and makes it his own. Neither of the two specially defined senses, 'the love of God for man,' or 'the love of man for God,' suits the context.

τετελ...ἐστίν] The resolved form (i. 4; contrast *v.* 17, ii. 5) emphasises the two elements of the thought: 'the love of God is in us'; 'the love of God is in us in its completest form.' It is through man that 'the love of God' finds its fulfilment on earth.

The ideas of the perfection of love

in the believer and of the perfection of the believer in love are presented in several different forms in the epistle. In c. ii. 5 the sign of the perfection of 'the love of God' in man is found in the watchful regard which the believer pays to His revelation (ὃς ἂν τηρῇ αὐτοῦ τὸν λόγον). Here it is found in the love of Christians for one another. The two signs explain and indeed include each other. Love is the fulfilment of divine obedience. The commandment of Christ was love (cf. c. iii. 23).

In *vv.* 17, 18 the perfection of love is presented under another aspect. The fruit of the possession of 'love' is shewn in regard to the believer himself. 'Love hath been perfected with us' to the end that 'we may have boldness in the day of judgment.' And for the present, 'he that feareth hath not been made perfect in love.' Obedience, active love, confidence, these three, point to the same fact. Where the one is the other is. The source of all is the full development of the divine gift of love.

This characteristic thought of St John is found in the Thanksgiving after the Eucharist in the *Doctr. App.* 10 Μνήσθητι, Κύριε, τῆς ἐκκλησίας σου τοῦ...τελειῶσαι αὐτὴν ἐν τῇ ἀγάπῃ σου....

13. ἐν τούτῳ γινώσκομεν...] *in hoc intellegimus* V., *in this,* the possession of the spirit of love, which flows from God, *we perceive,* we are severally conscious of the fact of the divine indwelling which has been affirmed generally (*v.* 12, *God abideth in us*); and that by continuous and progressive experience (contrast ἐγνώκαμεν, *v.* 16).

ἐν αὐτῷ μένομεν...] See Additional

πνεύματος αὐτοῦ δέδωκεν ἡμῖν. ¹⁴Καὶ ἡμεῖς τεθεάμεθα
καὶ μαρτυροῦμεν ὅτι ὁ πατὴρ ἀπέσταλκεν τὸν υἱὸν
σωτῆρα τοῦ κόσμου. ¹⁵ὃς ἐὰν ὁμολογήσῃ ὅτι Ἰησοῦς

13 δέδωκεν ℵB: ἔδωκεν A.   14 τεθεάμεθα ℵB: ἐθεασάμεθα A.
15 ὁμολογήσῃ: ὁμολογῇ A.   Ἰησοῦς: +Χριστός B.

Note on v. 15. The believer feels
in the enjoyment of this affection that
the centre of his life is no longer
within himself nor on earth; because
the spirit by which it is inspired, by
which alone it can be inspired, is the
Spirit of God.

ἐκ τοῦ πν.] de spiritu suo V., of
His Spirit, 'to each according to his
several ability.' Under different aspects it can be said that God gives to
Christians 'His Spirit' (1 Thess. iv.
8), or 'of His Spirit.' For the use of
ἐκ (contrast iii. 24) see John vi. 11, i.
16. In the Holy Trinity we conceive
of the perfect union of the Father
and the Son as realised through the
Spirit. So too it is through the same
Spirit that the 'many sons' are united
in the Son with God.

δέδωκεν] hath given. Contrast iii.
23, ἔδωκεν. The difference in tense
corresponds to the difference in the
sense of ἐκ τοῦ πνεύματος.

14. Καὶ ἡμεῖς τεθ....] Et nos vidimus V., And we have beheld.... The
emphatic pronoun (v. 6, i. 4; John i.
16) brings into prominence the experience of the Christian Society
gathered up in that of its leaders.
The apostle does not speak of himself
personally but as representing the
Church for which he had a special
work to do. His experience (John i.
14) was in another form the experience of all (John i. 16). The vision
and witness of the immediate disciples correspond with the knowledge and belief of the disciples in all
ages. Or to express the same truth
otherwise, that vision and witness
remain as an abiding endowment of
the living Body.

τεθεάμεθα] Strictly speaking the
immediate objects of τεθεάμεθα and
μαρτυροῦμεν are different. The object
of contemplation was the revelation
of the Lord's Life: the object of
witness, the declaration of its meaning. In a wider sense spiritual facts
can become the objects of direct
vision (comp. John i. 33, μένον). Here
however the thought is that the significance of the Lord's Mission was
made known to those who carefully
regarded His Life and observed the
necessary tendency of all His actions.
In this respect His Life was the object of contemplation (θεᾶσθαι) and
not of vision. Compare John i. 34
(ἑώρακα) with John i. 32 (τεθέαμαι).
See also c. i. 1, 2.

The use of τεθεάμεθα carries the
mind back to v. 12, θεὸν οὐδεὶς τεθέαται. Though God Himself had not
been the object of direct human regard, yet Christian faith rests upon a
historic revelation of His Nature.

τεθεάμεθα καὶ μαρτυροῦμεν] Comp.
i. 2, ἑωράκαμεν καὶ μαρτυροῦμεν, iii. 11,
32, and contrast John i. 34, ἑώρακα καὶ
μεμαρτύρηκα, xix. 35. The continuous
witness was based upon the abiding
experience.

ὁ πατήρ] Comp. v. 10 (ὁ θεός) note.

ἀπέσταλκεν] hath sent. The testimony is borne not simply to the historic fact (v. 10, ἀπέστειλεν), but (as
in v. 9) to the permanence of Christ's
mission. Of this believers have direct
knowledge. Comp. Additional Note
on c. iii. 5.

σωτῆρα τοῦ κ.] salvatorem mundi
V. (sœculi F.), as Saviour of the
world. The full title occurs once
again in the N. T. as the confession

[Χριστός] ἐστιν ὁ υἱὸς τοῦ θεοῦ, ὁ θεὸς ἐν αὐτῷ
μένει καὶ αὐτὸς ἐν τῷ θεῷ. ¹⁶Καὶ ἡμεῖς ἐγνώκαμεν

of the Samaritans, John iv.
42 ; and the thought which it conveys is expressed in John iii. 17. St John
nowhere else uses the title σωτήρ,
which in other apostolic writings is
applied both (1) to 'God': 1 Tim. i.
1 θεὸς σωτὴρ ἡμῶν καὶ Χ. 'Ι.; Tit. i. 3
ὁ σ. ἡμῶν θ., ii. 10, iii. 4 ; Jude 25
μόνος θεὸς σωτήρ ; and more expressly
1 Tim. ii. 3 ὁ σ. ἡ. θ. ὃς πάντας ἀνθρώπους θέλει σωθῆναι, iv. 10 θεὸς ζῶν,
ὅς ἐστιν σωτὴρ πάντων ἀνθρώπων, μά-
λιστα πιστῶν (comp. Luke i. 47); and
(2) to Christ: Luke ii. 11 ἐτέχθη ὑμῖν
σ. ὅς ἐστιν χριστὸς κύριος ; Acts v. 31
['Ιησοῦν] ὁ θεὸς ἀρχηγὸν καὶ σωτῆρα
ὕψωσεν, xiii. 23 ὁ θεὸς...ἤγαγεν τῷ 'Ισ-
ραὴλ σωτῆρα 'Ιησοῦν ; 2 Tim. i. 10 ὁ σ.
ἡ. Χ. 'Ι.; Tit. i. 4 Χ. 'Ι. ὁ σ. ἡ. (comp.
v. 3), ii. 13 ὁ μέγας θεὸς καὶ σ. ἡ. Χ. 'Ι.,
iii. 6 'Ι. Χ. ὁ σ. ἡ.; 2 Pet. i. 11 ὁ κύριος
ἡ. καὶ σ. 'Ι. Χ., ii. 20, iii. 18 (comp. iii.
2 ὁ κ. καὶ σ.); and more particularly
Phil. iii. 20 σ. ἀπεκδεχόμεθα κύριον 'Ι.
Χ. (Eph. v. 23 αὐτὸς σωτὴρ τοῦ σώματος is doubtful). Thus the title is
confined (with the exception of the
writings of St Luke) to the later writings of the N. T., and is not found in
the central group of St Paul's Epistles. The double application in Tit.
i. 3 f. is very instructive.

The title is applied to God not unfrequently in the LXX.: Deut. xxxii.
15 θεὸς σ. (צוּר יְשֻׁעָתֽו) a Deo salutari
V.); Ps. xxiv. (xxiii.) 5 ; xxv. (xxiv.) 5
(Deus salvator meus V.); xxvii. (xxvi.) 9
(אֱלֹהֵי יִשְׁעִי Deus salutaris meus V.);
lxv. (lxiv.) 6; lxxix. (lxxviii.) 9 ; xcv.
(xciv.) 1 ‖ Deut. xxxii. 15; Is. xvii. 10;
xlv. 15 (מוֹשִׁיעַ salvator V.). Comp.
Wisd. xvi. 7 ; Ecclus. li. 1 ; 1 Macc. iv.
30. It is used also of human deliver-
ers: Jud. iii. 9, 15 (מוֹשִׁיעַ salvator V.);
and of the promised salvation (Saviour): Is. lxii. 11 (יֵשַׁע salvator V.).

In Classical writers the title is used
of many deities, especially of Zeus ;
and it was given under later Greek
dynasties to princes and benefactors.
Comp. Pearson On the Creed, pp. 72 f.
(136 ff.) notes, and Wetstein on Lk.
ii. 11 for numerous examples. It
had no Latin equivalent in Cicero's
time. Cicero commenting on the title
as applied to Verres adds : Hoc quantum est? ita magnum est ut Latine
uno verbo exprimi non possit. Is est
nimirum soter qui salutem dat (in
Verr. ii. 2, 63).

The accus. (σωτῆρα) describes what
Christ is and not simply what He is
designed to be. Compare ii. 2 ἱλασμός
ἐστιν, v. 10 ἀπέστειλεν ἱλασμόν. That
which is yet partly future in its human
application (Phil. iii. 20 σωτῆρα ἀπεκδεχόμεθα) is complete in the divine idea.

It is worthy of notice that the words
σώζειν and σωτηρία are not found in
the Epistles of St John.

15. ὃς ἐάν] See ii. 5 note. There
is no limitation in the will of God
(1 Tim. ii. 3).

ὁμολογήσῃ] See ii. 23 note; v. 2
note. The different forms of the confession require to be studied together.
He that confesseth the Son hath the
Father also (ii. 23); Every spirit
that confesseth Jesus Christ come in
the flesh is of God (iv. 2); Whosoever
confesseth that Jesus [Christ] is the
Son of God, God abideth in him and
he in God. The exact point of the
confession here prepares for the conclusion. The recognition of the revelation of God is the sign of the presence of God (comp. 1 Cor. xii. 3).
The fruit of the confession characterised in v. 2 is now described fully.

ὁ υἱὸς τοῦ θ.] See c. iii. 8 note.

ὁ θ. ἐν αὐ...αὐ. ἐν τῷ θ.] God in him
...he in God. See Additional Note.
The two clauses mark two aspects

καὶ πεπιστεύκαμεν τὴν ἀγάπην ἣν ἔχει ὁ θεὸς ἐν

16 πεπιστεύκαμεν ℵB (vg): πιστεύομεν A me.   ὁ θεός: –ὁ ℵ.

of the Christian's life. The believer has a new and invincible power for the fulfilment of his work on earth: 'God is in him.' And again he realises that his life is not on earth, that he belongs essentially to another order: 'he is in God.' The divine fellowship is complete and effective in each direction.

This complementary view of the fulness of the Christian life, as the believer lives in God and God in him, is presented by St John in several forms. *The love of God abideth in him* (iii. 17), and he *abideth in love* (iv. 16). *Eternal life abides in him* (iii. 15); and *this life is in the Son of God* (v. 11). *The Truth is in him* (i. 8; ii. 4), and he *walketh in the Truth* (2 Ep. 3). *The word of God is* and *abideth in him* (i. 10; ii. 14; cf. ii. 24), and he *abides in the word* (John viii. 31). He is and abides in the light (ii. 9 f.), and the unction of God abides in him (ii. 27), and guides him to all the Truth. Comp. Apoc. iii. 20.

Vicissim in se habitant qui continet et qui continetur. Habitas in Deo, sed ut continearis: habitat in te Deus, sed ut te contineat ne cadas (Aug., Bede).

16. Καὶ ἡμεῖς] *And we*, we who can speak from the fulness of Christian experience as confessors of Christ.... The case is taken from supposition (ὃς ἐὰν) to fact. For ἡμεῖς see *v.* 14 note.

ἐγνώκ. καὶ πεπιστ. τὴν ἀγ.] *cognovimus et credidimus caritati* V., *cogn. et credimus quam dilectionem Deus habet* Aug., *cogn. et credidimus in* [caritate] *quam habet Deus* F. The two verbs form a compound verb, in which the idea of belief qualifies and explains what is in this case the primary and predominant idea, know-

ledge. The Vulgate rendering throws the emphasis wrongly on *belief.* The same two verbs occur in John vi. 69 in the reverse order: ἡμεῖς πεπιστεύκαμεν καὶ ἐγνώκαμεν ὅτι σὺ εἶ ὁ ἅγιος τοῦ θεοῦ. Under different aspects knowledge precedes faith and faith precedes knowledge. We must have a true if limited knowledge of the object of faith before true faith can exist; and true faith opens the way to fuller knowledge. A general faith in Christ and self-surrender to Him prepared the disciples for a loftier apprehension of His character. The actual experience of love includes the promise of a larger manifestation of its treasures. This St John indicates here: 'We have perceived the divine love. To a certain extent we have realised what it is: but we have not exhausted its meaning. In knowing we have believed too; and in the conscious imperfection of knowledge we wait without doubt for future revelation.'

τὴν ἀγ. ἣν ἔχει ὁ θ. ἐν ἡμῖν] For the phrase ἀγάπ. ἔχειν see John xiii. 35 ἐὰν ἀγ. ἔχητε ἐν ἀλλήλοις; John xv. 13; 1 Pet. iv. 8 τὴν εἰς ἑαυτοὺς ἀγ. ἐκτενῆ ἔχοντες; 1 Cor. xiii. 1 ff.; Phil. ii. 2. It is clear from the context that the love here spoken of is the love which God has and shews towards man. But St John adds a second thought to that of God's love towards man (εἰς ἡμᾶς). The love of God becomes a power in the Christian Body (ἐν ἡμῖν). Believers are the sphere in which it operates and makes itself felt in the world (2 Cor. iv. 10 f.). Comp. *v.* 9 note.

3. *The activity of love* (16 b—21).

In the two preceding sections St John has shewn what love is in its essence and origin, and how it neces-

ἡμῖν.   Ὁ θεὸς ἀγάπη ἐστίν, καὶ ὁ μένων ἐν
τῇ ἀγάπῃ ἐν τῷ θεῷ μένει καὶ ὁ θεὸς ἐν αὐτῷ [μένει].

ἐν αὐτῷ μένει אB me the syrhl: – μένει A vg.

sarily becomes an inspiring power in
the believer, answering to a confession
of the Incarnation. He now developes
more fully the activity of love; and
this in two relations, as to the believer in himself (16 b—18), and as
to the believer in his dealings with his
fellow-Christians (19—21). On the
one side, it is by continuance in love
that the divine fellowship is realised
by the believer (16 b), while love is
perfected in the divine fellowship, so
that the last element of fear is cast
out of the soul of him who loves (17,
18). And on the other side love,
which is of a divine origin (19), must
be fulfilled after a divine type, in love
to the brethren (20), according to the
divine commandment (21).

Ambrose has traced in a famous
passage the progress of love till it
finds its consummation in complete
self-surrender. This he sees shadowed
out in three passages of Canticles (ii.
16 f.; vi. 2; vii. 10). First there is
the quickening of the divine affection
in the soul by the revelation of the
Word; next, the freedom of mutual
intercourse between the soul and the
Word; and at last the soul offers
itself absolutely to the Word that He
may rest there (Ambr. *de Isaac et
anima*, c. viii. § 68).

*God is love, and he that abideth in
love abideth in God and God* [*abideth*]
in him. ¹⁷ *In this love is perfected
with us, that we may have boldness in
the day of judgment; because even
as he is, so are we in the world.*
¹⁸ *There is no fear in love, but perfect love casteth out fear, because fear
hath punishment; and he that feareth is not perfected in love.*

The words of *v.* 8 *God is love*
are repeated as the subject of a new

development of thought. Before the
idea was of birth and knowledge, now
the idea is of growth and action.
The revelation of the Nature of God
as love calls out a response in answer
to that which is necessarily regarded
as a 'personal' call to men, and by
suggesting the idea of unlimited self-
communication as characteristic of
God, it sets a type for human action.
The nature of the believer must be
conformed to the Nature of God.

καὶ ὁ μένων...] *and he that abideth*
... From the very Nature of God it
follows as a necessary consequence
that the life of self-devotion is a life
in fellowship with Him. By the use
of the conjunction in place of simple
parallelism (*he that abideth*) the
unity of the complex idea is emphasised.

ὁ μένων ἐν τῇ ἀγ.] *he that abideth
in love* as the sphere in which his
life is fulfilled. Compare John xv.
9 f. μ. ἐν τῇ ἀγάπῃ τῇ ἐμῇ, μ. ἐν τῇ ἀγ.
μου. Here the feeling is regarded
absolutely without any further definition of its object, as God or man.
But the divine ideal made known
through Christ is present to the mind
of writer and reader.

Under different aspects St John
presents elsewhere 'the light' (c. ii.
10), and 'the word' (John viii. 31),
as the sphere in which the Christian
'abides,' 'loving his brother' and
'believing'; just as the unbeliever
'abides in darkness' (John xii. 46),
and 'he that loveth not,' 'in death'
(c. iii. 14).

ἐν τ. θ. μ. καὶ ὁ θ. ἐν αὐ. [μ.]] *abideth
in God and God* [*abideth*] *in him.*
See *v.* 15 Additional Note. He that
so abideth in love hath risen to the
heavenly order (Col. iii. 3) and found

¹⁷Ἐν τούτῳ τετελείωται ἡ ἀγάπη μεθ᾽ ἡμῶν, ἵνα παρ-

17 ἡ ἀγάπη: +τοῦ θεοῦ the (lat).   μεθ᾽ ἡμῶν: +ἐν ἡμῖν ℵ.

the power of divine fellowship for the accomplishment of earthly work.

It has been seen that this twofold blessing is connected with obedience (iii. 24) and confession (iv. 15). And love involves obedience (John xiv. 15 τηρήσετε, Rom. xiii. 10), and is the condition of fuller knowledge (John xiv. 21 ff.).

17. Ἐν τούτῳ...] *In this...*The reference has been variously explained. Some have connected *in this* with what follows, others with what precedes. In the former case two views have been held. The words have been taken closely with the second of the following clauses, ἐν τούτῳ...ὅτι...*in this...because...*, and again with the first, ἐν τούτῳ...ἵνα..., *in this...that* ... The former construction may be at once set aside. The intervening clause, ἵνα...κρίσεως, makes the connexion of ἐν τούτῳ with ὅτι most unnatural. The connexion of ἐν τούτῳ with ἵνα gives a true sense and is not foreign to St John's style, though the exact combination does not occur (not John xv. 8) in his writings; for it would not be strange that he should use a final particle (ἵνα) in place of a demonstrative particle (ὅτι), in order to bring out the idea of effort involved to the last in the realisation of confidence (comp. John xvii. 3; c. iii. 11 note). But the context and his general usage (comp. ii. 3 note) favour the conclusion that the reference is to that which precedes. The argument requires the affirmation of a fact from which a consequence is drawn, rather than a further explanation of how love is perfected. The fellowship of man with God and of God with man carries with it the consummation of love. *In this*—in this double communion—*love hath been perfected* already on the divine

side; and it is God's will that men should make its blessings their own in view of the close of earthly life.

Jerome has a strange inversion of the sense of the passage : In hoc perfecta est...caritas, si fiduciam habeamus...ut quomodo ille est sic et nos simus... (*c. Jovin.* i. c. 40).

τετελ. μεθ᾽ ἡμῶν] *perfecta est nobiscum* V., is (*hath been*) *perfected with us.* There can be no doubt that μεθ᾽ ἡμῶν is to be joined with the verb. The structure of the sentence is decisive against taking ἡ ἀγ. μεθ᾽ ἡμῶν together in the sense 'the love which is realised between Christians,' or 'the love of God shewn among us.' The unique form of expression appears to have been chosen in place of the simple 'hath been perfected in us' in order to place the perfection clearly in the realised fellowship of God and man. Love is not simply perfected in man (ἐν ἡμῖν) by an act of divine power, but in fulfilling this issue God works with man (μεθ᾽ ἡμῶν). Something of the same thought of cooperation is seen in Acts xv. 4, ὅσα ἐποίησεν ὁ θεὸς μετ᾽ αὐτῶν. Comp. 2 John 3 ἔσται μεθ᾽ ἡμῶν χάρις....

Philo calls attention to a use of the preposition not unlike in Gen. iii. 12 (LXX. ἡ γυνὴ ἣν ἔδωκας μετ᾽ ἐμοῦ): εὖ τὸ μὴ φάναι ἡ γυνὴ ἣν ἔδωκας ἐμοὶ ἀλλὰ μετ᾽ ἐμοῦ. οὐ γὰρ ἐμοὶ ὡς κτῆμα...ἔδωκας ἀλλὰ καὶ αὐτὴν ἀφῆκας ἄνετον καὶ ἐλευθέραν...(*Leg. Alleg.* iii. § 18; i. 98 M.).

τετελείωται] *v.* 12; c. ii. 5 note. The tense presents the perfection as dependent on a continuous fellowship between God and the Christian body. Contrast Clem. *ad Cor.* i. 50 οἱ ἐν ἀγάπῃ τελειωθέντες.

ἵνα παρρ. ἔχ.] *ut fiduciam habeamus* V. The fulness of love is given with a view to an end. The feeling

ρησίαν ἔχωμεν ἐν τῇ ἡμέρᾳ τῆς κρίσεως, ὅτι καθὼς

ἔχωμεν: ἔχομεν ℵ.   ἡμέρᾳ: ἀγάπῃ ℵ.

which is active now will have its fullest effect in the supreme trial of existence. St John, who habitually regards the eternal aspect of things, regards the boldness as something which is possessed absolutely (τετελείωται...ἵνα ἔχωμεν...). In an earlier passage (ii. 28), he enjoined abiding in God in Christ as the source of confidence at Christ's Presence. He now points out how the confidence is established. To abide in God is to share the character of Christ under the conditions of earth. The sense of spiritual harmony with Him which this abiding brings necessarily inspires boldness in the believer; and it is the purpose of God that it should do so. So God fulfils His counsel of love. Thus the whole train of thought is brought to a natural conclusion. "God is love : he that abideth in love abideth in God...In this communion love finds consummation, in order that 'by conscious conformity with Christ' the last trial of life may be overcome, when 'the last fear is banished.'"

παρρ. ἔχωμεν] c. ii. 28 note.

ἐν τῇ ἡμ. τῆς κρ.] in die judicii V., in the day of judgment, when Christ shall come to execute judgment on the world (c. ii. 28). The definite phrase is found here only. The indefinite phrase, 'a day of judgment' (ἡμ. κρ.), occurs in Matt. x. 15; xi. 22, 24; xii. 36; 2 Pet. ii. 9; iii. 7. Compare also Apoc. vi. 17 ἡ ἡμ. ἡ μεγάλη τῆς ὀργῆς αὐτῶν; Rom. ii. 5 ἡμ. ὀργῆς καὶ ἀποκαλύψεως τῆς δικαιοκρισίας τοῦ θεοῦ; 1 Pet. ii. 12 ἡμ. ἐπισκοπῆς. In the Gospel St John speaks of 'the last day' (ἡ ἐσχάτη ἡμ.); vi. 39, 40, 44, 54; xi. 24; xii. 48; which is elsewhere styled simply 'that day' (ἐκείνη ἡ ἡμ., ἡ ἡμ. ἐκ.), Matt. vii. 22; Luke vi. 23; x. 12; xxi. 34; 2 Thess.

i. 10; 2 Tim. i. 12, 18; iv. 8. The phrase 'the judgment' (ἡ κρίσις) is found Matt. xii. 41 f.; Luke x. 14; xi. 31 f.

It is of interest to notice that the privilege which is here attributed to love is, under another aspect, attributed also to faith; John iii. 18; v. 24. The two cannot be separated.

ὅτι καθὼς ἐκεῖνος...] because even as He (Christ, c. ii. 6 note] is... The ground of boldness is present likeness to Christ. He has 'passed out of this world' (John xii. 1), but His disciples are still 'in the world' (John xvii. 11), and have a work to do there (John xvii. 18). In fulfilling this work He is their ideal (c. ii. 6): conformity to Him is the rule of their judgment (John xv. 18 ff.). And the likeness of Christians to Christ is to His character as it is at present and eternally (καθὼς ἐκ. ἐστιν, comp. iii. 2, 7) and not to the particular form in which it was historically manifested (κ. ἐκ. ἦν).

The reference is not to any one attribute, as love or righteousness, but to the whole character of Christ as it is made known; and His highpriestly prayer serves as a commentary on the view which St John suggests of the position of Christians in the world.

Following Augustine (see iii. 7 note) Bede says forcibly: Non semper ad æqualitatem dicitur sicut, sed dicitur ad quandam similitudinem... Si ergo facti sumus ad imaginem Dei, quare non sicut Deus sumus? non ad æqualitatem sed pro modo nostro. Inde ergo nobis datur fiducia in die judicii, quia sicut ille est et nos sumus in hoc mundo, imitando videlicet perfectionem dilectionis in mundo cujus ille exemplum nobis quotidie præbet de cælo.

ἐκεῖνός ἐστιν καὶ ἡμεῖς ἐσμὲν ἐν τῷ κόσμῳ τούτῳ.
¹⁸φόβος οὐκ ἔστιν ἐν τῇ ἀγάπῃ, ἀλλ' ἡ τελεία ἀγάπη
ἔξω βάλλει τὸν φόβον, ὅτι ὁ φόβος κόλασιν ἔχει, ὁ

ἐσμέν: ἐσόμεθα ℵ.

καθὼς...καὶ ἡμεῖς...] The οὕτως in the second member of the comparison is sometimes replaced by καὶ: c. ii. 6, 18; John xvii. 18; xx. 21 (xv. 9 is doubtful); sometimes it is omitted: c. ii. 27; and especially when the order of the clauses is inverted: John v. 23; Rom. xv. 7.

καὶ ἡμ. ἐ. ἐν τῷ κ. τ.] The likeness is conditioned by the circumstances of the present state. 'This world' (ὁ κ. οὗτος), as distinguished from 'the world,' emphasises the idea of transitoriness. The phrase is not found elsewhere in the Epistles of John. See John i. 10 note.

18. The thought of boldness necessarily calls up that of its opposite, fear. There is fear in man naturally; but love ever tends to expel it. Fear finds no place in love, and it cannot therefore co-exist with perfect love which occupies the whole 'heart.' The ideas are expressed in a general form and hold good absolutely, but they necessarily are specialised mentally from the context.

φόβος.. ἐν τῇ ἀγ.] Love is the simple desire for the highest good of another or of others, and is the expression of a spirit of self-surrender. Fear therefore—the shrinking from another—cannot be an essential element in love. Here the reader at once feels that the abstract principle has found a typical embodiment in the self-sacrifice of Christ, towards the imitation of which Christians strive through His Spirit.

The fear of which St John speaks is, of course, not the reverence of the son (Hebr. v. 7 ff.), but the dread of the criminal or of the slave (Rom. viii. 15).

So Augustine says: Aliud est timere Deum ne mittat te in gehennam cum diabolo: aliud est timere Deum ne recedat a te.

ἀλλ'...] but, so far is it from being the case that fear has a place in love, it is of the nature of love to expel fear. Fear is an instrument of painful discipline; and when the end of perfect fellowship with God has been reached, the discipline is no longer needed. This sentence ἀλλ'...ἔχει is parenthetical.

ἡ τελ. ἀγάπη] perfect love, not 'perfected love' (ἡ τετελειωμένη ἀγ.). The thought is of love which is complete in all its parts, which has reached its complete development (Hebr. v. 14 note); of what it is and not of what it has become. Comp. James i. 4; iii. 2; Eph. iv. 13.

The arrangement ἡ τελ. ἀγ., which is common, for example, in 2 Pet., is unique in the Epistle (comp. 3 John 4 τὰ ἐμὰ τέκνα). See c. ii. 7 note. It expresses a shade of meaning, as distinct from ἡ ἀγ. ἡ τελ., which is evidently appropriate here.

ἔξω βάλλει] foras mittit V., casteth forth from the whole sphere of life. There is no longer scope for its operation. St John thus recognises the provisional presence of fear in the believer. It is found for a time with growing love, but mature love removes it. The phrase βάλλει ἔξω, which suggests the thought of a defined realm of spiritual activity (Apoc. xxii. 15), is more vivid than ἐκβάλλει. Comp. Matt. v. 13; xiii. 48; Luke xiv. 35 (βάλλειν ἔξω); John vi. 37; ix. 34 f.; xii. 31; xv. 6 (ἐκβάλλειν ἔξω).

ὅτι ὁ φ. κόλ. ἔχει] quoniam timor poenam (tormentum Aug.) habet V.,

δὲ φοβούμενος οὐ τετελείωται ἐν τῇ ἀγάπῃ. ¹⁹ Ἡμεῖς
ἀγαπῶμεν, ὅτι αὐτὸς πρῶτος ἠγάπησεν ἡμᾶς. ²⁰ ἐάν

19 ἡμεῖς ℵB me the syrhl: +οὖν A vg syrvg.   ἀγαπῶμεν AB: +τὸν θεόν
ℵ (vg) me syrr. (αὐτόν and invicem are also added.)   αὐτός ℵB me the syrr:
ὁ θεός A vg.

because fear hath punishment. Fear, which is the expression of disharmony and therefore the anticipation of suffering, at the same time must include suffering. And the suffering which comes from disharmony with God is divine punishment which has a salutary office: Hebr. xii. 11. Such punishment is not future only but present. Comp. John iii. 18.

κόλ. ἔχει] includes, brings with it punishment. Comp. Hebr. x. 35 (τὴν παρρησίαν) ἥτις ἔχει μεγάλην μισθαποδοσίαν. James ii. 17 (i. 4).

The word κόλασις occurs elsewhere in the N. T. only in Matt. xxv. 46. The verb κολάζεσθαι is found in Acts iv. 21; 2 Pet. ii. 9 (not ii. 4). The noun occurs in the LXX. of Ezekiel (for מִכְשׁוֹל): xiv. 3, 4, 7; xviii. 30 (xliii. 11); xliv. 12; and both the noun and verb occur not unfrequently in Wisdom: xi. 14, 17; xvi. 1, 2, &c.

The familiar classical distinction between τιμωρία which regarded the retributive suffering and κόλασις which regarded the disciplinary chastisement of the wrong-doer was familiar to the Alexandrine Greeks: e.g. Philo, de confus. ling. § 34 (i. 431 M.) ἔστι δὲ καὶ κόλασις οὐκ ἐπιζήμιον ἁμαρτημάτων οὖσα κώλυσις καὶ ἐπανόρθωσις.

ὁ δὲ φοβούμενος...] and he that feareth... This clause goes closely with the first clause of the sentence: 'there is no fear in love, but he that feareth hath not been made perfect in love.' That which is stated first as an abstract principle ('fear') is repeated in a personal form ('he that feareth'). St John, while he lays down the full truth, recognises the facts of life and deals with them. There are those

who fear while yet they love: so far their love though real is incomplete.

The second and third clauses of the verse illustrate well the distinction of ἀλλά (sed) and δέ (autem). The second clause (ἀλλ' ἡ τ. ἀ.) stands in sharp opposition to the first, while the third (ὁ δὲ φ.) deals with a limitation, or objection.

οὐ τετελείωται ἐν τῇ ἀγ.] This consummation of the believer is presented in two complementary forms. He is himself the sphere in which love finds its perfection; and love is the sphere in which he finds his perfection. Love is perfected in him (ii. 5): and he is perfected in love. Comp. Additional Note on v. 15.

Bengel in one of his unmatched epigrams gives a history of the soul through its relations to fear and love: Varius hominum status: sine timore et amore; cum timore sine amore; cum timore et amore; sine timore cum amore.

19—21. In the preceding verses St John has shewn what love brings to the believer. He now lays open the obligation which it imposes upon him. The love which is inspired by God must be manifested towards the brethren according to His commandment.

¹⁹ We love, because he first loved us. ²⁰ If any one say I love God, and hate his brother, he is a liar; for he that loveth not his brother whom he hath seen cannot love God, whom he hath not seen. ²¹ And this commandment have we from him that he who loveth God love his brother also.

19. Ἡμεῖς ἀγ.] Nos ergo diligamus invicem V. The absence of any title of

τις εἴπῃ ὅτι Ἀγαπῶ τὸν θεόν, καὶ τὸν ἀδελφὸν αὐτοῦ
μισῇ, ψεύστης ἐστίν· ὁ γὰρ μὴ ἀγαπῶν τὸν ἀδελφὸν

20　– ὅτι ℵ.

address and the addition of the personal pronoun distinguish this phrase
from *v.* 7 ἀγαπητοί, ἀγαπῶμεν ἀλλήλους, and seem to shew clearly that
the verb is an indicative (*We love*),
and not a conjunctive (*Let us love*).
It is worthy of notice that the Latin
and Pesh. Syriac which give the
hortatory rendering add a connecting
particle as many Greek authorities
(οὖν).

The indicative also suits the context better. The fact of love is assumed, and then it is shewn in its
workings. Comp. iii. 16.

According to the true reading the
idea of love is left in its full breadth
without any definition of the object,
as God (αὐτόν or τὸν θεόν), or man
(*invicem* V.). This is required by
what follows, where it is falsely urged
that the claims of 'love' can be satisfied by bare 'love of God.'

ὅτι αὐτὸς πρ. ἠγ. ἡμ.] Comp. *v.* 10.
The thought here is different from
that in the former context. There
love was regarded in its essence: here
it is regarded in its personal exercise.
Our love is the light kindled by the
love of God. And the divine origin
of love determines its character and
also assures its stability. Comp. John
xv. 16.

πρῶτος ἠγ.] *prior dilexit* V. Comp.
Rom. v. 8. The priority of the love
of God to all love on man's part
which is accentuated here, is a ground
for the spontaneous exercise of love
on the part of the believer towards
those who do not seem to invite it.

20, 21. The consequences of the
preceding statement are traced out
in two ways from the nature of the
case (*v.* 20), and from the direct commandment of God (*v.* 21). The love
of God, which is assumed to exist at

W.

least in profession, must include love
of the brethren, and so God has Himself enjoined. The thought of loving
God is here first discussed (comp. *v.*
10).

20. ἐάν τις εἴπῃ] The form of expression differs slightly from that in
i. 6 ff. (ἐὰν εἴπωμεν). There a view
was given of the general position of
Christians : here a particular case is
taken, involving personal feeling. Contrast also 'he that [saith]' and 'every
one that [saith],' c. iii. 3 note ; ii.
4 note.

εἴπῃ ὅτι Ἀγαπῶ...] For the use of
the recitative ὅτι see i. 6 note. The
claim is like those which have been
noticed in ii. 4, 9; i. 6 ff., by which
the faith is taken out of the sphere of
practical life.

It is worthy of notice that in the
Gospel of St John ἀγαπᾶν is not used
of the feeling of man for God (the
Father). It is so used in the other
Gospels in a quotation from the LXX.

μισῇ] *hate.* St John admits no position of indifference. See ii. 9 note.

ψεύστης ἐστίν] Comp. ii. 4 ὁ λέγων
ὅτι Ἔγνωκα αὐτὸν καὶ τὰς ἐντολὰς αὐτοῦ
μὴ τηρῶν ψεύστης ἐστίν... The claim
to the knowledge of God without
obedience, and the claim to the love
of God without action, involve not
only the denial of what is known to
be true (ψεύδεσθαι), but falseness of
character. Comp. i. 10 note, and v.
10. See also John viii. 44, 55; and
c. ii. 22.

ὁ γὰρ μὴ ἀγαπῶν...] *for he that
loveth not...* The particular statement
(ἐάν τις εἴπῃ) is refuted by a general
principle. Sight is taken as the sign
of that kind of limitation which brings
objects within the range of our present powers. It is necessarily easier
to love that which is like ourselves

11

αὐτοῦ ὃν ἑώρακεν, τὸν θεὸν ὃν οὐχ ἑώρακεν οὐ δύναται
ἀγαπᾶν. ²¹καὶ ταύτην τὴν ἐντολὴν ἔχομεν ἀπ᾽ αὐτοῦ,
ἵνα ὁ ἀγαπῶν τὸν θεὸν ἀγαπᾷ καὶ τὸν ἀδελφὸν αὐτοῦ.

οὐ δύν. ℵB the syr hl: πῶς δύν. A vg me syr vg.   21 ἀπ᾽ αὐτοῦ: ἀπὸ τοῦ
θεοῦ A vg.

than that which we cannot grasp in
a finite form. And the title 'brother'
brings out the idea of that which is
godlike in man to which love can be
directed. He therefore who fails to
recognise God as He reveals Himself
through Christ in man (Matt. xxv. 40
ἑνὶ τούτων τῶν ἀδελφῶν μου τῶν ἐλα-
χίστων) cannot love God. He has
refused the help which God has provided for the expression of love in
action.

Philo traces the thought through
the natural love of children for parents: φασί τινες ὡς ἄρα πατὴρ καὶ
μήτηρ ἐμφανεῖς εἰσι θεοί...ἀμήχανον δὲ
εὐσεβεῖσθαι τὸν ἀόρατον ὑπὸ τῶν εἰς
τοὺς ἐμφανεῖς καὶ ἐγγὺς ὄντας ἀσεβούν-
των (de decal. § 23, ii. p. 204 M.). The
love of parents involves the love of
brethren.

τὸν θ. ὃν οὐχ ἑώρ.] John i. 18 note;
v. 12 (τεθέαται); 1 Tim. vi. 16. The
inverted order in the corresponding
clauses is singularly expressive. There
is also a more solemn pathos in the
direct negative οὐ δύναται than in the
more rhetorical phrase of the common text πῶς δύναται.

ἑώρακεν...οὐχ ἑώρακεν...] videt...
non videt... V., hath seen...hath not
seen... It might have seemed more
natural to say 'seeth...cannot see...';
but the two perfects mark the fact
that a revelation with abiding consequences has and has not been made
in the two cases. The vision of 'the
brother' may in any particular case

be clouded but he has been seen, and
the idea of brotherhood abides for
constant use.

21. καὶ ταύτην τ. ἐ.] That which is
a spiritual necessity is also an express
injunction. The commandment of
love which has been implied in the
preceding verses is now defined.
Comp. c. iii. 23.

ἀπ᾽ αὐτοῦ] a Deo V., ab ipso Lat.
Vet., from Him, from God. The context makes it probable that, though
the Divine Person is not clearly defined, the reference is to the Father
(v. 19), Who by sending His Son
shewed the way of love. The commandment was given in substance by
Christ (John xiii. 34), but it came
from God (ἀπό) as its final source.
Compare i. 5; ii. 27 notes; and contrast the use of παρά Apoc. ii. 27;
John viii. 26, 40; x. 18.

ἵνα...] that... The final particle
gives more than the simple contents
of the commandment. It marks the
injunction as directed to an aim; and
implies that the effort to obtain it
can never be relaxed (ἵνα...ἀγαπᾷ).
Comp. John xiii. 34 note.

Augustine (on c. v. 3) uses the
words of the ascended Lord to Saul
to illustrate and enforce the lesson:
Persecutori Saulo [Christus] dixit de-
super: Saule, Saule, quid me perse-
queris? Ascendi in cælum, sed adhuc
in terra jaceo. Hic ad dexteram patris sedeo: ibi adhuc esurio, sitio et
peregrinus sum.

Additional Note on the reading of iv. 3.

The first clause in this verse is given in several different forms in existing Greek authorities. These are

π. πν. ὃ μὴ ὁμολογεῖ τὸν Ἰησοῦν   AB.

π. πν. ὃ μὴ ὁμολογεῖ Ἰησοῦν Κύριον ἐν σαρκὶ ἐληλυθότα ℵ.

π. πν. ὃ μὴ ὁμολογεῖ τὸν Ἰησοῦν Χριστὸν ἐν σαρκὶ ἐληλυθότα L, &c.

π. πν. ὃ μὴ ὁμολογεῖ Ἰησοῦν Χριστὸν ἐν σαρκὶ ἐληλυθότα K, &c.

General view of the variations.

To these variations must be added another, which is represented by the Vulgate reading:

π. πν. ὃ λύει   τὸν Ἰησοῦν.

The main interest centres on the alternatives μὴ ὁμολογεῖ and λύει.

As the direct evidence now stands, μὴ ὁμολογεῖ is read by

   (1) All Greek MSS, uncial and cursive,

   (2) All the versions except the Latin, and by one important Old Latin MS (*Fris.*),

   (3) The Greek Fathers who quote the passage with the exception of Socrates, from Cyril downwards, to whom Polycarp must probably be added: πᾶς γὰρ ὃς ἂν μὴ ὁμολογῇ Ἰησοῦν Χριστὸν ἐληλυθέναι ἀντίχριστός ἐστι (*ad Phil.* 7).

External evidence for (i) μὴ ὁμολογεῖ,

On the other hand

   (1) Socrates gives λύει as having been the reading in 'the old copies.'

   (2) All Latin MSS, with one exception, read *solvit*; and

   (3) This reading, with the variant *destruit*, prevails in the Latin Fathers, being universal in the later writers.

(ii) for λύει.

The evidence of Socrates, the only Greek authority for λύει, is contained in a passage which presents several difficulties. Speaking of the error of Nestorius and of his general self-sufficiency and contempt for accurate learning, he goes on to say: 'for example he was ignorant of the fact that in the Catholic Epistle of John it was written in the ancient copies that *every spirit which divideth* (λύει) *Jesus is not from God*. For they that desired to separate the deity from the man of the dispensation [i.e. Christ Jesus] removed this thought [the condemnation of those who 'divide Jesus'] from the ancient copies. Wherefore also the ancient interpreters noted this very fact, that there were some who had tampered with the epistle wishing to divide the man from God[1].'

The evidence of Socrates.

---

[1] H. E. vii. 32, αὐτίκα γοῦν ἠγνόησεν ὅτι ἐν τῇ καθολικῇ Ἰωάννου γέγραπτο ἐν τοῖς παλαιοῖς ἀντιγράφοις ὅτι πᾶν πνεῦμα ὃ λύει τὸν Ἰησοῦν ἀπὸ τοῦ θεοῦ οὐκ ἔστι. ταύτην γὰρ τὴν διάνοιαν ἐκ τῶν παλαιῶν ἀντιγράφων περιεῖλον οἱ χωρίζειν ἀπὸ τοῦ τῆς οἰκονομίας ἀνθρώπου βουλόμενοι τὴν θεότητα· διὸ καὶ οἱ παλαιοὶ ἑρμηνεῖς αὐτὸ τοῦτο ἐπεσημήναντο, ὥς τινες εἶεν ῥᾳδιουργήσαντες τὴν ἐπιστολήν, λύειν ἀπὸ τοῦ θεοῦ τὸν ἄνθρωπον θέλοντες.

It will be seen that Socrates does not say that the reading was found in copies which he had himself seen, but only that it once was found in the text: he writes that it 'had been written' (γέγραπτο) and not that 'it is written' (γέγραπται). Again it is a sign that he is not quoting any Greek MS that he writes ἀπὸ τοῦ θεοῦ for ἐκ τοῦ θεοῦ, a variant which has no Greek authority. His language is in fact perfectly satisfied by the supposition that he was acquainted with the Latin reading and some Latin commentary[1].

Quotations in texts of Greek Fathers.

In the Latin translation of IRENÆUS 2 John 7 and 1 John iv. 3 are quoted as from the same epistle (Iren. iii. 16, 8). After the quotation of the former passage the text continues...Johannes in prædicta epistola fugere eos præcepit dicens...*omnis spiritus qui solvit Jesum non est ex Deo sed de (ex) Antichristo est.* The context shews clearly in what sense Irenæus understood St John's words, but it is not decisive as to the reading which he had in his Greek text.

The Latin translation of CLEMENT'S *Outlines* (Ὑποτυπώσεις) on 2 John gives as part of the substance of this Epistle: adstruit in hac epistola... ut nemo *dividat Jesum Christum,* sed unum credere *Jesum Christum venisse in carne.*

The reading 'solvit Jesum' is found in the Latin translation of ORIGEN: Hæc autem dicentes non solvimus suscepti corporis hominem, cum sit scriptum apud Johannem *omnis spiritus qui solvit Jesum non est ex Deo,* sed unicuique substantiæ proprietatem servamus (*in Matt. Com. Scr.* § 65). But the character of the translation is such as to give no satisfactory assurance that Origen's Greek text read λύει.

There is no indication, as far as I am aware, that the reading λύει was accepted by or known to any other Greek or Eastern father.

Latin Patristic evidence.

Yet the fact remains that the reading was found at a very early date. TERTULLIAN uses the phrases 'solvere Jesum' (*adv. Marc.* v. 16) and 'solvere Jesum Christum' (*de Jejun.* 1). In the former passage he appears to combine the language of 1 John iv. 3 and 2 John 7, as is done in the Latin translation of Clement: Johannes dicit processisse in mundum præcursores antichristi spiritus, *negantes Christum in carne venisse et solventes Jesum;* and it may be observed that the close connexion of the two verses in some of the Latin renderings (which give *venisse* for ἐρχόμενον in 2 John 7) makes it difficult to decide to which of the two reference is made in particular cases. The words of Tertullian *de Carne Chr.* 24 qui *negat Christum in carne venisse hic antichristus est; de Præscr. hær.* 33 in epistola sua [Johannes] eos maxime antichristos vocat *qui Christum negarent in carne venisse et qui non putarent Jesum filium Dei esse* (comp. *c. Marc.* iii. 8 negantes Christum in carne venisse); and of Cyprian (*Testim.* ii. 8) qui autem negat in carne venisse de Deo non est sed est de antichristi spiritu[2] were probably moulded by the passage in the second epistle.

AUGUSTINE in his explanation of the epistle first quotes the passage at length with the reading '*qui non confitetur Jesum Christum in carne venisse,*' which he explains (referring to c. ii. 19), and then without any

---

[1] Socrates was acquainted with Latin: *H. E.* i. 12.

[2] All. *de Deo natus non est sed est Antichristus.*

remark he passes on to explain 'solvere': Adeo ut noveritis quia ad facta retulit: *Et omnis spiritus*, ait, *qui solvit Jesum;* and again afterwards he unites both phrases: *'solvis Jesum et negas in carne venisse.'*

FULGENTIUS[1] and TICHONIUS[2] combine phrases from the two epistles with even greater freedom.

It is remarkable that BEDE, who was aware of the substance of Socrates' criticism, supposes that those who tampered with the epistle left out the whole clause: In tantum ex Deo non sunt ut quidam...hunc...versiculum quo dicitur *et omnis spiritus qui solvit Jesum ex Deo non est*, ex hac epistola eraserint, ne scilicet per auctoritatem beati Joannis convinceretur error eorum. Denique Nestorius nescire se prodidit hanc authenticis exemplaribus inditam fuisse sententiam...

This strange assertion is repeated by FULBERT of CHARTRES[3], and HINCMAR[4]. Such a misunderstanding offers a memorable example of the way in which critical statements are unintelligently perverted and made the ground of unjust charges.

From this review there can be no question as to the overwhelming weight *Internal* of external evidence in favour of μὴ ὁμολογεῖ. To set this aside without the *evidence.* clearest necessity is to suspend all laws of textual criticism. No reading supported by such authority as λύει is, I believe, more than a very early gloss. And on careful consideration it seems that the internal evidence is not more favourable to λύει Ἰησοῦν than the external. It is scarcely possible that such a phrase could be used for separating the divine and human natures in Christ. The name Ἰησοῦς brings prominently forward the humanity of the Lord. Socrates evidently felt this, for he defines λύειν by the addition ἀπὸ τοῦ θεοῦ.

The language of Polycarp shews that St John's teaching upon the subject was current in various forms. It seems likely that he used two main phrases λύειν Ἰησοῦν Χριστόν and μὴ ὁμολογεῖν τὸν Ἰησοῦν (answering to Κύριος Ἰησοῦς Rom. x. 9). This being so, the λύει in the former phrase was added as a gloss on the phrase μὴ ὁμολογεῖ of the epistle in some early copies, and so passed into the Latin version[5]. The additions to Ἰησοῦν are

---

[1] *Ad Trasim.* i. c. 5. De qua veritate...ille qui de pectore ipsius sapientiæ mysteriorum cælestium meruit intelligentiam illuminatus haurire fiducialiter dicit: *omnis spiritus qui confitetur Jesum Christum in carne venisse ex Deo est. Omnis spiritus qui non confitetur Jesum Christum in carne venisse ex Deo non est; et hic est Antichristus. Ep.* xvii. c. 10 Joannes...testatur quia *omnis spiritus qui solvit Jesum ex Deo non est, et hic est antichristus.*

[2] *Reg.* IV. Super Joannem *multi pseudoprophetæ prodierunt in hunc mundum. In isto cognoscite spiritus Dei. Omnis spiritus qui solvit Jesum et negat in carne venisse de Deo non est sed hic de* Antichristo est. *Quod audistis quoniam venit et nunc in isto mundo præsens est.*

[3] *Ep.* v. (i) Cujus [Arii] auditores quoniam Spiritum Sanctum Deum esse negabant de Evangelio eraserunt illud quod Salvator ait *Spiritus est Deus,* et de epistola Joannis eraserunt *et omnis spiritus qui solvit Jesum ex Deo non est.* Sicut Nestorius...

[4] *Opusc. et Epist.* xviii. (Migne, *Patr. Lat.* cxxvi. p. 351) quidam etiam de epistola Joannis eraserunt *et omnis spiritus qui solvit Jesum ex Deo non est.* The whole paragraph is very instructive.

[5] A passage of Cyril of Alexandria will shew how naturally the gloss

easily intelligible, and the forms in which they occur shew that they are no part of the original text. At the same time it is not unreasonable to suppose that the unusual amount of variants indicates the influence of some traditional form of words upon the text. In 2 John 7 there is no variation in the corresponding phrase; nor is the characteristic word of that passage (ἐρχόμενον) introduced here by any authority.

Additional Note on iv. 8. The revelation of God.

Tendencies towards two conceptions of God in the Apostolic age, abstract and concrete. Jewish thought in the age of St John represented in striking forms the two chief tendencies of religious speculation on the Being of God. On the one side there was the philosophic, theoretic tendency which leads to an abstract conception; and on the other the popular, practical tendency which leads to a concrete conception. The former found an exponent in Philo: the latter was embodied in the current creed of Palestine, which more and more reduced the God of the Covenant to the position of the God of the Jews.

St John unites them. St John unites the truths which gave force to these tendencies, the transcendental and the personal truth, in a perfect harmony. He wholly avoids the Alexandrine terms—τὸ ὄν, ἐπέκεινα πάσης οὐσίας and the like—and yet he preserves the thoughts at which they aimed. He recognises most emphatically the privileges of Israel, and at the same time he places the 'One God' in a living, loving connexion with 'the world.'

His teaching rests on the Old Testament. The foundation of his teaching lies in the Monotheism of the O. T., which is not rigid, sterile, final, like the Monotheism of Islam, but vital and progressive. The unity which it affirms is not numerical but essential (John x. 30 ἐγὼ καὶ ὁ πατὴρ ἕν ἐσμεν: comp. xvii. 3; 1 John v. 20).

Opposed to In this sense the thought of 'the only God' (John v. 44) is opposed to all forms of Dualism, Polytheism, Pantheism. He is the One source of life (John v. 26); and through the Word, 'the Son,' to Whom 'he gave to have **Dualism,** life in himself' (John l.c.), 'all things came into being' (John i. 3). All notion of coeternal matter or of a coeternal principle of evil, as antagonistic to or limiting the divine action, is set aside. God 'loved the world' (John iii. 16; comp. 1 John ii. 2) not as strange but as His own. All men need (John iii. 3) and all men are capable of (John xii. 32) union with Him. The devil left his first place 'in the Truth' (John viii. 44); and Christ 'came to undo his works' (1 John iii. 8) by taking 'flesh,' which could not therefore have been in essential opposition to His Nature.

Polytheism, The allusions to Polytheism in St John are naturally less prominent than those in St Paul. Once in general terms he warns against 'the idols' which

might be introduced. He quotes the passage: πᾶν πνεῦμα ὃ μὴ ὁμολογεῖ τὸν Ἰησοῦν ἐκ τοῦ θεοῦ οὐκ ἔστι and then in his interpretation adds ὁ τοίνυν οὐ λέγων θεὸν εἶναι ἀληθῶς τὸν Χριστὸν διαιρῶν δὲ καὶ κατασμικρύνων τὴν δόξαν αὐτοῦ τὸ τοῦ Ἀντιχρίστου πνεῦμα ἔχων ἁλώσεται (de recta fide ad reg. p. 94). The Greek version of Leo's Letter to Flavian (c. v. p. 830) gives πᾶν πνεῦμα τὸ διαιροῦν Ἰησοῦν Χριστὸν ἀπὸ θεοῦ οὐκ ἔστι καὶ οὗτός ἐστιν ὁ Ἀντίχριστος as the rendering of the Latin omnis spiritus qui solvit Jesum ex Deo non est et hic est Antichristus.

usurp the place of 'the true God' (1 John v. 21); and in the Apocalypse he marks the connexion between the empire and idolatry (xiii. 14 f.; and comp. xxi. 8; xxii. 15). But his teaching is directed rather against the spirit than against the form of polytheism. 'The only true God,' God revealed as Father in the Son, excludes polytheism of necessity both within and without the Christian Body.

St John, like St Paul, places Creation in close relation with the Creator, Pantheism. but he affirms the reality of the relation which the words imply. God is present in all things but He transcends them. They answered to His will in their beginning (Apoc. iv. 11), and are supported by His working (John v. 17).

For the most part St John, like the other writers of the Bible, leaves St John's the reader to form his conception of God from what is recorded of His three action; but in three phrases he has laid down once for all the great outlines state- within which our thoughts on the Divine Nature must be confined. The ments as first sentence is in his narrative of the Lord's words: '*God is spirit*' (John to the iv. 24); the two others are in his first Epistle: '*God is light*' (1 John i. 5 note) Nature. and '*God is love*' (1 John iv. 8, 16).

To these may be added a fourth, in which he speaks of the revelation of 'Him that is true' made in 'Jesus Christ His Son': 'this,' he says, 'is the true God and eternal life' (1 John v. 20). So he passes from the idea of God to the revelation of God to man.

The three phrases which have been quoted do not simply specify properties of God (as 'God is loving'), but, so far as we can apprehend them, essential aspects of His Nature. The first, if we may venture to distinguish them, is metaphysical and describes God in Himself, in His Being: He is Spirit. The second is moral, and describes God in His character towards all created things: He is Light. The third is personal, and describes God in His action towards self-conscious creatures: He is Love. In this order they offer a progress of thought: each statement is taken up and developed in that which follows.

i. *God is spirit* ($\pi\nu\epsilon\hat{\upsilon}\mu\alpha$ $\hat{o}$ $\theta\epsilon\acute{o}s$). The statement obviously refers to the i. God is divine nature and not to the divine personality. The parallel phrases are spirit. a sufficient proof of this. God is not 'a spirit,' as one of many, but 'spirit.' As spirit, He is absolutely raised above all limitations of succession (time and space) into which finally all thoughts of change and transitoriness are resolved.

There is no anticipation of this idea in the O.T. The 'Spirit of God' is constantly spoken of; but the loftiest descriptions of the Divine Majesty are always relative to space (Is. lxvi. 1; 1 K. viii. 27; Jer. xxiii. 24).

It follows that God as God is not cognisable by the senses (John i. 18; 1 John iv. 12). The Theophanies of the O.T. were not manifestations of 'God' but of the Son of God (John xii. 41; Is. vi. 1; comp. Apoc. iv. 2 ff.).

But while the material vision of God is impossible, there is a spiritual and a moral vision of God through Christ (John xiv. 9; comp. xii. 45) and through love, which leads up to the transfiguring contemplation of the Divine Presence (1 John ii. 2).

ii. *God is light* ($\hat{o}$ $\theta\epsilon\grave{o}s$ $\phi\hat{\omega}s$ $\acute{\epsilon}\sigma\tau\acute{\iota}\nu$). This statement again is absolute ii. God is as to the Nature of God, and not as to His action (not 'a light' or 'the light.

light of men'). The phrase expresses unlimited self-communication, diffusiveness. Light is by shining: darkness alone bounds. And further, the communication of light is of that which is pure and glorious. Such is God towards all finite being, the condition of life and action. He reveals Himself through the works of creation which reflect His perfections in a form answering to the powers of man, and yet God is not to be fully apprehended by man as He is.

The idea is not distinctly expressed in the O. T., though it underlies the thought of the Divine 'glory' (Ex. xxiv. 17; Hab. iii. 3 f.). Compare also Is. x. 17; Ps. xxxvi. 10; civ. 2; Ezek. i. 27. It is indicated in Wisdom (vii. 26), and Philo uses the very words of St John: de Somn. i. p. 632, πρῶτον μὲν ὁ θεὸς φῶς ἐστί...καὶ οὐ μόνον φῶς ἀλλὰ καὶ παντὸς ἑτέρου φωτὸς ἀρχέτυπον μᾶλλον δὲ ἀρχετύπου πρεσβύτερον, καὶ ἀνώτερον, λόγον ἔχων παραδείγματος. Compare also Philo de nom. mut. i. 579; de sacrif. ii. p. 254; one remarkable phrase which Philo uses deserves to be quoted: ὁ θεὸς ἑαυτοῦ φέγγος ὢν δι᾽ αὐτοῦ μόνου θεωρεῖται (de præm. et pœn. ii. 415).

The idea of Light, it may be added, passes into that of Fire; but this thought is not brought out by St John (Hebr. xii. 29: Deut. iv. 24).

iii. God is love.

iii. *God is love* (ὁ θεὸς ἀγάπη ἐστίν). In this declaration the idea of 'personality' is first revealed, and in the case of God necessarily of a self-sufficing personality (see Additional Note on v. 20). The idea of God is not only that of an unlimited self-communication, but a self-communication which calls out and receives a response (1 John iv. 7 ff.), which requires the recognition not only of glory but of goodness. And this love is original, and not occasioned (1 John iv. 10). It corresponds to the innermost nature of God, and finds its source in Him and not in man (1 John iv. 19, iii. 1). It is not like the love which is called out in the finite by the sense of imperfection (ἔρως Plat. *Sympos.* pp. 201 ff.), but is the expression of perfect benevolence. The only earthly image which answers to it is the love of parents for children (Eph. iii. 15), while that of Christ for the Church is compared to the love of husband for wife (Eph. v. 25); compare the view of the relation of Jehovah to Israel in the Old Test. (Jer. ii.; Hos. ii.).

As answering to this love of God, Creation in its essence and destiny reveals not only the will but also the nature of God. As yet there is conflict and disorder, and St John does not, like St Paul (1 Cor. xv. 28), distinctly contemplate the end. He lays down the eternal truths which must find fulfilment.

For the same reason the thoughts of judgment and vengeance which are prominent in the Apocalypse fall into the background in the Gospel and Epistles. These lie, so to speak, rather in the necessity of things so far as they are apart from God than in the will of God.

In the O. T. love is an attribute of God, one of many exercised in particular relations: Deut. iv. 37, vii. 8, 13, xi. 15, 18, xxiii. 5; 2 Sam. xii. 24; Is. xli. 8, xliii. 4, xlviii. 14; Mal. i. 2. In the N. T. first love can be shewn to be the very Being of God as answering to the Revelation in Christ; and we may see a certain fitness in the fact that this crowning truth is brought out in the latest of the apostolic writings.

In other passages St John speaks of God as 'living' (John vi. 57 ὁ ζῶν πατήρ), 'true' (ἀληθής John viii. 26, iii. 33; comp. 1 John i. 10), 'faithful' (πιστός 1 John i. 9; Apoc. i. 5, iii. 14, xix. 11), 'righteous' (δίκαιος John xvii. 25; 1 John i. 9; comp. Apoc. xvi. 5), 'holy' (ἅγιος John xvii. 11; comp. Apoc. vi. 10). And he records how His character is shewn to us in His action in Nature (John v. 17), History (ii. 3, xix. 11), and Grace (vi. 44 f.). Comp. John xii. 28, x. 29, xi. 41 f.

Additional Note on iv. 9. The use of the term μονογενής.

The term μονογενής is derived from the vocabulary of the LXX. It occurs there altogether eight times, three times in the Psalms, three times in Tobit, once in Judges and once in the book of Wisdom. The use of the word in Tobit is quite simple. Tobit and Sarah are two μονογενεῖς, *only children* of their parents (viii. 17): Sarah is μονογενής (or μία iii. 10) the *one daughter* of her father (iii. 15; cf. vi. 11 where the reading is doubtful). In the book of Wisdom the meaning of the term is less easy to express. It is said (vii. 22) that in Wisdom *there is a spirit intelligent, holy,* μονογενές, *manifold, subtle, versatile...* The epithet evidently describes the essential nature and not the derivation of this spirit : it is something absolutely one, unique (*unicus* in Latt.)

The use of μονογενής, i. in the LXX.

In the three passages of the Psalms, as in Jud. xi. 34, the word represents the Hebrew יָחִיד, twice as a significant title of the soul, the *one single* irreparable life of man (Ps. xxii. (xxi.) 21 ; xxxv. (xxxiv.) 17, *unicam meam* Lat. Vet. ; *solitariam meam* V.), and once of the sufferer left *alone and solitary* in his distress (Ps. xxv. (xxiv.) 16 *unicus* Lat. Vet. ; *solus* V. ; and so Aquila rightly in Ps. lxviii. (lxvii.) 6 [LXX. μονοτρόπους], but in the three other places he gives μοναχός, which is the rendering of Sym. and Theod. here.)

In six other places the same original word (יָחִיד) is represented by ἀγαπητός (Gen. xxii. 2, 12, 16; Jer. vi. 26; Amos viii. 10; Zech. xii. 10), which also carries with it the notion of 'an only child'; once by ἀγαπώμενος, Prov. iv. 3. In Jud. xi. 34 Cod. A. gives the duplicate rendering μονογενής, ἀγαπητή.

In the New Testament μονογενής has the same meaning *only* (Lk. viii. 42 *unica*), or *only child* (Lk. vii. 12 *unicus*; ix. 38 *id.*; Hebr. xi. 17, *unicus* Vet. Lat. *unigenitus* V., comp. John i. 14, *unici* Tert., *unigeniti* most); and so the word is used of the Lord (John iii. 16 *unicus* Vet. Lat.; *unigenitus* V. ; 1 John iv. 9 *unicum* Vet. Lat.; *unigenitum* V.; comp. John i. 14), and once, according to the most ancient authorities in connexion with the word 'God' (John i. 18 μονογενὴς θεός ; *unicus filius*, Adim. ap. Aug. ; *unigenitus filius* (Deus), rell.).

ii. in the N. T.

The one instance of the use of the word in the sub-apostolic writings gives exactly the same sense. Clement speaks of the Phœnix (*Ep.* i. 25) as μονογενὲς ὑπάρχον, a bird 'absolutely unique, the only one of its kind.' (Comp. Bp. Lightfoot *ad loc.*)

iii. in later writings.

The word next appears prominently in the system of Valentinus. The Mind (Νοῦς) the offspring of the ineffable Depth (Βυθός) and Silence (Σιγή), which alone embraced the greatness of the First Father, itself 'the Father and beginning of all things,' was also called ὁ Μονογενής, the only-born. And from this Being 'like and equal' to its Author, in conjunction with Truth the other Æons proceeded (Iren. i. 1, 2).

These mystical speculations fixed attention upon the term ; but perhaps at the same time they checked its technical use in the Church. It does not in fact occur in the earlier types of the Creed, which are found in Irenæus, Tertullian and Novatian; and in Tertullian the corresponding Latin term *unicus* is used of God (the Father): *de virg. vel.* 1 ; *adv. Prax.* 2. But it is worthy of notice that in the confession of Ignatius before Trajan, which follows the great lines of a Baptismal Symbol, the phrase is found : εἷς ἔστιν θεὸς...καὶ εἷς Χριστὸς Ἰησοῦς ὁ υἱὸς τοῦ θεοῦ ὁ μονογενής (*Ignat. Mart.* 2; comp. *Polyc. Mart.* 20). And it was apparently from Antioch that the term spread as an element of the expression of the Catholic Faith.

Confessions of Faith. In the second half of the third century the word appears in the Confessions of Syria and Asia Minor (*Syn. Ant.* A.D. 269, Routh, iii. p. 290; Greg. Thaum. ap. Greg. Nyss. 3, p. 912 ; Lucian, Socr. 2, 10, 7 ; *Apost. Const.* 7, 41 ; Marcellus, Epiph. *Hær.* 72, p. 836); and from that time it gradually obtained a permanent place in the Creeds of the East and the West.

The earliest certain example of the word in this connexion brings out its force very plainly. The Synod of Antioch (269), which condemned Paul of Samosata, in giving the exposition of their ancient belief which they addressed to him, write : 'We confess and proclaim the Son as begotten, ' an only Son (γεννητόν, υἱὸν μονογενῆ), the image of the unseen God, the ' firstborn of all creation, the Wisdom and Word ànd Power of God, who was ' before the ages not by foreknowledge but by essence and subsistence, ' God, Son of God, having recognised Him as such both in the Old and New ' Testament' (Routh, *Rell. Sacr.* iii. 290; comp. Alex. Alexandr. ap. Theodor. *H. E.* 1. 4. 45, φύσις μονογενής).

The point which is emphasised by the word here is evidently the absolute oneness of the Being of the Son. He stands to the Father in a relation wholly singular. He is the one only Son, the one to whom the title belongs in a sense completely unique and peculiar. The thought is centred in the Personal existence of the Son, and not in the Generation of the Son. That mystery is dealt with in another phrase. Consistently with this view the earliest Latin forms of the Creed uniformly represent the word by *unicus*, the *only son*, and not by *unigenitus* the *only-begotten son*, and this rendering has maintained its place in the Apostles' Creed and in our English version of it. But towards the close of the fourth century in translations from the Greek *unigenitus* came to be substituted for *unicus*, and this interpretation has passed into our version of the Constantinopolitan Creed (*only-begotten*).

The sense of *only Son* is preserved by the Syriac versions of the Nicene Creed, which go back to the original word which was rendered in the LXX. μονογενής and ἀγαπητός (ܚܒܝܒܐ) following in this the example of the Syriac translation of the N. T., where the word μονογενής is so rendered uniformly : Caspari, pp. 101, 116.

The exact phraseology of the true Nicene Creed separates distinctly these two thoughts of the generation of the Son, and of the unique being of the Son. 'We believe...in one Lord Jesus Christ, begotten of the Father an only Son' (γεννηθέντα ἐκ πατρὸς μονογενῆ)[1], where the uniqueness of nature is further defined by the addition 'that is to say of the essence of the Father.' And this proper sense of the word μονογενής, as marking the oneness of the sonship, preserves a close affinity in idea with ἀγαπητός well-beloved, the second translation of יָחִיד. Both words define that which is essentially singular in filial relationship : ' Only son and well-beloved,' Athanasius writes, 'are the same' (Or. c. Ar. iv. 24).

But in the interval which elapsed before the council of Constantinople Later in-the important distinction between the sonship and the generation of the terpreta-Son was beginning to be obscured, and μονογενής was treated as equivalent tions. to μόνος γεννηθείς, so as to include both the fact of the uniqueness of the Nature of the Son and the ground (if we may so speak) of His uniqueness[2].

In this way the grand simplicity of the original idea of the word was lost. Other thoughts, true in themselves, were gathered round it, and at last the sense was given by Gregory of Nazianzus as describing 'not the only Son of an only Parent, at one only time, but also that He was (be-gotten) in a singular way (μονοτρόπως)' (Orat. xxx. 20). And this conception, with which no fault can be found except that it is not contained in the word, became popularly current afterwards and was admirably expressed by John of Damascus : Μονογενὴς δὲ ὅτι μόνος ἐκ μόνου τοῦ πατρὸς μόνως ἐγεννήθη (De Fid. Orthod. i. 8. 135).

One other use of the word μονογενής, which is at first strange to our The ears, remains to be noticed. The true reading in John i. 18 is in all proba- phrase bility μονογενὴς θεός (unigenitus Deus), and this phrase occurs in some of μονογενὴς θεός. the Confessions of the fourth century. Thus it appears in a copy of the Nicene Creed addressed by Eustathius to Liberius (c. 366), (Socr. iv. 12, 14), and in a Creed set forth by the council of Antioch in 341 (πιστεύομεν …εἰς ἕνα Κύριον Ἰν. Χν. τὸν υἱὸν αὐτοῦ τὸν μονογενῆ θεόν…τὸν γεννηθέντα… Socr. ii. 10, 12 ; Athan. de Syn. 23), which was said in fact to be the Creed of Lucian the Martyr ; and again in the Synodical letter of the Synod of Ancyra (358) (Sozom. 3, 5, 9; Epiph. Hær. 73, 8).

The phrase is common in patristic writings both in connexion with the passage in St John's Gospel and independently. Didymus sets the phrase μονογενὴς θεὸς λόγος parallel with εἷς θεός. Alexander, who reads ὁ μονο-γενὴς υἱός in John i. 18 speaks afterwards of the 'ineffable subsistence of God the only Son' (θεὸς μονογενής Theod. 1, 4, §§ 15, 19). Gregory of Nyssa, who uses it most frequently, says 'the sum of the Christian religion is to believe in God the only Son (τὸν μονογενῆ θεόν) who is the Truth and the true Light and the Power of God and the Life' (c. Eunom. 12, p. 913, Migne).

On the relation of μονογενής to πρωτότοκος as applied to the Son see Lightfoot on Col. i. 15 ; and the typical passage of Athanasius : Orat. c. Ar. ii. 21 § 9. In connecting πρωτότοκος with the Incarnate Lord, I

---

[1] There can be no doubt that in this sentence μονογενῆ is (so to speak) a secondary predicate, and not a fresh epithet. The clause is so rendered in the Syriac version; Caspari, p. 101.

[2] The word μονογεννητός does not occur. The instance quoted by Bing-ham (3, 359) from Ussher is simply a false conjunction of the words…μονο-γενῆ τόν… See Heurtley, pp. 79, 82.

believe that the great Greek fathers wished to guard the truth which I have sought to express in the Essay on ' The Gospel of Creation.' For the use of the phrase μονογενὴς θεός see Dr Hort's *Two Dissertations*, Cambridge, 1876.

Additional Note on iv. 12. On the use of θεός and ὁ θεός.

Difference of ὁ θεός and θεός.

A careful examination of the passages, relatively few in number, in which θεός is used without the article in St John's writings leads to the conclusion that the difference between ὁ θεός and θεός is such as might have been expected antecedently. The former brings before us the Personal God Who has been revealed to us in a personal relation to ourselves : the latter fixes our thoughts on the general conception of the Divine Character and Being.

i. Use in St John, θεός without the article.

i. Θεός occurs without the article (exclusively of cases where it occurs with a preposition) in the following passages :

John   i.   1   θεὸς ἦν ὁ λόγος.
  „   12   τέκνα θεοῦ. So 1 John iii. 1, 2.
  „   18   θεὸν οὐδεὶς ἑώρακεν. 1 John iv. 12 θεὸν οὐδεὶς πώποτε τεθέαται.
  „   vi. 45   διδακτοὶ θεοῦ (LXX).
  „   viii. 54   λέγετε ὅτι θεὸς ὑμῶν ἐστίν.
  „   x.   33   ποιεῖς σεαυτὸν θεόν.
  „   34 f. εἶπα θεοί ἐστε (LXX).
  „   xix. 7   υἱὸν θεοῦ ἑαυτὸν ἐποίησεν.
1 John iii. 1, 2   (above John i. 12).
  „   iv. 12   (above John i. 18).
2 John 9   θεὸν οὐκ ἔχει.
Apoc. vii. 2   σφραγῖδα θεοῦ ζῶντος (comp. 1 Thess. i. 9; 2 Cor. iii. 3, vi. 16; 1 Tim. iv. 10; Hebr. ix. 14, x. 31, xii. 22).
  „   xxi. 3   ὁ θεὸς μετ' αὐτῶν ἔσται [αὐτῶν θεός].
  „   7   ἔσομαι αὐτῷ θεός.

It is clear that in these passages ὁ θεός either could not be used, or could only be used with a serious change of sense.

Use with prepositions.

The use of ὁ θεός and θεός with prepositions presents some marked results.

   1. ἀπό.

   (a) With article :

   Apoc. xii. 6 τόπον ἡτοιμασμένον ἀπὸ τοῦ θ.
     „   xxi. 10 (πόλιν) καταβαίνουσαν ἐκ τοῦ οὐρανοῦ ἀπὸ τοῦ θ.

   (β) Without article :

   John iii. 2 ἀπὸ θ. ἐλήλυθας.
     „   xiii. 3 ἀπὸ θ. ἐξῆλθεν.
     „   xvi. 30 ἀπὸ θ. ἐξῆλθες.

   2. εἰς.

   John xiv. 1 πιστεύετε εἰς τὸν θ.

3. ἐκ.

(a) With article:

γεννηθῆναι ἐκ τοῦ θ. 1 John iii. 9, v. 1, 4, 18.

εἶναι ἐκ τοῦ θ. John vii. 17, viii. 47 ; 1 John iii. 10, iv. 1 ff., 6 f., v. 19; 3 John 11.

John viii. 42 ἐκ τοῦ θ. ἐξῆλθον.

Apoc. xi. 11 πνεῦμα ζωῆς ἐκ τοῦ θ.

(β) Without article :

John i. 13 ἐκ θεοῦ ἐγεννήθησαν.

4. ἐν.

(a) With article :

1 John iv. 15 αὐτὸς [μένει] ἐν τῷ θ.

„ 16 ἐν τῷ θ. μένει.

(β) Without article :

John iii. 21 ἐν θ. ἐστὶν εἰργασμένα.

5. παρά.

(a) With article:

John vi. 46 ὁ ὢν παρὰ [τοῦ] θ.

„ viii. 40 ἣν ἤκουσα παρὰ τοῦ θ.

(β) Without article :

John i. 6 ἀπεσταλμένος παρὰ θ.

„ ix. 16 οὐκ ἔστιν οὗτος παρὰ θ.

„ 33 εἰ ἦν παρὰ θ.

2 John 3 εἰρήνη παρὰ θ. πατρός.

6. πρός.

Uniformly with the article :

John i. 1 ἦν πρὸς τὸν θ.

„ xiii. 3 ὑπάγει πρὸς τὸν θ.

1 John iii. 21 παρρησίαν ἔχομεν πρὸς τὸν θ.

Apoc. xii. 5 ἡρπάσθη πρὸς τὸν θ.

„ xiii. 6 βλασφημίας πρὸς τὸν θ.

Throughout it will be seen that in θεός the general conception of divinity is dominant, and in ὁ θεός that of the One Being in personal relation to others.

ii. The same general difference is observable in the use of the terms in the other Books of the N. T. Thus it may be noticed that the article is uniformly found

ii. Use in other Books, with prepositions.

(1) with ἐνώπιον (ἔναντι, κατενώπιον, κατέναντι) (31 times) except 2 Cor. ii. 17.

(2) with πρός acc. (19 times).

(3) with ὑπό gen. (13 times) except Rom. xiii. 1 ; Gal. iv. 9.

On the other hand the article is never used with κατά acc. (6 times), while it is used in the two places where κατά is used with gen.

A few illustrations will serve to make this difference felt :

Examples of usage.

Acts v. 4 οὐκ ἐψεύσω ἀνθρώποις ἀλλὰ τῷ θεῷ.

„ 29 πειθαρχεῖν δεῖ θεῷ μᾶλλον ἢ ἀνθρώποις.

„ vii. 55 εἶδεν δόξαν θεοῦ καὶ Ἰησοῦν ἑστῶτα ἐκ δεξιῶν τοῦ θεοῦ.

„ xiv. 15 ἐπιστρέφειν ἐπὶ θεὸν ζῶντα.

Acts xv. 19 τοῖς ἀπὸ τῶν ἐθνῶν ἐπιστρέφουσιν ἐπὶ τὸν θεόν.
Comp. 1 Tim. iv. 10 and 2 Cor. i. 9.
Acts xx. 21 τὴν εἰς θεὸν μετάνοιαν.
„ xxiv. 15 ἐλπίδα ἔχειν εἰς τὸν θεόν.
1 Thess. i. 9 ἐπεστρέψατε πρὸς τὸν θεὸν ἀπὸ τῶν εἰδώλων δουλεύειν θεῷ ζῶντι καὶ ἀληθινῷ.
„ ii. 13 εὐχαριστοῦμεν τῷ θεῷ...ὅτι παραλαβόντες λόγον ἀκοῆς... τοῦ θεοῦ ἐδέξασθε οὐ λόγον ἀνθρ. ἀλλά...λόγον θεοῦ.
1 Cor. iii. 19 μωρία παρὰ τῷ θεῷ ἐστίν.
„ vii. 24 ἐν τούτῳ μενέτω παρὰ θεῷ.
Rom. ii. 17 καυχᾶσαι ἐν θεῷ.
„ 11 καυχώμενοι ἐν τῷ θεῷ.

In this connexion also, though other considerations come in here, the following parallel phrases deserve notice : εὐαγγέλιον θεοῦ Rom. i. 1 ; τὸ εὐαγγ. τοῦ θ. Rom. xv. 16 ; δικαιοσύνη θεοῦ 2 Cor. v. 21 ; ἡ δικ. τοῦ θ. Rom. x. 3 ; ὀργὴ θεοῦ Rom. i. 18 ; ἡ ὀργὴ τοῦ θ. John iii. 36, Eph. v. 6 ; ἀλήθεια θεοῦ Rom. xv. 8 ; ἡ ἀλήθ. τοῦ θ. Rom. i. 25, iii. 7.

Additional Note on iv. 15. Divine Fellowship.

The fact of the divine fellowship is presented by St John in different forms.

1. Sometimes it is set forth in its reciprocal fulness :

iii. 24, *he that keepeth* (ὁ τηρῶν) *His commandments abideth in Him* (ὁ θεός) *and He in him.*

iv. 13, *hereby we perceive that we abide in Him and He in us, because He hath given us of His Spirit.*

iv. 15, *whosoever shall confess that Jesus [Christ] is the Son of God, God abideth in him and he in God.*

iv. 16, *God is love, and he that abideth in love abideth in God, and God [abideth] in him.*

With these passages in which the divine fellowship is described as a fellowship with 'God,' must be compared those in which it is described as a fellowship with Christ :

John vi. 56, *he that eateth* (ὁ τρώγων) *my flesh and drinketh my blood abideth in Me and I in him.*

John xiv. 20, *in that day ye shall know* (γνώσεσθε) *that I am in my Father, and ye in Me, and I in you.*

John xv. 5, *he that abideth in Me and I in him, the same beareth much fruit.*

It will be observed that, with one exception (c. iv. 15), the 'dwelling' or 'being' of man in God is placed first (iii. 24, iv. 13, 16; comp. ii. 24; John vi 56, xiv. 20, xv. 5). The ascension to heaven, if we may so speak, generally precedes the transfiguration of earth.

2. Sometimes again the divine fellowship is regarded in one of its two aspects :

(a) The abiding (being) of man in God (or Christ) :

ii. 5, *in this we know (γινώσκομεν) that we are in Him.*

ii. 6, *he that saith he abideth in Him ought himself also to walk even as He walked.*

iii. 6, *every one that abideth in Him sinneth not.*

v. 20, *we know (οἴδαμεν) that the Son of God hath come...and we are in Him that is true (ἐν τῷ ἀληθινῷ).*

Compare John xv. 4 (ye cannot bear fruit) *except ye abide in Me.*

ii. 28, *abide in Him that if He shall be manifested we may have boldness...*

(β) The abiding (being) of God (or Christ) in man :

iii. 24, *hereby we know (γινώσκομεν) that He abideth in us, from the Spirit which He gave us.*

iv. 12, *if we love one another God abideth in us...*

John xvii. 22 f., *the glory which Thou hast given Me I have given unto them ; that they may be one, even as We are one ; I in them, and Thou in Me...*

John xvii. 26, *I made known unto them Thy Name...that the love wherewith Thou lovedst Me may be in them and I in them.*

It is of interest to examine these several passages as illustrating the efficient cause, the conditions, the sign, the results of this fellowship of man with God.

(a) The efficient cause : the recognition of the revelation of God in Christ, of the Glory and the Name of the Father : John xvii. 22 f., 26, xiv. 20 ; 1 John v. 20.

(β) The conditions : confession, iv. 15 ; obedience, iii. 24, ii. 6 ; love, iv. 16. These are summed up in the thought of participation in Christ's Humanity, John vi. 56.

(γ) The sign : the possession of the Spirit of God, iii. 24 ; which shews itself as the source of obedience, ii. 5 ; and of love, iv. 12 f.

(δ) The results : fruitfulness, John xv. 4 f. ; confidence, 1 John ii. 28 ; guilelessness, iii. 6.

The use of the terms 'abiding' and 'being' is also suggestive :

(a) abide : ii. 6, 28, iii. 6, 24, iv. 12 f., 15 f. ; John vi. 56, xv. 4 f.

(b) be : ii. 5, v. 20 ; John xiv. 20, xvii. 23, 26.

In this connexion Basil's remark is of interest that the Spirit is spoken of 'as the place of those that are sanctified.' 'The Spirit,' he goes on to say, 'is the place of the saints ; and the saint is a place appropriate to the Spirit...' (*de Spir. S.* xxvi. § 62).

V.   ¹ Πᾶς ὁ πιστεύων ὅτι Ἰησοῦς ἐστιν ὁ χριστὸς

II. The Power of the Christian Life: the Victory and Witness of Faith (v. 1—12).

The whole of this section is closely connected, but two main thoughts, 'Faith' and 'Witness,' respectively prevail in the opening and closing verses. Thus it may be divided into two parts,

1.   *The victory of Faith* (1—5).
2.   *The Divine Witness* (6—12).

1.   *The victory of Faith* (v. 1—5).

In the last section it has been seen that the love of 'the brethren' is enjoined as an essential accompaniment of the love of God. St John now traces the foundations of spiritual kinsmanship. 'Brethren' are united by a common Divine Father. The human condition of this union is faith in Jesus as the Christ. This faith is able to overcome and has potentially overcome every force of the world. The succession of thought is clearly marked. Faith is the sign of a new life, and the presence of this life involves love for all who share it (1). The reality of this love is shewn by active obedience (2, 3). Such obedience is made possible by the gift of a Divine life, a truth which is affirmed in the abstract, and also in regard to the Life of Christ (4), and in regard to the experience of the believer (5).

¹ *Every one that believes that Jesus is the Christ is begotten of God, and every one that loveth him that begat loveth him that is begotten of him.* ² *In this we know that we love the children of God, when we love God and do his commandments;* ³ *for this is the love of God, that we observe his commandments, and his commandments are not grievous;* ⁴ *because everything that is begotten of God overcometh the world; and this is the victory that overcame the world, even our faith.* ⁵ [*Yea,*] *who is he*

that overcometh the world but he that believeth that Jesus is the Son of God?

1.   The transition from the former section lies in the thought of brotherhood. Brotherhood is founded on the vital apprehension of the revelation of Christ given by God. It is not then an arbitrary command that he who loves God love his brother also. He must do so. For he consciously shares with every brother the principle of his new being.

Πᾶς ὁ πιστεύων] Comp. c. iii. 3.
The verb πιστεύειν is here used for the first time in the epistle in its full and definite sense. In iv. 16 it describes a general position with regard to the Divine purpose. In iii. 23 it expresses a belief in the truth of the revelation as to Christ. Here it presents that belief in a direct and personal form. 'He that believeth that Jesus is the Christ' not only admits an intellectual truth but enters into a direct relation with the powers of a spiritual order. 'The command' of God (iii. 23) finds so far an individual accomplishment.

In the former chapter (iv. 2, 15; comp. ii. 23), St John has spoken of the 'confession' of Christ in relation to society: here he speaks of faith in relation to the single believer. The main thought there was of the recognition, here of the essence of the children of God. The forms of confession are given in the most explicit form. The article of faith is given more simply. A living faith carries with it more than the exact terms of specific belief convey (John xi. 27).

Compare *vv.* 5, 10, 13.

Such faith involves the present action of a new and Divine life, which must have a Divine origin. Comp. 1 Cor. xii. 3. Faith here is regarded simply as the sign of the life which has been given. Nothing is said of the relation between the human and

ἐκ τοῦ θεοῦ γεγέννηται, καὶ πᾶς ὁ ἀγαπῶν τὸν γεννήσαντα ἀγαπᾷ τὸν γεγεννημένον ἐξ αὐτοῦ. ²ἐν τούτῳ

1 ἀγ. τὸν γεγ. B vg the: ἀγ.+καί' τὸν γεγ. (אּ) A syrr.　　τὸν γεγ.: τὸ γεγ. אּ.

the Divine—the faith of man, and 'the seed of God' (iii. 9)—in the first quickening of life. Comp. John i. 12 note.
ὅτι 'I. ἐστὶν ὁ χριστός] Comp. v. 5 ὅτι 'I. ἐστὶν ὁ υἱὸς τοῦ θεοῦ. John xx. 31 ὅτι 'I. ἐστὶν ὁ χριστὸς ὁ υἱὸς τοῦ θεοῦ. For the choice of the exact terms of belief here, see ii. 22.

ἐκ τοῦ θ. γεγ.] See c. iii. 9 note.

καὶ πᾶς ὁ ἀγ. τ. γεννν.] et omnis qui diligit eum qui genuit V., and every one that loveth Him that begat... It is assumed that the child will have love for the Author of his being. Love follows directly from life. And in this spiritual connexion love must be directed to the character, and not to the Person apart from the character. It follows therefore that it will be extended to all those to whom the character has been communicated.

ὁ ἀγαπῶν] Augustine brings out the necessary connexion between faith and love (faith in action): cum dilectione, fides Christiani: sine dilectione, fides dæmonis.

τὸν γεννν.] The word is used also of the human agent, Philem. 10.

τὸν γεγεννν. ἐξ αὐτοῦ] eum qui natus est ex eo V., him that hath been begotten of Him, the child who draws from Him the abiding principle of his life. The singular (contrast 'the children' v. 2) emphasises the direct relation of Father and child, and also of brother and brother. This relation, as here regarded, is personal and not social. Throughout the Epistle St John individualises: ii. 4 ff., 9 ff., 15, 17, 22 f., 29; iii. 3 ff., 9 f., 15, 17. The idea of Augustine that the reference is to Christ is foreign to the context.

2. What then, it may be asked, is the sign of this spiritual love which

is essentially different from a natural preference? The love of the children of God, such is the answer, is attested by the love of God, that is, by obedience to God. At first sight this answer seems simply to invert the terms of the statement which has been made already. The love of God and the love of the children of God do in fact include each the other. It is equally true to say 'He who loves God loves the children of God,' and to say 'He who loves the children of God loves God.' Either form of love may be made the ground or the conclusion in the argument. But in reality the test of the love of the brethren given here introduces a new idea. The will of Christians is essentially the will of God (comp. iii. 22). The effort to fulfil the commandments of God is consequently the effort to do that which our 'brethren' most desire to be done: the proof of love.

Bede says well: Ille solus recte proximum diligere probatur qui et Conditoris amore flagrare conspicitur.

It will also be further observed that the passage stands in close connexion with c. ii. 3 in this we perceive that we know Him if we keep His commandments; and with iii. 23 this is His commandment that we believe the Name...and love one another... (comp. iv. 20).

Obedience to the manifold commandments of God (αἱ ἐντολαί), the active fulfilment of Christian duty, is the sign of a knowledge of God: and knowledge of God is love of God.

And again, the one commandment of God (ἡ ἐντολή) is that we believe the Name of His Son and love one another.

Here the love of God and obedience in detail, which is identical with

W.

γινώσκομεν ὅτι ἀγαπῶμεν τὰ τέκνα τοῦ θεοῦ, ὅταν
τὸν θεὸν ἀγαπῶμεν καὶ τὰς ἐντολὰς αὐτοῦ ποιῶμεν·

2 ποιῶμεν B vg (me the syrr): τηρῶμεν ℵ (lat).   2, 3 om. ποιῶμεν...αὐτοῦ A.

it (*v.* 3), is given as the sign of the reality of love for the brethren, who are the children of God.

This thought that the love of God is obedience to His commandments is the uniting thought in the three passages. It is clearly seen through this how we can say (now more completely than before): 'We love God and keep His commandments, and therefore we love the brethren'; or 'We love the brethren, and therefore we love God and keep His commandments.' Whichever proposition is established, the other follows from it. Comp. c. i. 3.

At the same time the transference of the test of the love of the brethren to a spiritual region enables the believer to discern (γινώσκομεν) the reality of his love in spite of the many differences which separate him from the object of it under the conditions of earthly life.

ἐν τούτῳ...] *in this...* The perception comes not as a conviction drawn from a state of obedient love (ἐκ τούτου, *from this*), but in the very exercise of the feeling. The 'this,' as elsewhere, seems to look backward at once and forward, to the fact and to the manifestation of the love of God. Comp. ii. 3 note.

γινώσκομεν] *cognoscimus* V., *we know, perceive.* The conviction is brought home to us in the present interpretation of the facts of life. Compare ii. 3 note, 5, 18; iii. 24 (V. *scimus*); iv. 13 (V. *intellegimus*); and contrast the use of οἴδαμεν in iii. 2, 5, 14 f.; v. 15, 18 ff. (V. *scimus, scitis*). See *v.* 18 note. The use of ὅταν brings into prominence the immediate and continuous exercise of this power of knowledge.

ἀγαπῶμεν] The love which is spoken

of is that of Christian for Christian as Christian, a feeling which has to be distinguished from human affection. Of this love, which belongs to the spiritual sphere, love to God, that is obedience to God, is necessarily a final criterion.

τὰ τέκνα τοῦ θ.] *natos Dei* V., *the children of God.* Comp. iii. 1 note. St John does not say 'brethren' here, because the argument turns upon the relation of Christians to God and not upon their relation to one another. At the same time the plural follows naturally on the singular of *v.* 1. Then the thought was of the individual realisation of the divine sonship: here the thought is of the general, social, duty.

This is the only place where ὅταν occurs in the Epistles of St John. With the present conj. it expresses either an action repeated indefinitely (John viii. 44, ix. 5, &c.), or an action at an indefinite time regarded as actually going on (John vii. 27 ἔρχηται, contrast *v.* 31 ἔλθῃ; xvi. 21 τίκτῃ followed by γεννήσῃ). Comp. 1 Cor. xv. 24 (παραδιδοῖ, καταργήσῃ).

ὅταν...ἀγαπῶμεν] *cum...diligamus,* V. The literal rendering 'whenever we love' makes the meaning clear. Each act of love to God, that is practically, each act of obedience, carries with it the fresh conviction of true love to the children of God. Ἐάν (c. ii. 3; John xiii. 35) gives the general condition: ὅταν, the particular and repeated fulfilment of it.

The change of order (comp. iii. 4) in the objects (ἀγαπ. τὰ τέκνα, ὅταν τὸν θ. ἀγαπ. καὶ τὰς ἐντ. ποι.) corresponds with a natural change in emphasis: 'We know that we love the brethren, when God is the end of our affection and His commands the guide of our

³αὕτη γάρ ἐστιν ἡ ἀγάπη τοῦ θεοῦ ἵνα τὰς ἐντολὰς
αὐτοῦ τηρῶμεν, καὶ αἱ ἐντολαὶ αὐτοῦ βαρεῖαι οὐκ εἰσίν,
⁴ὅτι πᾶν τὸ γεγεννημένον ἐκ τοῦ θεοῦ νικᾷ τὸν κόσμον.

action.' In other cases where the object stands before the verb a similar shade of meaning is seen : *e.g.* ii. 20; iv. 9, 12; v. 9.

καὶ τὰς ἐντ. αὐτοῦ ποι.] *et mandata eius faciamus* V., *and do His commandments*. This clause brings the love of God into the region of active life. The phrase itself is unique (Apoc. xxii. 14 is a false reading); and seems to be chosen in order to express the active energy of obedience as positive and not only negative. Comp. c. i. 6 π. τὴν ἀλήθειαν note.

Augustine follows out his false interpretation of 'him that is begotten of Him' in *v.* 1 by a striking application here: Filios Dei dixit qui Filium Dei paulo ante dicebat, quia filii Dei corpus sunt unici Filii Dei ; et cum ille caput nos membra unus est Filius Dei.

He also adds a wider application of the principle: Omnes homines, etiam inimicos vestros, diligatis, non quia sunt fratres, sed ut fratres sint; ut semper fraterno amore flagretis sive in fratrem factum, sive in inimicum ut frater fiat diligendo.

3. αὕτη γάρ...] *for this...* The words give an explanation of the second clause (*and do His commandments*) in the former verse. Love of God can only be shewn in the effort to fulfil His will. Comp. John xiv. 15, 21, 31.

ἵνα...τηρῶμεν καὶ...] *ut custodiamus* V. The love of God is not simply the keeping (τήρησις, τὸ τηρεῖν) of the commandments of God, but rather a continuous and watchful endeavour to observe them. Comp. John vi. 29 ἵνα πιστεύητε, xvii. 3 ἵνα γιν.: 2 John 6. And the nature of the commandments is not such as to crush the freedom and spontaneity of love. They are not *grievous*, heavy (βαρεῖαι, *gravia* V.), an oppressive and exhausting burden. Compare Matt. xi. 30 τὸ φορτίον μου ἐλαφρόν ἐστιν, and contrast Matt. xxiii. 4 δεσμεύουσιν φορτία βαρέα.

4. ὅτι...] *because...* Comp. ii. 19 note. The fact that the divine commandments are not a burden is not established by a consideration of their character. In themselves they are difficult (Acts xiv. 22; John xvi. 33). To love the brethren is not a light thing. But with the commandment comes also the power of fulfilment. Natural taste, feeling, judgment may check spiritual sympathy; but every faculty and power which is quickened by God is essentially stronger than 'the world' and realises its victory at once.

In the development of the thought St John passes from the abstract πᾶν τὸ γεγενν.) to the concrete and personal (τίς ἐστιν ὁ νικῶν), through the decisive history in which the truth was once for all absolutely realised (ἡ νίκη ἡ νικήσασα).

πᾶν τὸ γεγ.] St John chooses the abstract form (contrast *v.* 1 τὸν γεγ.) in order to convey an universal truth. The thought is not so much of the believer in his unity, nor of the Church, but of each element included in the individual life and in the life of the society. Compare John iii. 6 τὸ γεγ. and John iii. 8 πᾶς ὁ γεγ.

νικᾷ τὸν κ.] *conquers the world*— not 'hath conquered' (c. ii. 13 f., iv. 4), nor yet 'will conquer'—in a struggle which is present and continuous. Under the title 'the world' St John gathers up the sum of all the limited, transitory powers opposed to God which make obedience difficult. It

καὶ αὕτη ἐστὶν ἡ νίκη ἡ νικήσασα τὸν κόσμον, ἡ πίστις
ἡμῶν· ⁵τίς ἐστιν [δὲ] ὁ νικῶν τὸν κόσμον εἰ μὴ ὁ
πιστεύων ὅτι Ἰησοῦς ἐστιν ὁ υἱὸς τοῦ θεοῦ;

5 τίς ἐστιν δέ B (lat): τίς δέ ἐστιν ℵ (lat) syrhl me: τίς ἐστιν A vg.

is by the introduction of the spiritual, the eternal, that we obtain a true standard for things, and so can overcome the temptations which spring out of a narrow, earthly, temporal estimate. And this holds good not only of man as a whole but of each power and faculty with which he is endowed. Comp. John xvi. 33.

καὶ αὕτη...] The certainty of the victory of that which partakes of the Divine is illustrated by a view of the nature of the victory itself. The victory which the Christian is ever winning is the individual appropriation of a victory gained once for all.

ἡ νίκη...ἡ πίστις ἡμῶν] *the victory ...our faith.* The word νίκη occurs here only in the N.T., and πίστις here only in St John's Epistles. Πίστις is not found in St John's Gospel. It occurs in the Apocalypse: ii. 13, 19; xiii. 10; xiv. 12. In ii. 13, xiv. 12 it appears to be used objectively for 'the faith of Christ,' as embodied in a confession ('fides quæ creditur'): in ii. 19, xiii. 10, it is the subjective spirit of the true believer ('fides qua creditur'). Here the sense is fixed by the context. 'Our faith' is the faith which is summed up in the confession that Jesus is 'the Christ, the Son of God.' The Life represented by that creed was the victory over the world as Christ Himself interpreted it (John xvi. 33). To hold that faith, to enter into the meaning and the power of that conquest through apparent failure, is to share in its triumph. Our faith is not merely victorious: it is the embodiment of *the victory which overcame the world.* Thus the aorist (ἡ νικήσασα, *quæ vincit* V., inadequately) receives its full

force. The victory of Christ was gained upon a narrow field, but it was world-wide in its effects. Comp. Ign. *ad Sm.* 10 ἡ τελεία πίστις, Ἰησοῦς Χριστός, and Col. ii. 2 εἰς ἐπίγνωσιν τοῦ μυστηρίου τοῦ θεοῦ, Χριστοῦ.

5. τίς ἐστιν...] At length the question becomes directly personal. St John appeals to the experience of those whom he addresses. The single believer (ὁ νικῶν) takes the place of the abstract element (τὸ γεγεννημένον), and of the absolute force (ἡ πίστις). The victory of the divine principle is, as he triumphantly claims, actually realised in the victory of the Christian.

τίς...εἰ μή...] Compare ii. 22. The personal victory is regarded in its course (ὁ νικῶν), as the representative victory was regarded in its completion (ἡ ν. ἡ νικήσασα).

ὅτι Ἰ. ἐστὶν ὁ υἱ. τοῦ θ.] Comp. *v.* 1. By the use of the title 'the Son of God' in connexion with the human name, *Jesus,* the antithesis involved in the faith is expressed in the sharpest form. There is a similar passage from 'the Christ' to 'the Son' in ii. 22 ff.

2. *The Divine Witness* (v. 6—12).

The victory of Faith has been shewn to lie in the confession of Jesus as the Son of God. St John now goes on to unfold the character (6—8), and the effectiveness (9—12), of the witness by which this confession is sustained and justified.

6—8. The character of the witness to the substance of the Christian Faith is laid open by a consideration of the historical witness which is offered to men in the Life of Christ, and

^{6} Οὗτός ἐστιν ὁ ἐλθὼν δι' ὕδατος καὶ αἵματος, Ἰησοῦς

6 καὶ αἵματος B vg syr vg: +καὶ πνεύματος אA (lat) me the syrhl (others substitute πν. for αἷμ. and some read καὶ πν. καὶ αἷμ.).   Ἰς Χς אAB: Χς Ἰς the:
Ἰς ὁ Χς ς syrhl. See Additional Note.

in the life of the Church (6 a, b);
of the divine principle of witness
(6 c); and of the personal witnesses
⟨7, 8⟩.

^{6} *This is He that came by water
and blood, Jesus Christ; not in the
water only, but in the water and
in the blood. And the Spirit is that
which beareth witness, because the
Spirit is the Truth.* ^{7} *Because three
are they that bear witness,* ^{8} *the Spirit
and the water and the blood; and the
three are for the one.*

6. The two parts of the historical
witness to Christ are distinguished
by the different forms in which the
common outward symbols are used in
corresponding clauses. He came '*by
water and blood*,' and again '*not in
the water only, but in the water and
in the blood*.'

Οὗτος...] The pronoun goes back to
the subject of the last sentence.
"*This* 'Jesus,' who has been affirmed
to be 'the Son of God,' *is He that
came....*" The compound title at the
end of the clause, *Jesus Christ*, emphasises the truth which is established by the manner of the 'coming'
of 'Jesus': '*This is He that came...*'
and whose Divine Office is expressed
by the full name which He bears,
even *Jesus Christ*.

ὁ ἐλθών...] *He that came...* The
verb is used with a clear reference to
the technical sense of 'he that cometh'
⟨ὁ ἐρχόμενος Matt. xi. 3; Luke vii.
19 f.; comp. John i. 15, 27; vi. 14;
xi. 27; xii. 13; see also John i. 30;
x. 8). Thus 'He that came' is equivalent to 'He that fulfilled the promises to the fathers, as the Saviour
sent from God.' Comp. ii. 18 note.

δι' ὕδατος καὶ αἵματος] *per aquam et*

sanguinem V., *by (through) water
and blood.* The sense of '*He that
came*,' which distinctly points to a
past historic fact, determines that
these terms also must have a historic
meaning, and refer to definite events
characteristic of the manner in which
the Lord fulfilled His office upon
earth. 'He came — He was shewn
to be the Christ—by water and blood.'
'Water' and 'blood' contributed in
some way to reveal the nature and
the fulfilment of His work.

There can be no doubt that the
Death upon the Cross satisfies the
conception of 'coming by blood.'
By so dying the Lord made known
His work as Redeemer; and opened
the fountain of His life to men. Comp.
Additional Note on i. 7.

The 'coming by water,' which naturally corresponds to this final act of
sacrifice, is the Baptism, whereby
the Lord declared His purpose '*to
fulfil all righteousness*' (Matt. iii.
15). The water, by Christ's voluntary
acceptance of the Baptist's ministry,
became the means through which the
divine purpose was fulfilled (Matt. iii.
17). The Baptist was sent baptizing
in water that Christ might be made
manifest (John i. 31). Even in the
case of the Lord Baptism is shewn to
have been the external condition of
the 'descent and abiding of the Holy
Spirit' (John i. 33 f.); and by His
Baptism Christ fulfilled for the humanity which He took to Himself,
though not for Himself, the condition
of regeneration.

But we cannot stop at the reference to the cardinal events in the
Lord's Life whereby He 'came by
water and blood' in the fulfilment of

His historic work. While He hung upon the Cross, dead in regard to mortal life, but still living (see John xix. 34 note), He came again 'by water and blood.' The issue of 'blood and water' from His side evidently indicated that He henceforth became for men the source of blessing symbolised by the twofold stream, and realised in His own human life by Baptism and Death upon the Cross. The one historic coming was shewn to be the foundation of a continuous spiritual coming; and St John saw in this the subject of the crucial testimony which he had to give (John xix. 35).

Compare the fragment of Claudius Apollinaris (Routh, *Rell.* i. 161) ὁ ἐκχέας ἐκ τῆς πλευρᾶς αὐτοῦ τὰ δύο πάλιν καθάρσια ὕδωρ καὶ αἷμα, λόγον καὶ πνεῦμα (the Gospel of the Incarnate Word and the sanctifying presence of the Spirit).

This exceptional note of the Evangelist seems to place the reference here to the significant fact recorded in the Gospel beyond question. The readers of the Epistle could not but be familiar with the incident either from the oral or from the written teaching of the Apostle; and conscious of the stress which he laid upon it, as the confirmation of Christian faith, they could not fail to recall it here.

Compare Bede: Nec reticendum quod in hoc quoque sanguis et aqua testimonium illi dederunt quod de latere mortui vivaciter effluxerunt, quod erat contra naturam corporum mortuorum, atque ob id mysteriis aptum et testimonio veritatis fuit congruum, videlicet insinuans quia et ipsum Domini corpus melius post mortem esset victurum resuscitatum in gloria et ipsa mors illius nobis vitam donaret.

Such an extension of the meaning of 'water and blood' appears to be implied in the words that follow: *not in the water only, but in the water and in the blood,* followed by the reference to the present witness of the Spirit. The change of the preposition, the use of the article, and the stress laid on actual experience, shew that St John is speaking of a continuation of the first coming under some new but analogous form. Further it is to be noticed that what was before spoken of in its unity (δι' ὕ. καὶ αἵ.) is now spoken of in its separate parts (ἐν τῷ ὕ. καὶ ἐν τῷ αἵμ.). The first proof of the Messiahship of Jesus lay in His complete historical fulfilment of Messiah's work once for all in bringing purification and salvation: that proof is continued in the experience of the Church in its two separate parts.

Thus we are led to the ideas which underlie the two sacraments, and which are brought home to us in and through them: the ideas which in their most general form are laid open in John iii., vi. It is through Christ's 'coming by water and blood,' and His Life through Death, that the life of the Spirit and the cleansing and support of our human life in all its fulness are assured. The actual experience of these blessings is the abiding witness of the Church to Him.

Bede, probably following Augustine, whose Commentary is not extant after *v.* 3, well combines the historic and sacramental references: *Qui venit per aquam et sanguinem,* aquam videlicet lavacri et sanguinem suæ passionis: non solum baptizari propter nostram ablutionem dignatus est, ut nobis baptismi sacramentum consecraret ac traderet, verum etiam sanguinem suum dedit pro nobis, sua nos passione redimens, cujus sacramentis semper refecti nutriremur ad salutem.

διά...ἐν...] The historic Mission of Christ—the pledge of His Presence— was established 'through' the cardinal events of His Ministry. The abiding Presence of Christ—the issue of His Mission—is realised 'in' that which is appointed to perpetuate

Χριστός· οὐκ ἐν τῷ ὕδατι μόνον ἀλλ᾽ ἐν τῷ ὕδατι καὶ
ἐν τῷ αἵματι· καὶ τὸ πνεῦμά ἐστιν τὸ μαρτυροῦν, ὅτι τὸ

μόνον: μόνῳ B.   αἵματι ℵB vg me the syrr: πνεύματι A (some add πνεύματι,
others read αἵματι...πνεύματι).   τὸ πνεῦμα (2°): Χριστός vg. Perhaps xpc for sps.
(Not Ambr. Fulg.)

the power of His work. The one
preposition marks the means by
which Christ's office was revealed:
the other the sphere in which He
continues to exercise it.

δι᾽ ὕδατος καὶ αἵμ.] The order is
significantly changed from that in
the Gospel (*blood and water*). The
order in the Gospel is (so to speak)
the order of the divine gift: the full
power of human life comes first: that
in the Epistle is the order of the
human appropriation of the gift.

The symbolism of 'blood' as representing the natural human life
sacrificed and so made available for
others, has been already touched
upon. In contrast with this, 'water'
represents the power of the spiritual
life: John iii. 5; iv. 14; vii. 38 (Zech.
xiv. 8). Comp. Apoc. xxi. 6; xxii. 1,17.

οὐκ ἐν τῷ ὕδ. μ.] *not in the water
only.* The reference is probably to
such teachers as Irenæus mentions
(i. 26, 1): [Cerinthus docuit] post
baptismum descendisse in eum (Iesum)
ab ea principalitate quæ est super
omnia Christum figura columbæ; et
tunc annunciasse incognitum Patrem
et virtutes perfecisse: in fine autem
revolasse iterum Christum de Jesu et
Jesum passum esse et resurrexisse;
Christum autem impassibilem perseverasse, existentem spiritalem. In
some form or other the same kind of
error is always repeating itself. The
spiritual life is exalted into an undue
supremacy, to the neglect of the redemption of the earthly life.

For this reason St John says οὐκ
ἐν τῷ ὕδ. μόνον, and not οὐ δι᾽ ὕδ. μόνον.
He contradicts a false view of Christ's
abiding work and not only a false
view of Christ's Person in Himself.

καὶ τὸ πν....] *and the Spirit...* In
the words which immediately precede
St John has indicated a present action
of Christ. He now shews how the
reality of that action is established.
The Spirit—the Divine Spirit—*is
that which witnesseth,* not 'which
witnessed' (3 John 6), or 'which hath
witnessed' (*v.* 9). His testimony is
given now and uninterruptedly. Such
'witness' is the peculiar office of the
Spirit (John xiv. 26; xv. 26; xvi.
8 ff.). By this it is that men are
enabled to pierce beneath the external phenomena and the external
rites to their innermost meaning.
Nothing is said of the substance of
the witness or of those to whom it is
given. These details are included in
the idea of the Spirit's witness. He
speaks of Divine Truth; and He
speaks to the souls of believers.

Thus there is, as will be seen,
a striking parallelism between the
office of Christ and the office of the
Spirit. *Jesus is He that came,* once
for all fulfilling the Messiah's work;
and *the Spirit is that which beareth
witness,* ever applying and interpreting His Mission and His gifts.

ὅτι τὸ πνεῦμα...] *quoniam* (*quod*)
Christus V., *because the Spirit...* The
conjunction (ὅτι) has been interpreted
both as giving the substance (*that*)
and as giving the reason (*because*) of
the testimony. The former translation
gives no tolerable sense unless the
Latin reading of *Christ* for *the Spirit*
is adopted. But the sense thus gained
is foreign to the context. While then
we take the translation *because* as certainly right, the meaning of the word
is ambiguous here. It may mean:
The Spirit gives the witness (1) *be-*

πνεῦμά ἐστιν ἡ ἀλήθεια. ⁷ὅτι τρεῖς εἰσιν οἱ μαρτυροῦντες, ⁸τὸ πνεῦμα καὶ τὸ ὕδωρ καὶ τὸ αἷμα, καὶ οἱ

7 τρεῖς: οἱ τρεῖς ℵ.   7, 8 See Additional Note.

cause it is essentially *fitted* to do so:
or (2) *because* by its essential nature
it is *constrained* to do so. Perhaps
the one idea passes into the other, so
that it is not necessary to distinguish
them sharply. In that which is Divine, nature and office coincide.

τὸ πν. ἐστιν ἡ ἀλ.] *the Spirit is the
Truth.* Just as Christ is the Truth
(John xiv. 6), so the Spirit sent in
Christ's name is the Truth. The Spirit
cannot but make known, as men can
bear the revelation, that which is
eternal and absolute in changing phenomena. That which 'is' is in virtue
of the Spirit, in virtue of Christ (Col.
i. 15 ff.).

Bede has a vigorous note on the
Latin reading (*Christus est veritas*):
Quia ergo Spiritus Jesum Christum
esse veritatem testatur, ipse se veritatem cognominat, Baptista illum veritatem prædicat, Filius tonitrui veritatem evangelizat: taceant blasphemi
qui hunc phantasma esse dogmati-
zant; pereant de terra memoriæ eorum qui eum vel Deum vel hominem
esse verum denegant.

7, 8. ὅτι τρεῖς εἰσίν...] *Because
three are they...* This clause appears
to give the reason for the main proposition in *v.* 5, that 'Jesus is the
Son of God,' a truth briefly expressed
and affirmed by His full Name, 'Jesus
Christ.' What has been said in *v.* 6
—*this is He that came*—prepares
the way for the assertion of this
complete personal testimony, adequate according to the human standard: Deut. xix. 15; comp. John viii.
17 ff. The stress laid by the order
upon 'three' emphasises this thought
of the fulness of the number of the
witnesses, and the consequent certainty of that which they affirm. The
faith in Jesus as 'the Christ, the Son

of God' is reasonable according to the
ordinary laws of belief.

It seems to be less natural to regard
the clause as a confirmation of the
words which immediately precede.
The ground of the Spirit's witness
is given perfectly in the declaration
of His Nature and Office as 'the
Truth.' Yet it is possible that the
ὅτι may simply explain the addition
of the Spirit: "besides 'the Water'
and 'the Blood' there is yet another
witness; *because three are they that
bear witness.*"

τρεῖς...οἱ μαρτυροῦντες] The passage
from the neuter τὸ μαρτυροῦν to the
masculine οἱ μαρτυροῦντες marks the
different aspect under which the
witness is now regarded, as a personal witness. The transition is made
through the Spirit, who is regarded both as a power and as a person: comp. John xiv. 26; xv. 26,
τὸ πνεῦμα...ὅ...ἐκεῖνος. Just as the
Spirit is found to be personal in His
work with men, so also 'the water'
and 'the blood' speak personally
through those in whom their efficacy
is realised.

οἱ μαρτ.] The participle, as distinguished from the noun οἱ μάρτυρες
(Acts i. 8; ii. 32, &c.), expresses the
actual delivery of the witness, and
this as a present, continuous, action.
The witness here is considered mainly
as the living witness of the Church
and not as the historical witness of
the Gospels. Through believers these
three, 'the Spirit and the . Water
and the Blood,' perform a work not
for believers only but for the world
(John xvii. 20 ff.).

8. τὸ πνεῦμα] The Spirit has a twofold office, one corresponding with
that of Christ (οὗτός ἐστιν ὁ ἐλθών...
τὸ πνεῦμά ἐστιν τὸ μαρτυροῦν...); and

τρεῖς εἰς τὸ ἕν εἰσιν. ⁹Εἰ τὴν μαρτυρίαν τῶν ἀνθρώπων
λαμβάνομεν, ἡ μαρτυρία τοῦ θεοῦ μείζων ἐστίν, ὅτι
αὕτη ἐστὶν ἡ μαρτυρία τοῦ θεοῦ ὅτι μεμαρτύρηκεν περὶ

9 τῶν ἀνθρ.: τοῦ θεοῦ ℵ*.   ὅτι (2°) ℵAB vg me the: ἦν ϛ.

the other coordinate with that of the
power of spiritual life and the power
of redemption brought by Christ (τὸ
πν., τὸ ὕδωρ, τὸ αἷμα). In this latter
connexion it must be remembered that
the Spirit is the sign of the glory of
the Risen Christ; John vii. 39; xvi.
7; Acts ii. 32 f. Thus the Spirit,
with the Water and Blood, completes
the witness to the Incarnation as a
Fact no less than as an open source
of blessing. For the witness of the
Spirit see Acts v. 32.

οἱ τρεῖς εἰς τὸ ἕν εἰσιν] *the three are
for the one.* The subject is emphatically repeated to mark the unity of
the object. 'The three personal witnesses are turned to the one absolute end,' to establish the one Truth
(τὸ ἕν, *the one,* not simply *one*), that
definite Truth which is everywhere
present through the Epistle. The
idea is not that of simple unanimity
in the witnesses (εἰς ἓν εἶναι), but that
of their convergence (so to speak)
on the one Gospel of 'Christ come in
the flesh,' to know which is eternal
life.

With the phrase εἰς τὸ ἕν εἶναι may
be contrasted ἓν εἶναι John x. 30;
xvii. 21 f.; 1 Cor. iii. 8; τελειοῦσθαι εἰς
ἕν John xvii. 23; συνάγειν εἰς ἕν
John xi. 52.

9—12. St John goes on from considering the character of the witness
to Christ to consider its effectiveness.
It is a divine witness (9): it is a
human, internal witness (10): it is a
witness realised in a present life (11),
in fellowship with the Son (12).

⁹ *If we receive the witness of men,
the witness of God is greater, because
this is the witness of God, that He
hath borne witness concerning His*

Son. ¹⁰ *He that believeth on the Son
of God hath the witness in himself:
he that believeth not God hath made
Him a liar, because he hath not believed on the witness which God hath
borne concerning His Son.* ¹¹ *And
this is the witness, that God gave us
eternal life, and this life is in His
Son.* ¹² *He that hath the Son hath
the life: he that hath not the Son of
God hath not the life.*

9. Εἰ τὴν μ. τ. ἀνθρ. λαμβ.] *Si...
accipimus* V., *If we receive...* This is
assumed as unquestioned: c. iii. 13.
The threefold witness of which St
John has spoken, simply as being
threefold, satisfies the conditions of
human testimony. Much more then,
he argues, does a threefold divine
witness meet all claims; and such a
witness, it is implied, we have in the
witness of the Spirit, the water and
the blood. This witness therefore is
'greater' than the witness of men in
regard to its authority: John v. 36.
Comp. c. iii. 20; iv. 4.

For μαρτ. λαμβ. see John iii. 11,
32 f.; v. 34.

The form of the argument is irregular. Instead of completing the sentence on the same type as he began,
'much more shall we receive the witness of God,' St John states that which
is the ground of this conclusion, 'the
witness of God is greater.'

ὅτι αὕτη ἐ....ὅτι...] *quoniam hoc est
...quia...* V., *because this is...that...*
The words look backward and forward. This triple witness which has
been described, and which is now
defined further to be a witness of God
concerning His Son: this is the final
form of the witness of God.

The witness was open and visible

τοῦ υἱοῦ αὐτοῦ. ¹⁰ὁ πιστεύων εἰς τὸν υἱὸν τοῦ θεοῦ
ἔχει τὴν μαρτυρίαν ἐν αὐτῷ· ὁ μὴ πιστεύων τῷ θεῷ

10 τὴν μαρτ. ℵB the syrr: +τοῦ θεοῦ A vg me.   αυτω AB: ἑαυτῷ ℵ.
τῷ θεῷ ℵB me syrr: τῷ υἱῷ A vg syrhlmg (others read τῷ υἱῷ τοῦ θεοῦ, τῷ υἱῷ
αὐτοῦ, and Cod. Am. omits by the first hand).

to the world in the general effect of
Christ's death and the pouring out of
the Spirit: so much was unquestionable.

The first conjunction (because)
does not give the ground of the
superior authority of the divine witness, that is taken for granted, but
the ground for appealing to it. Such
a witness has been given, and therefore we appeal to it.

The second ὅτι is ambiguous. It
may be (1) parallel with the former
one: 'because this is the witness of
God, because, I say, He hath borne
witness...'; or, it may be (2) explanatory of the μαρτυρίαν: 'because this
is the witness of God, even that He
hath borne witness...'; or again (3)
the word may be the relative (ὅ τι):
'because this is the witness of God,
even that which He hath witnessed....'

No one of the explanations is without difficulty. Against (2) it may be
urged that it is strange to insist on
the idea that the witness of God lies
in the fact that He hath witnessed
concerning His Son.

The usage of St John and of the
Apostolic writers generally is against
(3); though perhaps reference may be
made to iii. 20; John viii. 25. [In
Matt. xviii. 28 εἴ τι.]

The usage of St John (c. i. 5; v.
11, 14) is equally against (1).

On the whole it is best to take the
clause as explanatory of αὕτη: 'because
this is the witness of God, even the
fact that He hath borne witness concerning His Son.' God has spoken;
and His message is the witness to the
Incarnation. Comp. v. 11.

μεμαρτύρηκεν] testificatus est V.,

hath witnessed. The form is to be
distinguished from 'witnesseth' and
'witnessed.'

μεμαρτύρηκα John i. 34; iii. 26; v.
33, 37; xix. 35. (Hebr. xi. 5; 3 John
12.)

ἐμαρτύρησα John i. 32; iv. 44;
xiii. 21; Acts xv. 8; 1 Cor. xv.
15; 1 Tim. vi. 13; 3 John 6; Apoc.
i. 2; Hebr. xi. 2, 4, 39.

It may be added that vv. 6—9
contain a testimony to the Holy
Trinity in the several works of the
Divine Persons: Christ 'comes,'
the Spirit 'witnesses,' God (the
Father) 'hath witnessed concerning
His Son.'

10. The witness is not of external
testimony only, but internal also.
Absolute self-surrender to the Son of
God brings to the believer a direct
consciousness of His Divine Nature
and work. *He that believeth on the
Son of God hath the witness in himself.* That which for others is external
is for the believer experimental. The
witness of Spirit and water and blood
becomes an inner conviction of life
and cleansing and redemption. The
title of divine dignity (*the Son o
God*) points to the assurance of this
effect. Moreover it is to be noticed
that here the condition laid down is
belief in the Person of Christ (πιστ.
εἰς), and not belief in a fact (πιστ. ὅτι
v. 1).

ὁ μὴ πιστ. τῷ θ.] *he that believeth
not God.* The direct antithesis to
'believing on the Son' is 'not believing God.' This follows from the fact
that 'believing on the Son' comes from
'believing God,' that is, welcoming
His testimony.

For the phrase μὴ πιστεύειν τῷ θεῷ

ψεύστην πεποίηκεν αὐτόν, ὅτι οὐ πεπίστευκεν εἰς τὴν
μαρτυρίαν ἣν μεμαρτύρηκεν ὁ θεὸς περὶ τοῦ υἱοῦ αὐτοῦ.
¹¹καὶ αὕτη ἐστὶν ἡ μαρτυρία, ὅτι ζωὴν αἰώνιον ἔδωκεν

οὐ πεπίστευκεν ςB: οὐκ ἐπίστευσεν A (οὐκ ἐπίστευκεν אּ).   μεμαρτ.: ἐμαρτύρηκεν אּ.

(as distinguished from μὴ π. εἰς τὸν θ.)
see John v. 24; vi. 29 f.; viii. 30 f.
Comp. c. iii. 23 n.

ψεύστην πεπ. αὐ.] *mendacem facit*
V., *hath made Him a liar*, false in
all His dealings with men. See i.
10 n. The word marks the general
character and not only falsity in the
particular case. Comp. John viii. 44;
c. ii. 4, 22; iv. 20. The form of expression suggests the idea of an inward
conflict. A voice has been heard and
it has been deliberately rejected.

πεποίηκεν...πεπίστευκεν] These two
perfects definitely connect the present
position of the unbeliever with a past
act. When the crisis of choice came
he refused the message : he made
God a liar : he did not believe on
His testimony : and the result of that
decision entered into him and clings
to him. Compare, for a similar use of
πεπίστευκα, John iii. 18; vi. 69 (c. iv.
16); xi. 27 ; xvi. 27 ; xx. 29 ; 2 Tim.
i. 12 ; Tit. iii. 8.

ὅτι οὐ πεπίστ.] The negative expresses the direct fact. Contrast John
iii. 18 ὅτι μὴ πεπίστ. which presents
the conception. See John vi. 64.

οὐ πεπίστ. εἰς τὴν μαρτ.] *non cre-
didit in testimonium* V., *hath not
believed on the witness*, not simply
'believed the witness.' The phrase
is unique. Belief in the truth of the
witness (πιστ. τῇ μαρτυρίᾳ, compare
John v. 47) is carried on to personal
belief in the object of the witness,
that is, the Incarnate Son Himself.
The phrase is illustrated by πιστεύειν εἰς τὸ ὄνομα (v. 13 n.), in which
the 'name' represents the Person
under the particular aspect which it
expresses. In one other case πιστεύ-

ειν εἰς is used with an object not
directly personal, John xii. 36 πιστεύειν
εἰς τὸ φῶς, but here φῶς is used with
immediate reference to John viii. 12 ;
ix. 5.
So it stands out that the ultimate
object of faith is not a fact or a dogma
but a Person.

ἣν μεμαρτ....] It might have seemed
simpler to say 'the witness of God'
(v. 9); but St John repeats at length
what he has shewn that witness to be,
a witness concerning His Son.

11, 12. The witness, which has
been shewn to be divine and internal,
points also to the presence of a divine
life, which, given once for all, is enjoyed by fellowship with the Son.

11. καὶ αὕτη...] 'The witness of God'
(v. 9) is in part unfolded : the witness
that He hath given concerning His
Son is this, that He gave us eternal
life. The Mission of His Son, which
He attested, was the gift of life (John
x. 10, 28 ; xvii. 2), of life in His Son
(John xx. 31, ἐν τῷ ὀνόματι).

ζ. αἰ. ἔδωκεν] *gave eternal life*, not
hath given. Compare c. iii. 23 f.
(ἔδωκεν) with c. iii. 1; iv. 13; v. 20
(δέδωκεν). The reference is to the
historic facts by which this life was
communicated to humanity. That
which before Christ's coming was a
great hope, by His coming was realised and given. The gift, as far as
St John here regards it, was made to
Christians (ἡμῖν), who appropriate it.

ζωὴν αἰώνιον] vv. 13, 20 ; c. iii. 15.
This form is to be distinguished from
ἡ ζ. ἡ αἰών. (c. i. 2, note) and ἡ αἰώνιος
ζ. which occurs only John xvii. 3.
It simply defines the character of the
life, and does not identify it with the
only true life.

ὁ θεὸς ἡμῖν, καὶ αὕτη ἡ ζωὴ ἐν τῷ υἱῷ αὐτοῦ ἐστίν.
¹²ὁ ἔχων τὸν υἱὸν ἔχει τὴν ζωήν· ὁ μὴ ἔχων τὸν υἱὸν
τοῦ θεοῦ τὴν ζωὴν οὐκ ἔχει.   ¹³ Ταῦτα ἔγραψα

11 ὁ θ. ἡμ. B (the) syr hl : ἡμ. ὁ θ. ℵA vg me syr vg.   αὕτη ἐστὶν ἡ ζ. A.

ἐν τῷ υἱῷ] The life is not separate
from God but in God. Believers united
with Christ are in Him united with
God. Comp. Rom. vi. 23; 2 Tim.
i. 1.

12. ὁ ἔχων...] The variations from
exact parallelism in the two members
of the verse are significant. In the
second member τὸν υἱὸν τοῦ θεοῦ
stands for τὸν υἱόν, and the position
of τὴν ζωήν is changed.

ὁ ἔχων τὸν υἱὸν] He that hath the
Son, in Whom the Father is known.
Comp. c. ii. 23; 2 John 9; and for
the use of ἔχειν, John iii. 29; iv. 17.

ἔχει τὴν ζ.] hath life, or rather
the life which God has given. Contrast v. 13; iii. 15; John v. 26;
x. 10; xx. 31. Comp. Col. iii. 4.

In the spirit of these words Ignatius speaks of Jesus Christ as τὸ
ἀδιάκριτον ἡμῶν ζῆν 'our inseparable
life' (Eph. 3); and τὸ ἀληθινὸν ἡμῶν
ζῆν, 'our true life' (Smyrn. 4). Comp.
Magn. 5; Trall. 9.

ὁ μὴ ἔχων τ. υἱ. τοῦ θ.] he that hath
not the Son of God. The fuller title
seems to mark emphatically the necessity of failure in such a case. God
is the only source of life.

For the combination of the positive
and negative see c. i. 5; ii. 4, 27;
John i. 3; iii. 16.

III. THE ACTIVITY AND CONFIDENCE
OF THE CHRISTIAN LIFE: EPI-
LOGUE.

This last section of the Epistle is
symmetrical in structure:

1. The aim re-stated (13).
2. The confidence of spiritual
   action (14—17).
3. The certainty of spiritual
   knowledge (18—20).

4. A final warning (21).
The progress of thought is clear.
Having reached the close of his
writing St John recals the main
purpose of writing it (i. 4), which he
has fulfilled (v. 13); and then illustrates the confidence of the Christian
life under two aspects (1) as it finds
expression in spiritual action (14—17),
and (2) as it is realised in inward conviction (18—20). He concludes by a
warning against everything which
usurps the place of God (21).

1. The aim of the Epistle re-
stated (13).

¹³ These things have I written, that
ye may know that ye have eternal life,
to you who believe on the name of the
Son of God.

13. Ταῦτα ἔγραψα] These things
have I written (I wrote)... In reviewing his Epistle St John indicates
the fulfilment of his purpose (i. 3, 4).
The consciousness of eternal life brings
divine fellowship and completed joy.
Comp. John xx. 30 f.

For the use of ἔγραψα (contrast
γέγραφα John xix. 22) see c. ii. 12
—14 note. The Apostle looks back
upon his work, and records the aim
which he set before himself.

ἵνα εἰδῆτε] ut sciatis V., that ye
may know with a knowledge final and
certain. Compare ii. 29 note; iii. 14
note. The eternal life may be present and yet not realised in its inherent power. The fruits may not be
referred to their source; and again
they may be delayed. But there is a
knowledge of life which is independent of external signs; and this St
John seeks to quicken.

The order ζωὴν ἔχ. αἰών. is not found

ὑμῖν ἵνα εἰδῆτε ὅτι ζωὴν ἔχετε αἰώνιον, τοῖς πιστεύουσιν
εἰς τὸ ὄνομα τοῦ υἱοῦ τοῦ θεοῦ. ¹⁴καὶ αὕτη ἐστὶν ἡ
παρρησία ἣν ἔχομεν πρὸς αὐτόν, ὅτι ἐάν τι αἰτώμεθα

13 ὑμῖν ℵAB vg me the syrr: +τοῖς πιστεύουσιν εἰς τὸ ὄνομα τοῦ υἱοῦ τοῦ θεοῦ ς.
ἔχ. αἰών. AB vg syrhl: αἰών. ἔχ. ℵ.   τοῖς πιστεύουσιν ℵ*B syrr: οἱ πιστεύοντες ℵcA vg me the: καὶ ἵνα πιστεύητε ς.   14 ἔχομεν: ἔχωμεν A.   ὅτι
ἐάν τι ςℵB syrhl the: ὅτι ἄν A: ὅτι ὃ ἐάν vg syrvg.

elsewhere: the epithet comes as an afterthought: 'that ye have life—yes, eternal life.'

τοῖς πιστεύουσιν] to you who believe. The dative, which is added as a kind of afterthought, defines the character of the persons who are addressed: 'to you, yes, to you who believe...' Compare John i. 12; v. 16. The present activity of faith (πιστεύουσιν) is the sign of life (iii. 23 note).

τοῖς πιστ. εἰς τὸ ὄν....] qui creditis in nomine...V., who believe in the name of..., who believe in Him who is revealed to us under this title as being the Son of God. Contrast iii. 23 note (πιστ. τῷ ὀν.); and compare John i. 12 note; ii. 23 note; iii. 18. For similar uses of ὄνομα see c. ii. 12 (διὰ τὸ ὄνομα αὐτοῦ) note; 3 John 7 (τὸ ὄνομα) note.

τοῦ υἱοῦ τοῦ θεοῦ] the Son of God, vv. 5, 10, 12, 20; iii. 8 note; iv. 15. The title is the pledge of the certainty of the possession of life.

2. The confidence of spiritual action (14—17).

The consciousness of a divine life brings to the believer perfect boldness in prayer, that is, in converse with God (14, 15); and this boldness finds characteristic expression in intercession for the brethren (16, 17).

¹⁴ And this is the boldness which we have towards Him, that, if we ask anything according to His will, He heareth us. ¹⁵ And if we know that He heareth us whatsoever we ask, we know that we have the petitions which we have asked from Him.

¹⁶ If any one see his brother sinning a sin not unto death, he shall ask, and He (he) will give him life, even to them that sin not unto death. There is sin unto death: I do not say that he should pray for that: ¹⁷ all unrighteousness is sin, and there is sin not unto death.

14. καὶ αὕτη...] It is implied that the knowledge which the Christian can gain is not for mere passive possession, nor yet for himself alone. It finds scope in corresponding expression. The life is fruitful.

ἡ παρρησία ἣν ἔχομεν...] fiducia quam habemus... V., the boldness of speech, utterance, which we have as the consequence of our possession of life. See c. ii. 28 note. The gift of eternal life enables the believer to come directly before God (Hebr. iv. 16) and speak every thought without reserve. This he has strength to do in the present trials of life (c. iii. 21); and he looks forward to a like openness of trust 'at the presence of Christ' (ii. 28), and 'in the day of judgment' (iv. 17).

πρὸς αὐτόν] ad eum V., towards Him, that is, God, the main subject of the passage.

αὕτη...ὅτι...ἀκούει...] this...that ...He heareth] The fact (that He heareth) and not the conviction of the fact ('we know that He heareth'), is identified with the feeling. Our boldness is not simply a belief, but indeed a certainty, an experience.

ἐάν τι αἰτώμεθα] quodcunque petierimus V., if we ask anything. The distinction between the middle (αἰ-

κατὰ τὸ θέλημα αὐτοῦ ἀκούει ἡμῶν. ¹⁵ καὶ ἐὰν οἴδαμεν
ὅτι ἀκούει ἡμῶν ὃ ἐὰν αἰτώμεθα, οἴδαμεν ὅτι ἔχομεν
τὰ αἰτήματα ἃ ᾐτήκαμεν ἀπ᾽ αὐτοῦ. ¹⁶ Ἐάν τις ἴδῃ τὸν

θέλημα: ὄνομα A.   15 καὶ ἐὰν (ἂν B) οἴδαμεν (ἴδωμεν אᶜ me) ὅτι ἀκ. ἠ. ς
(אᶜ) B syrr (me) the: et scimus vg: om. א*A.   ἔχομεν: ἔχωμεν א (ἐὰν ἔχ. א*).
ἀπ᾽ αὐτοῦ אB: παρ᾽ αὐτοῦ ςA.

τεῖσθαι) and the active (αἰτεῖν) is not
sharply drawn; but generally the
personal reference is suggested by
the middle while the request is left
wholly undefined as to its destination
by the active. Compare John xvi.
24, 26; xiv. 13, 14; xv. 16 with xv.
7; James iv. 2, 3. For αἰτεῖσθαι see
Matt. xxvii. 20 (and parallels), 58 (and
parallels); Acts iii. 14.

κατὰ τὸ θέλημα αὐ.] according to
His will. Comp. 1 Pet. iv. 19; Gal.
i. 4; Eph. i. 5, 11. This will finds
expression in the soul: John xv. 7;
and is the continuous manifestation
of the divine nature through Christ.
Thus asking 'according to the will of
God' is equivalent to asking 'in
Christ's name': John xiv. 13 note.

'The will of God' regards the
spiritual consummation of man (c. ii.
17; Rom. ii. 18), and all external
things only so far as they are contributory to this.

ἀκούει ἡμῶν] Compare John ix. 31;
xi. 41 f. This sense of 'hearing' is
peculiar to St John. The 'hearing'
of God, like the 'knowledge' of God,
carries with it every perfect consequence. For the thought see c. iii. 22.

15. καὶ ἐὰν οἴδαμεν...] Et scimus V.,
si scimus F., And if we know... The
force of this unusual construction appears to be to throw the uncertainty
upon the fact of the presence of the
knowledge and not upon the knowledge itself. The sense required is
not 'and should we know,' but 'and
should it be that we know.'

ὃ ἐὰν αἰτώμεθα] whatsoever we ask.
This universal phrase can be substituted for the limited phrase which

was used before (ἐάν τι αἰτ. κ.τ.θ.). The
believer would not make his own
any prayer which is not according
to God's will. And since he has made
God's will his own will, he has all he
truly seeks in immediate and present
possession (Mark xi. 24) though the
visible fulfilment may be delayed.

τὰ αἰτήματα] petitiones V., the petitions (Phil. iv. 6; Luke xxiii. 24):
the substance of the requests, if not
necessarily the actual things asked
for (τὰ αἰτηθέντα).

ἀπ᾽ αὐτοῦ] from Him. These words
go perhaps more naturally with 'have'
(c. ii. 20) than with 'asked.' Yet see
Matt. xx. 20 (ἀπ᾽ αὐτοῦ).

16, 17.   That boldness of access to
God, which finds expression in prayer,
finds its most characteristic expression in intercessory prayer. Fellowship with God involves fellowship
with man (i. 3). The energy of
Christian life is from the first social.
Hence St John passes naturally from
the general thought of prayer to that
of prayer for the brethren. And in
doing this he fixes attention on the
failures of Christians. These are the
sorest trial of faith.

The prevailing power of intercession
corresponds with the Christian revelation of the unity of the Body of Christ.
When this power is exercised for
others it is exercised in a true sense
for ourselves, and not, arbitrarily as
it were, for those apart from us. Apostolic teaching recognises a mysterious
dependence of man upon man in the
spiritual order like that which is now
being shewn to exist in the physical
order; and throughout the Epistle

ἀδελφὸν αὐτοῦ ἁμαρτάνοντα ἁμαρτίαν μὴ πρὸς θάνατον,
αἰτήσει, καὶ δώσει αὐτῷ ζωήν, τοῖς ἁμαρτάνουσιν μὴ

16 αἰτήσει...δώσει: αἰτήσις (-ήσεις)...δώσεις ℵ*.   τοῖς ἁμαρτ. μή: τοῖς μη
ἁμαρτάν. ἁμαρτίαν μή A.

St John assumes the reality of this
inner fellowship among those whom
he addresses, and he bases his arguments upon it.
Compare 1 Pet. iv. 8 τὴν εἰς ἑαυτοὺς
ἀγάπην; id. 10 εἰς ἑαυτοὺς αὐτὸ δια-
κονοῦντες; Eph. iv. 32; Col. iii. 13
χαριζόμενοι ἑαυτοῖς; Col. iii. 16 νουθε-
τοῦντες ἑαυτούς.

16. Ἐάν τις ἴδῃ...] If any one see
... The duty, the instinct, is universal in the Christian Society. At
the same time the character of the
sin towards which the duty is exercised is clear even outwardly. It is
not a matter simply of suspicion or
doubt.

τὸν ἀδελφὸν αὐτοῦ] his brother.
The end of prayer is the perfection of
the whole Christian body. The Christian prays for himself only as a member in the society. The sight of sin
in 'a brother'—a fellow Christian
(c. ii. 9 note)—and it is only with
Christians that St John is dealing—
necessarily stirs to intercession. Comp.
Clem. ad Cor. i. 2 ἐπὶ τοῖς παρα-
πτώμασι τῶν πλησίον ἐπενθεῖτε· τὰ
ὑστερήματα αὐτῶν ἴδια ἐκρίνετε.

ἁμαρτ. ἁμαρτ.] peccare peccatum
V., sinning a sin. The form of expression (ἁμαρτάνοντα, inadequately
rendered in the Latin) emphasises
the outward present character of the
act. There is no exact parallel in
N. T. to the phrase. Comp. c. ii. 25.
Winer iii. § 32, 2.

μὴ πρὸς θάνατον] not unto death.
Life is fellowship with Christ (v. 12).
Death is separation from Him. All
sin tends to make the fellowship less
complete. Yet not all equally; nor
all in a fixed and unalterable degree.
The thought is not of the definite

external characteristics of particular
acts, as having an absolute value, but
of acts in relation to the man's whole
nature and life.
The clause 'not unto death' goes
both with the participle and with the
noun, as is shewn separately afterwards.
For the conception of 'death' see
c. iii. 14 (the only other place in the
Epistles where the word occurs),
John v. 24 (viii. 51 f.; vi. 50; xi. 26;
viii. 24). The thought is evidently
not of physical death as James v. 14
ff. Compare, in another connexion,
John xi. 4 αὕτη ἡ ἀσθένεια οὐκ ἔστι
πρὸς θάνατον. The subjective negative (μὴ πρὸς θ.) naturally follows
from the supposition (ἐάν τις). It is
otherwise in v. 17.

αἰτήσει] petit (-at) V., postulabit F.,
he shall ask. This will be his natural
and spontaneous action. There is no
need of a command.

καὶ δώσει] and he will give. The
subject has been taken to be (1) the
intercessor, or (2) God (dabit ei vitam
Dominus Tert. de Pudic. 19; but
dabitur ei, id. 2). In favour of the
first view the continuity of the construction (αἰτήσει, δώσει) and the parallel James v. 20 have been urged.
The second view is that which is at
first suggested by the language of
Scripture generally. To 'give life'
is elsewhere treated as a divine prerogative; John vi. 33; x. 28; xvii. 2 ;
v. 11. But there is nothing unscrip-
tural in the thought that the believer
does that which God does through
him; James v. 20. Still on the whole
it seems more natural to see here
a reference to the direct action of
God.
If 'God' be the subject of 'give'

πρὸς θάνατον. ἔστιν ἁμαρτία πρὸς θάνατον· οὐ περὶ
ἐκείνης λέγω ἵνα ἐρωτήσῃ. ¹⁷πᾶσα ἀδικία ἁμαρτία

ἐρωτήσῃ: +τις vg syrvg.   ἐρωτήσῃς אᵒ.

then αὐτῷ may be the 'ethical'
dative, and τοῖς πιστ. the direct
object of δώσει: 'God shall give life
to those that sin not unto death for
him, in answer to his prayers.' This
however seems to be artificial. The
αὐτῷ is most naturally the sinning
brother in any case.

δ. ζωήν] give life. The sinner is
not 'dead,' nor yet 'sinning unto
death,' but his life is, as it were, sus-
pended in part. Comp. John x. 10.

τοῖς ἁμαρτ.] even to them that...
The single case (ἁμαρτάνοντα) is now
generalised. Comp. v. 13.

The apposition of a personal plural
to an abstract noun is not strictly
parallel; 1 Cor. i. 2.

ἔστιν ἁμ. πρὸς θ.] Est peccatum ad
mortem V., There is sin unto death.
The translation 'a sin' (ἁμαρτία τις)
is too definite. The thought is not
of specific acts as such, but of acts
which have a certain character:
'There is that which must be described as sin unto death; there is
that which wholly separates from
Christ.' The phrase, it must be remembered, comes in a passage which
deals with the prayer of Christians
for Christians and not for heathen.
See Additional Note.

οὐ περὶ ἐκείνης λέγω ἵνα...] non pro
illo dico ut roget quis V., not concerning that do I say that... The
sin unto death is isolated and regarded in its terrible distinctness
(ἐκείνη). The words περὶ ἐκείνης
may be connected either with λέγω or
with ἐρωτήσῃ. Perhaps it is best to
connect them with ἐρωτήσῃ. Comp.
John xvi. 26; xvii. 9, 20.

The construction λέγω ἵνα is not
common: Acts xix. 4.   Comp. εἰπεῖν
ἵνα Matt. iv. 3, &c.; ἐρρήθη ἵνα Apoc.
vi. 11, &c.

ἐρωτήσῃ] make request. The change
of the verb from αἰτεῖν (V. petere),
(αἰτεῖσθαι), to ἐρωτᾶν (V. rogare),
cannot but be significant. Ἐρωτᾶν
is the word which is used of Christ's
prayer to the Father (John xiv. 16;
xvi. 26; xvii. 9, 15, 20; comp. 1 Thess.
iv. 1; 2 John 5). It seems to mark
the request which is based upon
fellowship, upon a likeness of position. Here then it would naturally
express the prayer of brother for
brother as such, to the common
Father. Such a prayer is not enjoined by the apostle. At the same
time he does not forbid it. It does
not lie within his scope[1].

17. πᾶσα ἀδικία...] omnis iniquitas... V., all unrighteousness... The
words are added to shew the wide
scope which is given for the exercise
of Christian sympathy and intercession. Apart from such sins as are
open manifestations of a character
alien from God, there are other sins
which flow from human imperfection
and infirmity, and in regard to these
Christian intercession has its work.
All unrighteousness (c. i. 9), all failure
to fulfil our duty one to another, is
sin; and in this ample field there is
abundant opportunity for the exercise
of prayer. There is a sin not unto
death, of which the consequences may
be removed by the brother's petition.

The statement that 'all unrighteousness is sin' must be compared

---

[1] It is interesting to notice that ἐρωτᾶν
is used in this sense of Christian prayer
for Christians in a very early inscription
in the Roman Catacombs: ΖΗСΗС ЄΝ
ΚѠ ΚΑΙ ЄΡѠΤΑ ΥΠЄΡ ΗΜѠΝ (Northcote and Brownlow, Roma Sotterranea,
ii. 159).

ἐστίν, καὶ ἔστιν ἁμαρτία οὐ πρὸς θάνατον.   ¹⁸ Οἴδαμεν ὅτι πᾶς ὁ γεγεννημένος ἐκ τοῦ θεοῦ οὐχ ἁμαρ-

17 οὐ πρός: om. οὐ vg syrhl the Tert.

with the comprehensive definition of sin in c. iii. 4 *lawlessness is sin,* and conversely *sin is lawlessness.* Sin is the most general term and is used in regard to the will of God for man. By whatever act, internal or external, man falls short of this will, as it is spiritually apprehended, he 'sins.' The will of God may be conceived of as embodied in 'law,' in respect of the whole constitution of things, or in 'right,' in respect of the claims made by others. So it is that all violation of law and all violation of right is sin looked at in a special aspect. Unrighteousness is one manifestation of sin. Comp. Rom. vi. 13 ὅπλα ἀδικίας τῇ ἁμαρτίᾳ.

3. *The certainty of spiritual know-ledge* (18—20).

The thought of sin, of sin among the brethren, of sin unto death, forces the Apostle to recal once more the assurance of faith. In spite of the sad lessons of daily experience he re-affirms the truths which the Christian knows: the privileges of the divine birth (18); the fact of the divine kinsmanship (19); the advance in divine understanding issuing from divine fellowship (20).

The threefold repetition of οἴδαμεν, *we know* (18, 19, 20), gives a rhythmic form to the paragraph.

¹⁸ *We know that everyone who is begotten of God sinneth not, but He that was begotten of God keepeth him and the evil one toucheth him not.*

¹⁹ *We know that we are in God and the whole world lieth in the evil one.*

²⁰ *We know that the Son of God hath come and hath given to us un-derstanding that we may know Him*

W.

that is true; and we are in Him that is true, even in His Son Jesus Christ. This is the true God and life eter-nal.

18. The power of intercession to overcome the consequences of sin might seem to encourage a certain indifference to sin. Therefore St John re-affirms the elements of Christian knowledge. From this point of sight the first truth of which the Christian is assured is that, in spite of the ab-normal presence of sin even among the brethren, the child of God 'sin-neth not.' He has a watchful Pro-tector stronger than his adversary.

Οἴδαμεν] *Scimus* V., *We know.* St John uses this appeal to absolute knowledge in two forms : ' we know,' and 'ye know.' The former occurs :

iii. 2 οἴδαμεν ὅτι ἐὰν φανερωθῇ ὅμοιοι αὐτῷ ἐσόμεθα, ὅτι ὀψόμεθα αὐτὸν καθώς ἐστιν.

iii. 14 ἡμεῖς οἴδαμεν ὅτι μεταβεβή-καμεν ἐκ τοῦ θανάτου εἰς τὴν ζωὴν, ὅτι ἀγαπῶμεν τοὺς ἀδελφούς.

v. 18 οἴδαμεν ὅτι πᾶς ὁ γεγεννημένος ἐκ τοῦ θεοῦ οὐχ ἁμαρτάνει.

v. 19 οἴδαμεν ὅτι ἐκ τοῦ θεοῦ ἐσμέν.

v. 20 οἴδαμεν ὅτι ὁ υἱὸς τοῦ θεοῦ ἥκει καὶ δέδωκεν ἡμῖν διάνοιαν ἵνα γινώ-σκομεν τὸν ἀληθινόν.

In contrast with these appeals to fundamental knowledge, St John else-where appeals to the knowledge brought by actual experience (γινώ-σκομεν): *v.* 2 note.

St Paul uses the same form (οἴδα-μεν) not unfrequently : 1 Cor. viii. 1, 4; 2 Cor. v. 1; Rom. ii. 2; iii. 19; vii. 14; viii. 22, 28; 1 Tim. i. 8.

Οἴδατε is found :

ii. 20 οἴδατε πάντες...τὴν ᾽λήθειαν.

iii. 5 οἴδατε ὅτι ἐκεῖνος ἐφανερώθη ἵνα τὰς ἁμαρτίας ἄρῃ.

13

τάνει, ἀλλ' ὁ γεννηθεὶς ἐκ τοῦ θεοῦ τηρεῖ αὐτόν, καὶ
ὁ πονηρὸς οὐχ ἅπτεται αὐτοῦ. ¹⁹οἴδαμεν ὅτι ἐκ τοῦ
θεοῦ ἐσμέν, καὶ ὁ κόσμος ὅλος ἐν τῷ πονηρῷ κεῖται.

18 ὁ γεννηθείς: *generatio* vg.

iii. 15 οἴδατε ὅτι πᾶς ἀνθρωποκτόνος οὐκ ἔχει ζωὴν αἰώνιον ἐν αὐτῷ μένουσαν. πᾶς ὁ γεγενν, ἐκ τοῦ θ.] *omnis qui natus est ex Deo* V. Comp. c. iii. 9 note.

οὐχ ἁμαρτάνει] Comp. iii. 9 note (ἁμαρτίαν οὐ ποιεῖ). While St John states this without reserve he yet recognises 'the brother'—brother as son of the one Father—'sinning a sin not unto death' (v. 16). The paradox remains unsolved.

ἀλλ' ὁ γεννηθεὶς...τ. αὐ.] *sed generatio (nativitas* F.) *Dei conservat eum* V., *but He that was Begotten of God keepeth him.* He does not depend on his own strength or vigilance. He has an active Enemy (ὁ πονηρός), but he has also a watchful Guardian.

The phrase ὁ γεννηθεὶς ἐκ τοῦ θεοῦ is unique. Standing as it does in close juxtaposition with ὁ γεγεννημένος ἐκ τοῦ θεοῦ it is impossible to regard it as identical in reference, and the mention of the great adversary naturally suggests the thought of the Son of God. The peculiar expression is probably used to emphasise the connexion of the Son with those whom He 'is not ashamed to call brethren' (Hebr. ii. 11 ἐξ ἑνὸς πάντες); while the difference of γεννηθείς from γεγεννημένος suggests that difference in the sonship of the Son from the sonship of men which is marked in John v. 26 τῷ υἱῷ ἔδωκεν ζωὴν ἔχειν ἐν ἑαυτῷ.

The remarkable Latin reading appears to represent the Greek ἡ γέννησις τοῦ θεοῦ (Matt. i. 18).

τηρεῖ] The verb is used of persons Matt. xxvii. 36, 54; (xxviii. 4); John xvii. 11, 15 (note); Apoc. iii. 10; Jude 21 (ἑαυτοὺς τηρήσατε). It expresses a watchful regard from without rather than safe custody.

αὐτόν A*B vg: ἑαυτόν אA**.

ὁ πονηρός] *malignus* V. See c. ii. 13 note.

ἅπτεται] *tangit* V. The verb occurs elsewhere in St John only in John xx. 17. It describes 'a laying hold on,' more than a mere superficial touch (θιγγάνειν). Even when it is used of simple physical contact, a deeper connexion is indicated, as when the Lord 'touched' the sick. See Col. ii. 21 μὴ ἅψῃ μηδὲ γεύσῃ μηδὲ θίγῃς. Compare Ps. cv. 15 μὴ ἅψησθε τῶν χριστῶν μου. The ground of safety is revealed in John xiv. 30 ἐν ἐμοὶ οὐκ ἔχει οὐδέν. As yet the principle of evil is without.

19. From the general statement of the privilege of Sons of God St John goes on to the affirmation of the personal relation in which he and those whom he addresses stand to Him (ἐκ τοῦ θεοῦ ἐσμέν).

The structure of the verse is expressive. The absence of the personal pronoun (contrast iv. 6) in the first clause throws all the emphasis upon the divine source of life: 'We know that it is from God we draw our being.' In the second clause the emphasis is changed. Over against the Christian Society, only faintly indicated in the preceding words, stands 'the whole world,' and on this attention is fixed. The relation of the Church to God is widely different from that of the world to the Evil One.

This difference is brought out in the two corresponding phrases ἐκ τοῦ θεοῦ εἶναι and ἐν τῷ πονηρῷ κεῖσθαι. The first describes the absolute source of being: the second the actual (but not essential) position.

ἐκ τοῦ θ. ἐ.] See Additional Note on iii. 1.

καὶ ὁ κ. ὅ.] This clause like the

²⁰ οἴδαμεν δὲ ὅτι ὁ υἱὸς τοῦ θεοῦ ἥκει, καὶ δέδωκεν ἡμῖν διάνοιαν ἵνα γινώσκομεν τὸν ἀληθινόν· καί ἐσμεν ἐν τῷ

20 οἴδαμεν δέ ℵB me: καὶ οἴδαμεν A vg syrr the.   ἥκει: +et carnem induit nostri causa et passus est et resurrexit a mortuis; adsumpsit nos et dedit....(Latt.). δέδωκεν: ἔδωκεν A.   γινώσκομεν ℵAB*: γινώσκωμεν ϛ.   τὸν ἀλ.: τὸ ἀλ. ℵ* the: +θεόν A vg me (Latt.).   ἐσμέν: simus vg.   ἐν τῷ ἀλ.: om. me: in vita the.

corresponding clauses in vv. 18 (ἀλλὰ ὁ γεvv.), 20 (καί ἐσμεν), is an independent statement and not dependent on ὅτι. The Christian is able to look upon the saddest facts of life without being overwhelmed by them.

The order ὁ κόσμος ὅλος suggests a slightly different conception from ὅλος ὁ κόσμος (c. ii. 2): 'the world, the organization of society as alien from and opposed to God, is wholly, in all its parts and elements, placed in the domain of...' The two thoughts of the world, and of the entirety of it, are given separately. The same form occurs Matt. xvi. 26 and parallels; and the same order in Matt. xxvi. 59; Lc. xi. 36; John iv. 53; Acts xxi. 30; 1 Cor. xiv. 23; Apoc. iii. 10; vi. 12; xii. 9; xvi. 14. There is a similar difference of colour given by the corresponding position of πᾶς: John v. 22; xvi. 13; Matt. x. 30; xiii. 56; xxvi. 56; Acts xvi. 33; Rom. xii. 4; xvi. 16; 1 Cor. vii. 17; x. 1; xv. 7; xvi. 20, &c.

ἐν τῷ πον. κ.] in maligno positus est V., lieth in the evil one, is placed in the sphere of his influence. There is no question here of the Evil One 'laying hold on' (ἅπτεσθαι) the world, as from without (v. 8): it has been placed 'in him.' The phrase answers to the εἶναι ἐν τῷ ἀληθινῷ which follows, and to the characteristic Pauline ἐν χριστῷ. Comp. c. iii. 24, iv. 15 note. The connexion shews beyond question that τῷ πονηρῷ is masculine, and the converse of κεῖσθαι ἐν τ. π. is given in John xvii. 15 ἵνα τηρήσῃς ἐκ τοῦ πονηροῦ.

A close parallel to the expression is found in Soph. Œd. Col. 247 ἐν ὑμῖν

ὡς θεῷ κείμεθα τλάμονες. Comp. Œd. R. 314; Alc. 279.

20. The third affirmation of knowledge is introduced by the adversative particle (οἶδ. δέ). There is, this seems to be the line of thought, a startling antithesis in life of good and evil. We have been made to feel it in all its intensity. But at the same time we can face it in faith. That which is as yet dark will be made light. There is given to us the power of ever-advancing knowledge and of present divine fellowship. We can wait even as God waits. The particle δέ is comparatively unfrequent in St John's writings: c. i. 7; ii. 2, 5, 11, 17; iii. 12, 17; iv. 18; 3 John 14.

ἥκει, καὶ δέδωκεν] hath come and hath given. Faith rests on the permanence of the fact and not upon the historic fact only. Comp. John viii. 42 note.

δέδωκεν] c. iii. 1, iv. 13. Contrast iii. 23, 24; v. 11 (ἔδωκεν) note.

διάνοιαν] sensum V., understanding. This is the only place in which the term occurs in St John's writings; and generally nouns which express intellectual powers are rare in them. Thus St John never uses γνῶσις, nor is νοῦς found in his Gospel or Epistles. Διάνοια, as compared with νοῦς, represents the process of rational thought. Comp. Eph. iv. 18 ἐν ματαιότητι τοῦ νοὸς αὐτῶν, ἐσκοτωμένοι τῇ διανοίᾳ ὄντες (the first principles of the Gentiles were unsubstantial, and they had lost the power of right reasoning). Exclusive of quotations from the LXX, διάνοια is found: 1 Pet. i. 13 ἀναζωσάμενοι τὰς ὀσφύας τῆς διανοίας; 2 Pet. iii. 1 διεγείρω τὴν εἰλικρινῆ διάνοιαν;

13—2

ἀληθινῷ, ἐν τῷ υἱῷ αὐτοῦ Ἰησοῦ Χριστῷ. οὗτός ἐστιν

Ἰ. Χ.: om. A vg.

and, in a more concrete sense, Lc. i.
51 διανοίᾳ καρδίας; Col. i. 21 ἐχθροὺς
τῇ διανοίᾳ; Eph. ii. 3 τὰ θελήματα τῆς
σαρκὸς καὶ τῶν διανοιῶν.

That with which 'the Son of God'
Incarnate has endowed believers is
a power of understanding, of interpreting, of following out to their right
issues, the complex facts of life; and
the end of the gift is that they may
know, not by one decisive act (ἵνα
γνῶσιν) but by a continuous and progressive apprehension (ἵνα γινώσκωσι),
'Him that is true.' Thus the object
of knowledge is not abstract but personal: not the Truth, but Him of
Whom all that is true is a partial
revelation.

It is evident that the fact of the
Incarnation (υἱὸς τοῦ θ. ἥκει) vitally
welcomed carries with it the power
of believing in and seeing little by
little the divine purpose of life under
the perplexing riddles of phenomena.

The language in which Ignatius describes this gift is remarkable: διὰ τί
οὐ πάντες φρόνιμοι γινόμεθα λαβόντες
θεοῦ γνῶσιν, ὅ ἐστιν Ἰησοῦς Χριστός;
τί μωρῶς ἀπολλύμεθα ἀγνοοῦντες τὸ χάρισμα ὅ πέπομφεν ἀληθῶς ὁ Κύριος;
(ad Eph. xvii.).

ἵνα γινώσκομεν] This clause finds a
remarkable commentary in John xvii.
3. Eternal life is the never-ending
effort after this knowledge of God.
Compare John x. 38, ἵνα γνῶτε καὶ
γινώσκητε ὅτι ἐν ἐμοὶ ὁ πατὴρ κἀγὼ ἐν
αὐτῷ.

It seems likely that γινώσκομεν is
to be regarded as a corrupt pronun-
ciation of γινώσκωμεν. It is remarkable that in John xvii. 3 many authorities read γινώσκουσιν for -ωσιν. Comp.
Winer, iii. § 41. 1.

τὸν ἀληθινόν] verum Deum V.,
quod est verum F. (i.e. τὸ ἀλ.), Him
that is true, Who in contrast with

all imaginary and imperfect objects
of worship completely satisfies the
idea of Godhead in the mind of man,
even the Father revealed in and by
the Son (John i. 18, xiv. 9). Christ
is also called ὁ ἀληθινός, Apoc. iii. 7;
compare also Apoc. iii. 14 (vi. 10). For
ἀληθινός see John i. 9, iv. 23, xv. 1
notes. Comp. 1 Thess. i. 9 θεὸς ζῶν
καὶ ἀληθινός.

καί ἐσμεν...Ἰ. Χρ.] et simus (as depending on ut) in vero filio eius V.
St John adds a comment on what he
has just said. Christians are not only
enabled to gain a knowledge of God:
they are already in fellowship with
Him, 'in Him.' We are in Him
that is true, even in His Son, Jesus
Christ. The latter clause defines and
confirms the reality of the divine
fellowship. So far as Christians are
united with Christ, they are united
with God. His assumption of humanity
(Jesus Christ) explains how the union
is possible.

οὗτός ἐστιν...] As far as the gram-
matical construction of the sentence
is concerned the pronoun (οὗτος) may
refer either to 'Him that is true' or
to 'Jesus Christ.' The most natural
reference however is to the subject
not locally nearest but dominant in the
mind of the apostle (comp. c. ii. 22;
2 John 7; Acts iv. 11; vii. 19). This is
obviously 'He that is true' further
described by the addition of 'His
Son.' Thus the pronoun gathers up
the revelation indicated in the words
which precede (comp. John i. 2 note):
This Being—this One who is true,
who is revealed through and in His
Son, with whom we are united by
His Son—is the true God and life
eternal. In other words the revelation of God as Father in Christ
(comp. ii. 22 f.) satisfies, and can alone
satisfy, the need of man. To know

ὁ ἀληθινὸς θεὸς καὶ ζωὴ αἰώνιος.   ²¹ Τεκνία, φυλάξατε
ἑαυτὰ ἀπὸ τῶν εἰδώλων.

θεός: om. (Latt.).   ζωή al. ℵAB: ἡ ζ. al. ϚϚ: ἡ ζ. ἡ al. all.: +et resurrectio
nostra (Latt.).   21 ἑαυτά ℵ*B: ἑαυτούς ℵᶜA.   εἰδώλων: +ἀμὴν Ϛ.

God as Father is eternal life (John
xvii. 3); and so Christ has revealed
Him (c. i. 2).

ὁ ἀληθ. θ.] Comp. Is. lxv. 16 (LXX).
Compare the famous words of Ignatius : εἷς θεός ἐστι ὁ φανερώσας ἑαυτὸν
διὰ Ἰησοῦ Χριστοῦ τοῦ υἱοῦ αὐτοῦ, ὅς
ἐστιν αὐτοῦ λόγος ἀΐδιος, ἀπὸ σιγῆς
προελθών, ὃς κατὰ πάντα εὐηρέστησεν
τῷ πέμψαντι αὐτόν (ad Magn. viii.).

οὗτος...ζωὴ αἰών.] The phrase is not
exactly parallel with those which describe (as far as we can apprehend it)
the essential nature of God (John iv.
24, c. i. 5, iv. 8). See Additional Note
on iv. 8. It expresses His relation to
men, and so far is parallel with Hebr.
xii. 29 (Deut. iv. 24).
On 'Eternal life' see Additional
Note.

4. A final Warning (21).

From the thought of 'Him that is
true' St John turns almost of necessity
to the thought of the vain shadows
which usurp His place. In them the
world asserted its power. They forced
themselves into notice on every side
in innumerable shapes, and tempted
believers to fall away from the perfect
simplicity of faith. One sharp warning
therefore closes the Epistle of which
the main scope has been to deepen
the fellowship of man with God and
through God with man.

²¹ Little children, guard yourselves
from idols.

21. Τεκνία] Once again the anxiety
of the Apostle calls up the title of
affection which has not been used
since iv. 4. See ii. 1 note.

φυλάξατε ἑαυτά] custodite vos V.,

guard yourselves. The exact phrase
is not found again in the N. T. Compare τηρεῖν ἑαυτόν Jude 21 ; and with
an adj. James i. 27; 2 Cor. xi. 9 ; 1
Tim. v. 22. This 'guarding' of the
Christian answers to the 'keeping' of
Christ (v. 8). The use of the active
with the reflexive pronoun as distinguished from the middle (Lc. xii. 15
φυλάσσεσθε ἀπὸ π. πλεονεξίας) emphasises the duty of personal effort.
The use of the neuter (ἑαυτά) in direct
agreement with τεκνία seems to be
unique. For the use of ἑαυτά with
the second person see c. i. 8 n. The
aorist imp. (φυλάξατε) is remarkable :
compare 1 Pet. ii. 17 for its exact
force. Elsewhere in the Epistle (except iii. 1) St John always uses the
present.

ἀπὸ τῶν εἰδ.] a simulacris V. The
word εἴδωλον is comparatively in-
frequent in the N. T., and elsewhere
it is always used literally (e.g. 1 Thess.
i. 9). But 'idolatry' (Col. iii. 5) and
'idolater' (Eph. v. 5) have a wider
sense in St Paul; and the context
here seems to require a corresponding
extension of the meaning of the term.
An 'idol' is anything which occupies
the place due to God. The use of the
definite article calls up all the familiar
objects which fall under the title.
The command to Christians is not
generally to keep themselves from
such things as idols (ἀπὸ εἰδ.) but
from the well-known objects of a false
devotion. Compare 2 Cor. vi. 16 μετὰ
εἰδώλων with Rom. ii. 22 ὁ βδελυσσ.
τὰ εἴδωλα.

This comprehensive warning is probably the latest voice of Scripture.

Additional Note on v. 1.   *The use of the term 'the Christ.'*

The use
of the
term 'the
Christ' in
the Apo-
stolic age
not from
the Old
Testa-
ment.

The history of the title 'Messiah,' 'Christ' (הַמָּשִׁיחַ, ὁ χριστός, 'the Anointed One') is very remarkable.   It is not a characteristic title of the promised Saviour in the O. T.   It is not even specifically applied to Him, unless perhaps in Dan. ix. 25 f., a passage of which the interpretation is very doubtful.   And still in the apostolic age it was generally current among the Jews in Judæa, Galilee, Samaria, and in the Dispersion; and it was applied by them to the object of their religious and national hope (Matt. ii. 4, xvi. 16, xxii. 42; John i. 20, 41, iv. 25, xii. 34; Acts ix. 22, xvii. 3, xviii. 28, xxvi. 23).   The Hebrew word had been clothed in a Greek dress, and was current side by side with the Greek equivalent (Μεσσίας John i. 42, iv. 25).

The use
of the
term in
(i) the
Law,

The word מָשִׁיחַ, 'anointed,' occurs several times in the Book of Leviticus in the phrase הַכֹּהֵן הַמָּשִׁיחַ : Lev. iv. 3 (ὁ ἀρχιερεὺς ὁ κεχρισμένος), v. 16; vi. 15 (ὁ ἀρχ. ὁ χριστός).   Comp. 2 Macc. i. 10 (ἀπὸ τοῦ τῶν χριστῶν ἱερέων γένους).

(ii) the
Historical
Books,

In the Historical Books the word is used of the representative kings of the theocratic nation : Of Saul :

    1 Sam. xii. 3, 5 מְשִׁיחוֹ, ὁ χριστὸς αὐτοῦ.

    1 Sam. xxiv. 6, 11 ; xxvi. 16 ; 2 Sam. i. 14, 16 מְשִׁיחַ יְהוָה, LXX. ὁ χριστὸς κυρίου.

    1 Sam. xxvi. 9, 11, 23 מְשִׁיחַ יְהוָה, LXX. χριστὸς κυρίου.

    Comp. 2 Sam. i. 21 בְּלִי מָשִׁיחַ בַּשֶּׁמֶן, LXX. οὐκ ἐχρίσθη ἐν ἐλαίῳ.

Of David :

    1 Sam. xvi. 6 מְשִׁיחוֹ, LXX. ὁ χριστὸς αὐτοῦ.

    2 Sam. xix. 21 מְשִׁיחַ יְהוָה, LXX. ὁ χριστὸς κυρίου.

    2 Sam. xxiii. 1 מְשִׁיחַ אֱלֹהֵי יַעֲקֹב, LXX. χριστος θεοῦ Ἰακώβ.

    2 Sam. xxii. 51.

    Ps. xviii. 50.

Of Solomon :

    2 Chron. vi. 42 מְשִׁיחֶךָ, LXX. ὁ χριστός σου.

Of Jehu :

    2 Chron. xxii. 7 LXX. πρὸς Ἰηοὺ...χριστὸν κυρίου, אֲשֶׁר מְשָׁחוֹ יְהוָה.

    Compare the wider use in :

    1 Sam. ii. 10 יְהוָה...וְיָרֵם קֶרֶן מְשִׁיחוֹ, LXX. ὑψώσει κέρας χριστοῦ αὐτοῦ.

    „ ii. 35 לִפְנֵי מְשִׁיחִי, LXX. ἐνώπιον χριστῶν (χριστοῦ) μου.

    1 Chron. xvi. 22.

    Ps. cv. 15.

(iii) the
Prophets,

In the Prophets the word is used of Cyrus :

    Is. xlv. 1 כֹּה אָמַר יְהוָה לִמְשִׁיחוֹ לְכוֹרֶשׁ, LXX. οὕτως λέγει κύριος ὁ θεὸς τῷ χριστῷ μου Κύρῳ.

In the second passage where it occurs it is doubtful whether it is used in a personal or national sense:

Hab. iii. 13 לְיֵשַׁע אֶת־מְשִׁיחֶךָ, LXX. τοῦ σῶσαι τοὺς χριστούς σου.

It occurs twice in a difficult passage of the Book of Daniel:

Dan. ix. 25 מָשִׁיחַ נָגִיד,   Theod. χριστὸς ἡγούμενος.

„   26 יִכָּרֵת מָשִׁיחַ,   Theod. ἐξολεθρεύσεται χρίσμα.

Compare also:

Amos iv. 13 LXX. ἀπαγγέλλων τὸν χριστὸν αὐτοῦ.

Hebr. מַגִּיד...מַה־שֵּׂחוֹ.

In the Psalms the Divine King who is the type of 'the Christ' is spoken (iv) the of as 'the anointed of the Lord'; and there can be no doubt that it was Hagio-from the Psalms, and especially from Ps. ii., that the word passed into grapha. common use in the special technical sense.

Ps. ii. 2 עַל יְהֹוָה וְעַל מְשִׁיחוֹ, LXX. κατὰ τοῦ κυρίου καὶ κατὰ τοῦ χριστοῦ αὐτοῦ.

Ps. xviii. 50 לִמְשִׁיחוֹ לְדָוִד, LXX. τῷ χριστῷ αὐτοῦ τῷ Δαυείδ.

Ps. xx. 6 מְשִׁיחוֹ, LXX. (ἔσωσεν κύριος) τὸν χριστὸν αὐτοῦ.

Ps. xxviii. 8 מָעוֹז יְשׁוּעוֹת מְשִׁיחוֹ הוּא, LXX. ὑπερασπιστὴς τῶν σωτηρίων τοῦ χριστοῦ αὐτοῦ ἐστίν.

So Ps. lxxxix. 38, 51, cxxxii. 10, 17.

Compare Ps. lxxxiv. 10 מְשִׁיחֶךָ, אֱלֹהִים, LXX. ὁ θεός...τὸν χριστόν σου.

It occurs in the plural:

Ps. cv. 15, 1 Chron. xvi. 22 מְשִׁיחָי, LXX. οἱ χριστοί μου.

The full phrase is found:

Lam. iv. 20 מְשִׁיחַ יְהֹוָה, LXX. χριστὸς κύριος.

Compare Luke ii. 11.

It will be observed that in all these passages, with the exception of those in Leviticus, 2 Sam. i. 21, Dan. ix. 25 f., the Anointed One is always spoken of as the Anointed of the Lord or of God.

The title χριστός occurs in connexion with κύριος Ecclus. xlvi. 19 The use of ἐπεμαρτύρατο ἔναντι κυρίου καὶ χριστοῦ.   the term in later

It occurs several times also in the *Psalms of Solomon:*   books.

xvii. 36 (there shall be no unrighteousness, because) πάντες ἅγιοι Psalms of καὶ βασιλεὺς αὐτῶν χριστὸς κύριος.   Solomon.

xviii. 8 (happy are they who are) ὑπὸ ῥάβδον παιδείας χριστοῦ κυρίου ἐν φόβῳ θεοῦ αὐτοῦ ἐν σοφίᾳ πνεύματος καὶ δικαιοσύνης καὶ ἰσχύος.

xviii. 6 ... εἰς ἡμέραν ἐκλογῆς ἐν ἀνάξει χριστοῦ αὐτοῦ (τοῦ θεοῦ).

It is found in the Book of Henoch: Henoch.

c. 48, 10...they have denied the Lord of Spirits and His Anointed.

c. 52, 4 All these things which thou hast seen minister to the rule of His Anointed that he may be strong and mighty upon the earth.

And it occurs twice in the Targum of Onkelos on the Pentateuch: Targums.

Gen. xlix. 10 עַד דְּיֵיתֵי מְשִׁיחָא דְּדִילֵיהּ הִיא מַלְכוּתָא, *until Messiah come, whose is the kingdom.*

Num. xxiv. 17 כד־יקום מלכא מיעקב ויתרבא משיחא מישׂראל, *when a king shall arise from Jacob, and a Christ from Israel shall rule.*

and commonly in the Targum of Jonathan.　Comp. Buxtorf *Lex.* s. v.

It may be added that it is found also in 4 Esdras vii. 28 f. *my Son Christ* (comp. xii. 32).

And in the Apocalypse of Baruch: cc. xxiv, xxx, xxxix, xl, lxx, lxxii.

The use of the term in the New Testament a result of the study of Old Testament.　From this general view of the use of the word it appears that the limited application of the title to the Divine King and Saviour of Israel is, with the possible exception of the passage of Daniel, post-Biblical.　And it is likely that the combination of the ideas of a coming of the Lord to judgment and of the establishment of a Divine Kingdom in Daniel served to concentrate attention on the scriptural language in regard to 'the Anointed of the Lord' (Luke ii. 26) which was seen to transcend any past application.　Thus it could not but be felt that every one anointed to a special function in the divine economy pointed to One greater in whom all that he foreshadowed should find a final accomplishment.　The offices of king and priest and prophet were concentrated upon 'the Christ'; and now one office and now the other became predominant according to the tempers of men.

Use of the term by St John.　With regard to the usage of St John it may be observed that ὁ χριστός is without question uniformly an appellative ('the Christ,' 'the Anointed') in the Gospel: i. 20, 25, iii. 28, iv. 29, vii. 26 f., 31, 41 f., x. 24, xi. 27, xii. 34, xx. 31 (compare also the use of χριστός: i. 41, iv. 25, ix. 22).　So it is also in the first epistle: ii. 22, v. 1.　This large collection of examples seems to decide that the same sense must be adopted in 2 John 9; Apoc. xx. 4, 6, where otherwise the title might have seemed to be a proper name.

Additional Note on v. 6.　References to the facts of the Gospel.

Reference to the fact of the Gospel in the Epistles of St John.　The Epistles of St John are permeated with the thoughts of the Person and work of Christ but direct references to the facts of the Gospel are singularly rare in them.　In the third Epistle there is nothing in the language which is distinctively Christian except the pregnant reference to 'the Name' (*v.* 7).　The Baptism is not spoken of plainly ; nor yet any one of the crucial events of the Life of the Lord which were included in the earliest Confessions of faith, the Birth of the Virgin Mary, the Crucifixion, the Resurrection, the Ascension, the Session at the right hand of the Father, the Coming to Judgment.

But though these facts are not expressly mentioned they are all implied, and interpreted.　Without them the arguments and language of St John are unintelligible.

(1)　The Birth of the Virgin Mary : iv. 2 *Jesus Christ came in flesh.*

(2)　The Baptism : v. 6 *This is He that came by water.*

(3) The Passion: iii. 16 *He laid down His life for us*—v. 6 *This is He that came...by blood.*

(4) The Resurrection, Ascension and Session at the right hand of the Father: ii. 1 *we have an Advocate with the Father, Jesus Christ.* Comp. 2 John 7...*confess that Jesus Christ cometh in flesh ;* 1 John i. 3.

(5) The coming to Judgment: ii. 28 *that we may have boldness and not be ashamed before Him at His presence ;* iii. 2 *If He should be manifested we shall be like Him, for we shall see Him as He is.* 2 John 7.

In addition to these allusions to articles of the Baptismal Creed the first Epistle assumes a general knowledge of the Life and Teaching of Christ: ii. 6 *He that saith he abideth in Him ought himself also to walk even as He walked;* iii. 1 *The world knoweth us not because it knew Him not ;* ii. 25 *the promise which He promised;* iii. 23 *as He gave us commandment.* Compare also i. 1 note.

The revelation of the purpose and issue of Christ's work is made with singular fulness :

iii. 5 *He was manifested to take away sins.*

— 8 *The Son of God was manifested that He might destroy the works of the devil.*

iv. 9 [*God*] *hath sent His Son, His only Son, that we may live through Him.*

— 10 [*God*] *sent His Son, as a propitiation for our sins.* Comp. ii. 2.

— 14 *The Father hath sent the Son as Saviour of the world.*

v. 20 *The Son of God is come and hath given us an understanding that we may know Him that is true.*

Comp. i. 7 ; v. 18.

Additional Note on the readings in v. 6 f.

The variations of the three chief Greek MSS in the passage οὗτος...μαρτυροῦντες deserve to be studied in detail. Happily in this case the common text follows in the main that of B.

B.	ℵ.	A.
οὗτός ἐστιν ὁ ἐλθὼν	οὗτός ἐστιν ὁ ἐλθὼν	οὗτός ἐστιν ὁ ἐλθὼν
δι' ὕδατος καὶ αἵματος	διὰ ὕδατος καὶ αἵματος	δι' ὕδατος καὶ αἵματος
	καὶ πνεύματος	καὶ πνεύματος
Ἰησοῦς Χριστός·	Ἰησοῦς Χριστός·	Ἰησοῦς Χριστός·
οὐκ ἐν τῷ ὕδατι μόνῳ	οὐκ ἐν τῷ ὕδατι μόνον	οὐκ ἐν τῷ ὕδατι μόνον
ἀλλ' ἐν τῷ ὕδατι	ἀλλ' ἐν τῷ ὕδατι	ἀλλὰ ἐν τῷ ὕδατι
καὶ ἐν τῷ αἵματι	καὶ τῷ αἵματι	καὶ ἐν τῷ πνεύματι
καὶ τὸ πνεῦμα...	καὶ τὸ πνεῦμα...	καὶ τὸ πνεῦμα...
ὅτι τρεῖς εἰσιν	ὅτι οἱ τρεῖς εἰσιν	ὅτι τρεῖς εἰσὶν
οἱ μαρτυροῦντες...	οἱ μαρτυροῦντες...	οἱ μαρτυροῦντες...

For τὸ πνεῦμα the Latin Vulgate gives *Christus*.

Additional Note on the readings in v. 7, 8.

The interpolated gloss.

The words which are interpolated in the common Greek text in this passage (ἐν τῷ οὐρανῷ ὁ πατὴρ ὁ λόγος καὶ τὸ ἅγιον πνεῦμα· καὶ οὗτοι οἱ τρεῖς ἕν εἰσι. καὶ τρεῖς εἰσιν οἱ μαρτυροῦντες ἐν τῇ γῇ) offer an instructive illustration of the formation and introduction of a gloss into the apostolic text without any signs of bad faith. Happily the gloss was confined within narrow limits till the age of printing. If it had been known in the East in the sixth or seventh century, it is not rash to suppose that it would have found wide acceptance just as it did in the printed editions of the Greek text, and the evidence would have been complicated though essentially unchanged. In this respect the history of the Vulgate reading is of singular importance. The mass of later Latin copies which contain the interpolation obviously add nothing to the evidence in favour of the authenticity of the words, and do not even tend to shew that they formed part of Jerome's text.

The state of the external evidence can be summed up very briefly.

Summary of external evidence.

The words are not found

(1) In any independent Greek MS (more than 180 MSS and 50 lectionaries are quoted). Both the late MSS which contain it have unquestionably been modified by the Latin Vulgate [1].

(2) In any independent Greek writer. The very few Greek writers who make use of the words derived their knowledge of them from the Latin (not in Ir Cl.Al Orig Did Athan Bas Greg.Naz Cyr.Al) [2].

(3) In any Latin Father earlier than Victor Vitensis or Vigilius Tapsensis (not in Tert Cypr Hil Ambr Hier Aug Leo I [3]).

(4) In any ancient version except the Latin; and it was not found (*a*) in the Old Latin in its early form (Tert Cypr Aug), or (*b*) in the Vulgate as issued by Jerome (*Codd. am fuld*) or (*c*) as revised by Alcuin (*Cod. vallicell**) [4].

On the other hand the gloss is found from the sixth century in Latin Fathers; and it is found also in two copies which give an old Latin text, in some early copies of the Vulgate and in the great mass of the later copies and in the Clementine text.

It becomes of interest therefore to observe how the words originally

[1] The *Codex Ravianus* which was formerly quoted as a MS authority has been shewn to be a copy made from printed texts, chiefly from the Complutensian, which it follows in this passage. Comp. Griesbach, N.T. I. ii. *App.* 4 f. The clause is also written on the margin of a Naples MS 173 'manu recenti, unius ut mihi videtur ex bibliothecariis, sæc. fine 17' (Tischdf.).

[2] The gloss of Claudius Apollinaris, quoted in the note on the text, shews that he connected 'the word' and 'the spirit' with *v.* 8 in a different sense.

[3] Compare Griesbach *l. c.* 13 ff.

[4] The words are found in the Theodulfian Recension (Paris *Bibl. Nat.* Lat. 9380) in the following form: quia tres sunt qui testimonium dant in terra spiritus aqua et sanguis et tres unum sunt; et tres sunt qui testimonium dicunt in cælo pater *et filius*, et spiritus sanctus et hi tres unum sunt (Prof. Wordsworth).

found a place in the Latin texts, and were carried from that source into the Greek text, and into the printed editions of other versions.

The words are not, as has been already stated, found in any early Latin Father; but a passage of Cyprian, which shews that he was not acquainted with them as part of the apostolic text, shews at the same time how natural it was to form a distinct gloss on *v.* 7 according to their tenor: Dicit dominus : *Ego et Pater unum sumus;* et iterum *de* Patre et Filio et Spiritu Sancto scriptum est; *et tres unum sunt* (*de Eccles. unit.* c. 6; comp. *auct. de rebapt.* cc. 15, 19). The force of this application of 'the spirit and the water and the blood' with the false reading 'unum sunt' for 'in unum sunt' (εἰς τὸ ἕν εἰσιν) is made clear by a later reference to it in Facundus:...De Patre et Filio et Spiritu Sancto sic dicit : *Tres sunt qui testimonium dant in terra, spiritus, aqua et sanguis, et hi tres unum sunt;* in spiritu significans Patrem, sicut Dominus mulieri Samaritanæ... loquitur...in aqua vero Spiritum Sanctum significans sicut in eodem Evangelio exponit (John vii. 37)...in sanguine vero Filium...Quod... Johannis apostoli testimonium beatus Cyprianus...in epistola sive libro quem de Unitate scripsit de Patre Filio et Spiritu Sancto dictum intelligit (*Pro def. tr. Cap.* i. 3). The same mystical interpretation is found in Augustine (*c. Maxim.* ii. 22), and Eucherius (*Instruc.* i. *ad loc.* Migne, *Patr. Lat.* l. 810); and Augustine supplies the word 'Verbum,' which is required to complete the gloss : Deus itaque summus et verus cum Verbo suo et Spiritu Sancto, quæ tria unum sunt, Deus unus et omnipotens (*de Civ.* v. 11[1]).

The gloss which had thus become an established interpretation of St John's words is first quoted as part of the Epistle in a group of writings which come from Africa in the last quarter of the fifth century :

(1) Ut adhuc luce clarius unius divinitatis esse cum Patre et Filio Spiritum Sanctum doceamus, Joannis Evangelistæ testimonio comprobatur. Ait namque *Tres sunt qui testimonium perhibent in cælo, Pater, Verbum et Spiritus Sanctus, et hi tres unum sunt* (*Prof. Fid.* ap. Vict. Vit. *de Persec. Vand.* iii. 11[2]).

(2) Pater est ingenitus, filius vero sine initio genitus a patre est, spiritus autem sanctus processit (Casp. procedit ?) a patre et accipit de filio

The origin of the Latin gloss.

The gloss inserted in the text.

---

[1] It is by no means unlikely that the mystical interpretation of *v.* 8 may have taken a definite shape in Africa from a very early time. The language of Tertullian, which shews conclusively that he was not acquainted with the words *tres unum sunt* as a scriptural phrase, indicates the beginning of its growth: *adv. Prax.* 25...connexus patris in filio et filii in paracleto, tres efficit cohærentes, alterum ex altero. Qui tres unum sunt non unus ; quomodo dictum est *ego et pater unum sumus* (John x. 30) ad substantiæ unitatem, non ad numeri singularitatem. It is possible that the gloss may have found a place in copies of the Latin Version as soon as it was definitely shaped; but there is no evidence that it was found in the text of St John before the latter part of the 5th century.

[2] The authorship of this 'Exposition of the Faith' is uncertain. It is perhaps a later addition to the history of Victor (Papencordt, *Gesch. d. Vand. Herrsch.* 369 n.); but in no case does it prove more than that the words were found in the copy of the Epistle used by the writer.

sicut evangelista testatur, quia scriptum est: Tres sunt qui dicunt testimonium in cœlo, pater, verbum et spiritus, et hæc tria unum sunt, in Christo Jesu. Non tamen dixit: unus est in Christo Jesu[1].

It was not unnatural that in the stress of the Arian persecution words which were held to give the plain meaning of St John's words as they were read should find their way from the margin into the text, or if they had already obtained a place in the text of any copies should gain wider currency. But still the form is fluent:

(3) [Johannes Evangelista] ad Parthos: *Tres sunt,* inquit, *qui testimonium perhibent in terra, aqua sanguis et caro, et tres in nobis sunt; et tres sunt qui testimonium perhibent in cœlo, Pater Verbum et Spiritus...et hi (ii) tres unum sunt (c. Varim.* 5). And again:

(4)...dicente Joanne Evangelista in epistola sua: *Tres sunt qui testimonium dicunt in cœlo, Pater et Verbum et Spiritus; et in Christo Jesu unum sunt,* non tamen unus est, quia non est in his una persona (*de Trin.* i. p. 206; Migne, *Patr. Lat.* lxii. 243).

From this time the words seem to have maintained partially their position in the text. They are quoted by Fulgentius (c. 550) as St John's in the form: *Tres sunt qui testimonium perhibent in cœlo, Pater, Verbum et Spiritus; et tres unum sunt (Resp. c. Arian.* p. 68, Migne, *Patr. Lat.* lxv. 224); though the same writer in another place (*c. Fabian. fragm.*) speaks of the application of the clause *et tres unum sunt* to 'the Father, Son and Holy Spirit' as established by argument, a process wholly unnecessary if the gloss had been admitted as part of the text.

On the other hand the language of Cassiodorus (c. 550) seems to me to shew that he did not find the gloss in his text of St John, though he accepted it as a true interpretation of the apostle's words. Cui rei [quia Jesus est Christus], he writes, testificantur in terra tria mysteria, aqua sanguis et spiritus, quæ in passione Domini leguntur impleta; in cælo autem Pater et Filius et Spiritus Sanctus; et hi tres unus est Deus (*Complex. in Epp. ad loc.* Migne, *Patr. Lat.* lxx. pp. 1372 f.)[2].

Expressly affirmed to be authentic.
Not long afterwards the addition was expressly defended in 'a Prologue to the seven canonical Epistles' issued under the name of Jerome, which seems to have been written with this express purpose: [In prima Johannis Epistola] ab infidelibus translatoribus multum erratum esse a fidei veritate comperimus, trium tantum vocabula, hoc est, aquæ sanguinis et spiritus, in ipsa sua editione ponentibus et Patris, Verbique ac Spiritus testimonium omittentibus; in quo maxime et fides catholica roboratur et Patris ac Filii ac Spiritus Sancti una divinitatis substantia comprobatur (Migne, *Patrol. Lat.* xxix. 829 f.).

This Prologue is found in one of the earliest copies of the Vulgate (*Codex Fuldensis*) written in 546, though the gloss itself is not found in the text of the Epistle.

---

[1] This remarkable form of the gloss has been printed by Caspari in an *Expositio fidei* preserved in the Ambrosian MS which contains also the Muratorian fragment on the Canon (*Kirchen-*   hist. Anecdota, pp. xxiv. 305 and notes).

[2] The passage of Cassiodorus is well discussed by Bp Turton in his *Vindication of Porson*, pp. 279 ff.

But the gloss is found in early MSS both of the Old Latin and of the The earliest Vulgate, and in substantially the same form, so that it must have been MS au- introduced into both from the same source. These are (*a*) (of the old Latin) thority a *Speculum* (a classified series of Scriptural passages) *m* (sæc. viii. or ix.) for it. and a Munich fragment *q* (*cod. Fris.* sæc. vi. or vii.); (*b*) of the Vulgate, the Spanish (Visigothic) MSS *Cod. Cav.* (sæc. ix.) and *Cod. Tol.* (sæc. x.).

The whole passage appears in these authorities in the following form:

Cod. Fris.[1]	*Spec. (m).*	*Codd. Cav. Tol.*
quoniam tr	*quoniam* tres sunt qui testimonium *dicunt*	*quia* tres sunt qui testimonium *dant*
in terra	in terra	in terra
spiritus *et* aqua et sa	spiritus aqua et sanguis;	spiritus *et* aqua et sanguis;
	et hi tres unum sunt in Christo Jesu.	et hi tres unum sunt in Christo Jesu.
	Et tres sunt	et (om *Tol*) tres sunt
tificantur	qui testimonium dicunt	qui testimonium dicunt
in caelo	in caelo	in caelo
pater *e*	Pater verbum et spiritus	pater verbum et spiritus
tres unum sunt.	et hi tres unum sunt.	et hi tres unum sunt.

Here, it will be observed, the testimony on earth is placed first, so that the heavenly testimony retains its position as an interpretative gloss[2]. And there is also a second similar though shorter gloss *in Christo Jesu* which is even older than that which follows; for it is indicated in the Latin translation of the *Outlines* of Clement of Alexandria: *et hi tres unum sunt:* in salvatore quippe istæ sunt virtutes salutiferæ, et vita ipsa in ipso Filio ejus existit (p. 1011 P.).

After a time the second gloss *in Christo Jesu* was omitted; and the Modifica- two clauses were transposed; so that the passage assumed the form which tion of the was generally current in the fourteenth and fifteenth centuries, and was text. finally pronounced authentic in the Sixtine and Clementine editions of the Vulgate. The main forms in which the passage appears in the Latin texts are given in the following table:

---

[1] The MS is unfortunately mutilated. About half of each line is lost. The lines of the MS so far as they are preserved run thus:

> quiaspsestueritas qmtr
> in terra . spsetaquaetsa
> tificanturincaelop tere
> tresunumsunt sitestim

There is room in each line for about 21 more letters. It is not possible therefore that the words *et hi tres unum sunt in Christo Jesu* could have formed part of the text. It is further to be noticed that this MS reads *spiritus* in *v.* 6 for *Christus*.

[2] Another form of the reading preserved in the St Gall MS: Quia tres sunt qui testimonium dant spiritus et aqua et sanguis, et tres unum sunt. *Sicut* in cælo tres sunt, Pater Verbum et Spiritus, et tres unum sunt (Dobbin, *Codex Montfort.* p. 45), points clearly to the original gloss-form of the addition. This reading is given in a MS in the British Museum (Add. 11,852. See Dict. of Bible, *Vulgate*, p. 1713 n. q). A Greek MS has notes in v. 8 τουτέστι τὸ πνεῦμα τὸ ἅγιον καὶ ὁ πατὴρ καὶ αὐτὸς ἑαυτοῦ and on ἕν εἰσι: τουτέστι μία θεότης, εἷς θεός (Tischdf. ad loc.).

Cod. Cav.	*Cod. Vallicell.***	Common Text.
quia tres sunt qui testimonium dant in *terra,* spiritus et aqua et sanguis; et *hi* tres unum sunt *in Christo Jesu* et tres sunt qui testimonium *dicunt* in *caelo,* pater verbum et spiritus; et hi tres unum sunt.	*quoniam* tres sunt qui testimonium dant in *terra,* spiritus aqua et sanguis; et tres unum sunt *sicut* tres sunt qui testimonium *dant* in *caelo,* pater verbum et spiritus sanctus; et tres unum sunt.	*quoniam* tres sunt qui testimonium dant in *caelo,* pater verbum et spiritus sanctus; et *hi* tres unum sunt. et tres sunt qui testimonium *dant* in *terra,* spiritus et aqua et sanguis; et hi tres unum sunt[1].

The first appearance of the words in Greek.

Here the history of the Latin interpolation ends: we have to notice how it passed into the Greek text. It appears first in a Greek version of the Acts of the Council of Lateran held in 1215, coeval with the Council. The Latin text is: Quemadmodum in canonica Johannis epistola legitur: *Quia tres sunt qui testimonium dant in cœlo, Pater, Verbum et Spiritus Sanctus; et hi tres unum sunt.* Statimque subjungitur: *et tres sunt qui testimonium dant in terra, spiritus aqua et sanguis; et tres unum sunt,* sicut in quibusdam codicibus legitur[2]. For this the corresponding Greek, as far as it has been preserved, is: ὃν τρόπον ἐν τῇ κανονικῇ τοῦ Ἰωάννου ἐπιστολῇ ἀναγινώσκεται ὅτι τρεῖς εἰσιν οἱ μαρτυροῦντες ἐν οὐρανῷ, ὁ πατὴρ, λόγος καὶ πνεῦμα ἅγιον· καὶ τοῦτοι (sic) οἱ τρεῖς ἕν εἰσιν. εὐθύς τε προστίθησι *** καθὼς ἕν τισι κώδηξιν εὑρίσκεται.

The clause was quoted afterwards incompletely by Manuel Calecas (sæc. xiv.), and perhaps by Jos. Bryennius (sæc. xv.), who both wrote under Latin influence; and at last it found a place in a Græco-Latin MS of the Epistle (*Cod. Vat. Ottob.* 162) of the fifteenth century, and in a Greek MS of the sixteenth century (*Cod. Montfort. Dubl.* 34, the *Codex Britannicus* of Erasmus). The Greek text in both these MSS has been adapted in other places to the Latin Vulgate; and in this passage both follow a late Latin text in omitting the εἰς τὸ ἕν εἰσι after the earthly witness. The language of both, especially that of *Cod. Montfort.*, shews decisively that the Greek is a translation of the Latin[3].

The passage is thus given in the two MSS:

[1] This last clause is omitted in many late MSS. Some account of the Latin MSS known up to his time is given by Bp Turton, *l. c.* pp. 141 f. Griesbach *l. c.* 12 calculates that the gloss is omitted by 50—60 MSS of the Vulgate. In collections which he mentions it is omitted by 18 MSS out of an aggregate of 234.

[2] This remark refers to the last words *et tres unum sunt* which were omitted by many late MSS of the Vulgate.

[3] It has been shewn by Dr Dobbin that *Cod. Montf.* is 'a transcript with arbitrary and fanciful variations' of the MS in Lincoln College, Oxford 39, in which the gloss is not found (*Codex Montfortianus*, p. 57).

Cod. Montf. (34).		Cod. Vat. Ottob. (162).
ὅτι τρεῖς εἰσὶν	quia tres sunt	ὅτι τρεῖς εἰσὶν
οἱ μαρτυροῦντες	qui testimonium dant	οἱ μαρτυροῦντες
ἐν τῷ οὐρανῷ,	in caelo,	ἀπὸ τοῦ οὐρανοῦ,
πατὴρ λόγος καὶ πνεῦμα	pater verbum et spiri-	πατὴρ λόγος καὶ πνεῦμα
ἅγιον·	tus sanctus:	ἅγιον·
καὶ οὗτοι οἱ τρεῖς	et hi tres	καὶ οἱ τρεῖς
ἕν εἰσι·	unum sunt.	εἰς τὸ ἕν εἰσι·
καὶ τρεῖς εἰσὶν	et tres sunt	καὶ τρεῖς εἰσὶν
οἱ μαρτυροῦντες	qui testimonium dant	οἱ μαρτυροῦντες
ἐν τῇ γῇ,	in terra,	ἐπὶ τῆς γῆς,
πνεῦμα ὕδωρ καὶ αἷμα·	spiritus aqua et san-	τὸ πνεῦμα τὸ ὕδωρ καὶ
	guis	τὸ αἷμα·
εἰ τὴν μαρτυρίαν...	si testimonium.	εἰ τὴν μαρτυρίαν...

The Complutensian editors introduced another translation of the Vulgate similar to that in *Cod.* 162, into their text[1]. Meanwhile Erasmus had published his first edition giving the whole passage as he found it in his Greek MS with the note: In Græco codice tantum hoc reperio de testimonio triplici ὅτι τρεῖς εἰσὶν οἱ μαρτυροῦντες τὸ πνεῦμα καὶ τὸ ὕδωρ καὶ τὸ αἷμα; and on the clause *et hi tres unum sunt*, which he retained in his translation, he writes: *Hi* redundat : Neque est *unum* sed *in unum*, εἰς τὸ αὐτό. i. sive *in idem*. In his third edition, in fulfilment of a promise which he had made to insert the clause if it could be shewn to exist in a single Greek MS, he inserted the words on the authority of the *Cod. Montfort.* retaining however the words καὶ οἱ τρεῖς εἰς τὸ ἕν εἰσιν. *(margin: The introduction of the gloss into the printed Greek text.)*

The words were afterwards brought into a more correct shape without any manuscript authority; and at last the passage assumed the form which is given in the texts of Stephanus in 1550 and Elzevir of 1633 ('text. rec.'), and from them has assumed general currency.

The chief forms in which the whole passage appears in early printed texts are given in the following table:

Erasm. Ed. 1, 1516.	Erasm. Ed. 3, 1522.	Erasm. Ed. 4, 1527.
ὅτι τρεῖς εἰσὶν	ὅτι τρεῖς εἰσὶν	ὅτι τρεῖς εἰσὶν
οἱ μαρτυροῦντες	οἱ μαρτυροῦντες	οἱ μαρτυροῦντες
* *	ἐν τῷ οὐρανῷ,	ἐν τῷ οὐρανῷ,
* *	πατὴρ λόγος καὶ	ὁ πατὴρ, ὁ λόγος, καὶ
	πνεῦμα ἅγιον·	τὸ πνεῦμα ἅγιον·
* *	καὶ οὗτοι οἱ τρεῖς	καὶ οὗτοι οἱ τρεῖς
* *	ἕν εἰσι.	ἕν εἰσι.
* *	καὶ τρεῖς εἰσὶν	καὶ τρεῖς εἰσὶν
* *	οἱ μαρτυροῦντες	οἱ μαρτυροῦντες
	ἐν τῇ γῇ	ἐν τῇ γῇ,
τὸ πνεῦμα καὶ τὸ ὕδωρ	πνεῦμα καὶ ὕδωρ καὶ	πνεῦμα καὶ ὕδωρ καὶ
καὶ τὸ αἷμα·	αἷμα·	αἷμα·
καὶ οἱ τρεῖς	καὶ οἱ τρεῖς	καὶ οἱ τρεῖς
εἰς τὸ ἕν εἰσιν.	εἰς τὸ ἕν εἰσιν.	εἰς τὸ ἕν εἰσιν.
εἰ τὴν μαρτυρίαν...	εἰ τὴν μαρτυρίαν...	εἰ τὴν μαρτυρίαν...

[1] The ἀπὸ τοῦ οὐρανοῦ in the Greek text of *Cod.* 162 is very peculiar. Is it possible that ἐπί has been misread ἀπό, as was done in the corresponding clause, and that the translator intended ἐπὶ τοῦ οὐρανοῦ to answer exactly to ἐπὶ τῆς γῆς?

Ed. Compl. 1514 (Cod. Rav.).	Erasm. Ed. 3, 1522.	Ed. Steph. 1550; Elz. 1633 (text rec.).
ὅτι τρεῖς εἰσὶν οἱ μαρτυροῦντες ἐν τῷ οὐρανῷ ὁ πατὴρ καὶ ὁ λόγος καὶ 　τὸ ἅγιον πνεῦμα καὶ οἱ τρεῖς εἰς τὸ ἕν εἰσι. καὶ τρεῖς εἰσὶν οἱ μαρτυροῦντες ἐπὶ τῆς γῆς τὸ πνεῦμα καὶ τὸ ὕδωρ 　καὶ τὸ αἷμα[1]. 　　＊　＊ 　　　＊　＊ εἰ τὴν μαρτυρίαν...	ὅτι τρεῖς εἰσὶν οἱ μαρτυροῦντες ἐν τῷ οὐρανῷ πατὴρ λόγος καὶ πνεῦ- 　μα ἅγιον καὶ οὗτοι οἱ τρεῖς ἕν εἰσι. καὶ τρεῖς εἰσὶν οἱ μαρτυροῦντες ἐν τῇ γῇ πνεῦμα καὶ ὕδωρ καὶ 　αἷμα. καὶ οἱ τρεῖς εἰς τὸ ἕν εἰσιν. εἰ τὴν μαρτυρίαν...	ὅτι τρεῖς εἰσὶν οἱ μαρτυροῦντες ἐν τῷ οὐρανῷ ὁ πατὴρ ὁ λόγος καὶ τὸ 　ἅγιον πνεῦμα καὶ οὗτοι οἱ τρεῖς ἕν εἰσι. καὶ τρεῖς εἰσὶν οἱ μαρτυροῦντες ἐν τῇ γῇ τὸ πνεῦμα καὶ τὸ ὕδωρ 　καὶ τὸ αἷμα. καὶ οἱ τρεῖς εἰς τὸ ἕν εἰσι. εἰ τὴν μαρτυρίαν...

When the gloss had gained a place in the Greek text it naturally influenced the texts of other versions. Gutbir and Schaaf introduced with very slight modifications a translation which had been made by Tremellius into their printed texts of the Peshito[2]. It was introduced into editions of the Armenian and Slavonic Versions; and into the modern European versions.

The supposed dogmatic importance of the gloss has given a value to the evidence in its favour out of all proportion to its critical weight. The MS authority, for example, for the spurious *Epistle to the Laodicenes* is essentially the same. This also is supported by *m*, and by the *La Cava* and *Toledo* MSS and by a multitude of later MSS of the Vulgate. In the preceding verse (*v.* 6) of the Epistle almost all Latin authorities read *Christus*

---

[1] A note is added which seems to shew that the editors found the following clause καὶ—εἰσίν in their Greek MSS: Sanctus Thomas in expositione secundæ decretalis de sermone Trinitate et Fide Catholica tractans istum passum contra Abbatem Joachim viz. *Tres sunt qui testimonium dant in cælo, pater verbum et spiritus sanctus,* dicit ad litteram verba sequentia. Et ad insinuandam unitatem trium personarum subditur, *et hii tres unum sunt.* Quod quidem dicitur propter essentiæ unitatem. Sed hoc Joachim perverse trahere volens ad unitatem charitatis et consensus inducebat consequentem auctoritatem. Nam subditur ibidem: *et tres sunt qui testimonium dant in terra S. spiritus aqua et sanguis.* Et in quibusdam libris additur: *et hii tres unum sunt.* Sed hoc in veris exemplaribus non habetur: sed dicitur esse appositum ab hæreticis Arrianis ad pervertendum intellectum sanum auctoritatis præmissæ de unitate essentiæ trium personarum. Hæc beatus Thomas ubi supra.

This is, as far as I have observed, the only note of the kind in the New Testament. The treatment of the passage is wholly exceptional; for elsewhere the Edition marks prominently in the Greek text the absence of Latin additions: *e.g.* Acts viii. 37, ix. 5, 6, x. 6, xiv. 7, xv. 41; 1 John ii. 23; 2 John 11; and conversely the absence of words found in the Greek text from the Latin: *e.g.* Acts x. 21, 32, xv. 24; 1 Pet. iii. 12, iv. 14; 1 John v. 13.

[2] Gutbir's note is worth quoting: Cum notum sit Arrianos nec ipsi Græco Textui nec Versionibus Orientalibus hic pepercisse, ex Notis Tremellii hunc versum in aliis E. E. desideratum adscripsimus. Schaaf's note is to the same effect.

for *Spiritus* (τὸ πνεῦμα). A remarkable group of ancient authorities of the same type including *Cod. Tol.* add to c. ii. 17 *quomodo Deus manet in æternum.* In c. v. 20, *m* and *Cod. Tol.*, with Hilary substantially, add a clause very similar in character to the gloss on *v.* 8; and in the same verse *m Cod. Montf.* with the Lat vg (Hil Ambr Vigil Fulg Leo) read *simus* (ὦμεν).

It will also have been observed that the gloss itself sprang from a false reading *unum* for *in unum,* a change due to an omission which was equally easy in Greek (τρεῖς εἰς) and in Latin.

Additional Note on v. 16. Sin unto death.

The phrase 'sin unto death' is introduced as one which was familiar to the readers of the Epistle and is evidently borrowed from current language. And so in fact the distinction of 'sins unto death' and 'sins not unto death' is common among Rabbinic writers (Schoettgen *ad loc.*) and represents, it cannot be doubted, an old traditional view. *[The phrase 'sin unto death' in use among Jews.]*

1. In the first and simplest sense a 'sin unto death' would be a sin requiring the punishment of natural death: comp. Num. xviii. 22 ἁμαρτία θανατηφόρος[1]. Death in such a case was final exclusion from the Divine Society. *[A sin punishable by death.]*

2. It was a natural extension of this meaning when the phrase was used for an offence which was reckoned by moral judgment to belong to the same class. Words very closely resembling those of St John are used *Test. xii. Patr.* Issach. 7 οὐκ ἔγνων ἐν ἐμοὶ (al. ἐπ' ἐμέ) ἁμαρτίαν εἰς (for πρὸς) θάνατον. Comp. 1 Cor. v. 11. *[A sin of the same class.]*

3. If now the same line of thought is extended to the Christian Society, it will appear that a sin which in its very nature excludes from fellowship with Christians would be rightly spoken of as a 'sin unto death.' Such a sin may be seen in hatred of the brethren (c. iii. 15), or in the selfishness which excludes repentance, the condition of forgiveness (i. 7), or in the faithlessness which denies Christ, the One Advocate (*v.* 21; iv. 2). But in each case the character of the sin is determined by the effect which it has on the relation of the doer to God through Christ in the Divine Society. We are not to think of specific acts, defined absolutely, but of acts as the revelation of moral life. *[A sin carrying exclusion from the Christian society if persisted in.]*

4. It must be noticed further that St John speaks of the sin as 'tending to death' (πρὸς θάνατον) and not as necessarily involving death. Death is, so to speak, its natural consequence, if it continue, and not its inevitable *[Death the tendency not the necessary issue.]*

[1] Origen identifies the two phrases: ἐπὶ ἁμαρτήμασι τοῖς μὴ πρὸς θάνατον ἢ ὡς ὠνόμασεν ἐν Ἀριθμοῖς ὁ νόμος τοῖς μὴ θανατηφόροις (in Matt. T. xiii. § 30). In another passage he treats the infliction of death as the complete expiation of the crime for which it is inflicted: Absolvitur peccatum per pœnam mortis, nec superest aliquid quod pro hoc crimine judicii dies et pœna æterni ignis inveniat (*Hom. in Lev.* xiv. § 4).

W.

issue as a matter of fact.   Its character is assumed to be unquestionable, and its presence open and notorious.

The mode of dealing with such a sin.

5.   The question then could not but arise, How is such flagrant sin in a brother—a fellow Christian—to be dealt with ?   For it must be remembered that the words of the apostle are directed to those who are members of the Christian Church, sharing in the privileges of the common life.   The answer follows naturally from a view of the normal efficacy of Christian intercession.   The power of prayer avails for those who belong to the Body (comp. John xiii. 10).   But for those who are separated from the Body for a time or not yet included in it the ordinary exercise of the energy of spiritual sympathy has, so far as we are taught directly, no promise of salutary influence.   The use of common prayer in such cases is not enjoined; though it must be observed that it is not forbidden.   St John does not command intercession when the sin is seen, recognised by the brother, in its fatal intensity ; but on the other hand he does not expressly exclude it.   Even if the tenour of his words may seem to dissuade such prayer, it is because the offender lies without the Christian Body, excluded from its life but yet not beyond the creative, vivifying power of God.

In some cases uttermost chastisement necessary.

6.   We can understand in some degree how such sins, either in men or in nations, must be left to God.   Chastisement and not forgiveness is the one way to restoration[1].   The book of the prophet Jeremiah is a divine lesson of the necessity of purification through death for a faithless people.   And the fortunes of Israel seem to illustrate the character of God's dealings with men.

Patristic comments.

7.   The patristic comments upon the passage offer an instructive subject for study.

CLEMENT OF ALEXANDRIA.

CLEMENT of Alexandria in discussing the different kinds of voluntary and wrong action (*Strom.* ii. 15, § 66) refers to the language of St John as shewing that he recognised differences in sin (φαίνεται...τὰς διαφορὰς τῶν ἁμαρτιῶν ἐκδιδάσκων), and quotes as illustrating the kind of distinction to which he refers Ps. i. 1, but he gives no classification of specific offences.

TERTULLIAN.

TERTULLIAN naturally lays down a clear and definite interpretation: ' Who, he asks, can escape from the sin of rash anger...of breaking engage-

[1] The truth finds a noble expression in Browning's *The Ring and the Book:* *The Pope,* 2116 ff.

For the main criminal I see no hope
Except in such a suddenness of fate.
I stood at Naples once, a night so dark
I could have scarce conjectured there
    was earth
Anywhere, sky or sea or world at all:
But the night's black was burst through
    by a blaze—
Thunder struck blow on blow, earth
    groaned and bore,
Through her whole length of mountains

visible :
There lay the city thick and plain with
    spires,
And, like a ghost disshrouded, white
    the sea.
So may the truth be flashed out by
    one blow,
And Guido see, one instant, and be
    saved.

With this compare Guido's last words,
    Abate—Cardinal—Christ—Maria—
    God—
    Pompilia, will you let them murder
    me ?

'ments, of speaking falsely through shame or necessity...so that if there
'were no pardon for such acts, no one could be saved. Of these then there
'will be pardon through Christ, our Advocate with the Father.   There are
'however offences of a different character, heavier and deadly, such as admit
'no pardon, murder, idolatry, fraud, denial [of Christ], blasphemy, and
'assuredly also adultery and fornication, and every other violation of the
'temple of God.   For these Christ will no longer plead: these he who has
'been born of God will absolutely not commit, as he will not be a son of
'God, if he has committed them [1].'

ORIGEN speaks with wise reserve; after referring to 1 Cor. iii. 15, Matt. ORIGEN.
xvi. 26, he continues, 'There are some sins which are to loss (ad damnum)...
'some to destruction (ad interitum)...What kind of sins however are sins
'to death, what not to death but to loss, cannot, I think, easily be deter-
'mined by any man' (*Hom. in Ex.* x. § 3[2]).

HILARY brings out an important aspect of the truth. 'There is,' he HILARY.
says, 'a limit to mercy (*misericordiæ*), and justice must be used in shewing
'pity.   We can feel sorrow for those whose crimes are great, but there is
'no room for mercy.   For mercy turns to ask pardon of God for that which
'is done; but to give pardon to wrong deeds is not to shew mercy but not
'to observe justice in mercy.   This consideration the apostle John observed
'most carefully saying: *Si quis scit fratrem suum delinquere sed non ad*
'*mortem, petat et dabit illi Deus vitam.   Est enim peccatum ad mortem*
'*sed non pro eo dico*' (*in cxl. Psalm.* § 8).

AMBROSE regards the direction of St John as applying to the general AMBROSE.
action of the Church but not as excluding absolutely all intercession. 'He
'did not speak to a Moses (Ex. xxxii. 31 f.) or a Jeremiah (Jer. xiv. 11; vii.
'16; Baruch iii. 1 f.; v. 1), but to the people, who required to employ
'another to pray for their own sins; for whom it is enough if they pray

---

[1] *De pudic.* 19, Cui enim non ac-
cidit aut irasci inique et ultra solis
occasum, aut et manum immittere,
aut facile maledicere, aut temere ju-
rare, aut fidem pacti destruere, aut
verecundia aut necessitate mentiri;
in negotiis, in officiis, in quæstu, in
victu, in visu, in auditu, quanta
tentamur; ut si nulla sit venia istorum nemini salus competeret. Horum
ergo erit venia per exoratorem patris
Christum. Sunt autem et contraria
istis, ut graviora et exitiosa, quæ veniam non capiant, homicidium, idolo-
latria, fraus, negatio, blasphemia, utique et mœchia et fornicatio....Horum
ultra exorator non erit Christus. Hæc
non admittet omnino qui natus ex
Deo fuerit, non futurus Dei filius si
admiserit. The classification is instructive. In an earlier chapter (c. 2)
he divides sins into 'remissible' and
'irremissible': the former are fit subjects of intercession, the latter not,
and he concludes: Secundum hanc
differentiam delictorum pœnitentiæ
quoque conditio discriminatur. Alia
erit quæ veniam consequi possit, in
delicto scilicet remissibili; alia quæ
consequi nullo modo possit, in delicto
scilicet irremissibili.

[2] Comp. *in Joh.* Tom. II. (IV. p. 62
R.). In *Hom. in Lev.* IV. § 5 Origen
compares with 1 John v. 16 the words
in 1 Sam. ii. 25; and in the treatise
On Prayer (§ 28) he follows out the
comparison, implying that sins of
idolatry, adultery and fornication are
not to be remitted by the prayer and
offerings of the Church.

'God for lighter faults, and think that the pardon of graver must be re-
'served for the prayers of the just' (*de pœnit.* i. 10).

JEROME.

JEROME combines the language of 1 Sam. ii. 25 with that of St John,
when he is insisting on the different degrees of the heinousness of sins.
'*Qui scit fratrem suum peccare peccatum non ad mortem, petat, et dabit
'ei vitam peccanti non ad mortem.   Qui vero peccaverit ad mortem quis
'orabit pro eo?*' 'You see,' he continues, 'that if we pray for smaller sins we
'obtain pardon; if for greater, the obtaining pardon is difficult; and that
'there is a great interval between some sins and others' (*adv. Jovin.* ii. § 30).

AUGUS-
TINE.

The interpretation of AUGUSTINE is of great interest.   His commentary
on the verse of St John's Epistle is not preserved, but in his treatise on the
Sermon on the Mount (c. A. D. 393) he treats of the passage, and says:
Aperte ostendit esse quosdam fratres pro quibus orare non nobis præcipi-
tur, cum Dominus etiam pro peccatoribus nostris orare jubeat...Peccatum
ergo fratris ad mortem puto esse cum post agnitionem Dei per gratiam
Domini nostri Jesu Christi quisque oppugnat fraternitatem et adversus
ipsam gratiam qua reconciliatus est Deo invidentiæ facibus agitatur (*de
Serm. Dom.* i. 22, 73)[1].   In reviewing this passage afterwards in his *Retrac-
tationes* (c. A. D. 426—7) he writes: Quod quidem non confirmavi, quoniam
hoc putare me dixi: sed tamen addendum fuit, si in hac tam scelerata
mentis perversitate finierit hanc vitam; quoniam de quocunque pessimo in
hac vita constituto non est utique desperandum, nec pro illo imprudenter
oratur de quo non desperatur (*Retract.* i. 19, 7).

He develops this idea of deliberate persistence in evil in treating of
the sin against the Holy Spirit:

Hoc [peccatum in Spiritum Sanctum] est duritia cordis usque ad finem
huius vitæ qua homo recusat in unitate corporis Christi, quod vivificat
Spiritus Sanctus, remissionem accipere peccatorum....Huic ergo dono
gratiæ Dei quicunque restiterit et repugnaverit vel quoquo modo fuerit ab
eo alienus usque in finem vitæ non remittetur ei neque in hoc sæculo
neque in futuro; hoc scilicet tam grande peccatum ut eo teneantur cuncta
peccata quod non probatur ab aliquo esse commissum nisi cum de corpore
exierit (*Epist.* clxxx. v (1), xi. § 49).   No one can be pronounced guilty of it
while life still continues: Hæc blasphemia Spiritus, cui nunquam est ulla
remissio,... non potest in quoquam, ut diximus, dum in hac adhuc vita est
deprehendi (*Serm.* lxxi. 3, 21).

The fatal consequences of the sin are, he points out, involved in its
essential character:

Ille peccat in Spiritum Sanctum qui, desperans vel irridens atque con-
temnens prædicationem gratiæ per quam peccata diluuntur et pacis per
quam reconciliamur Deo, detrectat agere pœnitentiam de peccatis suis et

---

[1] Bede silently quotes this interpretation in his Commentary; and afterwards a singular alternative: Potest
etiam peccatum *usque* ad mortem ac-
cipi, pro quo rogare quempiam vetat,
quia scilicet peccatum quod in hac vita
non corrigitur ejus venia frustra post
mortem postulatur. But he prefers
Augustine's view.

in eorum impia atque mortifera quadam suavitate perdurandum sibi esse decernit et in finem usque perdurat (*in Ep. ad Rom.* § 14 ; comp. § 22).

Quisquis igitur reus fuerit impœnitentiæ contra Spiritum in quo unitas et societas communionis congregatur Ecclesiæ nunquam illi remittetur ; quia hoc sibi clausit ubi remittitur...(*Sermo* lxxi. 21, 34).

For chastisement is the way to restoration : Plane si in tantas ieris iniquitates ut repellas a te virgam verberantis, si repellas manum flagellantis et de disciplina Dei indigneris et fugias a Patre cædente et nolis eum Patrem pati quia non parcit peccanti, tu te alienasti ab hæreditate, ipse te non abjecit; nam si maneres flagellatus non remaneres exhæreditatus (*in Psalm.* lxxxviii. *Serm.* ii. § 3).

CHRYSOSTOM, like several earlier writers, connects the passage in St John with the words of Eli (1 Sam. ii. 25), and finds the description of the sin in Ps. xlix. 18 ff.   The fatal consequences which it brings are due to the accompanying wilful impenitence.   'How,' he adds, 'can (God) forgive 'one who does not allow that he has sinned, and does not repent?   For 'when we ask medicine from the physician we shew him the wound' (*in Ps.* xlix. § 7). CHRYSO-
STOM.

In a letter attributed to GELASIUS the issue of the sin in death is made to lie wholly in impenitence.   He has spoken of the sin of here- tics against the Holy Spirit which was incapable of forgiveness as long as they persisted in it; and then he goes on : 'As the passage of the apostle 'John runs in like sense : *Est peccatum ad mortem, non dico ut oretur* '*pro eo ; et est peccatum non ad mortem, dico ut oretur pro eo.*   There is 'a sin unto death when men abide in the same sin : there is a sin not 'unto death when men abandon the same sin.   There is no sin for the 'remission of which the Church does not pray, or which it cannot absolve 'when men cease from it in virtue of the power given to it from God'... (*Cod. Can. Eccles.* xlvii. § 5 ; Migne, *Patrol. Lat.* lvi. p. 622). GELASIUS.

ŒCUMENIUS, in the same spirit, when commenting upon the passage sees the ground of the apostle's instruction in the absence of all signs of repentance in him 'who sins a sin unto death.'   The brother is not to pray for such an one, he says, 'for he will not be heard, because he asks amiss, 'speaking for one who shews no intention ʼof return (περὶ τοῦ μηδεμίαν 'ἐπιδεικνυμένου ἐπιστροφήν).   For this sin is alone unto death that has no 'regard to repentance (ἡ μὴ πρὸς μετάνοιαν ἀφορῶσα), from which Judas 'suffered and was brought under the eternal death' (*ad loc.*)[1]. ŒCUME-
NIUS.

8.   The language of St John gave occasion to the current distinction of sins as 'mortal' and 'venial.'   In Augustine this distinction occurs fre- quently under the contrast of 'crimina' (*in Joh.* xli. 9 crimen est peccatum gravi accusatione et damnatione dignissimum) and 'peccata': c. *duas Epp. Pel.* i. § 28; *in Ps.* cxviii. 3, 2; *de perfec. Just. Hom.* ix. 20 ; *Enchirid.* Distinc-
tion of
'venial'
and
'mortal'
sins.

---

[1] In the Council of Troyes A.D. 879 it was forbidden to mention the names of those who had died under excom- munication on the ground of this pas- sage.   Peccatum enim ad mortem, it is said, est perseverantia in peccato usque ad mortem (*Conc. Tric.* II. § 3). This widespread interpretation came from the ambiguity of the Latin prepo- sition.   See Bede above.

c. lxiv. So he writes: Non peccata sola sunt illa quæ crimina nominantur, adulteria, fornicationes, sacrilegia, furta, rapinæ, falsa testimonia : non ipsa sola peccata sunt. Attendere aliquid quod non debebas peccatum est ; audire aliquid libenter quod audiendum non fuit peccatum est ; cogitare aliquid quod non fuit cogitandum peccatum est (*Serm.* cclxxi. 9, 9).

The later technical distinction is well summed up by RICHARD of St Victor who discussed the difference in a brief tract : Mortale peccatum, quantum mihi videtur, triplici recte ratione distinguitur. Mortale est quod a quovis non potest committi sine grandi corruptione sui. Item mortale est quod non potest committi sine gravi læsione proximi. Mortale nihilominus quod non potest committi sine magno contemptu Dei. Cetera vero omnia videntur mihi venialia (Migne, *Patrol. Lat.* 196, p. 1193).

Additional Note (1) *on* v. 20. *The idea of Life.*

The idea of 'Life' in St John has been already touched upon in the note on i. 1 ; but it requires to be discussed somewhat more in detail. For the characteristic message which St John gives is of a life through which fellowship with man and God—the end of human existence—is perfectly realised.

i. *The Source of Life.*

The Father the source of life.

Of the Father alone it is said that He 'hath life in Himself' as the absolute final source of all life. This is the last limit of thought : John v. 26 ὁ πατὴρ ἔχει ζωὴν ἐν ἑαυτῷ, *the Father hath life in Himself* (comp. 1 Tim. vi. 16).

At the same time it is made known that the Father communicated to the Son the absolute possession of life : in this is expressed the idea of Sonship. The Son 'hath life in Himself,' but not as the final source of life. John v. 26 ὥσπερ ὁ πατὴρ ἔχει ζωὴν ἐν ἑαυτῷ, οὕτως καὶ τῷ υἱῷ ἔδωκεν ζωὴν ἔχειν ἐν ἑαυτῷ, *as the Father hath life in Himself, even so gave He to the Son also to have life in Himself.* Compare John vi. 57 ζῶ διὰ τὸν πατέρα, and Apoc. i. 17. But men have not 'life in themselves,' either originally or by divine gift. Their life is a life of necessary, continuous, essential dependence (ἐν Χριστῷ 'in Christ,' according to St Paul's phrase). This must remain so to the end. Even when they participate in the virtue of Christ's humanity, they have life through Him and not in themselves : John vi. 57 (ὁ τρώγων), xiv. 19.

ii. *The Nature of Life.*

Terms for 'life' and 'living' in St John.

Three terms are used by St John to describe 'life' under different aspects :

(1) ἡ ζωή (the life), ' life which is truly life' : c. iii. 14 note.

(2) ζωὴ αἰώνιος, 'eternal life' (not in Apoc.) : c. i. 2 note.

For the shade of difference between ζωή and ζωὴ αἰώνιος see John iii. 36 (1 John iii. 14 f. ; John v. 24).

(3) ἡ αἰώνιος ζωή (John xvi. 3 ; comp. Acts xiii. 46 ; 1 Tim. vi. 12) ; ἡ ζωὴ ἡ αἰώνιος (1 John i. 2, ii. 25), 'the eternal life' : c. i. 2 note.

In connexion with those terms the following verbal phrases must also be noticed:

(1) ζῆν to live: John v. 25, vi. 57, xi. 25, xiv. 19; 1 John iv. 9 (Apoc. xx. 5). Comp. 1 Pet. iv. 6; 1 Thess. v. 10; 2 Cor. xiii. 4; Rom. viii. 13; Hebr. xii. 9.

(2) ζῆν εἰς τὸν αἰῶνα, 'to live for ever': John vi. 51, 58. Comp. Apoc. iv. 9, 10, xv. 7 ὁ ζῶν εἰς τοὺς αἰῶνας τῶν αἰώνων (peculiar to St John in N. T.).

(3) ἔχειν ζωήν, 'to have life': John x. 10, xx. 31; 1 John v. 12 (τὴν ζ.) (peculiar to St John in N. T.).

(4) ἔχειν ζωὴν αἰώνιον, 'to have eternal life': John iii. 15 f., 36, v. 24, vi. 40, 47, 54; 1 John v. 13 (iii. 15). Comp. Matt. xix. 16.

In considering these phrases it is necessary to premise that in spiritual things we must guard against all conclusions which rest upon the notions of succession and duration. 'Eternal life' is that which St Paul speaks of as ἡ ὄντως ζωή, 'the life which is life indeed' (1 Tim. vi. 19), and ἡ ζωὴ τοῦ θεοῦ, 'the life of God' (Eph. iv. 18). It is not an endless duration of being in time, but being of which time is not a measure. We have indeed no powers to grasp the idea except through forms and images of sense. These must be used; but we must not transfer them as realities to another order. *Eternal life essentially excludes time.*

Life for a finite creature is union with God (comp. Col. i. 16, 17 ἐν αὐτῷ ἐκτίσθη τὰ πάντα...τὰ πάντα ἐν αὐτῷ συνέστηκεν; Acts xvii. 28 ἐν αὐτῷ ζῶμεν). Such union is for a rational being involved in a real and progressive knowledge of God in Christ. For spiritual knowledge is not external but sympathetic; and necessarily carries with it growing conformity to God. Hence 'the eternal life,' which Christ is and gave, is described as lying in the continuous effort to gain a fuller knowledge of God and Christ (John xvii. 3 ἵνα γινώσκωσιν); or, as the apostle writes out the Lord's words more fully: '*the Son of God hath come and hath given us understanding that we may* '*know* (ἵνα γινώσκωμεν) *Him that is true; and we are in Him that is true,* '*in His Son Jesus Christ*' (1 John v. 20). So it is that Christ's words are 'words of life' (John vi. 68; comp. vi. 63; viii. 51; xii. 50; James i. 18; Acts v. 20 is different). Real knowledge rests on fellowship and issues in fellowship. *Life lies in knowledge of, that is fellowship with, God.*

Under this aspect all being is a revelation of life to man (John i. 4), which may become intelligible to him. The thought is one which is especially needed in an age of scientific analysis. We are tempted on all sides to substitute the mechanism, or the part, for the whole: the physical conditions or accompaniments for the vital force. The life is not in us only but in the world. *Universal life.*

Under another aspect it can be said that the Gospel is 'the revelation of life,' and that in the Incarnation 'the life was made manifest.' By the personal coming of the Word in flesh the worth of individual life is shewn. He who 'lives' is conscious of power and office, and so far as he lives uses his power and fulfils his office. *Individual life.*

This view of life corresponds with and completes the former. All power is finally the gift of God: all office is for the accomplishment of His will. Life therefore is the use of the gifts of God according to the will of God. *The two lives one.*

Or, to combine both notions, we are brought back to the original idea: life is fellowship with God, which includes fellowship with man, and this fellowship is realised in Christ.

iii. *Christ the Life.*

Christ is the Life in Creation and in the New Creation.

Christ is 'the life' and that both in regard to the individual (John xi. 25 ἐγώ εἰμι ἡ ἀνάστασις καὶ ἡ ζωή *I am the Resurrection and the Life*) and in regard to the whole sum of being (John xiv. 6 ἐγώ εἰμι ἡ ὁδὸς καὶ ἡ ἀλήθεια καὶ ἡ ζωή, *I am the Way and the Truth and the Life*). Even before His Coming in flesh, the Creation which He sustained by His presence was a divine revelation (John i. 4); and by His Coming 'the life was manifested' and men recognised it (1 John i. 2).

He came that men may have life and the fulness of all that life needs (John x. 10 ζωὴν περισσὸν ἔχειν). The life which He gives is not and cannot be separated from Himself. Therefore, as things are, His Coming was crowned by His Passion and Exaltation (John iii. 15), whereby His Life was made available for others through Death (John xii. 32 (24)).

His offer of Life is universal (John vi. 51 ὁ ἄρτος ὃν ἐγὼ δώσω ἡ σάρξ μου ἐστὶν ὑπὲρ τῆς τοῦ κόσμου ζωῆς, *the bread which I will give is my flesh for the life of the world*). And the offer is made of the pure love of God (John iii. 16; 1 John iv. 10). The new creation is a work of spontaneous divine love even as the first creation, while it answered, necessarily answered, to the fulfilment of the divine idea (John i. 17 ἐγένετο).

In one sense the gift of life is made and complete (1 John v. 11 ζ. αἰ. ἔδωκεν ἡμῖν); but under another aspect it is still offered, promised, given (John x. 28 δίδωμι αὐτοῖς ζ. αἰ.; xvii. 2 ἵνα...δώσει ζ. αἰ.; 1 John ii. 25 ἐπαγγελία). The spiritually sick, if living in one sense, require 'life' (1 John v. 16 δώσει αὐτῷ ζωήν, τοῖς ἁμαρτάνουσιν μὴ πρὸς θάνατον: comp. John iv. 50). Comp. § v.

iv. *The Life of the Believer.*

The life of the believer is the possession of the Living Son.

The universal gift of life offered by Christ has to be personally appropriated (John vi. 35, 50 f., 58). In this process it comes through Christ, as the agent (1 John iv. 9 ἵνα ζήσωμεν δι' αὐτοῦ, V. *per eum*: comp. John v. 40); and it comes for the sake of Christ, as the ground of quickening (John vi. 57 ζήσει δι' ἐμέ, V. *propter me*), because He is what He is (1 John ii. 12). In other words the life of the believer follows from the life of Christ (John xiv. 19 ὅτι ἐγὼ ζῶ καὶ ὑμεῖς ζήσεσθε, where the future is used in regard to the completer fulness of Christ's working; comp. 2 Cor. iv. 10 f.; Col. iii. 4; Eph. ii. 5), and is realised in (that is, by union with) Him (John iii. 15; 1 John v. 11: comp. Rom. vi. 23; 2 Tim. i. 1), as He has been made known (John xx. 31 ζ. ἐχ. ἐν τῷ ὀνόματι αὐτοῦ). For the life is in the Living Son (1 John v. 11) and not in the letter of the Law (John v. 39); so that the possession of the Son is the possession of life (1 John v. 12, comp. Rom. v. 10 κατηλλάγημεν...διὰ τοῦ θανάτου...σωθησόμεθα ἐν τῇ ζωῇ αὐτοῦ). And he who is one with Christ is one with God (John xvii. 21 ἵνα ἐν ἡμῖν ὦσιν: comp. 1 John ii. 24 f.; John vi. 56 f.).

In the realisation

For the believer the transition from death to life has been made (John v. 24; 1 John iii. 14 μεταβεβήκαμεν ἐκ τοῦ θανάτου εἰς τὴν ζωήν:

comp. 1 John v. 12). But the consequences of the transition are realised, of life
as the transition itself is conditioned, by the activity of faith (John iii. 16, 36, man
vi. 47, xx. 31; 1 John v. 13 [ὁ πιστεύων, οἱ πιστεύοντες]; John vi. 40 ὁ unites
θεωρῶν καὶ πιστεύων)[1]. So man in a true sense works with God; and in with God
John i. 12 the human and divine elements in the beginning, the growth by faith.
and the issue of life are set side by side in a striking parallelism (ἐγεννήθησαν, ἐξουσίαν, τέκνα—ἔλαβον, πιστεύουσιν, γενέσθαι). By this energy of
faith the believer finds union with Christ's humanity (John vi. 51, 54, 58:
comp. vi. 35, 56, 58, x. 10).

v. *Life present and future.*

The life which lies in fellowship with God in Christ is, as has been Eternal
seen already, spoken of as 'eternal' life in order to distinguish it from the life,
life of sense and time under which true human existence is veiled at
present. Such a life of phenomena may be 'death' (1 John iii. 14: comp.
v. 16). But 'eternal life' is beyond the limitations of time: it belongs to
the being of God (1 John i. 2 ἦν πρὸς τὸν πατέρα), and finds its consummation in the transforming vision of the Son seen as He is (1 John iii. 2;
John xiv. 23, 2 f.). For us now therefore it is spoken of as both present
and future.

1. The 'life eternal' is essentially present, so far as it is the potential present
fulfilment of the idea of humanity (John iii. 36, v. 24, vi. 47, 54, xx. 31; and
1 John v. 12); and the possession of life may become a matter of actual
knowledge (1 John v. 13: comp. 1 John iii. 15).

This thought of the present reality of 'eternal life' is characteristic of
St John, and in its full development is peculiar to him (but comp. Gal. ii. 20).

2. At the same time the life is regarded as future in its complete future.
realisation, so far as it is the fulfilment of Messianic promises (John iv. 14, 36,
vi. 27, xii. 25, v. 25, vi. 57, xi. 25, xiv. 19, vi. 54: compare 1 John ii. 25,
iii. 2; and also Mark x. 30; Gal. vi. 8).

Hence it is intelligible how 'eternal life' is spoken of as 'the commandment' of the Father (John xii. 50); and again as the progressive
knowledge of the Father in the Son (1 John v. 20). For the commandment of God is represented to us in the work of Christ; and to embrace
this in faithful obedience is to 'have life in His name' (John xx. 31), on
which we believe (1 John v. 13) with growing intelligence.

If now we endeavour to bring together the different traits of 'the
eternal life' we see that it is a life which with all its fulness and all its
potencies is *now:* a life which extends beyond the limits of the individual,
and preserves, completes, crowns individuality by placing the part in connexion with the whole: a life which satisfies while it quickens aspiration:
a life which is seen, as we regard it patiently, to be capable of conquering,
reconciling, uniting the rebellious, discordant, broken elements of being on

---

[1] In all these places the force of the present participle is conspicuous. St John uses the aor. partic. once only: John xx. 29. The force of the present can be seen by contrast with the aorist: [Mark] xvi. 16 f.; Luke i. 45, viii. 12; Acts iv. 32, xi. 21, xix. 2; 2 Thess. i. 10, ii. 12; Eph. i. 13; Hebr. iv. 3; Jude 5; and again with the perfect: Acts xv. 5, xvi. 34; [xviii. 27, xix. 18;] xxi. 20, 25; Tit. iii. 8.

which we look and which we bear about with us: a life which gives unity
to the constituent parts and to the complex whole, which brings together
heaven and earth, which offers the sum of existence in one thought.   As
we reach forth to grasp it, the revelation of God is seen to have been
unfolded in its parts in Creation; and the parts are seen to have been
brought together again by the Incarnation.

Additional Note (2) on v. 20.   'The true God.'

'The true
God' an-
swers to
the words
'God is
love.'

When St John speaks of God as 'He that is true' (ὁ ἀληθινός), He who
alone (John xvii. 3 ὁ μόνος ἀληθινὸς θεός) and absolutely fulfils the idea
of God which man is constituted to form, and then in significant and
mysterious words identifies union with 'Him that is true,' with union ' with
His Son Jesus Christ,' he explains in the terms of historical revelation that
which is involved in the statement 'God is love.' He indicates in what
way the 'personality' of God is to be held and guarded from false con-

'Person-
ality' as
applied to
God.

clusions. St John, as all the biblical writers, everywhere uses language of
God which assigns to Him 'action' and 'will.' But, as far as our human
observation reaches, 'will' implies resistance, and 'action' implies succession. Such limitations can find no place in the idea of God.   The conception of 'personality' which we can form therefore expresses only a
fragment of the truth, that side of it which assures us of the possibility of
approach to God on our part as to One Who loves and may be loved.

Love in-
volves a
'tri-per-
sonality.'

But we cannot rest here.   When we endeavour to think of God Himself
we are necessarily led to inquire whether Scripture does not help us to
rise to a thought in which we can see represented from the divine side
that which is in the Divine Being the analogue of sole-personality in a finite
being. This thought we find in the words 'God is love.' The phrase, as we
have seen, describes the essence and not an attribute of God. It presents
to us, as far as we can apprehend the truth, something of God in Himself.
It must hold good of God in His innermost Being, if we may so speak,
apart from creation. Now love involves a subject and an object, and that
which unites both. We are taught then to conceive of God as having in
Himself the perfect object of love and the perfect response of love, completely self-sufficing and self-complete. We thus gain, however imperfect
language may be, the idea of a tri-personality in an Infinite Being as correlative to a sole-personality in a finite being. In the Unity of Him Who
is One we acknowledge the Father, the Son and the Holy Spirit, in the
interaction of Whom we can see love fulfilled.

This fact
indicated
in the
opening
words of
the Gos-
pel, and
of the
Epistle.

The language in John i. 1, where we have opened a unique view of the
Divine Being without any regard to a revelation to man, indicates the
same thought. The relation of 'the Word' to 'God' is described as a
relation of active love: ὁ λόγος ἦν πρὸς τὸν θεόν, the personal energy of
the Word was directed towards, and (so to speak) regulated by 'God,'
while the Word Himself 'was God.' In the Epistle the thought is presented differently. There it is 'the Life' and not 'the Word' which is

spoken of. The conception of 'the Life' is wider in its range than that of 'the Word,' though it is through 'the Word' that 'the Life' is revealed. This life is 'the life eternal.' It is not of this temporal order though it is made known in it, under its limitations. It is a life which essentially finds its original in the Godhead: ἦν πρὸς τὸν πατέρα, it was realised in the intercommunion of the Divine Persons, when time was not. Thus we have in this twofold revelation of an activity of 'the Word' towards 'God,' of a fulfilment of 'Life' towards 'the Father,' beyond time, such a vision as we can look upon of the fulness of the Being of God in Himself. And when 'the Word' and 'the Life' are brought within the sphere of human existence, this action is characteristically described: 'the Life was manifested': 'the Word became flesh.'

Nothing is said in either passage directly of the Holy Spirit. But His action is involved in the phrase ἦν πρός in such a connexion. He is, so to seek a definite expression for the idea, the Mediating Power through Whom the love that goes forth is perfectly united with the love that answers. He gives unity to the Life, which we can only conceive of in fragments.

It will be evident that this view of the nature of God prepares the way for revelation. The Word, Who is God (θεός and not ὁ θεός as in Sabellian teaching), has a personal Being and can make the Father known (1 John ii. 22 ff.). The Spirit, Who is God, has a personal Being, and can make the Son known (John xiv. 26, xvi. 14). At the same time, while this fulness of life fulfilled in God Himself is disclosed to us, the divine unity is maintained as essential and not numerical. The Word and the Spirit are both spoken of in personal relations to 'God' (John i. 1; 32 f.). That is when the Persons in the Godhead are recognised, the unity of God is simultaneously affirmed. *This tri-personality opens the way for revelation.*

Such glimpses are opened to us of the absolute tri-personality of God as preparatory to the account of the historical Gospel by St John, but elsewhere, like the other apostolic writers, he deals with the Trinity revealed in the work of Redemption (the 'Economic Trinity'). The Father is spoken of in His relation to the Incarnate Son, and through Him to men. The Son is spoken of as manifested to men through the Incarnation in the union of the two natures (yet comp. John v. 26). The Holy Spirit is spoken of as 'proceeding' on His Mission to the Church (John xv. 26 note), sent by the Father and by the Son; and taking of that which is the Son's to declare to men (John xiv. 26, xv. 26, xvi. 14; 1 John ii. 20 f., 27). The truths are stated side by side in connexion with our creation, redemption, sanctification; and we are enabled to see that they answer in some way, which we have no power to determine adequately, to the very Being of God as He is in Himself. *Elsewhere St John speaks of 'the Economic Trinity.'*

The maintenance of the supreme Sovereignty of One God (μοναρχία) in this tri-personality has to be guarded against a twofold tendency to error: (1) towards a distinction in essence between God and Christ (the Father and the Son); and (2) towards a confusion of the Persons of the Father and the Son and the Spirit. The first error found its typical expression in Arianism: the second in Sabellianism. The first has affinities with Polytheism by introducing the idea of a subordinate Divinity. The second has affinities with Pantheism, as seeing in things transitory manifestations *Two errors to be avoided: Arian, and Sabellian.*

of the Person of God. Both rest upon a false Neo-Judaic conception of Monotheism.

The authority of St John has been brought forward in support of each of these views : for the first John xiv. 28 (see note, and compare Athanas. *de Syn.* § 28); and for the second John x. 30 (see note, and compare Tertull. *adv. Prax.* cc. xx. xxii.). It must however be noticed that the great Greek Fathers understood the first passage of the Personal Subordination of the Son as Son to the Father in the one equal and absolute Godhead. And this view, which has been obscured in the West by the teaching of Augustine, is of the highest importance; for it leads to the apprehension of the fitness of the mediatorial and consummative work of the Son. The assumption of humanity and the laying aside of the divine conditions of existence by the Son are everywhere spoken of by St John as voluntary acts. They correspond therefore to the Being of the Son as Son, for we cannot conceive of the Father or of the Spirit as Incarnate. In other words the unchanged and unchangeable ' I ' of the Word, the Son, includes either the potentiality or the fact of the Incarnation, the union with the finite.

The dualism of the subordination of the Son in Person not in essence.

ΙΩΑΝΟΥ Β

ΙΩΑΝΟΥ Β

Ο ΠΡΕϹΒΥΤΕΡΟϹ ἐκλεκτῇ κυρίᾳ καὶ τοῖς τέκ-

The structure of the letter is simple and natural. It consists of (1) the salutation (1—3); (2) the counsel and warning (4—11); (3) the conclusion (12, 13). Whatever may be the interpretation of the individual address in *vv.* 5, 13, the main part of the letter is addressed to more readers than one (*v.* 6 ἠκούσατε, περιπατῆτε, *v.* 8 βλέπετε ἑαυτούς, *v.* 10 πρὸς ὑμᾶς, *v.* 12 ὑμῖν, πρὸς ὑμᾶς, ἡ χαρὰ ὑμῶν).

1. *The Salutation* (1—3).

The salutation is framed on the usual type: ὁ πρεσβύτερος ἐκλεκτῇ κυρίᾳ... ...χάρις ἔλεος εἰρήνη παρὰ θεοῦ πατρός, καὶ παρὰ Ἰησοῦ Χριστοῦ...But this outline is filled up by successive amplifications as the apostle dwells on each word which he writes in relation to the circumstances of the case. In this respect the Salutation may be compared with that in the Epistle to the Galatians, where in like manner St Paul expands his usual formula in view of the peculiar condition of the Churches which he is addressing.

¹ *The Elder to one who is an elect lady and her children, whom I love in truth; and not I only but also all they that know the truth;* ² *for the truth's sake which abideth in us—and it shall be with us for ever:* ³ *grace, mercy, peace, shall be with us from God the Father, and from Jesus*

Christ the Son of the Father, in truth and love.

1. ὁ πρεσβύτερος] *Senior* V. *The elder.* The definite form of the title marks the writer as completely identified by it. In this connexion there can be little doubt that it describes not age simply but official position. The writer was recognised by the receiver of the Epistle as 'the Elder.'

The title 'elder' appears to have had special currency in the Asiatic Churches, where it was used of a particular class (Papias ap. Euseb. *H. E.* iii. f.; Iren. v. 33. 3; 36. 2); yet not without a recognition of the Apostles as 'the elders' in point of time (Papias, *l. c.*). It is easy to see why St John would choose such a title, which, while it described official position, suggested also a fatherly relation, and perhaps even pointed to intercourse with Christ (1 Pet. v. 1). For the history of the word πρεσβύτερος see Lightfoot, *Philippians*, pp. 228 f.

ἐκλεκτῇ κυρίᾳ] *electæ dominæ* V. The rendering of the phrase is beset by the greatest difficulties. No interpretation can be accepted as satisfactory.

The difficulty seems to have been felt from a very early time. Two distinct views have found support, that the title describes a person, and that it describes a society.

νοις αὐτῆς, οὓς ἐγὼ ἀγαπῶ ἐν ἀληθείᾳ, καὶ οὐκ ἐγὼ

1 καὶ οὐκ ἐγώ ℵB vg me the syrhl: οὐκ ἐγω δέ A.

The first view has been held in several different forms. The Latin fragments of the *Hypotyposes* of Clement ot Alexandria represent the letter as written 'to a certain Babylonian (comp. 1 Pet. v. 13) Electa by name' (ad quandam Babyloniam Electam nomine); 'it signifies however' (that is, this proper name, *Electa*), Clement adds, 'the election of the holy Church.'

Others again (so the [late] Syrian version) have regarded Κυρία as a proper name (' to the elect Kyria'). Such a name is found (see Lücke, 444 n.); but if Κυρία were so used here it is in the highest degree unlikely that St John would have written ἐκλεκτῇ Κυρίᾳ, and not Κυρίᾳ τῇ ἐκλεκτῇ as *v.* 13; 3 John 1; Rom. xvi. 13.

It has also been supposed that the two words form a compound proper name (' to Electa Kyria'). This view removes the difficulty of the construction ; but the combination is at least very strange.

On the other hand it is not easy to suppose that the letter was addressed to an unnamed person, a single Christian 'lady' ('To an elect lady,' so Vulg.); though this is the most natural rendering of the text (comp. 1 Pet. i. 1).

All these notions of a personal address moreover are unsupported by such allusions in the letter as might be expected to mark an individual relationship.

Feeling these difficulties many from the time of Jerome (*Ep.* cxxiii. (xi.) § 12 *ad Ageruchiam*) have taken the title, the 'elect lady,' to be applied to some particular Christian society (Schol. ap. Matt. ἐκλεκτὴν Κυρίαν λέγει τὴν ἐν τινι τόπῳ ἐκκλησίαν ὡς τὴν τοῦ Κυρίου διδασκαλίαν ἀκριβῆ φυλάττουσαν...), or even to the whole Church: 'to her who is a chosen Lady, a

Bride of Him who is the Lord.' But of such a use of Κυρία no example is quoted.

On the whole it is best to recognise that the problem of the address is insoluble with our present knowledge. It is not unlikely that it contains some allusion, intelligible under the original circumstances, to which we have lost the key. But the general tenour of the letter favours the opinion that it was sent to a community and not to one believer.

τοῖς τέκνοις αὐ.] *natis eius* V., *her children*. The phrase can be understood either literally, 1 Tim. iii. 4; or spiritually, 1 Tim. i. 2; Gal. iv. 25. Comp. Apoc. ii. 23. The context here and the use of the term in *vv.* 4, 13 (comp. 3 John 4) favour the spiritual sense.

οὓς ἐγὼ ἀγ.] *whom*, mother alike and children, *I love*. It seems better to take this comprehensive sense than to refer the relative to the children only.

The emphasis which is laid upon the apostle's feeling (ἐγὼ ἀγ.) points to some unknown facts (compare 3 John 5). Both the shorter letters imply the existence of divisions in the societies to which they were directed; and St John brings his authority to bear against those from whom the persons addressed may have suffered.

ἐν ἀληθείᾳ] *in truth*, that is with a feeling which rightly deserves the name; see John xvii. 19 note; Col. i. 6.

καὶ οὐκ ἐγὼ μόνος...] *and not I alone* (*solus* V.), a single person, *but also all that have come to know the truth*. The love is directed to a character. Wherever the character exists, the love exists. This is made clear by the words which follow. The love felt by St John and by those whom he describes is felt 'for the truth's sake...'

μόνος ἀλλὰ καὶ πάντες οἱ ἐγνωκότες τὴν ἀλήθειαν, ²διὰ
τὴν ἀλήθειαν τὴν μένουσαν ἐν ἡμῖν, καὶ μεθ' ἡμῶν ἔσται
εἰς τὸν αἰῶνα· ³ἔσται μεθ' ἡμῶν χάρις ἔλεος εἰρήνη παρὰ

2 μένουσαν: ἐνοικοῦσαν A.　　3 ἔσ. μεθ' ἡμῶν (ὑμῶν me): om. A.　　παρὰ
θ. : ἀπὸ θ. א*.

μόνος] Luke xxiv. 18; Hebr. ix. 7.
Contrast 2 Tim. iv. 8 οὐ μόνον ἐμοί
(1 John ii. 2); Rom. iii. 29.

ἐγνωκότες] 1 John ii. 3 note. John
viii. 32. Contrast 1 John ii. 21 οὐκ
οἴδατε τὴν ἀλ.

τὴν ἀλ.] the truth, which is identical
with Christ's message (John i. 17),
and with Christ's Person (John xiv. 7).
Comp. 1 John i. 6, 8, notes.

2. The common acknowledgment
of the eternal Truth is the certain
foundation of love.

διὰ τὴν ἀλ.] The words recal ἐν ἀλ.
The Truth makes true love possible.
This Truth is not said to abide 'in
you' or 'in them,' but 'in us.' The
apostle at once identifies himself with
the whole society of the faithful.
Compare v. 5 ἵνα ἀγαπῶμεν. 1 John i.
4 (ἡμῶν).

τὴν μένουσαν ἐν ἡ.] See 1 John iii. 15
note.

καὶ μεθ' ἡ. ἔσται] and with us it
shall be. The position of μεθ' ἡ. emphasises the peculiar privileges of
those whom St John identifies with
himself. The change of construction
from the participle to the finite verb
(μένουσαν...ἔσται) answers to a pause
during which the writer contemplates
the fact which he has affirmed, and
then solemnly confirms the fulness of
his faith in it. Compare 1 John iii.
1 καὶ ἐσμέν, i. 2 note.

μεθ' ἡμῶν] with us and not only
in us. The Truth itself has through
Christ a personal power. Comp. 1
John iv. 17. The different relations
of the Paraclete to believers are described in John xiv. 16 f. by μετά,
παρά, ἐν.

εἰς τὸν αἰῶνα] See 1 John ii. 17
note.

W.

3. ἔσται μεθ' ἡμῶν...] There shall
be with us... This unique form of
salutation seems to have been determined by the preceding clause (μεθ'
ἡμῶν ἔσται): 'with us truth shall be
...yes, there shall be with us...' The
wish passes into assurance. In the
Epistles of St Paul no verb is expressed in the salutation (e.g. 1 Thess. i.
1, χάρις ὑμῖν καὶ εἰρήνη). In 1, 2
Peter, Jude πληθυνθείη is added (1
Pet. i. 1 χάρις ὑμῖν καὶ εἰρήνη πληθ.).

μεθ' ἡμῶν] v. 2. The readers are
identified with the writer.

χάρ. ἔλ. εἰρ.] The succession 'grace,
mercy, peace' marks the order from
the first motion of God to the final
satisfaction of man. 'Mercy' defines
as it were the manifestation of the
divine 'grace' and prepares for the
restoration of 'peace' to man's disordered life.

The same combination occurs in
salutations in 1 Tim. i. 2; 2 Tim. i. 2
(Ign. ad Smyrn. 12). Χάρις καὶ εἰρήνη
is found in Apoc. i. 4; 1 Pet. i. 2;
2 Pet. i. 2, and in all the other
Epistles of St Paul. In St Jude 2
the salutation is ἔλεος καὶ εἰρήνη καὶ
ἀγάπη. (Comp. Mart. Pol. Inscr.)

χάρις ἔλεος...] The word χάρις occurs elsewhere in St John only in
3 John 4; John i. 14, 16, 17; Apoc.
i. 4; xxii. 21; and the absence of the
cognate forms (χαρίζομαι, χάρισμα) from
his writings is worthy of notice. Ἔλεος
is not found elsewhere in his writings
nor yet ἐλεεῖν.

In regard to the divine action
'grace' points to the absolute freedom of God's love in relation to man's
helplessness to win it; and 'mercy' to
His tenderness towards man's misery.

εἰρήνη] John xiv. 27; xvi. 33; xx.

θεοῦ πατρός, καὶ παρὰ Ἰησοῦ Χριστοῦ τοῦ υἱοῦ τοῦ
πατρός, ἐν ἀληθείᾳ καὶ ἀγάπῃ.

om. παρά (2°) א*.   Ἰησοῦ AB vg the: +κυρίου' Ἰ. ꜱא me syrhl.   τοῦ
π.: +αὐτοῦ τοῦ π. א*.

19, 21, 26. The peace which is the gift of 'the God of peace' (1 Thess. v. 23; Rom. xv. 33; xvi. 20; Phil. iv. 9; Heb. xiii. 20) answers to all the disharmonies of being in man himself, in his relation to his fellow-men and to God, and in creation generally. Compare especially Rom. viii. 6; Eph. ii. 14 ff.

παρά...παρά...] The repetition of the preposition in such a form is unique. It serves to bring out distinctly the twofold personal relation of man to the Father and to the Son. Elsewhere in parallel cases the preposition used is always ἀπό: e.g. Rom. i. 7; 1 Cor. i. 3, &c. Comp. 2 Tim. i. 18.

θεοῦ πατρός] God the Father: more commonly God our Father (θ. π. ἡμῶν), e.g. Rom. i. 7; 1 Cor. i. 3 &c. Comp. 1 Tim. i. 2; 2 Tim. i. 2; Tit. i. 4; Eph. vi. 23; Col. iii. 17. Special stress is laid upon the revelation of God in this absolute character. Comp. v. 9.

Ἰ. Χρ. τοῦ υἱοῦ τοῦ π.] The phrase is unique. It seems to have been chosen to connect the revelation of the Father as definitely as possible with the Son. Comp. 1 John ii. 22 f.; and 1 John i. 3; Col. i. 13.

It may be noticed that the title 'Lord' (κυρίου Ἰ.), which is added by some early authorities, is not found in the Epistles of St John, though it occurs in every other book of the N.T. except the Epistle to Titus.

ἐν ἀλ. καὶ ἀγ.] The threefold divine gift is realised perfectly both in regard to thought and in regard to action. Truth and love describe an intellectual harmony and a moral harmony; and the two correspond with each other according to their subject-matter. Love is truth in human action; and truth is love in regard to the order of things.

The combination is not found elsewhere.

2. *Counsel and warning* (4—11).

The rise of false teachers, who seem to have affected superior knowledge (v. 9 προάγων), and neglected moral duties (comp. 1 John ii. 4), leads St John to emphasise the duty of active love, which is the sum of the divine commandments (4—7); and then to insist upon the necessity of guarding inviolate 'the teaching of Christ,' the historic Gospel which conveys the revelation of 'the Father and the Son' (8—11).

4—7. Past faithfulness is made the foundation for the apostle's counsel (v. 4). He enjoins practical love because deceivers have arisen who by denying the coming of Jesus Christ in flesh deprive earthly life of its divine significance (5—7).

4 *I rejoice greatly that I have found of thy children walking in truth, even as we received commandment from the Father.* 5 *And now I pray thee, Lady, not as writing a new commandment to thee, but that which we had from the beginning, that we love one another.* 6 *And this is love, that we should walk according to His commandments. This is the commandment even as ye heard from the beginning, that ye should walk in it* (love). 7 *Because many deceivers are gone out* (went out) *into the world, even they that confess not Jesus Christ coming in flesh: this is the deceiver and the antichrist.*

⁴Ἐχάρην λίαν ὅτι εὕρηκα ἐκ τῶν τέκνων σου περι-
πατοῦντας ἐν ἀληθείᾳ, καθὼς ἐντολὴν ἐλάβομεν παρὰ
τοῦ πατρός. ⁵καὶ νῦν ἐρωτῶ σε, κυρία, οὐχ ὡς ἐντολὴν
γράφων σοι καινὴν ἀλλὰ ἣν εἴχαμεν ἀπ᾽ ἀρχῆς, ἵνα

4 ἐλάβομεν : ἔλαβον ℵ.　　　　παρά: ἀπό A.　　　　του π.: om. τοῦ B.
5 γράφων σοι καινήν B the: καινὴν γρ. σοι ℵA vg me.　　ἀλλά: +ἐντολήν ℵ
(+an old commandment syrhl).

4. Ἐχάρην...ὅτι εὕρηκα] *I rejoiced
...that I have found...* The joy is
referred to its initial moment : the
ground of it still continues.

For the precedence given to the
expression of joy compare St Paul's
thanksgivings : I Thess. i. 2; 2 Thess.
i. 3; 1 Cor. i. 4; Rom. i. 8; Phil. i.
3 f.; Eph. i. 16; Col. i. 3; Philem. 4.

εὕρηκα] Comp. 3 John 3; and John
i. 44, note.

ἐκ τῶν τ. σ.] V. *de filiis tuis. Some
of thy children.* For ἐκ see John xvi.
17.

The words appear to refer to an
experience of the writer in some other
place than that to which the 'Lady'
belonged.

περιπ. ἐν ἀλ. καθώς...] *walking in
truth even as...* The phrase (περιπ.
ἐν ἀλ. 3 John 3) is not identical with
walking in the truth (περιπ. ἐν τῇ
ἀλ. 3 John 4). Comp. John xvii. 17,
19. It describes the general character of the life as conducted 'in
truth,' really and in very deed in a
certain fashion, even after the commandment of God.

ἐντ. ἐλάβ.] John x. 18; Acts xvii.
15; Col. iv. 10.

παρὰ τοῦ π.] *from the Father* in
the Person of Christ. The preposition
(*v.* 3) marks the directness of the
divine injunction : Apoc. ii. 27.

5. καὶ νῦν] *and now,* looking back
upon that former feeling (*v.* 4) of joy...
The words may mark simply a logical
connexion : 1 John ii. 28.

ἐρωτῶ] *I pray thee,* in the exercise of the full privilege of Christian
fellowship. Comp. 1 John v. 16, note.

The request is directly personal and
not a general exhortation (παρακαλῶ).
It is remarkable that the words παρα-
καλεῖν, παράκλησις, do not occur in the
writings of St John. The singular
address (σέ) occurs again in *v.* 13.
In the intermediate verses the plural
is used.

οὐχ ὡς ἐντ....] *not as writing a new
commandment...* The order is significant (ἐντ. γράφων σ. κ.). The prayer
is first distinguished from a command
generally : 'I pray thee, not as writing
a command to thee ;' and then the
command is more exactly described ;
which is indeed the substance of the
prayer. Comp. 1 John ii. 7.

εἴχαμεν] *we had.* Contrast 1 John
ii. 7 *ye had.* Throughout the apostle
identifies himself with those to whom
he is writing, Christian with Christians.

ἵνα ἀγαπῶμεν...] *that we love...* The
words seem to depend upon *I pray
thee* (John xvii. 15), the intervening
clause being parenthetical. The apostle includes himself in the object of
his prayer (*that we,* not *that ye*). It
is possible that the form in which the
request is thus shaped is occasioned
by the reference to 'the command
which we had.'

ἐρωτῶ σε...ἵνα...] *I pray thee...that...*
The infinitive and a final particle are
both used by St John after ἐρωτᾶν:
(1) *infin.* John iv. 40 ‖ Luke v. 3 ; viii.
37; Acts iii. 3; x. 48; xvi. 39; xviii.
20; xxiii. 18; 1 Th. v. 12. (2) ἵνα
John iv. 47; xix. 31, 38 ‖ Mk. vii. 26;
Luke vii. 36 (vii. 3 ; xi. 37 ὅπως); xvi.
27 (Acts xxiii. 20 ὅπως).

15—2

ἀγαπῶμεν ἀλλήλους. ⁶καὶ αὕτη ἐστὶν ἡ ἀγάπη, ἵνα
περιπατῶμεν κατὰ τὰς ἐντολὰς αὐτοῦ· αὕτη ἡ ἐντολή
ἐστιν, καθὼς ἠκούσατε ἀπ᾽ ἀρχῆς, ἵνα ἐν αὐτῇ περιπατῆτε. ⁷ὅτι πολλοὶ πλάνοι ἐξῆλθαν εἰς τὸν κόσμον, οἱ

6 αὐτοῦ: + ‘ἵνα καθώς’ א* (by the omission of a line of the archetype in
copying).   ἡ ἐντ. ἐ. AB (vg) syrhl: ἐ. ἡ ἐντ. ℭא me the.   ἡ ἐντ.: +αὐτοῦ א.
καθώς…ἵνα ἐν αὐτῇ… B syrhl: ἵνα καθώς…ἵνα ἐν αὐτῇ… אA: ἵνα καθώς…ἐν αὐτῇ
(vg) (me) (the).   περιπατῆτε: περιπατήσητε א.   7 ἐξῆλθαν: εἰσῆλθον ℭ.

6. The two thoughts of ‘commandment’ and ‘love’ are taken up in the inverse order: ‘this is love’, ‘this is the commandment.’ In treating them St John appears to reason in a circle. ‘Love,’ he says, ‘is the effort to walk according to the divine commandments’; and again, ‘The divine commandment is that we endeavour to walk in love.’ The key to this difficulty lies in the difference between ‘commandments’ and ‘commandment.’ Love strives to realise in detail every separate expression of the will of God. The summary expression of the will of God is that men should walk in love, the spirit of sons (1 John iii. 1).

καὶ αὕτη ἐ. ἡ ἀγ.] And this is love… The description of love is simply joined to the request to realise it: 1 John v. 4, 11. ‘Love’ is left completely undefined. Love to God and love to man are not finally distinguished. Comp. 1 John iii. 16; iv. 10, 16—18.

αὕτη…ἵνα…] See 1 John v. 3, note. περιπ. κατὰ τὰς ἐ. αὐ.] walk according to… Compare Mk. vii. 5 περιπ. κατὰ τὴν παράδοσιν…; 2 Cor. x. 2; Rom. viii. 4 κατὰ σάρκα (πνεῦμα) περιπ.; Rom. xiv. 15 κατὰ ἀγάπην περιπ.; 1 Cor. iii. 3 κατὰ ἄνθρωπον περιπ. Elsewhere the construction is περιπ. ἐν (1 John i. 6, note). The two constructions stand side by side 2 Cor. x. 2 f.

αὕτη ἡ ἐντ. ἐ.…] this is the commandment which gathers up in one the many commandments. Compare 1 John iii. 22, 23. The change of order

from the first clause is significant (αὕτη ἐστ. ἡ ἀγ., αὕτη ἡ ἐντ. ἐ.).

ἠκούσατε…περιπατῆτε…] ye heard …ye walk… The second person is required by the definite reference to the first teaching of the Church: 1 John ii. 7, note.

ἵνα ἐν αὐτῇ περιπ.] that ye walk in it, that is in love, which is the main subject of the sentence (comp. Eph. v. 2). No adequate sense is gained by supplying in the commandment (in eo V., sc. mandato). The complete identification of the life of love with the fulfilment of all the commandments of God is characteristic of St John: 1 John v. 2, 3.

7. The peril which arises from false teachers moves St John to stir believers to the active exercise of love one with the other. Love so realised is a safeguard against error. On the other hand the failure to realise the Lord's true humanity in the present imperils the love of man for man. There is a passage here from ‘love’ to ‘truth’ (v. 3 ἐν ἀλ. καὶ ἀγ.).

πλάνοι] seductores V., seducers, deceivers, who lead to wrong action, and not only to wrong opinion. Comp. 1 John ii. 26 οἱ πλανῶντες. 1 Tim. iv. 1 πνεύμασι πλάνοις. 2 Cor. vi. 8 ὡς πλάνοι; Matt. xxvii. 63.

ἐξῆλθαν] went out. The tense (1 John ii. 19) appears to mark a particular crisis. They went out from the bosom of the Christian society to fulfil their work.

πολλοί…οἱ μὴ ὁμολ.] The participial clause does not only assert a

μὴ ὁμολογοῦντες Ἰησοῦν Χριστὸν ἐρχόμενον ἐν σαρκί·
οὗτός ἐστιν ὁ πλάνος καὶ ὁ ἀντίχριστος. ⁸Βλέπετε
ἑαυτούς, ἵνα μὴ ἀπολέσητε ἃ ἠργασάμεθα, ἀλλὰ μισθὸν

ὁ ἀντίχρ.: om. ὁ ℵ.　　8 ἀπολέσητε ἃ ἠργασάμεθα…ἀπολάβητε B the (syrhl):
ἀπολέσητε ἃ εἰργάσασθε …ἀπολάβητε (ℵ) A vg me (syrhl): ἀπολέσαμεν ἃ εἰργα-
σάμεθα…ἀπολάβωμεν ϛ.　　ἀπόλησθε ℵ*.

definite fact as to these deceivers (οὐχ
ὁμολογοῦντες), but marks the character
of the class (comp. 1 John iv. 3):
'even they that confess not.' See Mk.
xv. 41 ἄλλαι πολλαὶ αἱ συναναβᾶσαι.

οἱ μὴ ὁμ.] they who confess not…
The frank and open confession of the
truth is required. Not to make confession, even when this does not take
the form of denial, becomes practically
identical with it. Comp. John i. 20;
1 John iv. 2, 3.

'I. Χρ. ἐρχ. ἐν σ.] Jesus Christ coming in flesh. The thought centres
upon the present perfection of the
Lord's Manhood which is still, and is
to be manifested, and not upon the
past fact of His coming, 1 John iv. 2
(ἐληλυθότα): 1 John v. 6 (ὁ ἐλθών).
Comp. John xiv. 3, note; i. 9 ἦν—
ἐρχόμενον. Apoc. xxii. 20. Cf. ἡ
ὀργὴ ἡ ἐρχ. 1 Thess. i. 10; Col. iii. 6.

οὗτός ἐστιν…] this is… The general
description is individualised. He that
offers this character is the deceiver—
the typical deceiver—and the antichrist. We might perhaps look for
other marks: these are decisive.
Comp. v. 9; 1 John ii. 22; v. 6, 20.

ὁ ἀντίχρ.] the antichrist, of whom
the readers had already heard. 1 John
ii. 18, note.

The idea of the 'deceiver' is mainly
relative to men: that of 'antichrist'
to the Lord.

8, 9. The action of false teachers
imposes upon believers the duty of
self-examination. The danger which
they embody is internal as well as external. There must be a careful watch
within; and this necessity is shewn to
be more urgent by the consideration

that what seems and claims to be progress may be fatal error.

⁸Look to yourselves, that ye may
not lose (destroy) the things which
we wrought, but may receive a full
reward. ⁹Every one that goeth forward and abideth not in the teaching
of Christ hath not God: he that
abideth in the teaching, the same
hath both the Father and the Son.
¹⁰If any one cometh unto you, and
beareth not this teaching, receive him
not into your house, and give him no
greeting; ¹¹for he that giveth him
greeting hath fellowship with his evil
works.

8. Βλέπετε ἑαυτ.] Videte vosmet ip-
sos V., Look to yourselves that… Mark
xiii. 9; 1 Cor. xvi. 10.

ἵνα μὴ ἀπολ.…] ne perdatis…V., that
ye may not lose (or destroy) what we
wrought, the manifold results of our
labours among you, which were as
talents entrusted to your charge for
use.

For the confidence of the apostle
see 1 John iv. 6; but the word ἠργασάμεθα appears to refer to the apostolic teachers generally.

ἀλλά…ἀπολ.]accipiamus V.,but may
receive, receive back, from the Great
Judge… Comp. Luke vi. 34; xv. 27;
xvi. 25; xxiii. 41; Rom. i. 27; Gal. iv.
5 (non accipiamus sed recipiamus,
Aug.).

μισθ. πλ.] mercedem plenam V., a
full reward, in which no one element
is wanting (Ruth ii. 12, LXX, &c.).
Comp. Mk. iv. 28 πλ. σῖτος; 2 Chron.
xv. 17 καρδία πλ. (שָׁלֵם). For the idea
of μισθός see Apoc. xi. 18; xxii. 12;

πλήρη ἀπολάβητε. ⁹πᾶς ὁ προάγων καὶ μὴ μένων ἐν
τῇ διδαχῇ τοῦ χριστοῦ θεὸν οὐκ ἔχει. ὁ μένων ἐν τῇ
διδαχῇ, οὗτος καὶ τὸν πατέρα καὶ τὸν υἱὸν ἔχει. ¹⁰εἴ
τις ἔρχεται πρὸς ὑμᾶς καὶ ταύτην τὴν διδαχὴν οὐ φέρει,
μὴ λαμβάνετε αὐτὸν εἰς οἰκίαν καὶ χαίρειν αὐτῷ μὴ

9 προάγων ℵAB vg me the: παραβαίνων ⲋ.   μένων (2°): +'καὶ μή' ℵ* (as the
copyist looked back three lines in the archetype to προάγων).   διδαχῇ:
+τοῦ χριστοῦ ⲋ me.   τὸν π. καὶ τὸν υἱ. ℵB me the syrhl: τὸν υἱ. καὶ
τὸν π. A vg.

John iv. 36; Matt. v. 12 and parallels;
1 Cor. iii. 8.

9.   πᾶς ὁ προάγων καὶ μ. μ.] omnis
qui præcedit et non m. V., Every one
that goeth forward and abideth not...
every one that advances in bold confidence beyond the limits set to the
Christian Faith. True progress includes the past. These false teachers
proposed to enter on new regions of
truth leaving the old. The two characteristics are taken together (ὁ πρ.
καὶ μὴ μ.).

μένων ἐν] abideth in...John viii. 31;
2 Tim. iii. 14.

ἐν τῇ διδ. τοῦ χρ.] in the doctrine of
Christ, the doctrine which Christ
brought, and which He brought first
in His own person, and then through
His followers (Hebr. ii. 3). This sense
seems better than the doctrine of
(concerning) the Christ, and the usage
of the N.T. is uniformly in favour of
it: Apoc. ii. 14, 15 ; John xviii. 19;
Acts ii. 42. Ἡ διδ. is used absolutely
(as below) in Tit. i. 9 (Rom. xvi. 17).

θ. οὐκ ἔχει] hath not God, Whom he
claims to know more perfectly. Comp.
1 John ii. 23 (οὐδέ) note.

ὁ μένων...οὗτος...] The pronoun emphasises the definition given. Comp.
John vi. 46; vii. 18; xv. 5. Faithful
continuance in 'the doctrine' brings a
living possession of God as He is revealed in the fulness of His Fatherly
relation in 'the Father and the Son.'
The change from the abstract title

'God' in the former clause is significant. Comp. 1 John ii. 22 f.

10, 11. Not only is there danger
within, but false teaching may come
from without under a friendly guise.
The confession of the revelation in 'the
Father and the Son' is the indis-
pensable test of fellowship.

10.   εἴ τις ἔρχεται...] If any one
cometh... The form of expression is
not found elsewhere in the Epistles
or Gospel of St John. It assumes the
case, and does not simply regard it as
possible (ἐάν τις). By 'cometh' is to
be understood an official 'coming.'
St John is not dealing with the casual
visit of a stranger but with that of a
teacher who claims authority.

The picture of the itinerating 'prophet' in the Διδαχή is a vivid illustration of the scene present to St John's
mind (§§ 11 f.).

πρὸς ὑμᾶς] 'the lady and her children' vv. 1, 12.

ταύτ. τ. δ. οὐ φ.] and beareth not
as his message, this doctrine of Christ
which declares the Father and the
Son, the decisive revelation of the
Gospel. For φέρειν compare John
xviii. 29; Acts xxv. 18; 2 Pet. ii. 11.
See also 2 Pet. i. 17, 18, 21; 1 Pet. i.
13. The negative is not affected by
εἰ, because it goes closely with the
verb.

μὴ λαμβ....] nolite recipere...nec ave
ei dixeritis V., receive him not...and
give him no greeting.... These words

λέγετε· ¹¹ὁ λέγων γὰρ αὐτῷ χαίρειν κοινωνεῖ τοῖς
ἔργοις αὐτοῦ τοῖς πονηροῖς.

¹²Πολλὰ ἔχων ὑμῖν γράφειν οὐκ ἐβουλήθην διὰ
χάρτου καὶ μέλανος, ἀλλὰ ἐλπίζω γενέσθαι πρὸς ὑμᾶς
καὶ στόμα πρὸς στόμα λαλῆσαι, ἵνα ἡ χαρὰ ὑμῶν

11 ὁ λέγων γάρ: ὁ γὰρ λ. ϛ.　　12 ἔχων: ἔχω א*Α*.　　γράφειν: γράψαι Α.
ἀλλὰ ἐλπίζω אB the syr hl: ἐλπ. γάρ Α vg me.　　γενέσθαι: ἐλθεῖν ϛ the.
στόμα (1°): +τι א*.　　ὑμῶν AB vg me: ἡμῶν א syrhl (my the).

are to be interpreted with the limitation suggested by the character of the
'coming': 'Do not receive such a
teacher as one who can justly claim
the privilege of Christian hospitality
as a brother; and do not even welcome
him with a greeting of sympathy.' In
the N. T. χαίρειν is always used of the
greeting of first address (Acts xv. 23;
xxiii. 26; James i. 1); otherwise the
context would perhaps suggest that
the thought here is of the greeting of
farewell: 'Do not entertain such a
one: do not send him on his way with
good wishes.' Clement adds: arbi-
tror autem quia et orare cum talibus
non oportet, quoniam in oratione quæ
fit in domo postquam ab orando sur-
gitur salutatio gaudii est et pacis in-
dicium (Fragm. *Hypotyp.* p. 1011 P.).
Whatever may be thought of the application the picture of family devotion is of singular interest.

11. κοινωνεῖ τ. ἔ....] *communicat
operibus illius malignis* V. Comp.
1 Tim. v. 22. The word κοινωνεῖν
implies more than participation in the
definite acts. It suggests fellowship
with the character of which they are
the outcome.

τοῖς ἔ....τοῖς πον.] Comp. 1 John ii.
7 note. John iii. 19; 1 John iii. 12;
Col. i. 21; 2 Tim. iv. 18.

3. *The conclusion* (12, 13).
The main request and the main
warning have been spoken. Other
subjects St John reserves for a per-

sonal interview. A general salutation closes the letter. Comp. 3 John
13—15.
¹² *Though I have many things
to write to you, I would not write
them with paper and ink; but I
hope to be present with you, and to
speak face to face, that your joy may
be fulfilled.*
¹³ *The children of thine elect sister
salute thee.*

12. II. ἔ. ὑμῖν γρ.] The pronoun (*v.*
10) stands in a position of emphasis
(contrast 3 John 13): the special circumstances of those addressed suggested topics to the apostle.

οὐκ ἐβουλ.] *nolui* V., *I would not*
communicate them.... The aorist regards the letter as complete: the decision is made. Comp. 1 John ii. 14
note. Some general word such as
'communicate' must be supplied from
'write.'

διὰ χ. καὶ μέλ.] *per chartam et atra-
mentum* V. Jer. xxxvi. 18.

ἀλλὰ ἐλπ. γ. πρ. ὑ.] *spero enim me
futurum apud vos* V., *but I hope to
be present with you.* The delay in
the communication was to be but
brief. For γεν. πρ. ὑ. see 1 Cor. ii. 3;
xvi. 10.

στόμα πρὸς στόμα] *face to face*,
פֶּה אֶל־פֶּה (Num. xii. 8, LXX. στόμα
κατὰ στόμα). Comp. 1 Cor. xiii. 12.

ἵνα ἡ χ. ὑ. πεπλ. ᾖ] *that your joy
may be fulfilled.* Comp. 1 John i. 4
note.

πεπληρωμένη ᾖ. ¹³Ἀσπάζεταί σε τὰ τέκνα τῆς ἀδελφῆς σου τῆς ἐκλεκτῆς.

πεπλ. ᾖ (א) B: ᾖ πεπλ. A.   ἦν א*.   13 ἐκλεκτῆς: +ἀμήν ς syrhl.

13. Ἀσπ. σε] v. 5. The singular
pronoun answers to τῆς ἀδελφῆς.
τῆς ἀδ....τῆς ἐκλ.] 1 John ii. 7 note.
The adj. ἐκλεκτός is found in St John's
writings elsewhere only in v. 1 and
Apoc. xvii. 14. The verb ἐκλέγεσθαι
occurs in the Gospel: vi. 70; xiii. 18;
xv. 16, 19.

No sure argument as to the individual or corporate interpretation of
κυρία (v. 1) can be drawn from the occurrence of τὰ τέκνα τῆς ἀδ. without ἡ
ἀδελφή. On the whole however the
general tenour of v. 13 seems to favour
the corporate view.

ΙΩΑΝΟΥ Γ

ΙΩΑΝΟΥ Γ

Ο ΠΡΕΣΒΥΤΕΡΟΣ *Γαίῳ τῷ ἀγαπητῷ, ὃν ἐγὼ ἀγαπῶ ἐν ἀληθείᾳ.*

The letter is marked throughout by personal circumstances, and is broken up into short paragraphs which are severally suggested by these. After the salutation (*v.* 1) St John (1) expresses in general terms his joy at the tidings of Gaius which he hears (2—4); and (2) specially approves his hospitality towards missionary brethren (5—8). In contrast with this generosity (3) he condemns the ambitious self-assertion of Diotrephes (9, 10); and then (4) gives his witness in favour of Demetrius (11, 12); and so (5) concludes (13—15).

1. *The salutation.*

The salutation stands in contrast by its brevity with the salutations in the other personal letters of the New Testament. The wish of blessing is transposed in another form to the following verse.

¹*The Elder to Gaius the beloved, whom I love in truth.*

1. ὁ πρεσβύτερος] 2 John 1 note.
Γαίῳ τῷ ἀγ.] The name 'Gaius' (Caius) occurs Acts xix. 29 (a 'Macedonian'); xx. 4 ('of Derbe'); 1 Cor. i. 14 (a Corinthian); Rom. xvi. 23 (a Corinthian). There is nothing to identify this Gaius with any one of these. Another is mentioned as having been made bishop of Pergamum by St John (*Const. Ap.* vii.

46). The position which Gaius occupied in the church to which he belonged is not shown by the letter. The epithet 'beloved' is afterwards used as a title of address (*vv.* 2, 5, 11). It occurs several times in salutations of St Paul: Rom. xvi. 12; Philem. 1 ('the beloved'); Rom. xvi. 5, 8, 9, ('my beloved'); 2 Tim. i. 2 ('my beloved child').

ὃν ἐγὼ ἀγ.] The emphatic personal pronoun (2 John 1) seems to point to some gainsayers with whom the apostle contrasts himself. Compare 'thou' (σύ) in *v.* 3.

ἐν ἀληθ.] Comp. 2 John 1 note. ἐν ἀληθείᾳ ἀγαπᾷ ὁ κατὰ Κύριον ἀγαπῶν (Œcumen.).

2. *The teacher's joy* (2—4).

St John, having much ground for sorrow and disappointment, begins with the expression of joy (comp. 2 John 4). Some of his own children (comp. 2 John *l.c.*), Gaius among them, were loyal to the Truth. He could wish him nothing better than that all his circumstances should correspond to his spiritual progress.

The salutation is completed, after the common model, in *v.* 1. The second verse adds what corresponds to the fuller Christian greeting (2 John 3).

²*Beloved, I pray that in all things*

²Ἀγαπητέ, περὶ πάντων εὔχομαί σε εὐοδοῦσθαι καὶ
ὑγιαίνειν, καθὼς εὐοδοῦταί σου ἡ ψυχή. ³ἐχάρην γὰρ
λίαν ἐρχομένων ἀδελφῶν καὶ μαρτυρούντων σου τῇ ἀληθείᾳ, καθὼς σὺ ἐν ἀληθείᾳ περιπατεῖς. ⁴μειζοτέραν

3 ἐχάρην γάρ ABC me syr.: om. γάρ ℵ vg the.   μαρτυρούντων: μαρτυρουν B
(at the end of a line).   καθὼς σύ: om. σύ A.

thou mayest prosper and be in good
health even as thy soul prospereth.
³For I rejoiced (rejoice) greatly when
brethren came (come) and bore (bear)
witness to thy truth, even as thou
walkest in truth. ⁴I have no greater
grace than these tidings, that I may
hear of mine own children walking
in the truth.

2. Ἀγαπητέ] carissime V. (vv. 5, 11).
For the use of the plural see 1 John
ii. 7 note.

περὶ π. εὐχ. σε εὐοδ....] de omnibus
orationem facio prospere te ingredi
V. In all things I pray that thou
mayest be prosperous... The phrase
περὶ πάντων is remarkable. It may
go with εὐοδοῦσθαι or with the sentence generally (comp. 1 Cor. xvi.
1). The sense 'above all things' is
not justified by any parallel in the
N. T. or LXX.; and the context points
to a contrast between 'the soul' and
other things. The thought appears
to be of the public and social work of
Gaius as distinguished from his personal progress, though ὑγιαίνειν may
point to some illness.

εὔχομαι] The word is rare in N.T.:
2 Cor. xiii. 7, 9; Acts xxvi. 29; xxvii.
29.

εὐοδ. καὶ ὑγιαίνειν] The elements of
progress and vigour are combined.
For εὐοδοῦσθαι see 1 Cor. xvi. 2;
Rom. i. 10. In St Paul ὑγιαίνειν is
always used metaphorically of sound
doctrine; but it occurs in the literal
sense of sound health in St Luke: v.
31, vii. 10, xv. 27.

καθὼς...ψυχή] sicut prospere agit
anima tua V. Ψυχή expresses here
the principle of the higher life ('soul')

(Hebr. vi. 19, x. 39, xiii. 17; 1 Pet. ii.
11, iv. 19). The nearest approach to
this sense elsewhere in St John's
writings is John xii. 27 (x. 24). In
other places he uses it only of the
principle of the 'natural' life.

3. ἐχάρην γάρ...] Comp. 2 John 4.
The joy which the apostle felt at the
tidings of the action of Gaius is given
in explanation of his far-reaching wish
for his welfare, and not only as an
assurance of his spiritual well-being.
The words evidently point to some
difficulties from false teaching which
Gaius had boldly met, though as yet
the issue of his work was uncertain.

ἐρχομ. ἀδ.] when brethren came not
on one occasion only (ἐλθόντων) but
from time to time, though all these
visits belonged definitely to the past
(ἐχάρην) when the apostle wrote. The
words give a vivid picture of continued troubles even in the apostolic
church.

ἀδελφῶν] vv. 5, 10. Comp. 1 John
iii. 14 addit. note.

μαρτ. σ. τῇ ἀλ.] testimonium per-
hibentibus veritati tuæ V., bore witness to thy truth, attested the perfect
and sincere loyalty with which you
maintain the fulness of the Christian
faith in life. Christian thought and
Christian action are inseparable.

καθὼς σύ...] even as thou walkest
in truth, truly. Comp. 2 John 4.
The emphatic pronoun (σύ) suggests
a contrast with others as (for example) Diotrephes. Gaius walked not
only in word but really (ἐν ἀληθ. 1
John iii. 18) according to the standard
of the Christian revelation (ἐν τῇ ἀλ.
'in the Truth'). The clause seems to

τούτων οὐκ ἔχω χάριν, ἵνα ἀκούω τὰ ἐμὰ τέκνα ἐν
τῇ ἀληθείᾳ περιπατοῦντα.　⁵Ἀγαπητέ, πιστὸν

4 τούτων οὐκ ἔ. χ. ℵAB: τούτων χ. οὐκ ἔ. C.　ἔχω: ἔχων B*.　χάριν
B vg me: χαρὰν ⸤ℵAC the.　τῇ ἀλ. ABC*: om τῇ ⸤ℵ.

be one of those personal comments
in which St John pausing on what is
written, as it were, thinks aloud:
'They witnessed to thy truth; yes,
and when the vision of vain profes-
sions rises before me I know that
thou at least livest indeed as thou
teachest.'

4. μειζοτέραν...χάριν, ἵνα...] majorem horum non habeo gratiam quam
ut...V. I have no greater grace
—favour from God—than these tidings, that I may hear... The plural
τούτων 'these things' does not refer
to what follows ('that I may hear')
but to what precedes, the manifold
testimonies which St John received of
the courageous resolution with which
Gaius maintained the Truth in the
face of difficulties. The end assured
by such tidings was the open acknowledgment of the fidelity of disciples
('that so I may hear'). Even if St
John had himself no doubt of the
fact, it would be a joy to know that it
was also observed by others. For the
construction see John xv. 13 note.

For the form μειζότερος compare
ἐλαχιστότερος Eph. iii. 8.

ἔχω χάριν] The use of χάρις is remarkable; but χάρις makes the 'joy'
(χαρά) of the common text itself a
divine gift. The word is very rare
in St John (2 John 3 note). Here
it expresses the divine favour in a
concrete form. So it is used of the
gracious gift of men: 1 Cor. xvi. 3.
'To have grace' (or 'a grace') here
corresponds with 'giving' (Rom. xii.
6, &c.) and 'receiving' grace (Rom. i.
5). Ἔχειν χάριν is used elsewhere in
different constructions and senses:
ἔχειν χάριν τινί Luke xvii. 9; 1 Tim. i.
12; ἔ. χ. πρός τινα Acts ii. 47.

τὰ ἐμὰ τ.] mine own children

(Philem. 10), not simply τὰ τέκνα μου.
Those Christians to whom the apostle
had been the human author of spiritual life: 1 Cor. iv. 14, 17; 1 Tim. i.
2, &c.; 2 John 1, 13. Τεκνία, the title
of affection, would be used of all to
whom he at present stood in the position of father: 1 John ii. 1, note.

ἐν τῇ ἀλ. περιπ.] The phrase is not
found elsewhere in N. T. Comp. ἐν τῷ
σκ. (ἐν τῇ σκ.) π. 1 John i. 6; ii. 11;
ἐν τῷ φωτὶ π. 1 John i. 7; ἐν αὐτῇ (τῇ
ἀγάπῃ) π. 2 John 6. For the image
see 1 John i. 6, note.

3. The duty of generosity to the
brethren (5—8).

Gaius appears to have incurred the
displeasure of some in his Church
by entertaining strange brethren. St
John emphatically approves what he
had done, and enforces such hospitality as a Christian duty.

In this brief notice we have a vivid
sketch of the work and of the difficulties of the first 'Evangelists': Eph.
iv. 11. Compare Doctr. of App. 11 ff.

⁵Beloved, thou makest sure whatsoever thou doest unto the brethren and
strangers withal, ⁶who bore witness
to thy love before the church; whom
thou wilt do well to help forward
on their journey worthily of God;
⁷for they went out for the Name's
sake, taking nothing from the Gentiles.
⁸We therefore ought to welcome such
that we may be fellow workers with
the truth.

5. πιστὸν π.] fideliter facis V. The
phrase is commonly interpreted: 'thou
doest a faithful work,' a work which
answers to thy faith: so Œcum. ἄξιον
πιστοῦ ἀνδρός. No parallel is quoted
in support of such a sense of πιστός.
The more natural rendering is rather

ποιεῖς ὃ ἐὰν ἐργάσῃ εἰς τοὺς ἀδελφοὺς καὶ τοῦτο ξένους,
⁶οἳ ἐμαρτύρησάν σου τῇ ἀγάπῃ ἐνώπιον ἐκκλησίας, οὓς
καλῶς ποιήσεις προπέμψας ἀξίως τοῦ θεοῦ· ⁷ὑπὲρ γὰρ

5 ἐργάσῃ: ἐργάξῃ A.   καὶ τοῦτο ℵABC vg me the syrr: καὶ εἰς τοὺς ϛ.
6 οὓς: ου B*.   ποιήσεις προπέμψας: ποιήσας προπέμψεις C (lat).

'thou makest sure'; that is, such an act will not be lost, will not fail of its due issue and reward (Apoc. xxi. 5). This sense falls in well with the context (comp. Apoc. xiv. 13), and explains the use of the two verbs, ποιεῖν, ἐργάζεσθαι, which are combined also in Col. iii. 23.

ὃ ἐὰν ἐργ.] The indefinite form (ὃ ἐάν as contrasted with ὅ) marks the variety of service. For ἐργάζομαι see John vi. 28, ix. 4; and for ἐργ. εἰς, Matt. xxvi. 10.

καὶ τοῦτο ξ.] et hoc in...V., and strangers withal. The fact that this detail is emphasised in the commendation of the hospitality of Gaius seems to imply that it had been made the occasion of unjust blame. For καὶ τοῦτο compare 1 Cor. vi. 6; Phil. i. 28; Eph. ii. 8. Viewed rightly the fact that these brethren were strangers gave them a more pressing claim upon the common ties of brotherhood. Comp. Hebr. xiii. 2 note.

6. οἳ ἐμαρτ....] Those who in one particular case experienced the habitual hospitality of Gaius bore open testimony to his character in a public assembly of the church where the writer was, gathered together, as it may seem, to receive their report: comp. Acts xiv. 26 ff. For ἐνώπιον ἐκκλ. (not τῆς ἐκκλ.) compare ἐν ἐκκλ. 1 Cor. xiv. 19, 35: ἐν συναγωγῇ John vi. 59, xviii. 20. Doctr. Ap. iv. 14 ἐν ἐκκλησίᾳ ἐξομολογήσῃ τὰ παραπτώματά σου.

οὓς κ. π. προπέμψας] quos benefaciens deduces (benefacies ducens) V. Those who had before found help from Gaius now again required it for a special work. The future implies a wish which, it is assumed, will at once

be fulfilled. Comp. Rom. vi. 14. For προπέμψας see Acts xv. 3; Tit. iii. 13. The latter passage suggests that the word includes some provision for the journey as well as sympathetic attendance: Acts xxi. 3. St John regards the act in its completeness (προπέμψας) and not in process (προπέμπων). This makes the combination of the aor. and fut. natural. For προπ. compare Polyc. Phil. 1 συνεχάρην ὑμῖν...προπέμψασιν ὡς ἐπέβαλεν ὑμῖν τοὺς ἐνειλημμένους τοῖς ἁγιοπρέπεσι δεσμοῖς.

καλῶς ποι.] Acts x. 33; James ii. 8 (19); 2 Pet. i. 19; 1 Cor. vii. 37 f.; Phil. iv. 14.

Compare Ign. Smyrn. 10 Φίλωνα καὶ Ῥέον Ἀγαθόπουν, οἳ ἐπηκολούθησάν μοι εἰς λόγον θεοῦ, καλῶς ἐποιήσατε ὑποδεξάμενοι ὡς διακόνους Χριστοῦ θεοῦ.

ἀξ. τ. θ.] worthily of their dedication to the service of God: John xiii. 20. Comp. 1 Thess. ii. 12; Col. i. 10 ἀξ. τοῦ κυρίου.

7. ὑπὲρ γὰρ τ. ὀν.] pro nomine enim V., for the Name's sake, that is, to make the Name better known: Rom. i. 5.

'The Name' is used absolutely Acts v. 41 (comp. v. 40 ἐπὶ τῷ ὀν. Ἰησοῦ). Comp. James ii. 7. It is also found in the letters of Ignatius: ad Eph. 7 τὸ ὄνομα περιφέρειν: ad Philad. 10 δοξάσαι τὸ ὄνομα. Comp. ad Eph. 1 δέδεμαι ὑπὲρ τοῦ κοινοῦ ὀνόματος καὶ ἐλπίδος: id. 3 εἰ...δέδεμαι ἐν τῷ ὀνόματι οὔπω ἀπήρτισμαι ἐν Ἰησοῦ Χριστῷ. From the contexts it is evident that 'the Name' is 'Jesus Christ' ('the Lord Jesus'), or, as it is written at length, 'Jesus Christ, the Son of God' (John xx. 31; 1 John iv. 15). This 'Name'

τοῦ ὀνόματος ἐξῆλθαν μηδὲν λαμβάνοντες ἀπὸ τῶν
ἐθνικῶν. ⁸ἡμεῖς οὖν ὀφείλομεν ὑπολαμβάνειν τοὺς τοι-
ούτους, ἵνα συνεργοὶ γινώμεθα τῇ ἀληθείᾳ.

7 ὀνόματος: +αὐτοῦ Elz.   ἀπὸ τῶν: om. τῶν C.   ἐθνικῶν: ἐθνῶν ⸋.   8
ὑπολαμβάνειν: ἀπολαμβάνειν ⸋.   γινώμεθα: γινόμεθα C.   ἀληθείᾳ ℵBC vg:
ἐκκλησίᾳ ℵ*A.

is in essence the sum of the Christian
Creed (comp. 1 Cor. xii. 3; Rom. x. 9).

When analysed it reveals the triune
'Name' into which the Christian is
baptized, Matt. xxviii. 19. Compare
also 1 Pet. iv. 16 ἐν τῷ ὀνόματι τούτῳ
i.e. *Christian*.

With the absolute use of 'the
Name' may. be compared the absolute use of 'the Way'; Acts ix. 2, xix.
9, 23, xxiv. 22.

See Additional Note.

ἐξῆλθαν] *profecti sunt* V., *they went
forth* from some Church, well known
to the apostle and Gaius, on a mission
of Truth, as others went forth on a
mission of error (2 John 7; 1 John ii.
19). Comp. Acts xv. 40.

μηδὲν λαμβ....] *taking nothing* as
their habitual rule. This trait is given
not as a simple fact (οὐδὲν λαμβ.), but
as a mark of character. These teachers
refused to receive hospitality from
Gentiles who were unconverted. Many
reasons may have recommended such
a rule. St Paul alludes frequently to
difficulties which arose even from that
reasonable provision by the Church
which St John here claims: 1 Thess.
ii. 6 ff.; 1 Cor. ix. 14 f.; 2 Cor. xii. 16 ff.
For λαμβ. ἀπὸ see Matt. xvii. 25.

ἀπὸ τῶν ἐθνικ.] *a gentilibus* (*genti-
bus*) V., *from the Gentiles* to whom
they carried the Gospel. The form
used (ἐθνικός) describes character rather than mere position: Matt. v. 47,
vi. 7, xviii. 17. It does not seem to
be found in the LXX.

8. ἡμεῖς οὖν...] *We therefore*, as
fellow Christians, *ought* (are bound,
1 John ii. 6 note) *to receive* (support)
such. The word ὑπολαμβάνειν (*sus-*

cipere V.) gives the notion of welcoming with hospitable support.

ἵνα συν. γιν. τῇ ἀλ.] *ut cooperato-
res simus veritatis* V. The phrase is
ambiguous. The fellowship may be
either with the teachers: 'that we
may be fellow-workers with them in
support of the truth'; or with the
truth, the substance of their teaching:
'that we may help the truth which is
effective through them.' The word
συνεργός is not used elsewhere in the
N. T. or LXX with the dat. It is
used with the gen. of the person with
whom the worker cooperates (*e.g.*
Rom. xvi. 21 ὁ συν. μου, 1 Cor. iii. 9
θεοῦ συνεργοί), and with the gen. of
the object, 1 Cor. iii. 9 συνεργοὶ τῆς
χαρᾶς, 1 Macc. xiv. 5. It is also used
with εἰς (Col. iv. 11 συν. εἰς τὴν βασιλείαν) and πρός (2 Macc. viii. 7 πρὸς
τὰς...ἐπιβουλὰς συν.) of the object.
The verb is used with the dat. of that
which is helped, James ii. 22 συνήργει
τοῖς ἔργοις, 1 Macc. xii. 1; and this
construction is sufficient to support
the connexion of συν. with τῇ ἀλ.

4. *The temporary triumph of ambition* (9, 10).

As yet St John had not succeeded in
removing the opposition from which
Gaius suffered; but he makes it clear
that the issue cannot be doubtful.

⁹*I wrote a few words to the
Church; but he that loveth to have
the preeminence among them, Diotrephes, doth not receive us.* ¹⁰*For
this cause, if I come I will call to
remembrance his works which he
doeth, prating of us with evil words;
and, since he is not content therewith,*

⁹Ἔγραψά τι τῇ ἐκκλησίᾳ· ἀλλ᾽ ὁ φιλοπρωτεύων
αὐτῶν Διοτρέφης οὐκ ἐπιδέχεται ἡμᾶς. ¹⁰διὰ τοῦτο,
ἐὰν ἔλθω, ὑπομνήσω αὐτοῦ τὰ ἔργα ἃ ποιεῖ, λόγοις
πονηροῖς φλυαρῶν ἡμᾶς, καὶ μὴ ἀρκούμενος ἐπὶ τούτοις

9 ἔγραψα אּ*AC: ἔγραψα ἄν אּᶜ vg syrr: ἔγραψας B.　ἔγρ. τι: om. τι 5אּᶜ vg syrr.
10 ἡμᾶς: εἰς ἡμᾶς C.

neither doth he receive the brethren himself and them that would he hindereth and casteth out of the Church.

9. Ἔγραψά τι] scripsissem forsitan V., I wrote a few words. The use of τι to express 'something of importance' is foreign to the N. T. and unsuitable to the context. St John treats his letter lightly. The letter, which may be regarded as the type of a class, has not been preserved. To escape from the difficulty supposed to be involved in the loss of an apostolic letter several early authorities introduced ἄν (as V.).

τῇ ἐκκλησίᾳ] to the Church to which Gaius belonged, as well as now to Gaius himself. St John had by this time heard that his letter had for the present failed. This is the only passage in his Epistles (v. 6 is different) in which St John speaks of 'a Church.' The word ἐκκλησία does not occur in his Gospel. In the Apocalypse (as here) 'the Church' is always used of the special society in a particular place (comp. Apoc. xxii. 16 ἐπὶ ταῖς ἐκκλησίαις); so that St John nowhere gives a distinct expression to the thought worked out in Eph. i. 22, v. 23 ff.; though he records the gift of its new life, John xx. 21 ff.

ὁ φιλοπρ....Δ.] is qui amat primatum gerere in iis D. V., he that loveth to have the preeminence among (or over) them... The word φιλόπρωτος occurs in late Greek (Polyb. Plut.), but φιλοπρωτεύειν is not quoted from any other passage. The idea of πρωτεύειν governs the gen. αὐτῶν, which answers

to ἡ ἐκκλησία (comp. 1 Cor. i. 2 τῇ ἐκκλ., ἡγιασμένοις). It is of interest to compare the two sources of failure noticed in the two Epistles, προάγειν (2 John 9) and φιλοπρωτεύειν, the undue claims to intellectual progress and to personal authority. There is nothing to indicate that Diotrephes held false opinions : his ambition only is blamed. Comp. Herm. Tim. viii. 7, 4 ἔχοντες ζῆλόν τινα ἐν ἀλλήλοις περὶ πρωτείων καὶ περὶ δόξης τινός : id. 7.

οὐκ ἐπιδέχ. ἡ.] In v. 10 the word is used of the literal welcome of visitors : here it is naturally understood of the recognition of the apostle's wish as authoritative. Comp. 1 Macc. x. 1 ἐπεδέξαντο αὐτόν (as sovereign); xii. 8, 43 ; x. 46 ἐπεδ. λόγους; Ecclus. vi. 26 ἐπεδ. παιδείαν. By the use of ἡμᾶς (contrast ἔγραψα v. 1 ἐγώ) St John removes the question from a personal issue. He identifies himself with the society (vv. 8, 12 ἡμεῖς, 1 John iv. 6 ; v. 14 f.).

10. διὰ τοῦτο...] St John implies that his personal presence will be decisive. By using the form ἐὰν ἔλθω there is no doubt thrown on the main fact of his coming (v. 14). Comp. 1 John ii. 28.

ὑπομν. αὐτ. τ. ἔ.] commoneam ejus opera V., I will call to remembrance his works, I will bring them to his notice and to the notice of others. Ὑπομιμνήσκειν is used with the acc. of the person (2 Pet. i. 12) and of the thing (2 Tim. ii. 14), and of both (John xiv. 26).

λ. πον. φλ. ἡ.] verbis malignis garriens in nos V., prating of us with

οὔτε αὐτὸς ἐπιδέχεται τοὺς ἀδελφοὺς καὶ τοὺς βουλομένους κωλύει καὶ ἐκ τῆς ἐκκλησίας ἐκβάλλει.
¹¹Ἀγαπητέ, μὴ μιμοῦ τὸ κακὸν ἀλλὰ τὸ ἀγαθόν.
ὁ ἀγαθοποιῶν ἐκ τοῦ θεοῦ ἐστίν· ὁ κακοποιῶν οὐχ
ἑώρακεν τὸν θεόν.   ¹²Δημητρίῳ μεμαρτύρηται ὑπὸ πάν-

βουλομένους: ἐπιδεχομένους C the.   ἐκ τῆς ἐκκλ.: om. ἐκ ℵ.   11 ὁ κακοπ.:
ὁ δὲ κακοπ. ⸊ me.

evil words (Matt. v. 11; Acts xxviii.
21). The adj. φλύαρος occurs 1 Tim.
v. 13.

μὴ ἀρκ. ἐπὶ τ.] quasi non ei ista
sufficiant V., and since he does not
rest content therewith... Ἀρκεῖσθαι is
used with the simple dat. Luke iii.
14; Hebr. xiii. 5; 1 Tim. vi. 8.

οὔτε...καί...] nec...et... V.   John iv.
11.

κωλύει...ἐκβάλλει] The verbs do not
necessarily express more than the
purpose and effort: comp. John x.
32 (Matt. iii. 14). It is difficult to
realise the circumstances of the case.
It may perhaps be reasonably conjectured from ὁ φιλοπρωτεύων that
Diotrephes regarded the reception of
the brethren as an invasion of his
authority.

ἐκβάλλει] Luke vi. 22; John ix. 34 f.

5.   The witness to the faithful disciple (11, 12).

Self-seeking may have its tempting
successes, but they rest on no secure
foundation. The faithful are supported
by many converging testimonies.
¹¹ Beloved, imitate not that which
is evil but that which is good. He
that doeth good is of God; he that
doeth evil hath not seen God. ¹²De-
metrius hath witness borne to him
by all and by the truth itself: yea
we also bear witness; and thou
knowest that our witness is true.

11. Ἀγαπητέ...] The transition lies
in the thought of the power which
Diotrephes had won by wrong means.
μὴ μιμοῦ] noli imitari V. Comp.
2 Thess. iii. 7, 9; Hebr. xiii. 7. The
W.

noun μιμητής occurs several times: e.g.
1 Cor. iv. 16; Eph. v. 1.

τὸ κ....τὸ ἀγ....] malum...quod bonum est V. Rom. xii. 21.

ἀγαθ....κακοπ....] Mk. iii. 4; Luke
vi. 9; 1 Pet. iii. 17.

ἐκ τοῦ θ. ἐ....οὐχ ἑώρ. τ. θ....] The
two stages of divine relationship correspond with the two characters. He
who does good proves by his action
that his life springs from God as its
source (εἶναι ἐκ τ. θ. Addit. Note on
1 John iii. 1): he who does evil has not
made the first step towards participation in the Divine Nature (1 John
iii. 6 note). In one sense the vision of
God (the Father) in Christ (John xiv.
9) is the condition of fellowship with
Him: in another sense the vision of
God as God lies beyond the power of
man (John i. 18).

It is likely that here, as elsewhere,
St John points to men who professed
to have deeper insight into truth and
disparaged the importance of virtuous
action.

12. Δημητρίῳ μεμαρτ.] From the
unfaithful St John turns to the faithful: from the 'evil' to the 'good.' It is
likely from the context that Demetrius
was the bearer of the letter. For μαρτ.
τινί see John iii. 26; Luke iv. 22;
Acts xv. 8; and in pass. Acts vi. 3; x.
22; xvi. 2; xxii. 12; 1 Tim. v. 10, &c.

St John appeals to a threefold witness given in favour of Demetrius (1)
ὑπὸ π. by all, that is the general witness of men arising out of the experience of life; (2) ὑπ᾽ αὐτ. τ. ἀλ. by
the Truth itself, so far as the ideal of
Christianity was seen to be realised by

16

τῶν καὶ ὑπὸ αὐτῆς τῆς ἀληθείας· καὶ ἡμεῖς δὲ μαρτυροῦμεν, καὶ οἶδας ὅτι ἡ μαρτυρία ἡμῶν ἀληθής ἐστιν.

¹³ Πολλὰ εἶχον γράψαι σοι, ἀλλ᾽ οὐ θέλω διὰ μέλανος καὶ καλάμου σοι γράφειν· ¹⁴ἐλπίζω δὲ εὐθέως σε
ἰδεῖν, καὶ στόμα πρὸς στόμα λαλήσομεν. ¹⁵Εἰρήνη σοι.
ἀσπάζονταί σε οἱ φίλοι. ἀσπάζου τοὺς φίλους κατ᾽
ὄνομα.

12 τῆς ἀληθείας: τῆς ἐκκλησίας καὶ τῆς ἀλ. C: τῆς ἐκκλησίας A* (?).　οἶδας: οἴδατε
ς.　ἡ μαρτ. ἡ. ἀλ. ἐστ.: ἀλ. ἡ. ἐστ. ἡ μαρτ. C.　　13 γράψαι σοι: γράφειν ς.
οὐ θέλω: οὐκ ἐβουλήθην A (2 John 12).　　σοὶ γρ. אBC: γρ. σοι A vg me the syrr.
γράφειν: γράψαι ς.　　14 σε ἰδεῖν ABC vg: ἰδεῖν σε ςא me.　　πρός: πρό B*.
15 οἱ φίλοι: οἱ ἀδελφοί A.　　ἀσπάζου: ἀσπασαι א.

him; (3) καὶ ἡμ. δὲ μαρτ. *yea and we
also bear witness:* St John and those
with him spoke with the authority of
the Church.

For the combination μεμαρτ., μαρτυροῦμεν see John v. 33, 36. The
witness given in the past was still
effective while it was also complete:
the witness of St John came with
present fresh force.

ὑπὸ π.] *by all.* It is possible that
these words are to be taken quite
generally: 1 Tim. iii. 7; though it is
not necessary to extend them beyond
the circle of Christians.

καί...δέ...] See 1 John i. 3.

καὶ οἶδας] The words in John xxi.
24 sound like an echo of this sentence.
This verse serves the purpose of 'a
commendatory letter' (συστατικὴ ἐπιστολή 2 Cor. iii. 1).

6.　*The conclusion* (13—15).

¹³*I had many things to write to
thee, howbeit I will not write to thee
with ink and pen;* ¹⁴*but I hope to
see thee shortly, and we will speak
face to face.*

¹⁵*Peace be to thee: the friends*

*salute thee: salute the friends by
name.*

13. εἶχον] The writer goes back to
the time when the letter was begun.
See 2 John 12. The variations in
form are worth notice: ἔχων οὐκ
ἐβουλήθην, εἶχον ἀλλ᾽ οὐ θέλω—ὑμῖν
γράφειν, γράψαι σοι—διὰ χάρτου καὶ μέλανος, διὰ μέλανος καὶ καλάμου—γενέσθαι πρὸς ὑ., εὐθ. σε ἰδεῖν—λαλῆσαι,
λαλήσομεν. If the second Epistle was
addressed to a Church it would not
be difficult to shew that there is a
fitness in the subtle differences in
tone.

15. εἰρήνη σοι] *Peace be to thee:*
1 Pet. v. 14. As a formula of greeting:
Luke x. 5; xxiv. 36; John xx. 19, 21,
26. And so (in combination with
other words) in epistolary salutations:
2 John 3 note.

οἱ φίλοι] *our friends.* The word
does not occur again in the Epistles in
this connexion. Comp. Acts xxvii. 3.
It gives a faint glimpse of personal
relationships. Comp. John xv. 13 ff.

κατ᾽ ὄνομα] *per nomen* V. Comp.
John x. 3 (xx. 16). Polyc. *Phil.* 13
ἀσπάζομαι...πάντας κατ᾽ ὄνομα.

Additional Note on v. 7.   The Divine Name.

The idea of the 'Name' (שֵׁם, ὄνομα) has a far deeper significance in Biblical language than in our own. As applied to God it expresses that which has been made known of Him ; or, more exactly to distinguish the two factors in the revelation, that which He has made known of Himself, and which man can apprehend as addressed to him. Thus the Name of God does not represent His Essence as He is in Himself but the manifestation of Himself which He has been pleased to give : that view of His Being and Character by which it is His will to be known, and under which He authorises man to address Him (comp. Gen. xvi. 13, xxxii. 29 ; Ex. vi. 3). And as applied to men the new name symbolises a new state, a new work and new powers for its fulfilment (Apoc. ii. 17, iii. 12, xxii. 4). *The Divine Name in the O. T.*

Under this aspect the Name of God is used in two ways. It may express some particular revelation, expressed by one definite title (*El-Shaddai, Jehovah, Father*), or the whole sum of these manifold revelations taken together as one supreme revelation (ὁ θεός, *God*).

Hence it comes to pass that the 'Name' often stands for God Himself so far as it brings Him before man: Ex. xxiii. 21 (my Name is in Him, *i. e.* the Angel of the Covenant); 1 K. viii. 29 (the place of which Thou hast said: My Name shall be there); Is. xxx. 27 (Behold the Name of the Lord cometh from far).

'To blaspheme the Name' was the same as 'blaspheming the Name of the Lord' (Lev. xxiv. 11, 16), that is blaspheming God as He had revealed Himself through Moses to His people (comp. Ex. vi. 3). And in the Acts (iii. 13, 16) it is said that the Name of 'Jesus, the Servant of the God of Abraham and Isaac and Jacob' gave strength to the lame man (comp. Acts iv. 30, 12).

It follows as a natural consequence that the Divine Names in the Bible give in a broad outline the course of revelation.

There is first the general name *El, Elohim*, which expresses man's feeling after God, apart from any special revelation.

Then follows the patriarchal title *El-Shaddai*, which indicates the exercise of the sovereign might of God for the fulfilment of His counsel.

Then the covenant name *Jehovah*, which is developed in the titles 'the Holy One,' 'the Lord of Hosts.'

Then follows a silence, when the Divine Name is unspoken.

At last the revelation of the Father is given: 'ὁ πατὴρ μου καὶ πατὴρ ὑμῶν καὶ θεός μου καὶ θεὸς ὑμῶν' (John xx. 17).

Two names present the two main views of God in the O. T., *Elohim* and *Jehovah*. The former, the generic name, gathers up what St Paul speaks of as τὸ γνωστὸν τοῦ θεοῦ...ἡ ἀΐδιος αὐτοῦ δύναμις καὶ θειότης (Rom. i. 19 f.), all that man is made to recognise little by little from the study of his own constitution and the world without. The latter, the proper name, gathers up all that God made known of Himself in His dealings with His people during the discipline of the first Covenant. Speaking generally

16—2

Elohim describes the God of Nature, *Jehovah* the God of revelation. The former includes the ideas of the creation, preservation, and general fixed government of finite things: the latter, the idea of living, progressive intercourse with men, of whom Israel were for the time the representatives. The great confession of the chosen people was to declare that the God of revelation is the God for Whom man's soul craves, One in His infinite perfections: Deut. vi. 4. '*Jehovah* our *Elohim* (or is our *Elohim*), *Jehovah* is One' (comp. 1 John v. 20).

The Divine Name in the N. T. Not to dwell in detail here upon the Divine Names in the O. T. it must be noticed that the idea of 'the Name' is no less prominent in the N. T. Thus the Lord characterises His own Mission as a 'Coming in the Name of His Father' (John v. 43); and the Mission of the Holy Spirit as a Mission in His Name (John xiv. 26 ὃ πέμψει ὁ πατὴρ ἐν τῷ ὀνόματί μου). He glorified His Father and manifested His Father's Name to men (John xvii. 4, 6); and it is the work of the Holy Spirit to glorify Him, and to take of His and declare it to His disciples (John xvi. 14). In the one case, if we may so speak, the Name of the Father was completely shewn: God was made known perfectly in this relation by the fact of the Incarnation. In the other case the Church is learning little by little the Name of the Son.

The most complete expression of the Divine Name is that given in Matt. xxviii. 19 τὸ ὄνομα τοῦ πατρὸς καὶ τοῦ υἱοῦ καὶ τοῦ ἁγίου πνεύματος, but the essence of this Name so written at length is the simple Name 'Jesus Christ' or 'the Lord Jesus,' or even 'Jesus' alone, when the context determines the office attached to it : ὄν. Ἰ. Χρ. (Acts ii. 38, iii. 6, iv. 10, viii. 12, x. 48, xvi. 18; ὄν. τοῦ κυρίου Ἰ. Acts viii. 16 (ix. 14) (xv. 26), xix. 5, 13, 17, xxi. 13; ὄν. Ἰ. iv. 18 (30), v. 20, ix. 27, xxvi. 9).

In the Epistles the Name of revelation, the Lord's Name, occurs in several forms: 'the Name of Christ': 1 Pet. iv. 14 (16) ; 'the Name of the Lord': James v. 14 (? contrast v. 10); 'the Name of our Lord Jesus': 2 Thess. i. 12; 'the Name of our Lord Jesus Christ': 1 Cor. i. 2, 10; (v. 4, vi. 11 ;) Rom. i. 5; Eph. v. 20; (Col. iii. 17;) 'the Name of Jesus': Phil. ii. 10. Compare Additional Note on 1 John iii. 23.

The phrase 'the Name of God' is found in the Epistles only in 1 Tim. vi. 1, besides quotations from the LXX. (Hebr. vi. 10, xiii. 15), and the context explains its use. In the Apocalypse it occurs xvi. 9 (comp. iii. 12).

The characteristic Name of God in the N. T. is 'the Father' (Matt. vi. 9; John xii. 28 ; comp. Additional Note on i. 2).

From what has been said the full force of the phrases 'to believe in the name' (πιστεύειν εἰς τὸ ὄν. 1 John v. 13 note), 'to ask in the name' (John xiv. 13 note), 'to be gathered in (into εἰς) the name' (Matt. xviii. 20), 'to have life in the name' (John xx. 31) becomes evident. In every case the Name brings before the mind that aspect of the Divine Person which is realised by faith in each action of the spiritual life.

In close connexion with the idea of the Divine Name is that of the Divine Glory (Introd. to Gosp. of St John pp. xlvii. ff.). The Name expresses the revelation as it is apprehended and used by man. Man is called by the Name and employs it. The Glory expresses rather the manifestation of the Divine as Divine, as a partial disclosure of the Divine Majesty not directly intelligible by man (comp. Ex. xxxiii. 18 ff.). In this relation it is of interest to notice that while St John's Gospel is, in one aspect, a record of the unfolding of the Divine Glory in Christ, there is no mention of Glory in his Epistles. This is the more remarkable since the idea of Glory is found in the Apocalypse and in all the other Epistles except that to Philemon.

THE TWO EMPIRES:

THE CHURCH AND THE WORLD.

ὁ κόσμος παράγεται, καὶ ἡ ἐπιθυμία αὐτοῦ.

THE TWO EMPIRES.

I.   The foundation of the two Empires contemporaneous.
     The idea of the kingdom of God in the New Testament.
          ,,   ,,   in the subapostolic age.
     The contrast of the two Empires.

II.   The Christian Church a necessary object of persecution.
     The necessity, though not realised at first, lies in the claims of Christianity.

    1. Christianity universal.
        Roman religion national.
        Roman religious policy.
          View of Celsus.
          Corresponding idea of toleration.
            No toleration for personal conviction.
        Ancient idea of a national religion.

    2. Christianity absolute.
        Contrast with polytheism.
        No compromise possible.

    3. Christianity aggressive.
        Patristic view of idolatry.
        Idolatry to be met in social and domestic life.

    4. Christianity spiritual.
        Heathen confusion of temporal and spiritual powers.

III.   The Christian idea of the World embodied in the Emperor.
     Emperor-worship the climax of the imperial system.
     Growth of hero-worship.
     Two elements in emperor-worship.
       The worship of the Genius.
       The worship of power.
     Consecration of Julius Caesar.
       Rites of consecration.
     Worship of Augustus at Rome.
           ,,   ,,   in the Provinces.
     Later consecrations.

    1. The effect of the Apotheosis.

    2. The effect of the worship of the Genius.

    3. The law of treason.

THE TWO EMPIRES: THE CHURCH AND THE WORLD.

I.

The two Empires founded at the same epoch.

THE coincidence of the establishment of the Roman Empire with the rise of Christianity has always attracted the attention of modern historians. Even the early apologists saw a certain significance in the fact. Melito addressing Marcus Aurelius describes the Christian faith as a blessing of good omen (αἴσιον ἀγαθόν) to the reign of Augustus. 'And as his successor,' he adds, 'thou wast welcomed by 'the prayers of the people, and wilt be welcomed if thou protectest 'the religious system (φιλοσοφία) which like a foster-sister grew with 'the Empire and commenced with him[1]'. The view thus given is however essentially false in its estimate of the relation of the two systems. Christianity was destined by its very nature not to save but to destroy the Empire: at the same time their outward correspondence was not less full of meaning. All that was progressive in the old world was united under one supreme head at the time when the new faith was revealed which should bind the universe together in a sovereign unity. Peace won by arms ushered in Him who revealed the peace of life in God. So it was that the only two powers which have claimed absolute dominion over mankind appeared together. For three centuries each followed the necessary law of its development. Then at last the Empire was seen to have

---

[1] Melito *ap*. Euseb. *H. E.* iv. 26, 8.

failed; and the Church was seen to contain the forces which could regenerate and rule the world. Diocletian when he finally organised the old power of the State with the greatest political genius gave the occasion for the concentration of the power of the Church and prepared the way for its victory.

The coincidence becomes more striking when account is taken of the form under which Christianity was first presented to men. The message of the Gospel was essentially the proclamation of a Kingdom, 'a Kingdom of heaven,' 'a Kingdom of God,' 'a Kingdom of the Son of Man.' The coming of the Kingdom was the keynote of the preaching of John the Baptist and of Christ Himself. The disciples were the 'sons of the Kingdom.' As a King Christ died. During the great forty days He spoke of 'the things pertaining to the Kingdom.' When the faith was first carried beyond the limits of Judæa Philip announced in Samaria 'the Gospel of the Kingdom of God.' The burden of St Paul's first teaching in Europe was that there was 'another King than Cæsar, even Jesus.' The same apostle when he sums up his work describes himself as having gone about 'preaching 'the Kingdom of God'; and the last glimpse which is given of his labours at Rome shews him there still preaching the Kingdom.

Christianity proclaimed as a Kingdom.
Matt. iii. 2; iv. 17.
Matt. xiii. 38.
Acts i. 3.
Acts viii. 12.
Acts xvii. 7.
Acts xx. 25.
Acts xxviii. 31.

Everywhere the same idea is prominent in the history of the Acts and in the Apostolic letters. At one time it excites the hostility of unbelievers; at another time it gives occasion to mistaken hopes in Christians. But however the truth was misrepresented and misunderstood, however much it gave occasion to unjust attacks and visionary expectations, it was still held firmly. The idea may have grown somewhat unfamiliar to us now, but it is clearly impressed upon the New Testament. The distinctness with which we have learnt to realise our personal responsibility and personal relationship to God in this last age of the Church has brought with it some drawbacks, and this is one of them, that the sense of a visible Kingdom of God on earth established in righteousness and embracing all the fulness of humanity has been deadened.

This idea pervades the New Testament, though less familiar now.

Still the two aspects of the Faith—the individual and social—

are not only reconcilable : they are complementary. Each is necessary to the completeness of the other. The individual view tends to
selfishness and isolation, when the larger scope of redemption is
neglected ; the social view tends to enthusiastic dreams, when the
Illustra-
tions of
the belief
in the
next age. need of the transfiguration of every power of man is forgotten. So
it was that the early millenarian extravagancies gained currency.
But not to notice these, one or two illustrations will shew how the
faith in Christ's Kingdom in various shapes was a leading thought
in the subapostolic age. It was natural that this belief should be
most vivid in Palestine. Not long after the destruction of Jerusalem
the kinsmen of Christ being of the race of David were brought before
Domitian. He asked them, it is said, about Christ and His Kingdom,
its character, and the place and time of its appearance, and when he
heard that it was heavenly and spiritual and to be established at the
consummation of the age he released them as poor and contemptible
enthusiasts[1]. A generation later the belief in Christ's Kingdom
became more formidable. The Jewish zealots found the Christian
teachers formidable opponents of their spurious patriotism. The
Roman governors confounded both as forming a dangerous and
disloyal body ; and Symeon the son of Clopas, being accused by
certain heretical teachers before the Roman Governor as a Christian
and of the race of David, was crucified[2]. To descend only one step
further, Justin Martyr writing to Antoninus Pius says 'when you
'hear that we look for a Kingdom you inconsiderately suppose that we
'mean a human Kingdom, while we mean a Kingdom with God, as is
'evident from the fact that when we are examined by you we confess
'that we are Christians, though we know that death is the penalty
'of confession. For if it had been a human Kingdom for which we
'look, we should have denied in order to save our lives and have
'endeavoured to remain undetected that we might obtain what we
'look for ; but since our hopes do not rest upon the present order, we
'do not heed those who take our lives, since in any case we must
'die[3].'

---

[1] Hegesippus, *ap.* Euseb., *H. E.*,
iii. 20.

[2] Hegesippus, *ap.* Euseb., *H.E.* iii. 32.
[3] Just. M. *Apol.* i. 11.

Even in this latest expression of the belief, the faith in 'Christ a _{Chris-}
'King'—the terms are practically synonymous—is still retained, and ^{tianity must have}
so it must always be. The Christian creed cannot stop short of a a social
social realisation. It deals with men not as isolated units but as ^{embodi-} ment.
members of a commonwealth. Opinions may differ as to the form
in which the society will be revealed, but the fact that Christianity
must issue in the perfection of social life, and must manifest its
power in dealings with social relations, cannot be lost sight of without
peril to the dignity and essence of the Faith.

It is, then, quite true to say that two Empires, two social organi- The con-
zations, designed to embrace the whole world, started together in the ^{trast of the two}
first century. The one appeared in the completeness of its form: the Empires.
other only in the first embodiment of the vital principle which
included all after-growth. But the two Empires had nothing in
common except their point of departure and their claim to universality. In principle, in mode of action, in sanctions, in scope, in
history they offer an absolute contrast. The Roman Empire was
essentially based on positive law ; it was maintained by force ; it
appealed to outward well-doing ; it aimed at producing external
cooperation or conformity. The Christian empire was no less essentially based on faith : it was propagated and upheld by conviction :
it lifted the thoughts and working of men to that which was spiritual
and eternal : it strove towards the manifold exhibition of one
common life. The history of the Roman Empire is from the first
the history of a decline and fall, checked by many noble efforts
and many wise counsels, but still inevitable. The history of the
Christian Empire is from the first the history of a victorious
progress, stayed and saddened by frequent faithlessness and self-
seeking, but still certain and assured though never completed.

II.

It is in the reality of this contrast, though it was but seldom _{Christian-}
consciously apprehended, that the final necessity of the persecution ^{ity neces-}
which was directed by the Empire against the Church must be ^{sarily per-} secuted.

found. For a time the waxing power might not seem sufficiently
great to awaken the jealousy of that which was upon the wane.
But sooner or later a conflict for existence was unavoidable ; and for
this supreme struggle the earlier encounters were a preparation,
revealing the character of the rival forces and shewing what interests
were substantially at stake.

*The ne-
cessity not
realised at
first,*
At first, however, the nature of the contrast was not fully understood.   The apologists constantly ask why a freedom of life and
worship should be refused to the Christians which was granted to
others.   'We say the same as the Greeks,' Justin Martyr writes,
'and yet we alone are hated for the name of Christ, and while we do
'no wrong are put to death as sinners, though men in different
'places worship trees and rivers and mice and cats and crocodiles...'[1]
'In the Roman Empire,' Athenagoras writes to Marcus Aurelius,
'men observe various customs and laws, and no one is prevented by
'law and fear of punishment from devotion to his national obser-
'vances even if they be absurd...But for us Christians you have
'taken no care, and you allow us though we are guilty of no crime...
'to be harassed and plundered and persecuted...[2]' 'Yet it is great
'folly to plead that we do not approach and admit the same gods as
'our several cities do.   In fact the men who accuse us of not
'believing in any gods, because we do not hold the same as they
'acknowledge, do not agree amongst themselves about the gods...
'If then we are impious because we do not share their religion, all
'cities and all nations are impious ; for they do not all admit the
'same gods[3].'

*and dis-
sembled.*
The same kind of argument has been used with a different
purpose by other authors.   It is argued that some strange change
must have come over 'the mild indifference of antiquity' if we are to
receive the popular accounts of the persecutions.   Appeal is made
to 'the universal toleration of polytheism' as if that would have
naturally admitted Christianity at least to the privilege of conni-
vance.   Insinuations are thrown out that if the Christians suffered
they were themselves to blame.

[1] Justin M. *Apol.* i. 24.   [2] Athenagoras, *Leg. pro Christ.* c. 1.   [3] *id.* c. 14.

There is certainly a sense in which these statements are true. The
The policy of heathenism was changed, because it had to deal with necessity lay in the
an antagonistic and not with a co-ordinate belief.   The martyrs might unique claims of
have escaped tortures and death by the affectation or semblance of Chris-
conformity to popular customs, but such conformity would have tianity.
involved a complete sacrifice of their faith.   Christians were not
contented with permission to exercise their personal religion without
molestation : they demanded freedom for expansion and conquest.
If indeed a distinct conception be formed of what Christianity is, it
will be evident that a sincere and zealous pagan could not but persecute it.   The Christian Faith is universal: it is absolute: it is aggressive; and once more it is spiritual and not only temporal.   On all
these grounds it necessarily came into collision with the Roman laws.

1. Christianity is universal. This characteristic places it at 1. Chris-
once in opposition with every form of polytheism. Polytheism is tianity universal.
distinctively national. The gods which receive the honour of any
state are connected with it by special ties. Among the Romans this Nationa-
belief was bound up with the whole history of their empire. The lity of Roman
pledge of their dominion was the venerable monument of their religion.
ancient faith. The permanence of traditional rites was held to be
the condition of the prosperity of the family and of the State.
'Sacra privata perpetuo manento'[1] was the principle which underlay
the continuity of domestic life. 'Sacra majorum perire nefas'[2] was
the comprehensive rule which animated and controlled civil policy.
In these two maxims that 'natural piety' which gave coherence and
unity to the growing commonwealth found a natural and effective expression. Victory was the gift of the national gods : disaster
was the retribution for neglecting them. 'I have found that some,'
writes Arnobius, 'who believe that their conclusions are very wise
'affect the airs and language of inspiration, and say, as if they were
'quoting an oracle, that since the race of Christians has come into the
'world the whole earth has been ruined, that mankind has been visited

[1] Cic. de Legg. ii. 9.   [2] Serv. Aen. iii. 104.

'with manifold disasters, that the very gods have abandoned their
'customary functions, wherein they once used to bestow care on our
'affairs, and have been banished from the realms of earth....Nay more,
'exasperated by the wrongs and insults of Christians they send, it is
'said, pestilences and droughts, wars, dearth, locusts, mice and hail
'and other noxious pests by which the conduct of life is plagued[1].' A
hundred and fifty years of Christian supremacy could not eradicate
the feeling which survived the faith out of which it had grown; and
in the last and, in some respects, the greatest of the Apologies
Augustine laboured to shew that the desolation of Italy was not due
to the abandonment of the old national worship[2].

Roman policy as to religion. The conviction which was thus inwrought into the popular mind
was adopted and used by statesmen. The language which Mæcenas
is said to have addressed to Augustus when he set before him his
views on the right administration of the Empire exactly expresses
what a thoughtful Roman would feel on the claims of religion :
'Everywhere and in every way show reverence for the divine power
'(τὸ θεῖον) yourself according to the rites of your fathers (κατὰ τὰ πάτρια)
'and compel all others to honour it. Those who introduce any
'strange opinion on the subject (τοὺς ξενίζοντάς [cf. Acts xvii. 20] τι
'περὶ αὐτό) visit at once with hatred and chastisement, not only for
'the sake of the gods, though he who despises them would not re-
'gard anything else, but because such men by introducing strange
'divinities (καινά τινα δαιμόνια) in place of the old persuade many
'men to adopt foreign laws, and from this cause conspiracies and
'combinations and societies are formed, which are by no means ex-
'pedient for a monarchy. Do not tolerate then anyone who dis-
'believes in the gods (ἄθεος) or practises superstitious arts (γόης)[3].'

The form of the words, which Dion uses, seems to have an oblique
reference to what he had heard of the Christians of his own time, but

---

[1] Arnob. *adv. Nat.* i. 13.
[2] For example, after enumerating
some of the disasters of the Empire
in præ-Christian times, Augustine asks:
Talis itaque vanitas qualem ferimus
eique respondere compellimur, quid
horum non Christianae relligioni tri-
bueret si temporibus Christianis vide-
ret? Et tamen diis suis non ista tri-
buunt; quorum ideo cultum requirunt
ne ista vel minora patiantur cum ea
majora pertulerint a quibus antea cole-
bantur (Aug. *de Civ.* iii. 31).
[3] Dion Cass. lii. 36.

their spirit is perfectly consonant with that of the Augustan age. National usage was the criterion of worship. The sanctity which age brings to ceremonies and temples is exactly proportioned to their antiquity[1]. 'Religious respect,' to use the words of a later writer, ' is not lessened but increased by time.'

Such views were eminently characteristic of Roman policy, but they were not peculiar to it. The same thoughts were emphatically set forth as a general principle by Celsus in his work against Christianity. 'Each nation,' he says, 'observes its national rites whatever 'they may happen to be. And this custom is advantageous, not only 'in so far as different people have conceived the idea of different 'institutions, and men ought to keep what has been ratified for 'common use; but also because, in all probability, the different parts 'of the earth were originally assigned to different presiding powers '(ἐπόπται) and distributed according to certain sovereignties, and are 'so administered. Consequently the observances in each nation 'will be rightly conducted if they are directed according to their 'several views; and it is impious (οὐχ ὅσιον) to abrogate what has 'been originally instituted in each particular place[2].' A universal religion, he says elsewhere, is absolutely inconceivable. 'If anyone 'supposes that it is possible that the inhabitants of Asia and Europe 'and Africa, Greeks and barbarians, should agree to follow one law, 'he is hopelessly ignorant[3].'

The same feeling expressed by Celsus.

From these passages it is easy to see what was the corresponding idea of toleration. It was toleration based upon the mutual recognition of partial claims. Its symbol and monument was the Pantheon. As nation after nation was incorporated in the victorious body, new forms of worship received a limited sanction for the protection of those who are already devoted to them. The conquerors accepted together with the province the duty of reverence to the unseen powers under whose guardianship it had been placed. In the striking words of a pagan advocate 'they did homage to the 'vanquished deities while still inflamed with the wild passion of

Corresponding idea of toleration.

---

[1] Minuc. Fel. *Oct.* 6.   [2] Celsus ap. Orig. *c. Cels.* v. 25.
[3] *id.* ap. Orig. l. c. viii. 72.

W.   17

'victory : they sought for strange gods and made them their own....
'They took upon themselves the religious services of every nation in
'the world, and so deserved and won the sovereignty of all (dum
'universarum gentium sacra suscipiunt etiam regna meruerunt)[1].'
But this manifold worship was based upon the co-ordination and not
upon the confusion of rites. It recognised a variety of obligations
and not a freedom of choice: fixity and not indifference of form. No
individual Roman could claim the personal right of adopting the
tolerated ritual. The venerable law of the Twelve Tables remained
unrepealed : 'No one shall have gods for himself alone at his own
'pleasure, and men shall not worship in private new or foreign gods
'unless they be adopted by the State[2] (separatim nemo habescit deos,
'neve novos sive advenas nisi publice adscitos privatim colunto).'
Nor did it remain unenforced. When from time to time under the
Republic great calamities drove the people to look for help in strange
ceremonies, the government vindicated the purity of the national
religion and forbade the worship of foreign gods or of Roman gods in
a novel manner[3]. Under the Empire, when the confusion of ritual
was more widespread, the same principle was not unfrequently
asserted and general restrictions were placed upon the celebration of
strange ceremonies. Augustus would not allow 'Egyptian rites' to
be performed within the pomœrium, and when the rule was broken
removed them a mile further from the city[4]. Tiberius acted with
greater severity when, as we may suppose, the forbidden worship
was spreading among the Roman population. He suppressed 'the
'Egyptian and Jewish rites' throughout Italy by a decree of the
senate, banished four thousand of the class of freedmen who were
'infected with that superstition' and required all who held it to
abjure before a certain day on pain of banishment from Italy[5]. A
definite penalty was attached to the crime of proselytising. 'If any
'one,' it was enacted, 'introduces new rites (relligiones) unknown in

---

[1] Minuc. Fel. *Oct.* c. 6. Macrobius
(iii. 9) gives the formula of invocation
addressed to the deities of a besieged
city.
[2] Cic. *de Legg.* ii. 9.

[3] Liv. iv. 30; xxv. 1; xxxix. 18.
Comp. Val. Max. i. 3.
[4] Dion Cass. liii. 2; liv. 6.
[5] Tac. *Ann.* ii. 85. Comp. Suet.
Tib. 36; Josephus, *Ant.* xviii. 5 (4).

' use or principle (usu vel ratione), if he be of a higher station he
' is banished (honestiores deportantur): if of a lower he is put to
' death[1].'

There were exceptional circumstances under which the State
sanctioned the worship of strange deities, in which case any citizen
might practise the foreign rites without reproach. Even Isis and
Serapis found at last an acknowledged place in the public service[2];
and it was the popular belief among Christians at the end of the
second century that Tiberius and perhaps Hadrian, like Alexander Severus at a later date, had designed to extend this recognition to Christ[3]. But this coordination of new deities with the
old brought no relief from the original obligations of the Roman.
He could no more legally divest himself of his religion than of his
country. To refuse homage to the gods of the State was essentially
treason.

It is obvious that Christianity could not under any circumstances
claim protection from toleration, if it can be so called, based on
such principles as these. It came forward as a universal religion.
It could not take a place as one among many; and this was the
utmost which ancient modes of thought could concede to it. The
idea of toleration as expressing a respect for personal conviction was
utterly unknown to the statesmen of the old world. It found no
clear expression in the new world till the seventeenth century.
The toleration of the Empire was in effect not unlike toleration in
Russia now: it accepted diversities which had established themselves
by actual existence, but it allowed no change away from the national
faith. And yet more than this at its first appearance Christianity
could receive no benefit which such toleration as this could confer.
It was a rebellion against the principle on which the toleration was
founded. It was a new faith and therefore absolutely to be condemned. Judaism had at least the attribute of antiquity. But no
crime could be greater in the eye of a Roman legislator than to call
again into question what had once been settled and gained general cur-

*No tole-
ration till
recent
times for
personal
convic-
tion.*

[1] Jul. Paul. *Sent. Rec.* v. 21, § 2.   Lamprid. *Commodus*, 9.
[2] Spartian. *Caracalla*, 9. Comp.   [3] Euseb. *H. E.* ii. 2.

rency[1]. As time went on, however, the Christian Faith was gradually
delivered from this accusation of novelty, though the rise of various
forms of heresy frequently exposed the orthodox to the charge of
innovation and fresh unsettling of the minds of men.   The arguments
of the apologists may have produced some effect by shewing that it
answered to the earliest instincts of humanity.   They could plead
that in the consideration of eternity nothing is to be called late: that
when there is no beginning and no end, nothing is before its time or
behind it : that the divine counsels are one and fixed, manifested in a
definite order and liable to no change[2].   But even when Christianity
had won by heroic endurance some consideration for age, when it was
no longer condemned without a hearing for the fatal defect of recent
origin, it stood none the less necessarily in antagonism with the
spirit of the Empire.   It maintained, as we have seen, one universal
form of religion against many national forms.   And the consequences
of the antagonism will be found to be more far reaching, if we consider a little more in detail what the Roman theory of a national
religion was.

The an-
cient idea
of national
religion.

According to this the national religion was a part of the historical development and habits of the nation, a mode of expressing
certain thoughts and convictions which could no more be changed
than language.   The augurs might not believe their own art :
generals might despise it, but still Cicero adds : 'Those who put to
'sea against the auspices deserve any punishment.   They were bound
'to obey the claims of religion : they ought not to have set aside by
'arbitrary self-will the custom of their ancestors[3].'   'No man's spirit,'
says Cotta in another place[4], 'be he learned or unlearned, will ever
'move me from the opinion which I have received from my ancestors
'about the worship of the immortal gods.'   Varro in treating of the

[1] Dioclet. ed. adv. Manich: Dii im-
mortales providentia sua ordinare et
disponere dignati sunt, quæ bona et
vera sunt, ut multorum et bonorum
et egregiorum virorum et sapientissi-
morum consilio et tractatu illibata
probarentur et statuerentur: quibus
nec obviam ire nec resistere fas est,
neque reprehendi a nova vetus religio
debet. Maximi enim criminis est re-
tractare quæ semel ab antiquis statuta
et definita suum statum et cursum
tenent ac possident (Cod. Greg. Lib.
xiv. [yit. iv.]; Haenel, pp. 45 ff.).

[2] Arnob. adv. gentes, ii. 75.
[3] Cic. de Div. ii. 33.
[4] Cic. de Nat. Deor. iii. 2, 5.

Roman mythology admitted, according to Augustine, that his own judgment did not approve it, but said that 'since it existed in an old 'people he ought to maintain it as it was received from the ancients, 'and that his writings and investigations were directed to that end 'that the common people might be more willing to worship the gods 'than to despise them[1].' Nor is Augustine unjustly severe when he sums up the teaching of Seneca on the popular belief in the following words: 'The man whom philosophy in some sense had made free, 'still because he was a dignified senator of the Roman people, 'worshipped that which he blamed, did that which he arraigned, 'adored that with which he found fault. Philosophy, we must con- 'clude, had taught him a famous lesson, not to be superstitious in 'the world, but for the sake of the laws of the State and the 'manners of men to recognise the duty of imitating an actor in the 'temple though he was not to perform his part upon the stage; and 'yet he was exposed to more just condemnation in that he played 'his false part so that the people thought he was in earnest, while 'the player rather gives pleasure by illusion than leads astray by 'deceit[2].'

2. Here then lies the second difference between imperial pa- ganism and Christianity which made persecution inevitable. Christi- anity is absolute. It can admit no compromise. It is essentially grounded upon personal conviction and not accepted as an accident of descent. It is embodied in a Church which is held together by unity of faith; and not in a Nation which represents at least unity of race.

2. Christianity absolute.

Nothing struck the apologists with more amazement than the first natural consequence which followed from this difference between the Christian and heathen conceptions of religion. They saw the popular gods held up to mockery upon the stage, degraded in the works of poets, ridiculed by philosophers[3], and they could not recon- cile such license and sarcasm with resolute devotion. But to the

---

[1] Varro. ap. Aug. *de Civ.* iv. 31, 1.
[2] Aug. *de Civ.* vi. 10, 3.
[3] Just. M. *Apol.* i. 4; Theoph. *ad Autol.* iii. 3, 8; Tertull. *Apol.* 46.

polytheist of the empire—and to all later polytheists—the offices of
worship were an act of public duty and not of private confession.
Outward conformity in act was owed to the State, complete freedom
in opinion and word was allowed to the worshipper.   There was no
complete and necessary correspondence between the form and the
thought.   With the Christian it was otherwise.   His religion in
every detail was the expression of his soul.   So it was that the
Christian confessor would make no compromise.   This phenomenon
was a novel one ; and we can see in the records of the martyrdoms
how utterly the magistrates were incapable of understanding the
difficulty which Christians felt in official conformity.   In their judgment it was perfectly consistent with religious faith to drop the
morsel of incense on the fire, and still retain allegiance to Christ.
All that they required was the appearance of obedience and not the
distinct expression of conviction.   'Have regard for thy gray hairs'
or, 'for thy tender youth' was the common appeal of a merciful
judge, who failed to apprehend that the faith of the Christian like his
own being was one.   "What harm is it to say 'O Lord Cæsar' and to
"sacrifice and be saved," was the well-meant expostulation which
was addressed to Polycarp on his way to trial[1].   When Dionysius
of Alexandria was brought before the magistrate he was urgently
pressed to do honour to the gods who were the saviours of the
Empire.   'We believe in one God and Maker of all things,' was his
reply, 'who gave the empire into the hands of Valerian and Gallienus;
'Him we reverence and worship; and to Him we pray constantly
'that their empire may remain undisturbed.'   'Who prevents you
'then,' was the answer, 'from worshipping Him also if indeed he is a
'god together with the natural gods[2]?'

We have passed now into a region of religious thought so different
from that of polytheism, that it is perhaps difficult for us to feel the
sincerity of such words.   Still undoubtedly they were sincere ; and to
refuse to listen to them was held to be, as Pliny said, criminal obstinacy.
But the concession which seemed reasonable to the polytheist was
impossible to the Christian, because his faith was personal.   To

[1] Euseb. *H. E.* iv. 15, 13.   [2] Euseb. *H. E.* vii. 11, 6.

abandon wilfully the least fragment of it was to abandon all. When the father of Perpetua, an African martyr, sought to turn her from confession by consideration for his own sorrow, 'My father,' she said, 'do you see this vessel lying here, a flagon or the like?' 'I see it,' he said. 'Can it then be called by any other name than what it is?' And he said, 'No.' 'So I,' she continued, 'cannot say that I am anything 'but what I am, a Christian[1].' Thus the acceptance of the faith was personal, and the faith itself was personal. It sprang from the devotion of the whole soul: it was directed to one who was known to be a loving Lord. 'Do you suppose,' said the præfect Rusticus to Justin, 'that you will ascend up to heaven to receive some recom-'pense there?' 'I do not suppose,' was the martyr's ready correction, 'but I know it (οὐχ ὑπονοῶ ἀλλ' ἐπίσταμαι καὶ πεπληροφόρημαι)[2].' When the proconsul urged Polycarp to reproach Christ he could but make one answer: 'Eighty and six years have I continued to serve 'Him, and He has done me no wrong. How then can I speak evil 'of my King who saved me[3]'? Even a young boy could declare when the offer of pardon and favour was made to him on the condition of renouncing Christ, 'I am Christ's servant. I confess Him with 'my mouth. I bear Him in my heart. I worship Him without 'ceasing[4].' Out of this personality of faith, consecrated by the opera-tions and ordinances of one Spirit, grew a body greater and nobler than a nation. 'There was a time,' Tertullian says to his heathen readers, 'when we also laughed at the doctrines which we now teach. 'We come from among your number. Christians are made Chris-'tians and not born Christians (fiunt non nascuntur Christiani)[5].' The words which are true now in a spiritual sense were true to a large measure literally in the first centuries. In this way the con-ception of the grandest visible communion of men was gradually defined. If lineage has no authoritative power to impose a creed, there must be a society beyond the state answering to the free harmony of spiritual fellowship. At present it is sufficient simply

[1] *Acta SS. Perpet. et Felic.* § i. 2.
[2] *Acta S. Justini*, § 5.
[3] *Mart. Polyc.* § 6. Euseb. *H. E.*
v. 15, 16.
[4] *Acta S. Felic.* § 3.
[5] Tertull. *Apol.* 18.

to notice the necessity of this last antagonism of the Church and the Empire. We shall have to consider afterwards the form in which it was manifested.

3. Christianity aggressive.

3. Since Christianity claimed in this way to be a universal and absolute religion, it was necessarily aggressive. Not only was the Christian unable to admit that the old faiths ought to receive any respect from himself: he felt also that they were positively false and pernicious. They must be assailed and not tolerated. 'We affirm,' writes Justin Martyr, 'that the spirits (δαίμονας) who did [what is 'recorded in the heathen mythologies] not only were not gods but 'were evil and unholy spirits whose actions are not like those even 'of men whose heart is set on virtue. For that cause we are called 'atheists; and we confess that we are atheists in respect of such gods 'as are popularly received, but not in respect of Him who is the 'most true God, the Father of justice and temperance and every other 'virtue, untouched by evil[1].' So it was that one of the first popular cries against the Christians was 'Away with the atheists[2].' 'We 'are guilty,' Tertullian pleads, 'if you can prove that your gods are 'gods. But we appeal from yourselves to your own conscience. I am 'content for that to judge us, to condemn us, if it can deny that all 'your vaunted gods were men[3].'

Idolatry inspired by evil spirits.

But, as we have already seen, while the Christian affirmed that the heathen gods were no gods, he attributed to them and to their worship a malignant spiritual power. It was in this way, he held, that the evil spirits—demons—tried to thwart the counsels of God, enslaving men to themselves, deceiving them by false prodigies, diverting them from the sources of truth, bringing discredit on the faith, stirring up persecution, and that with the greatest success because they knew much of the divine scheme[4]. These, it was argued, invested with a semblance of life the worship of the dead,

---

[1] Just. *Apol.* i. 5: for μὴ ὀρθούς read μὴ θεούς. Comp. § 13.

[2] *Mart. Polyc.* § 9. Euseb. *H. E.* iv. 15, 15.

[3] Tertull. *Apol.* 10. Comp. Athenag. *Leg. pro Christ.* 4 ff.

[4] Just. M. *Apol.* i. 14, 12; *Apol.* ii. 19, 8.

and the worship of idols, striving to keep men from searching for the true God. 'It is not men who persecute us of themselves,' Lactantius writes, 'for they have no cause of anger against the innocent; but 'those stained and lost spirits, who know the truth and hate it, 'introduce themselves into their minds and goad them unwittingly 'to madness... ...seeking either to diminish through suffering the 'faith of those who believe, or to remove them wholly from the 'earth......'[1].

This conviction gave a stern reality to the conflicts of the martyrs. Their struggle was not against mere phantoms and names, but against actual powers of darkness. 'Who art thou,' Trajan is reported to have said to Ignatius, 'that strivest to trans-'gress our ordinances, thou man of an evil spirit (κακοδαίμων)?' 'No 'one,' Ignatius replies, 'misnames the man who bears God within 'him a man of an evil spirit: for the spirits depart from the ser-'vants of God. But if thou callest me evil towards the spirits 'because I vex them, I accept the title; for since I possess Christ 'the heavenly King, I destroy their devices[2].' 'I have already told 'you,' said Symphorian to the judge before whom he was accused 'of dishonouring the statue of Cybele, 'I am a Christian. I worship 'the true God who reigns in heaven. The image of a demon I 'not only do not worship, but if you allow me at my own risk I 'will dash it to pieces[3].'

The intensity of this belief could not but manifest itself in all the details of life. The pagan temples were to Christians like unclean sepulchres, of which they were tempted to shew their loathing openly[4]. 'How long,' said a bishop when he passed by a temple erected to the Genius of the emperor whom he had just left, 'how long shall this tomb stand[5]?' 'A Christian,' Celsus says, 'argues, Lo I stand by the statue of Zeus, or Apollo or whatever 'God it may be, and revile it and smite it and it takes no vengeance 'on me[6].' And though Origen condemns such conduct as lawless and

The martyrs contended with personal powers of evil.

Constant antagonism in social and

---

[1] Lactant. *Instit.* v. 22. Comp. ii. 17.   Oct. 8.
[2] Mart. Ign. § 2.   [5] Amm. Marcell. xxii. 11.
[3] *Acta S. Symphor.* § 2.   [6] Orig. *c. Cels.* viii. 38.
[4] Tertull. *de idol.* 13. Minuc. Fel.

rude, it is easy to see that zeal would often be carried beyond the limits of reason and good order. Heathenism indeed was so mixed up with the ordinary routine of society and home that the believer would be forced to stand in a position of continual protest. The proceedings of the courts, the public ceremonies, the ordinary amusements were more or less connected with idolatrous forms or observances. The smoking altar constantly called for some sign of abhorrence[1]. The universal presence of the images of the gods made watchful caution a necessity for the believer. The common language of familiar conversation often required a disclaimer of the superstition on which it was framed[2].

in domestic life.

Thus it was that in the ordinary conduct of social intercourse, and in the closer relationships of life, collisions between Christian conviction and heathen practice were necessarily more frequent and more perilous. Tertullian has left a lively and well-known picture of the difficulties which from hour to hour beset a Christian wife married to a heathen. 'She certainly cannot,' he writes, 'satisfy the Lord when she has beside her a slave of the devil, 'an agent of his master to hinder the objects and duties of the 'faithful; so that if she has a station to keep, her husband makes 'an appointment early to meet her at the baths: if a fast is to 'be observed, her husband on the same day has a feast: if she 'has to go out, then above all other times engagements with her 'household interfere...' 'Will you be unobserved,' he continues addressing the woman, 'when you sign [i.e. with the cross] your 'couch, your person, when you express outwardly your abhorrence '(flatu explodis) of something unclean, when you rise up even by 'night to pray? and will you not seem to be engaged in some rite 'of magic? Your husband will not know what you taste in secret 'before every meal; and if he learns that it is bread, he does not 'believe that it is that which it is said to be. And while he is 'ignorant on this, will he in each case be ready simply to admit 'your explanation, without an expression of sorrow, without a sus-'picious question whether it be bread or poison[3]?'

[1] Tertull. *de idol.* 11.   [2] *Id.* 21.   [3] Tertull. *ad uxor.* ii. 4, 5.

Under such circumstances the Christian could not but be The feeling kept alive by exceptional acts. brought frequently into direct opposition to the popular faith, however carefully he might avoid positions of danger, and however liberally he might interpret the law of charity. The cases might be rare where the conscript refused to serve in the army or accept the badge of his enlistment[1], where the soldier refused to imitate his comrades in wearing the crown which he interpreted as the symbol of slavery to a heathen power[2], where the yearly banquet on the emperor's birthday stirred the conscience of the centurion and moved him to cast off the symbol of his profession[3]; but these kept the idea of the conflict present to the minds of men, and invested the smaller divergences in thought and conduct with their real importance.

4. In this way Christianity challenged persecution. It was 4. Christianity spiritual. universal and therefore it could not acquiesce in a place beside national religions : it was absolute and therefore it could not yield the tribute of conformity to the state worship : it was aggressive, because it was universal and absolute, and therefore it could not in the end fail to come into conflict with the civil power. These characteristics are all consequences or special forms of one fundamental characteristic, Christianity was spiritual and not temporal. For the Christian the state was not the highest power. He owed allegiance to a greater Sovereign than the Emperor.

This essential difference between the two Kingdoms may be Confusion of spiritual and temporal powers in the empire. expressed in another form. In the Empire the spiritual and temporal powers, the ideas of worship and law, of progress and order, were completely confused : in Christianity they are distinctly separated. Just as all the various functions of government were concentrated in the Emperor, so also the traditional reverence for natural ties, for all that in which the ancestral ' pietas ' found scope, was directed to him. As the gods were removed further

---

[1] *Acta S. Maximiliani*, Ruinart, p. 300.

[2] Tertull. *de cor. mil.* 1.

[3] *Acta S. Marcelli*, Ruinart, p. 302.

from the affairs and thoughts of men, the state became the symbol of that which was permanent and sovereign; and in the Emperor the state was personified. The principle was laid down from the first but it was only realised by degrees. It was natural that Augustus should refuse the title of 'Lord[1]:' it was hardly less natural that Domitian should claim to be styled 'Our Lord and God[2].'

III.

The World embodied in the Emperor.

The claim of Domitian is a startling illustration of a fact which has an important bearing on apostolic thought and language. The position assumed by the Roman Emperor gave a distinctness to the conception of 'the world' in the first age which it is very difficult for us now to realise. 'The world' was not then an abstraction but, to take an obvious illustration, the most definite power which received worship at Ephesus in the time of St John. The inscriptions which decorated the places of public resort could not fail to keep before the inhabitants of that city this clear and intelligible service in which that which is earthly obtained consecration in its earthliness. In the Emperor 'the world' found a personal embodiment and claimed divine honour.

Emperor-worship the climax of the imperial system.

The growth of the worship of earthly sovereignty is a singular episode in the history of the Empire, or rather it is the essential moral of it. As the faith which was founded upon sacrifice grew to be a supreme power, so on the other side men found in triumphant force that which could command their immediate

[1] Suet. Oct. 53.
[2] Suet. Domit. 13. There are two coins of Aurelian which bear the inscriptions: Deo et domino nato (comp. Bullet. di Arch. Christ. N. s. 1883 pp. 61 f.) and Deo et domino nostro. The head of the Emperor is rayed and on the reverse is the inscription: Restitut . orbis. Eckhel, vii. 482. There are three types of coins of Carus with the inscription : Deo et Domino Caro. Eckhel, vii. 508. These coins seem to have

been struck during the lifetime of the Emperors. Eckhel, l.c. There is a consecration coin of the latter Emperor with the inscription : ΘΕω ΚΑΡω CEB and on the reverse ΑΦΙΕΡωCΙC : Eckhel, vii. 509.

On the use of the titles Dominus and Deus on coins see Spanheim, De præst. et usu nummorum, ii. 482 ff.; 489 ff. Compare also Tert. Apol. 34 and on the other hand Dion Cass. lv. 12 (δεσπότης).

homage. On a selfish view of life, where the visible is the measure
of hope and aspiration, this is indeed the necessary end to which
worship comes. That which may have been the worship of heroes
degenerates into the worship of conquerors. The idolatry of service
passes into the idolatry of success.

The later period of Grecian history shews the transition from
the adoration of the unseen to the adoration of the seen, from the
conception of gods to the conception of divine men, whose divinity
was recognised first in true nobleness and then in mere strength[1].
The certain symptoms of the change are found in the time of the
Peloponnesian War, but as yet the feeling which guided it was
generous. The honours which the people of Amphipolis paid to
Brasidas were at least given to one who had died for the independence of their city[2]; and Lysander to whom first religious
honours were paid while still living had crowned his country with
a decisive victory[3]. Even in the next stage the magnificent exploits
of Alexander might seem to offer some excuse for the assumption
of more than human dignity; but with his successors in Syria
and Egypt simple selfishness was consecrated[4]. The old beliefs

The growth of hero-worship.

---

[1] It is said that Darius the father of
Xerxes first received from the Egyp-
tians the title of 'God' in his lifetime. Diod. Sic. i. 95.

[2] Thucyd. v. 12. So the Syracusans
gave to Dion 'the honours of a hero:'
Diod. Sic. xvi. 20. Herodotus gives
an earlier example of hero-worship,
which he says was unprecedented, in
the case of Philippus of Crotona, a
victor at Olympia, and the hand-
somest man of his time. After his
death, he says, the Egestæans, διὰ
τὸ ἑωῦτοῦ κάλλος ἐπὶ τοῦ τάφου αὐτοῦ
ἡρῷον ἱδρυσάμενοι θυσίῃσι αὐτὸν ἱλάσκον-
ται (Herod. v. 47).

[3] Plut. *Lysander*, 18. Comp. Athenag. *Leg.* 14, who gives other examples.
Honours similar to those paid to Lysander were paid to T. Quinct. Flami-
ninus at Chalcis in the time of Plutarch
(ἔτι καὶ καθ' ἡμᾶς). This was the close
of the Pæan sung at the sacrifice in his
honour:

μέλπετε, κοῦραι,
Ζῆνα μέγαν Ῥώμαν τε Τίτον θ' ἅμα
Ῥωμαίων τε πίστιν.
Ἰήιε Παιάν, ὦ Τίτε σῶτερ.
Plut. *Titus*, c. 16.

Suetonius speaks of the erection of
temples in honour of proconsuls as
an ordinary honour: Templa quamvis
sciret [Augustus] etiam proconsulibus
decerni solere, in nullâ tamen provin-
cia nisi communi suo Romæque nomine recepit (*Oct.* c. 52). So Cicero
takes credit to himself for having declined the compliment : *Ep. ad Att.* x.
21. 7 ; *ad Quint. fr.* i. 1, 26. But in
such cases the temple was not erected
to the officer, but in honour of him,
though the transition from the one
thought to the other became easy a-
mong degenerate races.

[4] For the worship of the Ptolemies
see Theocr. *Id.* xvii.

It was with better reason that Demetrius obtained divine honours at Si-

had died out. Euhemerus had laboured to shew that the persons
of the popular mythology were mortal heroes, and there was no
longer any faith behind, which such beings could embody and represent.   It was then only a step to substitute a power present at
least and real for that which was not different in kind and obscured
by time.   Great sovereigns were felt to be more powerful than the
ancient gods; and the language in which Tertullian describes the
popular feeling of his own time in Africa was already true three or
four centuries earlier in the kingdoms of Alexander's successors.
Atheism was a less serious charge than disloyalty.   The majesty of a
god was less august than that of a monarch; 'for,' he adds, saying
of his countrymen what was equally applicable to the subjects of an
Antiochus or a Ptolemy, 'you regard the Emperor with a greater
'dread, and more calculating fearfulness than Olympian Jove himself
'...you would sooner forswear yourselves by all the gods than by the
'single genius of Cæsar[1].'

Extends to
Rome.
  The general unbelief in spiritual powers which thus grew up in
the Greek kingdoms of the East after the conquest of Alexander soon
spread to the West.   The speculations of Euhemerus found an
advocate at Rome in the poet Ennius[2].   At the same time however
the national Italian faith in the gods of the family — the Lares,
the Manes, the Genius—modified the results which they were
calculated to produce.   Such a faith declared that in man there is
something more than what is called human.   The life of the family,
of the clan, of the state was acknowledged to be Divine, and to have
a connexion with an unseen order.   'Roma' was already worshipped
as a goddess, and assumed before long the figure and attributes of
Pallas[3].   If the belief in the ancient divinities was gone, some con-

cyon : τιμῶν ἰσοθέων ἔτυχε παρὰ τοῖς εὖ
παθοῦσι (Diod. Sic. xx. 102).

[1] Tertull. Apol. 28. Minuc. Fel. Oct.
29. Compare the song in Athen. vi. 63.

[2] Cic. de Nat. Deor. i. 42, 119.

[3] The Smyrnæans claimed to be the
first who erected a temple to Rome
B.C. 195 (Tac. Ann. iv. 56). The worship spread even to Britain. In the
Library of Trinity College there is an
inscription on an altar found at 'Ro-
'chester in Rhedesdaile' which bears
at the head the letters D . R . S . (D[eæ]
R[omæ] S[acrum]). Comp. Mommsen,
Iscrr. Latt. vii. 179, No. 1037.

Some interesting representations of
Rome on coins are given in the Thesaurus Morellianus : see Havercamp's
Index s. v. (ed. 1734). How soon Rome
appeared as Pallas is disputed.

ception of the Divine still lingered. ' For a mortal to help a mortal,' writes the elder Pliny, 'is the essence of deity (Deus est mortali juvare mortalem), and this is the way to eternal glory. By this 'path it was the chiefs of Rome advanced: by this it is'—so he adds coming to his own time—' Vespasian, the greatest ruler of any 'age, is now proceeding with his children, in a heavenly course, 'succouring the exhausted Empire. And the oldest form of return-'ing gratitude to benefactors, is that such men should be enrolled 'among the deities [1].'

Thus in the consecration of the Emperors[2] two distinct elements were combined, the national faith in the Genius and the eastern adoration of power. The homage which one citizen might yield in servile adulation to a supreme lord, might be rendered by another to that which he looked upon as a spirit of the state. Such a combination of thoughts was present to the mind of the first emperors. Augustus during his lifetime would not allow any temple to be erected to himself alone, but only to ' Rome and Augustus [3].'

Two elements in the idea of Emperor-worship.

Yet even so there were some men left in the republic who felt that the first assumption of divine prerogatives by Cæsar justified his death[4]. But Cæsar had himself measured more accurately the true

The consecration of Julius Cæsar.

[1] Plin. *Hist. Nat.* ii. 7. The same kind of feeling runs through the fragment of Cicero's treatise *De consolatione* (ap. Lactant. *Instit.* i. 15) in which he proposes to render divine honours to Tullia: te omnium optimam doctissimamque, approbantibus diis immortalibus ipsis, in eorum cœtu locatam ad opinionem omnium mortalium consecrabo.

[2] The subject of *Apotheosis* has been treated at length by J. D. Schoepflin in a special dissertation (*De apotheosi*... Argentor. 1729). References to later literature are given in Pauly, *Real-Encykl. s. v.*

Boissier discusses the Apotheosis of the Roman Emperors with special reference to that of Julius Cæsar and Augustus in considerable detail (*La Religion Romaine*, i. 122—208).

[3] Inscriptions of this form are found

as at Mylasa: ὁ δῆμος αὐτοκράτορι Καίσαρι θεοῦ υἱῷ Σεβαστῷ ἀρχιερεῖ μεγίστῳ καὶ θεᾷ 'Ρώμῃ (Boeckh, *Inscr. Gr.* No. 2696); at Cyme in Mysia: ἐπὶ ἱερέως τᾶς 'Ρώμας καὶ αὐτοκράτορος Καίσαρος θέω υἱω, θέω Σεβάστω...Παλάμωνος (*id.* No. 3524); and at Athens: θεᾷ 'Ρώμῃ καὶ Σεβαστῷ Καίσαρι (*id.* No. 478).

Elsewhere the name of Augustus stands alone, as at Malta: ἀμφιπολεύσας θεῷ Αὐγούστῳ (*id.* No. 5754); and Ilium: αὐτοκράτορα Καίσαρα θεοῦ υἱόν, θεὸν Σεβαστόν... (*id.* No. 3604). Comp. *id.* No. 4474, ψήφισμα τῆς πόλεως πεμφθὲν θεῷ Αὐγούστῳ (Syria). See also Nos. 2087, 3285, 4238; and Appian, *Bell. Civ.* v. 132, καὶ ἦν ὁ Καῖσαρ ἐτῶν ἐς τότε ὄκτω καὶ εἴκοσι, καὶ αὐτὸν αἱ πόλεις τοῖς σφετέροις θεοῖς συνίδρυον.

[4] Suet. *Jul. Cæsar*, c. 76. Non enim honores modo nimios recepit...sed et ampliora etiam humano fastigio de-

spirit of his age, though he fell a victim to the few. No sooner
was he dead than the Senate decreed to him ' every honour divine
' at once and human[1];' and he was placed in the number of the gods
not only ' by the word of those who passed the decree, but also by
' the conviction of the people. A comet appeared for seven days in
' succession at the first celebration of the games which Augustus
' exhibited in his honour, and it was believed that it was the soul of
' Cæsar admitted into heaven[2].'

Worship of
Augustus
at Rome,

When the beginning was once made the descent was rapid[3].
Augustus resolutely refused to receive divine honours publicly at

cerni sibi passus est : sedem auream in
curia et pro tribunali, thensam et fer-
culum Circensi pompa, templa, aras,
simulacra juxta deos, pulvinar, flami-
nem, lupercos, appellationem mensis e
suo nomine. Comp. c. 88 in deorum
numerum relatus est non ore modo
decernentium sed et persuasione vulgi.

[1] Id. c. 84. Comp. Dion Cass. xlvii.
19.

[2] Id. c. 88. The language of the
poets is well known and not without
deep significance, before it had become
conventional. Comp. Ovid, Met. xv.
840 ff., and Burmann's note ; Fasti
iii. 701 ff.; Lucan, Phars. i. 45 ff.
The language used in an inscription at Ephesus in honour of Jul.
Cæsar (A. U. C. 706—7), which St John
may have read, is worth quoting :
...Γάϊον 'Ιούλιον, Γαΐου υἱὸν Καίσαρα,
τὸν ἀρχιερέα καὶ αὐτοκράτορα καὶ τὸ δεύ-
τερον ὕπατον, τον ἀπὸ "Αρεως καὶ 'Αφρο-
δείτης θεὸν ἐπιφανῆ καὶ κοινὸν τοῦ ἀν-
θρωπίνου βίου σωτῆρα... Boeckh, Inscr.
Gr. No. 2957.

[3] The rite was variously described
by Latin writers as dicari caelo, con-
secrari, inter divos referri, in deorum
numerum referri (Suet.), divus appellari.
Thus Eutropius says of Claudius :
post mortem consecratus est divusque
appellatus (vii. 13), and of Antoninus
Pius : inter divos relatus est et merito
consecratus (viii. 8). His notice of the
consecration of Diocletian is remarkable : Contigit igitur ei, quod nulli
post natos homines, ut cum privatus
obisset inter divos tamen referretur.

The Greek historians use the terms
ἀποθέωσις (Tertull. Apol. 34) and ἐκ-
θειάζειν.
Herodian has given a detailed description of the ceremony in connexion
with the consecration of Septimius
Severus (Herodian, iv. 2). The last
sentence is worth quoting. The structure on which the figure of the deceased was placed in order to be con-
sumed is built, he says, 'like a Pharos'
in diminishing stages. When the pile
is lighted an eagle is let loose from
the highest and smallest, 'as from a
' battlement, to ascend with the fire
' to the sky. This is believed by the
' Romans to carry the soul of the Em-
' peror from earth to heaven ; and from
' that time he is worshipped (θρησκεύε-
' ται) with the rest of the gods.' However difficult it may be to believe that
such an exhibition was made in the
first age of the empire, Dion relates
that this ceremony was performed at
the burning of Augustus : ἡ μὲν [πυρὰ]
ἀνηλίσκετο, ἀετὸς δέ τις ἐξ αὐτῆς ἀφεθεὶς
ἀνίπτατο ὡς καὶ δὴ τὴν ψυχὴν αὐτοῦ ἐς
τὸν οὐρανὸν ἀναφέρων (lvi. 42) ; and Suetonius relates that one was found, a
man of prætorian rank, who swore
that he saw his form (effigiem) ascend
from the pyre to heaven : Oct. 100.
Compare also Dion Cass. (Xiphil.)
lxxiv. 5 (an eagle rose from the pyre
of Pertinax).
The Apotheosis is represented on
two important works of art, on the
' Tiberian Agate,' and on the base of
the column of Antoninus Pius. There

Rome[1] though he accepted the title (*Augustus*, Σεβαστός) which seemed to challenge them[2]; but at his death his feeling, at least, was sufficiently notorious to be made a ground of reproach[3]. In this respect the description which Ovid gives of the private worship which he paid to the members of the imperial family at his place of exile on the Euxine may probably serve as a type of the popular practice even during the emperor's lifetime :

> 'Nec pietas ignota mea est: videt hospita tellus
>   In nostra sacrum Cæsaris esse domo.
> Stant pariter natusque pius, conjuxque sacerdos,
>   Numina jam facto non leviora Deo...
> His ego do toties cum ture precantia verba
>   Eoo quoties surgit ab orbe dies[4].'

After the death of Augustus divine honours were solemnly decreed and paid to him in the capital. The Senate decreed to him 'a temple and divine rights (caelestes relligiones)'[5]. A sacred college (sodales Augustales) was established afterwards to provide for the due performance of the ceremonies connected with his worship[6]. And the crowning rite of the 'apotheosis' sanctioned and defined the religious honours which he had received and which were yet due to him[7].

In the provinces the enthusiasm of the devotees of the Empire *in the provinces.* was allowed free scope. The only limit placed upon it was that which has been already mentioned : Augustus required that the name of Rome should be joined with his own. In obedience to this command temples were dedicated at Athens[8] and Pola[9] to Rome and

---

are good outlines on a small scale and descriptions of both in Millin's *Galerie Mythologique*, pll. clxxix, clxxx, and also in Schoepflin, *Tab.* i. A large engraving of the sculpture on the base of the column of Antoninus is given in the *Museo Pio Clement.* V., tav. xxix; and of the 'Tiberian Agate' in Montfaucon, *L'Antiquité expliquée*, v. 153. The Apotheosis of Faustina is represented on a bas-relief from the Arch of M. Aurelius. Parker, *Phot.* 1686.

To these works may be added a group at Madrid symbolising the Apotheosis of Claudius, in which an eagle is represented bearing the bust of the Emperor, who has a rayed crown

and nimbus: Montfaucon, *l. c.* p. 161: Schoepflin, *Tab.* ii.

[1] Suet. *Oct.* 52.
[2] See below, p. 280, n. 1.
[3] Tac. *Ann.* i. 10.
[4] Ovid, *Ep. ex Pont.* iv. 9, 105 ff. Other passages of the Augustan poets are worth study : Virg. *Ecl.* i. 6 ff.; *id. Georg.* i. 24 ff.; iii. 16 ff.; Hor. *Od.* iii. 25; iv. 5, 32.
[5] Tac. *Ann.* i. 11 ; Dion Cass. lvi. 46.
[6] Tac. *Ann.* i. 54; *Hist.* ii. 95.
[7] Dion Cass. lvi. 34, 42.
[8] Comp. Suet. *Oct.* 60. Boeckh, *Inscr. Gr.* No. 478.
[9] Stuart and Revett, *Athens...* iv. (ed. 1816).

Augustus; and Herod the Great placed two images to these kindred powers in the temple which he built at his new Cæsarea[1]. The cities of Asia Minor vied with one another in paying him the same kind of honour. He was celebrated in temples at Pergamum[2], at Nicomedia, at Mylasa[3], at Cyrene, in his lifetime. At Sparta he seems to have had a temple alone like Julius Cæsar which was seen by Pausanias[4]. There were temples to him also at Cyzicus, Nysa, Apollonia in Pisidia, and Assos. The Augusteum at Ancyra has preserved the famous record of his achievements which was inscribed upon its walls[5]. The Augusteum at Alexandria was one of the most splendid buildings in the city[6]. In the West temples were raised to him at Tarragona in Spain[7], at Narbonne, Vienne and Lyons in Gaul[8]. And Philo could say that the whole world decreed honours to Augustus equal to those paid to the Olympian gods[9].

Later consecrations. It is unnecessary to trace at length the repetition of similar honours in the case of the following Emperors. The example once given was steadily followed with such variations as were due to the individual character of those who claimed or gave them. Tiberius imitated the reserve of Augustus. He only allowed a single temple

---

[1] Jos. *Ant.* xv. 10 (13) ; *id. B. J.* i. 21 (16). He placed in it a statue of Augustus 'as large as that of Zeus at Olympia, of which it was an imitation, and another of Rome equal to that of Hero at Argos' (Jos. *loc. post.*).

Augustus, under the form of Jupiter and Livia, with the attributes of Rome, are represented on a famous cameo at Vienna : Millin, *Galerie Mythologique*, clxxxi. 676; compare *id.* clxxviii. 661.

[2] Tac. *Ann.* iv. 38, 55.

[3] Boeckh, *Inscr. Gr.* No. 2696.

[4] Pausan. iii. 11, 4. This may have been erected after his death like that at Nola : Suet. *Tib.* 40.

[5] On this Augusteum compare E. Guillaume, *Revue Archéologique*, 1871, pp. 347 ff.

[6] Philo, *Leg. ad Cai.* ii. p. 567.

[7] Tac. *Ann.* i. 78. Comp. Spartian. *Traj.* c. 12.

[8] Suet. *Claud.* 2. Guillaume, *Rev. Archéol.* 1871, p. 348.

[9] Philo, *l. c.* ii. pp. 567 f.

At Tentyra he was called Ζεὺς ἐλευθέριος. Boeckh, *Inscr. Gr.* No. 4715.

Ephesus claimed to be νεωκόρος of the Augusti and of Artemis : Inscrr. Nos. 3, 7, 13, 15 from the Great Theatre, No. 15 from the site of the Temple, No. 12, 15 from the city and suburbs, in Wood's *Discoveries at Ephesus*, 1877.

On the Temples of Augustus see Guillaume, *l. c.*

On Roman consecration coins he is styled generally *Divus*, but once on a coin of Gallienus *Deus ;* and this title is found on provincial pieces (DEO AVGVSTO) : Eckhel, vi. 125.

The following inscriptions are taken almost at random : at Perugia, NVMINI AVGVSTI SACR. (Orelli, 608) : at Verona, DEO AVG...(id. 609) : at Herculaneum, DIVO AVGVSTO AVGVSTALES (id. 610) : at Fano, DIVO AVGVSTO...PIO PATRI DOMINORVM.

to be erected to himself in connexion with the Senate in Asia; and refused to sanction a like honour in Spain[1]. It is said that Caius when he was warned that he had gone beyond the dignity of emperors and kings, immediately claimed the majesty of the gods, replacing by his own likeness the heads of famous statues, and offering himself for the adoration of the citizens between the figures of Castor and Pollux[2]. A temple erected to Claudius at Camulodunum, to enforce, as it appeared, an endless dominion over the Britons, is given as one of the causes of the revolt of Boadicea[3]. Nero after the conspiracy of Piso went further than his predecessors and allowed a temple to be decreed to himself at Rome with the epithet 'Divus' though some at the time regarded the assumption of such a title as an omen of speedy death[4].

When the chiefs of the state were thus invested with a divine character, it was natural to extend celestial honours to the principal members of the imperial family. Accordingly wives and children of the emperors received the stamp of divinity[5]. Caius consecrated his sister[6] and Trajan his father[7]. The license of such power was not exhausted, till Hadrian carried the profanation of worship to the furthest limit, and offered his unworthy favourite, Antinous, who was not even a Roman, as a new Bacchus or Apollo or Pan, for the adoration of the world. 'And all men,' in the in-

---

[1] Tac. *Ann.* iv. 15, 55 f. ; 37 f.

[2] Suet. *Cal.* 22.

[3] Tac. *Ann.* xiv. 31. Comp. *id. Ann.* xii. 69; xiii. 2.

[4] Tac. *Ann.* xv. 74. Comp. Tert. *Apol.* 34.

On contemporary coins he bears the titles of Zeus, Apollo and Hercules; and one coin in his honour is inscribed τῷ σωτῆρι τῆς οἰκουμένης: Eckhel, vi. 278 f.

[5] Thus the wives of Augustus (Livia), Vespasian (Domitilla), Trajan (Plotina), Hadrian (Sabina), Antoninus Pius (Faustina), M. Aurelius (Faustina Pia), Septimius Severus (Julia Augusta), Maximinus (Paulina), Valerian (Mariniana), received divine honours.

See Schoepflin, pp. 54 ff. The first lady of the imperial family who was consecrated was Drusilla, the sister of Caius: Suet. *Calig.* 24.

Nero gave divine honours to his daughter Claudia Poppæa who died an infant: Tac. *Ann.* xv. 23.

Those who had been consecrated were often represented under the form of the old deities, Livia, for example, as Juno, Julia as Ceres, Faustina as Cybele (Schoepflin, pp. 90 f.).

In the *Mus. Pio Clement.* V., Tav. xxvi. there is a striking representation of Hadrian in the character of Jupiter.

[6] Comp. Suet. *Calig.* 24.

[7] Plin. *Paneg.* 10 f.

dignant words of Justin, 'were eager to reverence him as a god through fear, though they knew who he was and whence he sprung[1].'

Two elements in the embodiment of Emperor-worship.

These details, a few only out of many which are preserved on coins and inscriptions as well as in the scattered notices of historians, will indicate how deeply the belief in the superhuman character of the Emperor was inwrought into the popular mind in the first and second centuries, and how welcome it was to the mass of men, as offering them at least a definite object for worship, though the more thoughtful might shrink from some of the consequences which such an opinion carried with it. If we now endeavour to look at the belief more closely we shall see that as it was based upon two ideas originally, so it was manifested in two forms. We have to distinguish the position of the Emperor during his lifetime, and his position after death: the apotheosis and the inherent sacredness of the head of the state. These two elements are by no means necessarily connected. Many emperors like Caius and Nero and Domitian who had claimed and received while living divine honours were not reckoned among the gods after their death. The apotheosis was a deliberate act of the state performed through the Senate: the sacredness of the Emperor followed from the simple possession of power. Practically it was the latter which made a stumblingblock to the Christian. The recognition of the divinity of the Emperor found expression in many of the acts of daily life. The apotheosis once accomplished

---

[1] Just. M. *Apol.* i. 29. Orig. *c. Cels.* iii. c. 36.

Eckhel (*Doctr. Numm.* viii. 463) gives a list of members of the imperial family whose consecration is witnessed by coins, 48 in all, including 15 females. Compare also Schoepflin, pp. 15—57.

The divine worship paid to Antinous may serve as a striking example of popular fanaticism or profanity. Among the inscriptions on coins struck in his honour by Greek cities—'none 'were struck at Rome or in Roman 'colonies'—are the following: ΑΝΤΙ-ΝΟΟС ΙΑΚΧΟС (Adramyttium), ΝΕω

ΙΑΚΧω and ΝΕω ΠΥΘΙω (Tarsus), ΟСΤΙΛΙΟС ΜΑΡΚΕΛΛΟС ΙΕΡΕΥС ΤΟΥ ΑΝΤΙΝΟΟΥ (Corinth), ΑΝΤΙΝΟΟΝ ΘΕΟΝ (Hierapolis, Nicopolis), Η ΠΑΤΡΙС ΑΝ-ΤΙΝΟΟΝ ΘΕΟΝ (Bithynium), ΠΑΝΙ ΑΝ-ΤΙΝΟω (Arcadia?) One inscription may be added: ΑΝΤΙΝΟωΙ СΥΝΘΡΟ-ΝωΙ ΤωΝ ΕΝ ΑΙΓΥΠΤωΙ ΘΕωΝ Μ. ΟΥΛΠΙΟС ΑΠΟΛΛωΝΙΟС ΠΡΟΦΗΤΗС (Gruter, p. 86. 1).

These examples are taken from Eckhel, *Doctr. Numm.* vi. 528 ff.

The worship of Antinous was still continued in Egypt in the time of Clement (*Protr.* iv. p. 14 P.).

only added one more to the list of deities who had no strong hold even upon the thoughts of the heathen.

1. The essential divinity of the sovereign power was the main religious thought of the Empire, but at the same time the ceremony of the apotheosis gave distinctness to the conception of divinity in the living Emperors. The various emblems proper in the gods which were attributed to the deceased on works of art—the rayed crown, the pure wand, the nimbus, the sacred car, the eagle—appealed to the imagination and brought the idea of deity nearer to the earth. Moreover the apotheosis was not necessarily the reward of signal virtues. If it had been so the rite might have lessened the respect which was rendered to a vicious sovereign. But as it was the exceptions were not sufficient to disturb the belief that apotheosis was the natural issue of an ordinary reign[1]. The language of Pliny is undoubtedly rhetorical, but still there is some truth in his contemptuous explanation of the motives which had led to earlier apotheoses in order to extol the wisdom of Trajan. 'Tiberius consecrated Augustus, but he did so in 'order that he might introduce the charge of treason : Nero conse-'crated Claudius, but that he might mock [the ceremony], Titus 'consecrated Vespasian, and Domitian, Titus, but the former that he 'might appear to be the son, the latter that he might appear to be 'the brother of a god. You have raised your father to heaven not to 'inspire fear into the citizens, not to insult the deities, not to gain 'honour for yourself, but because you believe him to be a god[2]'. Such a belief however was not required even from the noblest Emperors. It is reckoned among the most distinguished merits of M. Aurelius that he dissembled or defended the profligacy of his colleague Verus, though it was most repulsive to him, and procured for him all the honours of consecration[3]. On the other hand it is said that the consecration of Marcus himself was something more

The wide effect of the Apotheosis.

---

[1] Plin. *Paneg.* 11.
[2] Comp. Spart. *Hadr.* 27. Suet. *Domit.* 2 [Titum] defunctum...nullo præterquam consecrationis honore dignatus...carpsit...edictis.
[3] Capitol. *M. Aur.* 15.

than a pageant. No one thought that he should be lamented as one who was lost. Death had simply restored him to the gods who had lent him for a time to men. Not to have his statue in the house, if a person's position allowed or required it, was sacrilege; and some believed that he continued to care for his people and revealed to them the future in dreams[1]. But such cases on either side were rare and the mocking words with which Vespasian recognised the progress of his fatal illness sufficiently describe the general feeling. 'Woe is me: I suppose I am on the point of becoming a god[2].'

[1] Capitol. *M. Aur.* 18 parum sane fuit quod illi honores divinos omnis ætas omnis sexus omnis conditio ac dignitas dedit, nisi quod etiam sacrilegus judicatus est qui eius imaginem in sua domo non habuit, qui per fortunam vel potuit habere vel debuit. Comp. *id. Ant. P.* 13.

[2] Suet. *Vesp.* 23.

It is said by Eutropius (x. 15, 17) that Constantius and Jovian were consecrated (*inter divos relati*); and the title *Divus* was given to the deceased Emperors in formal documents to the close of the Western Empire (Schoepflin, pp. 50 f.). The title was transferred to later sovereigns even during their lifetime; and John of Salisbury, in a passage referred to by Schoepflin, remarks on the misuse of the word in his time: Suos quoque imperatores quos de more Romanus populus fideliter jugulabat, deificavit fidelis inani solatio...eosque mentiebantur in sortem transiisse numinum ac si caelo suo mundoque regendo, nisi tyrannis ascitis, omnipotentis non sufficiat manus. Facti sunt ergo divi indigetes aut, ut aliis placet, heroes, quos nec etiam humana sorte dignos Romanorum perfidia reputavit. Tractum est hinc nomen quo principes virtutum titulis et veræ fidei luce præsignes se divos audeant nedum gaudeant appellari, veteri quidem consuetudine etiam in vitio et adversus fidem catholicam obtinente (Polycr. iii. 10; Migne, *Patrol. Lat.* cxcix. 496). Charles the Great had already condemned the custom. After reproving Constantine and

Irene for their assumption of the title and for the use of the corresponding word *divalia* in regard to their decrees, he says: Cesset igitur, cesset falsi nominis ambitio, destituatur antiqui erroris vestigium, facescat cæcæ superstitionis vocabulum, abdicatur procacis nominis supercilium, pellatur a fidelibus in divos transferendorum hominum gentile mendacium (*Libr. Carol. cap. de imag.* i. 4).

The Consecration Coins form an interesting study. The mode in which the old idea is translated into a Biblical form in the consecration coin of Constantine is of singular interest. The head of the Emperor is covered with the usual veil, but on the reverse the eagle which before symbolised the removal of the soul above no longer appears. In its place the Emperor is represented in a chariot drawn by four horses with uplifted head and outstretched hands, and from heaven the Divine Hand is stretched to raise the believer.

In this connexion an earlier coin may be mentioned, which seems to express simply the Christian thought of 'consecration.' This is one struck by Gallienus in honour of his wife Salonina. It bears the empress seated with an olive-branch in her hand and the legend AVGVST . IN PACE. The last two words can scarcely have a different meaning from that which they bear on monuments. They shew almost beyond question that Salonina was a Christian, and that the coin was struck by the Emperor in memory

2. The apotheosis gave definiteness to the idea of the imperial divinity by the consequent array of priests and sacrifices and temples; but it was, as has been said, the practical belief in the essential sacredness of the Emperor as such which forced the Christian into direct antagonism with the state[1]. He could not, like his fellow-citizens, acknowledge the 'Genius' of the Emperor: he could not give divine honour to the Emperor himself. The Genius or Fortune of the Emperor symbolised the spiritual energy which through him was supposed to direct the whole system of the commonwealth. To swear by this was to recognise the reality of a power which the Christian either denied to exist or held to be malignant[2]. And it was equally impossible for him to attribute to a man any of the prerogatives which he held to belong to God. 'We render honour to the Emperor,' writes Tertullian[3], 'in such a way as is lawful for us and expedient for him, 'as to a man who stands next to God, and who has obtained what-'ever he is from God, and is less than God only...And so we offer 'sacrifices for the safety of the Emperor, but to our God and his, and, 'as God has enjoined, with simple prayer.' And however extravagant

The genius of the Emperor.

---

of his wife after her death. Comp. King, *Early Christian Numismatics,* pp. 44 ff.; and on the whole subject of Consecration Coins Eckhel, *Doctr. Numm.* viii. 456 ff.

[1] The representation of the Genius is found sparingly on the coins of the early Emperors: *e.g.* GENIO AUGUSTI (Nero: Eckhel, vi. 272); GENIO P. R. (Augustus: *id.* vi. 97 f.); GENIUS P. R. (Vitellius: *id.* vi. 317). Towards the close of the third century the Genius appears much more commonly and in different forms. It is significantly characteristic of the reign of Diocletian. The following types of inscription are given in Bandurius: GENIUS AUGUSTI, G. AUGUSTORUM, G. AUGG. ET COSS., G. CÆSARIS, and GENIUS EXERCITUS, G. EXERCITUS ILLYRICIANI, G. ILLYRICI, G. IMPERATORIS, G. POPULI ROMANI. The GENIUS AUGUSTI, G. IMPERATORIS, G. POPULI ROMANI appears on coins of Constantine. The only later example which I have observed is on a coin of

Julian : GENIO ANTIOCHENI.

Inscriptions in honour of the Genius of a particular place, or society or person are very frequent. Among the Roman inscriptions Mommsen gives examples of dedications: GENIO CEN-TURIÆ, G. TURMÆ, G. SANCTO CASTRO-RUM, G. HORREORUM, G. DECURIÆ, G. EXERCITUS, &c. (*Inscrr. Latt.* vi. 1, 208 ff.). In Britain inscriptions are found GENIO LOCI, G. CENTURIÆ, G. COHORTIS, G. VALLI, G. TERRÆ BRITAN-NICÆ, &c. *id.* vii. The corresponding phrases ΤΥΧΗ CEBACTOY and ΤΥΧΗ ΠΟΛΕωC are found on Greek coins : Eckhel, iv. 60; ii. 455. It would be of deep interest to compare the ideas of ΤΥΧΗ and GENIUS.

There is an impressive figure of the Genius of Augustus in the *Mus. Pio Clement.* iii. Tav. 11.

[2] Orig. *c. Cels.* viii. 65.

[3] Tert. *ad Scap.* 2. Comp. Theoph. *ad Autol.* i. 11.

the pretensions may appear which Tertullian here sets aside they were
a necessary consequence of the conception of the Empire. The very
title 'Augustus' was rightly felt from the first to separate him to
whom it was assigned from other men, and, so to speak, to conse-
crate him while still on earth[1]. So Ovid rightly contrasts the name
with the most glorious titles which the heroes of Roman history
had won, and adds:

> ' Sed tamen humanis celebrantur honoribus omnes :
> Hic socium summo cum Jove nomen habet.
> Sancta vocant augusta patres : augusta vocantur
> Templa, sacerdotum rite dicata manu[2].'

If the Empire was one and had one life, if the centre of life was in
the sovereign, if the many deities of polytheism were supposed to
exercise local and circumscribed authority it is evident that the
Emperor alone could offer to all his subjects a common object for
adoration. In him all that affected their outward well-being was
visibly gathered up. No member of the popular Pantheon presented
a similar point of convergence for hope. If unity could be gained
under polytheism it could exist only through an actual, temporal
head. And this unity it was, constructed artificially and set forth
for the acceptance of men in the person of an Emperor, that the
Roman system expressed.

Essential-
ly opposed
to the idea
of Chris-
tianity.

In such a view of humanity the Christian found the complete
antithesis to that which had been revealed to him. He held indeed
most firmly the unity of humanity, but this was assured to him in
the Incarnation. Unity resting on that which is outward seemed to
him necessarily to be partial and worthless. He reached forward to
another order for the resolution of all the discords of life. He could
not acknowledge in the Emperor the centre of that larger being
which he had found in all its fulness in Christ. He could not invoke
the Genius—the demon—the spiritual essence of a power which

---

[1] On the title compare Eckhel, *Doctr.*
Numm. viii. pp. 355 ff. The words of
Dion Cassius (liii. 16) state the case
plainly: Αὔγουστος ὡς καὶ πλεῖόν ἢ
κατὰ ἀνθρώπους ὢν ἐπεκλήθη, πάντα γὰρ
τὰ ἐντιμότατα καὶ τὰ ἱερώτατα αὔγουστα
προσαγορεύεται· ἐξ οὕπερ καὶ Σεβαστὸν

αὐτὸν καὶ ἑλληνίζοντές πως ὥσπερ τινὰ
σεπτὸν ἀπὸ τοῦ σεβάζεσθαι προσεῖπον.

[2] Ovid, *Fasti,* i. 607 ff. Comp. Suet.
Octav. 7; Florus, ii. 34. On the Ephe-
sine inscriptions φιλοσέβαστος occurs
not unfrequently as a regular official
epithet.

stood forth as a rival of that to which he was devoted. He could not admit any of the prerogatives of absolute and irresponsible power in the person of one who represented the principles and authority of the visible order. Thus the opposition of Christianity and Imperialism was complete and irrevocable. The two Empires, when regarded in their principles, were seen to be utterly irreconcilable.

3. One practical consequence of momentous importance followed from the concentration of all the dignity of the state in the single supreme head. An offence against the Emperor was not an offence against a man but against the commonwealth. Pliny, as we have seen, does not scruple to affirm that Tiberius procured the consecration of Augustus, that he might introduce the law of treason (*majestas*, ἀσέβεια). The statement may be an exaggeration, but it is evident that the two ideas closely correspond; and no one can study the early history of the Empire without feeling that the novel conception of the law of treason expresses in a most striking form the change which had passed over the constitution of the state.

The effect of the law of Treason.

Even to a Roman this application of an old law—based on the exceptional position of the Emperor—often seemed to be intolerably vexatious. To shew that a man had been condemned for treason was held in the next reign to be, as Tacitus implies, a presumption of his innocence[1]. On the other hand Pliny remarks that it was a crime which a tyrant could plead against those who were free from every other[2]. At one time the sale of a statue of the reigning Emperor was supposed to furnish ground for an impeachment: at another the conversion of such a statue into vessels for ordinary use. It was treason to speak evil of Augustus: it was treason to call Cassius the last of the Romans[3]. Caius, it is said, put men to death because they expressed a poor opinion of his shows, or never swore by his genius[4].

---

[1] Tac. *Hist.* i. 77.
[2] Plin. *Paneg.* 42. Comp. Tac. *Ann.* iii. 38.
[3] Tac. *Ann.* i. 73; ii. 50; iii. 70; iv. 34.
[4] Suet. *Calig.* 27. Comp. *id. Claud.*

In such a state of things it will be evident how liable Christians would become to the charge of treason, and how impossible it was for them to render the homage to the Emperor which was the test of loyalty. They could not offer sacrifices for his safety: they could not invoke his genius: they could not give him titles which seemed to trench upon the majesty of the one Lord. And while this was so it was vain for them to appeal to their secret prayers for his well-being: to pledge their wishes for his safety: to call him 'a man second to god[1].' They did not dissemble that they owed supreme allegiance to another Master: that they waited for the establishment of another Kingdom: that they must fix for themselves the limits of their obedience. They were forced to stand as witnesses to the reality of an unseen world. They felt, it may have been indistinctly as yet, that in a firm hold on that they had a pledge of a nobler freedom than had ever been realised among men: that the belief in God, as made known to them in Christ, was the one safeguard against utter slavery. And because they believed in His Kingdom as more sure than all things, they knew that the faith which was committed to them was for all men, and not for Jew or Greek or Roman: they knew that it covered the whole area of life and could not leave any fragment of it to be occupied by a strange power: they knew that their work was not one of silence only but of might: and in that knowledge they were armed for the final conflict for life or death.

[1] Tert. *Apol.* 28 ff., 32.

THE GOSPEL OF CREATION.

ὁ θεὸς ἀγάπη ἐστίν.

ὃ ἦν ἀπ᾽ ἀρχῆς...περὶ τοῦ λόγου τῆς ζωῆς.

THE GOSPEL OF CREATION.

I.   Humanity created for union with God.
Conception of the normal progress towards union, apart from sin.

II.   The subject belongs to a late period in the history of Theology
prominent in scholastic discussions.
Illustrations of its treatment
> Rupert of Deutz.
>> Movements in the xiiith Cent.
> Alexander of Hales.
> Albert the Great.
> Thomas Aquinas.
> Bonaventura.
> Duns Scotus.
> Gabriel Biel.
> John Wessel.
> Picus of Mirandola.
> Naclantus.
> Andr. Osiander.
> Servetus.
> F. Socinus.
> Calvin.
>> Latin Calvinists.

III.   Right mode of approaching the question.
Two main questions

     1. The relation of man to God and the world.

     2. The consequent aspect of the Incarnation.

     1. Man as created.

        i. In the image of God.

           (a) The individual.
                Need of Mediation.

           (b) The race.
                Need of unity.
                Relation of Christ to the Church.

        ii. The representative of Creation.
           Differentiation the law of progress.
           Reunion.

     2. The necessities of man and men independent of the Fall.
Consummation answers to Creation.
The Gospel of Creation not an arbitrary speculation.
The general silence of Scripture natural.
The truth practical, and helpful for our needs.

THE GOSPEL OF CREATION.

I.

Conditions under which the inquiry is permissible. IN attempting to speak of such a mystery as the Gospel of Creation, that is of the promise of the Incarnation which was included in the Creation of man, it is evident that we have need of watchful and reverent care lest we should strive to go beyond the limits which bound the proper field of our powers. It is necessary also that we should guard ourselves against the danger of using human language, not only (as we must do) to represent as clearly as possible our conceptions of the divine, but as the legitimate foundation for secondary conclusions. If however we do devoutly recognise that in such speculations we are entering on holy ground; if we steadily refuse to admit deductions as absolute which are derived from the conditions under which we apprehend the Truth made known to us; then it is well for us to look for a time towards the loftiest heights and the deepest foundations of faith. If we essay something without 'pre-'sumption and in submission to the judgment of the Church'—to borrow words spoken on the subject three hundred years ago—'and 'supported by the light of the divine word give expression to our 'thoughts humbly to the best of our power with stammering lips, 'not only do we not offend God, but we do Him reverence, and not 'unfrequently profit the weaker members of the Church[1].'

---

[1] Et si Divinæ mentis arcana in patria pertingemus illustrius, ubi in lumine gloriæ lumen nostræ videbimus felicitatis; immo cum cogitationes Dei longe diversæ sunt a cogitationibus nostris, mirum non est si nobis, dum hic agimus, magna sunt ex parte recondita; attamen cum sine præsumptione subque censura, prout facimus, sacrosanctæ ecclesiæ aliquid attentamus et

In this spirit then we must attempt to define our meaning when Conception of the progress of sinless humanity towards union with God. we express the belief that the true Protevangelium is to be found in the revelation of Creation, or in other words that the Incarnation was independent of the Fall. All our present ideas of human life necessarily involve thoughts of pain and suffering and weakness. Such thoughts however are wholly excluded from the conception of that manhood which we regard as predestined in the eternal and absolute counsel of God for union with the Word, or (to look at it from the other side) as answering to Him of whom it was, in some sense which we cannot strictly define, the image, related as a copy to the archetype. In order to gain, however imperfectly and transiently, this conception, we endeavour to present to ourselves humanity made in God's image and advancing in harmonious cooperation with His Grace towards His likeness. We look upon men and man, upon the race as well as upon the individual, as far as we can, growing perfect as God is perfect, holy as God is holy. We follow this progress to its consummation; and then having so gained a conception of manhood, answering to what is made known of the divine idea of man, we go on to say that it is most consonant to what God has revealed to believe that it was His pleasure that humanity, so consummated in its proper development in many parts, should find its true personality by union with His Son. According to this view man's self-will by which he fell was not the occasion of the supreme manifestation of the love of God in 'the taking of manhood unto God.' That was the end of Creation from the beginning. The Fall, and here lies the greatest mystery of divine love, did not frustrate this end which it might seem to have made unattainable consistently with that truth and justice which define omnipotence.

There is no question on any side that everything of suffering and All idea of humiliation excluded from such a union. shame connected with the Incarnation was due to the Fall: there is no question that in our imagination the voluntary endurance of these by the Son of God makes His love appear greater. But indeed

luce Divini verbi suffulti illud pro nostro captu humiliter balbutimus, non solum Deum non offendimus sed veneramur et ecclesiæ imbecillioribus membris non raro proficimus (Naclantus, *Opera*, p. 37).

nothing finite can appreciably alter the love manifested in the Incarnation which is essentially infinite; and it can be fairly maintained that we are led by Scripture to regard the circumstances of the Incarnation as separable from the idea of the Incarnation, and to hold that the circumstances of the Incarnation were due to sin, while the idea of the Incarnation was due to the primal and absolute purpose of love foreshadowed in Creation, apart from sin which was contingent.

II.

The idea of a Gospel of Creation not discussed in the first ages of the Church.

The subject as it is thus presented belongs properly to the later ages of the Church. It may perhaps be truly said that the thought of an Incarnation independent of the Fall harmonizes with the general tenor of Greek Theology[1]. Some patristic phrases seem to imply that the thought was distinctly realised here and there, and perhaps discussed. But the question was not formally raised, at least not so as to come into prominence, till the xith or xiith century. The circumstances of the primitive church adequately explain this silence on a point of speculation, which was not suggested and was even put out of sight by the work to be done in the first ages. The intensity of the conflict with heathenism was a necessary hindrance to the realisation of the unity of humanity; and physical research had not within its own sphere forced the thought of such a unity upon men's minds. Under such circumstances it was natural that Christian teachers should concentrate their efforts upon bringing out the truth of the redemption of a Church from fallen humanity rather than enter upon the theoretical investigation of the original relation of man and humanity to God.

Stages in the history of the question.

There is indeed a divine order in the progressive apprehension of the fulness of truth by the Christian consciousness. So the first work of conquest, the conquest of the old world, was accomplished by the Church in due time. And when the controversies of the fourth century were decided, a period of mainly traditional theology followed during

[1] See below, pp. 306 ff.

the conquest of the northern nations (590—1050). Then at length a fresh energy of life was quickened in the West in the eleventh century, and scholars began to venture on independent lines of thought in many directions. Among other subjects the absolute idea and motive of the Incarnation appears then first to have received attention. The topic is handled by Rupert of Deutz († 1135), but in such a way as to indicate that he is dealing with it tentatively and without having either received or gained a firm and consistent opinion on the subject[1].

From the beginning of the thirteenth century the question 'whether Christ would have been incarnate if Adam had not sinned,' became one of the recognised questions of the schools. In the period of the Reformation it was debated by representatives of the chief parties of Christendom ; and now again in quite recent times, after falling out of sight, the subject has been, and is likely to be, keenly discussed.

The course of the controversy, the arguments used on the different sides, the grounds of decision and of doubt alleged by the great teachers, afford a most instructive study in theology, the more instructive perhaps because the subject itself is not complicated with considerations of orthodoxy, for it has been generally allowed that both decisions on the point in dispute are allowable. If it were only for the purpose of examining in one detail the method of the schoolmen, it would be well worth while to consider what they have written upon a subject not uncongenial to their spirit, and one in which they are brought near to ourselves. Many of the arguments which they use appear to us frivolous and pointless. It requires a serious effort to enter into them with a sympathetic intelligence. But the effort is worth making. Conclusions which rest upon arbitrary assumptions as to the symmetries of things witness in an

The subject offers an interesting study of this scholastic method.

---

[1] In the attempt to trace the outline of the history of the doctrine, I have derived great assistance from the references in Gerhard (Joh.) *Uberior explicatio*, loc. IV. cap. vii. §§ 142 ff. ; Quenstedt (J. A.) *Syst. Theol.* III. 109 ff.;

Thomassin (L.), *De dogmatibus: De Incarn.* ii. 17, 7 ff. There is a slight review of the history in Dorner's *Doctrine of the Person of Christ*, ii. vol. I. pp. 361 ff. (Eng. Transl.).

W.

imperfect fashion to a deep sense of a divine order in creation; and
we do injustice to those who draw them if we allow even the
greatest errors of expression and form to blind us to the nobility of
the conception which they embody most inadequately.

RUPERT OF
DEUTZ.

The first writer however whom we have to notice, RUPERT OF
DEUTZ, was not either in spirit or in form a schoolman. The contemporary of Bernard of Clairvaux, he gave himself even more completely than Bernard to the study of Holy Scripture and looked to
the immediate guidance of the Spirit for the understanding of it. His
early years were spent at Liège. In 1120 he was called to be Abbat
of Deutz, and died there in 1135. His numerous works rest almost
exclusively on interpretations of books or passages of the Bible; and
even where he gives way to a license of allegorising he preserves and
enforces the conviction that the Word of God is still directly
addressed to man through the writings of prophets and apostles.

It is very startling that the main argument of Rupert in favour
of the absolute divine purpose of the Incarnation is based upon a
false reading of the Latin text of Hebr. ii. 10. This he quotes with
the passive *consummari* for *consummare*[1], and thus obtains the sense
that it was fitting that He for Whom were all things and through
Whom were all things—even the Son of God—in bringing many sons
to glory, should Himself be made perfect through suffering. 'The
'first thing to inquire here,' he goes on to say, 'is whether the Son
'of God spoken of in this place would have become man or not even
'if sin, for which we all die, had not intervened.' All are agreed,
he continues, that in that case He would not have become a mortal
man. 'The question is whether God would have become man as the
'Head and King of all as He now is, and whether this was in some

---

[1] Decebat enim eum propter quem
omnia et per quem omnia, qui multos
filios in gloriam adduxerat, auctorem
salutis eorum per passionem consummari. So also Ambrose, Rufinus,
Sedulius, Vigilius Tapsensis. Comp.
Sabatier *ad loc.* Rupert, *Comm. in*
Matt. Lib. xiii. p. 696 (Migne, *Patrol.*
Lat. clxviii. p. 1628). The Commentary is referred to the year 1126. In
the treatise *De glorif. Trin.* i. § 6 the
text gives *consummare*, but the line of
argument requires *consummari*.

'sense necessary for the human race.' The elect saints would certainly have been born, if man had not fallen, as Augustine shews
(*De civ. Dei* xiv. 23), in accordance with the blessing at creation
(Gen. i. 28 *Increase and multiply*).   It is then absurd to suppose that
sin, which was not necessary for their birth, was necessary for the
Head and King of all elect angels and men, in order that He should
become man, who was destined to have 'the delights of His love with
'the sons of men' (Prov. viii. 31)...'It is marvellous,' he concludes,
'and worthy of devout gratitude (*adoratione*) that sin coming in the
'way did not make of none effect (*evacuarit*) that purpose of so
'great love,' in which God had purposed that the Word of God
should take delight with the sons of man, by having a form limited
according to human nature in the midst of angels and men; 'nay,
'then came to pass the saying... *Where sin abounded grace did much
'more abound* (Rom. v. 20)...seeing that the Son became without sin
'such as we had become for sin; that is, not only did He not shrink
'from our nature which He had purposed to assume, but for our
'sake descended even unto death...as the Apostle says, *For it became
'Him...to be made perfect through suffering* (Hebr. ii. 10).'

In another work written not long after Rupert, in answer to the
opinion that man was created to fill up the gap made in the angelic
orders by a Fall, says[1]: 'It is more right to say not that man was
'made for the sake of angels, but that the angels, as every thing
'else, were made for a particular man, according to the witness of the
'Apostle : *For it became Him* [i.e. Christ, the Son of man] *for Whom
'are all things and through Whom are all things.*'   And after referring
to John i. 3 f. (with the Latin reading *quod factum est in ipso vita erat*)
he goes on to Prov. viii. 31, and asks 'what else is this than if he had
'said : "Before God made anything from the beginning, and when He
"was making this or that, this was His purpose that I the Word of
"God, the Word God (*verbum Deus*) should become flesh, and dwell
"among men with great love and great humility, which are true
"delights." 'Therefore we say that it is not so likely that man was
'made to fill up the number of angels as that both angels and men

[1] *De glorif. Trin.* iii. §§ 20 f. (Migne *Patrol. Lat.* clxix. pp. 71 ff.).

'were made for the sake of one man Jesus Christ; that as He, one
'and the same, was both God, born of God, and destined to be born
'man, He might have a family prepared on both sides, of angels
'and of men, and might Himself, God and man, rise aloft Lord and
'Creator of angels, Lord and Creator and Saviour of the saints, Lord,
'I say, among them as in His own house, King in His own nation,
'God in His own majesty, because, as has been already said, *all*
'*things are both for Him and through Him.*'

Thus Rupert regards the Incarnation as essentially independent
of Sin and the Fall, and still he argues that the Fall did in fact
redound to this glory of Christ. The humiliation of love which it
called out was followed by a more exceeding glory (Phil. ii. 9). And
thus, he says[1], when the trembling sinner looks to Christ in His
majesty, he may fancy that he hears Him answer: 'I should not
'have been such as I am and so great, except for thy sake for
'the sins of the human race (*causa tui propter peccata generis
'humani*).... *We see*, the Apostle says, *the Lord Jesus Christ for
'suffering crowned with glory and honour* (Hebr. ii. 9). Therefore
'the godless and the wicked were the cause that He is crowned and
'seated at the right hand of God, crowned with the glory of the
'kingdom, with the honour of the priesthood. He therefore owes
'much to the godless who are turned through faith in Him to godli-
'ness: He owes much to enemies who through Him were reconciled
'to God.'

In a later work the same thought is expressed if possible in a
bolder paradox[2]. 'Let believing sinners, penitent sinners,' he writes,
'reply in answer to the accusations of their Judge: "If we owe much
"to Thee, O God Christ, because Thou wast made man, yet Thou on
"the other hand owest much to us, O man Christ, because for us
"Thou wert taken into God. For unless we had been sinners there
"would have been no reason why Thou shouldest have been taken
"into God."' The penitent sinner must look therefore, he argues,
not at Christ's sufferings only, but at His exaltation. 'Unless the

[1] *Comm. in Matt.* xii. 697 (Migne, *Patrol. Lat.* clxviii.).

[2] *De medit. mortis* ii. p. 249 (Migne, *Patrol. Lat.* clxx. p. 387).

'slaves had sinned the nature of the slave would not have been taken
'into the Lord God.   For the Lord did not receive more outrages
'for the rebellious and wicked slaves than glory for the same.'

The two views thus expressed are inconsistent only in appearance.
The Incarnation as absolute in idea is in some way contrasted with
the Incarnation as conditioned by sin in fact.   Christ by taking upon
Himself man's nature, when man had fallen, and bearing all the
consequences of sin was more highly exalted, it is argued, than if the
union of man and God had been otherwise made.   The circumstances
of the Incarnation have actually made the issue of it more glorious
for Christ.   The thoughts are evidently written down without
careful guarding against misconception.   New lights flash across the
thinker's soul and he hardly pauses till they have settled into the
calm of the perfect day.

It is difficult to trace the history of the question during the century which followed the death of Rupert.   It does not appear to have
been discussed in the school of St Victor at Paris, where it might
have been expected to attract attention.   The teaching of Hugh of
St Victor († 1141) and Richard of St Victor († 1173) seems to
connect the Incarnation exclusively with the Fall[1].   Meanwhile the
system of scholastic theology was being reduced to a definite shape.
Anselm († 1109) had proved in controversy and in original speculation the power of a logical method.   The recovery of the direct Latin
translation of Aristotle stimulated and guided independent thought.
The translation of the treatise of John of Damascus, *On the Orthodox
Faith* into Latin (c. 1146), gave a model to the West for the construction of a general view of Christian doctrine.   Several 'Systems'
(*Summæ Theologiæ*) were compiled, one by our own Stephen Langton
(c. 1205), and *Books of Sentences*.   But supreme among these by
its masterly completeness of form and lasting influence was the great

The growth of Scholasti-cism.

[1] Ecclesia fidelium cum omni fiducia canat: O certe necessarium Adæ peccatum et nostrum quod morte Christi deletum est.   O felix culpa quæ talem ac tantum meruit habere redemptorem.   Ric. a S. Victore, *de Verbo Inc.* 8 (Migne, *Patrol. Lat.* cxcvi. p. 1003).

work of Peter Lombard of Novara, the scholar of Abélard, and afterwards Bishop of Paris († 1164), *Sententiarum Libri* iv., which practically determined once for all the outlines of the various mediæval systems of doctrine, and through them has influenced the direction of the currents of thought over to the present day.

Outline of the *Books of Sentences* of PETER LOMBARD.

The *first* book of the Sentences treats of the questions which concern the mystery of the Godhead : of the Trinity and Unity : of the Divine Persons : of the Divine attributes and will.

The *second* book treats of finite being : of Creation and creatures : of angels : of the work of the six days : of the fall : of free-will and grace : of sin and sins.

The *third* book treats of the Incarnation : of the Human nature of Christ and its relation to the Divine : of the nature and necessity of redemption : of Faith, Hope and Charity : of the four cardinal virtues (Justice, Courage, Prudence, Temperance) : of the seven gifts of the Holy Spirit : of the ten commandments.

The *fourth* book treats of the Sacraments and Eschatology : of Baptism, Confirmation, the Eucharist, Penance, Extreme Unction, Orders, Marriage : of the Resurrection, the Last Judgment, the Future State[1].

ALEXANDER OF HALES.

The question of the absolute motive of the Incarnation is not raised by Peter Lombard, but when it appears next it has evidently been already made the subject of careful inquiry from many sides. About the year 1243 Innocent IV. commissioned Alexander of Hales (Alexander Alensis, Alesius), a Franciscan, who had won for himself the titles of ' Fountain of Life ' and ' *Doctor irrefragabilis*,' to compose ' a Body of Theology[2].' This he did on the general lines of the

[1] The history of scholasticism is commonly divided into three periods. The first extends to about 1250; the second to about 1330; the third to the close of the 15th century. I have taken ALEXANDER OF HALES as the representative of the first: ALBERT THE GREAT, THOMAS AQUINAS, BONAVENTURA, and DUNS SCOTUS, as the representatives of the second, the heroic age of the schoolmen; and GABRIEL BIEL, as the representative of the last age, the age of the decline and dissolution of their system.

[2] Alexander cannot have been educated as is universally stated in the Cistercian [not Franciscan] Abbey of Hailes in Gloucestershire. This was

Sentences in four parts; and the work, which was approved by a Bull of Alexander IV. in accordance with the solemn judgment of seventy Theologians, is a marvellous monument of learning and thought.

The third Part treats of the Incarnation. The first two questions discussed are ' *On the Necessity of the Incarnation* ' and ' *On the* '*fitness (convenientia) of the Incarnation.*' The last topic (*membrum*) which is considered under the second head (and the twelve preceding topics shew singular fertility and subtlety of thought), is ' whether if ' human nature had not fallen through sin there would still have ' been reason and fitness for the Incarnation of Christ ? (*an si humana* ' *natura per peccatum lapsa non esset adhuc fuisset ratio et conve-* ' *nientia ad Christi Incarnationem ?*)'

This Alexander affirms (*sine prœjudicio concedendum est*) ; and he brings forward four reasons in support of his view :

1. The highest good is necessarily diffusive and perfectly diffused. It must therefore be extended to the creature; for otherwise we could imagine a more complete diffusion. And this diffusion would not be complete unless He who is the highest good were united with the creature, that is, with man the representative of creation.

2. All blessedness is in God; and the creature is capable of blessedness in all its parts. A man therefore, a rational creature made up of body and mind, is capable of being blessed in sense as well as in understanding.

He must then be blessed in God in both (*secundum sensum et secundum intellectum*).

But he cannot be blessed in God in Himself as far as sense. Therefore God must assume a corporeal nature to bring this blessedness to him, and, if so, a human nature.

---

not founded till 1246, the year after his death. Rudder, in his *History of Gloucestershire*, suggests that he was educated at Hales Owen in Shropshire, which was commonly called Hales, where there was a convent of Præmonstratensian Monks founded in the reign of John. It is said that Alexander reckoned among his pupils Bonaventura and Thomas Aquinas. Zealous Dominicans deny that Thomas heard him, but the tradition is supported with strong evidence by Wadding, *Annales*, iii. pp. 133 ff.

3. There are three Persons in unity of substance (in the Holy Trinity) : there are three persons in three substances (as three angels or three men).

Hence to complete the possible combinations, that there may be perfection in the universe, we conclude that there will be three substances in one Person.

This can only be realised by the union of the divine nature with the twofold human nature (spiritual and corporeal).

4. We find unity of Nature in three Persons (in God); we find also unity of Person in two natures (in man): if this plurality of natures belongs to the perfection of persons it must be possible for God. We must suppose therefore that one divine Person (and if so the Son) was destined absolutely to be united in time to human nature[1].

[1] Alex. Alensis *Summæ Theol. Pars* iii., *Quæst.* iii., *Membr.* xiii......dicit Dionysius *Bonum est diffusivum sui esse*......Ergo si summum bonum existente creatura non se diffundit in creaturam, adhuc erat cogitare majorem diffusionem......Sed hæc diffusio non potest intelligi summa nisi ipse [Deus] uniatur creaturæ; ergo convenit quod Deus uniatur creaturæ, et maxime humanæ...Ergo posito quod ipsa non esset lapsa, adhuc ei uniretur summum bonum.

ITEM, non est beatitudo nisi in Deo; et creatura rationalis tota est beatificabilis...ergo et secundum sensum et secundum intellectum; ergo oporteret quod in Deo beatificaretur quantum ad utrumque...Sed in Deo secundum se considerando et in propria natura non potest beatificari sensus sed solum intellectus...Si ergo totus homo debet beatificari in Deo, oportet Deum esse corporalem et sensibilem. Sed non est conveniens, ut assumat quamlibet corporalem naturam, sed solum humanam, ut dictum est.

ITEM, contingit intelligere tres personas in unitate substantiæ; et ex opposito tres substantias in unitate personæ; et inter hæc duo tres personas in tribus substantiis. Si ergo unum extremorum est in rerum natura ...et medium...contingit ponere tertium, videlicet unam personam in tribus substantiis; sed hoc non potest fieri nisi per unionem divinæ naturæ ad humanam, quia in nulla alia creatura est ponere duas substantias quam in homine, scilicet spiritualem et corporalem...Convenit ergo quod sit unio divinæ naturæ ad humanam in unitate personæ; ut sit in rerum universitate perfectio; ut sicut tres personæ in una natura, et tres personæ in tribus naturis, ita tres naturæ in una persona, scilicet divinitas, corpus, et anima.

ITEM, nos invenimus unitatem naturæ in pluribus personis...ut in Deo: Item...unitatem personæ in pluribus naturis, ut in homine. Si ergo de perfectione naturæ est quod est in pluribus personis ergo et de perfectione erit quod potest esse in pluribus naturis. Si ergo semper quod est perfectius Deo tribuendum quantum ad naturam et quantum ad personam... convenit...quod uniatur divina natura naturæ creatæ in persona divina, sed non......cuilibet .....sed solum humanæ; nec etiam cuilibet personæ in Trinitate nisi filio...Relinquitur ergo quod circumscripto lapsu humanæ naturæ adhuc est convenientia unionis in persona filii.

In support of this view Alexander quotes a passage ascribed to Bernard, in which it is said that envy at the prospect of man's destined union with the Son of God led to the fall of Lucifer; and that he planned the temptation to hinder the union which he foresaw[1]; and another passage from [a work falsely ascribed to] Augustine. ' God was therefore made man to bless the whole of man in ' Himself, that whether man went within by intellect, or went ' without by sense, he might find pasture in his Creator, pasture ' within in the knowledge of the Godhead, pasture without in the ' flesh of the Saviour[2].' This reason, he adds, remains even if the fall of human nature be excluded.

On the other side he brings forward ' the authority of the ' Church' ' in the preface to the [Easter] candle' (*nihil nasci profuit nisi redimi profuisset*). This objection he removes by shewing that the words refer to man as fallen, and not to man absolutely.

ALBERT THE GREAT, who was a Dominican, of a noble German family and at last Bishop of Ratisbon, approached the question from a different side. In commenting upon the section of the Sentences in which Peter Lombard[3] shews ' that God could have freed man ' otherwise than He did,' and then points out ' why He chose to free ' him in that particular way,' he comes to speak of the words : ' What ' so much rouses our minds and frees them from despair of immor- ' tality as that God esteemed us so highly that the Son of God ' remaining in Himself what He was, unchangeably good, and re- ' ceiving from us that which He was not, deigned to enter into ' fellowship with us and bear our ills by dying.' On this view, he says, it appears that if man had not sinned [God] would not have challenged us so powerfully to His love as He does now. This, he continues, is implied in the words of the sequence :

ALBERT
THE
GREAT,
1205
(1193)—
1280.

> O culpa nimium beata
> ·Quâ redempta est natura:
> Deus qui creavit omnia
> Nascitur ex femina[4]:

[1] The passage is referred to *Hom. super Jon.* 2, and it is probably a free adaptation of part of it.

[2] *De an. et spir.* § 9 (quoted freely). The treatise was probably written by Alcher, a monk of Clairvaux. The passage in *De Civ.* x. 27 is quite different in tone.

[3] Sent. iii. Dist. xx. Art. 4.

[4] Daniel, *Thesaurus Hymnol.* ii. 3.

which as much as say that because the guilt was incurred God was made man. And further, he adds, in some Churches a hymn is used at the blessing of the Easter Candle which contains the phrase, *O felix culpa quæ tantum ac talem meruit habere redemptorem*[1], in which the Incarnation is distinctly made to depend upon the Fall. The same conclusion, he continues, is drawn from Rom. viii. 28 (*all things work together for good*). For the only good which sin can be said to have wrought is in the Incarnation, which must therefore be supposed to have depended upon it. And further, if there had been no sin we should not have needed a teacher, or liberator, or redeemer.

These are the arguments which Albert gives in support of the common opinion that the Incarnation was dependent on the Fall. On the other side he alleges the following arguments :

1. Good is diffused (see above, p. 295).

2. There are four conceivable modes of birth, and if any one of them, as the birth from a virgin, had been wanting, the order of production would not have been perfect.

3. The Incarnation was foreseen from eternity, and so must have taken place under any circumstances.

4. Man was created capable of being united to God, and this capability must have been satisfied.

5. Sin in point of fact did not make man more fitted to be united to God, but less fitted.

6. The perfection of the universe consists in a circular figure. It was fitting therefore that the two extremes of being, God and man, should be united.

7. The greatest love is shewn in union. Since God therefore has the greatest love for man, His union with man cannot have been contingent.

'We must allow,' he says in summing up, 'that the solution of 'this question is uncertain, but as far as I can form an opinion

[1] Daniel, *l. c.* 303, and notes. The clause, together with the words which precede 'O certe necessarium Adæ peccatum, quod Christi morte deletum est' is omitted generally in German and French MSS, while it is found in Italian MSS. See p. 293, n.

'I believe that the Son of God would have been made man even if 'sin had never been.   Still I say nothing positively on this point, 'but I believe this which I have said to accord better with the piety 'of faith [than the contrary opinion].'   He then examines in detail the answers which can be made to the arguments on both sides, and rightly remarking that the language of the Hymn is 'very inexact' (*locutiones valde impropriæ*), in the end reaffirms his judgment.

The great pupil of Albert, THOMAS, COUNT OF AQUINUM (*Doctor angelicus*), who declined the Archbishopric of Naples, himself also of noble birth, treats the question with singular reverence and moderation.   In his early commentary on the Sentences (c. 1255) he proposes four questions on the Incarnation (Sent. iii. Dist. i. Quest. 1): (1) Whether it was possible for God to be incarnate; (2) Whether it was suitable (*congruum*); (3) Whether the Incarnation would have taken place if man had not sinned; (4) On the time of the Incarnation.   In discussing the third of these points he states at length the main arguments on both sides, and then concludes that 'He alone can know the truth of this ques-'tion Who was Born and Offered because He willed...Since the 'redemption of man from the slavery of sin is assigned in Holy 'Scripture as the sole cause of the Incarnation many say with good 'reason (*probabilitas*) that if man had not sinned, the Son of God 'would not have been man...Others however say that since by the 'Incarnation of the Son of God there was accomplished not only the 'liberation from sin, but also the exaltation of human nature, and 'the consummation of the whole universe, for these reasons even if 'sin had not existed the Incarnation would have taken place.   And 'this also can be maintained with good reason.'

As time went on Thomas appears to have yielded more and more to what he held to be the teaching of Scripture on a great mystery[1];

THOMAS AQUINAS, 1224— 1274.

---

[1] In his commentary on 1 Tim. i. 15 (*Lect.* iv.) he says: Sed si nullus fuis-set peccator numquid incarnatus non fuisset? Videtur quod non: quia venit peccatores salvos facere. Non ergo fuisset necessaria incarnatio. Item

Glossa: Tolle morbum, et medicinæ non opus erit.
Respondeo. Dicendum est quod ex verbis sanctorum satis (?) hoc patet. Sed hæc quæstio non est magnæ auc-toritatis: quia Deus ordinavit fienda

300 THE GOSPEL OF CREATION.

and in his latest work (the *Summa*, c. 1270) he speaks with tolerable distinctness on the main issue, yet so as to recognise the validity of some (at least) of the grounds on which the contrary opinion had been maintained.

The first Question in the Third Part of his *Summa* is on 'the Fitness (*convenientia*) of the Incarnation.' The first three Articles, under which it is discussed, deal with the following topics : (1) Whether it was fitting (*conveniens*) that God should be incarnate ; (2) Whether it was necessary for the reparation of the human race that the Word of God should be incarnate ; (3) Whether if man had not sinned, God would have been incarnate.

His conclusion on the first point is that 'since the nature of God 'is the essence of goodness, and it pertains to the character (*rationem*) 'of good that it communicates itself to others; it is clear that it 'became God in the highest degree to communicate Himself to His 'creatures, which was fulfilled in the work of the Incarnation.'

The force of this argument (as we have seen before) is evidently wholly independent of the consequences of the Fall. So far therefore it might seem that Thomas was inclined to hold that this divine fitness would have been realised in the Incarnation apart from sin. But the discussion of the second Article brings into prominence the adaptation of the Incarnation to the wants of fallen man. And thus when he reaches the third Article he decides that 'Although God 'might have been incarnate if sin had not existed, yet it is said more 'fittingly that if man had not sinned God would not have been

secundum quod res fiendæ erant. Et nescimus quid ordinasset si non præscivisset peccatum. Nihilominus tamen auctoritates videntur expresse sonare quod non fuisset incarnatus si non peccasset homo in quam partem ego magis declino.

Comp. *Quæst. de Ver.* xxix. 3, 4. (If we admit that Christ would not have been Incarnate if man had not sinned, He would have been Head of the Church in His Divine Nature only.) The passage is characteristic: Supposita illa opinione quod Christus non fuisset incarnatus si homo non pec-

casset, Christus ante peccatum fuisset caput ecclesiæ secundum divinam naturam solum ; sed post peccatum oportet quod sit ecclesiæ caput etiam secundum humanam. Nam per peccatum natura humana vulnerata est et ad sensibilia demersa, ut ad invisibilem Verbi gubernationem non sit sufficienter idonea. Unde oportuit medicinam vulneri adhiberi per humanitatem Christi per quam Christus satisfecit, et oportuit quod visibilem naturam assumeret ut per visibilem gubernationem ad invisibilia homo revocaretur.

'incarnate, since in Holy Scripture the ground (*ratio*) of the Incar-
'nation is everywhere set down as springing from the sin of the first
'man (*ex peccato...assignetur*).'

This opinion he holds to be more probable because we can know
that which depends on the will of God from Scripture only; and
Scripture presents the Incarnation as the Divine remedy for sin.
Sin, he goes on to say, may have been the occasion for the greater
elevation of the human race; for God permits evil to happen that
He may bring a greater good out of it. And thus he quotes without
disapprobation the sequence, which his master Albert had criticised,
'*O felix culpa.*'

GIOVANNI DI FIDENZA, who is known by the name of BONAVEN- BONAVEN-
TURA from the exclamation of Francis of Assisi on the occasion of TURA, 1221
—1274.
his restoration to health when a child, combined the schoolman and
the mystic in a character of singular beauty. His master, Alexander
of Hales, is said to have remarked that 'Adam did not sin in Bona-
'ventura.' Even Luther gave him special praise; and the popular
judgment was expressed in his title '*doctor seraphicus.*' Bonaventura entered the order of the Franciscans (1248), and he became
doctor on the same day and died in the same year as his Dominican
contemporary Thomas Aquinas. He deals with the subject of the
absolute motive of the Incarnation more fully and (if possible) more
reverently than his more famous rival. Indeed it was said that the
third Book of the Sentences, the Doctrine of the Incarnation, was
his peculiar field[1].

In treating of the whole subject he first examines[2] the question of
the possibility of the union of the divine and human natures: he
then examines the question of the suitableness (*congruitas*) of the

[1] Compare: Non itaque absque causa
tantam admiratus est in operibus ejus
doctrinam et eruditionem S. Thomas
Aquinas ut petierit a Bonaventura sibi
ostendi libros ex quibus tam multipli-
cem atque adeo magnam eruditionis
ubertatem hauriret. Is vero Christi
Domini Cruci affixi imaginem demon-
stravit, e quo fonte uberrimo se accipere professus est quicquid vel legeret
vel sentiret (Wadding, *Annales*, IV.
139).

[2] III. *Dist.* i. *Quæst.* 2. There are
considerable variations in the texts
of Bonaventura which I have used,
but they do not affect the general scope
of his arguments.

union. Under the latter head he raises four points. ' 1. Whether
' it was suitable that God should become incarnate. 2. Whether
' the cause of the Son of God coming into the world was the restora-
' tion (*reparatio*) of the human race; whether, that is, if man had not
' sinned Christ would have been Incarnate. 3. Whether it was
' suitable that of the three Persons the Son should be Incarnate.
' 4. Whether the Son of God was Incarnate at a suitable time.'

He approaches the second point as Thomas also did, from the side
of Scripture, and gives the negative arguments first. The general
language of the Bible and the current glosses, so he states the argument, represent the coming of Christ as being for the redemption of
man (Gal. iv. 4; Hebr. ii. 14; Ps. lxix. (lxviii.) 2).

Further, Christ assumed human nature either for its dignity or
its necessity. But it could not have been for the former seeing that
the nature of angels is nobler. And man's necessity came from
sin.

Further, the Incarnation is a work of grace; but the grace is
greater as the object of it is more unworthy.

Having thus given summarily the arguments in favour of the
current opinion, Bonaventura states the reasoning on the opposite
side at greater length.

1. He first gives the argument from the Pseudo-Augustine
which was urged by Alexander of Hales. 'Man required to be
' made wholly blessed (*debebat totus beatificari*), and that as fully if
' he had not fallen as after he had fallen.

2. 'The union with a Divine Person is not given to the nature
' of angels (Hebr. ii. 16). If therefore...nothing has been given to
' human nature in vain, such a dignity would not have remained
' unfulfilled (*vacua*), but it would still have been united with the
' Divine nature.'

3. 'It became God as much to manifest His infinity and per-
' fection and bountiful love (*liberalitas*) if man had stood as if he
' had fallen...'

4. 'It is a work of as great difficulty and nobility to lay claim
' to and gain (*vindicare et acquirere*) an infinite good, as to make

'satisfaction for an offence against an infinite good. If therefore
'man could not by himself make satisfaction for the offence com-
'mitted against God, neither could he by himself earn the possession
'of God (*mereri habere Deum*). Therefore as it was seasonable
'(*opportunum*) that the Son of God should be incarnate on the fall of
'man, to make satisfaction for man, so it seems seasonable that the
'Son of God should be incarnate, if man had remained unfallen
'(*homine stante*), that man through Him might earn [the divine
'union].'

5.   'If the Incarnation took place primarily (*principaliter*) for
'the expiation of sin, then the soul of Christ[1] was made not of
'primary purpose (*principali intentione*) but contingently (*quadam
'occasione*); if therefore it is incongruous (*inconveniens*) that the
'noblest object of creation should have been brought into being con-
'tingently (*occasionaliter esse introductum*), while an agent primarily
'purposes the noblest works, it seems to be incongruous to say that
'the Incarnation took place only for the restoration (*reparationem*)
'of man.'

6.   'In the Incarnation of the Son of God human nature is most
'highly exalted. If therefore God was Incarnate because human
'nature sinned; it appears that man gains an advantage from his
'wickedness...'

7.   'Christ is the Head of the Church not only in His Divine
'Nature, but also in His human Nature ..But if man had not sinned
'the Body of the Church would still have existed.   Either therefore
'the Son of God would have become Incarnate or the Church would
'have remained without a Head.'

8.   'If man had not fallen the sacrament of marriage would have
'existed....If therefore man had remained unfallen, either the sacra-
'ment of marriage would have been a false sign (Eph. v. 32) or the
'Son of God would have been Incarnate.   But the first supposition
'is impossible.'

9.   There are four ways in which we can conceive of man being
produced: (1) of man and woman, (2) without man or woman

[1] Comp. p. 291.

(Adam), (3) of man without woman (Eve), (4) of woman without man (Christ). Unless this fourth possibility had been realised the universe would not have been perfect.

10. Yet further Bonaventura goes on to consider the assumption of human nature, as distinguished from the assumption of mortality by the Son of God, as belonging to the perfection of man, and by consequence to the perfection of the universe, both in regard to nature, and grace, and glory.

Having thus set out both views, he concludes : ' Which of these 'two modes [of regarding the question] is the better, He knows ' Who was Incarnate for us. Which of them is to be preferred 'it is difficult to see, inasmuch as each is in accordance with 'the catholic faith and is supported by catholic men. Moreover 'each excites the soul to devotion on different grounds. The first 'view however seems to be more consonant with the judgment of ' reason : the second, as it appears, is more consonant with the piety ' of faith. First because it is in closer agreement with [the letter of] ' Holy Scripture, the authority of Saints...and secondly because it ' gives greater honour to God...since the other view makes God in ' some sense dependent on the universe...Thirdly...because an excep- 'tional cause is assigned for an exceptional mystery...Fourthly ' because it kindles the affection of faith more ardently...'

Having thus stated his general conclusion he suggests answers to the arguments which he had given in favour of the view which he finally sets aside. They deserve to be indicated in outline :

1. The beatitude of man which comes through the Incarna- tion, and from the corporeal vision of Christ, is accidental and not essential.

2. There are many potencies in creation which are not brought to act ; but these are not in vain.

3. These attributes of God are adequately manifested in crea- tion.

4. Even allowing the premiss, the blessing of divine fellowship might have been secured by the mission of the Holy Spirit into the soul without the mission of the Son into the flesh.

5. God foreknew the fall and provided for it from eternity.

6. The Incarnation was not from (*ex*) man's wickedness, but from God's goodness. The obedience of Christ pleased Him more than the disobedience of Adam displeased Him.

7. The Church would not have been without a Head. As God is the Head of man, so He would have been the Head of the Church of men, as He is the Head of the Church of angels.

8. The sign of marriage would still have marked the union of Christ with the Church by love.

9. The fourth mode of production is beyond the perfection of the universe (Jer. xxxi.) ; moreover the man so produced need not have been also the Son of God.

After this reply he concludes : 'These statements I desire to be 'made (*dicta sint*) without prejudice. For I do not wish to confine 'the goodness of God, but to commend the excess of His love 'towards fallen man, that our affections may be roused to love Him 'while we mark the extremity of His exceeding love.'

The transition from the calm and eloquent tenderness of Bona- DUNS SCO-
ventura to the stern roughness of DUNS SCOTUS is most abrupt. TUS,†1308,
Duns Scotus (*doctor subtilis*) is simply the dialectician, without grace, without sympathy, inexhaustible in ingenuity, and unhesitating in decision. He is the master without the softening experiences of the ecclesiastic. In affirming that the Incarnation was independent of the Fall, he dwells mainly on the conceivable order of thoughts in the divine counsel, a form of argument which was only lightly touched before.

'The Incarnation of Christ was not foreseen as a contingent event '(*occasionaliter prævisa*), but was seen by God directly (*immediate*) 'as an end from eternity : so Christ, in His human Nature, since He 'is nearer to the end than other things, was predestined before 'them...[1].'

And again : 'If the Fall was the cause of the Incarnation of 'Christ, it would follow that the greatest work of God was con-'tingent only (*occasionatum tantum*), because the glory of all things

[1] *Opus Oxoniense*, iii. *Dist.* xix.; Wadding, vii. 1, p. 415.

W.   20

'will not be so great (*intensive*) as that of Christ, and it seems to be
'very irrational to suppose that God would have left undone (*dimi-*
'*sisset*) so great a work because of Adam's right action, that is, if he
'had not sinned[1].'

The thought is set out more fully in the following passage:

'[God] wills grace and glory to any other being soever before He
'foresees the opposites of those habits...that is sin and condemnation.
'Therefore from the first He wills the glory of the soul of Christ
'before He foresees that Adam will fall...Redemption, we allow,
'would not have required to be made if man had not sinned. But it
'was not for this reason only that God seems to have predestined
'that soul to so great glory, seeing that redemption, or the glory of
'redeeming the soul is not so great a good as is that glory of the soul
'of Christ, nor is it likely that the sovereign good in being (*tam*
'*summum bonum in entibus*) was only contingent, that is dependent
'on a less good...[2].'

GABRIEL
BIEL.

No fresh arguments appear to have been added on either side
after Duns Scotus. GABRIEL BIEL, 'the last of the schoolmen' who
assisted in the foundation of the Gymnasium at Tübingen (1477),
in his lectures on 'the Sentences' which were delivered there gives

---

[1] *Opus Parisiense*, iii. *Dist*. vii.
Quæst. 4; Wadding, xi. p. 451: Si
lapsus esset causa prædestinationis
Christi sequeretur quod summum opus
Dei esset occasionatum tantum, quia
gloria omnium non erit tanta intensive
quanta erit Christi; et quod tantum
opus dimisisset Deus per bonum factum Adæ, puta, si non peccasset, videtur valde irrationabile.

Dico igitur sic: Primo Deus diligit
se: secundo diligit se aliis (?), et iste
amor est castus; tertio vult se diligi
ab alio qui potest eum summe diligere, loquendo de amore alicujus ex-
trinseci: et quarto prævidit unionem
illius naturæ quæ debet eum summe
diligere etsi nullus cecidisset.

[2] *Opus Oxoniense*, iii. *Dist*. vii.
Quæst. 3; Wadding, vii. 1, p. 202
...[Deus] prius cuilibet alteri vult
gratiam et gloriam quam prævideat

opposita istorum habituum...scilicet
peccatum et damnationem. Ergo a
primo prius vult animæ Christi gloriam quam prævideat Adam casurum
...Sed nec redemptio fuisset facienda
nisi homo peccasset. Sed non propter
solam istam causam videtur Deus
prædestinavisse illam animam ad tantum gloriam. Cum illa redemptio sive
gloria animæ redimendæ non sit tantum bonum quantum est illa gloria
animæ Christi; nec est verisimile tam
summum bonum in entibus esse tantum occasionatum, scilicet propter
minus bonum... Compare *Dist*. xix (p.
405) Incarnatio Christi non fuit occasionaliter prævisa sed sicut finis immediate videbatur a Deo ab æterno, ita
Christus in natura humana, cum sit
propinquior fini, ceteris prius prædes-
tinabatur loquendo de his quæ prædes-
tinantur...

a general review of opinion upon the subject, and leaves the decision in suspense. He starts from the teaching of Thomas Aquinas, which he quotes at length, and gives in the course of his lecture an account of the opinions of Alexander of Hales, and Duns Scotus, justly remarking in reply to his argument from the priority of the pre-destination of Christ to glory in relation to the Fall, that in such questions we cannot speak of 'before' and 'after.' This criticism he supports by the authority of Occam. 'The problem therefore remains 'doubtful'—this is his conclusion—'...until the Lord shall deem it 'right to make a revelation[1].'

Still one other writer, JOHN WESSEL, must be noticed before we leave the 15th century. Wessel was born at Gröningen about 1419 and died in the same place in 1489. In spirit and pursuits and doctrine he belongs to a period of transition. Like Rupert of Deutz, the first mediæval writer whom he noticed, he expresses the striving after a new and direct approach to the source of truth. Like Rupert he also based his doctrine with absolute devotion upon Holy Scrip-ture; and he is described in his epitaph as justifying his claim to teach by a knowledge of Hebrew and Greek. His relation to Rupert is still closer than that of a kindred character. Hardenberg, his early biographer, relates that while studying at Cologne he grew weary of the mere repetition of the teaching of Thomas Aquinas and Albert the Great, and often crossed the Rhine to the Abbey of Deutz, where he found in the works of Rupert fresher and more congenial thoughts. From these writings he transcribed many passages, to which he added other extracts and comments of his own. This collection of notes and fragments he afterwards arranged and called his ' *Mare magnum.*' The collection itself has perished ; but the two essays *de causis Incarnationis* and *de magnitudine Passionis Domini*, with which we are chiefly concerned, are said to have been derived in great part from it ; and it is not difficult to see

---

[1] iii. *Dist*. ii. *Quæst*. 1.

how the speculations of Rupert have influenced the views which Wessel maintains in them.

Wessel approaches the subject of the Incarnation characteristically from a comparison of two passages of the Old Testament[1], '*I am* '*God, I change not*' (Mal. iii. 6), and '*I am he that I am*' (Ex. iii. 14). The latter translation is, he says, inadequate, though he believes that it was by a divine purpose that the LXX and Jerome preserved the present tense. The true rendering, he maintains, is: '*I will be the man I will be*' (*ero homo qui ero*). There is then an antithesis to be reconciled in this twofold revelation of the Divine nature; and the antithesis is reconciled for us, he argues, in the Incarnation.

The language of St Paul in Rom. ix. 28, as represented in the Vulgate, furnishes Wessel with his next illustration[2]. '*Verbum abbreviatum et consummatum,*' he says, '*fecit Deus super terram.*' And this was done in three ways. The divine Word, remaining in Himself unchangeable, was brought within limits (*abbreviatum*) at the Creation, but not consummated. He was also brought within limits in Holy Scripture, as it is said '*day unto day uttereth Word,*' but still the Word was not consummated in the written Word '*quantumlibet liquescentis veritatis claritate resplendens.*' Once again therefore the Word was brought within limits and consummated by the Incarnation.

Here then, he continues[3], is a fitting place to inquire why God was made man: *Cur Deus homo?* Again and again he repeats Anselm's famous question, and answers it by paraphrases of passages of Scripture which he quotes. The whole section is so full of thought, and offers so vivid a picture of Wessel's mode of interpreting the Bible that it must be quoted entire.

'*Why was God made man?* Why, but that that holy and fair body, the universal Church of the triumphant saints might not be maimed but rejoice in its proper head. Eph. i. 22; Col. i. 18, ii. 10.

'*Why was God made man?* That the building of the Holy Temple might have its corner-stone in which the two walls of men

---

[1] *De causis Incarn.* c. iv.   [2] *Id.* c. v.   [3] *Id.* c. vi.

and angels might meet and find their foundation. Ps. cxviii. 22 ; Acts iv. 11 [referred to St Stephen]; 1 Cor. iii. 11, 1 Cor. x. 4.

'*Why was God made man?* That all creation (*creatura*) might have a Mediator common to God and creation. Gal. iii. 19; 1 Tim. ii. 5.

'*Why was God made man?* That the whole host (*militia*) of God, and all the people of God might have their King. Luke i. 33; Apoc. xix. 16.

'*Why was God made man?* That the School of God might have its Teacher. Joel ii. 23 (*doctorem justitiæ* as mg. A.V.).

'*Why was God made man?* That the city of Jerusalem might have its Temple. Apoc. xxi. 22.

'*Why was God made man?* That the temple of the heavenly Jerusalem might have its High Priest. Ps. cx. 4; Hebr. v. 4.

'*Why was God made man?* That all the daughters of God might find their Bridegroom and the pattern (*paradigma*) of their love. John iii. 29; Matt. ix. 15.

'*Why was God made man?* That all who sacrifice in the Temple of God might have their sacrifice (*hostia*). Hebr. ix. 13 f. And if all do not offer sacrifices or victims for the present, still part do for the past, and all for preservation (*de præservato*) offer sacrifices and victims and offerings for sin and ignorance, and tithes and first fruits and peace offerings. All whether men or angels offer whole burnt offerings and incense in this Temple.

'*Why was God made man?* That all the sheep of God's pasture might have their common shepherd. John x. 2, 9. He left His ninety and nine sheep on the mountains, going away to seek the one which had strayed. A common shepherd then had been destined and predestined for this and for those, as He had been before foreseen and hated (*prævisus et invisus*) by Lucifer who pursues the Lamb.

'*Why was God made man?* That all the sons of God and all creation might have their first-born brother. Rom. viii. 29; Col. i. 15.'

It is easy to anticipate the answer which Wessel gives to the next question which he asks: '*Whether God the Word would have*

'assumed flesh even if man had not sinned?' His answer however
rests mainly upon another form of argument akin to that of Duns
Scotus. He regards the humanity assumed by Christ (*creaturam*
illam beatam a Verbo adsumptam in unionem hypostaticam) as so full
of grace, and righteousness and glory, that its fulness alone outweighs
in the judgment of God all the fulness of the whole remaining
creation. 'God therefore loved Christ more from eternity than the
'whole of the rest of the Church, and before it.' 'Nay the rest of
'the body would not have been destined [to glory], except it had
'been [included] in the dignity of the Sacred Head[1].'

'We must consequently use great care (*reverentia*) in dealing with
'the phrase in the Nicene Creed ' *who for us men*...,' as if the Word
'was made Flesh for our sakes, when otherwise He would not have
'been so made. For in final causes, which are essentially coordinated,
'the order is not that the better are for the worse...[2].'

Even the angels who had not fallen were, as Wessel teaches,
immeasurably blessed by the Incarnate Christ. 'Whence he con-
'cludes theirs is an unworthy question who ask 'Whether if Adam
''had not sinned the Word would have been made flesh?' For that
'wise designer (*destinator*) of the holy city Jerusalem had purposed
'(*destinaverat*) to grant union and perfection among its citizens, that
'the natural union of the head and members is inadequate to express
'it. It is then like asking in the case of an ulcerated arm or leg,
'whether if the arm had not been ulcerated the head would have
'been given to the combination of members to heal the arm or not[3]?'

This figure presents an impressive view of Wessel's general
teaching, which he sums up in a series of brief propositions, tracing
the fulfilment of the divine counsel from the creation to the consummation of all things[4]. This series concludes thus: 'God destined
'and regarded (*intendit*) the Lamb as first and the first-fruits of all
'creation. He destined that the Lamb should become man. He
'destined the Lamb as King of a blessed state. It was fitting (*con-*
'*gruebat*) that the Man-Lamb being King should have men as
'citizens of His kingdom.

---

[1] *De causis Incarn.* c. vii.   [2] *Id.* c. vii.   [3] *Id.* c. xiv.   [4] *Id.* c. xv.

' The Lamb has the promise from the Father that men should be
' given Him at His request as His inheritance.

' If neither angel nor man had fallen the Lamb in bliss would no
' less have reigned over them.

' Still truly ' for us men and for our salvation He came down from
' ' heaven.'

' He was truly made man for our salvation, suffered, died, was
' buried.'

' He was not however wholly or entirely (*non penitus non prorsus*)
' made man for our salvation.'

' For our salvation wholly He suffered, died, was buried, being
' made a sacrifice and victim. It was not wholly to restore (*curare*)
' us from destruction, that He was made an offering (*sacrificium*), a
' holocaust, incense.

' That most holy [human] soul [of Christ] was inflamed and
' borne to God by the impulse of its own love. It [or Christ] lived
' more for God and for itself [as directed] towards good than for
' saving all of us.'

Thus there were in Christ three 'forms.' The form of God,
which is eternal; and in this He is equal in all things to the
Father: the form of a slave, which He assumed for the sake of
sinners, which was temporal, and in this He emptied Himself: the
form of the supreme creature (*supremi plasmatis*), which He would
have assumed even if man had not sinned. In the second form He
will receive a kingdom which afterwards He will give back to the
Father. The kingdom which He has in the third form will be for
ever and ever (Luke i. 32 f.)[1].

Thus wrote the Dutch mystic from his northern home. About PICUS OF
MIRANDO-
the same time Picus, count of Mirandola, the most brilliant type of LA, †1494.
the universal scholarship of the Renaissance, maintained the same
doctrine from a different point of view. 'It was fitting,' he writes,
' that He who is the image of the invisible God, the first-born of all
' creation, in whom all things (*universa*) were created, should be
' united in an ineffable union to him (*i.e.* man) who was made after

---

[1] *De causis Incarn.* c. xvii.

'the image of God, who is the bond of all creation, in whom all
'things are included (*conclusa*). And if the whole of nature was
'imperilled by man, its loss was not to be disregarded, or to be
'repaired by any other than by Him by Whom all nature had been
'framed[1].'

In the age of the Reformation the question was still debated.
Among the Romanist divines who maintained that the Incarnation
was independent of the Fall, GIACOMO NACHIANTI, bishop of Chiozza
(Jacobus Naclantus, *Ep. Clodiensis*, or *Clugiensis*), a Dominican, is
the most conspicuous[2]. His general spirit is characterised by a
remark in the preface to his commentary on the Epistle to the
Ephesians, in which he gives as the reason for discussing that
Epistle before the Epistle to the Romans, that it suggests in its
'loftier and more mysterious revelations, which are truly brought
'from the third heaven, many thoughts which are necessary for the
'understanding of the latter.'

The argument by which Naclantus supports his opinion is an
analysis of the divine counsel of creation as man can apprehend it.
In this he argues that man was marked out as the object of the
Divine love, and that in regard to him an end absolutely perfect

[1] *In Hept.* v. 7.

I do not observe among the theses of
PICUS any one on this subject, as there
is commonly said to be.

WICLIF appears to regard the Incarnation as lying in some sense
eternally in the Nature of the Word:
assumpsit [Verbum] in unitatem personæ humanitatem integram, faciendo
se esse illam personam hominis quæ
æternaliter prius fuit, quia secundum
naturam Verbi æternaliter prius fuit
(*Trialogus*, iii. 27, p. 224).

[2] The glimpses which are gained of
Nachianti at the Council of Trent are
full of interest. He spoke warmly
against placing traditions on the same
footing as Scripture: Nemo enim
ignorat contineri in sacris libris ea
omnia quæ ad salutem pertinent...Quod
vero etiam ecclesiasticæ traditiones re-

cipiantur et eorum mentio in decreto
fiat nullo modo probare possum, cum
tot indictiones jejuniorum, tot cere-
moniæ, quæ plerumque frustratoriæ
sunt, nimis Christianum populum
gravant (Theiner, *Acta Conc. Trident.*
I. 58 f.). And again: Non possum
pati ut sæpe dixi, s. synodum pari
pietatis affectu suscipere traditiones et
libros sanctos; hoc enim, ut vere
dicam quod sentio, impium est. Neque
placet quod ponatur anathema in ipsis
traditionibus... A lively scene followed
these bold words, which ended in an
explanation and an apology (*id.* 85).
Comp. pp. 76, 82. The words of Nachianti were condemned by the Council,
and Card. Pole joined in the condemnation: 'sed posset, inquit, defendi,
quia dixit, "mihi videtur"' (*id.* p. 85).

must have been prepared before the means towards the end. This end regarded man's spiritual and eternal state; and therefore his approach to God and his union with God. And when it is said that man was the crown of creation, we mean in particular Christ as man, by whom as God and man, in the divine counsel, and therefore truly man, even before the Incarnation, it was predestined that the world should be made, preserved and consummated[1]. The effect of the Fall then was that He who 'was determined to be man, but not 'passible, ordained the Maker of the world, appointed Heir of the 'universe, chosen as King of all things, given as Head to the 'peculiar possession (*peculio*) of God the Father, should in due 'season be sent down, lowered (*dejici*), emptied, that clothed in 'passible flesh' He might make atonement for sin[2].

Whence Naclantus concludes, 'it is not only consonant to reason 'but to Holy Scripture, that although the decree for the assumption 'of flesh follows the decree for the permission of sin, so that if Adam 'had not sinned there would have been no need of Christ as a 'Physician, yet the decree of the assumption of man precedes not 'only the decree of the permission of sin, but even the determination 'of the creation of the world[3].'

The same general conclusion that 'the Son of God would have 'been Incarnate if sin had not entered into the world,' was maintained in the Lutheran Church by ANDR. OSIANDER[4]. This singularly ANDR. OSI-ANDER, †1552.

---

[1] Eodem constitutum est decreto ut per eundem Deum et hominem CHRISTUM (hoc est) verbum definitione Dei ad induendum hominem determinatum, et ob id hominem vere apud Deum effectum non solum quælibet conderetur, servaretur, ac promoveretur creatura...sed...in longe feliciorem statum ...certo transferretur tempore...p. 38.

[2] Decretum......Unigenitum summi Patris, jam quidem hominem sed non passibilem definitum, Opificem orbis ordinatum, Hæredem universorum institutum, in Regem omnium rerum selectum, Peculio Dei patris donatum, et eidem uti caput ascriptum; tandem (sed opportuno tempore) eousque demitti, dejici, exinaniri: ut eo passi-

bilem carnem induto......mortem execrabilem passo, impensa tanti sacrificii crimen expiaretur læsæ majestatis Dei... p. 39.

[3] Qua de re, si non fallor, facile ex præmissis habetur : non modo consonum esse rationi sed et Scripturis Sanctis : quod etsi decretum assumptionis carnis decretum subsequitur permissionis culpæ, propter quod si Adam non peccasset CHRISTO medico opus non fuisset : decretum tamen assumendi hominem non tantum præcedit permissionem peccati sed et definitionem creationis Mundi (*ib.* 39 f.).

[4] The title of the work in which he discusses the question is: *An Filius Dei fuerit incarnandus si peccatum*

vigorous and original thinker[1] brought the doctrine into connexion
with his peculiar views on justification. Man, he taught, is justified
by the indwelling in him of the Divine Word ' our Lord and Saviour
' and only Mediator, Jesus Christ, Son of God and Son of Mary,
' very God and very man... And since the one eternal and divine
' essence of the Father, Son and Holy Spirit is indivisible, the Father
' and the Holy Spirit also dwell in us[2].' The divine likeness, for
which man was made, according to his original constitution, involved
the union of God and man as presented in the Incarnation. This
opinion was fiercely assailed as ' new, useless, and impious.' The
most interesting feature in the arguments by which Osiander supports his teaching is the form of his biblical proof. He was specially
devoted to the study of Scripture, and thought that the confirmation
of the doctrine was to be sought there rather than in authority.
And such confirmation he found primarily in the account of Creation,
wherein man is revealed to have been ' made in the image of God.'

    This statement then formed the starting point of his discussion.
What, he asks, is ' the image of God'? The answer, he replies, is to
be found in the words of Christ : ' He that hath seen Me hath seen
' the Father' (John xiv. 9). ' Therefore our Lord Jesus Christ, the
' Son of God and the Son of Mary is the image of the Father....The
' Word made flesh, the Word of life which was from the begin-
' ning, which the apostles heard and handled with their hands, as
' John bears witness (1 John i. 1)[3].' In other words ' He in whom
' the fulness of Godhead (Father, Son and Spirit) dwells, Jesus Christ,
' or the humanity of Christ, embracing the divinity,...is the real ob-
' jective image of God[4].'

non introivisset in mundum. Item de
imagine Dei quid sit ex certis et eviden-
tibus sacræ Scripturæ testimoniis et
non ex philosophicis et humanæ rationis
cogitationibus deprompta explicatio.
Monteregio Prussiæ 1550. I have been
unable to obtain access to a copy of
the book which is not, as far as I can
find, in any of our great libraries. I
can therefore quote it only from Grau's
Essay (de And. Osiandro doctrinæ com-

mentatio...scr. R. F. Grau, Marb.
1860). There is a good and sympathetic account of Osiander's views in
Möller's life (Andreas Osiander...von
Dr W. Möller, Elberfeld, 1870).
  [1] ' Homo αὐτοδίδακτος nulliusque Aca-
demiæ discipulus,' as Quenstedt dis-
paragingly remarks (p. 110).
  [2] Grau, p. 27.
  [3] Grau, l. c. p. 5.
  [4] Osiander ap. Grau, p. 7.

Thus Christ was destined to be naturally the image and glory of God; and God made man, the whole man and not any part of him, capable of becoming like Christ through His pure grace and goodness. Man, that is, was created to be as it was already determined eternally that Christ should be[1].

This being the Destiny of man, the Incarnation, Osiander argues, was necessarily independent of the Fall. The image of God in which man was created was first realised in the Incarnation. Looking forward to this, in the language of time, God created man. Otherwise man could not have been created in God's image which would have had no existence[2].

Further the relation of Christ to the Church as its Head cannot be supposed to be dependent on man's sin. And this, Osiander thinks, was already shadowed forth in the record of Creation before the Fall (Gen. ii. 23 f.; comp. Matt. xix. 4 f.; Eph. v. 31 f.).

In a word all things were created for the Son, Who was to be incarnate (comp. Col. i. 13—20).

Osiander rests his conclusion on Scripture, but he finds support for it also in the language of the Nicene Creed. 'Christ came down 'from heaven for us men and for our salvation.' Here, he says, we have two distinct thoughts. He was Incarnate 'for us men' as men created for Him and in His image ; and 'for our salvation' as having fallen through sin[3].

Among those who had wandered far from the Catholic faith SERVETUS, SERVETUS and F. SOCINUS maintained that the coming of Christ in †1553. the flesh was independent of the Fall. 'Adam,' the former writes, 'was made after the pattern, form, figure and image of Christ, in

---

[1] Osiander's reasons are given at length by Grau, pp. 12 ff., and Möller, pp. 394 ff.

[2] Si filius Dei non fuisset incarnandus nisi Adam peccasset, sequeretur aliud absurdum, nempe quod Adam non Imagine Christi sed Christus Imagine Adami esset factus (Osiander, ap. Grau, p. 13).

[3] Quis non videat Spiritum Sanctum hic duas inter sese longe diversissimas causas ostendere propter quas Filius

Dei descenderit de cælis et homo factus sit? Quarum prior est quia nos homines eramus homines, propter ipsum et imagine eius conditi, qui conditi nunquam fuissemus nisi ipse quoque voluisset homo fieri et inter nos versari (Prov. viii). Posterior causa est quia per peccatum corrueramus in mortem, unde nos eruere et salutem nobis restituere dignatus est (ap. Grau, p. 15).

'body and soul[1].' And again 'Christ Himself before Adam sinned
'was already in the Word with God, destined to be true man. If
'Adam had not sinned Christ would have been Incarnate so as not
'to die, and would have provided for our change while living to
'heavenly glory without any form of death[2].'

F. Soci-
NUS,
†1604.

F. SOCINUS, on the other hand, held that man was created
without the gift of immortality. Hence in discussing 1 Pet. i. 20
he maintains that 'Christ came, after men had sinned, to do away
'their sins, but that He would have come even if men had not
'sinned. For He was destined to come to give us immortality which
'the first man did not possess at the beginning of creation...[3].'

CALVIN,
1509—
1564.

CALVIN attacked the doctrine and arguments of Osiander with
considerable severity in the remodelled edition of his *Institutes*
(1559). He characterises the opinion 'that Christ should have been
'man although there had been no need of His interposition to redeem
'mankind,' as one of those 'wandering speculations that ravish
'unto them light spirits.' 'I allow,' he says, 'that in the first order
'of creation, and while nature was undisturbed by the fall, [Christ]
'was set over angels and men, whereupon He is said by Paul to be
'the first-born of every creature (Col. i. 15). But since all Scripture
'declares that He was clothed with flesh to become Redeemer, it is
'an act of exceeding rashness to imagine another cause or another
'end.' He then quotes and examines Is. liii. 4 f.; John i. 9 f., 14,
iii. 16, v. 25; Matt. xviii. 11, ix. 12, &c.; and continues: 'If any
'object that some of these considerations are not opposed to the belief

[1] *Christianismi Restitutio*, 1553. *De Trin.* III. p. 104: Ad exemplar igitur, formam, figuram, et imaginem Christi est factus Adam, secundum corpus et animum.

[2] *Id. De orb. perdit.* I. p. 382: Christus ipse antequam Adam peccaret jam in verbo erat apud Deum, futurus verus homo. Si Adam non peccasset citra mortem fuisset Christus incarnatus, nos ad gloriam cælestem viventes immutaturus absque aliqua morte.

[3] *Prælect. Theol.* x. 8 (*Opera*, I. 549):

Ceterum quia certum est Deum ante mundum conditum de mittendo Christo decrevisse, ne quis ex eo hominum peccata prævisa fuisse colligat, sciendum est Christum quidem postquam homines peccaverant ad ipsorum peccata delenda venisse sed venturum tamen fuisse etiamsi homines non peccassent. Venturus enim erat ad immortalitatem nobis dandam, qua...ab ipso creationis initio primus homo caruit... Comp. *De statu primi hominis ante lapsum*, ii. 263 ff.

'that Christ who redeemed men under condemnation might have
'shewn His love to them while still safe and fallen by putting on
'flesh, the answer is short : since the Spirit proclaims that by the
'eternal decree of God these two facts were united together, that
'Christ should be our Redeemer, and partaker of the same nature
'with us, it is not right to inquire farther.... This modesty Osian-
'der unjustly assails, who at the present time has again unhappily
'discussed this question which was before slightly mooted by a
'few[1].'

Some Calvinists however maintained, and this touches close upon
the essence of the doctrine, that unfallen men needed the mediatorial work of Christ for the support of their union with God. A
single illustration will be sufficient. POLANUS thus expresses the
thought : 'From the beginning of the world [Christ] was and is the
'Mediator between God and the sons of God, as rational creatures
'made in the image of God, through Whom alone they had in the
'beginning and have blessedness, that is communion with and
'fruition of God as the highest good[2].'

III.

The long line of authorities which we have examined shews The Gos-
beyond question that 'the Gospel of Creation' is a just subject for pel of
discussion. The belief that the Incarnation was in essence inde- Creation a
pendent of the Fall has been held by men of the most different topic of
schools, in different ways and on different grounds. All however in inquiry.

---

[1] *Instit.* ii. 12, 4—7. He concludes:
Quas hactenus refutavi nænias, pro
firmissimis oraculis ducit Osiander,
nempe ut suarum speculationum dul-
cedine inebriatus ridiculos pæanas de
nihilo efflare solet.

[2] *Syntagma*, vi. 27. Comp. Zan-
chius *in Hexaem.* iii. *Lib.* iii. *c.* 2.
Docemus etiam in statu ante lapsum
[Adamum] opus habuisse Christo me-
diatore, non per quem reconciliaretur
Patri...sed per quem præservaretur a
peccato... Bucanus (*Instit. Theol.* Art.

x. 3, p. 106) uses almost the same
words. I have not seen that the English Reformers touched upon the question; and I cannot find Willett's book
de statu hominis, to which Gerhard
refers (*Loc. Theol.* iii. p. 444), in the
Library of the British Museum or in
the Cambridge University Library.

Bp. Bull's Discourse on '*The State
of Man before the Fall*' (Works ii.
52 ff.), contains many suggestive
thoughts which illustrate some aspects
of the problem.

the main agree in this, that they find in the belief a crowning promise of the unity of the Divine order; a fulfilment, a consummation, of the original purpose of creation; a more complete and harmonious view of the relation of finite being to God than can be gained otherwise.

The sense of theological formulas must change.

In every age the theory of the Divine economy, if we may so speak, will present itself under an aspect corresponding with the general aspect under which the whole finite order, so far as it comes under human observation, presents itself. It cannot but be that the views which are entertained of the relations of man to the earth on which he lives, of the earth to the universe, of the period of human life to the measurable period of the existence of the objects of sense, should affect our views of the Redemption and Consummation of man, not in essence but in the mode of apprehension. It is impossible for us now to understand a formula which deals with man and the world in the sense in which it was understood when the earth was regarded as the centre of the system of material creation, and the human race as having existed for five or six thousand years. The effect upon the mind of the words in which it is expressed must be different even if we use the same words. And the sovereign preeminence of Scripture as the vehicle of spiritual knowledge lies in this, that it finds fuller interpretation from growing experience. The Scripture does not change, but our power of entering into its meaning changes.

Two questions: 1. The relation of man to God and the world; 2. The consequent aspect of the Incarnation.

If then we endeavour to consider the question before us from the position in which we are placed in regard to the teaching of Scripture, we shall be led (1) to examine what Scripture teaches or indicates as to the essential relations of man to God and to the world, so far as we can now apprehend the revelation which is made of them; and then (2), looking at the whole revelation of the Divine purpose recorded in the Bible, to determine, as far as may be, the motives, if such a word may be used, to which the Incarnation is to be assigned.

1. The relations of man to God and to the world, as laid down in Scripture, may be expressed in two brief propositions. In relation to God, man was made in His image (i). In relation to the world, man is the representative of the visible creation (ii).

1. Man, (i) made in the image of God; (ii) the representation of the visible creation.

(i) The truth that man was 'made in the image of God' admits of two distinct developments. It may be viewed (a) in regard to the individual, or (b) in regard to the race. In both respects man was created to gain a divine ideal. It is true indeed that neither the race nor the individual can be properly considered apart : each is dependent upon the other for the attainment of its perfection. But much is gained both in clearness and fulness of view by considering them separately.

(i) Man as the image of God to be regarded (a) individually, and (b) socially.

(a) It is wholly unnecessary to inquire in what exact sense man was 'made in the image of God.' We have no faculties for the investigation. There is however no authority for limiting the image to any particular part of his nature. For us the individual man in his complex being is one; and as man he was made in God's image to gain His likeness.

(a) The individual man.

In this work he had constant need of Divine help. As he was made he was not at once capable of union with God. To reach this consummation he required discipline and training. In the Divine order men are 'first made men and then afterwards gods[1].'

If then man had fulfilled the law of his being, he would still, so far as we can see, have stood in need of a Mediator through whom the

Man as created needed a Mediator.

---

[1] Irrationabiles igitur omni modo qui non exspectant tempus augmenti, et suæ naturæ infirmitatem adscribunt Deo...Jam volunt similes esse factori Deo, et nullam esse differentiam infecti Dei, et nunc facti hominis, qui plus irrationabiles sunt quam muta animalia. Hæc enim non imputant Deo, quoniam non homines facit ea...Nos enim imputamus ei, quoniam non ab initio Dii facti sumus, sed primo quidem homines, tunc demum Dii...(Iren. iv. 38, 4 : the whole passage is worthy of careful study: comp. iii. 10, 2 ; iii. 19, 1).

The thought, which is startling at first to us, finds frequent expression in Athanasius: *de Inc. Verbi* § 51, p. 75 αὐτὸς γὰρ [ὁ τοῦ θεοῦ λόγος] ἐπηνθρώπησεν ἵνα ἡμεῖς θεοποιηθῶμεν· καὶ αὐτὸς ἐφανέρωσεν ἑαυτὸν διὰ σώματος ἵνα ἡμεῖς τοῦ ἀοράτου Πατρὸς ἔννοιαν λάβωμεν· καὶ αὐτὸς ὑπέμεινε τὴν παρ' ἀνθρώπων ὕβριν ἵνα ἡμεῖς ἀθανασίαν κληρονομήσωμεν. *De decr. Syn. Nic.* § 14, p. 173 ὁ λόγος σὰρξ ἐγένετο ἵνα...καὶ ἡμεῖς ἐκ τοῦ πνεύματος αὐτοῦ μεταλαβόντες θεοποιηθῆναι δυνηθῶμεν, ἄλλως οὐκ ἂν τούτου τυχόντες εἰ μὴ τὸ κτιστὸν ἡμῶν αὐτὸς ἐνεδύσατο σῶμα. Compare Newman, Note on *the Second Discourse against the Arians* § 21, p. 380, for other references ; and the Index under θεοποίησις ; and Suicer *s. v.* θεοποιέω.

relation of fellowship with God might have been sustained, and deepened, and perfected. Nor is it easy to suppose that this fellowship could have been made stable and permanent in any other way than by the union in due time of man with God, accomplished by the union of man with Him who was the Mediator between God and man, and in whose image man was made[1].

Irenæus has given a striking expression to this truth. He starts indeed from the consideration of man as fallen, but his argument passes into an absolute form. Speaking of the necessity of the Incarnation he says: 'If man had not conquered the adversary of 'man, the enemy would not have been justly conquered. And 'again, if God had not bestowed salvation, we should not have 'possessed it surely. And if man had not been united to God, he 'could not have partaken of incorruption. For it was necessary 'that the Mediator of God and men by His own essential relation-'ship with both should bring both together into friendship and 'concord, and on the one hand present man to God and on the other 'make God known to man[2].'

---

[1] This thought is clearly expressed by many Calvinistic theologians, though they do not follow it out to its full breadth. Hominum integrorum Mediator [fuit Christus] respectu primæ illius unionis ante lapsum, quia homines integri non per seipsos sed per Filium Dei erant Deo uniti et conjuncti, quamdiu ipsi visum fuit largiri illis gratiam persistendi in amicitia cum Deo...Inde ab initio mundi fuit atque est inter Deum et filios Dei, seu creaturas rationales ad imaginem Dei conditas, Mediator per quem solum illæ statum initio habuerunt et habent beatitudinem, hoc est, communionem et fruitionem Dei tanquam summi boni (Polanus *Syntagma*, vi. 27). Compare p. 317.

[2] Iren. iii. 18, 7 Εἰ γὰρ μὴ ἄνθρωπος ἐνίκησε τὸν ἀντίπαλον τοῦ ἀνθρώπου, οὐκ ἂν δικαίως ἐνικήθη ὁ ἐχθρός. Πάλιν τε, εἰ μὴ ὁ θεὸς ἐδωρήσατο τὴν σωτηρίαν, οὐκ ἂν βεβαίως ἔσχομεν αὐτήν. Καὶ εἰ μὴ συνηνώθη ὁ ἄνθρωπος τῷ θεῷ, οὐκ ἂν ἠδυνήθη μετασχεῖν τῆς ἀφθαρσίας. Ἔδει γὰρ τὸν μεσίτην θεοῦ τε καὶ ἀνθρώπων, διὰ τῆς ἰδίας πρὸς ἑκατέρους οἰκειότητος, εἰς φιλίαν καὶ ὁμόνοιαν τοὺς ἀμφοτέρους συναγαγεῖν· καὶ θεῷ μὲν παραστῆσαι τὸν ἄνθρωπον, ἀνθρώποις δὲ γνωρίσαι τὸν θεόν.

Compare v. 16, 2 Ἐν τοῖς πρόσθεν χρόνοις ἐλέγετο μὲν κατ' εἰκόνα θεοῦ γεγονέναι τὸν ἄνθρωπον, οὐκ ἐδείκνυτο δέ· ἔτι γὰρ ἀόρατος ἦν ὁ λόγος, οὗ κατ' εἰκόνα ὁ ἄνθρωπος ἐγεγόνει. διὰ τοῦτο δὴ καὶ τὴν ὁμοίωσιν ῥᾳδίως ἀπέβαλεν. ὁπότε δὲ σὰρξ ἐγένετο ὁ λόγος τοῦ θεοῦ, τὰ ἀμφότερα ἐπεκύρωσε· καὶ γὰρ καὶ τὴν εἰκόνα ἔδειξεν ἀληθῶς, αὐτὸς τοῦτο γενόμενος ὅπερ ἦν ἡ εἰκὼν αὐτοῦ· καὶ τὴν ὁμοίωσιν βεβαίως κατέστησε, συνεξομοιώσας τὸν ἄνθρωπον τῷ ἀοράτῳ πατρί [per visibile Verbum].

iv. 33, 4 πῶς ἄνθρωπος χωρήσει εἰς θεόν, εἰ μὴ ὁ θεὸς ἐχωρήθη εἰς ἄνθρωπον. The form ἐχωρήθη in this connexion is strange (comp. iv. 38, 2). The Latin translation has nothing to correspond to it. The Greek is preserved by Theodoret, *Dial.* ii. p. 129 (Migne *Patr. Gr.* lxxxiii. 171).

Moreover, if we regard the predestined humanity of the Son of God as the archetype of humanity[1], light is thrown upon the doctrine of the Atonement. It becomes in this case in some degree intelligible how Christ could fitly (if we may so speak) take man's nature upon Him, and suffer for man, inasmuch as He took upon Himself a nature which was not alien in its idea, but one which in some mysterious sense was in its propriety partially an image of His own though it had fallen.

The relation of this idea to that of the Atonement.

So far then the essential constitution of man suggests at least the belief that the Incarnation, by which we understand in this case the taking of sinless and perfected humanity into God, was part of the Divine counsel in creation.

(b) These considerations which apply to the individual man obtain greater weight if they are extended to the race. We cannot but believe that under any circumstances, and wholly apart from the Fall, there would have been a progress in the race, as well as in the individual, towards the gradual fulfilment of the idea of humanity. All that was potentially included in man in his various relations to being would have been realised in many parts. In this way the whole conception of humanity would have been broken up and distributed, so to speak, through countless separate personalities. There would then have been need of some power by which at last all the scattered elements of manhood should be brought together into a personal unity. In other words the endeavour to follow out the normal development of the human race leads us to look for that

(b) The human race.

---

[1] Compare Tertull. *de Resurr. Carn.* 6 Quodcunque enim limus exprimebatur Christus cogitabatur homo futurus, quod et limus, et sermo caro, quod et terra tunc. Sic enim præfatio patris ad filium: *Faciamus hominem ad imaginem et similitudinem nostram: et fecit hominem Deus.* Id utique quod finxit ad imaginem Dei fecit illum, scilicet Christi. Et Sermo enim Deus qui in effigie Dei constitutus *non rapinam existimavit pariari Deo.* Ita limus ille jam tunc imaginem induens Christi futuri in carne non tantum Dei opus erat sed et pignus. *Id. adv. Prax.* 12 Denique sequens scriptura distinguit inter personas *et fecit Deus hominem, ad imaginem Dei fecit illum.* Cur non *suam* si unus qui faciebat et non erat ad cujus faciebat? Erat autem ad cujus imaginem faciebat, ad filii scilicet; qui homo futurus certior et verior imaginem suam fecerat dici hominem qui tunc de limo formari habebat, imago veri et similitudo.

which answers to the Incarnation, by which the completed body might be brought into a final unity in fellowship with God.

All the varieties of the race to be brought to a unity.   For Christ, as we are taught, supplies that which gives a common life to all the members. He is the Head of the Body. All the differences of men, so far as they correspond with a true growth, are reconciled in Him, and shewn to be contributory to the manifestation of His perfection[1].

The relation of Christ to the Church.   In this respect the argument which was drawn from Eph. v. 31 f., by several early writers deserves more consideration than we are at first inclined to give to it. The main idea in the passage seems to be that the Church, the representative of perfected humanity, of that which the race would in the end have been if sin had not intervened, is related to a Head, just as in the typical record of Creation woman is related to man. The Church and woman are severally regarded as derived, and yet belonging to the completeness of that from which they are derived, and so destined finally to be restored to perfect fellowship with it. Man ideally is not man only but man and woman; Christ, such appears to be the thought, however unfamiliar it may be to us, unites with the Godhead the idea of perfected humanity, and that not accidentally but essentially. The personal relation of sex regarded in typical individuals, represents, as we should express the view, beyond itself a corporate relation which exists in respect to the race. Just as the individual union is necessary for the fulfilment of the idea of woman; so the corporate union is necessary for the fulfilment of the idea of humanity. Christ is the true Adam : the Church is the true Eve. And both these relations, the individual relation and the corporate relation, are independent of the Fall. The Fall has disturbed and disordered each, but it was not the occasion for the first existence of either[2].

[1] Eph. i. 22 f. αὐτὸν ἔδωκε κεφαλὴν ὑπὲρ πάντα τῇ ἐκκλησίᾳ, ἥτις ἐστὶ τὸ σῶμα αὐτοῦ, τὸ πλήρωμα τοῦ τὰ πάντα ἐν πᾶσιν πληρουμένου. I cannot but believe that in the last clause πληρουμένου is (as elsewhere) passive, so that everything which is is represented as serving for the manifestation of the glory of God (Col. ii. 19), Who is ' fulfilled in all things in all '.

[2] The thought finds a confused expression in a very remarkable passage of the Homily which is known as the Second Epistle of Clement. In this the writer speaks of a spiritual Church, corresponding to the spiritual Christ, and of an earthly Church corresponding with the earthly Christ; and he

(ii) So far we have regarded man only, the individual and the race. We venture to go yet further, and to look upon man as the representative of Creation. This thought appears to be distinctly suggested in the records of the Creation, and of the Fall, and of the new Creation. The dominion of man (Gen. i. 28) was such that his realm shared the consequences of his sin (Gen. iii. 17). His destiny therefore has not yet been accomplished (Ps. viii.; Hebr. ii. 5 ff.). But in its promised fulfilment lies the hope of the material world. For that something is in store which answers to the redemption of man's body (Rom. viii. 22 ff.[1]).

It will at once be obvious how this wider view of the relations of man to Creation tends to confirm what has been already said of the inherent fitness of the Incarnation in relation to the plan of Creation, as we are enabled to look upon it. In all parts of the natural order, and not in humanity only, in the very course of progress, there is constant division, dispersion, differentiation, of elements ; and at the same time clearer glimpses are opened of a unity to which all the parts appear to tend. This separation, this unity, as far as we can see, belong alike to the essence of things. The separation has been, it is true, influenced by the Fall, but, as a condition of growth, it is not due to it. The idea of the Incarnation therefore satisfies

finds in this relation the fulfilment of the words of Genesis: ἐποίησεν ὁ θεὸς τὸν ἄνθρωπον ἄρσεν καὶ θῆλυ· τὸ ἄρσεν ἐστὶν ὁ Χριστός, τὸ θῆλυ ἡ ἐκκλησία (2 Clem. xiv.).

Compare Hermas i. Vis. ii. 4 Τὴν πρεσβυτέραν παρ' ἧς ἔλαβες τὸ βιβλίον, τίνα δοκεῖς εἶναι; ἐγώ φημι Τὴν Σίβυλλαν. Πλανᾶσαι, φησίν, οὐκ ἔστι. Τίς οὖν ἐστι; φημί. Ἡ ἐκκλησία, φησίν. εἶπον οὖν αὐτῷ Διὰ τί οὖν πρεσβυτέρα; Ὅτι, φησίν, πάντων πρώτη ἐκτίσθη, διὰ τοῦτο πρεσβυτέρα, καὶ διὰ ταύτην ὁ κόσμος κατηρτίσθη.

[1] Iren. iii. 16, 6. Unus igitur Deus Pater quemadmodum ostendimus, et unus Christus Jesus Dominus noster, veniens per universam dispositionem et omnia in semetipsum recapitulans. In omnibus autem est et homo, plasmatio Dei; et hominem ergo in semetipsum recapitulans est, invisibilis visi-

bilis factus, et incomprehensibilis factus comprehensibilis, et impassibilis passibilis, et Verbum homo, universa in semetipsum recapitulans: uti sicut in supercoelestibus et spiritalibus et invisibilibus princeps est Verbum Dei, sic et in visibilibus et corporalibus principatum habeat, in semetipsum primatum assumens, et apponens semetipsum caput ecclesiæ universa attrahat ad semetipsum apto tempore.

Comp. Theod. Mops. fragm. Lib. xiv. de Incarn. (Migne Patr. Gr. lxvi. p. 990) οὐδὲ γὰρ ἂν ὁ θεὸς οὕτως ἁπλῶς καὶ ἄνευ τινὸς χρησίμου λόγου ἄνθρωπον μὲν ἐλάμβανε καὶ ἤνου πρὸς ἑαυτὸν προσκυνεῖσθαι παρὰ τῆς κτίσεως παρασκευάζων ἁπάσης, τὰς δέ γε νοητὰς φύσεις προσκυνεῖν, ἐδικαίου, εἰ μὴ τὰ περὶ αὐτὸν γεγονότα κοινὴ πάσης ἦν εὐεργεσία τῆς κτίσεως.

the aspiration towards the vaster unity to which the full development of Creation points. The restoration of unity to man carries with it the promise of the restoration of unity to all finite being.

2. Motives for the Incarnation.

2. If we regard the subject from the opposite point of sight we obtain the same general result. Reasons have been alleged for thinking that man's constitution as unfallen, required the personal union of humanity with God for his consummation individual and social and for the consummation of the world through Him. It appears also that the Incarnation necessarily included in itself consequences which were irrespective of the Fall, and which yet, so far as we can see, cannot be regarded as contingent in the Divine Counsel.

These not limited by the Fall.

Theologians have classed the objects or results of the Incarnation —for in this case the motive and the effect are identical—under three heads, the Revelation of God, the benefit of man, the conquest of Satan. Of these in their essential nature the first is wholly and the second partly irrespective of the Fall. It is not possible upon reflection to exclude all other conceptions from the Incarnation except those of satisfaction and atonement. These thoughts naturally rise at once to our minds in connexion with it from the conditions of suffering and sin under which we live; but these conditions do not belong to humanity but to fallen humanity. And if the consequences of the Fall be set aside, there yet remain those characteristics of a finite nature which require what they have received from God's love in the Incarnation for their true fulfilment. We must look to the perfection and not only to the redemption of man. The arguments which we have heard pressed on this point by many writers seem to me to be of very great weight. We cannot conceive that a being capable of knowing God and of being united with Him should not have been destined to gain that knowledge, to realise that union. We cannot suppose that the consummation of man and of humanity and the realisation of Christ's kingdom which have been brought about by the Incarnation are dependent on the Fall: we cannot suppose that they could have been brought about in any other way than in that according to which they are now revealed to us in their supreme glory[1].

It will perhaps be said that the view which has been indicated makes the action of God dependent on creation. So far as there is force in this argument it extends not only to the perfection of creation but to creation itself. The very act of Creation is a self-limitation of Omnipotence. And as far as we dare speculate on such subjects it is easier for us to suppose that the crowning act of love, the consummation of all finite being, was included in the one creative act, than that it was contingent on man's conduct. Or to put the thought in another way, it is in every way more consonant with the idea of God's action which is given to us in Scripture to suppose that the union of man with God was predestined in relation to man as answering to the Divine idea of man, than to suppose that it was first designed for man as he made himself by his sinful self-assertion.

No limitation of the action of God on this view not included in Creation.

And here again I would repeat that we must carefully guard the conception of the Incarnation, as we thus endeavour to view it in the absolute Divine Counsel, from every thought of humiliation. We must conceive, if I may so represent the idea, that in that case glorified humanity would have been raised up to heaven and not that the Son of God would have come down to earth.

It may again be urged that this is merely speculation on matters too high for us where Scripture is silent. I reply that we cannot but speculate : that we are so made that we must strive after some view of the relations and end of the system in which we are placed : that the advance of partial knowledge forces upon us more and more

The Gospel of Creation not an arbitrary theory.

---

[1] Hippolytus, regarding the Incarnation in its actual effects, points out how it wrought not only the redemption of fallen beings, but the sure establishment of unfallen beings. Man even if unfallen would have needed this divine confirmation. Hipp. *c. Ber. et Hel.* ii. (Migne *Patr. Gr.* x. p. 833) διὰ τοῦτο γέγονεν ἄνθρωπος ὁ τῶν ὅλων θεὸς ἵνα σαρκὶ μὲν παθητῇ πάσ- χων ἅπαν ἡμῶν το τῷ θανάτῳ πραθὲν λυτρώσηται γένος, ἀπαθεῖ δὲ θεότητι διὰ σαρκὸς θαυματουργῶν πρὸς τὴν ἀκή- ρατον αὐτοῦ καὶ μακαρίαν ἐπαναγάγῃ ζωὴν ἧς ἀπέπεσεν τῷ διαβόλῳ πειθόμενος· καὶ τὰ κατ᾽ οὐρανοὺς ἅγια τάγματα τῶν νοερῶν οὐσιῶν στομώσῃ πρὸς ἀτρεψίαν τῷ μυστηρίῳ τῆς αὐτοῦ σωματώσεως, ἧς ἔργον ἡ τῶν ὅλων ἐστὶν εἰς αὐτὸν ἀνακε- φαλαίωσις.

the duty of looking for a more comprehensive synthesis : that even if Scripture were silent the real question would be, Is the view consistent with Scripture ? that Scripture gives us facts, and above all the one Fact, which must be for us the sovereign expression of the Divine will ; that if circumstances prompt the inquiry, we are bound to inquire with reverence whether that Fact illuminates the position which we occupy in face of the thoughts and discoveries of the time. The Fact is final, but the Spirit sent in Christ's name enables men to see more and more of its meaning.

Nor is the general silence of Scripture, at least so far as direct statements are concerned, on this absolute view of the Incarnation in any way surprising. The view belongs properly to an order which has ceased to be. The Gospel is a message to man as he is. It is perfectly natural therefore that Scripture should for the most part contemplate the actual state of things and speak of the Incarnation as dealing with man fallen. It is perfectly natural that the Creeds (and the same remark applies to early patristic writings) dealing with the actual history of the Incarnation should state that Christ 'came down from heaven for us men and for our salvation.' The very words 'came down' and all corresponding phrases belong exclusively to the Incarnation as the assumption of possible humanity in consequence of sin. But this language is in no way inconsistent with the belief that what was accomplished under certain conditions due to sin would have been accomplished otherwise if man had remained sinless. There is force in Osiander's remark[1] that the two phrases 'for us' and 'for our salvation' express two distinct ideas. And yet more : the revelation of love involved in the Divine purpose is included in the revelation of love given in the Divine act. And while we cling most firmly to the ideas of 'salvation', of 'the seeking and saving that which was lost', we must also bear in mind that 'salvation' is far more than deliverance from the consequences of evil. It expresses also the final preservation of that which truly belongs to the saved ; to the fulness of human nature as

The general silence of Scripture natural.

---

[1] See p. 315.

well as to the condition of fallen nature. There is 'a making perfect' which is correlative with 'salvation[1].'

But in one passage at least we seem to be admitted by St Paul to look upon the Truth as it is in the divine counsel with regard to Creation and re-creation. In Col. i. 13 ff. he presents a view of the work of 'the Son of God's love' in the creation, preservation (ἔκτισται; ἐν αὐτῷ συνέστηκεν, 16), redemption, consummation (v. 20) of finite being. The whole work is fulfilled by one Person (13—20), who is before Creation, and is also the source of peace 'through the Blood of His Cross'. This view is satisfied by the theological conception that the personality of Christ is in His Divine Nature. But at the same time His human nature is taken into account (v. 19 f.); and when He is spoken of as the 'image of the invisible God,' He is presented as the archetype of humanity in creation even as He is also 'the firstborn from the dead'.

Doubts however may still remain as to the interpretation of this mysterious passage. But at least it cannot be said that a belief in the absolute purpose of the Incarnation is at variance with Scripture. Nor does it in any way derogate from the infinite love of God. If it is 'most consonant to the judgment of reason' it seems to be also 'most consonant to the piety of faith'. It adds to every motive of devout gratitude which is suggested by the circumstances of the Incarnation, a further motive of gratitude in the contemplation of that primal love which the selfwill of man could not thwart. For if the common view moves us to devotion as we look at the individual—the one sheep which was lost—this view teaches us to draw in addition new causes for fuller adoration from the thought of the whole—of the ninety and nine who have not strayed—who are no less near to the great Shepherd's love. Nothing is lost, and for those who cannot but turn from time to time with anxious questionings from the contemplation of the vastness, the complexity, the contradictions, the earnest expectation, as we are encouraged to call it, of

The idea of the Gospel of Creation gives a new ground for man's gratitude.

---

[1] The thought of τελείωσις is characteristic of St John and the Epistle to the Hebrews. Comp. John xvii. 23; Hebr. vii. 11 and notes.

the world, to Holy Scripture, much is gained by the thought that from the first it was the purpose of God to gather up all things in the Son of His love[1].

A practical doctrine.

The subject on which we have touched is not, I believe, a mere matter of speculation, or a curious fancy of a past age.   If I had so regarded it, I should not have thought it fitting to give here sketches of reasoning which must in many cases appear strange and obscure. But I have chosen to dwell upon it because I think that I have found in the opinions which I have ventured to maintain, support and light in the face of great problems which seem likely to grow more urgent every day.   The thought that the Incarnation, the union of man with God, and of creation in man, was part of the Divine purpose in Creation, opens unto us, as I believe, wider views of the wisdom of God than we commonly embrace, which must react upon life.

It presents to us the highest manifestation of Divine love as answering to the idea of man, and not as dependent upon that which lay outside the Father's Will.

It reveals to us how the Divine purpose is fulfilled in unexpected and unimaginable ways in spite of man's selfishness and sin.

It indicates, at least, how that unity to which many physical and historical researches point is not only to be found in a dispersive connexion of multitudinous parts, but is summed up finally in one life.

It helps us to feel a little more, and this is the sum of all, what the Incarnation is, what it involves, what it promises, what it enforces, what it inspires; that Fact which we strive to believe, and which is ever escaping from us ; that Fact which sets before us with invincible majesty Christ's 'power to subdue all things to Himself[2]'.

[1] Comp. Eph. iii. 9 ff.; iv. 10.   [2] Phil. iii. 21.

THE RELATION OF CHRISTIANITY
TO ART.

ἐκ μεγέθογο καλλονῆο κτιομάτων ἀναλόγωο
ὁ γενεοιογργὸο αγτῶν θεωρεῖται.

Wisd. xiii. 5.

THE RELATION OF CHRISTIANITY TO ART

The relation of Christianity to Art a practical question for the student of
the New Testament.
Apparent contrast.

1. Man made to seek beauty.
   Nature needs interpretation.
   Moral importance of the interpretation.
   Sense needs discipline.
2. Art not directly recognised in the New Testament.
   The use of Art in the Old Testament not a sufficient sanction.

The principle of reconciliation.

I. Contrast of Shemitic and Hellenic tendencies.

1. No free pursuit of imitative Art among the Jews.
   Art consecrated.
2. Imitative Art treated as absolute by the Greeks.
   Necessary decline of Greek Art.
   Christianity necessarily antagonistic to classical Art in the Apostolic
   age.

II. The task of Christian Art.
Early literary evidence as to Christian Art.
      Tertullian : Clement Alex.: Origen.

1. *Painting.*
   Cemeteries at Rome.
                 Naples.
   The Synod of Elvira.
   The judgment of Eusebius Cæs.
   Change of feeling in the Fifth Century.
   Paulinus of Nola.
       Gregory of Nyssa : Asterius : Nilus : Augustine.
2. *Sculpture.*
   Scanty remains.
3. *Architecture.*
   The Church of Paulinus at Tyre.
              of Constantine at Jerusalem.
   Mosaics.

THE RELATION OF CHRISTIANITY TO ART.

No student of the apostolic writings can fail to find himself Does Christianity leave scope for Art? sometimes confronted by the question Does the teaching of the New Testament cover all the interests of human life? and more particularly Does the New Testament, does Christianity as laid down there in its broad outlines, leave scope for the free development of Art? This latter question deserves consideration. It is not enough that it should have been practically answered by general consent: the answer thus given includes many elements which tend at least to create misgivings as to its soundness; and it is, superficially at least, in conflict with the most prominent utterances of early Christian feeling. The main issue is not whether the Christian spirit encourages that temper which is the strength of the artist, but whether it recognises his work as contributory to the fulfilment of man's destiny. There can be no doubt that truth, sympathy, reverence, will characterise all effort which deserves the name of Christian; but it is not at once obvious that in the face of the overwhelming moral problems of life Christian effort can be properly directed to the pursuit of Art.

Thus there is the suggestion if not the distinct appearance of a conflict between man's constitution and the Gospel. He is born with artistic instincts and powers; and these, it may be alleged, are not directly taken into account by the records of the Faith.

The apparent contrast requires to be stated a little more in Apparent contrast. detail.

On the one side it is certain that Art corresponds with essential 1. Man so constituted as to seek beauty. parts of our nature. Men universally seek particular combinations of form, colour, sound, and the pleasure which these give can be

deepened and extended through the study of the principles by which
they are ruled. Men can be trained to a keener and finer perception
of beauty. There is then here a force of influence which cannot be
overlooked in the discipline of life.

External nature needs interpretation. And more than this, the complex scene in which we are placed
requires to be revealed to us. We are not at once able to enter into
the manifold aspects of Nature which we can recognise when they
are pointed out. There is something of disorder and disproportion
in the impression which we first receive from the world about us.
The 'form' of things needs some interpretation; and the particular
interpretation which we adopt has helped and will help to make us
what we are and what we shall be.

The interpretation of nature by Art has a powerful moral effect. For the physical effects which Art produces exercise a profound
moral and spiritual influence upon character. It is unnecessary to
attempt to make any comparison of the relative power of external
nature and society upon the education of the soul. It is enough
that both have their due office in moulding the ideal man. Remove the discipline of one or the other, and the man is weaker and
poorer however successfully he cultivates the self-centred virtues on
which he has concentrated himself. It may be necessary to 'cut off
the right hand' or to 'pluck out the right eye', but he who is forced
to do so enters into life 'maimed'.

Sense specially needs discipline. This expressive image seems to carry with it a full recognition of
the manifold activities of eye and hand, of the power of seeing
beauty and setting it forth, as belonging to the completeness of
man. And if under the actual conditions of life it is through sense,
which Art uses as its organ, that the most obvious and universal
dangers come to men, the natural conclusion seems to be that this
fact shews convincingly the paramount importance of the study of
Art. In this region we need peculiarly to be trained in order that
we may enjoy rightly; and not be called upon to sacrifice that
which was capable of ministering to a richer service.

2. But Art not directly recognised in N. T. Such reflections, indicated in the briefest summary, serve to shew
that Art justly claims a permanent place in the highest training of
men; but on the other hand it may be urged that, with the excep-

tion of music, there is no recognition of the office of Art in the New Testament. One or two illustrations from engraving (Hebr. i. 3) or painting (Hebr. viii. 5; x. 1) are all that it contains. The imagery of the Apocalypse—as the cubic city (Apoc. xxi. 16)—is symbolic and not pictorial.

And not only so, but it seems as if representative Art were Apparently excluded. distinctly condemned. It is difficult to give any sense to 'the desire of the eyes,' which St John declares to be 'not of the Father but of the world' (1 John ii. 16), which shall not include works of sculpture and painting; and at first sight the revelation of the transitoriness of that out of which they spring appears to carry with it the sentence of their rejection.

Nor can any stress be laid upon the partial recognition of the The use of Art in O. T. not a sufficient recognition. service of Art in the Old Testament. The system of the old Covenant was essentially external. It spoke through symbols. But it might be argued, not unreasonably, that, as Christianity is essentially spiritual, it is likely that it would be independent of all illustrations from Art.

These are the elements of the contrast which have to be recon- The principle of reconciliation. ciled. The reconciliation, to anticipate the result of our inquiry, lies in the central message of Christianity 'the Word became flesh.' By that fact the harmony between the seen and the unseen which had been interrupted was potentially restored. Creation in all its parts was made known as a revelation of Him through whom it was called into being. But the reconciliation here as elsewhere lies in transfiguration. The passage to life is through death. The old had to pass away that the new might find its proper place. This truth has even now not been fully mastered; but it will be seen more clearly if we first consider the position of Art in relation to Christianity in the apostolic age (I), and the character of Christian Art in the first four centuries (II), and then attempt to determine the relation of Christianity to Art (III), and the peculiar office of Art (IV).

I.

Contrast
of Shem-
itic and
Hellenic
tenden-
cies.
The position of the early Christian teachers towards Art was determined under two powerful and conflicting influences. In no other region of human activity were the Shemitic and Hellenic tendencies more directly at variance. Each bore witness to a partial truth; and in the apostolic age each had reached its complete development.

1. No free
exercise of
imitative
Arts
among the
Jews.
For the Jews imitative Art had practically no public existence. In the absence of satisfactory evidence it is impossible to say how far Architecture and Music found free and characteristic expression. But in spite of the very narrow range within which Jewish Art was confined it embodied a principle which enters into the life of Art. The commandment which forbade the making of graven image or likeness was not observed in the Sanctuary itself. By this exception it was made evident that the enactment was directed against accidental abuses of imitative Art and not against the Art itself. At the same time the manner in which Art was employed served to embody another thought. The description of the decorations of the Tabernacle and of the Temple brings out plainly the idea that representations of outward things, and the manifold combination of materials, which found place there, were designed to suggest more than the simple figure or effect. Whatever there was of grandeur or beauty in 'the ordinances of divine service' pointed beyond itself. Natural forms and elements were used to indicate the unseen. How this could be is still powerfully shewn in the works of Egyptian Art, which constrain the spectator to rise beyond that which he looks upon to something which can find no adequate expression externally. The figures of gods and men alike—Pasht or Rameses—are above all things symbols of character. They cannot be taken simply as efforts to present direct and complete portraitures of the beings whom they call up before the soul. Later experience indeed proved that there were possibilities of deep corruption in the promiscuous use of such images of the mysteries of life as were presented in the

accompaniments of Egyptian worship. The conception was noble but it was unfitted for common use. So it was that the sacred legislation of Israel kept the conception and guarded it jealously. The employment of the symbolic figures in the sanctuary of the Temple, by emphasizing this exception to the general law[1], kept the Jew from the desecration of the symbol, and preserved for him in its purity the thought which it enshrined. He learnt from the records of the Old Testament that it was the Divine will that in the unapproachable darkness of the Holy of Holies the costliest works of Art should render service before the revealed Presence of the Lord. No human eye could rightfully ever again trace the lineaments of those cherubim and palm trees and open flowers when they were once placed in the oracle, but it was enough to know that they were there. In no other way could the Truth be more eloquently or solemnly enforced that the end of Art is to witness to the inner life of Nature and to minister to God. The repetition of the forms in the Holy place kept the memory of them fresh in the minds of the priests[2]. Their significance could not be mistaken. By that offering of the best which he could command simply for the Divine glory Solomon declared to his people for all time the consecration of Art, and he declared not obscurely that it is the office of Art to reveal the meaning of that which is the object of sense. Circumstances delayed for ages the fruitfulness of the idea; but it remained and remains still; and few can think of all that was implied by the adornment of that august chamber lighted only by the splendour of a manifested Presence of God or the glow of the kindled incense (Apoc. v. 8) without feeling that it has a lesson for those to whom Art is appointed work. Philosophers and poets have dwelt often upon the veiled statue at Sais: there is an open secret in the sacred gloom of the Holy of Holies more sublime and more inspiring.

Art consecrated.

[1] The twelve oxen which supported the Molten Sea in Solomon's Temple (1 K. vii. 25; 2 Chron. iv. 4 f.; Jer. lii. 20) are a perplexing exception to the law. The twelve lions on the steps of the royal throne (1 K. x. 18 ff.; 2 Chron. ix. 18 f.) form a corresponding exception in the civil use of Art. The Brazen Serpent was a work of a wholly different order; as also was 'the Teraphim' of David (1 Sam. xix. 13).

[2] According to 2 Chron. iii. 14, cherubim were wrought on the veil.

2. Imitative Art treated as absolute by the Greeks.

The Jewish repression of imitative Art, which the Law still hallowed for the highest service, corresponded with the spiritual conception of God which was the endowment of His 'people'. Spiritual Religion could not at this stage of its development admit the habitual use of painting or sculpture. With the Greeks on the other hand imitative Art was the characteristic embodiment of the Nature worship which underlay their life. The form of beauty was for them not the symbol but the direct representation of the godlike. The statue was the final expression of the artist's thought, and his consummate skill enabled the spectator to rest in it. Humanity was made the measure of the divine; and under these conditions anthropomorphism became a fatal temptation. At the same time Greek Art, if premature and perilous in regard to the complete spiritual training of man, witnessed to a part of the truth affirmed in the record of Creation which is most commonly forgotten. The form of man, the visible expression of what he is essentially embodied under the conditions of time, answers to 'the image of God' in which he was made. So far the Greek was right in seeking for traits of divinity in human beauty. The source of error, from which flowed the stream of later corruption, was that he regarded these as fixed and final. He failed, necessarily failed in the way of nature, to claim recognition for the fulness of the truth that man made in the image of God has to grow into His likeness: that all that is noblest in form or present embodiment is preparatory to something yet unseen and higher: that Art in its greatest achievements must be prophetic, must not rest in a victory but reveal that which is unattained[1].

The necessary decline of Greek Art.

It would be difficult to overrate the skill with which Greek sculpture of the best period represents strength in majestic repose, and feeling under sovereign control; but all, so to speak, lies within the figure before us. 'The Gods have come down to us in the likeness of men'; and we look no further. At first the spiritual, reli-

[1] This is only one application of the general law that man cannot find rest in the finite. The key to the understanding of Ecclesiastes lies in the recognition of this truth which the Book illustrates from many sides. Comp. Eccles. iii. 11.

gious, element is supreme, as in all living Art; but with the decay of faith that which is sensuous usurps the place of the spiritual, and Art which takes man as the standard of the divine cannot but fall. A single illustration will be sufficient to indicate my meaning. This is given in a crucial shape by the treatment of Aphrodite in the earlier and later schools. The physical beauty of the Medicean Venus has lost all the pure sovereign majesty of the Aphrodite of Melos, which is worthy to be an ideal of 'woman before the Fall[1].'

It is unnecessary to trace the decay of Greek Art. It retained to the last the gift of physical beauty, but in the apostolic age it had become the servant of the luxury of the Empire. Starting from a human ideal it became enslaved to man. So far as it had a place in popular worship it brought down the divine to the level of a corrupt life.

This being so the antagonism of early Christians to contemporary Art was necessarily essential and absolute. Before Art could be placed in its true position there was need of a complete change of centre. For this the stern discipline of Judaism had made provision. The lesson of consecration which had been kept in silent witness for long ages could be applied now that 'the Word had become flesh.' By that fact a new meaning was given to the beauty which the Greek artist had felt for, and an immeasurable scope was opened for the ministry of nature to God which the Jewish legislator had declared in symbols. But death is the condition of resurrection. There is indeed a continuity through death; but a formal severance from the past was the prelude to the new birth of Christian Art. *Christianity essentially antagonistic to Art as it was.*

II.

It will be seen from what has been already said that Christianity had to recognise and reconcile the partial and contrasted aspects of imitative Art which had found expression in Judaism and Hellenism. Christian Art embodies the twofold conception of the spiritual destiny *The task of Christian Art,*

[1] Kraus (F. X.), *Die Christliche Kunst,* s. 22.

of the visible, and of a spiritual revelation through the visible. The central fact of the Christian Faith gives a solid unity to both truths.

fulfilled slowly. The realisation of such an idea of Art can of necessity only come slowly and through the course of life, not by any definite and conscious effort but in the gradual conquest of humanity. The beginning was made when St Paul established Christian Churches in Ephesus, Athens, Corinth, and Rome. The end is still far off, even if it has come from age to age more clearly into view. When the Church first appeared openly in the Empire it had already the outlines of a system of Art which had been drawn in the times of darkness and suffering. In the first stage of such a progress the inspiring thought is supreme: the perfection of form comes later.

It is however extremely difficult to trace the course of Christian **Scanty literary evidence.** Art in the ante-Nicene age. The literary evidence is extremely scanty; and it naturally deals for the most part with the dangers and abuses of popular Art. Even in the present age little could be gathered as to the place which is occupied by Art in ordinary Christian life from the works of theological controversy and general **Tertullian.** instruction. But the stern warnings of a man like Tertullian are evidently directed against influences and practices which he felt to be powerful if not dominant. Christian artists did not scruple to continue their profession even when they were admitted to the ministry[1]. The painter Hermogenes is condemned for the use which he made of his art, but the art itself is not proscribed[2]. It may also be fairly concluded from the denunciations of female luxury that other adornments of life besides rich dresses and jewels found admission into Christian households; and excess and extravagance imply a temperate use. It is also of interest to notice that Tertullian mentions incidentally 'paintings on chalices'[3], and in

[1] Tertull. *de idol.* 3 ff., adleguntur in ordinem ecclesiasticum artifices idolorum. Comp. *de spectac.* 23. A Christian sculptor is represented at his work on a sarcophagus assigned by De' Rossi to the third century. See Northcote and Brownlow, ii. p. 236.

The subject was first engraved by Fabretti *Inscr. Ant.* N. cii. p. 587, who describes the sarcophagus as 'ex cœmeterio Helenæ.'

[2] Tertull. *adv. Hermog.* i. pingit illicite, that is, by painting pagan subjects.

[3] *de Pudic.* c. 7 picturæ calicum.

especial the image of 'the Shepherd,' which he speaks of as a usual subject[1].

The scanty notices of Christian Art at Alexandria are of the same character as those in Tertullian. The language of Clement shews clearly that many Christians did not scruple to wear heathen gems; and when he defines the subjects which might rightly be admitted in consideration of their typical significance, he accepts a principle which is capable of a very wide application[2]. *Clement of Alexandria.*

At the same time it is evident from Origen's eloquent vindication of the spiritual service of Christians—the spiritual altar, and sacrifices and images of God—that no religious use was as yet publicly made of imitative Art[3]. Nor can it be doubted that the feeling of the great teachers of the African Churches was decidedly adverse to the pursuit of Art[4]. The influence of Judaism was so far prevailing. Local circumstances probably in this case checked what might have been expected to be the natural result of Alexandrine thought. *Origen.*

The position of the Italian, and specially of the Roman Church, seems to have been somewhat different. Among the earliest Italian converts were members of noble families who brought with them the influence of cultivated taste, and at once found a place for the ministry of Art. But here again the evidence is limited in range. It is derived almost exclusively from paintings in the Catacombs, and mainly from the Catacombs of Rome; so that the simplest remains of Christian Art are necessarily confined in scope. They throw no light upon its domestic use, nor do they furnish any measure of its actual extent in subject or in prosecution. Moreover many of the paintings have been retouched at later times and some which are commonly reckoned among the earliest are of uncertain antiquity. *The Italian Churches.*

In spite of these drawbacks however the paintings in the Catacombs appear to give a fair representation of the character and spirit of Christian Art in Italy. They extend in date over the whole history of the early Church, though the earliest works are *1. Painting.*

---

[1] *id.* c. 10 pastor quem in calice depingis.

[2] Clem. Alex. *Pæd.* iii. 11, § 59, p. 289 P.

[3] Orig. *adv. Cels.* viii. 17 ff. Comp. *de Orat.* 17.

[4] Clem. Alex. *Protr.* i. § 62, p. 54 P.

very few, from the beginning of the second century onwards, and
include works of the greatest rudeness and of high artistic merit.

Cemetery of Domitilla. The earliest Roman example which is known, the decorations of
the most ancient part of the cemetery which bears the name of
Flavia Domitilla, are, as it appears, a unique monument of the
primitive patrician Church of the Imperial City. In this case it
may be supposed that the converts had the means for readily
securing the services of a good artist, and an impartial judge pronounces the work to be such as would not discredit a painter of the
best age[1]. Both in general style and subject these decorations
closely resemble contemporary pagan works, but there are sufficient
traces of characteristic subjects to establish their Christian origin[2].

Catacombs of St Januarius at Naples. The decorations of the Catacombs of St Januarius at Naples
and of chambers in the cemetery of St Callixtus at Rome are even
more completely classical in treatment. The artist acting under
Christian instruction has followed as far as he could the custom
of his time, using freely conventional ornaments, birds and flowers
and masks, which were consistent with Christian feeling, and introducing subjects which marked the faith of those for whom he
worked[3].

[1] Mommsen, *Cont. Rev.* May 1871, p. 170.
[2] Northcote and Brownlow, ii. 120 ff. Garrucci, *Storia dell' Arte Cristiana* I. 19.
[3] Schultze, *Die Katakomben*, 90 ff.; Garrucci, Tavv. 90—98.
Northcote and Brownlow, ii. pp. 18 ff. Garrucci, Tav. 26. Compare Garrucci, Tavv. 13, 20, 37, 38, 88 for other examples of a classical type, and the beautiful pagan decorations of the tomb in the Via Latina (Parker, *Tombs*, pl. xiv. ff.).
The following classical subjects may be specially noticed:
ORPHEUS.
S. Domitilla, Northcote and Brownlow, p. 31.
S. Callixtus, North. and Br. *Pl.* xviii. 2 (as Good Shepherd).
Bottari, lxxi.

The figure occurs also on a Lamp, D.C.A. 922.
PSYCHE.
S. Domitilla, North. and Br. 33; Schultze, *Die Katakomben*, 98.
S. Gennaro, Naples. Schultze, *Tab.* v.; id. *Die Kat.* s. 93.
Compare North. and Br. p. 239 (sarcophagus).
DIOSCURI.
Arles; sarcophagus. Le Blant, *Les sarc. chrét. d'Arles* xxiii.
ULYSSES and the SIRENS.
Crypt of Lucina: sarcophagus: North. and Br. p. 240.
A very remarkable series of scenes from the Gospel History is found in the Catacomb of Prætextatus. They are unfortunately only imperfectly known. From the drawings published by Garrucci, they appear to represent (1) Christ and the woman of Samaria;

The other examples of painting in the Roman Catacombs are of inferior artistic merit, being provided by poorer converts. But the same general features are preserved throughout. Christians used as far as they could the resources of popular art, and even adopted some current subjects which were capable of a Christian interpretation. There was no chasm of separation between Christianity and Art except that which was fixed by the ordinary subservience of Art to idolatrous purposes[1].

Other examples.

At the beginning of the fourth century, when the Christian Society had emerged from obscurity and begun to erect dignified places for worship, it was natural that Christians should introduce into their churches the Art which had decorated their tombs. The famous Canon of the Synod of Elvira was evidently not directed against a prospective or imaginary danger, but against an actual and probably a growing practice. There can be no real doubt as to its meaning, whatever opinion may be held as to its wisdom and its authority. The Synod absolutely forbids the painting of pictures on the walls of churches, in order to guard against the representation of the objects of worship[2]. Primitive feeling shrank, most justly, I

The canon of Elvira.

(2) The healing of the woman with the Issue; (3) The Baptism. The last subject is debated, but De' Rossi's idea that it represents the striking of the Lord with the reed is wholly at variance with the cycle of subjects in early Art, and with the appearance of the Dove in the picture.

The drawing seems to be singularly good; and the figure of the Lord is of a youthful classical type. Schultze, *Die Kat.* 145; North. and Br. 143 ff.

Schultze points out that Christian artists borrowed ornamental figures from classical myths which embodied beliefs about the dead: a. a. O. 98 ff.

[1] E.g. Garrucci, Tavv. 8, 12. None of the groups of figures seem to shew real artistic merit, unless it be the Madonna in the Cemetery of Priscilla as interpreted in Northcote and Brownlow, ii. pl. vii.; yet contrast the photograph in Parker's *Catacombs*, pl. ii.

The marvellously beautiful group of the Shepherd and Sheep in the tomb of Statilius Taurus (B.C. 30) is wholly unapproached by any Christian work. Parker, *Tombs in and near Rome*, pl. xix.

There are examples of decorations in Jewish and Mithraic tombs closely analogous to those of the Christian tombs: Garrucci, Tavv. 493 ff.

[2] *Conc. Illib.* Can. 36. *Ne picturæ in ecclesia fiant.* Placuit picturas in ecclesia esse non debere, ne quod colitur et adoratur in parietibus depingatur. Comp. Dale, *Synod of Elvira*, p. 289 n.

The Canon is most strangely quoted by Northcote and Brownlow (ii. p. 4) as 'one which forbad "pictures to be placed in a church, or that which is worshipped and adored to be painted on the walls."'

believe, from the portraiture of Divine Persons. Perhaps there
were already symptoms that this reserve was likely to be broken.
So it seemed better to exclude pictures from the churches altogether
than to run the risk of injuring the sensibility of faith.

There was perhaps something of the sternness of African Christianity in the Canon of Elvira. It may have been called for by
peculiar local perils. It is therefore of more interest to notice a
similar expression of feeling from an opposite quarter. This is found
in a letter addressed by Eusebius of Cæsarea to the Empress Constantia, which was brought forward at the second Council of Nicæa.
In this Eusebius seems to speak according to the general feeling of
the time. The empress had requested a likeness (εἰκών) of Christ.
What do you mean by a likeness of Christ? is the answer of Eusebius.
Not of course the image of Him as He is truly and unchangeably ;
nor yet of His human nature as it has been glorified, of which the
overpowering splendour of the Transfiguration offered some pledge
and likeness. It must then be an image of the frail mortal flesh
which He bore before His Ascension. But such images are forbidden
by the Mosaic Law. They are nowhere to be found in churches ;
and it is notorious that with us alone they are forbidden. 'Some
'poor woman', he goes on to say, 'brought to me two painted
'figures, like philosophers, and ventured to say that they represented
'Paul and the Saviour; I do not know on what ground. But to save
'her and others from offence, I took them from her and kept them
'by me, not thinking it right in any case that she should exhibit
'them further (εἰς ἑτέρους ὅλως ἐκφέρειν), that we may not seem like
'idolaters to carry our God about in an image.' The images of
Simon Magus and Mani may be worshipped by their followers.
'But such objects are forbidden us. Since we confess that our
'Saviour is God and Lord we prepare ourselves to see Him as God,
'using all zeal to purify our own hearts, that if so be when purified
'we may see Him. For *Blessed are the pure in heart because they
'shall see God*. And if in addition to this hope (ἐκ περιουσίας) before
'that vision which shall be "face to face" you set high value on the

'images of the Saviour, what better artist can there be than the 'God-Word Himself[1]?'

Such judgments were however unable to stem the tide of popular feeling which soon set in. The revolution in the Empire, which was marked and crowned by the conversion of Constantine, introduced new and perilous elements into the Christian body. The intense spirituality of the first ages was lost. Paganism passed not yet wholly conquered under the yoke of the Church. Within less than a century the representations of sacred scenes obtained for good and evil a recognised place in Christian sanctuaries. The innovation was not accomplished without resistance. The familiar anecdote of Epiphanius († 402) is a kind of summary of the controversy. This zealous and rigid bishop when visiting a village church in Palestine found there a veil 'bearing a fanciful image of Christ (imaginem 'quasi Christi) or of some Saint', for this detail he could not remember. He at once tore it asunder, and ordered the guardians of the church where it hung to use it for the shroud of a pauper. Nor was any further remonstrance made than that he should supply a new one, which he did through the Bishop of Jerusalem, begging him to warn the priest in charge of the church not to hang there veils 'which are contrary to the Christian religion[2].' *A revolution of feeling.*

But in spite of such isolated action, and the traditional practice by which it was supported, pictures found a recognised place in sacred buildings even in the lifetime of Epiphanius. Three illustrations will be sufficient to shew how far their use was extended in the West and in the East. Paulinus († 431), who was a scholar of Ausonius and of consular rank, devoted himself and his fortune to the service of the Church. He took for his special hero Felix, a martyr of Nola, whose grave he decorated with noble buildings while he celebrated his praises in a long series of poems. In one of these he describes in some detail the pictures with which he had adorned the cloister of the church[3]. The series included the events of the *Paulinus.*

---

[1] Euseb. *Ep. ad Const.* Migne, *Patrol. Gr.* xx. 1515 ff.

[2] Epiph. *Epist. ad Joann. Hier.* § ix. (iii. 390 ed. Migne).

[3] xxvii. (*De S. Felice carm. natal.* ix.) 511 ff.

Nunc volo picturas fucatis agmine longo

history of the Pentateuch, Joshua and Ruth[1]. By means of these representations he hoped to attract and instruct the crowds of ignorant rustics who visited the shrine of St Felix[2]. Each scene had, as he describes it, a certain fitness for enforcing some particular lesson, the new creation, the offering of Isaac, the continence of Joseph, the overthrow of Pharaoh[3], the separation of Ruth and Orpah[4]. He admits that the experiment was an unusual one[5]; and it does not appear that he introduced into his decorations any scenes from the Gospel history. His language indeed implies that he shared to some extent the feeling expressed by Eusebius as to representations of the Lord[6].

Porticibus videas, paulumque supina
    fatiges
Colla, reclinato dum perlegis omnia
    vultu.
[1] Qui videt hæc vacuis agnoscens vera
    figuris
Non vacua fidam sibi pascet imagine
    mentem.
Omnia namque tenet serie pictura
    fideli
Quæ senior scripsit per quinque vo-
    lumina Moses,
Quæ gessit Domini signatus nomine
    Iesus...
Jam distinguentem modico Ruth
    tempora libro,
Tempora Judicibus finita et Regibus
    orta,
Intentis transcurre oculis: brevis ista
    videtur
Historia, et magni signat mysteria
    belli...   id. 514 ff.
[2] Propterea visum nobis opus utile,
    totis
Felicis domibus pictura illudere
    sancta ;
Si forte attonitas hæc per spectacula
    mentes
Agrestum caperet fucata coloribus
    umbra,
Quæ super exprimitur titulis ut lit-
    tera monstret
Quod manus explicuit...
                        id. 580 ff.
[3] De genesi, precor, hunc orandi col-
    lige sensum,

Ne maneam terrenus Adam...
Hostia viva Deo tanquam puer of-
    ferar Isac...
Sit mihi castus amor, sit et horror
    amoris iniqui...
Sit mihi ab Aegypto bonus exitus...
                        id. 607 ff.
[4] Nonne, precor, toto manet hæc dis-
    cordia mundo,
Parte sequente Deum, vel parte
    ruente per orbem?
                        id. 537 f.
[5] Forte requiratur quanam ratione
    gerendi
Sederit hæc nobis sententia pingere
    sanctas
Raro more domos animantibus ad-
    simulatis.
                        id. 542 ff.
[6] Hæc tibi, Christe Deus, tenui faci-
    lique paratu
Pro nobis facimus; nec enim te,
    summe Creator,
Facta manu capiunt, toto quem cor-
    pore mundus
Non capit.
In his restoration of the old Basilica
Paulinus introduced 'the two Testa-
ments,' but his language is very ob-
scure:
        tribus in spatiis duo Testa-
    menta legamus;
Hanc quoque cernentes rationem
    lumine recto,
Quod nova in antiquis tectis, antiqua
    novis lex

The contemporary evidence of Gregory of Nyssa († c. 400) shews Gregory of Nyssa. that in some places at least the range of subjects had been already enlarged. In commemorating Theodorus he has given a description of a picture of his martyrdom, which in its intense realism no less than in its subject is foreign to the spirit of early Christian Art. The artist, he says, had imaged in glowing colours the heroic acts of the martyr, his struggles, his pains, the brutal forms of his persecutors, their insults, the flaming furnace, the blessed consummation of the soldier of Christ. Painting, he adds, even in silence can speak upon the wall, and do great service[1].

About the same time Asterius, bishop of Amasea, gives a strange Asterius. description of popular extravagance. Men and women wore robes embroidered with all kinds of subjects 'as if it were not enough to have the walls of their houses decorated with pictures'. The more pious, he adds, choose scenes from the Gospels, and think that in so doing they dress themselves in a way to please God. 'If they follow 'my advice, let them sell such garments and honour the living 'images of God. Do not paint Christ, for the one act of humility of 'His Incarnation, which He voluntarily undertook for us, is suffi-'cient, but bear in thy soul and carry about spiritually (νοητῶς) the 'incorporeal Word[2].'

Not long afterwards there is evidence that still more remarkable Nilus. freedom was used in ecclesiastical ornament. Olympiodorus consulted Nilus († 430) on the decorations which he proposed to place in a great church to be erected in honour of the martyrs. It was his design to represent on both sides of the Sanctuary (ἱερατεῖον)

Pingitur; est etenim pariter decus utile nobis
In veteri novitas, atque in novitate vetustas.
Compare also xxviii. 22—27.
In the apse of the Basilica at Funda he represented the idea of the Passion as it is found on sarcophagi:
Sanctorum labor et merces sibi rite cohærent,
Ardua crux pretiumque crucis sublime corona.

Ipse Deus, nobis princeps crucis atque corona,
Inter gloriferi cæleste nemus paradisi,
Sub cruce sanguinea niveo stat Christus in agno,
Agnus ut innocua injusto datus hostia leto. (*Ep.* xxxii. 17.)
[1] Greg. Nyss. *de S. Theod. Mart.* iii. p. 733 (ed. Migne).
[2] Hom. *de div. et Laz.* p. 167, Migne (*Patrol. Gr.* xl.).

scenes of hunting and fishing, with representations of various animals
and fish; and to erect in 'the common house' 'a thousand crosses,
and histories (ἱστορίας) of all kinds of birds and beasts and reptiles
and plants.' 'In answer to your letter', so Nilus writes, 'I should
'say that it would be puerile and childish that the eye of the faithful
'should wander over such subjects. It befits a strong and manly
'character to fashion one single cross at the east of the most sacred
'precinct (τοῦ θειοτάτου τεμένους)...and to fill the holy sanctuary (τὸν
'ναὸν τὸν ἅγιον) on both sides with histories of the Old and New
'Testament by the hand of a skilful artist, in order that those...who
'are unable to read the divine Scriptures may by looking at the paint-
'ings call to mind the courage of men who have served the true
'God and be stirred to emulation of their heroic exploits[1].'

AUGUS-
TINE.

In the time of Augustine the African Church had yielded to the
growing fashion. Speaking of the Sacrifice of Isaac he says 'that it
was sung in many tongues, painted in many places[2].' And he bears
witness that the fashion had brought the results which earlier
Christians had dreaded: 'I know many', he writes, 'who worship
tombs and pictures[3].'

2. Sculp-
ture.

The remains of early Christian Sculpture are singularly few.
This may be due partly to the costliness of such works, and still
more to the nature of the Art itself. Sculpture far more than paint-

Statues.

ing was identified with idolatry. The aversion from 'the graven
image' has perpetuated itself in the Greek Church[4], and even to the

---

[1] Nilus, *Epp.* iv. 61. The letter was
brought forward at the Second Council of Nicæa. In the following letter
Nilus speaks of a young monk who
recognised a martyr who appeared to
him from having seen him often represented 'in the paintings' (ἐκ τοῦ πολ-
λάκις τὸν χαρακτῆρα τοῦ ἁγίου ἐπὶ τῶν
εἰκόνων τεθεᾶσθαι). The phrase sounds
like one of a later time. But Chrysostom bears witness to the custom in his
Homily on Meletius (ii. 2, p. 516, ed.
Migne); he says that the portrait of
that Saint was drawn on 'rings, seals,
bowls, and chamber walls.'

[2] *c. Faust.* xxii. 73. Compare also

de cons. evv. i. x. 16, Sic omnino errare
meruerunt qui Christum et apostolos
ejus non in sanctis codicibus sed in pic-
tis parietibus quæsierunt; nec mirum
si a pingentibus fingentes decepti sunt.

[3] *de Mor. Eccles. Cath.* i. 34 (75)
novi multos esse sepulcrorum et pic-
turarum adoratores. The famous phrase
'picturæ (imagines) sunt idiotarum
libri' is often referred to Augustine,
but, as far as I know, wrongly.

[4] I am informed that statues are
used as ornaments of Russian churches,
as (for example) on the outside of the
Isaac Church at St Petersburgh. I
may add here that a friend, who has

present time Sculpture is for the most part inspired by the spirit of the old world. A single ideal figure, the Good Shepherd of the Vatican, which seems to have been suggested by the type of the Hermes Kriophoros, is referred to the fourth century[1]; part of a single portrait statue, that of Hippolytus, is referred to the fifth century. To these two works may be added a small statue of the Good Shepherd found at Seville, and perhaps the famous bronze statue of St Peter; and the list of the extant Christian statues of the first five centuries is complete[2]. The other early works of sculpture are sarcophagi, one of which belongs to the third century[3].

In spite of the limited scope which sarcophagi offered to the artist the sculptures which they present are of great interest as confirming the general impressions conveyed by the remains of early

The character of the sepulchral subjects.

given a considerable amount of study to the monuments of early Celtic hagiology, especially of the Scoto-Irish school, informs me that, as far as his reading has extended, he 'cannot remember meeting with any 'mention of a sacred picture or image, 'unless it be in one passage in the 'Life of Brigid by Cogitosus, a work 'which Colgan attributes to the last 'quarter of the sixth century. It is 'there stated that in the church of 'Kildare, in which the body of Brigid 'was still lying buried in the time of 'the author, the *paries tabulatus*, which 'separated the eastern part from the 'twin naves, was *decoratus et imagi-* '*nibus depictus, ac linteaminibus tec-* '*tus* (Cogitosus, *cap.* xxxv., in the '*Trias Thaumaturga*, p. 523). But 'what subjects these *imagines* depicted, 'is not hinted: it is possible that only 'flowers, or, at most, figures of angels, 'are meant.'

[1] According to Eusebius (*Vit. Const.* iii. 497) Constantine set up in the market at Constantinople 'the representation of the Good Shepherd familiar to students of Scripture (τὰ τοῦ καλοῦ ποιμένος σύμβολα, τοῖς ἀπὸ τῶν θείων λογίων ὁρμωμένοις γνώριμα), and a gilded bronze figure of Daniel with the lions.'

[2] The two other figures of the Good

Shepherd which remain (Appell, *l. c.* p. 5) are hardly so early. A statuette of St Peter (Appell, p. 6) which was once at Berlin appears to be of early date; but is known only by engravings.

[3] It is dated 273. See Le Blant, *Étude sur les Sarcophages Chrétiens de la ville d'Arles*, p. iv; and compare *id.* pl. xxxiv. Le Blant assigns to the same age the sarcophagus of Livia Primitiva, which bears a rude representation of the Good Shepherd between two sheep, a fish and an anchor: *l.c.* Bottari, T. xxxv. 2.

Garrucci's fifth volume contains the sarcophagi. A very careful and valuable list and description is given by Dr Appell, *Monuments of Christian Art* ...1872.

Prof. Ramsay has shewn me a drawing of a most interesting relief which is probably the oldest remaining specimen of Christian sculpture. It is found on a monument erected by 'Abercius a deacon, to himself, his wife, and his children,' and represents a small figure with one arm laid across the breast standing between two profiles of a man and a woman executed on a larger scale. These profiles are evidently portraits, and that of the woman has considerable artistic merit. Prof. Ramsay places the work c. 200.

Christian painting. The sarcophagi of Helena and Constantine, the mother and daughter of Constantine, are perfectly classical in character. The vine and wine-making which are represented on the latter recall the earliest wall-paintings. Such objects lend themselves readily to a Christian interpretation while they are not distinctively Christian. In other cases classical imagery is found to which a Christian meaning can only be given with difficulty[1]. But for the most part the same scenes are found as in the Catacombs, and they are treated in the same manner. The sculptor brought to his work the experience and the traditions of ancient art, as far as they still survived, and used them for the expression of new ideas[2].

3. Architecture. Meanwhile Christian Architecture had made vigorous progress. When the persecution of Diocletian broke out at Nicomedia (A. D. 303), 'a most lofty temple' there was one of the first objects of destruction. At that time it is evident that the religious buildings of Christians were of considerable importance; and the church which **Paulinus.** Paulinus erected at Tyre not many years afterwards (A. D. 313) probably only reproduced the type of earlier works of which no detailed description has been preserved. Eusebius has fortunately given an account of this which proves beyond question that Christians were ready to devote the costliest work to purposes of Divine worship[3]. The central door was decorated 'with plates of bronze and reliefs' (παραπήγμασί τε χαλκοῦ σιδηροδέτοις καὶ ποικίλμασιν ἀναγλύφοις).' Elaborate carvings of wood were freely used. The roof was made of cedar. And Eusebius taxes the powers of his rhetoric to represent the splendour of the effect produced both by the costliness of the materials and by the beauty of the workmanship. The external

---

[1] *E.g.* The figures of the Dioscuri on a sarcophagus at Arles. Le Blant, pl. xxiii. pp. 38 ff. On the use of classical details see Le Blant, *l. c. Introduction*, pp. x. f.; 19.

[2] Some examples shew considerable artistic merit. For example a sarcophagus in the Lateran Museum, given in Northcote and Brownlow, ii. 255; Parker, pl. xvii.; Bottari, T. xxxiii. The sarcophagus of Junius Bassus

(A.D. 359) shews thoughtful work. It is hard to understand how other engravings come to represent Daniel as nude, according to all but universal custom, while Parker's engraving 'taken from a photograph' (pl. xiii.) represents him as fully clothed. Dr Appell says that the figure is modern. (*Monuments of Christian Art*, p. 10.)

[3] *H. E.* x. 4.

magnificence was indeed designed, if we may believe him, to attract passers by and lead them to enter the sacred precincts[1].

The church of Paulinus was a genuine expression of Christian feeling.   Less stress can be laid on the evidence furnished by the works of Constantine at Jerusalem.   These so impressed Eusebius that he suggests that they may have been prefigured by the prophets in their description of the New Jerusalem[2].   No kind of rich decoration was spared.   The interior walls were encrusted with variegated marbles.   The carved ceiling was gilded throughout.   The semicircular apse was adorned with twelve columns, supporting as many silver vases which the Emperor 'presented as an offering to his God.' And Eusebius says that he could not enumerate the other gifts ' of gold and silver and precious stones' with which the building was enriched[3]. *(margin: Constantine.)*

The works of Constantine at Rome seem to have been of a similar type; and the drawings of the original Basilica of St Peter which have been preserved are so full of beauty that it is difficult not to feel that the present building has been dearly purchased by the loss of the greatest of his churches.

The development of Christian Architecture gave occasion to the first original effort of Christian Art, the application of Mosaic on a large scale to wall-pictures.   The earliest remaining examples are in the churches of St Constantia and St Maria Maggiore at Rome; and one of the most beautiful in the tomb of Galla Placidia at Ravenna[4]. This form of art, it is obvious, lends itself naturally to conventional representation; and it is not unlikely that the later Mosaics preserve unchanged the earliest types as they were successively fixed. *(margin: Mosaics.)*

One example deserves to be specially noticed, that on the apse of

---

[1] Euseb. l. c. ὡς ἂν μὴ παρατρέχῃ τις ὅτι μὴ τὴν ψυχὴν καταυγεὶς πρότερον μνήμῃ τῆς τε πρὶν ἐρημίας καὶ τῆς νῦν παραδόξου θαυματουργίας, ὑφ᾽ ἧς τάχα καὶ ἑλκυσθήσεσθαι κατανυγέντα καὶ πρὸς αὐτῆς τῆς ὄψεως ἐπὶ τὴν εἴσοδον προτραπήσεσθαι ἤλπισεν.

[2] Vit. Const. ii. 33.

[3] Id. 34—40. Bingham (Antiqui-

ties, viii. § 5) has given an interesting early inventory of Church vessels.

[4] There is a drawing of this Mosaic in D. C. A. ii. 6, 1328, and a large coloured drawing at South Kensington. It is excellently described in Woltmann and Woermann, Hist. of Painting, London, 1880, i. 167 f.

the church of St Pudentiana at Rome.   No existing work gives a better idea of the peculiar spirit and power of early Christian Art. The treatment is conventional without being lifeless.   A spiritual purpose is dominant without destroying the natural dignity of the figures and the grouping.   The spectator is forced by the beauty of that which he sees to look beyond to that which is suggested[1].

Domestic
Art.

There are very few traces of the domestic Art of the early Christians.   Clement of Alexandria gives a list of subjects which might properly be engraved on rings; and existing specimens present nearly all the types which he allows[2].   Many early Christian lamps are works of considerable merit[3].   And one of the gold coins of Constantine offers a unique and most beautiful embodiment of a Christian

[1] There are valuable representations of early Mosaics in the South Kensington Museum. See *Christian Mosaic Pictures* by J. W. Appell, Ph. D., 1877. Garrucci devotes his fourth volume to Mosaics.

[2] For the history and remains of early Christian glyptic Art see C. W. King, *Antique Gems and Rings*, ii. § vii. pp. 24 ff. London, 1872; and Dr Babington's article *Gems* in D. C. A.

A simple enumeration of the subjects of the small collection of early Christian gems in the British Museum will give a fair idea of the general character of these works.

1.   A dove, olive branch and star (ruby).
2.   A fish, olive, pastoral staff.
3.   A fish and anchor, with the word ЄΠΙΤΥΝΧΑΝΟΥ (D. C. A. p. 714).
4.   A cross, fish and dove (D. C. A. p. 713).
5.   Two fish (ascending and descending) and a bowl.
6.   An anchor between two dolphins with the letters Α. Π. Λ.
7.   An anchor between two fish.
8.   ΙΧΘΥC enclosed between two olive branches (sard).
9.   An anchor-cross with two doves resting on the arms, two fish (ascending and descending), and two palms.
10.   Good Shepherd under an olive with two doves (hæmatite).

11.   Good Shepherd between two sheep : very rude.
12.   Good Shepherd with ΙΗ ΧC : very rude.
13.   Good Shepherd, with sheep and two lambs, under a tree with a dove : very rude.
14.   Good Shepherd and Jonah cast out by the monster: a dove with olive branch: a palm and gourd with a star between : in the centre the monogram.
15.   Two parts: above, the Good Shepherd and Jonah under the gourd : below, an anchor, dove, branches, fish, figures kneeling, a figure floating above.
16.   A Cross, which has become a living tree, with a dove resting upon it.   (This is a singularly interesting device.)
17.   Two sheep between two palms : very well executed.
18.   Chariot with two horses and angel.
19.   Four sheep with collars.
20.   The temptation.
21.   Cross with the Chrisma (sapphire).
22.   Palm between two branches.
23.   Palm tree, two branches and two birds with inscription : very rude.

[3] See Dr Babington's article in D. C. A.

thought. The Emperor is represented as 'looking upwards in the attitude of prayer': so, Eusebius says, he wished to express his faith[1].

The rapid sketch which has been given of the progress of Christian Art in different directions will be sufficient to indicate the circumstances under which it gained finally a recognised place in Christian life, and especially in Christian worship. It was, as we have seen, fashioned on classical models; it inherited the use of classical methods; it incorporated some of the familiar subjects of classical use[2]; but at the same time it embodied, even if only in an elementary form, the power of a new life. It was conventional and it was symbolic. By these characteristics it claimed effectually the office of interpreting the invisible through the visible, of giving predominance to the spiritual idea over the external appearance, of advancing from within outwards, from the thought to the expression. The means adopted for securing these ends belong, no doubt, to the infancy of Christian Art. Efforts which were arrived at directly and simply in the first stage of the new artistic life can be secured now without any sacrifice of the freedom or of the fulness of the artist's labours. But this fact does not deprive the earliest works of their distinctive meaning and importance.

Characteristics of Christian Art.

---

[1] *Vit. Const.* iv. 15. An engraving of the coin, which does not do it justice, is given in D. C. A. *Money*, Fig. 23. Dr Babington (D. C. A. i. p. 720) refers to an agate in which the Emperor is represented in the same way.

Some other coins of Christian emperors deserve mention as illustrating the symbolism of Christian Art. Most conspicuous among these is the small 'third brass' coin of Constantine, bearing on the reverse the words *spes publica* with the labarum, the spiked end of which pierces the serpent (D. C. A. *s.v. Labarum* and *Money*, fig. 16). A variation of this design Constantine is said to have set over the portal of his palace (Euseb. *Vit. Const.* iii. 3). The old device of the

phœnix with the legend *Felix temporum reparatis* occurs on coins of Constans and Constantius. On coins of the two Eudoxias Victory is represented inscribing the letters of the sacred monogram on a shield. On a coin of Valentinian III., which has the common legend *Victoria Augusti*, Satan takes the place of the barbarian whom the Emperor treads under his feet. At last the head of the Lord, of a singularly dignified type, appears on a gold coin of Justinian II. Compare C. W. King, *Early Christian Numismatics*, pp. 35 ff.

A very complete account of the interesting Christian glass work is given by Dr Babington in D. C. A. (*Glass*). See also Garrucci, Tom. iii.

[2] See p. 343, n. 1.

W.

Early Christian Art is conventional. This is true both as to the
choice and as to the treatment of subjects. It is indeed necessary to
remember that our illustrations are chiefly drawn from the Catacombs, from tombs and sarcophagi. But when allowance is made
for the limitation of the artist's freedom by the nature of his work,
it seems certain that other influences must have kept him within
the narrow circle of subjects to which he confined himself. He made
a new departure in Art, though perhaps unconsciously, and strove
to call attention to the divine element in life. For this purpose
it was necessary to take a few familiar subjects which could easily
be made to express a universal spiritual truth. Scenes and figures
came in this way to express great thoughts; and when this correspondence between facts and ideas was established in a few cases,
a lesson of wide application was surely taught.

Thus it is that a few subjects from the Old Testament and a few
from the New Testament are repeated both in painting and sculpture
with almost wearisome monotony. Among these three scenes from
the history of Jonah ((a) Jonah cast out of the ship; (b) disgorged by
the sea-monster; (c) resting under the gourd), Daniel between two
lions, Noah in the ark, the feeding of the multitudes and the Raising
of Lazarus are perhaps the most frequent in early works; and next to
these the Fall, Moses striking the rock, the three Children in the
furnace, Job in his distress, the sacrifice of Abraham, the ascension
of Elijah, the adoration of the Magi, the miracle of Cana[1]. It
is very remarkable that only one representation of David is referred
to by the historians of early Christian Art[2].

The treatment of these subjects offers little variation. Jonah is
always represented nude, and the sea-monster seems to have been
modelled on the type of that found in representations of Andromeda.

---

[1] Lists of examples of these different subjects are given in various
writers. It is sufficient to refer to
Canon Venables' articles *Fresco*, and
Old Testament in D. C. A., and Mr
Tyrwhitt's article in the same work on
the different subjects. See also C. J.
Hemans, *The Church in the Catacombs*, Cont. Rev. Oct. 1866.

How great was the tendency of the
subjects to become fixed is shewn by
the identity of the decorations of two
sarcophagi, one at Rome (Bottari,
xxiv.) and the other at Arles (Le
Blant, ix.).

[2] See p. 357, n. 5.

Daniel, nearly always nude, stands in the attitude of prayer between two lions placed symmetrically. Lazarus is drawn like a mummy, and his tomb commonly appears like a small chapel, while the Lord holds a rod in hand. The Magi are dressed in Persian (Phrygian) costume. The treatment of the Good Shepherd offers a partial exception to the general uniformity. In addition to the commonest type in which He bears the lamb over His shoulders, the Shepherd is represented with the pipe, and leaning on His staff, and with goats[1]; and on a sarcophagus He appears in three separate forms[2]. It is not difficult to see the special colouring which is given in each case to the common thought. Elsewhere there is little change; and anyone who examines the work of Garrucci will feel the truth of the words used at the second Council of Nicæa, 'the making of 'pictures is not the invention of artists but the admitted legislation 'and tradition of the Catholic Church[3].'

This view as it was maintained by the artists of the Greek Church was necessarily fatal to Art. The conventionalism of early work was no more than a first step in the new life. Conventionalism was the condition of Symbolism, that is of the simplest assertion of the spiritual purpose of Art. But when the end was gained, the provisional restriction of subjects ceased to be necessary.

Christian Art symbolic.

We are thus brought to the second characteristic of early Christian Art: it was symbolic. There is no doubt some exaggeration in the theory, which has gained the support of De' Rossi, that Christian artists worked under the direction of theologians and embodied definite schemes of doctrine in their pictures. But it is impossible to study the cycle of subjects in connexion with early Christian literature and not feel that the artists embodied thoughts which their religious services brought before them. Scenes in the Old Testament shadowed forth truths of the Gospel and illustrated the reality of the one purpose underlying all life. By repeating these it was not

[1] Compare Northcote and Brownlow, ii. p. 24. Bottari, lxxviii., lxxx., xcvii., ciii., cv., cxiii., cxvi., cxviii., cxliii., cxlv., clv., clxxii., clxxix.

[2] Bottari, clxiii.

[3] Οὐ ζωγράφων ἐφεύρετις ἡ τῶν εἰκόνων ποίησις ἀλλὰ τῆς καθολικῆς ἐκκλησίας ἔγκριτος θεσμοθεσία καὶ παράδοσις. Conc. Nic. II. Act. vi. (Concil. viii. 1085 ed. Colet.)

difficult to suggest the thought of the correspondence between different stages in the fulfilment of the divine will, of the inner meaning of ordinary events, of the way in which things are set 'one over against another.' The offering of Isaac indicated as much as the early believer thought could be safely indicated, in a direct representation, of the Lord's Passion. The deliverance of Noah from and by the waters was an eloquent symbol of salvation in the Church 'through water.' The four rivers of Paradise suggested thoughts of the streams of grace flowing to the Church through the Gospel and the Gospels. The domestic feast, and the feeding of the multitudes called up recollections of the provision which the Lord had made and still continues to make for the material and spiritual sustenance of His people. Above all the familiar figure of the Good Shepherd brought together the imagery of the Old Testament and the experience of daily life, and in some degree perhaps symbolic forms of ancient art[1]. In one subject at least the imagination of the old world was allowed its full right. The myth of Orpheus expressed with far-reaching pathos the faith of man in a restored order of creation; and the Christian artist gladly accepted the pictured parable of which his faith gave the meaning.

The symbolism of figures recognised in the works. The reality of this symbolic meaning is placed beyond all question by the direct testimony of the monuments themselves. In several cases St Peter, 'the leader of the New Israel,' is represented under the figure of Moses striking the rock. Not only is the figure of Moses commonly given in the conventional type of St Peter, but the identification is completed by the addition of the name, Peter[2]. In other examples Christ Himself appears as Moses[3] and again as Abraham[4]. Elsewhere, as when a young Christian man in the attitude of prayer occupies the place of Noah in the ark, the lessons taught by the experience of the old saints are brought down into actual life[5].

[1] On the relation of the Good Shepherd to the Hermes Kriophoros see Northcote and Brownlow, ii. pp. 26 ff.
[2] Compare Northcote and Brownlow, ii. frontispiece, and p. 180; Le Blant,

Sarc. Chrét. p. xxii.; pp. 36 f.
[3] Garrucci, lv. 2; xliii. 1.
[4] Garrucci, T. xliii. 1.
[5] It is enough simply to refer to the unquestioned symbolism of 'the Fish'

An illustration of a different kind is furnished by the sarcophagus of Bassus. On this, in the small reliefs which fill the spandrils of the arcade, a sheep occupies the place of the divine representation in the familiar cycle of subjects. A sheep receives the Law, strikes the rock, administers Baptism, multiplies the loaves, raises Lazarus. So the unity of the working of God throughout the Old and New Testaments is vividly brought out[1].

When the general principle is once recognised it is scarcely possible to overlook the combination of thoughts which is indicated by definite groupings of types, such as Moses striking the rock and the raising of Lazarus[2]; Moses striking the rock and Baptism[3]; Christ teaching in the centre, and grouped round the sacrifice of Abraham, the feeding of the multitudes, Moses striking the Rock, Noah, the three children[4]; and again, Orpheus in the centre, and around David with the sling[5], Moses striking the Rock, Daniel, the raising of Lazarus, separated by four pastoral scenes[6]; yet again, the Good Shepherd in the centre, and around the raising of Lazarus, Moses striking the rock, the healing of the Blind, Job[7]. In one example Daniel, the Good Shepherd, and Jonah cast to the whale occur in a continuous picture[8].

Symbolism of groups.

(ΙΧΘΥC). Except in scenes of 'fishing' this figure hardly comes within the proper scope of Art, though it illustrates the attitude of the artist. Compare D. C. A. s. v. The most remarkable use of 'the Fish' which I have seen is in a picture from Cyrenaica where several distinct kinds of fish are combined with a figure of the Good Shepherd (Garrucci tav. 105 c). Fishing and Baptism are combined: Garrucci, vii. 2. Figures of some very curious gems with the 'Fish' are given in D. C. A. i. p. 713. Le Blant (*Sarc. Chrét. Intr.* § 5) has pointed out the remarkable correspondence between the subjects on sarcophagi and the historical references in the Offices for the dead. His last words are well worth quoting: Mais, je le répète, ce qui me semble dominer dans le cycle des représentations figurées sur les tombes, c'est l'idée même dont s'in-

spirent les liturgies funéraires et qui fit mettre aux lèvres du preux Roland ce cri suprême: O notre vrai Père, toi qui ressuscitas saint Lazare d'entre les morts et qui défendis Daniel contre les lions, sauve mon âme et protége-la contre tous périls (p. xxxix).

[1] Compare Northcote and Brownlow, ii. p. 260.

[2] Bottari, T. cxxix.

[3] Le Blant, xv.

[4] Bottari, T. lix.; Garr. xxiv.

[5] Bottari says that this is the single representation of David with which he is acquainted in early art (p. 32). May not the figure really be that of the Sower?

[6] Bottari, lxiii.; Garr. xxv.

[7] Bottari, xci., Garr. xl. Other examples are given Garrucci xliii.; xlviii.; li. (Bottari, cxviii).

[8] Bottari, T. clxx.

The reserve of early Art. The symbolism of Christian Art is one expression of another mark by which it is distinguished, its reserve. This characteristic is specially illustrated by the treatment of subjects from the Gospels, and especially of the Person of the Lord. As early as the second century Gnostic sects had alleged portraits of the Lord[1]. Such representations were foreign to the mind of the Church. They do not occur in works connected with the Catholic Communion till the fourth century at the earliest, and then in conventional types[2]. At the same time the figures of the Lord which appear commonly on sarcophagi shew Him as a youthful figure of a pure classical form with no attempt at realistic portraiture[3]. It is no doubt due to the reverent shrinking from all representations of the Lord in His human Presence that scenes from the Gospel history were with very few exceptions carefully avoided.

A rude sketch of the Nativity is found upon a fragment of a sarcophagus dated A.D. 343[4]. There are representations of the visit of the Magi of as early a date[5]. Other scenes, except the Raising of Lazarus, are very rare and of isolated occurrence.

The treatment of the Passion. In this connexion the early treatment of the Passion is of the deepest interest. One of the earliest representations of the subject

[1] Iren. i. 24, 25. Compare D. C. A. Gems, i. p. 721.

[2] Compare Northcote and Brownlow, ii. 216 ff.; Pearson On the Creed, p. 88 note; and the articles by Mr Tyrwhitt and Archd. Cheetham in D. C. A. i. pp. 874 ff.
The famous statue at Cæsarea (Euseb. vii. 18) cannot in any case be regarded as contravening the general statement.
I do not enter on the question of the date of the legendary portraits of the Lord. The two specimens on 'cloth' reproduced by Mr Heaphy in his work on The Likeness of Christ (edited by W. Bayliss, London, 1880), from the originals at St Peter's at Rome, and St Bartholomew's at Genoa, are most remarkable works. I know nothing in early Christian Art at all resembling the former in style. Those who have

seen 'the Holy Face' at Lucca speak of it as being no less impressive.

[3] A very fine example is found on the sarcophagus of Junius Bassus. Appell, p. 9; Bottari, xv.; Parker, xvii. See also Bottari, xxxiii. Another remarkable example is given in Bottari liv. With these may be compared the corresponding figures of the bearded Christ: Le Blant, pl. iv.; Bottari xxi., xxii., xxiii., xxv., xxviii. The distinction which has been drawn between the beardless and bearded figures as expressing the human and divine aspects of Christ's Person (see Le Blant, p. 25) does not seem to hold good.

[4] Northcote and Brownlow, ii. 235.

[5] The occurrence of the Star in the group noticed above, p. 343, n. 2, seems to shew that that really represents the visit of the Magi.

is of singular beauty and impressiveness. It is found on a sarco-phagus preserved in the Lateran and referred to the fourth century[1]. The face of the sarcophagus is divided by columns into five compart-ments. The two end compartments shew on one side Christ, a youthful figure, led by a soldier, and Pilate washing his hands ; on the other Christ crowned by a soldier with a crown not of thorns but of flowers, and Simon the Cyrenian bearing His Cross[2]. In the centre is the Cross terminated by the sacred monogram encircled by a wreath. On the arms of the Cross two doves are resting, and beneath are two figures of the Roman guards, one watching and one sleeping. So the whole story of sadness and joy, of suffering and glory, of death and triumph, is eloquently told.

This representation of the Passion was widely spread, though without the accompanying scenes[3].

In one example below the Cross, in the place commonly occupied by the two guards, the Lord is represented appearing to two women[4]. In another the crowned Cross is the object of devout contemplation to the apostles, who stand six on each side with their right hands upraised, while from above out of the starry heaven a hand places a crown upon the head of each[5].

Another treatment of the idea of the Passion, which occurs on the sarcophagus of Anicius Probus, who died in 395, is scarcely less beautiful. In this case also the face of the sarcophagus is divided into five compartments. The two on either side are occupied each by two disciples. In the centre one, which is wider, the Lord appears between St Peter and St Paul. He stands, a graceful youthful figure, upon a mound from which flow the four streams of the new

---

[1] Appell, p. 21 ; Parker, xv. ; North-cote and Brownlow, ii. 253. Compare Paulinus *Ep.* xxxii. 17, quoted above, p. 346 n.

[2] This is well pointed out by Le Blant, *Sarc. Chrét.* p. 18. His en-graving p. xxxiii. 3 is admirable. The smaller size and dress of the figure bearing the Cross leave no doubt as to the artist's meaning.

Le Blant observes that this is the single example in which any incident of the Passion subsequent to the ap-pearance before Pilate is represented in early art (*l. c.*).

[3] Examples are given by Garrucci, Tavv. 349—353 ; 403.

[4] Bottari, T. xxx.; Garrucci, T. cccl.

[5] Le Blant, pl. xiv. A small en-graving of this work is given in D. C. A. i. p. 108.

Paradise: in His left hand He holds the roll of the Gospel, and in the right a jewelled cross[1].

The full meaning of this representation is brought out more clearly in other examples, where the Lord stands on the mound, and by Him a Lamb bearing the Cross upon its head[2]. The same thought is indicated by a Lamb standing in front of the Cross; or by a Lamb with a cruciform nimbus which stands upon a mound from which issue the four rivers[3]; and less distinctly by a Cross or the Chrisma between two lambs[4].

Yet more significant and touching is a representation of the Passion which is found on a slab preserved in Wirksworth Church, Derbyshire. The slab was found some years ago buried under the floor of the Chancel. The work is rude, and was probably executed by some English sculptor of the ixth or xth century, but the design is of a much earlier date, and may reasonably be referred to an Italian artist of the vith or viith century.

The larger portion of the slab which remains is in good preservation, and contains scenes from the Life of the Lord, among others less distinct, the Nativity and the Ascension in a most suggestive juxtaposition, the Feet-washing and the Burial, and between these a symbolic image of the Passion. On the centre of a plain Greek Cross is laid the figure of a dead lamb. As far as I can learn the conception is unique[5]. The drooping head and the bent legs of the victim tell of death with eloquent force; and under this limited

---

[1] Bottari, T. xvi. A similar group with the addition of two palm trees is found in another sarcophagus: Bottari, T. xxxv.

[2] Bottari, Tavv. xxi., xxii., 1. With this may be compared the rude, almost startling, figure of Christ throned with the Chrisma upon His head: Le Blant, pl. xxvii.

[3] Garrucci, T. ccclvi.; T. 355.

[4] Garrucci, Tavv. 10, 303, 337, 345, 389, 393, 422, 426.
On the cover of an Evangelarium at Milan are several typical scenes from the Lord's Life; but there is no Crucifixion. In place of this there is a

Lamb in the centre with a wreath: Labarte, Hist. des Arts industriels... 1864; pl. vi.; Garrucci, T. 454.

[5] The image of the Living Lamb is found on the centre of the Vatican Cross (D. C. A. 1, 513) and elsewhere. A very striking example occurs in a bas-relief on the Ciborium at St Mark's, Venice: Grim. de St Laurent, Iconographie de la Croix...in Didron's Annales Archéologiques xxvi. p. 213 (Paris, 1869). It is said that the Face of the Lord is represented as the intersection of the arms of the Cross in the Transfiguration at Ravenna: D. C. A. p. 494.

aspect it is perhaps allowable to present for contemplation the Dead Christ [1]. No one, I think, can regard it without feeling that we have lost greatly by substituting a literal representation for such a symbol [2].

The same spirit of reserve which led Christian artists to shrink from direct representations of the Lord's sufferings, kept them also from representing the sufferings of His martyrs. A single painting in the Cemetery of St Callixtus is supposed to portray the trial of Christian confessors [3]. And a single gem, a new-year's gift, of unusually good execution, which is referred to the age of Constantine, represents an actual martyrdom, perhaps that of St Agnes [4]. It seemed enough for the most part to represent the death and deliverance of martyrs by the type of the three Children.

Representations of martyrdom avoided.

In correspondence with the reserve of early Christian Art we may also notice its joyousness. The reserve was a natural consequence of the vivid realisation of spiritual truth : the aim of the artist was, so to speak, to let earth speak of heaven and not to confine heaven in forms of earth. The joyousness was another manifestation of the same faith. In spite of appearances the Christian believed that the victory over sin and death was already won ; and he gave expression to his conviction. The characteristic words ' in pace ' which marked the ' rest ' of the believer were reflected in all the associations of death. The painful literalism which deforms many of the monuments of the xvth and xvith centuries found no place in the vth and vith, and still less in earlier times. The terrible pictures which Tertullian drew of the sufferings of persecutors, and the scarcely less terrible descriptions by Augustine of the sufferings of the wicked were not as yet embodied by Art. No attempt was

Joyfulness of Christian Art.

---

[1] I feel unable to believe that a gem representing the Dead Christ (D. C. A. i. p. 718) can be as early as the ivth century.

[2] This is not the place to enter on the history of the direct representations of the Crucifixion first ideal and then realistic. The subject is of deep theological importance, but it belongs

wholly to a later period than that with which we are concerned here. The essay of M. Grimouard de St Laurent referred to in note 5, p. 360, is a valuable contribution to the history, but by no means exhaustive.

[3] Northcote and Brownlow, i. pl. 8, ii. 173.

[4] D. C. A. i. p. 719.

made to give distinctness to the unseen world. It is doubtful whether there are any representations of angels earlier than the latter half of the fourth century, and it seems certain that there are no representations of powers of evil, other than the natural serpent, till a later date.

By that time the work of early Christian Art was ended.

III.

General relation of Christianity to Art. From what has been said it will appear that the relation of Christianity to Art is that which it holds generally to life. It answers to a fresh birth, a transfiguration of all human powers, by the revelation of their divine connexions and destiny. The pregnant words of St Paul, 'old things (τὰ ἀρχαῖα) passed away : behold, they have become new,' have an application here. There is no loss, no abandonment of the past triumphs of thought and insight and labour, but they are quickened by a new power, and disclosed in a new position with regard to the whole discipline of man. Christian Art is the interpretation of beauty in life under the light of the Incarnation. The ministry of the beautiful in every shape, in sound, in form, in colour, is claimed for God through man.

The relation slowly realised, The realisation of this idea must necessarily be slow, but it is impossible that the facts of the Incarnation and Resurrection can leave Art in the same position as before. The interpretation of Nature and the embodiment of thought and feeling through outward things must assume a new character when it is known not only that Creation is the expression of the will of God, and in its essence 'very good,' but also that in humanity it has been taken into personal fellowship with the Word, through whom it was called into being. Such a revelation enables the student to see in the phenomena of the visible order Sacraments, so to speak, of the spiritual and unseen, and free him from bondage to 'the world' while he devotes himself with devout enthusiasm to the representation of the mysterious beauty which it contains. The Old Testament teaches us to regard Creation as an embodiment of a Divine thought, marred by the self-assertion and fall of its temporal sovereign: the New Testament teaches us to see it brought again potentially to harmony with God through the Blood of Him who is its Eternal Author and Head (Col. i. 14—23).

The Gospel therefore seeks the service of Art in the sensible proclamation of its message. The spirit must clothe itself in some way, and the dress may help to emphasise salient features in that which it partly veils. No doubt it is true that the spirit can in any case illuminate that in which it is confined; but it is no less true that it has a necessary tendency to fashion its own shrine, even as the soul 'doth the body make [1].' but necessarily asserted.

The early controversy as to the outward appearance of the Lord illustrates this twofold truth [2]. Some argued from the description of 'the servant of the Lord' that the Son of man had 'no form or comeliness,' 'no beauty that we should desire Him.' And others replied that it could not but be that perfect holiness should become visible in perfect beauty. To the spiritual eye, we feel, there would be no final antagonism in the two statements. And Art by spiritual sympathy is able to guide the spectator to a right vision of that which is not naturally discerned. Illustration from the conflicting views as to the Lord's appearance.

Or, to present the same thought from the opposite side, as all Art brings the ideal, in some sense, before us in a material form, and preserves for earth a definite place in the present order, so Christian Art is characterised by the endeavour to present 'in many parts and in many fashions' that view of Creation wherein it is shewn in 'earnest expectation' 'waiting for the revelation of the sons of God' (Rom. viii. 19). In other words Christian Art treats its subject as that which has partly lost and is partly striving Art reveals the divine end.

---

[1] A remarkable and somewhat obscure passage of Athenagoras points to one aspect of this truth in the discussion of the objects of worship in præ-Christian times. After quoting the famous lines from the Melanippe of Euripides (ὁρᾷς τὸν ὑψοῦ τόνδ' ἄπειρον αἰθέρα...) he says τῶν μὲν γὰρ οὔτε τὰς οὐσίας, αἷς ἐπικατηγορεῖσθαι τὸ ὄνομα συμβέβηκεν, ὑποκειμένας ἑώρα...τὸν δὲ ἀπὸ τῶν ἔργων (sc. ἑώρα), ὄψει τῶν ἀδήλων νοῶν τὰ φαινόμενα ἀέρος, αἰθέρος, γῆς (Legat. pro Christ. c. 5). To the true spiritual eye natural phenomena reveal something of the Divine character more really than any creation of the imagination of man.

[2] On the appearance of the Lord compare the Oxford translation of Tertullian, note F, pp. 252 ff.

towards a divine type, not self-complete and not an end, and seeks
to make clear the signs of the true character and the true goal of all
with which it deals. It is directed not to humanity and nature
in themselves, but to humanity and nature as revelations of the
Divine.

Christian-
ity does
not alter
the range
of Art.

Such an effort is obviously of universal application. Christian
Art, like Christianity itself, embraces all life. The inspiration of the
new birth extends to every human interest and faculty. Christian
Art, as Christian, does not differ from classical Art in range of
subject but in its prevailing treatment. It will indeed happen again
and again that 'the soul naturally Christian' unconsciously fulfils
its high office of spiritual interpretation in classical works, but
Christian Art exists by and for this. And there is nothing to which
the office does not apply, nothing in which it does not find scope for
exercise. The joys and sorrows and energies of men, the manifold
forms and varying moods of nature, all have their 'religious' aspect,
if religion be, as it assuredly is, the striving towards the unity of
man, the world, and God. Music, which is, as it were, the voice of
the society, and architecture which is as its vestment, have in all
their applications a religious power. This Christianity affirms as its
postulate, and by affirming determines its relation to Art.

Opposing
influences.

The fulfilment of this universal claim, as has been already said,
will be necessarily slow. The conquest of life for Christ is gradual
and not without reverses. New forces are not subdued without a
struggle, and old forces, which have been subdued, not unfrequently
rise up again in dangerous rebellion. More than once the fanatical
iconoclasm of a false Judaism, and the sensual nature worship of a
false Hellenism, have troubled the development of Christian Art.
No struggle indeed has been fruitless ; but even now we cannot dare
to say that the office of Art is frankly acknowledged, or the exercise
of Art spiritually disciplined.

Unequal
advances
of Chris-
tian Art.

The development of Christian Art has been gradual, and it has
been unequal in different branches. The social Arts, if I may so
describe them, Music and Architecture, were soon welcomed by the
Church and pursued in characteristic forms. It is not too much to

say that modern Music is a creation of the Church; and the continuous and rich growth of Christian architecture up to the Renaissance in types of varied beauty is in itself a sufficient proof of the
power of the Faith to call out and train the highest genius in Art.
The advance of painting and sculpture was checked perhaps in a
great degree by the influence of Eastern asceticism.   Both were
treated as subsidiary to architecture, which was preeminently the
Art of the Middle Ages; but some of the single statues of the xiiith
century contain a promise, not yet fulfilled, of a Christian Art
worthy to crown that of Greece.   Meanwhile a new style of painting
was being prepared by the illumination of manuscripts, in which not
only scenes and persons but small natural objects, flowers and insects,
were treated with the utmost tenderness and care.   Here again the
Renaissance checked the direct development of the twofold promise
over which the student lingers in admiration and hope as he regards
at Bruges side by side the works of Van Eyck and Memling.

The forces of the Renaissance have not yet been completely Disturb-
assimilated.   The wealth of ancient material then poured at once ing effect of the Re-
before Christian Artists hindered their normal progress; but they naissance.
have moved since along their proper lines and the Past contains the
assurance that 'all things' are theirs.

So much at least the history of Christianity fairly shews, that
nothing which is human lies beyond its range.   It lays the greatest
stress upon practical duties, upon 'the good part' of moral discipline,
but none the less it finds place for the satisfaction of what we regard
as less noble instincts.   The single incident recorded in the Gospels
in which the Lord received a costly offering seems to illustrate the
principles which hallow even the simplest gratifications of sense.
When Mary lavished the precious spikenard over the Head and The Evan-
Feet of her Master, 'the house,' St John tells us, 'was filled with gelic sign.
the odour of the ointment.'   It was natural that the thought of the
apostles should find expression by the lips of Judas.   'Why was not
this ointment sold for three hundred pence and given to the poor?'
'To what purpose was this waste?'   And the judgment was given:
'Verily I say unto you, wheresoever this gospel shall be preached in

the whole world, there shall also this that this woman hath done, be told for a memorial of her.' The fragrance was most transitory, but it was diffusive : the waste was most complete, but it gave clear witness of love, of that highest love of which the chief reward is that it should be known that its object inspired the devotion of perfect sacrifice. So it is with every work of Christian Art. It aims not at a solitary but at a common enjoyment : it seeks to make it clear that all to which it is directed has a spiritual value able to command the completest service [1].

IV.

<small>Love the guide of Art.</small>

Christianity, it has been seen, claims the ministry of Art in the whole field of life. What then is the peculiar office of Art ? It is in a word to present the truth of things under the aspect of beauty, to bring before us the 'world as God has made it' where 'all is beauty.' The fulfilment of this office involves the exercise not only of insight but of self-control. Man and nature are evidently disordered. The representation of all the phenomena of life would not be the representation of their divine truth. Love therefore, a looking for the highest good of the whole, will guide and limit the search after beauty to which Art is directed.

<small>The peculiar office of Art seen most clearly in the imitative Arts.</small>

In the imitative arts, painting and sculpture, the effort to make visible the truth of God in man and in nature is immediate and direct. In the creative arts, music and architecture, the effort is to find an expression, an embodiment, harmonious with the truth of things for elementary emotions and wants. Men in society seek a common voice, a common home : the hymn and the temple belong to the first stage of the state. But in these arts there is necessarily more freedom and variety than in those which are directly imitative. The application of the general laws of Art to them is complicated by

---

[1] This is the lesson of the soul in *The Palace of Art*:

"Make me a cottage in the vale," she said,
  "Where I may mourn and pray.
Yet pull not down my palace towers,

    that are
So lightly, beautifully built:
Perchance I may return with others
  there
When I have purged my guilt."

many physical influences.   It is best then to endeavour to determine the office of Art by a consideration of the imitative arts, and specially of painting which is both richer than sculpture in its effects and wider in its range.

In three most suggestive studies of painters of the Renaissance Browning has marked with decisive power the mission of Art, and the grounds of its failure.   He has not crowned the series by a portraiture of the ideal artist, but it is not difficult to gather his lineaments from the sketches of the other three.   In 'Fra Lippo Lippi' the poet vindicates the universality of Art answering to the fulness of life, and yet plainly indicates the peril which lies in this frank recognition of 'the value and significance of flesh.'   In 'Andrea del Sarto' he shews the power of faultless execution neutralised by the deliberate acceptance of a poor and selfish motive.   In 'Pictor ignotus,' the loftiest ideal and the fullest power of imagination and execution are supposed to be combined, but the artist shrinks from facing a world sordid proud and unsympathising, and buries his work in obscurity.

Browning's revelation of failure in Art.

It would not be possible to describe the artist's feeling more truly than in Lippi's words :

Fra Lippo Lippi.

> This world's no blot for us
> Nor blank: it means intensely, and means good:
> To find its meaning is my meat and drink.

So it is that for him to see the world is to see

> The beauty and the wonder and the power,
> The shapes of things, their colours, lights and shades,
> Changes, surprises—and God made them all...
> ... paint any one, and count it crime
> To let a truth slip.

If it be said that nature is before us, and that the artist can neither surpass nor reproduce it, the answer is complete :

> we're made so that we love
> First when we see them painted, things we have passed
> Perhaps a hundred times nor cared to see ;...
> ... Art was given for that:
> God uses us to help each other so,
> Lending our minds out.

It is therefore faithless disloyalty to the Creator to seek to 'paint the souls of men' by disparaging their bodies. Even if such a thing as soulless beauty were possible, the devout spectator would 'find the soul he wants within himself, when he returns God thanks.'

These pregnant words describe the manifold field of Art, its peculiar interpretative power, and its moral effect, but in connexion with a perfect, an unfallen, world. They take no account of the sorrows and failures which come from 'what man has made of man'; and the circumstances under which they are spoken give powerful emphasis to the reality of that disorder in life which imposes on Art the necessity of discipline. There must indeed be no violent suppression of any part of true nature in the endeavour to gain the highest lesson of earth, but the divine meaning must be sought through the traces of the divine ideal, so that the artist 'makes new hopes shine through the flesh they fray.'

Andrea del Sarto.

The failure of Lippi springs from a reaction against conventionality. In the assertion of the divine glory of Nature he overlooks the reality of corruption. The failure and the success of Andrea del Sarto are of a different kind. There is in him no sense of an illimitable progress of Art as it 'interprets God to men.' 'I can do,' he says, 'do easily,

> what I know,
> What I see, what at bottom of my heart,
> I wish for, if I ever wish so deep.'

The last words give the clue to his position. He has deliberately, irrevocably, limited his ideal by an unworthy passion. In earth and in heaven, as he looks forward, he accepts defeat as the consequence : so he chooses. He has fettered himself and strives to think that 'God laid the fetter.'

But none the less he is conscious that his matchless power was given him for something nobler. He recognises truer greatness in pictures less perfect than his own. The complete fulfilment of his design is his condemnation :

> a man's reach should exceed his grasp,
> Or what's a heaven for? all is silver grey,
> Placid and perfect with my art—the curse !

He has said of the Madonna, which was but the image of his wife,

> It is the thing, Love! so such things should be—

but yet looking back to the early and unsullied days he thinks, addressing Lucrezia, how he

> could paint
> One picture, just one more—the Virgin's face,
> Not your's this time!

The artist has need of discipline : he has need of devotion to an unattainable ideal: he has need also of un-selfregarding courage. The pathos of earthly passion in the confession of Andrea is less touching than the self-effacement of 'the unknown painter,' who, conscious of power and purpose, keenly alive to the joy of triumphs which he might secure, yet shrinks from the cold hard criticism of the crowd, 'as from the soldiery a nun,' and chooses for his works silent unnoticed decay. He has failed to acknowledge the reality of his mission. The question for him was not how men would judge him, whether 'their praise would hold its worth,' but whether he had a trust to discharge, different from that monotonous task which he took to himself, painting

> ...the same series, Virgin, Babe and Saint,
> With the same cold, calm, beautiful regard.

It might have been that 'merchants would have trafficked in his heart'; but they could not have disguised the heart's teaching. It might have been that his pictures would have lived with those who

> count them for garniture and household-stuff,

but no dull eye could have extinguished the light of his interpretation of life. The work of the artist is a battle, not without loss and suffering, and he must bear its sorrows, just as he must exercise the patient self-control of one who has to recover an image partly marred and defaced, and to keep in vigorous activity his loftiest aspiration.

All nature, all life, so far as it can be presented under the form of beauty, is the field of Art. But the beauty which is the aim of Christian Art is referred to a divine ideal. It is not 'of the world,' as finding its source or its final measure there, but 'of the Father,' as corresponding to an unseen truth. The visible to the Christian eye is in every part a revelation of the invisible. The artist, like the

Pictor ignotus.

Beauty answering to a divine ideal the object of Art.

W.   24

poet, sees the infinite in things, and, under the conditions of his works, suggests it.

Positive value of artistic discipline.

So far the artist's pursuit of beauty is limited. The boundaries within which he is confined will not always be the same, but they will always have the same relation to moral discipline. They will correspond with the circumstances of the time. And the discipline of sense has a positive and not only a negative value. It brings into healthy action a power of goodness which a rigid asceticism keeps unused and tends to destroy. In this way Christianity is able to give back, as has been already indicated, what was lost by the corruption of the old Aryan passion for Nature. All that was at first referred to limited divinities is shewn to be essentially an expression of one Divine Will. The spiritual signs may be greatly obscured : they may not be in every case distinctly discoverable ; but the assurance of the significance and purpose of the whole cannot but illuminate the study of every part.

And while the field of Christian Art is in one sense limited by the recognition of a spiritual destiny of all its fruits, it is, in another sense, unlimited. The understanding of Nature is deepened and enlarged with the progress of life. Every discovery as to the history of creation, sooner or later, places new forces in the artist's hands. It may be some detail as to the formation of rocks, some law as to the arrangement of leaves and branches, some phenomenon of light or vapour, which has been more firmly seized; and shortly the painter's interpretation of the landscape will offer a fuller truth. The instructed eye will discern the importance of some minute effect and the artistic instinct will know how to convey it to the ordinary spectator [1].

The Artist interprets and embodies.

For the artist has both to interpret and to embody. He has to gain the ideal of his subject and then he has to present it in an intelligible shape. He has to give the right effect and to call out

---

[1] When the Turner Collection was first exhibited at Marlborough House, I remember examining a sketch-book which contained some studies of laurel bushes. At the side was a note to the following effect : 'N.B. The under-side of a laurel leaf does not shine.' It would be interesting to know how Turner conveyed the effect which he noticed.

the right feeling. He has, as it were, to enter within the veil, and coming forth again to declare his heavenly visions to men. He is not a mirror but a prophet. The work of the photographer may help him, but it in no sense expresses his aim, which is not reproduction but translation. He has abdicated the office of an artist who simply repeats for the mass of men what they see themselves. The artist bids them behold the ideal as it is his privilege to realise it. He strives to make clear to others what his keener sensibility and penetrating insight have made visible to him. There is, as in every true poem, an element of infinity in his works. They suggest something beyond that which they directly present: something to be looked for, and felt after, thoughts which they quicken but do not satisfy. So it is that

Art may tell a truth
Obliquely, do the thing shall breed the thought,
Nor wrong the thought.

This consideration places in a true light the danger of the popular realism in Art. There is a charm, no doubt, in being enabled to see some scene far removed from us in time or place as it would have presented itself to an ordinary observer; but exactly in proportion to the grandeur of the subject such a superficial portraiture is likely to be misleading. The spectator is tempted to rest in that which he understands at once; and the loftier though vague impression which he had before is lost and not assisted by the external details which profess to give the literal truth. Or, to put the truth in another light: the divine act was fitted to convey the divine meaning at the time of its occurrence, in relation to those who witnessed it, but a realistic representation could not give the same impression to a different age. *Peril of realistic Art*

This is signally the case with scenes in the Gospel History. The early Church by a right instinct refrained from seeking any direct representation of the Lord. It was felt that the realistic treatment of His Person could not but endanger the living sense of the Majesty which the Church had learnt to recognise. By no effort could the spectator in a later age place himself in the position of the disciples before the Passion and the Ascension. The exact repro- *in scriptural subjects.*

duction, if it were possible, of what met their eyes would not produce on him the effect which they experienced. The scene would require artistic interpretation in order that the idea might be preserved.

Illustrations from the treatment of the Madonna.

A great artist can alone determine what the law of interpretation must be, and even then he will not himself always obey it. Two illustrations taken from the commonest of sacred subjects, the Madonna and the Crucifixion, may serve to bring out the thought which I wish to emphasise. In the *Madonna della Seggiola* Raffaelle has given an exquisite natural group of a Mother and Child, overflowing with human tenderness, affection and proud joy, and we look no further: in the *Madonna di San Sisto* he has rendered the idea of divine motherhood and divine Sonship in intelligible forms. No one can rest in the individual figures. The tremulous fulness of emotion in the face of the Mother, the intense far-reaching gaze of the Child, constrain the beholder to look beyond. For him too the curtain is drawn aside: he feels that there is a fellowship of earth with heaven and of heaven with earth, and understands the meaning of the attendant Saints who express the different aspects of this

The Crucifixion.

double communion. It may well be doubted whether the Crucifixion is in any immediate shape a proper subject for Art. The image of the Dead Christ is foreign to Scripture. Even in the record of the Passion Death is swallowed up in Victory. And the material representation of the superficial appearance of that which St John shews to have been life through death defines and perpetuates thoughts foreign to the Gospel. The Crucifixion by Velasquez, with its overwhelming pathos and darkness of desolation, will shew what I mean[1]. In every trait it presents the thought of hopeless defeat[2]. No early Christian would have dared to look upon it. Very different is one of the earliest examples of the treatment of the Crucifixion on the Sigmaringen Crucifix[3]. In that life, vigour, beauty, grace, the open

---

[1] A small engraving is given in Mrs Jameson's *History of the Lord*, ii. 205.

[2] The Lord's words in the Gospel narrative speak of the uttermost conflict as over before the physical Death: ἵνα τί με ἐγκατέλιπες;

[3] Mrs Jameson's *History of the Lord*, ii. 330. It is, I fear, doubtful whether the youthful figure is correctly given.

eye, and the freely outstretched arm, suggest the idea of loving and victorious sacrifice crowned with its reward. This is an embodiment of the idea: the picture of Velasquez is a realisation of the appearance of the Passion.

If the view of Art which has been given is correct, its primary destination is public and not private, and it culminates in worship. Neither a great picture nor a great poem can be for a single possessor. So it has been at all times when Art has risen to its highest triumphs. But as an element of worship Art must be seen to be distinctly ministerial. In every form, music, painting, sculpture, it must point beyond the immediate effect. As long as it suggests the aspiration 'to Thy great glory, O Lord,' it is not only an offering, but a guide and a support. When it appears to be an end idolatry has begun.

Art ministerial, and not an end.

The artist, we have seen, must use every fresh help and discovery: he must make evident new thoughts or illuminate thoughts which are imperfectly understood. It is clear therefore that he cannot follow one constant method in the fulfilment of his office. His work will be accomplished according to the conditions of his time. He will choose that mode of presenting the truth that he sees which is on the whole likely to be most effective. As a teacher, with a limited and yet most noble range of subjects, he will consider how he can best serve his age. Nothing short of this conviction can overcome the influence of fashion, or sustain that resolute purpose which bears temporary failure.

The Artist a teacher.

I have touched only upon the highest forms of creative Art. The principles by which these are animated apply also with necessary modifications to the humbler types of decorative art. The problems which these raise are in many respects more difficult and of wider application than those connected with the artistic interpretation of nature and life. It is no affectation to speak of the moral influence of colours and shapes in the instruments and accessories of everyday life. Here also there is room for a manifold apprehension and embodiment of truth. If once thoughtfulness of workmanship could be placed in general estimation before richness of material, a legitimate and fruitful field would be opened for domestic art. When

Decorative Art.

Greek Art was greatest it was consecrated to public use; and one chief danger of modern society is lest the growth of private wealth should lead to the diversion of the highest artistic power from the common service, and at the same time leave the appropriate labours of domestic art unencouraged.

Summary.   This however is not the place to pursue the questions which are thus opened for inquiry. It is enough to have shewn that Christian Art is a necessary expression of the Christian Faith; that the early antagonism of Christianity to ancient Art was an antagonism to the idolatry, the limited earthliness, of which it was the most complete expression; that from the first beginnings of the Faith there were strivings after an Art which should interpret nature and life as a revelation of God, leading the student through the most patient and reverent regard of phenomena to the contemplation of the eternal; that the consecration of Art, involved in the facts of the Christian Creed, limits the artist only in the sense that a clear exhibition of the ideal saves the beholder from following wayward and selfish fancies.

The works of the greatest masters of the Middle Ages, of the greatest masters of the Renaissance, and the statement holds good still, shew how constantly foreign elements, fragments of the old life, not wholly transfigured, intrude themselves in that which as a whole belongs to a new order. Here perhaps traces of sensuousness, there traces of unlicensed satire, reveal disturbing forces in the artist's soul which are yet powerful enough to make themselves felt. But it is true, I believe, without exception that the noblest works, those on which we look with the deepest gratitude, drawing from them new powers of spiritual vision, new convictions of a spiritual world about us, are those which are most Christian.

INDEX.

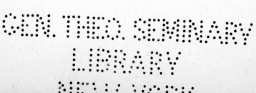

CAMBRIDGE: PRINTED BY C. J. CLAY, M.A. & SON, AT THE UNIVERSITY PRESS.

MESSRS MACMILLAN AND CO.'S PUBLICATIONS.

Works by THE RIGHT REV. J. B. LIGHTFOOT, D.D., D.C.L., LL.D.
BISHOP OF DURHAM.

St Paul's Epistle to the Galatians. A Revised Text, with Introduction, Notes, and Dissertations. Eighth Edition, revised. 8vo. 12s.

St Paul's Epistle to the Philippians. A Revised Text, with Introduction, Notes, and Dissertations. Eighth Edition, revised, 8vo. 12s.

St Clement of Rome. The two Epistles to the Corinthians. A Revised Text, with Introduction and Notes. 8vo. 8s. 6d.

St Clement of Rome. An Appendix, containing the newly-recovered portions. With Introductions, Notes, and Translations. 8vo. 8s. 6d.

St Paul's Epistles to the Colossians and to Philemon. A Revised Text, with Introductions, Notes, and Dissertations. Seventh Edition, revised. 8vo. 12s.

The Apostolic Fathers. Part II.: S. Ignatius—S. Polycarp. Revised Texts, with Introductions, Notes, Dissertations, and Translations. 2 vols. in 3. Demy 8vo. 48s.

St Paul's Epistle to the Thessalonians, Commentary on the Greek Text. By JOHN EADIE, D.D., LL.D. Edited by the Rev. W. YOUNG, M.A., with Preface by Professor CAIRNS. 8vo. 12s.

St Paul's Epistles to the Ephesians, the Colossians, and Philemon; with Introductions and Notes, and an Essay on the Traces of Foreign Elements in the Theology of these Epistles. By the Rev. J. LLEWELYN DAVIES, M.A. Second Edition, revised. Demy 8vo. 7s. 6d.

The Epistle to the Hebrews. In Greek and English. With Critical and Explanatory Notes. Edited by Rev. FREDERIC RENDALL, M.A., formerly Fellow of Trinity College, Cambridge, and Assistant-Master at Harrow School. Crown 8vo. 6s.

St Paul's Epistle to the Philippians. With Translation, Paraphrase, and Notes for English Readers. By C. J. VAUGHAN, D.D., Dean of Llandaff. Crown 8vo. 5s.

St Paul's Epistle to the Romans. The Greek Text with English Notes. By C. J. VAUGHAN, D.D., Dean of Llandaff. Fifth Edition. Crown 8vo. 7s. 6d.

Works by RICHARD CHENEVIX TRENCH, D.D.

Notes on the Parables of Our Lord. Fourteenth Edition, revised. 8vo. 12s.

Notes on the Miracles of Our Lord. Twelfth Edition, revised. 8vo. 12s.

Commentary on the Epistles to the Seven Churches in Asia. Fourth Edition, revised. 8vo. 8s. 6d.

Lectures on Medieval Church History. Being the substance of Lectures delivered at Queen's College, London. Second Edition, revised. 8vo. 12s.

Synonyms of the New Testament. Ninth Edition, revised. 8vo. 12s.

MACMILLAN AND CO.: LONDON.